ASSESSING THE NEW TESTAMENT EVIDENCE FOR THE HISTORICITY OF THE RESURRECTION OF JESUS

ASSESSING THE NEW TESTAMENT EVIDENCE FOR THE HISTORICITY OF THE RESURRECTION OF JESUS

William Lane Craig

WIPF & STOCK · Eugene, Oregon

Wipf and Stock Publishers
199 W 8th Ave, Suite 3
Eugene, OR 97401

Assessing the New Testament Evidence for the Historicity of the Resurrection of Jesus
By Craig, William L.
Copyright © 2002 by Craig, William L. All rights reserved.
Softcover ISBN-13: 978-1-6667-7269-2
Publication date 2/28/2023
Previously published by The Edwin Mellen Press, Ltd., 2002
Reprinted with permission of The Edwin Mellen Press
Apendix D reprinted with permission of *Philosophia Christi*.

This edition is a scanned facsimile of the original edition published in 2002.

*To
Bryan*

TABLE OF CONTENTS

Abbreviations — i

Preface — iii

PART I. THE EVIDENCE OF PAUL

Chapter 1. The Pre-Pauline Formula of I Corinthians 15:3ff — 3

Chapter 2. The Witnesses of the Resurrection Appearances — 39

Chapter 3. Indications of the Empty Tomb — 63

Chapter 4. The Nature of the Resurrection Body — 85

PART II. THE EVIDENCE OF THE GOSPELS

Chapter 5. The Burial Narrative — 117

Chapter 6. The Empty Tomb Narrative — 143

Chapter 7. The Appearance Narratives — 181

Chapter 8. Three Issues Raised by the Gospel Narratives — 223

PART III. ASSESSING THE EVIDENCE

Chapter 9. The Evidence for the Empty Tomb — 255

Chapter 10. The Evidence for the Resurrection Appearances — 275

Chapter 11. The Origin of the Christian Way — 295

Appendix A: From Easter to Valentinus and the Apostle's Creed Once More: A Critical Examination of James Robinson's Proposed Resurrection Appearance Trajectories — 307

Appendix B: John Dominic Crossan on the Resurrection of Jesus — 327

Appendix C: Visions of Jesus: A Critical Assessment of Gerd Lüdemann's Hallucination Hypothesis — 349

Appendix D: Dale Allison on Jesus' Empty Tomb, His Post-Mortem Appearances, and the Origin of the Disciples' Belief in His Resurrection — 381

General Index — 391

Scripture Index — 401

ERRATA

Several secretarial errors in the production of the typescript have found their way into the text. These have been marked by hand in the text. Below are the corrections.

p. 4:
קבל מן
מסר ל

p. 8:
נראה
איתחמי

p. 9:
מן
משיח

p. 10
אתמסר בעויתנא

p. 11
משיח
משיח
משיח
משיח
אתא

p. 12
משיח

p. 13
משיח
משיח
משיח

ABBREVIATIONS

AB	Analecta Biblica
AGAJU	Arbeiten zur Geschichte des antiken Judentums und des Urchristentums
ARGU	Arbeiten zur Religionsgeschichte des Urchristentums
ATANT	Abhandlungen zur Theologie des Alten und Neuen Testaments
AnchBib	Anchor Bible
BA	*Biblical Archaeologist*
BET	Beiträge zur evangelischen Theologie
BFCT	Beiträge zur Förderung christlischer Theologie
BGBE	Beiträge zur Geschichte der biblischen Exegese
BH	Biblische Handbibliothek
BHT	Beiträge zur historischen Theologie
BNTC	Black's New Testament Commentaries
BO	*Biblica et Orientalia*
BS	Biblische Studien
BU	Biblische Untersuchungen
BiLeb	*Bibel und Leben*
Bib	*Biblica*
CBQ	*Catholic Biblical Quarterly*
CGTC	Cambridge Greek Testament Commentary
CivCath	*Civilta Catholica*
CTM	Calwer theologische Monographien
DT	*Deutsche Theologie*
EBC	Expositor's Bible Commentary
EKKNT	Evangelisch-Katholischer Kommentar zum Neuen Testament
ETL	*Ephemerides Theologicae Lovanienses*
EvT	*Evangelische Theologie*
ExpTim	*Expository Times*
FRLANT	Forschungen zur Religion und Literatur des Alten und Neuen Testaments
FSOT	Forschungen zur systematischen und ökumenischen Theologie
FZPT	Freiburger Zeitschrift für Philosophie und Theologie
GBS/NT	Guides to Biblical Scholarship/New Testament
Greg	*Gregorianum*
HTKNT	Herders Theologischer Kommentar zum Neuen Testament
HTS	Harvard Theological Studies
ICC	International Critical Commentary
IKZ	*Internationale katholische Zeitschrift 'Communio'*
ITL	International Theological Library
IsrEJ	*Israel Exploration Journal*
JAAR	*Journal of the American Academy of Religion*
JBL	*Journal of Biblical Literature*
JR	*Journal of Religion*
JSNT	*Journal for the Study of the New Testament*
JTS	*Journal of Theological Studies*
KEKNT	Kritisch-exegetischer Kommentar über das Neue Testament
LD	Lectio Divina
NCB	New Century Bible
NIGTC	New International Greek Testament Commentary
NLC	New London Commentary

ABBREVIATIONS

NLCNT	New London Commentary on the New Testament
NT	*Novum Testamentum*
NTA	Neutestamentliche Abhandlungen
NTD	Neues Testament Deutsch
NTS	*New Testament Studies*
QD	Quaestiones Disputatae
RB	*Revue Biblique*
RScRel	*Revue des Sciences Religieuses*
RTPhil	*Revue de Théologie et de Philosophie*
SANT	Studien zum Alten und Neuen Testament
SBA	Sitzungsberichte der Berliner Akademie der Wissenschaften
SBFA	Studii Biblici Franciscani Analecta
SBL	Society of Biblical Literature
SBS	Stuttgarter Bibelstudien
SBT	Studies in Biblical Theology
SF	Studia Friburgensia
SHA	Sitzungsberichte der Heidelberger Akademie der Wissenschaften
SJT	*Scottish Journal of Theology*
SNT	Studien zum Neuen Testament
ST	*Studia Theologica*
TBl	Theologische Blätter
TBu	Theologische Bücherei
TGl	*Theologie und Glaube*
Theol	*Theology*
THKNT	Theologischer Handkommentar zum Neuen Testament
TQ	*Theologische Quartalschrift*
TRu	*Theologische Rundschau*
TS	*Theological Studies*
TSK	*Theologische Studien und Kritiken*
TT	Themen der Theologie
TvT	*Tijdschrift voor Theologie*
TW	Theologie und Wirklichkeit
TWiss	Theologische Wissenschaft
TWNT	*Theologisches Wörterbuch zum Neuen Testament*
TZ	*Theologische Zeitschrift*
UT	Urban-Taschenbücher
WMANT	Wissenschaftliche Monographien zum Alten und Neuen Testament
ZKG	*Zeitschrift für Kirchengeschichte*
ZKT	*Zeitschrift für Katholische Theologie*
ZNW	*Zeitschrift für die neutestamentliche Wissenschaft und die Kunde der älteren Kirche*
ZST	*Zeitschrift für systematische Theologie*
ZTK	*Zeitschrift für Theologie und Kirche*

PREFACE

Theology during the first half of the twentieth century was characterized by the subjectivism and scepticism which dominated the latter nineteenth century. Throughout the reign of Dialectical and Existential Theology, the question of the historicity of the resurrection of Jesus was viewed largely with apathy or antipathy. But in the second half of the past century, a remarkable transformation appears to have taken place in resurrection studies. The Marburg conference in 1953 marked a turning point against Bultmann's view of the irrelevancy of history for faith, and several of his pupils, notably Ernst Käsemann, began to seek new ways of retying the Christ of faith to the Jesus of history.[1] The so-called new quest for the historical Jesus spawned a fresh interest in the historicity of the events of Easter and the origins of the disciples' Easter faith. Hans von Campenhausen's *Der Ablauf der Osterereignisse und das leere Grab* (1952) and Hans Grass's *Ostergeschehen und Osterberichte* (1956) were landmarks in the renewed attempt to investigate and defend the historicity of the resurrection of Jesus. Von Campenhausen defended the essential historicity of the Markan narrative of the women's discovery of the empty tomb, while Grass, though rejecting the empty tomb, argued that the post-resurrection appearances of Jesus cannot be explained as subjective visions, but ought to be understood as objective (veridical) visions of the risen Lord. Together these works set the basis for subsequent discussion of the historicity of Jesus's resurrection.

Sceptical treatments of the resurrection continued, of course, to be published. But by the late 1960s the Barth/Bultmannian approach to the resurrection was a

---

[1] Ernst Käsemann, "Das Problem des historischen Jesus," *ZTK* 51 (1954): 125-153.

spent force, moving forward only by its own inertia. Scepticism reached its faltering apogee in Willi Marxsen's popular book *Die Auferstehung Jesu von Nazareth* (1968) and then began quickly to recede. On the self-reversal of scholarship in this area, Gutwenger comments:

> It appears that a few years ago the attack on Jesus's resurrection...reached its climax. This situation was created through modern rationalism, which wants to explain everything through immanent causes, through a weariness with the divine, and a massive, hedonistic materialism. Bultmann's poorly understood teaching of demythologization and the open confession of some theologians that they cannot believe in the resurrection of a corpse helped to bring about a crisis of faith in Easter...Reaction came, and from the Catholic as well as the Protestant side the theme of the resurrection of Christ was taken up anew.[2]

Throughout the 1970s a continuing stream of works in German, French, and English sought to re-examine the question of the historicity of the resurrection. Perhaps the most striking indication of the new appreciation of the historical credibility of the resurrection of Jesus was the declaration of one of the leading Jewish theologians of today, Pinchas Lapide, that he is himself convinced on the basis of the evidence that the God of Israel did raise Jesus from the dead.[3] Theologically speaking, equally significant has been Wolfhart Pannenberg's attempt to construct his entire Christology "from below," that is, based on the historical evidence for Jesus and his resurrection, a move that has been hailed as ushering in a new era in European Protestant theology.[4] After the predominance of the Barth/Bultmannian approach to the resurrection, Pannenberg's program is a surprising development that one would scarcely have held for possible in German theology. Not that this is all being taken in quietly: if I read the lay of the theological land correctly, it appears that we are now witnessing a re-assertion by sceptical critics of their viewpoint. Still it is not unfair to speak of a veritable resurrection of historical interest in and appreciation of the resurrection of Jesus.

---

[2] E. Gutwenger, "Auferstehung and Auferstehungsleib Jesu," *ZKT* 9 (1969): 32.
[3] Pinchas Lapide, *Auferstehung* (Stuttgart: Calwer Verlag, 1977; München: Kösel Verlag, 1977).
[4] Wolfhart Pannenberg, *Jesus: God and Man*, trans. L. L. Wilkins and D. A. Priebe (London: SCM Press, 1968). Pannenberg argues that the reports of Jesus's appearances and empty tomb are most plausibly accounted for by the explanation that he really did rise from the dead and that this supplies the foundation for faith. On the significance of this development, see B. A. Willems, "W. Pannenberg, *Grundzüge der Christologie*," *TvT* 7 (1967): 322; René Marlé, "Comincia un era nuova nella teologia protestante tedescal?" *CivCath* 119 (1969): 214-225; Daniel P. Fuller, "A New German Theological Movement," *SJT* 19 (1966): 160-175.

Preface

Despite the vastness and quality of the literature on the resurrection, there has not yet appeared in English a comprehensive treatment of the question of the historicity of Jesus's resurrection comparable in scope to, say, Grass's *Ostergeschehen und Osterberichte* or Beda Rigaux's *Dieu l'a ressuscité* (1973), both of which remain untranslated. In view of the several controversial and important issues yet unresolved, such a treatment is desirable, and it is with this intent that I offer the present volume.

II

According to the late Norman Perrin, the *meaning* which the evangelists give to the resurrection is more important than the question of what actually happened.[5] This raises the knotty question of the relationship between history and theology in the New Testament documents. Perrin maintains that because the gospels are primarily pieces of theology, the question, "What actually happened on that first Easter morning?" is alien to these ancient religious texts; none of the gospel writers is concerned to give historical information.[6] Questions of historicity and authorship are matters of "the most complete indifference" compared to the coherence and integrity of the theological viewpoint of the works themselves.[7]

Now I simply cannot bring myself to subscribe to such a viewpoint. However fine a theological synthesis an evangelist may present us, I cannot commit myself existentially to it unless I am also convinced that it is true. This is not to take the standpoint of theological rationalism with regard to the resurrection, for certainly God's Spirit may move in the hearts of men to persuade them of the truth apart from considerations of evidence. But it is to deny that a dead Jesus can be of decisive significance for my life today and that this situation is somehow reversed because the proclamation of this dead man's resurrection has theological meaning, though the proclamation is in fact historically false. I think this perspective is nearer the attitude of the New Testament writers than is Perrin's. Indeed, they seem very concerned, with their repeated emphasis on the witnesses to the events surrounding the resurrection, to assure us that the resurrection of Jesus is a historical fact and therefore is of life-changing significance.

---

[5] Norman Perrin, *The Resurrection according to Matthew, Mark and Luke* (Philadelphia: Fortress Press, 1977), p. 84.
[6] Ibid., p. 78.
[7] Ibid., pp. x, 6.

In this work, therefore, I am primarily interested in the question of the historical credibility of the resurrection accounts, not their theology, except insofar as the latter impinges upon the former. Hence, I am unashamedly pre-occupied with the question of what actually happened. This has its drawbacks, of course, but one must place limits somewhere, and therefore I must refer the reader interested primarily in the theology of the resurrection narratives to one of the many fine books on that subject.[8]

III

A final point ought to be discussed at the outset, and that is the question of presuppositions.[9] It is increasingly recognized that presuppositions play an important role in shaping one's conclusions apart from considerations of evidence. When it comes to a theologically-charged subject like the resurrection, it would be naive to think that any investigator comes to the subject without a point of view. But this fact alone need not vitiate profitable discussion of the issues so long as one does not reason circularly from the presuppositions to the truth of the hypothesis based on those presuppositions. For example, Bultmann's approach to the New Testament was guided by two underlying presuppositions: (1) the existence of a full-blown pre-Christian Gnosticism and (2) the impossibility of miracles. While he sought to provide evidence for (1), he simply assumed (2). Although these two points of view guided most of Bultmann's work, it would not be enough for a critic of the Marburger to dismiss his work by simply stating that his conclusions are determined by his presuppositions. Rather a critic must refute the specific arguments used by Bultmann to support any given position, even though Bultmann's view may have been determined in advance by one of his presuppositions. It is not why or how the hypothesis in question came to be formulated, but the evidence adduced in favor of the hypothesis that is crucial.[10] Consider spe-

---

[8] The best being perhaps the work of Grant Osborne, *The Resurrection Narratives: A Redactional Study* (Grand Rapids, Mich.: Baker, 1984); cf. his earlier "History and Theology in the Resurrection Narratives: A Redactional Study" (Ph.D. thesis, University of Aberdeen, 1974).
[9] I have profited in this regard from discussion with D. A. Carson.
[10] On this historiographical principle, see Maurice Mandelbaum, *The Problem of Historical Knowledge* (New York: Harper & Row, Harper Torchbooks, 1967), p. 184; Morton White, "Can History Be Objective?" in *The Philosophy of History in Our Time*, ed. Hans Meyerhoff (New York: Doubleday, Anchor Books, 1959), pp. 199-201; Raymond Aaron, "Relativism in History," in ibid., p. 160. For a critique of the view that one's *Weltanschauung* obviates scientific objectiv-

cifically Grass's *Ostergeschehen und Osterberichte*. It seems evident that Grass's scepticism concerning the empty tomb and bodily appearances of Jesus is largely determined in advance by a presuppositional rejection of the *"massiven Realismus"* of the gospel resurrection narratives; but woe to the critic who thinks that, having pointed this out, he has thereby refuted Grass's lengthy catalog of arguments against the empty tomb! By the same token, it would be invalid for a Bultmannian to dismiss the conclusions of a writer who defends the resurrection, say, Gerald O'Collins in his *The Easter Jesus* (1973), on the grounds that his conclusions are determined in advance because O'Collins is, after all, a Jesuit.

The point is that there is a difference between innocuous and vicious presuppositions. A presupposition remains innocuous so long as it does not enter into the verification of the hypothesis. Like a chemical catalyst, it guides the research but does not itself become a part of the argumentation in support of the hypothesis. Grass, for example, while having an aversion to nature miracles almost as great as Bultmann's, usually refrains from allowing this to be the grounds upon which he rejects an account as unhistorical; for this he is to be commended. His usual procedure is to adduce factual arguments in support of his hypothesis, although these hypotheses are no doubt largely shaped by his presupposition. A presupposition becomes vicious, however, when it actually enters into the argumentation and purports to be a ground for the acceptance of the hypothesis. For example, when Bultmann or Grass rejects an account as legendary because it is miraculous, then the presupposition has ceased to be innocuous. For it has become the ground for accepting the hypothesis it helped for formulate, which closes a vicious circle. Similarly were a conservative to accept the historicity of a resurrection account, say, on the authority of the Church's teaching, this presupposition would remain innocuous only so long as he, in contending for the historicity of that account, argues solely on the basis of the evidence without appealing to Church authority.

Now in this work, I have presuppositions of both Bultmann's first and second kinds. With regard to the first type I presuppose (1) Markan priority, (2) the independence of John from the synoptics, and (3) that Mk. 16:8 represents the original conclusion to that gospel. Were these assumptions shown to be false, that would substantially alter many of my conclusions. But in each case, the presup-

---

ity, see Frederick Suppe, "Introduction," in *The Structure of Scientific Theories*, 2nd ed., ed. F. Suppe (Urbana, Ill.: University of Illinois Press, 1977), pp. 208-217.

position represents the consensus of the majority of scholars today. With regard to the second type, I am committed theologically to the doctrine of inspiration and, hence, to the historical reliability of Scripture. This presupposition remains, however, innocuous, since in no place in this work do I argue for the credibility of an account on the basis that it is inspired and therefore authoritative.

IV

This book has been a long-term project, many years in the making. I wish to express my heartfelt thanks to the Alexander von Humboldt Stiftung, not only for their generous fellowship which funded my initial work several years ago at the Universität München and Cambridge University, but also for their warmth and personal concern for the comfort of my family during our two years in Germany. Over the course of time, certain portions of this work have appeared in preliminary article form, including "The Bodily Resurrection of Jesus," in *Gospel Perspectives* I (1980); "The Empty Tomb," in *Gospel Perspectives* II (1981); "The Guard at the Tomb," *NTS* 31 (1984): 273-281; "The Historicity of the Empty Tomb of Jesus," *NTS* 31 (1985): 39-67; "Paul's Dilemma in 2 Corinthians 5.1-10: A 'Catch-22'?" *NTS* 34 (1988): 145-147; and "Pannenberg's Beweis für die Auferstehung Jesu," *Kerygma und Dogma* 34 (1988): 78-104. I am grateful for profitable discussion and criticism of various parts of this work from John Alsup, Craig Blomberg, E. L. Bode, Bruce Chilton, Craig Evans, Robert Gundry, Ferdinand Hahn, I. H. Marshall, C. F. D. Moule, Wolfhart Pannenberg, M. E. Thrall, and David Wenham. For permission to use the cover illustration, I gratefully acknowledge the Colmar Museum of Unterlinden. Special thanks are due to my former secretary Bev Faugerstrom and to my wife Jan for their lengthy hours spent in producing the typescript and to Jan once more for entering the entire tome all over again into the computer and helping to prepare the camera-ready copy. I am also grateful to my former student Jennifer Jensen for bringing the typescript into its final form for Edwin Mellen Press.

William Lane Craig

Westmont College
Santa Barbara, California

Université Catholique de Louvain
Louvain, Belgium

PART I

THE EVIDENCE OF PAUL

CHAPTER 1

THE PRE-PAULINE FORMULA OF I CORINTHIANS 15

THE EXISTENCE OF A FORMULA

Undoubtedly one of the most important respects in which contemporary research on the historicity of the resurrection differs from that of previous centuries is with regard to the primacy of Paul. The discovery early in the twentieth century that I Cor. 15:3-7 contains an old, pre-Pauline formula of the primitive church[1] has made Paul's testimony to the fact and nature of the resurrection the logical *Ausgangspunkt* of virtually every modern discussion.

---

[1] The point was first elaborated by Alfred Seeberg, *Der Katechismus des Urchristentums*, with an Introduction by F. Hahn, TB 26 (Leipzig: A. Deichert, 1903; rep. ed.: München: Christian Kaiser, 1966), pp. 50-84. For discussion, see Karl Holl, "Der Kirchenbegriff des Paulus in seinem Verhältnis zu dem der Urgemeinde," in idem, *Gesammelte Aufsätze zur Kirchengeschichte*, 3 vols. (Tübingen: J. C. B. Mohr, 1928), 2: 44-67; Ferdinand Kattenbusch, "Die Vorzugstellung des Petrus und der Charakter der Urgemeinde zu Jerusalem," in *Festgabe von Fachgenossen und Freunden Karl Müller* (Tübingen: J. C. B. Mohr, 1922), pp. 322-351; Adolf von Harnack, *Die Verklärungsgeschichte Jesu: Der Bericht des Paulus (I Cor. 15,3ff.) und die beiden Christusvisionen des Petrus*, SBA (Berlin: Walter de Gruyter, 1922), pp. 62-80; Eric Fascher, "Die Auferstehung Jesu and ihr Verhältnis zur urchristlichen Verkündigung," *ZNW* 26 (1927): 1-26. More recent studies include Ernst Lichtenstein, "Der älteste christliche Glaubensformel," *ZKG* 63 (1950-51): 1-74; Ernst Bammel, "Herkunft und Funktion der Traditionselemente in I Kor. 15.1-11," *TZ* 11(1955): 401-419; P. Winter, "I Corinthians XV. 3b-7," *NT* 2 (1958): 142-150; Karl Heinrich Rengstorff, *Die Auferstehung Jesu*, 4th rev. ed. (Witten: Luther-Verlag, 1960), pp. 128-135; Hans Grass, *Ostergeschehen und Osterberichte*, 4th rev. ed. (Göttingen: Vandenhoeck & Ruprecht, 1970), pp. 94-112; Ulrich Wilckens, "Der Ursprung der Überlieferung der Erscheinungen des Auferstandenen," in *Dogma und Denkstrukturen*, ed. W. Joest and W. Pannenberg (Göttingen: Vandenhoeck & Ruprecht, 1963), pp. 56-95; Hans Werner Bartsch, "Die Argumentation des Paulus in I Cor. 15, 3-11," *ZNW* 55 (1964): 261-274; Ferdinand Hahn, *Christologische Hoheitstitel*, 3rd ed., FRLANT 83 (Göttingen: Vandenhoeck & Ruprecht, 1966), pp. 197-212; Hans Freiherr von Campenhausen, *Der Ablauf der Osterereignisse und das leere Grab*, 3rd rev. ed., SHA (Hei-

The classic statement of the argument for the existence of a formula in these verses belongs to Jeremias.² He observes: (1) The words παραλαμβάνειν and παραδιδόναι used by Paul to introduce vs. 3-7 correspond to the technical rabbinical terms קבל מן and מסר, which are used for the transmission of tradition (cf. I Cor. 11:23). (2) Besides this clear statement by Paul, the subsequent verses contain many non-Pauline traits: (a) ὑπὲρ τῶν ἁμαρτιῶν ἡμῶν: The word ἁμαρτία is used 64 times by Paul; but three of these are in the Pastorals and five more are in quotations from the Old Testament. Of the remaining 56 times, in 50 instances ἁμαρτία is singular and without the genitive case. In those six cases where it is plural or with the genitive, the influence of tradition is to be seen (I Cor. 15:3: kerygmatic influence; I Cor. 15:17: consequence of the kerygma; Gal. 1:4: Christological formula; Rom. 7:5; Eph. 2:1; Col. 1:14: un-Pauline formulations). (b) κατὰ τὰς γραφάς: The expression appears nowhere else in Paul; he always writes καθὼς γέγραπται. (c) ἐγήγερται: The perfect passive of this verb is also found only in vs. 12-14, 16, and 20 as a result of its appearance here in v. 4 and in II Tim. 2:8, which is a pre-Pauline confessional formula. (d) τῇ ἡμέρᾳ τῇ τρίτῃ: The *nachgestellte* ordinal number is unique for Paul in this verse. (e) ὤφθη: The word is found only in I Cor. 15:5-8 and in the confessional formula of I Tim. 3:16. (f) οἱ δώδεκα: Paul always writes οἱ ἀπόστολοι (Gal. 1:19; I Cor. 9:5; II Cor. 11:5; 12:11). To these considerations Conzelmann adds the following:³ (3) Similar formulas are found elsewhere in the New Testament (Mk. 8:13; 9:31; 10:32-34; Acts 10:42; II Tim. 2:8; I Pet. 2:21-25; 3:18-20). (4) The contents of

---

delberg: Carl Winter, 1966), pp. 8-10; Philipp Seidensticker, "Das Antiochenische Glaubensbekenntnis I. Kor. 15, 3-7 im Lichte seiner Traditionsgeschichte," *TGL* 57 (1967): 286-323; Josef Blank, *Paulus und Jesus*, SANT 18 (München: Kösel Verlag, 1968), pp. 133-143; Karl Lehmann, *Auferweckt am dritten Tag nach der Schrift*, QD 38 (Freiburg: Herder, 1968), pp. 68-157; J. Charlot, "The Construction of the Formula in I Corinthians 15, 3-15" (D.Theol. dissertation, Universität München, 1968); Jacob Kremer, *Das älteste Zeugnis von der Auferstehung Christi*, 3rd ed., SBS 17 (Stuttgart: Katholisches Bibelwerk, 1970); Leonhard Goppelt, "Die Auferstehung Jesu: Ihre Wirklichkeit und ihre Wirkung nach I. Kor. 15," in *Der auferstandene Christus und das Heil der Welt* (Witten: Luther-Verlag, 1972), pp. 98-111; Klaus Wengst, *Christologische Formeln und Lieder des Urchristentums*, SNT 7 (Gütersloh: Gerd Mohn, 1972), pp. 92-101; *TRE* (1979), s.v. "Auferstehung Jesu Christi. II/1. Neues Testament," by Paul Hoffmann, pp. 478-497; Jerome Murphy-O'Connor, "Tradition and Redaction in I Cor. 15:3-7," *CBQ* 43 (1981): 582-589.
² Developed through the successive editions, the argument summarized here is from Joachim Jeremias, *Die Abendmahlsworte Jesu*, 4th ed. (Göttingen: Vandenhoeck & Ruprecht, 1967), pp. 95-98. For a discussion of the development of the argument, see Lehmann, *Auferweckt*, pp. 87-113.
³ Hans Conzelmann, *Der erste Brief an die Korinther*, KEKNT 5 (Göttingen: Vandenhoeck & Ruprecht, 1969), p. 296.

these verses are appropriate to a formula. (5) What is cited in these verses exceeds that which needs to be proved, namely the resurrection. Taken together these considerations have persuaded virtually all New Testament scholars that vs. 3-7 do contain a pre-Pauline formula.

THE LENGTH OF THE FORMULA

More disputed has been the exact length of the formula.[4] Everyone agrees that v. 8, in which Paul reports his own vision of Christ, is an addition from the hand of the apostle himself. Bammel's suggestion, on the other hand, that the formula ends at ὤφθη, with no naming of witnesses has also been rejected by virtually all critics.[5] Although this would create a pleasant symmetry between ἐτάφη—ὤφθη, it would leave the formula incomplete, since the indirect object is implied in the verb itself, and would contradict the evidence of Acts that the mention of witnesses was part of the early kerygma.

Most critics hold that the formula ends at v. 6, since there is a definite break in the sentence structure and rhythm. Michaelis does caution that I Cor. 11:25 shows that Paul will break a tradition stylistically;[6] but it is difficult to see the analogy. Dodd asserts that the entire list of witnesses must have been a unity, for Paul says it was common to all missionaries, which was an important point for Paul, since James's followers were his greatest opponents.[7] But this seems to confuse the conditions for Paul's citation of the formula with the conditions for

---

[4] In addition to the entries in note 1, consult Eduard Norden, *Agnostos Theos* (Darmstadt: Wissenschaftliche Buchgesellschaft, 1956), p. 270; Martin Albertz, "Zur Formgeschichte der Auferstehungsberichte," *ZNW* 21 (1922): 259; Ethelbert Stauffer, *Die Theologie des Neuen Testaments* (Stuttgart and Berlin: Kohlhammer, 1941), p. 223; Hermann Strathmann, "Die Stellung des Petrus in der Urkirche," *ZST* 20 (1943): 240-241; Wilhelm Michaelis, *Die Erscheinungen des Auferstandenen* (Basel: Heinrich Majer, 1944), p. 10; Oscar Cullmann, *Die ersten christlichen Glaubensbekenntnisse* (Zürich: Evangelischer Verlag, 1949), p. 18; Walter Schmithals, *Das kirchliche Apostelamt*, FRLANT 81 (Göttingen: Vandenhoeck & Ruprecht, 1961), p. 65; Klaus Wegenast, *Das Verständnis der Tradition bei Paulus und in den Deuteropaulinen*, WMANT 8 (Neukirchen-Vluyn: Neukirchner Verlag, 1962), pp. 54-56; Peter Stuhlmacher, *Das paulinische Evangelium*, FRLANT 95 (Göttingen: Vandenhoeck & Ruprecht, 1968), pp. 268-269; C. F. Evans, *Resurrection and the New Testament*, SBT 12 (London: SCM Press, 1970), pp. 43-47; Reginald H. Fuller, *The Formation of the Resurrection Narratives* (London: SPCK, 1972), p. 11.

[5] Bammel, "Herkunft," pp. 402-403. For a critique, see Schmithals, *Apostelamt*, p. 65; cf. Günter Klein, *Die Zwölf Apostel*, FRLANT 59 (Göttingen: Vandenhoeck & Ruprecht, 1961), p. 40.

[6] Michaelis, *Erscheinungen*, p. 10.

[7] C. H. Dodd, "The Appearances of the Risen Christ: A study in form-criticism of the Gospels," in idem, *More New Testament Studies* (Manchester: Manchester University Press, 1968), p. 125.

the origin of the formula itself. Even if Paul wanted to prove that James's followers preach this gospel, that does not seem to imply that any such motive inspired the authors of the formula itself. And it is doubtful that Paul has Judaizing opponents in mind here when he includes James in the list, for these were not the source of the heresy at Corinth.[8] Besides, in saying all missionaries preach this gospel, Paul undoubtedly did not mean that the same specific names were always mentioned, but just that witnesses were adduced, as in Acts.

More compelling are the arguments of Stuhlmacher for the tradition's extending through v. 7.[9] He maintains that while v. 6b is typically Pauline, v. 6a is unPauline: ἐπάνω is *hapax legomenon* for Paul; ἐφάπαξ is here unPauline, meaning "at once," not "once for all" (as in Rom. 6:10; cf. Heb. 7:27; 9:12; 10:10). In addition to this, "all the apostles" was a pre-Pauline group. Therefore, vs. 3-7 is a tradition interrupted by v. 6b and appended with v. 8. In favor of Stuhlmacher's argument, it can be said that Paul's own understanding of the term "apostle" was quite broad and included himself, so that he would not write in his own terms that Christ appeared to "all the apostles," for this would exclude not only himself, but probably others as well from being apostles.[10] His own formulation would perhaps have qualified the term in some way: Christ appeared to the "first" apostles, or with some other modification. That v. 7 states "all the apostles" seems to indicate a pre-Pauline formulation that probably designated a restricted circle somewhat wider than the Twelve (as in Acts 1:21-23). It is this formulation that Paul quotes, not thinking to exclude himself from being an apostle, but merely from being a member of that early group which all Christian hearers of this familiar formula would recognize and not confuse with Paul's own wider group of latter day apostle-missionaries. It must be kept in mind that although the groups mentioned in this formula are vague to us, to the primitive church they were probably

---

[8] It is true that Schweizer contended that Paul's opponents at Corinth were ultra-conservative, Pharisaic types who believed that only those alive at the Parousia would be ushered into the Messianic age (Albert Schweizer, *Die Mystik des Apostels Paulus* [Tübingen: Mohr, 1930], pp. 92-94). But as Davies observes, Corinth was Gentile in character, and it would be strange to find ultra-conservative Jews there; certainly this is less plausible than alternative explanations of the source of the Corinthian error (W. D. Davies, *Paul and Rabbinic Judaism*, 2nd ed. [London: SPCK, 1965], p. 292).
[9] Stuhlmacher, *Evangelium*, pp. 268-269.
[10] Ironically, this is, I think, the correct implication of Kümmel's argument in Werner Georg Kümmel, *Kirchenbegriff und Geschichtsbewusstsein in der Urgemeinde und bei Jesus*, 2nd ed. (Göttingen: Vandenhoeck & Ruprecht, 1968), p. 6.

quite perspicuous and needed no identification.[11] Thus there would be no thought at all that by citing an appearance to an early, well-known group of "all the apostles," Paul was thereby implying that he and others were not also apostles. And it might be added that if the formula is very old, reaching back to the years before Paul's conversion, then it would be true that when the formula was drafted, Christ had appeared to "all the apostles," for there was as yet no wider circle of Christian missionaries. That was all the apostles there were, and in quoting the formula, Paul does not mean that since that time more have not been added to their ranks, as apostles in the wider sense of "ones sent out." But had Paul formulated this sentence himself, he would perhaps not have said that Christ appeared to *all* the apostles, for that would be manifestly untrue at the time of Paul's writing.

So it could be argued that vs. 6-7 are also part of the traditional formula. But there remains the break between vs. 5 and 6. It is possible that the formula proper extends to v. 6, but that vs. 6-7 also contain traditional material not formulated by Paul, but appended to the formula itself. It seems best to leave the question open and to regard the formula as extending at least through v. 5.

The Geographical Origin of the Formula

Even more disputed is the place of origin of the formula. Traditionally, under the influence of Heitmüller, Bousset, and Dibelius, the material in vs. 3-7 was thought to stem, not out of the Palestinian *Urgemeinde* (Jerusalem) but from a Hellenistic community of believers (like Damascus or Antioch).[12]

But Jeremias almost single-handedly overturned the opinion of New Testament scholarship with his argument for a Palestinian origin of the formula.[13] He argues that the highly semitized Greek of the formula points to a Semitic *Urtext* behind the Greek. In support of this contention, he argues: (1) The structure of the formula is a *parallelismus membrorum*. The first and third lines are longer, have the same construction (verb, closer modification, Scripture proof), have the phrase "according to the Scriptures" at the end, and are followed by a short sentence in-

---

[11] So Stuhlmacher, *Evangelium*, p. 275.
[12] Wilhelm Heitmüller, "Zum Problem Paulus und Jesus," *ZNW* 13 (1912): 331; Wilhelm Bousset, *Kyrios Christos*, 5th ed., FRLANT 4 (Göttingen: Vandenhoeck & Ruprecht, 1965), p. 76; Martin Dibelius, *Die Formgeschichte des Evangeliums*, 2nd ed. (Tübingen: Mohr, 1933), p. 17.
[13] Jeremias, *Abendmahlsworte*, pp. 96-97. For discussion of Jeremias's argument, see Lehmann, *Auferweckt*, pp. 102-113.

troduced by ὅτι, whose function is to secure the reality of the preceding statement. (2) The four-fold ὅτι is Semitic. (3) The absence of all particles except καὶ is Semitic. (4) The avoidance of God's name by the passive ἐγήγερται is Semitic. (5) The Aramaic Κηφᾶς is employed instead of Σίμωνι (Lk. 24:34). The face that Paul often uses Κηφᾶς (Gal. 1:18; 2:9, 11, 14; I Cor. 1:12; 3:22; 9:5) does not count against this, for the formula has already been proved to be pre-Pauline. (6) It is unusual in Greek to have the ordinal number *nachgestellt*, but in Semitic language this is the only possibility. (7) Semitic is the use of ὤφθη instead of ἐφάνη, for this harks back to the Hebrew נראה (Aramaic איתחמי), which has the double meaning "he was seen" or "he appeared." (8) Κηφᾷ stands as the logical subject in the dative case after the passive instead of the expected construction ὑπό + genitive. (9) The wording is independent of the LXX of Isaiah 53, which lacks ὑπὲρ τῶν ἁμαρτιῶν ἡμῶν. Finally, Jeremias adds, the reference in I Cor. 15:11 to the other apostles points to a Palestinian origin of the formula. Moreover, Paul did not himself formulate the kerygma, but it came from Jewish-Christian origins.

When Jeremias broke with the prevailing opinion of a Hellenistic origin for the tradition in vs. 3-7, other critics followed him in droves.[14] Not until 30 years later, in an essay by Conzelmann that threatened to turn the tables once again, was Jeremias's case seriously challenged.[15] Conzelmann first attempts to show that all the factors adduced by Jeremias can be explained on the basis of a semitized Greek text from a Greek-speaking, Jewish-Christian church, without resort to a Semitic *Urtext*. (1) The parallelism only shows the Jewish style of tradition, which characterizes all primitive Christian formulas. (2) The adversative καὶ at the beginning of the third line would be good Greek and may not necessarily be adversative. (3) The avoidance of God's name by the passive says nothing for the *Ursprache* (cf. Mt. 16:21 as a change of Mk. 8:31). (4) Cephas is a translation variant of Lk. 24:34. To say it proves an Aramaic *Urtext* presupposes the exact wording of the formula, which is never given in New Testament formulas; rather

---

[14] Among others, W. G. Kümmel, E. Lichtenstein, J. Gewiess, E. Bammel, F. Hahn, E. Lohse, J. Dupont, O. Cullmann, J. Schmitt, K. H. Schelkle, A. Vögtle, L. Cerfaux, K. H. Rengstorff, H. Grass, P. Winter, H. v. Campenhausen, J. R. Geiselmann, J. Kremer, W. Thüsing, F. Mussner, B. Gerhardsson, J. Roloff, B. Klappert, R. Deichgräber.

[15] Hans Conzelmann, "Zur Analyse der Bekenntnisformel I Kor. 15,3-5," *EvT* 25 (1965): 1-11. Conzelmann's statement of his argument also developed, and I summarize the final form in Conzelmann, *Korinther*, pp. 298-299.

they are variants of the same tradition. (5) The use of ὤφθη rather than ἐφάνη could come from the LXX. It is so used in Greek as well. And it is a kerygmatic word and thus says nothing about the *Ursprache*. (6) The *nachgestellte* ordinal number could come from the LXX (Hos. 6:2). It is also part of Christian tradition (cf. Mk. 10:34-Lk. 18:32; Jn. 2:1; Acts 13:33). (7) In the LXX of Isaiah 53 there is no ὑπέρ, but there is περί, which is closer than the Hebrew מן. The terms ὑπέρ and περί interchange in kerygmatic formulas: Mt. 26:28-Mk. 14:24; cf. I Pet. 3:18 (περί next to ὑπέρ); Heb. 10:26 (περί); I Jn. 2:2 (περί, but in 3:16 ὑπέρ); Tit. 2:14; 3:18 (ὑπέρ). Conzelmann then presents two positive arguments *against* a Semitic *Urtext*: (1) "Christ" as the subject at the beginning of a sentence is, if not impossible, at least unusual in Aramaic. On the other hand, it so occurs in Christian formulas (Gal. 3:13; Heb. 9:11; I Pet. 3:18). It also heads up relative clauses (Rom. 5:6; 6:9; 8:10; 14:15; I Cor. 8:11; 15:12, 14, 17; I Pet. 2:21; cf. Rom. 6:4; 14:9; Gal. 5:1). (2) There is no Aramaic equivalent to the expression "according to the Scriptures." Immediately scholars began to desert from the fold and join Conzelmann.[16]

Jeremias replied to his critics a year later in an important essay.[17] Vielhauer, who had asserted that the anarthrous use of "Messiah" was not customary in Palestinian Judaism, is buried in references from Strack-Billerbeck I.6, Targum, Midrash, Talmud, and Qumran;[18] Jeremias puts particular emphasis on Jn. 4:25: οἶδα ὅτι Μεσσίας ἔρχεται. Against Conzelmann, Jeremias notes that anarthrous משיח is used as the subject at the beginning of a main sentence in b Sanhedrin 98a, of a *nachgestellten* main sentence in b 'Erubin 43b (twice), of a relative clause (like I Cor. 15:3b) in Pesiqtha 149a, and of a conjunctive clause in b Sukka 52a Bar; b Sanhedrin 96b. In response to Conzelmann's other objection to a Semitic *Urtext*, he maintains that κατὰ τὰς γραφάς could be a rendering of כדכתיב ,ככתוב (Yoma 6:2); כמה שכתוב (Midrash Quoheleth 2:8); כשם שכתוב (Genesis R 53 to 21:16). At any rate, the "according to the Scriptures" probably does not belong to

---

[16] Philipp Vielhauer, "Ein Weg zur neutestamentlichen Christologie?" *EvT* 25 (1965): 24-72; Ernst Käsemann, "Konsequente Traditionsgeschichte?" *ZTK* 62 (1965): 137-152.
[17] Joachim Jeremias, "Artikelloses Χριστός, zur Ursprache von I Cor.15, 3b-5," *ZNW* 57 (1966): 211-215; cf. idem, *Abendmahlsworte*, p. 98. Two important earlier discussions include Rengstorff, *Auferstehung*, pp. 129-131; Hahn, *Hoheitstitel*, pp. 208-209.
[18] Tg Song 4.5; 7.4; Tg Hos. 3.5; Midrash Psalms 43:1; b Sukka 52a Bar; CD 12:23-13:1; 14.19; 19.10; 20.1. According to Jeremias both the span and age of these passages indicate a common Palestinian usage of New Testament times.

the earliest formula.[19] Jeremias then reiterates his argument that because the formula was preached by all the apostles, it must go back to the Aramaic or Hebrew languages. On the independence of the formula from the LXX, Jeremias contends the περί in Is. 53:4 changes nothing. Paul's formula is closest to the Targum text (cf. Mk. 14:12's citing Is. 6:9-10 in paraphrase). Jeremias points out that Rom. 4:25 παρεδόθη διὰ τὰ παραπτώματα ἡμῶν corresponds exactly to Tg Is. 53:5b אתמסר בְּחוֹבָנָא. This could also stand behind the rendering in I Cor. 15:3. Jeremias concludes that there are indications of a Semitic *Urtext* or at least of a Semitic *Urgestalt* (a more modest conclusion than that of *Abendmahlsworte*).

Berthold Klappert also sought to support Jeremias's case.[20] He argues that Rom. 4:25 cannot stem from LXX Is. 53:12 because the word order is reversed (διὰ τὰς ἁμαρτίας αὐτῶν παρεδόθη) and the LXX has αὐτῶν not ἡμῶν while παραπτώματα is altogether lacking. I Cor. 15:3 and Rom. 4:25 are probably translation variants of the same passage: Tg Is. 53:5ab. If Gal. 1:4 is also a translation of this passage, then this would support this conclusion. The words ὑπέρ and διά are alternate translations of ב. In response to Conzelmann's argument on the interchangeability of ὑπέρ and περί, Klappert notes that Mt. 26:28 has to do with a peculiarity of Matthew who has ὑπέρ + genitive only one time (5:44), but περί 20 times. While περί is often substituted for ὑπέρ the reverse is not the case. Only in late writings does περί ἁμαρτιῶν occur (I Pet. 3:18; Heb. 10:26; I Jn. 2:2). Turning to the argument concerning the placement of the ordinal number, Klappert rejoins that it is illegitimate to appeal to New Testament texts for τῇ ἡμέρᾳ τῇ τρίτῃ because these have been influenced by the kerygma. In classical Greek the construction does sound harsh.

In a meticulously researched study two years later Ehrhardt Güttgemanns attempted to turn back the force of Jeremias's citations for anarthrous "Messiah."[21] The references given in Strack-Billerbeck span the second to the twelfth centuries and thus do not clearly testify to first century use in Palestine. The references from Targum, the rabbinical writings, and Qumran are not to the point because

---

[19] See also Jeremias, *Abendmahlsworte*, p. 98. He suggests this to be a Hellenistic-Christian addition (Rom. 5:8; cf. I Thess. 5:9-10; II Cor. 5:15; Rom. 5:6; 14:15; I Pet. 3:18; Jn. 11:51; I Cor. 15:4 ~ Lk. 24:34).

[20] Berthold Klappert, "Zur Frage des semitischen oder griechischen Urtextes von I. Kor. XV. 3-5," *NTS* 13 (1966-67): 168-173.

[21] Ehrhardt Güttgemanns, "Χριστός in I. Kor. 15, 3b—Titel oder Eigenname?" *EvT* 28 (1968): 533-554.

either the grammar requires that there be no article or the word "Messiah" does not stand alone as a name, but appears as משיח בר דוד or משיח בר אפרים or משׁיח. The reference to Jn. 4:25 is invalid because it is Greek, and the original language may have been much different. In Jn. 1:41 "Messiah" appears with an article; for John it made no difference, since Messiah is a proper name. Siphre Deuteronomium 1:37 is also invalid because it is citing a fixed formula of the word "Messiah" with the word "come."

Güttgemanns concludes that: (1) over half of Jeremias's examples are anarthrous due to linguistic necessities, while others are non-Palestinian or too late; (2) there is no genuine use of משׁיח as a proper name; (3) there is no contemporary parallel to I Cor. 15:3; (4) the stereotyped use of משׁיח with אתא is no parallel to I Cor. 15:3; and (5) since Paul understands Χριστός as a personal name (I Cor. 15:12), it is questionable that the formula is a translation of a Semitic original.

Güttgemanns's conclusions were, however, questioned by Ina Plein, who argued that the "bar Ephraim" is determined by "Messiah," and so one would expect "Messiah" to be determined as well by an article.[22] Jeremias agrees with her that expressions like "son of David" ought to be understood as appositions and the passages are thus valid instances of anarthrous "Messiah."[23] He also points out that Number R 13-17:13 is a Palestinian use, and he then furnishes three additional texts (b Baba Bathra 75b; b Sanhedrin 97a; b Sanhedrin 93b). He concludes that use of משׁיח without the article was widespread in Palestine and that it is therefore no surprise that the pre-Pauline, Greek speaking church should use the anarthrous Χριστός.

The result of this debate appears to be that the opponents have each effectively criticized their opposition's viewpoint without being able to establish their own. Thus, Jeremias was forced to hedge on so many of his original points that the case for a Semitic *Urtext* no longer appears compelling. For example, in asserting that κατὰ τὰς γραφάς may be a loose rendering of the Aramaic original, he gives up any literal translation of a Semitic *Urtext*. But then the distinction between a Semitized Greek text as posited by Conzelmann and a loose Greek rendering of a

---

[22] Ina Plein, "Hinweise," *EvT* 29 (1960): 222-223. See also the reply by Ehrhardt Güttgemanns, "Hinweise," *EvT* 29 (1969): 675-676.
[23] Joachim Jeremias, "Nochmals: Artikelloses Χριστὸς in I Cor. 15, 3," *ZNW* 60 (1969): 214-219.

Semitic *Urtext* or even *Urgestalt* becomes fuzzy indeed. It would seem to make it virtually impossible to weigh the significance of the various Semitisms listed by Jeremias. The appeal to Tg Is. 53:5 is also not very compelling when one reads the context of the two words which are supposed to have been extracted: it concerns the temple whose destruction was the result of Israel's sins—it has nothing to do with death for sins or atonement whatsoever.[24] It is not impossible that this text afforded the words used in the formula, but one doubts whether the LXX Is. 53:12 is not equally as likely. While Klappert is certainly correct in rejecting Conzelmann's parallels for τῇ ἡμέρᾳ τῇ τρίτῃ within the New Testament, this does not nullify the point that the expression is a common Septuagintism and in conjunction with "according to the Scriptures" could very well reflect the LXX rendering of such a text.

On the other hand, the arguments against a Semitic *Urtext* appear to be no more compelling. Jeremias has succeeded in showing that Palestinian anarthrous use of משיח cannot be ruled out; this is all he must do to neutralize the objection. Güttgemanns's treatment of Jn. 4:25 seems also inadequate: the very fact that the Greek could be different from the original language is surely precisely the point. If John could translate the Aramaic into Greek with or without the article, then the absence of the article in I Cor. 15:3 ought to be no problem. In this sense, I think the hunt for an anarthrous משיח seems to be rather beside the point. The real question would appear to be whether משיח with the article could be translated into anarthrous Χριστός. Güttgemanns dismisses John's anarthrous Χριστός because it is for John a personal name; Conzelmann similarly states that in I Cor. 15 "Christ" is more a personal name, rather than the title "Messiah." But now the objection loses all force. For if John and Paul use anarthrous Χριστός as a personal name, then the reason that Jewish parallels are so hard to find is that the Jews probably did not use משיח as a personal name. Now if the formula in I Cor. 15 has a Semitic *Urtext*, then either those who drafted the formula understood משיח as a personal name or not. If they did, then the anarthrous Χριστός reflects such usage. But if they did not, then *ex hypothesi* at least the *translators* of the formula did so, and they have translated משיח with the article by Χριστός without the article. So whether the original formula understood משיח as a name or as a

---

[24] A point made by Conzelmann, *Korinther*, p. 299; Wengst, *Formeln*, p. 100; Stuhlmacher, *Evangelium*, p. 272.

title, those who translated it into Greek, since they understood Χριστός as a name, rendered it without the article. It cannot be urged that the translators were too early to know Χριστός as a name, for if the formula does not have a Semitic *Urtext*, then the persons I have called translators were properly authors and on this view did know Χριστός as a name. Hence, whether the original Aramaic formulators took משיח as a name or a title, writing it with or without the article, the point is that the Hellenistic translators of the formula understood Χριστός as a name and so translated it without the Greek article. If one wishes to deny that Χριστός in I Cor. 15:3 is a personal name, but rather a title, then again the objection is lost, since as a title it would properly translate משיח with the article. Thus it seems to me that wholly apart from Jewish references to anarthrous משיח—indeed, on the above account, we ought *not* to expect them—, the presence of Χριστός without the article in the formula says nothing against a Semitic *Urtext*.

As for Conzelmann's second objection, that "according to the Scriptures" has no Semitic parallel, all this would seem to prove is that the Greek translators have not given a literal, word for word translation but have rendered one of the Semitic expressions noted by Jeremias by a Greek equivalent. In saying this, however, one cannot avoid the problem that a free Greek rendering of a Semitic formula is virtually indistinguishable from one formulated in Semitized Greek. Wengst concludes that "...from linguistic considerations at hand no decision over the original language of the formula in I Cor. 15:3b-5 can be reached,"[25] and this judgment seems quite reasonable. It ought to be noted, too, that the presupposition of this entire debate on both sides is that the primitive Jerusalem church could not itself have drafted a formula *in Greek*—a presupposition which according to Stuhlmacher needs to be revised.[26] Thus, linguistic considerations alone cannot, it seems, determine the place of origin of the formula.

But now the question must arise whether there are nonlinguistic considerations which might prompt one to incline toward a specific place of origin for the formula. The question here is not the *Ursprache*, but rather the *Urgestalt* of the formula. What was almost an afterthought in Jeremias's case ought now to be more seriously considered: the fact that in I Cor. 15:11 Paul states that all the apostles preach this kerygma seems to point to Jerusalem as the place of origin of the for-

---

[25] Wengst, *Formeln*, pp. 99-100.
[26] Stuhlmacher, *Evangelium*, p. 272.

mula.[27] For when Paul speaks here of the apostles he undoubtedly includes Peter and the Twelve (and perhaps implicitly Jesus's brothers; cf. I Cor. 9:5), and for them to preach this kerygma, it seems that it must have stemmed originally out of Jerusalem.

This appears to be confirmed by more recent research establishing the Judaeo-Christian traditions behind the sermons in Acts.[28] The primitive *Schema* that lies behind the missionary speeches is the same as the *Urgestalt* of I Cor. 15:3-5. Writes Wilckens: "The formula of I Cor. 15:3f on the one hand and the kerygma of the speeches of Acts on the other hand presuppose a similar pattern (*ein gleichartiges Schema*) that stems out of the tradition of the passion and Easter reports."[29] Such a *Schema* could only have arisen in Palestine, not in a Hellenistic community, and thus points to Jerusalem as the place of origin of the formula.

According to Grass, Paul probably received the formula in Damascus immediately after his conversion.[30] For we know that three years after his conversion, Paul visited Jerusalem, where he met personally Peter and James (Gal. 1:18-19). It is unthinkable, says Grass, that the resurrection of the Lord would not have been a subject of discussion. Paul would thus have received at that time the information in vs. 6-7 which he appends to the formula at v. 5. Because he mentions both Cephas and James, we may assume personal contact behind these references. Paul probably received the formula mentioning the appearances to Peter and the Twelve in Damascus shortly after his conversion before he got to know Peter personally, and he doubtlessly served in missionary work both in Arabia and Damascus. In his later work he held on to the formula which he had received and did not replace it with a self-formulated expression, as he could have after his visit with Peter. The opposite is more improbable, that he would replace personal information from Peter during the visit to Jerusalem with a formula that first came to him later (in Antioch).

---

[27] Interestingly, it is the age of the formula and this consideration that swing Lehmann in favor of a Jerusalem origin of the formula (Lehmann, *Auferweckt*, pp. 112, 131). So also Fuller, *Formation*, pp. 10-11.
[28] See notes 67 and 75. This undermines the position of Hoffmann, who relies on Haenchen and the early Wilckens to hold that the Acts sermons are essentially Lukan constructions (*TRE*, s.v. "Auferstehung," p. 479).
[29] Ulrich Wilckens, *Die Missionsreden der Apostelgeschichte*, 3rd ed., WMANT 5 (Neukirchen-Vluyn: Neukirchner Verlag, 1974), p. 199.
[30] Grass, *Ostergeschehen*, p. 95.

Grass's reasoning makes good sense. It does seem likely that during his Jerusalem visit Paul would have spoken with Peter about Jesus's resurrection. One thinks of Dodd's famous quip, "We may presume that they did not spend all their time talking about the weather."[31] As a matter of fact, the very word used by Paul to describe this visit confirms this assumption: ἰστορῆσαι, used only here in the New Testament, is generally used elsewhere to designate fact-finding missions to well-known cities and other points of interest with a view toward acquiring first-hand information about them. Accordingly, it implies that Paul's visit to Cephas and Jerusalem was for the purpose of gaining information about the faith from first-hand witnesses.[32] But he may well have received the formula in Damascus prior to this visit. Since Paul says that he was in Damascus for three years after his conversion, he most likely received as a young Christian instruction in the faith during that time, and such a formula would be suitable for that purpose as well as for preaching the gospel.[33] It might be thought that this contradicts Paul's statement concerning the gospel which he preached: "For I did not receive it from man, nor was I taught it, but it came through a revelation of Jesus Christ" (Gal. 1:12). But the context of the verse makes it clear that "Paul's gospel" was the gospel of grace apart from the law (Gal. 1:6-9; 2:2-10, 14, 16) and does not exclude his learning the historical facts contained in the formula from persons older in Christ than him. In fact it is difficult to imagine Paul's not receiving at least the contents of this formula soon after his conversion, and, as Grass observes, had he not received the formula itself before or at least during the Jerusalem visit, it is difficult to imagine his adopting it later as a veteran preacher. This would seem to point to a Palestinian origin of the basic formula.

Finally, I think one other consideration weighs in favor of an origin of the *Urgestalt* of the formula in Jerusalem. According to Acts, Paul with Barnabas was largely responsible for grounding and teaching the church in Antioch (Acts 11:25-26), and Paul's activity there with Barnabas is confirmed by Paul's own

---

[31] C. H. Dodd, *The Apostolic Preaching and Its Developments*, 3rd ed. (London: Hodder & Stoughton, 1967), p. 26.

[32] G. D. Kilpatrick, "Galatians 1:18 ἰστορῆσαι κηφᾶν," in *New Testament Essays in Memory of Thomas Walter Manson*, ed. A. J. B. Higgins (Manchester: Manchester University Press, 1959), pp. 144-149.

[33] The fact that the formula may be catechetical (Stuhlmacher, *Evangelium*, p. 274; Wilckens, *Missionsreden*, pp. 195-200) is not mutually exclusive with its being a kerygmatic summary as well (C. K. Barrett, *A Commentary on the First Epistle to the Corinthians*, BNTC [London: Adam & Charles Black, 1968], p. 337).

testimony (Gal. 2:11, 13). But if this is so, then Paul could not have *received* (παρέλαβον, a word which denotes the reception of a prior tradition; cf. I Cor. 11:23; II Thess. 3:6) the formula from the church at Antioch, for he himself was the person responsible for the catechesis there. Given his role in the church, he would have been the one to have drafted the formula. But we have already seen that the formula is replete with un-Pauline characteristics. Therefore, it must have been drawn up beforehand elsewhere than Antioch.[34] Once again, we are drawn back to Jerusalem.

The solution that may best account for the data would be that the *Urgestalt* of the formula stems out of the mother church in Jerusalem and that Paul, after his conversion, received the formula itself as it was used in Damascus. This would satisfy the linguistic demands of both Jeremias and Conzelmann as well as the non-linguistic probabilities discussed. This conclusion is, of course, far from certain, but seems nevertheless the most plausible account of the matter.

PAUL'S PURPOSE IN CITING THE FORMULA

Why does Paul cite this formula in I Cor. 15? He states that he wants to remind the Corinthians of the content of the gospel which he preached to them (v. 1). The reason for this reminder is that some of the Corinthians were maintaining "...there is no resurrection of the dead" (v. 12). Paul saw that the logic of such a statement would imply that Christ himself did not rise from the dead, which would make the Christian faith a sham. If, however, Christ rose from the dead, then the general statement is false. The crux of Paul's argument, therefore, is to show that Christ did rise from the dead (v. 20). For this purpose, he cites the formula, which culminates in Jesus's resurrection and appearances, and adds his own comment in v. 6b, the appearance to himself in v. 8, and perhaps the appearances in vs. 6-7. Pannenberg draws attention to the fact that the method employed by Greek historians, such as Herodotus, in proving a historical event was the naming of witnesses, a method which Paul follows here.[35] With regard to Paul's com-

---

[34] This consideration militates against the view of Hoffmann that the formula reflects the Antiochian-Syrian missionary preaching which allegedly combined the simple formula "God raised Jesus from the dead" with the confession to Christ and the appearance of the Son of Man (*TRE*, s.v. "Auferstehung," pp. 485-489).
[35] Wolfhart Pannenberg, "Ist Jesus wirklich auferstanden?" in *Ist Jesus wirklich auferstanden? Geistliche Woche für Südwestdeutschland der Evang. Akademie Mannheim von 16. bis 23. Februar 1964* (Karlsruhe: Evangelische Akademie Mannheim, 1964), p. 24.

ment in v. 6a, Dodd observes, "There can hardly be any purpose in mentioning the fact that most of the 500 are still alive, unless Paul is saying, in effect, 'the witnesses are there to be questioned.'"[36] In short, Paul seems to be arguing historically for the resurrection of Jesus. "The intention of this enumeration is clearly to give proof by means of witnesses to the facticity of Jesus' resurrection," concludes Pannenberg; "...one will hardly be able to call into question Paul's intention of giving a convincing historical proof by the standards of that time..."[37]

Conzelmann's objection that Paul cannot be trying to prove the resurrection since the Corinthians already accepted the authority and content of the formula (vs. 1-2, 13)[38] misses the point. Of course, he is not now trying for the first time to convince the Corinthians of Jesus's resurrection, but he is *reviewing* the evidence which underlies the crucial assertion of v. 20. Weiss also appears to misunderstand Paul's argument, declaring it to be purely *ad hominem*: if Christ is not raised, then our faith is in vain; but this cannot be affirmed because our experience is too real.[39] Though Paul does draw out the disastrous consequences of de-

---

[36] Dodd, "Appearances," p. 128. Cf. Berthold Klappert, "Einleitung," in *Diskussion um Kreuz und Auferstehung*, ed. idem (Wuppertal: Aussaat Verlag, 1971), p. 10; Murphy-O'Connor, "Tradition and Redaction," p. 586.

[37] Wolfhart Pannenberg, *Jesus: God and Man*, trans. L. L. Wilkins and D. A. Priebe (London: SCM Press, 1968), p. 89. Cf. Trilling's judgment: "This entire testimony aims to establish the cause of Easter faith: Jesus has proven and shown himself to be alive" (Wolfgang Trilling, *Fragen zur Geschichtlichkeit Jesu* [Düsseldorf: Patmos Verlag, 1966], p. 153).

[38] Conzelmann, *Korintherbrief*, pp. 294-295, 313. Conzelmann asserts that because the credo is accepted in Corinth, Paul does not want to prove Christ is risen, but to draw out the meaning of "from the dead" (Ibid., p. 295). But Paul never does draw out the meaning of this phrase, which is not even found in the formula: the "from the dead" plays no special role in Paul's argument. It is the fact that Christ is risen that makes the difference and provides the key to the argument (I Cor. 15:20), for if he is risen, we shall rise also. The fact that Christ is risen is supported by the testimonial evidence of vs. 5-7. If Paul does not want to prove the resurrection, then why does he continue to pile up witnesses in vs. 6, 7 after the formula ends in v. 5? Conzelmann thinks the extra names are not listed as evidence for the resurrection because that would contradict vs. 12ff. There Paul argues "If..., then..." because the Corinthians accept the resurrection of Christ. This is no *formallogische Konsequenzmacherei*. The point is to show that the resurrection is temporally removed from us, as is the Parousia, and that we live in the *Zwischenzeit* (Ibid., pp. 304, 314). But it seems to me that the feared contradiction is imaginary. The "if..., then..." argumentation spells out the disastrous consequences of the Corinthian error; but the evidence of vs. 5-7 secures the fact of v. 20. Therefore, the disastrous results will not follow. The naming of extra witnesses is thus important to secure v. 20; but it would not be necessary to prove we live in the *Zwischenzeit*—Paul could have stopped the list at the 500 brethren in order to make that point.

[39] Johannes Weiss, *Der erste Korintherbrief*, 9th ed., KEKNT 5 (Göttingen: Vandenhoeck & Ruprecht, 1910), p. 355.

nying Christ's resurrection,[40] perhaps to bring home the gravity of just what the Corinthians were asserting, he does not then argue, "But our experience is too real...." Rather he states, "But in fact Christ has been raised from the dead..." (v. 20). He appeals, not to subjective experience, but to historical fact. On Weiss's view there would seem to be no reason to cite the formula at all; the chapter could have begun at v. 12. The logic of Paul's argument and his insertions and additions to the formula make it likely that he is recounting the historical testimony for the resurrection of Jesus in order to undergird his statement that Christ has been raised.

That this understanding of the passage is probably correct is reinforced, I think, by the famous Barth-Bultmann debate over I Corinthians 15.[41] Barth asserted, "...it must be emphasized that *neither* for Paul *nor* for the tradition, to which we see him appealing here, was it a question of giving...a 'historical proof of the resurrection.'"[42] The expression "according to the Scriptures" twice repeated would have no meaning in a historical proof. The "he was seen" is connected to the "he rose again" by "and," not "then," as would be the case if the passage aimed at historical demonstration. The most serious objection to the historical interpretation is that the historical fact of Jesus's resurrection, if it occurred, is according to verse 13 dependent upon the general resurrection of the dead. Barth asks incredulously, "What kind of historical fact is that reality of which (*sic*), ...is bound up in the most express manner with the perception of a general truth, which by its nature cannot emerge in history...?"[43] The point of the passage is actually to demonstrate the continuity of Paul's preaching with that of the primitive church.[44] Paul adduces the witnesses "*not* to confirm the fact of the resurrection of Jesus, not for that purpose at all, but to confirm that the foundation of the Church, so far as the eye can see, can be traced back to nothing else than appearances of the

---

[40] Chiefly three in number: (1) Christian faith would be in vain and we should still be in our sins, (2) the apostles would be liars, and (3) Christian loved ones who have died would be no more (cf. I Thess. 4:13-18).
[41] For an analysis, see Manfred Kwiran, *The Resurrection of the Dead*, TD 8 (Basel: Friedrich Reinhardt Kommissionsverlag, 1972), pp. 235-325; Adriaan Geense, *Auferstehung und Offenbarung*, FSOT 27 (Göttingen: Vandenhoeck & Ruprecht, 1971), pp. 13-33.
[42] Karl Barth, *The Resurrection of the Dead*, trans. H. J. Stenning (London: Hodder & Stoughton, 1933), p. 138. "Verses 5-7 have nothing whatever to do with supplying a historical proof..." (Ibid., p. 150).
[43] Ibid., p. 140.
[44] Ibid., p. 147.

risen Christ."[45] Barth means by "appearances," not optical phenomena, but the incomprehensible revelation of Christ.[46] Paul's mention of the 500, most of whom were still alive though some had died, was intended to show that though some of these men who had seen the Lord nevertheless died, the ultimate victory over death would be won through Christ's resurrection.

Bultmann responded that Barth's interpretation of I Cor. 15:1-11 was simply false exegesis.[47] In the mind of Paul and the whole Christian community, a historical account would be the more meaningful if it were "in accordance with the Scriptures." And since Paul also accepted the final resurrection of the dead as a historical event, the truth of Christ's resurrection could be said to depend on the fact of the resurrection of the dead. That Christ's appearances were localized is evident from the expressions "most of whom are still alive" and "last of all" (I Cor. 15:6, 7). Says Bultmann, "I can understand the text only as an attempt to make the resurrection of Christ credible as an objective historical fact."[48] Although Bultmann characterizes such historical argumentation as "fatal" because it tries to adduce proof for the kerygma,[49] he acknowledges that Paul does "think he can guarantee the resurrection of Christ as an objective fact by listing the witnesses who had seen him risen."[50]

---

[45] Ibid., pp. 150-151.
[46] Ibid., pp. 146-147. "Of what these eyes see it can really be equally said that it was, is, and will be, never and nowhere, as that it was, is, and will be, always and everywhere possible" (Ibid., p. 143).
[47] Rudolf Bultmann, *Faith and Understanding I*, 6th ed., trans. L. P. Smith, ed. with an Introduction by Robert W. Funk, Library of Philosophy and Theology (London: SCM Press, 1969), pp. 83-84.
[48] Ibid., p. 83.
[49] Rudolf Bultmann, "Reply to the Theses of J. Schniewind," in *Kerygma and Myth*, 2 vols., ed. H. W. Bartsch, trans. R. H. Fuller (London: SPCK, 1953), 1:112.
[50] Rudolf Bultmann, *Theologie des Neuen Testaments*, 7th ed., ed. Otto Merk (Tübingen: J. C. B. Mohr, 1961), p. 295; cf. p. 305. Referring specifically to Acts 17:31 and I Cor. 15:3-8, he admits, "Yet it cannot be denied that the resurrection of Jesus is often used in the New Testament as a miraculous proof" (Rudolf Bultmann, "New Testament and Mythology," in *Kerygma and Myth*, 1:39). The post-Bultmannian James M. Robinson disagrees: "...Paul explicitly recognized the rejection of such signs as inherent in the existential meaning of the *kerygma* (I Cor. 1:17-25)" (James M. Robinson, *A New Quest of the Historical Jesus*, BT 25 [London: SCM Press, 1959], p. 51). When Paul does discuss the signs legitimizing himself in II Cor. 10-13, he begins by listing the facts which demonstrate his superiority—"but all under the admission 'I am speaking as a fool,' *i.e.*, such a method is contrary to the *kerygma*"; but then he shifts to speaking of his humiliation, the only Christian way of speaking of one's self (Ibid). But Paul in no way rejects legitimizing signs for the kerygma and in fact appeals to them as its factual foundation. In I Cor. 1:17-2:13, Paul is not denying that his preaching has either miraculous attestation or wisdom; rather he is rejecting the ability of the natural man to reach God by his own religious or intellectual efforts

More recently, however, R. H. Fuller has resupported Barth's position.[51] He acknowledges that Paul uses the list of witnesses as evidence. But they are cited as proof, not of the resurrection, but of the appearances. Paul proves the appearances to show that his gospel is identical with the original disciples', who, the Corinthians insisted, preached a gospel with no future resurrection (I Cor. 1:12; 3:4).

But Fuller's distinction between appearances and resurrection seems to be artificial. The witnesses are cited as proof for the appearances—and *thereby* for the resurrection. Once it is known that a man "died" and "was buried," what better way to prove that he "was raised" than by adducing reliable testimony that he "appeared" alive to people after his death (cf. Acts 1:3)? Thus, in Acts to be a witness of the *appearances* is bluntly said to be a witness of the *resurrection* itself (Acts 2:32; 3:15; 5:30-32). Moreover, Paul's primary aim does not seem to be to show continuity with the disciples' doctrine, a tangential truth which appears only incidentally in v. 11. Paul's foremost aim appears to be a refutation of the Corinthian heresy by a step-by-step argument. His first point is to remind the Corinthians of the content of the gospel preached to them by Paul. Then from v.12 he proceeds to show that the content of this preaching would be false if the dead were not raised. If the content of the preaching is false, then all sorts of rueful consequences follow, with the final result that we are of all men most to be pitied. But the content of the preaching *is* true: "But in fact Christ has been raised from the dead" (I Cor. 15:20); therefore, the dead are raised: "...the first fruits of those

---

(cf. I Cor. 3:18-21). To the eye of unregenerate man the simple gospel of faith appears to be foolishness, and the notion of a crucified Messiah is a stumbling block. Nevertheless it is true, and Paul does not "dress it up" in any way to make it appear more respectable. But this does not mean Paul will not argue for its truth (cf. Acts 17:16-34) nor adduce signs on its behalf (I Cor. 15:3-8). Indeed in the very passage in question, Paul says that his preaching was "in demonstration of the Spirit and power" (I Cor. 2:4), which were the apostolic miracles: "The signs of a true apostle were performed among you in all patience, with signs and wonders and mighty works" (II Cor. 12:12; notice he says this after speaking of his humiliation). Robinson's assertion that Paul's interjection "I am speaking as a fool" means that the method of legitimizing signs is contrary to the kerygma seems groundless; Paul simply recognizes that self-centered boasting of one's own worth is contrary to the "meekness and gentleness of Christ" (II Cor. 10:1-2) and therefore to Christian character (II Cor. 10:12, 18; 12:11). But furnishing signs to legitimate the truth of the content of preaching has nothing to do with selfish boasting (as I Cor. 1:31-2:5 shows) and is not at all opposed to humility. Look at Paul's juxtaposition of the two: "Last of all, as to one untimely born, he appeared also to me. For I am the least of the apostles, unfit to be called an apostle, because I persecuted the church of God" (I Cor. 15:8, 9). Indeed the legitimation of the kerygma by Jesus's resurrection focuses the attention on *God's* act: "...we testified of God that he raised Christ..." (I Cor. 15:15b). Robinson seems to be guilty of reading his existentialist kerygma into, rather than out of, Paul.

[51] Fuller, *Formation*, pp. 28-30.

who have fallen asleep. For as by a man came death, by a man has come also the resurrection from the dead" (I Cor. 15:20b-21). Therefore, the rueful consequences do not follow either (I Cor. 15:22-28).[52] It is in establishing that the content of the preaching is not false (= Christ has been raised) that harks back to verses 5-8; it is the historical evidence for this fact upon which the entire argument depends. Hence, Paul is probably citing these witnesses as evidence for the resurrection.[53] Finally, there seems to be no evidence that the Corinthians believed that the other apostles preached no future resurrection. The bickering church described in the first chapter is so factional (with even Paul and Jesus parties) that the problems are probably not reducible to the rather black-and-white issue of whether the dead are raised. The source of the Corinthian heresy most likely lies in Greek secularism, not apostolic proclamation. The evidence, therefore, does not seem to support Fuller's exegesis, which appears to have been affected by the same theological assumption that inspired Barth's, namely, that the resurrection "is not an event within history."[54]

So whether we regard it as fatal or not, it seems that Paul, as Bultmann admitted, is arguing for the historicity of the resurrection in I Cor. 15. Dodd has drawn an interesting comparison between the gospels and Paul on this count: both wish to provide historical evidence to the resurrection, the gospels by appealing to corporate apostolic testimony, Paul by focusing on the availability of individuals to be questioned.[55]

---

[52] It might be said that Paul commits a logical fallacy in concluding that the rueful consequences do not follow, but this would be to treat his argument unsympathetically. His argument is logically equivalent to saying: if the car has an engine, it will run; the car does not have an engine; therefore, it will not run—technically fallacious, but hardly offensive in ordinary discourse. Conzelmann emphasizes that for Paul, Christ's resurrection was not an isolated fact but is causally connected with our personal resurrection. Hence, the Corinthians could not even have objected that Christ was an exception to the general rule that the dead do not rise (Conzelmann, *Korintherbrief*, pp. 313-314). Thus, implicit in Paul's reasoning is the assumption that if Christ is raised, then his redemptive work on our behalf is efficacious.

[53] On the logic of Paul's argument, see Archibald Robertson and Alfred Plummer, *First Epistle of Saint Paul to the Corinthians*, 2nd ed., ICC (Edinburgh: T&T Clark, 1967), p. 346; Ernst-Bernard Allo, *Première Épître aux Corinthiens* (Paris: Librairie Lecoffre, 1934), p. 401; Hans Lietzmann, *An die Korinther I, II*, 4th ed., rev. Werner Georg Kümmel, HNT 9 (Tübingen: J. C. B. Mohr, 1949), p. 79. Contrast Marxsen's misunderstanding of the argument (Willi Marxsen, *The Resurrection of Jesus of Nazareth*, trans. Margaret Kohl [London: SCM Press, 1970], pp. 108-109). I cannot recommend the various writings of T. G. Bucher on Paul's logic, though he agrees that Paul is arguing syllogistically here.

[54] Fuller, *Formation*, p. 23.

[55] Dodd, "Appearances," pp. 127-128.

The Unity and Tradition History of the Formula

So far we have assumed that the formula is a unity. Paul presents it as such, as a transmitted summary of the central points of the apostolic kerygma (vs. 1, 11, 12, 14, 15). The issue is important because if the formula is a unity, it is therefore probable that the adduction of witnesses for the resurrection was part and parcel of the earliest proclamation of the gospel. Fuller, however, has disputed that the kerygma entailed the naming of witnesses.[56] Drawing attention to the repetition of ὅτι before each of the four main statements in I Cor. 15:3-7, he, in dependence on Wilckens,[57] believes that ὅτι serves the function of modern quotation marks. Usually ὅτι is regarded simply as typical of credal formulas, but, according to Fuller, in the only multiple example of this (I Thess. 4:13-17) the three occurrences of ὅτι combine quite separate elements (a credal formula in 4:13, a dominical logion in 4:15, and an apocalyptic elaboration in 4:16) and therefore are used as quotation marks to combine *different* traditions. From this Fuller believes it follows that in I Cor. 15 we also have four different traditions combined by ὅτι. The first three statements summarize basic incidents in the act of salvation, whereas the fourth validates the third. The Semitized Greek suggests Damascus as the origin of the first three; the mention of Cephas and James suggests that Paul received the fourth while visiting Jerusalem. Thus the first three formulas are kerygmatic and catechetical, while the fourth consists of information gathered by Paul. The upshot of this is that the appearances formed no part of the primitive kerygma or catechesis. The earliest church did not prove the reality of the resurrection from appearances; it simply affirmed it kerygmatically (I Thess. 1:9). Paul began the use of witnesses as evidence.

Now a deductive chain of reasoning is only as strong as its weakest link, and Fuller's argument seems to me strained in many points: (1) Wilckens has shown only the possibility, by no means the necessity, of taking ὅτι as serving the function of quotation marks in I Thess. 4:13-17. As Lehmann has observed, ὅτι serves so many different functions that it is extremely questionable whether one may infer very much from its multiple occurrence.[58] He suggests that it would be better to leave the question open than to embrace interpretations which are very

---

[56] Fuller, *Formation*, pp. 13-14.
[57] Wilckens, "Ursprung," pp. 56-95; idem, *Missionsreden*, pp. 74-80.
[58] Lehmann, *Auferweckt*, pp. 73-77.

difficult to prove but which carry with them decisive consequences. Certainly Wilckens and Fuller seem to be guilty in this sense of trying to rest a pyramid on its point. (2) Neither Wilckens nor Fuller has justified the subsequent application, much less the probability, of the function of ὅτι in question to I Cor. 15:3-8. If the combination of quite separate elements is the criterion for discerning this function of ὅτι, then I Cor. 15:3-8 ought, it seems, to be ruled out, since we have here a smooth chronological and historical sequence of related events of a common subject, Χριστός (I Cor. 15:3). To support the weight of the conclusions he draws from the function of ὅτι in these verses, Fuller would need to demonstrate a strong probability that the ὅτι here combines originally disjointed elements, which has not been done.[59] The four-fold ὅτι in I Cor. 15:3-8 may well be intended, as Kramer and Mussner have suggested, simply to emphasize the equal importance of each successive event. Embarrassing for Fuller is that in his third edition of *Missionsreden*, Wilckens declared himself convinced that this interpretation is correct.[60] (3) The first three formulas cannot be convincingly placed over against the fourth as salvific, for in no sense can the burial of Christ be called a basic incident in the event of salvation (cf. Rom 4:24-25). Unlike the crucifixion and resurrection, it has no redemptive significance, certainly no more than the appearances so as to exclude the latter. (4) The names James and Cephas do not suffice to prove that the fourth statement was not also used in Damascus. They only show that the formula could be no *later* than Paul's Jerusalem visit, since then he would have heard from Cephas and James themselves what took place. It seems naive to think that the content of the first three formulas could be delivered to the believers in Damascus without mentioning the names of Jesus's disciples or that, given the free flow of information among the primitive Christian churches (Acts 9:13; Gal. 1:22-23), these two leaders of the Jerusalem church could remain

---

[59] We can agree with Hoffmann that the expression "God raised Jesus from the dead" (Acts 13:30; Rom. 4:24; 8:11; 10:9; I Cor. 15:15; Gal. 1:1; Col. 2:12; I Pet. 1:21, *etc.*) was an independent formula widespread in the early church, but there is no hard evidence that the formula of I Cor. 15:3-5 represents a significant evolution of such a formula or of baptismal formulas such as are found in Rom. 6. (*TRE*, s.v. "Auferstehung," pp. 479-489). There is just no reason to believe that a multiplicity of such formulated ways of speaking could not have been used simultaneously, just as they are so used by the New Testament writers. Hoffmann's evolutionary thesis entails giving the formula in I Cor. 15:3-5 a late date and a non-Palestinian origin and holding the abbreviated kerygma in I Thess. 1:9-10 to have been a different kerygma from the Jewish-Christian proclamation, both of which are implausible, as I argue in the text.

[60] Wilckens, *Missionsreden*, p. 228.

unknown in Damascus. (5) It seems highly unlikely that the formulas ever existed separately, for no conceivable function could be served by the bald statement "He was buried" in isolation from the other statements. While one could imagine the first and third, and even the fourth, formula existing alone, Fuller's hypothesis seems to founder on what Barth called the "unambiguous banal historical fact" "that he was buried."[61] It seems more plausible that the early church formulated a tradition that related in smooth succession the principal events of Jesus's death and resurrection, just as Paul delivers it, with all the events interconnected and complementary. (6) The remainder of the New Testament evidence indicates that the primitive church did not simply preach the resurrection without adducing the testimony of witnesses. I Thess. 1:9 does contain kerygmatic traces (as is evident from comparing it with Acts 14:15-17; 17:22-31),[62] but does not pretend to be a complete kerygmatic summary, since then the death of Christ would also have to be excluded from the kerygma. (7) A severe difficulty for Fuller's argument seems to be the fact that the formula far overreaches what Paul wants to prove in I Cor. 15, namely, the resurrection. If the formula contains four separate elements, then it is difficult to explain why Paul bothers to cite the first two at all, since they are extraneous to his argument. That Paul recites the whole formula, despite the fact that it overreaches his purpose, is a strong indication that the formula was received by Paul as a unity. Together these considerations make it likely, I think, that the formula is a unity and that the apostolic preaching did include the naming of witnesses. It is important to remember that what Paul says in I Cor. 15:3-8 is a *reminder* of what he preached to the Corinthians on his missionary tour which took him through Thessolonica, Athens, and Corinth. There is no reason to doubt his word that the gospel that he, like the other apostles, preached in all these cities included the fact that "he appeared to Cephas, then to the twelve...."

Wilckens himself pursued a somewhat different line of reasoning than Fuller.[63] As we have seen, he took the fourfold ὅτι as an indication of separate traditions. But he further argues that the appearance formula itself is not a unity, but a fusion of principally two legitimation formulas sanctioning the authority of the leaders of

---

[61] Barth, *Resurrection*, p. 142. So also Conzelmann, *Korintherbrief*, p. 301; Wengst, *Formeln*, p. 93.
[62] This is developed by Wilckens, *Missionsreden*, pp. 86-88; idem, "Ursprung," pp. 58-59.
[63] Wilckens, *Missionsreden*, pp. 73-81; idem, "Ursprung," pp. 70-81; idem, *Auferstehung*, pp. 26, 29.

the church. The appearance to the 500 did not belong to the original formula because it alone contains the words ἐπάνω and ἐφάπαξ, is less exact in content, and cannot be confirmed through comparison with other material. That leaves two parallel sets of appearances, each containing an appearance to an individual and then to a group. Since this obvious pattern is not likely to be chronological, Wilckens thinks that we have here two independent traditions, which probably arose consecutively as a historical description of the leadership of the Jerusalem church. Paul has brought these originally independent formulas together. The upshot of this is that the naming of witnesses was not, therefore, part of the early kerygma: "Thus the appearances were handed down, not really as *witnesses to the resurrection*, but much more as *legitimations* of the men who, because of their divine commission, had standing authority in the church."[64] Wilckens analyzes I Cor. 15:3-7 into six separate levels of (I) kerygmatic tradition and (II) catechetical tradition:

Ia.	I Cor. 15:3	formula on Christ's substitutionary death for our sins plus proof-text
b.	15:4a	mention of the burial
c.	15:4b	missionary preaching formula constituting the central point
IId.	15:5	oldest legitimation formula for Peter as the leader
e.	15:6	Paul's own summary of the legend of the founding of the first church
f.	15:7	legitimation formula from a somewhat later time when James was the leader

But Wilckens's argument, it seems to me, fares no better than Fuller's. (1) For it, too, appears to stand on the pebble of the fourfold ὅτι, and once this is removed

---

[64] Wilckens, *Auferstehung*, p. 147. Pesch, in dependence on Wilckens, takes a similar line (Rudolf Pesch, "Zur Entstehung des Glaubens an die Auferstehung Jesu," *TQ* 153 [1973]: 211-215). He objects that to allow multiple appearances runs contrary to the principle of economy of revelation (*offenbarungsökonomische "Sparsamkeitsprinzip"*). Rather I Cor. 15:3-5 is a legitimation formula and the early kerygma did not entail naming of witnesses. Even the "he appeared to Peter" cannot be taken as a vision, since this is merely a legitimation formula. It is hard to believe that Pesch thinks *a priori* principles on the economy of revelation can actually dictate what did and did not happen. The only value which such principles could have would be as generalizations based on, not imposed on, empirical facts. Pesch also assumes that legitimation and witness are mutually exclusive categories; the truth would seem to be that legitimation presupposes witness, as Hengel observes: "Only because Cephas or 'the Twelve' really experienced something extraordinary, because Jesus 'encountered' them as the risen one, could they thereby derive a legitimation..." (Martin Hengel, "Ist der Osterglaube noch zu retten?" *TQ* 153 [1973]: 264). Even Hoffmann, who stands very much under the influence of Wilckens and Pesch, is very sceptical about analyzing the form and use of the formula in terms of legitimation (*TRE*, s.v. "Auferstehung," p. 491-493).

the whole structure topples. With Wilckens's afore-mentioned repudiation of his earlier interpretation, points a–d in the analysis must all belong to the same formula, so that at least the appearances to Peter and the Twelve belonged to the kerygmatic tradition. The truth seems to be that in this context, the appearances were regarded primarily as authentications of the resurrection and only secondarily as legitimations of the men who saw them. After all, why were these men "legitimated?" Was it not precisely because they were witnesses? As Stuhlmacher points out, if one wishes to speak of legitimation, then one must say that they were legitimated and established as *witnesses* to the risen Lord.[65] (2) Wilckens may well be correct that the 500 brethren did not belong to the original formula, but his arguments for this are not convincing: (a) the mention of "more than" and "at one time" provides no clue of the appearance's not belonging to the formula, especially when one considers that the appearance to the apostles includes πᾶσιν; (b) to say this appearance is less exact than the others, especially the vaguely characterized group mentioned last, seems unwarranted; (c) neither can the appearance to James or all the apostles be definitely confirmed through comparison. (3) Paul seems to go to great lengths to spell out the chronological sequence of appearances. The appearances follow the chronological pattern of the death, burial, and resurrection of Christ and are guided by the pattern εἶτα...ἔπειτα...ἔπειτα...εἶτα and conclude with ἔσχατον δὲ πάντων. Paul apparently holds these appearances to be strictly chronological.[66] Now when we keep firmly in mind the astounding fact, at which we cease to wonder because of its familiarity, that we have here the testimony of a man who actually talked with Jesus's brother and one of his principal disciples, both of whom claimed to have personally seen Jesus risen again from the dead, during a two-week period in Jerusalem about six years after the event, then it must become clear that Paul makes no mistake here with regard to the succession of events. The order is intended to be chronological, and a theoretical discernment of patterns seems insufficient to overthrow this conclusion. But this undermines the legitimation theory: (a) For the only rationale for such a theory seems to be the perception of the individual/group pattern in the appearances. But it is possible that the mention of James

---

[65] Peter Stuhlmacher, "'Kritischer müssten mir die Historisch-Kritischen Sein!'" *TQ* 153 (1973): 250, in reply to Pesch, "Entstehung", p. 215.
[66] So von Campenhausen, "Ablauf," p. 11.

and the apostles could stem, like that of the 500 brethren, from single bits of information which Paul arranged chronologically. Any pattern could well be either simply fortuitous or the result of intentionally leaving out other single bits of information, such as the appearance to the women. (b) But what is especially troublesome for Wilckens's theory is that Paul says, *last of all to me*. For this means that the appearances to James and the apostles occurred before Paul's conversion, that is, *before* James became prominent (cf. Acts 8:14; 12:17b; Gal 1:19; 2:1, 9) and *before* any later body not comprised principally of the first apostles could arise and assume their name. (4) The age of the formula militates against its being a historical description of the leadership of the Jerusalem church. When Paul visited Jerusalem and spoke with Cephas, James was there. Fourteen years later he had become with Peter and John one of three pillars of the church (Gal. 2:1, 9). Even then he does not appear to be the sole leader of the church. But this takes us practically right up to the time of writing of I Corinthians. Since Paul's formula is probably very old, the notion of a legitimation formula for James is difficult since the formula threatens to ante-date James's ascension to power. Indeed, if Grass is correct that the formula can be no later than Paul's first visit, then a historical description of the church's leadership is simply excluded. To this may be added that if the formula is a late legitimation formula, it seems to become impossible to identify any group associated with James that could be called "all the apostles." That this is a later body of missionaries looking to James for authority is purely speculative; against it counts the consideration that the church would not be likely to lend much credibility to a supposed appearance so many years distant from the originals. (5) It needs to be asked whether the notion of a legitimation formula has sufficient basis in historical reality but is not rather a modern notion. In the early church not everyone who saw a resurrection appearance was invested with authority (the 500 brethren) and not everyone who was called an apostle had seen an appearance (Andronicus and Junias [Rom. 16:7], Barnabas [I Cor. 9:5, 6]). John and Luke are strikingly in accord in stating that a disciple belonged to the apostles, not so much because he had seen the risen Jesus, but because he had been with Jesus *from the beginning* (Jn. 15:27; Acts 1:21, 22). Paul did not explicitly ground his apostleship in the fact that Jesus had appeared to him, but rather that Jesus had *commissioned* him through this appearance (Rom. 1:1-5; 15:15, 16; I Cor. 1:1; 3:10; 9:1, 2, 16, 17; 15:8-11; II Cor. 1:1; 2:17; 5:18; Gal.

1:1; 2:15-16; Col. 1:1, 23-25; I Thess. 2:4-6; cf. Eph. 3:7-8). For Paul, apostleship was a spiritual gift (I Cor. 12:28; cf. Eph. 4:11), which was confirmed by signs and wonders (Rom. 15:19; II Cor. 12:12). In justifying his apostleship he usually appeals to his labors and sufferings, not just to the fact that he had seen an appearance of Christ (I Cor. 15:8-10; II Cor. 11:1-12:13). All this seems to make it at least questionable whether so-called legitimation formulas based on who had seen an appearance of Christ ever existed. The concept of legitimation and authority in the early church seems to have been much more complex than that.

In view of these considerations, the interpretation of the formula as a fusion of separate kerygmatic formulas plus legitimation formulas seems very dubious. That the formula is both a unity and a faithful summary of apostolic preaching, including the adduction of witnesses, is confirmed by its concordance with Luke's reconstructions of the apostolic sermons in Acts.[67] It is extremely instructive to

---

[67] The problem of the accuracy of Luke's reconstruction of the kerygma is still very hotly debated. (For histories of the problem consult A. J. Matill, Jr., "Luke as a Historian in Criticism since 1840" [Ph.D. Dissertation, Vanderbilt University, 1959]; W. Ward Gasque, *A History of the Criticism of the Acts of the Apostles*, BGBE 17 [Tübingen: Mohr 1975].) Martin Kähler was one of the first researchers who sought to demonstrate that the words of Peter's speeches were not Lukan but went back to a Palestinian origin (Martin Kähler, "Die Reden des Petrus in der Apostelgeschichte," *TSK* 46 [1873] pp. 492-536). C. C. Torrey championed the thesis that the first fifteen chapters of Acts are so filled with Aramaisms that it is probable that Luke has simply translated an early document into Greek and then added the final chapters himself (C. C. Torrey, *Composition and Date of Acts*, HTS 1 [Cambridge, Mass.: Harvard University Press, 1916]). J. de Zwaan critically reviewed Torrey's thesis and, although finding it exaggerated, did conclude that Torrey had a strong case for Acts 1-5:16 and 9:31-11:18 (J. de Zwaan, "The Use of the Greek Language in Acts," in *The Beginnings of Christianity*, Part I: *The Acts of the Apostles*, ed. F. J. Foakes Jackson & Kirsopp Lake [London: Macmillan & Co., 1922], II: 44-65). C. H. Dodd concluded that the Petrine speeches are based on material from the Aramaic-speaking church at Jerusalem. He observes that in Acts 10 the Greek is "notoriously rough and ungrammatical," "scarcely translatable," but when translated back into Aramaic becomes "grammatical and perspicuous;" therefore the speech to Cornelius is probably a translation of an Aramaic original and represents the "form of the kerygma used by the primitive church in its earliest approaches to a wider public" (Dodd, *Apostolic Preaching*, p. 26). Meanwhile Martin Dibelius had drawn attention to the primitive Christology of the speeches and to their harmony with Paul's summary of the kerygma as evidence of their great age. He argued that the earliest kerygma included an account of Jesus's life, sufferings, and resurrection, mostly under the emphasis of the disciples' role as witnesses (*meist unter Betonung der Zeugenschaft der Jünger*). He believed that not only the outline, but even core sentences of the kerygma, such as in I Cor. 15, were at Luke's disposal (M. Dibelius, *Die Formgeschichte des Evangeliums*, 3rd ed. [Tübingen: Mohr, 1959], pp. 12-18; M. Dibelius, *Aufsätze zur Apostelgeschichte*, ed. H. Greeven, FRLANT 60 [Göttingen: Vandenhoeck & Ruprecht, 1953], p. 142). The arguments of Dodd and Dibelius still constitute the principal case for the historical authenticity of the speeches of Acts: (1) the abundant Semitisms, (2) the primitive Christology, and (3) the harmony with the Pauline kerygma. Each of these questions is contested: (1) Critics of the Aramaic source theory contend that the Semitisms of Acts are really Septuagintisms, *i.e.*, expressions borrowed by Luke from the LXX to give the speeches an intentionally authentic coloring (H.

survey the development of Wilckens's assessment of this question. He first attempted to drive a wedge between the kerygma of I Cor. 15 and that of Acts: (1) Paul's kerygma stresses that Christ died "for our sins," while Acts sees Jesus's death merely as the Jews' evil mishandling of Jesus; (2) Paul has "Christ," not "Jesus" as the subject of the kerygma; (3) Paul makes no mention of the sufferings of Christ; (4) Paul recounts no life of Jesus in the kerygma; (5) what is "according to the Scriptures" is different: for Acts it is the fact, but for Paul it is the meaning of the fact; (6) Paul mentions "on the third day," a phrase found only in Acts 10, probably under the influence of a formula such as Paul's; and (7) Luke knows only the formula of the appearance to Peter (Lk. 24:34) in isolation from the others. Thus, it cannot be said that I Cor. 15 and Acts mutually confirm one another as to the content of the early preaching. In fact, in I Thess. 1 and Heb. 6 Wilckens finds a totally different kerygma; the only common element is the resur-

---

F. D. Sparks, "The Semitisms in Acts," *JTS* ns 1 [1950]: 16-28; Ernst Haenchen, "Schriftzitate und Textüberlieferung in der Apostelgeschichte," *ZTK* 51 [1954]: 153-167; Ernst Haenchen, *The Acts of the Apostles*, 14th ed.; trans. B. Noble, G. Shinn, and R. McL. Wilson [Oxford: Basil Blackwell, 1971], pp. 73-77). The question cannot be pronounced settled, for scholars remain divided on the problem: Grässer makes the interesting observation that the issue of Aramaisms in Acts is handled in Anglo-Saxon research with as great an optimism as it is in German research with scepticism (Erich Grässer, "Acta-Forschung seit 1960," *TRu* 41 [1976]: 181)! For the most outstanding work on the problem, consult Max Wilcox, *The Semitisms of Acts* (Oxford: Clarendon Press, 1965). (2) Wilckens has argued vigorously that the so-called primitive Christology of the speeches is really Luke's own, although Luke may occasionally use a traditional title to his own purposes (Wilckens, *Missionsreden*, 3rd ed., pp. 156-178, 237-240; cf. C. F. Evans, "The Kerygma," *JTS* ns 7 [1956]: 25-41). The majority of scholars, however, do see in the speeches evidence of an early christological tradition. (For a critique of Wilckens and Evans, see John A. T. Robinson, "The Most Primitive Christology of All?" *JTS* ns 7 [1956]: 177-189; Jacques Dupont, "Les discours missionaires des Actes des Apôtres d'après un ouvrage recent," *RB* 69 [1962]: 37-60.) This would tend to support the antiquity of the tradition in the speeches. (3) Wilckens has also attempted to sharply differentiate the Pauline kerygma from that of Acts (Wilckens, *Missionsreden*, pp. 72-81). So influential has Wilckens's argument been that Haenchen took it for granted that "Ulrich Wilckens...has proved against Dibelius and Dodd that Peter's speeches in the first part of Acts do not contain any old pattern of Jewish-Christian missionary preaching" (Haenchen, *Acts*, pp. 129-130). But in the third edition of *Missionsreden* Wilckens did an about face and took back all his objections to Dibelius's thesis, thus leaving Haenchen without a perch to roost on (Wilckens, *Missionsreden*, p. 1951). Nor is he alone in this, according to Grässer, "Acta-Forschung seit 1960," *TRu* 42 [1977]: 50. Stuhlmacher, for example, has argued that Acts 10 is not simply Luke's own gospel but follows a pattern of presentation (*Darbietungsschema*) that grows out of the same tradition as I Cor. 15 (Stuhlmacher, *Evangelium*, pp. 297-298). Bovon also researches the speech to Cornelius and finds a Christian kerygmatic tradition for a Jewish audience (François Bovon, "Tradition et rédaction en Actes 10.1-11.18" *TZ* 26 [1970]: 42), as does Burchard (Christoph Burchard, *Der dreizehnte Zeuge*, FRLANT 103 [Göttingen: Vandenhoeck & Ruprecht, 1970], p. 139). As a result of these and other studies, it seems fair to say that the weight of the evidence supports the Dodd/Dibelius thesis that Luke has accurately reproduced the substance of primitive Christian preaching.

rection, but even it has a different meaning: in I Thess. it is the ground for Jesus's coming again as Savior. This other kerygma is duplicated in Acts 14 and 17 and consists in (1) a call to the true God from lesser gods, (2) God's overlooking the past of ignorance, and (3) the resurrection as the basis for Jesus's coming as Judge. If this represents the true kerygmatic tradition, then it at once raises the question whether the type of preaching prior to Acts 14 is not then simply Luke's own invention. Wilckens answers in the affirmative. He contends, in dependence on Conzelmann's conception of Luke's program, that Luke's theological purpose is to ground the church age in the time of Jesus, and he does this through the instrumentality of eyewitnesses. Thus, the schema of the Jewish-Christian preaching is Lukan.[68]

> The theory of the twelve apostles as 'witnesses' directly commissioned by the Risen One in virtue of extensive eyewitness experience is conceived by Luke himself; the generalizing mention of the appearances, through which the witnesses are legitimized in salvation history, is also Lukan.
> ...*The apostolic speeches of the Acts are in an outstanding way summaries of his theological conception; they cannot be valued as witnesses of old or especially the oldest primitive Christian theology, but of Lukan theology of the expiring first century.*[69]

Now several of Wilckens's premises in this series of deductions need to be seriously questioned.

1. That the differences he discerns between the kerygma of I Cor. 15 and that of Acts are rather exaggerated and artificial seems evident. For example, difference (2) seems to be trivial, and (3) and (4) cannot be rigidly assumed because of the summary character of the formula cited by Paul. Difference (5) has more substance; but it seems doubtful that Paul's second reference to "according to the Scriptures" explicates the meaning and not the event of the resurrection (contrast Rom. 4:25), and it is not clear that the first reference does not also include the event of the death as well as its meaning. Meanwhile, in Acts it is sometimes the meaning of an event that is clarified by the Scriptures (Acts 2:34-36; 10:43; 13:33). Difference (6) appears to be question-begging, since both I Cor. 15 and Acts 10 could reflect an element of the primitive kerygma. Difference (7) shows only that Luke did not have a story to go with the appearance to Peter and, therefore, quotes only the kerygmatic exclamation. But he did have a story about the appearance to the Twelve and so is independent of the kerygma at this point. The

---

[68] Wilckens, *Missionsreden*, pp. 72-100.
[69] Ibid., pp. 150, 186.

order of events and appearances in Luke and I Cor. 15 are harmonious. This leaves difference (1), which seems to be really the major discrepancy between I Cor. 15 and Acts. Two things may be said here: (a) There can be no doubt that the kerygma did include Christ's dying "for our sins," for (i) the very age of the formula shows that this doctrine was held in the early church, (ii) this is a theme that is widespread in the New Testament and not of Pauline origin (Rom. 3:25; 5:9; Eph. 1:7; Col. 1:20; Heb. 9:12; 10:19; I Pet. 1:19; Rev. 1:5; 5:9), and (iii) otherwise we should have no choice but to say that Paul was quite simply lying when he asserts that this gospel is preached by all the apostles and was received by him and was approved by the Jerusalem apostles (Gal. 2:2, 9; this included the substitutionary death of Christ as the basis of breaking down the wall of partition between Jew and Gentile). (b) Luke does give hints of the death of Christ "for our sins," most obviously in the account of the Lord's Supper and in Acts 20:28 (interestingly a Pauline speech), which even Haenchen admits echoes the doctrine of vicarious atonement.[70] The Christological title "Servant" may reflect Is. 53, from which this doctrine could be inferred (cf. Acts 8:32-35). Indeed, the Acts speeches inevitably include an offer of forgiveness of sins through Jesus (Acts 2:38; 3:19; 4:12; 5:31; 10:43; 13:38-39), so that this doctrine may lie just beneath the surface. The difference between the kerygma of Acts and I Cor. 15 may therefore be simply one of emphasis; it alone cannot overturn the conclusion that Luke and Paul seem to be remarkably compatible in their representation of the early kerygma.

2. The "totally different" kerygmatic tradition inferred from I Thess. 1 and Heb. 6 may well be a different cast of the same kerygma. Heb. 6 is so sketchy that no kerygmatic reconstruction is feasible; I Thess. 1 and Acts 14 and 17 appear to represent a form of the kerygma appropriate to a Gentile pagan audience. It is noteworthy that the resurrection still plays the central role. Wilckens's assertion that its meaning has changed seems rather exaggerated: in the Gentile preaching the resurrection remains God's decisive act of vindication of Jesus, and even in the Jewish speeches, the magisterial and apocalyptical elements are clearly present (Acts 3:20-21; 10:42). There is no justification in taking the Jewish preaching as a Lukan invention and the Gentile preaching as the genuine kerygmatic tradition. Rather these represent different methods of *approach*, suited to the au-

---

[70] Haenchen, *Acts*, p. 92.

dience to be addressed. (Thus, there appears to be no reason to believe that Paul could not have given a speech like that of Acts 13 as well as that of Acts 17. Indeed, the correlation between the former speech and I Cor. 15 is astonishing: every element of the formula is *explicitly* mentioned except the "for our sins," and this seems implicit in Acts 13:38. That Paul was also familiar with the kerygmatic approach of the Jews' mishandling of Jesus is evident from I Thess. 2:14-15.)

3. Because Wilckens's interpretation of Luke's emphasis on eyewitnesses is dependent upon Conzelmann's construction of Luke's understanding of history, insofar as Conzelmann's construction succumbs to criticism, Wilckens's interpretation is undermined. Even Haenchen, who accepts Conzelmann's "*Mitte der Zeit*" construction, rebukes Wilckens for reading too much theory of history into Luke's work; a mighty arch of God's saving plan stretches from Abraham to the Parousia—"…there is no deep caesura between the time of Jesus and that which follows."[71]

4. The decisive consideration against Wilckens's interpretation, however, may be that the emphasis on witnesses is not at all exclusive Lukan property.[72] That the Twelve apostles are not a Lukan construction erected to serve as official witnesses is secured by Rev. 21:14, as well as Mk. 6:7, 30; Mt. 10:1, 2, 5, 19.[73] We have already seen Paul's use of confirmatory witnesses in preaching the resurrection. John also has an emphasis on witnesses nearly as great as Luke's. Gerald O'Collins underscores this point well:

> Luke and John…clearly interpret the post-Easter encounters of these witnesses as different in principle from experiences of the risen Lord which later Christians might enjoy. Luke represents Christ as ascending into heaven…. The events of the forty days (in which the risen Lord met, spoke and ate with that privileged group) differed fundamentally from all later encounters. John also carefully discriminates other Christians from those disciples to whom the risen Christ appeared. Thomas came to belief when he saw the Lord. His road to faith differed from that of later Christians…. the official witnesses to the resurrection did not enjoy some privileged form of faith. But they played a unique role in testifying to the 'signs,' so that others might 'believe that Jesus is the Christ, the

---

[71] Ibid., p. 132.
[72] See the outstanding work on this subject by Allison A. Trites, *The New Testament Concept of Witness*, SNT 31 (Cambridge: Cambridge University Press, 1977). Trites particularly emphasizes the accord between Luke and John on the role of the apostolic eyewitnesses in grounding faith.
[73] Cf. Haenchen, *Acts*, pp. 124-125.

Son of God' (John 20:29-31).... John invites those 'who have not seen' to believe in reliance on eye-witness testimony.[74]

This invitation is especially clear in I John, which in the Muratorian canon follows directly upon John as a postscript (while II and III John appear much later): "That...which we have seen with our eyes, which we have looked upon and touched with our hands, ...that which we have seen and heard we proclaim also to you..." (I Jn. 1:1, 3). There are many remarkable parallels between John and Luke with respect to the resurrection, and this mutual emphasis on eyewitness testimony as evidence is one of the most noteworthy. We also find the same concern in II Pet. 1:16: "For we did not follow cleverly devised myths when we made known to you the power and coming of our Lord Jesus Christ, but we were eyewitnesses of his majesty." Thus it seems quite clear that Luke did not—out of any motive, theological or otherwise—invent the theory of the disciples as witnesses to the resurrection. Rather what Paul and Luke affirm seems to be in fact the case: that the original apostolic preaching really did include as an important element the appeal to eyewitness testimony as historical evidence for the resurrection.

Most interesting is that in his third edition of *Missionsreden* Wilckens surrendered his case. Under the influence of O. H. Steck's investigation of Old Testament Jewish preaching,[75] Wilckens concedes that the kerygmatic outline of the Acts speeches is not Lukan, but belongs to Jewish-Christian tradition.[76] The speeches directed to the Gentiles are created from a broad Hellenistic-Jewish tradition of apologetic-missionary activity to pagans that goes back to the oldest time of Hellenistic missionary work, since Paul refers to it.[77] The speeches to the Jews, which Wilckens formerly ascribed to the creative hand of Luke, are now acknowledged to stem from the early traditions underlying I Cor. 15.[78] The seven differences between the kerygma of Acts and I Cor. 15 now, says Wilckens, really resolve into only one: Paul sees saving significance in Christ's death, while Luke regards it as the last abuse of the Jews' maltreatment of Jesus. But this tension, says Wilckens, may be explained as a result of the *Sitz im Leben*: for Paul the

---

[74] Gerald O'Collins, *The Easter Jesus*, 2nd ed. (London: Darton, Longman & Todd, 1980), p. 80.
[75] O. H. Steck, *Israel und das gewaltsame Geschick der Propheten*, WMANT 23 (Neukirchen-Vluyn: Neukirchner Verlag, 1967).
[76] Wilckens, *Missionsreden*, p. 3.
[77] Ibid., pp. 190-193.
[78] Ibid., pp. 193-200.

catechetical viewpoint of the salvific meaning of Jesus's death; for Luke the tradition, also found in the gospels, of the course of events of the passion and resurrection, showing the contrast between the Jews' mistreatment and God's vindication of Jesus. The firm conclusion is that I Cor. 15 and the kerygma of Acts presuppose a similar outline, which stems out of the passion and Easter reports, which is then filled out according to the respective *Sitz im Leben*. But more than that: in dependence on Steck, Wilckens proceeds to argue that Luke's employment of this material in the context of the Acts speeches is not his own, but reproduces the Christianized form of Jewish preaching.[79] "*Luke did not himself construct the pattern of the apostolic preaching addressed to the Jews as such, but took it over from the tradition of Jewish, Deuteronomic repentance preaching as mediated by the Christians.*"[80] This being the case, there seems to be no grounds left for denying that the mention of confirmatory witnesses to the resurrection was an integral part of the earliest Christian preaching. If Paul and Luke represent twin developments of the same tradition, and despite their differences in emphasis concerning the meaning of the events, they both testify that the apostolic preaching climaxed in the proclamation of the resurrection confirmed by eyewitnesses, then we seem to have no reason to doubt the authenticity of this feature of the primitive kerygma.

It seems, therefore, that we ought to regard the formula both as a unified piece of tradition and as an accurate presentation of the apostolic preaching. "Jesus is in fact risen from the dead, *because after his death he 'appeared' to definite witnesses*. That is the post-Easter argument of the Christian community," concludes Mussner.[81]

THE STRUCTURE OF THE FORMULA

Looking now at the formula as a whole, we have already noted its structure in terms of a *parallelismus membrorum*. But a word of caution is in order here. A great number of critics assert—often without argument—that the second and fourth lines of the formula are subordinated to the first and third lines and so serve

---

[79] Ibid., pp. 200-208.
[80] Ibid., p. 205.
[81] Franz Mussner, *Die Auferstehung Jesu*, BE 7 (München: Kösel Verlag, 1969), p. 58.

to underscore them or provide confirmation of the fact stated therein.[82] Inevitably such authors have the formula printed with the second and fourth lines indented underneath the first and third lines—it is no wonder that they appear to be *zugeordnet*! But this manner of exhibiting the formula biases the issue in advance; initially the formula ought to be printed simply in a line or, if in four lines, with the left margin even. When this is done, it is not so obvious that the second and fourth statements are meant to be subordinated.

It may be said that the first and third lines are parallel in construction and likewise the second and third lines; but this only shows parallelism, not logical subordination. It may be urged that the second and fourth lines are both short; but this is misleading, since the fourth is longer than the second (especially if the formula includes vs. 6a and 7) and at any rate only shows parallelism, not subordination. It is sometimes asserted that the existence of shorter, and presumably earlier, formulas consisting of only the first and third lines (Rom. 4:25) proves the second and fourth lines are later subordinated additions. At the most, however, this only proves that the second and fourth lines are later insertions perhaps of less *importance* that the first and third, but not that they are *logically subordinated* to them. And it needs to be seriously called into question whether "shorter" implies "earlier," especially given the probably very great age of the formula in I Cor. 15. It could be that various formulas were simultaneously in circulation or even that a shorter formula is an abbreviation of a longer. Which formula an author cites could be a matter of appropriateness in his context. If this is the case, then it is incorrect to say even that the second and fourth lines are later insertions. There appears to be nothing in the structure of the formula itself that suggests that the second and fourth lines are subordinated to the first and third.

In fact, the structure of the formula seems to count positively against it. I have reference here to the fourfold repetition of ὅτι before each event mentioned in the

---

[82] Harnack, *Verklärungsgeschichte*, p. 64; Lichtenstein, "Glaubensformel," pp. 7-8; Eduard Lohse, *Märtyrer und Gottesknecht* (Göttingen: Vandenhoeck & Ruprecht, 1955), p. 115; Rengstorff, *Auferstehung*, pp. 51-52; Grass, *Ostergeschehen*, p. 146; Conzelmann, "Analyse," p. 7; Ehrhardt Güttgemanns, *Der leidende Apostel und sein Herr*, FRLANT 90 (Göttingen: Vandenhoeck & Ruprecht, 1966), pp. 262-264; Von Campenhausen, *Ablauf*, p. 21; Hahn, *Hoheitstitel*, pp. 203-204; Jeremias, *Abendmahlsworte*, p. 96; Gerhard Delling, "The Significance of the Resurrection of Jesus for Faith in Jesus Christ," in *The Significance of the Message of the Resurrection for Faith in Jesus Christ*, ed. C. F. D. Moule, SBT 8 (London: SCM, 1968), p. 81; Lehmann, *Auferweckt*, pp. 69, 81; Edward Lynn Bode, *The First Easter Morning*, AB 45 (Rome: Biblical Institute Press, 1970), p. 98; Klappert, "Einleitung," pp. 16, 48; Pesch, "Entstehung," p. 214.

formula. Grammatically, it would have sufficed to place a single ὅτι at the head of the entire formula. But instead we have it repeated: that Christ died...that he was buried...that he was raised...that he appeared. Why this grammatically unnecessary four-fold use? Kramer asserts that it is used by Paul to emphasize the single statements serially.[83] Well and good; although there seems to be no reason to think that the ὅτι is from Paul's own hand. But what does this imply for the notion of subordination? Mussner explains,

> It is apparent therefore that all four statements about the subject Χριστός are significant and no one of them may at the expense of another be weakened or suppressed. The *Paradosis* formula has four important points to make about Christ, and therefore every one is introduced with the conjunction ὅτι. This four-fold ὅτι thus declares the four statements about Christ to be highly significant.[84]

The four-fold ὅτι thus serves the function of marking each statement as being of equal emphasis with the others in the series. This means that the second and fourth statements, being equally emphasized, are not subordinated to the first and third. Wilckens, who once held to the subordination view, writes, "...that the mention of the burial is meant merely to underline the reality of the death, so that death and burial belong closely together..., is excluded because the sentence despite its shortness is given the same, independent weight in the series of statements in the formula as the other three sentences."[85] Hence, the very structure of the formula seems to militate against the view that the shorter lines are subordinated to the longer.

Can considerations of content overthrow the conclusion suggested by structural considerations? This seems doubtful. Many authors assert that the burial is mentioned in close connection with the death in order to underscore it, as if to say Jesus was "dead and buried." But the evidence for this, I think, seems rather artificial. Grass adduces Lk. 16:22 and Acts 2:29 as parallels.[86] But in the first reference it is not apparent that the burial emphasizes the death; indeed, it may contrast the rich man's descent to Hades with Lazarus's ascent to Paradise. And in the second reference the burial clearly is meant to point to David's tomb which

---

[83] Werner Kramer, *Christos, Kyrios, Gottessohn*, ATANT 44 (Stuttgart and Zürich: Zwingli Verlag, 1963), p. 15.
[84] Mussner, *Auferstehung*, pp. 60-61. See also Joseph Schmitt, "Le 'milieu' littéraire de la 'tradition' citée dans I Cor., XV, 3b-5," in *Resurrexit*, ed. Édouard Dhanis (Rome: Liberia Éditrice Vaticana, 1974), p. 178.
[85] Wilckens, *Auferstehung*, p. 20.
[86] Grass, *Ostergeschehen*, p. 146.

is still with us to this day in contrast to Jesus's being raised; far from supporting Grass's view, this could suggest the burial is a *Hinweis auf* the empty tomb. Grass's further Old Testament texts (Gen. 25:8; 35:8; II Chron. 24:16) concerning persons who died and were buried are rather far removed from the formula of I Cor. 15. Grass's own statement that only "for our sins in accordance with the Scriptures" separates ἀπέθανεν καὶ ἐτάφη (he also failed to notice the important καὶ ὅτι) seems to expose sufficiently the artificiality of this purported parallel.

It is also often stated that the second and fourth lines serve as confirmation of the first and third.[87] But the burial does not seem to be mentioned here as evidence for the death in the same way that the appearances are evidence for the resurrection. Conzelmann says Paul wants to prove the death, not indeed for apologetics, but to "present the death as a salvific event."[88] I must confess that this is far too subtle for me. How ἐτάφη alone puts the death in a new light, I cannot see. But Conzelmann raises an interesting question: why *would* Paul want to prove the death? As far as I can see, there is no good reason; therefore, this is probably not his intention.

I think that a much more plausible explanation concerning the ordering of the events is, not that they are logically ordered so that one serves as evidence for another, but that they are chronologically ordered so that one historical event naturally follows another. Is not this a more natural and forthright explanation of why the burial follows the death than that the burial is subordinated to the death as a confirmation? The sequence of events here is simply chronological: Christ died, was buried, rose, and appeared. The order is linear and historical. The advantage of this understanding of the contents of the formula is that it best accords with the structure of the formula; each successive event is, as it were, listed in order: first, second, third, fourth, by the four-fold ὅτι as independent, equally emphasized events. Thus, analysis of both the structure (the four-fold ὅτι) and the content (the chronological sequence) suggests that the second and fourth statements are not to be subordinated to the first and third; the agreement of both structure and content imply that we have here four equally weighty statements describing chronologically successive events.

---

[87] See note 82.
[88] Conzelmann, *Korinther*, p. 301.

CHAPTER 2

THE WITNESSES OF THE RESURRECTION APPEARANCES

Let us now examine more closely the list of witnesses adduced for the appearances.

THE STRUCTURE OF THE LIST

In considering the structure of the list, we ought to dismiss at the outset Harnack's old theory that the list reflects two rival factions in the early church: Peter and the Twelve versus James and the Apostles.[1] The theory has been rightly rejected by all contemporary critics.[2] (1) The chronological order of presentation precludes seeing rival lists in the formula. (2) The parallelism is insufficient ground for the purely speculative theory of leadership contention between Peter and James. (3) There was not sufficient time for the competing lists to arise. (4) James's exclusive prominence in the church was touted only in certain Judaeo-Christian groups of second generation followers and has no applicability to Paul's first hand information during the initial years. The modern offshoot of Harnack's theory, namely, that what we have here are not rival lists, but legitimation formu-

---

[1] Adolf von Harnack, *Die Verklärungsgeschichte Jesu: Der Bericht des Paulus (I Kor. 15, 3ff.) und die beiden Christusvisionen des Petrus*, SBA (Berlin: Walter de Gruyter, 1922), p. 67.
[2] For a critique, see Hans Grass, *Ostergeschehen und Osterberichte*, 4th rev. ed. (Göttingen: Vandenhoeck & Ruprecht, 1970), pp. 96-98; Hans Freiherr von Campenhausen, *Der Ablauf der Osterereignisse und das leere Grab*, 3rd rev. ed., SHA (Heidelberg: Carl Winter, 1966), pp. 10-11; Hans Grass, *Christliche Glaubenslehre*, 2 vols. (Stuttgart: W. Kohlhammer, 1973), 1:102; Reginald H. Fuller, *The Formation of the Resurrection Narratives* (London: SPCK, 1972), p.12-13.

las, has already been criticized. The most plausible view of the list is that it presents a chronological enumeration of separate witnesses.

Most critics today do not seem bothered by the fact that Paul fails to list all the appearances mentioned in the gospels. It is usually pointed out quite correctly that because women were not regarded as legal witnesses their presence in the formula would be not only superfluous, but even counter-productive.[3] Michaelis makes the interesting comment that Paul's intention is not to list all the appearances, but all the witnesses.[4] Even that ought to be qualified, however, for it appears that the tradition names here only the most important witnesses. Although some critics want to assert that Paul intends the list to be complete,[5] there is no evidence for this, and the assertion seems to be unverifiable.

THE APPEARANCE TO PETER

The first appearance listed by Paul is that to Peter. It is ironic that although we have no appearance story to go with this incident, it is nevertheless a well-attested appearance of Jesus, one accepted by even the most skeptical investigators. It is mentioned here in a very old formula cited by a man who could personally vouch for its authenticity. A second reference to this appearance is Lk. 24:34, which contains the cry, "The Lord is risen, indeed, and has appeared to Simon!" Because of the awkward insertion of this verse in the Lukan narrative and its similarity to Paul's "he appeared to Cephas," most critics regard this exclamation as a pre-Lukan kerygmatic tradition which Luke, lacking an accompanying story, has

---

[3] See M. Rosh Ha-Shanah 1.8; M. Shebuoth 4.1; Josephus *Antiquities of the Jews* 4.8.15; Numbers Rabbah 10.159b; T J Yoma 6.2; and references in Paul Billerbeck, *Kommentar zum Neuen Testament aus Talmud und Midrasch*, 6 vols., ed. Hermann L. Strack (München: Beck, 1922-63), 2:441; 3:217, 251, 259. See also Archibald Robertson and Alfred Plummer, *First Epistle of Saint Paul to the Corinthians*, 2nd ed., ICC (Edinburgh: T & T Clarke, 1967), p. 335; Ernst-Bernard Allo, *Première épître aux Corinthiens* (Paris: Librairie Lecoffre, 1934), p. 392; Wilhelm Michaelis, *Die Erscheinungen des Auferstandenen* (Basel: Heinrich Majer, 1944), p. 14; Michael Ramsey, *The Resurrection of Christ* (London: Centenary Press, 1945), p. 42; Ernst Bammel, "Herkunft und Funktion der Traditionselemente in I Kor. 15:1-11," *TZ* 11 (1955): 403; Ethelbert Stauffer, *Jesus and His Story*, trans. D. M. Barton (London: SCM, 1960), p. 124; Joachim Jeremias, *Jerusalem in the Time of Jesus* (London: SCM, 1969), pp. 374-375; J. A. T. Robinson, *The Human Face of God* (London: SCM Press, 1973), p. 132; Josef Blinzler, "Die Grablegung Jesu in historischer Sicht," in *Resurrexit*, ed. Édouard Dhanis (Rome: Libreria Éditrice Vaticana, 1974), p. 67.
[4] Michaelis, *Erscheinungen*, p. 13.
[5] For example, von Campenhausen, *Ablauf*, p. 20.

inserted at this point.⁶ Thus, both Luke and Paul testify to the tradition of an appearance to Peter prior to that to the Twelve. It is very often urged that a third reference to the appearance to Peter is the allusion in Mk. 16:7: "But go, tell his disciples and Peter that he is going before you to Galilee; there you will see him, as he told you." It is thought that Mark must know of an appearance to Peter, otherwise he would not have mentioned his name (cf. Mt. 28:7). This seems, however, a tenuous assumption. The verse does not allude to an appearance to Peter alone, but to a collective body of disciples which may have included the women as well, depending on whether one takes this to be direct or indirect discourse. Peter is not singled out as the one who will see, but as the one to be told. Why should Peter be told in particular? Commentators on Mark usually suggest that this either is a note of reassurance mirroring Peter's denial, or reflects Peter's prominence as leader of the disciples and the church, or is both of these together. Of course, Peter's prominence in the church could be indirect evidence of an appearance to him, but that does not mean Mk. 16:7 refers to an appearance to Peter.

So strange is it that no story of such an important appearance of Jesus should have been handed down that many critics believe that it *must* be there, either in a dislocated narrative or hidden in another resurrection story (Mt. 16:17-19; Mk. 4:35-41; 6:45-52; 9:2-8; Lk. 5:1-11; Jn. 21:1-23).⁷ The problem with such a viewpoint is that most of these narratives are so firmly embedded in their context that no resurrection appearance to Peter is likely to be concealed therein.⁸ But even if we are left without a story of this appearance, we nevertheless possess two apparently early testimonies to Peter's having seen Jesus, as well as Paul's first-hand confirmation.

---

⁶ Stuhlmacher, for example, argues that Lk. 24:34 is equally as old as I Cor. 15:5: (1) the *passivum divinum* is Semitic; (2) the ὁ κύριος is a Palestinian cry, as in Maranatha (I Cor. 16:22; Acts 22:20); (3) Simon is an old Semitic equivalent for Peter. This goes to show, he adds, that this is no simple legitimation formula (Peter Stuhlmacher, "'Kritischer müssten mir die Historisch-Kritischen Sein!'," *TQ* 153 [1973]: 250).

⁷ For example, von Campenhausen, *Ablauf*, pp. 16-17; F. Gils, "Pierre et la foi au Christ ressuscité," *ETL* 38 (1962): 5-43; Oscar Cullmann, *Petrus: Jünger, Apostel, Märtyrer*, (Zürich: Zwingli Verlag, 1952), pp. 62, 202; Raymond E. Brown, *The Gospel According to John*, Anch Bib 29A (Garden City, N. Y.: Doubleday & Co., 1970), pp. 1085-1095; Raymond E. Brown, Karl P. Donfried, and John Reumann, *Saint Pierre dans le Nouveau Testament*, LD 79 (Paris: Les éditions du Cerf, 1974), pp. 141-147, 154-158.

⁸ C. H. Dodd, "The Appearances of the Risen Christ: A study in form-criticism of the Gospels," in idem, *More New Testament Studies* (Manchester: Manchester University Press, 1968), pp. 119-122; Fuller, *Formation*, pp. 160-167; John E. Alsup, *The Post-Resurrection Appearance Stories of the Gospel-Tradition*, CTM A5 (Stuttgart: Calwer Verlag, 1975), pp. 139-144.

Paul's evidence, and Luke's as well, indicates that this appearance was prior to that to the Twelve. Luke places the appearance in Jerusalem, but Paul's formula does not provide any indication of the geographical locale. If the expression "on the third day" is a genuine time indicator, then I should be inclined to agree with Michaelis that the proximity of the resurrection on the third day and of the appearance to Peter in the formula would naturally lead one to expect that the geographical locale is the same, namely, Jerusalem.[9] But, of course, the formula cannot be considered in isolation from the gospels and the Jerusalem/Galilee appearance traditions, the consideration of which would at this point lead us too far astray from I Cor. 15.

At any rate the evidence for an appearance of Jesus to Peter seems quite impressive. Paul's formula, which probably reaches back into the first five years after the crucifixion, mentions it, as does Luke's tradition, which may also be quite old. Paul himself spoke with Peter about six years after the event and vouches for its facticity. At the very least we must say that Peter must have experienced something which he believed was an actual appearance of Jesus; given the brevity of time available plus Paul's personal contact with Peter, it would be infeasible to regard these reports as legends.

The Appearance to the Twelve

The second appearance listed, that to the Twelve, is the best-attested postmortem appearance of Jesus. Not only is it mentioned here in the formula, but we have what are undoubtedly stories of this event in Lk. 24:36-43 and Jn. 20:19-23. It is also related in the longer ending to Mark (16:14-18), but it is disputed whether this represents independent tradition or is simply a catalogue compiled from the other gospels. Luke refers to the group as "the eleven" (Lk. 24:33) and John as "the twelve" (Jn. 20:24), which like Paul's term are clearly technical designations of a certain circle, not merely the number of people present (according to Luke the appearance was to "the eleven gathered together and those who were with them," while John reports, "Now Thomas, one of the twelve, ...was not with them when Jesus came"). Thus the circle of "the Twelve" in Paul's formula and in John corresponds to Luke's circle which he conscientiously calls "the Eleven," since Judas Iscariot had forfeited the apostolic office (Acts 1:20, 25). Luke and

---

[9] Michaelis, *Erscheinungen*, p. 57.

John's narratives of this appearance are generally regarded as independent, and yet their accord in what they relate is striking. There can be little doubt that Luke, John, and Paul's formula all refer to the same event.

More difficult is the relationship of the appearance mentioned in Mark and Matthew. Mark alludes to an appearance to a body of disciples which may have included not only the Twelve, but a number of women disciples as well (Mk. 15:40-41; 16:7), and Matthew briefly relates an appearance on a mountain to "the eleven disciples" (Mt. 28:16). If these are intended to be the same appearance as that which Paul's formula calls the appearance to "the Twelve," a term also used in Mark and less frequently Matthew (Mk. 3:14; 4:10; 6:7; 9:35; 10:32; 11:11; 14:10, 17, 20, 43; Mt. 10:5; 26:14, 47), then we should have further confirmation of this appearance, although the accuracy of the historical circumstances would have to be sacrificed at some points. This confirmation cannot be certain, however, for the presupposition of this identification is that Paul's formula intends to list *all* the appearances, which cannot be taken for granted. Further, if the formula lists witnesses, not appearances, then more than one appearance to the disciples cannot be ruled out. Indeed, both Luke and John insist that there were repeated appearances to the disciples after the initial meeting with the Twelve (Acts 1:3; Jn. 20:26-29; 21:1-14). So I think it best to regard the appearance to the Twelve mentioned in Paul's list as conclusively identical only with the accounts of Luke and John. As to the geographical location of the appearance, Paul gives us no clue, but Luke places it in Jerusalem on the same day as the appearance to Peter, and John is in accord with Luke.

The evidence, therefore, of an appearance of Jesus to the Twelve is even better than that for an appearance to Peter: we have the testimony of the old formula, Paul's personal confirmation through his contact with at least Peter, and independent traditions relating the appearance in at least Luke and John. Once again, it seems very probable that the disciples as a group experienced something which they interpreted as Jesus's being alive from the dead.

THE APPEARANCE TO THE 500 BRETHREN

At this point there is a break in the formula, and a new sentence begins with the astounding assertion that Christ next appeared to over 500 brethren at one time!¹⁰ Again one can only shake one's head in bewilderment that we should apparently possess no story, nor indeed any other mention at all, of so monumental an event. Of all the appearances, this one would seem to be the most difficult to accept historically. Yet here it is in a tradition related confidently by a man who had ample opportunity to confirm its historicity. To make the situation even more amazing, this man adds a personal comment of his own that most of these people are still alive, though some have died. This seems to show that he had personal knowledge concerning individuals who were present at this appearance and that the appearance was not merely hearsay for him nor a meaningless cipher in an ecclesiastical formula. Indeed, we have seen that the purpose of this remark may have been to draw attention to the availability of witnesses to be questioned. It thus seems idle to speak of this appearance as "the legend of the founding of the first church,"¹¹ since Paul personally knew of people who were still about who could relate first-hand the circumstances of this event. He could not have said this if the event had not taken place.

In mentioning that these persons are still living, Paul probably has the intention of strengthening the evidence for the resurrection. The facts of vs. 4-8 provide the groundwork for the assertion of v. 20, and Paul wants to make it as firm as he can. Conzelmann's interpretation that Paul is emphasizing, not that some are *alive* but that some are *dead*, artificially twists a perspicuous verse, as well as violates the context of the argument as a whole.¹² The fact that the brethren are *still* alive (ἕως ἄρτι), despite (δὲ) the fact that some have died shows clearly enough that it is the living witnesses to whom Paul draws attention.

---

¹⁰ The hypothesis that ἐφάπαξ means here "once for all" and that the appearance to the 500 was thus the only historical appearance (Philipp Seidensticker, "Das Antiochenische Glaubensbekenntnis I. Kor. 15,3-7 im Lichte seiner Traditionsgeschichte," *TGL* 57 [1967]: 313-321; idem, *Die Auferstehung Jesu in der Botschaft der Evangelisten*, SBS 26 [Stuttgart: Katholisches Bibelwerk, 1968], pp. 25-30) has nothing in its support and the weight of all the historical evidence for all the other appearances against it. For a critique, see E. Gutwenger, "Auferstehung und Auferstehungsleib Jesu," *ZKT* 91 (1969): 34-35.

¹¹ Ulrich Wilckens, "Der Ursprung der Überlieferung der Erscheinungen des Auferstandenen," in *Dogma und Denkstrukturen*, ed. W. Joest and W. Pannenberg (Göttingen: Vandenhoeck & Ruprecht, 1963), p. 80.

¹² Hans Conzelmann, *Der erste Brief an die Korinther* KEKNT 5 (Göttingen: Vandenhoeck & Ruprecht, 1969), p. 304.

Some scholars wish to identify this appearance with the experience of the 120 brethren at Pentecost.[13] But this has been rightly rejected by the majority of critics as bearing little parallel. It has also been suggested, though not so much recently, that the appearance to the 500 brethren is to be identified with the mountaintop appearance of Mt. 28.[14] A meeting of 500 persons would have to be in the open air, perhaps on a hillside, as Matthew relates. Unlike every other resurrection appearance, this encounter was, according to Matthew, not a sudden surprise, but by appointment (Mt. 28:16), and it would not be surprising that although Matthew concentrates on the Eleven, others should wait for the Lord with them. It may be that Matthew actually hints at this in the words of the risen Jesus to the women at the tomb: "Go and tell my brethren to go to Galilee, and there they will see me" (28:10). Whereas the command of the angel referred on the Markan pattern to "his disciples" (28:7), the percipients of this appearance in Jesus's command are described as brethren, a term broadly used in Matthew to designate more than just the twelve disciples, but any follower of Jesus (cf., 12:49-50; 23:8). Could it be that Matthew's reiteration of the angel's command, which otherwise seems such a pointless and insipid redundancy, is meant to make clear by this change that the appearance predicted in Mk. 16:7 in fact referred to an appearance to a wider group of Christian brethren than just the Eleven? In fact, it may be that the reference to the brethren is traditional (cf. Jn. 20:17), which means that Matthew knew of a tradition of an appearance to a wider group of disciples which he identifies with the mountaintop appearance. In fact, the Markan empty tomb narrative may itself attest to such a tradition. For as Schottroff points out, the angelic prophecy of a Galilean appearance indicates by the second person plural verb in v. 7 that the women were among the percipients of the Galilean ap-

---

[13] F. C. Burkitt, *Christian Beginnings* (London: University of London, 1924), pp. 90-91; Hans Lietzmann, *Geschichte der alten Kirche* (Berlin: Walter de Gruyter, 1932), I: 52; Jack Finnegan, *Die Überlieferung der Leidens und Auferstehungsgeschichte Jesu* (Giessen: Töplemann, 1934), p. 109; Emmanuel Hirsch, *Die Auferstehungsgeschichten und der christliche Glaube* (Tübingen: Mohr, 1940), pp. 34-35; Joachim Jeremias, *Neutestamentliche Theologie* (Gütersloh: Gerd Mohn, 1971), p. 292; Fuller, *Formation*, p. 35. For a critique, see Maurice Goguel, *La foi a la résurrection de Jésus dans le christianisme primitif* (Paris: Leroux, 1939), pp. 255-257; Werner Georg Kümmel, *Kirchenbegriff und Geschichtsbewusstsein in der Urgemeinde und bei Jesus*, 2nd ed. (Göttingen: Vandenhoeck & Ruprecht, 1968), pp. 8-9.
[14] Robertson and Plummer, *Corinthians*, p. 337; Allo, *Première épître*, p. 396; Michael Perry, *The Easter Enigma*, with an Introduction by Austin Farrer (London: Faber & Faber, 1959), pp. 76-77; D. A. Carson, *Matthew*, EBC 8 (Grand Rapids, Mich.: Zondervan, 1984).

pearance.¹⁵ She accordingly maintains that although Matthew changes the verb to the third person, the mountaintop appearance story he narrates probably included the women as well as the Eleven among its audience. So although he is interested in the Eleven, Matthew may well be aware of the presence of other Christians besides the Eleven. Indeed, when Matthew writes "...οἱ δὲ ἐδίστασαν." (Mt. 28:17), this hardly seems appropriate for the Eleven at this final moment of triumph in which the exalted Lord gives them his commission to go out into all the world carrying the gospel. It is sometimes urged that this doubt motif figures importantly theologically in the gospels, but this cannot be said for Matthew. Whereas the women in Mark tell no one of the angel's message (Mk. 16:8), in Matthew they run "with great joy" to tell the disciples, who do not doubt the women's report (as in Lk. 24:11), but proceed obediently to the appointed place whereupon they see Jesus and worship him (in contrast to Lk. 24:37; Jn. 20:20); only then does Matthew add the cryptic phrase "...οἱ δὲ ἐδίστασαν." What makes this doubly inappropriate with regard to the Eleven is that in Luke and John the whole point of the doubt motif is to show how doubt is triumphantly overcome by the risen Jesus, but Matthew leaves us with the doubt, which the other gospels do not, and at a point so inappropriate to the climax of the gospel and the great commission of vs. 18-20.¹⁶ It could be argued that the phrase may not be a redactional or theological device, but a historical reminiscence, referring to other Galilean disciples who had assembled with the Eleven. Recent discussions of the οἱ δὲ construction have shown that this expression can be used to refer to a group distinguishable within a larger group and that the subgroup can be either contained within the larger group or completely distinct from it. McKay concludes, "It is quite likely, in grammatical terms, that the *hoi de* in Mt. 28:17 were...a minority of the main group mentioned specifically, here the eleven; but in view of the distance of the whole group subject from the main verb it could be that *hoi de* were a minority of a larger group led by the eleven and did not neces-

---

[15] Luise Schottroff, "Maria Magdalena und die Frauen am Grabe Jesu," *EvT* 42 (1982): 19, 22.
[16] Dunn comments,
"But in Mt. 28:17...the doubt is not treated apologetically; Jesus neither addresses himself to it nor removes it. The words which follow (28:18-20) cannot be shown to serve any other function than that of commissioning.... The bare mention of doubt in Mt. 28:17 is best seen therefore as a genuine historical echo" (James W. D. G. Dunn, *Jesus and the Spirit* [London: SCM, 1975], p. 124).

sarily contain any of the eleven themselves."[17] Van der Horst goes even further, contending that the οἱ δὲ *cannot* refer to all the disciples; but he protests the suggestion that it refers to others present with them because, although that is grammatically possible, the disciples were alone.[18] But that is precisely the question (cf. Jn. 20:2; Lk. 24:12, 24 for resurrection narratives focusing on one person though an implicit plurality is present; cf. also Lk. 5:4-7)! The presence of a wider body than the Eleven could be implicit in the οἱ δὲ. It was in Galilee that, according to the gospels, the thousands had flocked to hear Jesus, and it cannot be ruled out that 500 persons should come together there. Although we are apt to picture Galilee in our minds as a rural land of tiny villages, Josephus informs us that Galilee contained many villages, the least of which possessed around 15,000 inhabitants.[19] Roman historian A. N. Sherwin-White explains that these κῶμαι were large communities of peasant cultivating population which congregated together because of the primary value and scarcity of agricultural land, the rarity of water, and the necessity of local defense.[20] In Palestine these were the "villages." In the vicinity of such a village a meeting of 500 disciples is not at all inconceivable. So if Matthew's account harks back to a historical incident, it is not impossible that this was the appearance to the 500 brethren.

The hypothesis that the appearance occurred in Galilee is attractive because this may explain why it is mentioned in neither Luke nor John and why we therefore hear so little of it. Could the appearance have occurred in Jerusalem? If so, it is very difficult to explain why Luke does not mention it, since it would accord wonderfully with his Jerusalem appearances. And it seems doubtful that prior to Pentecost the body of believers in Jerusalem was so large as 500. Grass suggests therefore that the appearance to the 500 brethren did not occur right away, but sometime after Pentecost.[21] This would give one about three years' leeway, since Paul's conversion came thereafter. But even then it is still difficult to explain why Luke should fail to mention so significant an incident in the life of the

---

[17] K. L. McKay, "The Use of *hoi de* in Matthew 28.17," *JSNT* 24 (1985): 71-72.
[18] P. W. van der Horst, "Once More: The Translation of οἱ δὲ in Matthew 28.17," *JSNT* 27 (1986): 27-30.
[19] Josephus *Jewish War* 3. 41-43. This figure is disputed; but recent archeological excavation of the remains of a first century 4,000 seat amphitheater at Sepphoris in Galilee seems to give ample evidence that an assembly of five hundred Christian brethren in Galilee is not at all implausible.
[20] A. N. Sherwin-White, *Roman Society and Roman Law in the New Testament* (Oxford: Clarendon Press, 1963), p. 132.
[21] Grass, *Ostergeschehen*, pp. 98-101, 109.

mother church in Jerusalem. He does not shy from relating visions to Stephen and Paul, and he could have treated this incident in the same way. If he knew of the incident, he would probably have related or mentioned it. But how could he not know of the incident, given Luke's research into the history of the early church (especially if this appearance was in the formula) and the hundreds of witnesses, most of whom were still alive in AD 55? Some critics claim that the appearance must have been in Jerusalem because Paul's mentioning of the witnesses available to be questioned assumes that they are together in one place.[22] The point has some weight, but could not a Galilean village be as suitable as Jerusalem?[23] And some of the Galilean disciples no doubt moved to Jerusalem. At any rate, this is all quite speculative and perhaps serves to obscure the fact that, regardless of where the event occurred, Paul's tradition and personal comment attest to the fact that there were literally hundreds of people about who were known in the early church and who had been at an assembly where they experienced an appearance of Jesus and who were ready to testify to that fact. It is quite amazing.

THE APPEARANCE TO JAMES

Next, according to Paul, Jesus appeared to James. Here is another remarkable event—Jesus appears after his resurrection to his own brother, for it is undoubtedly this James who is meant. Again we possess, sadly, no narrative of this event.[24] But Paul writes in Gal. 1:19 of his two week sojourn in Jerusalem three years after his conversion, during which he met James, the Lord's brother. If Paul had not heard of this appearance before that visit, he certainly would have learned of it then. So the report of this appearance is also only once removed from the

---

[22] Ibid., p. 122; Jeremias, *Theologie*, p. 292.
[23] Galilee is as probable as Jerusalem in the opinion of H. A. W. Meyer, *Handbuch über den ersten Brief an die Korinther*, 6th ed., rev. Georg Heinrici, KEKNT 5 (Göttingen: Vandenhoeck & Ruprecht's Verlag, 1881), p. 401; more probable, states von Campenhausen, *Ablauf*, pp. 13-15.
[24] Jerome records a fragment from the Gospel of the Hebrews which relates Jesus's appearance to James:
> "And when the Lord had given the linen cloth to the servant of the priest, he went to James and appeared to him. For James had sworn that he would not eat bread from that hour in which he had drunk the cup of the Lord until he should see him risen from among them that sleep. And shortly thereafter the Lord said: Bring a table and bread! And immediately it is added: he took the bread, blessed it, and broke it and gave it to James the Just and said to him: My brother, eat thy bread, for the Son of man is arisen from among them that sleep" (Jerome *De viris illustribus* 2).

But as historical evidence this is quite worthless and was probably invented precisely because of Paul's mention of an appearance to James.

original source. There can be little doubt that James did experience a resurrection appearance.

This becomes all the more remarkable when we consider that James as Jesus's own brother did not believe during Jesus's lifetime that his older brother was the Messiah or indeed anyone of special greatness (Mk. 3:21, 31-35; 6:3; Jn. 7:1-10). John relates the rather vicious story that Jesus's brothers, of whom James was apparently the eldest (Mk. 6:3), tried to goad him into a death trap by showing himself publicly at the Feast of Tabernacles in Jerusalem when the Jews were seeking to kill him. We hear little more of them until suddenly in Acts they crop up again surprisingly among the post-Easter fellowship of believers in the upper room (Acts 1:14). They are mentioned there only in passing as "his brothers;" we hear nothing of them again until Acts 12:17, where James is mentioned by name. But Paul reports that when he visited Jerusalem three years after his conversion he saw "none of the other apostles except James the Lord's brother" (Gal. 1:19). If Paul does not explicitly call James an apostle, he comes very close. James now seems to have a place of prominence in the primitive church: when Peter is miraculously delivered from prison, his instructions to the group assembled for prayer at Mary the mother of John Mark's house are extremely interesting: "Tell this to James and to the brethren" (Acts 12:17). When Paul and Barnabas return from their missionary activity among the Gentiles, it is James who stands up and pronounces the decisive verdict on the problem of Gentile converts' relation to the law (Acts 15:13). Paul reports that when he went up to Jerusalem with Barnabas 14 years after his first visit, James had become with John and Peter one of the "pillars" of the church (Gal. 2:9); some time later when a delegation from the Jerusalem church visited the fellowship at Antioch, Paul refers to them as "Men...from James" (Gal. 2:12). In Acts 21, one of the famous "we" passages, Paul and his companions upon returning to Jerusalem immediately report to James, who now appears to be the sole head of the church and of the council of elders (Acts 21:18). This is the last we hear of James in the New Testament, but from Josephus we learn that he was stoned to death under orders from the Sanhedrin for his faith in Jesus Christ during the 60s.[25]

---

[25] Josephus *Antiquities of the Jews* 20.200. Cf. the account by Hegesippus cited in Eusebius *Historiae ecclesiasticae* 2.33.

His younger brothers, too, became believers. Paul writes of them, "Do we not have the right to be accompanied by a wife, as the other apostles and the brothers of the Lord or Cephas?" (I Cor. 9:5). Eusebius records the church tradition that it was the brothers of Jesus who evangelized Galilee and Syria.[26] That there was a profound change in the lives of Jesus's brothers seems to be historically well-founded. Their role in the missionary activity and life of the community of believers guarantees this.

Some critics doubt the historicity of Acts 1:14, but it accords quite well with James's progressive rise to power. And if it were a late addition it could be such only because James and his brothers had, in fact, assumed prominent roles in the early church. That they were not believers in Jesus during his lifetime is also reasonably attested and quite plausible; but more than that, it is unlikely that, had they been loyal believers in Jesus during his lifetime and continued to serve in important ministries of the church after his death, the early church would have invented such ugly stories about them in the gospels. But if Jesus's brothers did undergo such a conversion, then the inference is certainly not far away that the reason was that "then he appeared to James." Certainly the crucifixion of their brother could not have brought this about, for though that might pierce their hearts, it could not cause them to worship him as Messiah and Lord as the early church did. Even Grass exclaims that one of the surest proofs of the resurrection of Jesus is that his own brothers came to believe in him.[27]

Where and when did this appearance occur? If one accepts the historicity of Acts 1:14, then the incident occurred prior to Pentecost, perhaps in Galilee, where James lived. This would necessitate that the appearance to the 500 brethren was also prior to Pentecost. If one rejects Acts 1:14, then the appearance to James could be placed anywhere during the three years prior to Paul's conversion. But all the gospels, especially Luke, give the impression that the appearances ceased shortly after the resurrection; this would count against a later appearance.

THE APPEARANCE TO ALL THE APOSTLES

Finally, he appeared to all the apostles. The identity of this group has constituted a great puzzle. Does it refer simply to the Twelve, or is this a latter-day

---

[26] Eusebius *Historiae ecclesiasticae* 1.7, 14.
[27] Grass, *Ostergeschehen*, p. 102.

group of apostle-missionaries, or is it something in between? That the group is identical with the Twelve seems unlikely. This would be a confusing repetition of the same body under two names. On the other hand, attempts to identify a later body of missionaries to whom Christ appeared have been unsuccessful. The appearance was no doubt a single event; it is not meant that all of the apostles saw Jesus separately and successively. But when and where did such a body ever come together prior to Paul's Damascus road encounter? We have no clue. In light of this it seems wisest to identify the apostles as a circle of original disciples who had been with Jesus from the beginning (Acts 1:21-22; cf. Jn. 15:27) and were therefore qualified to preach the gospel. They were thus a limited body, which was nevertheless larger than the Twelve.[28] In time the concept of apostle either broadened so as to include people like Barnabas, whom even Luke calls an apostle (Acts 14:4, 14), or else the word came to be used in a secondary sense as well so that such persons could be called apostles without implying that they were at the same time members of the narrower circle. The appearance, however, was to this originally limited circle.

Since according to Paul this was the last appearance prior to his own and his own was the last, this would suggest the identification of this appearance with the ascension (Lk. 24:50-51; Acts 1:2, 6-11). If this event is taken to be a wholly mythological or theological construction devoid of historical traces, then of course this identification would be impossible. But most of the gospels contain some sort of commissioning story, albeit in different words, of the disciples by Jesus (Mt. 28:18-20; Lk. 24:44-49; Jn. 20:21-23), and the appearance to all the apostles could have been some such event when a larger group of disciples, not simply the Twelve, were present.

The difficulty with placing the appearance in the post-Pentecost period is not only that the group in question then becomes unidentifiable, but also that such an appearance would be so discontinuous with the gospel appearances that it would probably have been regarded as a vision of the Lord rather than an appearance.[29]

---

[28] So Hans Lietzmann, *An die Korinther I, II*, 4th ed., rev. Werner Georg Kümmel, HNT (Tübingen: J. C. B. Mohr, 1949), p. 78. See also Kümmel, *Kirchenbegriff*, p. 7; cf. Klaus Wengst, *Christologische Formeln und Lieder des Urchristentums*, SNT 7 (Gütersloh: Gerd Mohn, 1972), p. 94.

[29] On the difference between visions and appearances of Christ, see the discussion by Grass, *Ostergeschehen*, pp. 189-207. Although Grass discounts most of the visions recorded in Acts as legendary, he nevertheless concludes, primarily on the basis of Paul's testimony, that the Easter appearances took place within a community that enjoyed visions, revelations, and ecstatic experi-

This was probably part of the apostle Paul's problem in justifying his apostleship, and he sturdily insisted in language reminiscent of the gospels that he, too, had "seen Jesus our Lord" (I Cor. 9:1: οὐχὶ Ἰησοῦν τὸν κύριον ἡμῶν ἑώρακα; cf. Jn.

---

ences (I Cor. 12-14; II Cor. 12:1-5; Gal. 2:1; Acts 16:9). The community recognized, however, that the appearances of Christ were restricted to a small circle designated as witnesses and that even to them Jesus did not continually re-appear but appeared only at the beginning of their new life. One cannot follow Grass, however, when he attempts to draw the essential distinction between an appearance of Christ and a vision as being solely in content, viz., in an appearance Christ was seen as exalted (Ibid., pp. 229-232). This is undoubtedly true, but surely a vision could be of the exalted Christ, too; indeed, how could a Christian believer have a vision of the unexalted Christ? Both the vision of Stephen and the book of Revelation show that visions of the exalted Lord which were not appearances were possible for the early church. It is of no matter whether Stephen's vision be an unhistorical embellishment as Grass thinks; the point is that the church of Luke's day was prepared to accept that Stephen saw a vision of Christ. Grass's argument that Revelation is not a vision but a picture story because of the many portraits of Christ seems to presuppose that visions must be monotone. At any rate, the point is Revelation presents itself as a vision, thus showing again that the church did not reject out of hand visions of the exalted Christ.

Nor can it be said that the distinguishing element in an appearance as opposed to a vision was the commissioning, for appearances were known which lacked this element (the 500 brethren). What then distinguished an appearance from a vision? It seems to me that the most natural answer to this question is that an appearance involved extra-mental phenomena, something's actually appearing, whereas a vision, even if caused by God, was purely in the mind. Certainly this seems to be the way in which the New Testament conceives of the distinction. Visions, even veridical visions sent by God, are exclusively mental phenomena, whereas Jesus's appearances always involve an extra-mental appearing in the real, external world. The resistance to this conclusion among contemporary critics seems largely due to a philosophico-theological rejection of the physicalism of the gospels. On this basis, Grass superimposes the form of heavenly visions onto the resurrection appearances, and contemporary scholarship has followed him in this. (See Alsup, *Stories*, pp. 32, 34, 54.) But if this is done, then—apart from its being exegetically unjustified—it seems to me impossible to differentiate between a vision and an appearance, which the early church clearly did. It might be said that a vision is, in modern parlance, a subjective vision, that is, a self-induced visionary seeing, but that an appearance is an objective vision, that is, a visionary seeing induced by God. This distinction, however, will not help to solve the problem, for so-called objective visions were experienced in the church and these were not ranked as appearances. For example, Peter's vision in Acts 10:9-17 was certainly "objective", for it was caused by God (10:28), but it was not in the same class of phenomena as the appearances of Jesus. More to the point, Stephen's vision of Jesus was probably "objective"—Luke does not want us to take it as a self-induced hallucination—, but this was not an appearance of Jesus. But what is the difference between what Stephen saw and what Paul experienced, such that the latter could be called an appearance of Jesus (Acts 9:17; contrast the vision to Ananias himself in 9:10 which was not an appearance)? What is the difference between Paul's opportunity on the Damascus road "to see the Just One and to hear a voice from his mouth" (22:14) and his subsequent experience in the temple when he fell into a trance and saw Jesus speaking to him (22:17)? It is of no help to speak of subjective vs. objective visions, for to the mind of the Jewish/Christian believer, all *genuine* visions were "objective"—anything else would be just an illusion. It seems to me, therefore, despite the modern antipathy to "physicalism," that the difference between a vision and an appearance of Jesus was that only in the latter did he actually appear in the external world. The support for this view is two-fold: (1) exegetically this is consistently the difference between the two; (2) if one rejects this view, then the distinction between an appearance and a vision which was made in the early church threatens to dissolve.

20:18: Εώρακα τὸν κύριον; Jn. 20:25: Εωράκαμεν τὸν κύριον). And it would be very puzzling, too, that Luke would not even mention such an incident, as it would be ideal for founding the Gentile mission in the book of Acts (cf. his use of Peter's vision, Acts 10:1-11:18). It seems most likely that this appearance occurred prior to Pentecost. Since the appearances listed by Paul hang together in chronological order, this would imply that the appearances to the 500 brethren and to James also occurred in the pre-Pentecost period. I see nothing inherently improbable in this, but of course one cannot be certain. In any case, we have yet another occurrence in which a group had an experience of seeing Jesus risen and which was part of Paul's tradition, for which he could personally vouchsafe from his contact with the apostles.

The Appearance to Paul

Having listed the witnesses to appearances of Christ which Paul had learned about from others, he adds his own personal experience to the list: last of all he appeared also to me. In including himself in the list, Paul implicitly asserts to have been the recipient of a genuine appearance of Jesus, not simply a vision. Paul was familiar with religious visions (II Cor. 12:1-7), and what he saw on the Damascus road was no mere vision.[30] His use of ἑώρακα (I Cor. 9:1) is not only

---

[30] Otherwise he would have begun II Cor. 12 with the appearance of Christ to him (Michaelis, *Erscheinungen*, p. 99). Cf. B. F. Wescott, *The Revelation of the Risen Lord*, 3rd ed. (London: Macmillan, 1884), p. 193; Weiss, *Korintherbrief*, p. 351; Walter Künneth, *The Theology of the Resurrection*, trans. J. W. Leitch (London: SCM Press, 1965), p. 84.

Some critics have taken the word ὤφθη as an indication that all the appearances were heavenly visions (Johannes Weiss, *Der erste Korintherbrief*, 9th ed., KEKNT 5 [Göttingen: Vandenhoeck & Ruprecht, 1910], p. 349; Robertson and Plummer, *Corinthians*, p. 340; Harnack, *Verklärungsgeschichte*, p. 70; Conzelmann, *Korinther*, p. 303). But, as Grass maintains, from vocabulary alone, one cannot determine the type of appearance. In fact, one cannot even say that ὤφθη is primitive, for Paul also uses ἑώρακα and ἀποκαλύψαι, and even if the gospels are late, they testify to a rich combination of different word groups: ὁρᾶν, ἰδεῖν, θεωρεῖν, βλέπειν, θεᾶσθαι, ὀπθάνεσθαι, φανερόω. The ὤφθη can be either passive or deponent ("was seen" or "appeared") and in the LXX is used of things that were hidden, people who let themselves be seen, and divine epiphanies. Here it underscores the activity and initiative of the one appearing but says nothing about the nature of the appearance (Grass, *Ostergeschehen*, pp. 186-189), except that it was an *appearance*. See also Michaelis, *Erscheinungen*, pp. 104-109; Karl Heinrich Rengstorff, *Die Auferstehung Jesu*, 4th rev. ed. (Göttingen: Vandenhoeck & Ruprecht, 1970), pp. 119-124; Josef Blank, *Paulus und Jesus*, SANT 18 (München: Kösel Verlag, 1968), pp. 156-163; Franz Mussner, *Die Auferstehung Jesu*, BH7 (München: Kösel Verlag, 1969), pp. 68-69; Bode, *Easter*, pp. 93-95; Fuller, *Formation*, p. 30; Dunn, *Jesus*, p. 133; cf. pp. 104-106.

More recently, Hoffmann, following Vögtle and Pesch, seems inclined to repeat this erroneous procedure all over again with ἀποκαλύψαι (*TRE* [1979], s.v. "Auferstehung II. Auferstehung Jesu Christi II/1. Neues Testament," by Paul Hoffmann, pp. 492-497; Anton Vögtle and Rudolf Pesch,

reminiscent of the language of the appearances but also indicates an event in the past with enduring consequences: the unrepeated event of seeing Christ and being commissioned as an apostle. His use of ἔσχατον δὲ πάντων (I Cor. 15:8) also indicates that the appearance to him was not repeated. The ἔκτρωμα in the same verse could also be an indication of the uniqueness of that event. Paul held that the resurrection appearances ceased with himself and that this event was therefore essentially different from his later "visions and revelations of the Lord" (II Cor. 12:1). Convinced that this was no mere vision, Paul seems eager to include himself among those who had received an appearance of the Lord, perhaps because his detractors denied or doubted his apostleship (I Cor. 9:1-2; II Cor. 11:5; 12:11) and his having seen Christ would be an argument in his favor (Gal. 1:1, 11-12, 15-16; I. Cor. 9:1-2; 15:8-9). A vision of Christ so much later than the appearance to the Twelve would naturally be regarded with suspicion,[31] and so Paul is anxious

---

Wie kam es zum Osterglauben? [Düsseldorf: Patmos Verlag, 1975], p. 58). He concedes that the range of subjects connected with ὤφθη in the Old Testament is so broad that only the context can determine what sort of appearance is meant but asserts that if the resurrection appearances are related to Old Testament theophanies, then, as Vögtle and Pesch have allegedly shown, there can be no doubt that ὤφθη presupposes the exaltation of Jesus to heaven. The *Urgemeinde* could only think of the Risen Christ as in heaven, and this fact is reflected in the perfect tense of I Cor. 15:4. So the more mundane uses of ὤφθη (*e.g.*, Mk. 9:4; Lk. 1:11; 22:43; Acts 2:3; 7:2, 26, 30, 35) do not refute this conclusion. Hoffmann appeals to Paul's use of ἀποκαλύψαι in Gal. 1:15 as evidence of the appearances' being eschatological, visionary experiences. But this train of inferences is multiply flawed: (i) the appearances' connection with Old Testament theophanies is a moot point (see pp. 231-235), (ii) more seriously, these theophanies and epiphanies themselves prove that heavenly visions were not always at issue, but very often earthly or anthropomorphic appearances, (iii) the *Urgemeinde* had no difficulty of conceiving of the Risen Christ as appearing in earthly parameters; indeed, this is implied in their characterizing what happened to Jesus as a resurrection rather than a translation (see pp. 302-304), (iv) the perfect tense in I Cor. 15:4 indicates that Christ's resurrection is a permanent state but affords no inference about where he first appeared to his disciples; (v) the uses of ὤφθη with regard to angels, Jesus's transfiguration, and other heavenly beings is decisive refutation of the view that a numinous context implies heavenly visions with no physical elements, and (v) the notion of "revelation" to characterize eschatological realities does not imply non-physicality either, unless pure visions are meant, in which case these are, as we said, sharply distinguished by Paul from resurrection appearances.

[31] Perhaps this is the force of "untimely born"(ἔκτρωμα)—that Paul realized he was abnormally discontinuous with the original appearances. But ἔκτρωμα always denotes a premature birth and so would seem inappropriate to describe Paul's later appearance (*TWNT*, s.v. "ἔκτρωμα," by Johannes Schneider; Conzelmann, *Korinther*, p. 306). Usually the word is taken to mean "miscarriage" and to refer to the violence or suddenness of Paul's conversion (Robertson and Plummer, *Corinthians*, p. 339; Allo, *Première épître*, p. 393; [Kümmel] Lietzmann, *Korinther I*, p. 192; C. K. Barrett, *A Commentary on the First Epistle to the Corinthians*, BNTC [London: Adam & Charles Black, 1968], p. 344) or to Paul's feeling of unworthiness of having seen Christ ([Heinrici-] Meyer, *Ersten Brief*, p. 403; Michaelis, *Erscheinungen*, p. 25; Grass, *Ostergeschehen*, p. 105) or to a derogatory term used by the enemies of the apostle (Weiss, *Korintherbrief*, p. 352; many of the above references). Dunn suggests the interesting view that ἔκτρωμα means Paul was

to include himself with the other apostles as a recipient of a genuine, objective appearance of the risen Lord.

This raises a very instructive point. In including himself in the list, Paul in no sense implies that the foregoing appearances were the same *sort* of appearance as the one to him.[32] He is concerned here, not with the *how* of the appearances, but with *who* appeared. He wants to list witnesses of the risen Christ, and the mode of the appearance is entirely incidental. But furthermore, in placing himself in the list, Paul is not trying to put the appearances to the others on a plane with his own; rather he is trying to level up his own experience to the objectivity and reality of the others.[33] He wants to say that what *he* saw was every bit as much a real appearance of Jesus as that which *they* saw. Hence, no inference can be made from the sort of appearance Paul received to the sort received by the earlier apostles. Paul affords no such deduction.

The appearance to Paul on the Damascus road is related three times in Acts (Acts 9:1-19; 22:3-16; 26:9-23) and is confirmed in its chief points by Paul's statements in his letters.[34] He tells us that he was a Pharisee blameless under the

---

spiritually born prematurely, without the normal spiritual gestation period, so that he might be in time to witness the last resurrection appearance before they ceased (Dunn, *Jesus*, pp. 101-102). The problem with such a view is that it assumes that the appearances to the 500 brethren, James, and all the apostles took place between Pentecost and Paul's conversion and that the series of appearances was still "open". It seems more probable that there were no appearances between Pentecost and Paul's experience and that the series was regarded as closed *de facto*. Von Campenhausen believes that Paul thought of the appearance to him as portentous because of the lateness and absolute improbability of this occurrence, when the church was already established and further appearances were not to be expected. Hence, ἔκτρωμα in all probability does mean untimely birth (Von Campenhausen, *Ablauf*, p. 19). Brown agrees: "Paul recalls the tradition of the appearances of Jesus to show that, even if he came out of time and last of all, he did see the risen Jesus, just as did the other well-known apostles" (Brown, *John*, p. 971).

[32] D. H. van Daalen, *The Real Resurrection* (London: Collins, 1972), p. 53. Even Fischer, who propounds the heavenly vision view, agrees that Paul does not concern himself with the kind or manner of the appearances, but with the unity of the apostolic testimony (Karl Martin Fischer, *Das Ostergeschehen*, 2nd ed. [Göttingen: Vandenhoeck & Ruprecht, 1980], p. 74).

[33] For good statements of this point, see Brooke Foss Wescott, *The Gospel of the Resurrection* (London: Macmillan, 1906), pp. 93-94; James Orr, *The Resurrection of Jesus* (London: Hodder & Stoughton, 1909), p. 39; P. Gardner-Smith, *The Narratives of the Resurrection* (London: Methuen, 1926), pp. 21-22; *Interpreter's Dictionary of the Bible*, s.v. "Resurrection in the New Testament," by J. A. T. Robinson. Dunn even hypothesizes that Paul's placing himself in the list could be a case of special pleading—interpreting a less distinctive religious experience as a resurrection appearance in order to boost his claim to apostolic authority (Dunn, *Jesus*, p. 99)! Dunn rejects the hypothesis in the end because the pillar apostles accepted Paul's claim without serious dispute (Ibid., p. 108).

[34] See helpful discussion in Xavier Léon-Dufour, "L'apparition du Ressuscité à Paul," in *Resurrexit*, pp. 281-282. Masson believes Luke may have even employed the Galatians account

law and extremely zealous for Judaism (Phil. 3:5-6; Gal. 1:14), that as a result he was involved in the persecution of the Christian movement, which he apparently pursued with a vengeance (Phil. 3:6; Gal. 1:13; I. Cor. 15:9), that as he was in or near Damascus (Gal. 1:17) Christ appeared to him (I Cor. 9:1; 15:8; Gal. 1:15-16) and commissioned him to preach the gospel (Gal. 1:16; Col. 1:25), and that after this event, which Paul always counted as his conversion (I Cor. 15:8; Phil. 3:7), he remained in Damascus for three years before launching out as a gospel preacher in other regions (Gal. 1:17-21). The Acts narrative differs primarily in adding more details. Even if these were fictitious, we should have more information from Paul's own letters concerning the appearance of Christ to him than we do for most of the other appearances in the list. But in fact most critics are quite willing to accept the historicity of much of the Acts versions of the incident.[35]

According to Luke's account, Paul was blinded by a light from heaven, brighter than the sun, which shone about him (Acts 9:3; 22:6, 11; 26:13), and he heard a voice which demanded, "Saul, Saul, why do you persecute me?" (Acts 9:4; 22:7; 26:14). In answer to Paul's question of the identity of the speaker, the voice replied, "I am Jesus" and gave him instructions what to do in Damascus (Acts 9:5-6; 22:8, 10; 26:15-18). The most confusing aspect of the story is the role of Paul's companions: the men with him stood speechless, hearing the voice but seeing no one (Acts 9:7); those with him saw the light but did not hear the voice (Acts 22:9); the light shone round Paul's fellow travellers and they all fell to

---

(C. Masson, "A propos de Act. 9. 19b-25. Note sûr l'utilisation de Gal. et de 2 Cor. par l'auteur des Actes," *TZ* 18 [1962]: 161-166).

[35] There are some really remarkable parallels between the story of Paul's conversion and the story of Heliodorus (II Macc. 3:1-39). Heliodorus was commissioned by the secular authorities to go to Jerusalem and confiscate the monies of the temple treasury. As he was about to do this, God, in response to the prayers of the people, sent an apparition which physically attacked him. He fell to the ground, thick darkness enveloped him, and he was carried away absolutely helpless and unable to speak. Later the apparition re-appeared and commanded him to publish abroad to all men the sovereign majesty of God. So Heliodorus offered sacrifice and testified to all men the deeds of God which he had witnessed. If we possessed only the accounts of Paul's conversion in Acts and his letters had been lost, no small number of scholars would probably regard the Acts account as a legendary tale based on this story. But the main parallels, remarkable as they are, appear to be purely coincidental, for from Paul's own testimony we know that he really was commissioned to persecute the faithful, that in the process of doing so he saw an appearance of Jesus which interrupted his mission, and that thereafter he did go about preaching the gospel. The details of the apparition are entirely diverse: Heliodorus saw a terrible horseman which threatened to trample him and two glorious youths who scourged him, inflicting physical wounds on him. All Paul saw was a light brighter than the sun, and he heard the Lord's voice reprimanding him and commanding him what to do. See also Grass, *Ostergeschehen*, pp. 217-218; Fuller, *Formation*, pp. 46-48.

the ground (Acts 26:13-14). This makes it evident that although Paul's experience involved visionary elements, such that Luke could refer to it as a "heavenly vision" (Acts 26:19), it cannot be characterized without further ado as purely visionary and subjective, for it is portrayed as involving extra-mental accompaniments, namely, the light and the voice.

Grass asserts that participation of Paul's companions in the experience is due to objectifying tendencies.[36] Had the experience been objective, then Paul and his companions should have all seen and been blinded by the light and all heard the voice. If they did not, then the experience must have been visionary. The difficulty in trying to eliminate the extra-mental aspects of Paul's experience, however, is two-fold. (1) For consider: either Luke had a tradition about Paul's companions' being involved in the event or not. If not, then why would he invent them? Grass's answer that these are objectifying tendencies seems inconsistent, for Luke does *not* want to objectify the post-ascension visions of Jesus; it is the pre-ascension appearances whose extra-mental reality Luke emphasizes. Had he no tradition that included Paul's companions, then we should have another vision like Stephen's, with the light and the voice's possessing no extra-mental manifestation. (2) Besides this, if Luke invented the details concerning Paul's companions, he would certainly have been more consistent. For anybody who reads these accounts can notice the difficulties, which harmonizers have struggled with for years.[37] We cannot assume therefore that as the author of these accounts Luke was not also aware of them. I think it unlikely, therefore, that Luke knew only

---

[36] Grass, *Ostergeschehen*, p. 222. So also Ernst Haenchen, *The Acts of the Apostles*, 14th ed. trans. B. Noble, G. Shinn, and R. McL. Wilson (Oxford: Basil Blackwell, 1971), pp. 322-323, who asserts that Luke was merely underlining the objectivity of the event and that for him it was a matter of indifference whether this was done by the voice or the light, since each makes sense in its own context.

[37] J. L. Lilly argues that the chief discrepancies, that between 9:7 and 22:9 concerning the voice, may be resolved by the different nuances of ἀκούειν plus the genitive or accusative in combination with the range of meaning of φωνή (J. L. Lilly, "The Conversion of Saint Paul: The Validity of his Testimony to the Resurrection of Jesus Christ," *CBQ* 6 [1944]: 180-204). In Acts 9:7 ἀκούειν τῆς φωνῆς means to hear the sound or noise. But in Acts 22:9 ἀκούειν τὴν φωνήν means to understand the voice, a rendering of φωνή which is reinforced by the additional phrase τοῦ λαλοῦντός μοι. It has been pointed out, however, (H. R. Moehring, "The Verb AKOYEIN in Acts IX.7 and XXII.9," *Nov T* 3 [1959]: 80-99; R. G. Bratcher, ἀκούω in Acts ix.7 and xxii.9," *Exp Tim* 71 [1960]: 243-245) that there is no evidence of this difference in meaning between ἀκούειν plus genitive or accusative, known in classical Greek, during the Hellenistic period. Even if Lilly is correct, however, the question would need to be asked whether this and other at least apparent discrepancies are Luke's invention or go back to Luke's sources, perhaps even to Paul himself.

Paul's experience, and he spun the companions' participation out of his own imagination. But if Luke did have tradition concerning the story which included the companions, then he either had one story which he varied on three occasions or he had multiple traditions which were somewhat inconsistent. If the former, then it is difficult again to explain the inconsistencies. For while he might vary the story, say, by leaving out Ananias in ch. 26, in order to make it appear that we have three really different occasions upon which Paul told his story, Luke would probably not construct such discrepancies as that the companions heard and did not hear the voice. Thus the conclusion presents itself that Luke had mixed information concerning the conversion story, perhaps more than one account of it, and hence the conflicting details concerning the companions.[38] In either case, however, the extra-mental phenomena were part of the tradition that Luke received. All the accounts agree that the companions did experience *something*, and it would be tendentious to conclude from the discrepancies that they therefore experienced *nothing*. That they all were not blinded by the light does not speak against this, for Luke understands this to be a supernatural blindness inflicted by God and instantly removed by the laying on of Ananias's hands (Acts 9:12, 17-18; 21:13), not a natural blindness caused by the glare of the light.[39] Now this does not establish the *truth* of the traditions which Luke received; it only shows that one cannot appeal to the discrepancies as an argument for a purely visionary experience by the apostle with no extra-mental manifestations; the data from Acts would seem to point in the opposite direction.

Grass further thinks that Luke had before him a tradition of Paul's appearance that could not be assimilated to the more physical experiences of the disciples and

---

[38] C. H. Dodd, *The Apostolic Preaching and its Developments*, 3rd ed. (London: Hodder & Stoughton, 1967), p. 18. Charles Hedrick argues that Luke's variation in chaps. 22 and 26 are meant to be understood by his readers as corrections of the traditional story he relates in chapter 9 (Charles W. Hedrick, "Paul's Conversion/Call: A Comparative Analysis of the Three Reports in Acts," *JBL* 100 [1981]: 415-432). If this was his intention, however, I cannot understand why he just did not correct the version in chapter 9 itself, instead of constructing a series of apparent inconsistencies, the purpose of which has remained opaque to subsequent generations of readers. In any case, Hedrick's hypothesis still precludes Grass's view because the extra-mental phenomena in chapter 9 at least are traditional. Against Haenchen, he urges that while the discrepant statements do make sense in their individual contexts, this is so only when they are read *in isolation* from each other. "When one reads them as supplementary accounts, however, there appears to be a clear contradiction. It is unclear why the contradictions would not trouble Luke, since he evidently intended each subsequent account to build on the preceding account(s)" (Ibid., p. 430).
[39] Grass acknowledges this point (Grass, *Ostergeschehen*, p. 200).

that therefore the tradition is probably reliable. But the participation of the companions in the experience Grass attributes to mythical or legendary influences.[40]

But as for the first point, one could argue that the opposite is true: that because the appearance to Paul is a post-ascension experience Luke is forced by the necessity of his physical realism to construe it as a heavenly vision and he presents it as such since Jesus has ascended.[41] So the "spiritualism" of the appearance does not in itself commend its historicity, given Luke's scheme. As to the second point, Grass's anthropomorphic parallels from Greek mythology seem far removed from Paul's experience: examples include Homer's *Iliad* α158 where Athena appears and speaks to Achilles while remaining invisible and unheard to others; Apollonius of Rhodes's *Argonauts* 4.852, where Hera appears and speaks with Peleus while remaining invisible and unheard to the others; and Homer's *Odyssey* π v. 161, where Athena appears as a virgin to Odysseus while remaining invisible to Telemachus; she silently beckons to Odysseus and takes him aside to speak with him lest Telemachus hear her. A final example is from the Acts of Thomas, which appears to copy Acts 9, where during the Lord's supper Jesus appears to a select few, while the others "heard his voice but did not see his form." Not only are these "parallels" very distant from the Acts accounts, but Grass provides no argument to show a genealogical link between the former and the latter.

Grass asserts that to allow the companions to take part in the appearance by experiencing either the voice or the light violates Acts 10:41a "God made him manifest, not to all the people but to us who were chosen by God as witnesses."[42] But the verse does not mean *manifest at the same time and place*; as Luke portrays the gospel appearances, if outsiders had been present on the occasion of a resurrection appearance, they surely would have seen and heard everything. If then one accepts the general historicity of Luke's tradition of Paul's conversion experience as a light and voice from heaven, it would seem arbitrary to exclude his companions from also experiencing some sort of visual or auditory phenom-

---

[40] Ibid., pp. 219-220.
[41] This is, in fact, the view of Peder Borgen, "From Paul to Luke," *CBQ* 31 (1969): 180; cf. C. F. Evans, *Resurrection and the New Testament*, SBT 12 (London: SCM Press, 1970), pp. 55-56, 66; Léon-Dufour, "Apparition," p. 294; Hedrick, "Paul's Conversion/Call," pp. 430-431. Borgen's argument that Luke rejected Paul's apostleship is not, however, very compelling in light of Acts 14:4, 14 and the prominence and heroic stature of Paul in the last half of the Acts. See Grant Osborne, "History and Theology in the Resurrection Narratives: a Redactional Study," (Ph.D. thesis, University of Aberdeen, 1974), pp. 371-378.
[42] Grass, *Ostergeschehen*, p. 219.

ena. In this case, one cannot reduce the appearance to Paul as described in Acts to a purely visionary experience: though visionary elements were involved, something actually happened "out there" in the external world such that visual and/or auditory phenomena were experienced by standers-by. What Paul saw, after all, was an *appearance* of Jesus, not a *vision* of Jesus.

Paul himself gives no firm indication of the nature of the appearance to him.[43] He says that Jesus appeared (ὤφθη) to him, that he saw (ἑώρακα) Jesus, and that God revealed (ἀποκαλύψαι) His Son to him (Gal. 1:16). It might be thought that Paul's saying ἐν ἐμοί in this last case instead of simply using the dative (as in I Cor. 2:10; 14:30; Eph. 3:5; Phil. 3:15) indicates the subjective, visionary character of the appearance. But even Dunn admits, "...Paul is not talking here about the visionary side of his conversion experience as such—ἀποκαλύψεως (Gal. 1:12) does not mean 'vision'...."[44] But, Dunn insists, Paul is describing his conversion experience; and he describes it as "a personal subjective experience."[45] But what conversion experience could not be described as a personal subjective experience? Paul is referring to what God did in his heart, not the mode of the appearance which he saw. At any rate, this could at the most indicate that the appearance had subjective elements, not that it was wholly subjective. Sometimes appeal is made to II Cor. 4:6, which is thought to refer to the blinding light on the Damascus road. But in fact the verse does not seem to have any connection with Paul's conversion experience: the light is the light of the gospel (v. 4) and is compared with

---

[43] How erroneous, therefore, is Robinson's assertion that Paul and John's experiences are the only two resurrection appearances recorded in the New Testament by eyewitnesses and that "both these authenticated visualizations of a resurrection appearance were of the luminous kind!" (James M. Robinson, "Jesus from Easter to Valentinus (or to the Apostle's Creed)," *JBL* 101 [1982]: 10). For as O'Collins rightly notes, the luminosity motif is found in Luke, not Paul; we have no direct reports from Paul of a luminous appearance. Moreover, John's experience in Rev. 1:13-16 is not a resurrection appearance at all, but a vision, a distinction to which Robinson seems oblivious (Gerald O'Collins, "Luminous Appearances of the Risen Christ," *CBQ* 46 [1984]:250-251). See also note 26. That means that one cannot appeal to Paul or John as proof of a tradition of luminous, heavenly appearances which is more primitive than the tradition of physical terrestrial appearances, also recorded by Luke and John.

[44] Dunn, *Jesus*, p. 105. Even Hoffmann concedes that the ἐν ἐμοί says nothing about the nature of the experience (*TRE*, s.v. "Auferstehung II/1," p. 494). His appeal to ἀποκαλύψαι to prove a visionary experience makes the crucial and unwarranted assumption that one cannot have an apocalyptic-eschatological experience of a physical object. Cf. O'Collins, "Luminous Appearances," p. 249. Brown points out that Paul could not have thought of the appearances in terms of internal sight for the simple reason that he speaks of Christ's appearing to 500 brethren (Raymond E. Brown, *The Virginal Conception and Bodily Resurrection of Jesus* [London: Geoffrey Chapman, 1973], pp. 91-92).

[45] Dunn, *Jesus*, pp. 105-106.

God's act of creation (Gen. 1:3). There appears to be no reason to think it refers to the Damascus road experience. But in any case, such an appeal would be counter-productive: for the light from heaven was precisely one of the extra-mental phenomena of the experience. Paul's reference to it here, therefore, would not underline the subjectivity of that experience, but on the contrary its objectivity, since it would confirm the Acts account with respect to one of the phenomena also experienced by Paul's companions. And again, it could not in any case show the experience to be wholly subjective. It might be urged that Paul's relative silence concerning the appearance to him is indicative of its subjectivity and ineffability; but such an argument from silence has little force. Given the accidental nature of the epistles, we should not be surprised not to find a description of the incident. Why should Paul relate it in his letters?[46] He certainly could have told the story of the light and the voice had he wanted to. In fact, if the traditions in Acts are reliable, Paul was not at all loath to relate his experience, but did so on several occasions. Paul did not appear to be so enamored with ineffable experience as some theologians would like to think: in II Cor. 12:2-4 he even tries to relate what really was an ineffable experience! Had he had occasion, there seems no reason to doubt that Paul would have related the story of Jesus's appearance to him. Hence, it seems to me, Paul's experience cannot be reduced to a mere vision on the basis of his testimony, nor of Luke's.

SUMMARY

In summary, given the age of these traditions concerning Christ's appearances and Paul's personal contact with the people involved, there would appear to be little doubt that these persons really did experience *something* and that they described it as Jesus's appearing to them alive from the dead. From Paul's list of witnesses, we know that these experiences occurred on multiple occasions and to individuals and groups of different sizes. They may have occurred in both Jerusalem (Peter) and Galilee (the 500 brethren). We know that they ceased with Paul,

---

[46] Paul evidently did not consider the appearance as powerful an argument for his apostleship as the signs of an apostle (I Cor. 2:4; II Cor. 12:12; Rom. 15:18-19) and the fruit of his ministry. After all, it must be remembered, witnessing an appearance of Christ did not *ipso facto* make one an apostle. Nor did Paul apparently regard the mode of the appearance to him as determinative for a doctrine of the resurrection body. So there was no need to relate in detail his experience; reference to it was enough.

and it is probable, I think, that the others were all pre-Pentecost. But what were these experiences? One thing we know for certain: they were not visions or any of the other ecstatic, spiritual phenomena experienced in the early church. Although many modern scholars like to talk about subjective and objective (veridical) visions, for the primitive church such a distinction would seem to reduce to the difference between a self-induced illusion and a vision sent by God, and the appearances of Christ were neither illusions nor visions. The appearances were something qualitatively distinct from anything in the later life of the church. If the suggestion is correct that the essential difference between an appearance and a vision is that the former involves an extra-mental reality while the latter does not, then Jesus's appearances must have involved manifestations in the external world. This is confirmed in the Acts accounts of the appearance to Paul. This conclusion, of course, runs counter to the conventional wisdom of German theology that the appearances were "objective visions" involving no extra-mental manifestations, but it is, I believe, the conclusion warranted by the evidence. The popularity of the "objective vision" understanding seems not infrequently due to contemporary prejudice against "physicalism." Unless a better differentiation between appearance and vision is forthcoming from the New Testament and unless Luke's account of the appearance to Paul is shown to be inaccurate with regard to the extra-mental manifestations, then the weight of the evidence suggests that the appearances experienced by the early believers involved phenomena occurring in the external world. Further than this Paul's information will not take us. The other appearances could have been like the one to Paul described in Acts (assuming Luke has not adapted it to his post-ascension framework) or they may not have been. The one thing we can know is that they were all *appearances*. Thus on the basis of Paul's information concerning the appearances of Jesus, we reach the remarkable conclusion that *on multiple occasions different individuals and groups experienced "appearances of Jesus" after his death which were at least in part objective and in the external world and which soon ceased, never to be repeated in the life of the church.*

CHAPTER 3

INDICATIONS OF THE EMPTY TOMB

Having examined Paul's testimony to the appearances of Christ, we may now wish to inquire if he bears any witness to the empty tomb. Grass considers the empty tomb to be the key to understanding the nature of Christ's resurrection,[1] but I think this needs to be carefully qualified. For while a closed or non-empty tomb would disqualify a physical resurrection body of Christ, an empty tomb does not automatically imply a physical resurrection body of Christ, for the corpse could be changed or annihilated by God so that the risen Jesus has no physical body. So while a closed tomb has definite implications for the nature of the resurrection, an empty tomb cannot be decisive. But does Paul bear witness to the empty tomb? Several questions here need to be kept carefully distinct. First we must decide: (1) does Paul *accept* the empty tomb, and (2) does Paul *mention* the empty tomb? It is clear that although (2) would imply (1), (1) does not imply (2). Therefore, although Paul may not mention the empty tomb, that does not mean he does not accept the empty tomb. Too many New Testament scholars have fallen prey to Bultmann's fallacy: "*Legenden sind die Geschichten vom leeren Grab, von dem Paulus noch nicht weiss.*"[2] Paul's citation of Jesus's

---

[1] Hans Grass, *Ostergeschehen und Osterberichte*, 4th rev. ed. (Göttingen: Vandenhoeck & Ruprecht, 1970), p. 139. Similarly O'Collins asserts that the empty tomb serves to guard against "spiritual," docetic, Platonizing interpretations of the resurrection (Gerald O'Collins, *The Easter Jesus*, 2nd ed. [London: Darton, Longman & Todd, 1980], p. 94).

[2] Rudolf Bultmann, *Theologie des Neuen Testaments*, 7th ed., ed. Otto Merk (Tübingen: J. C. B. Mohr, 1961), p. 48. Cf. Hans Grass, *Christliche Glaubenslehre*, 2 vols. (Stuttgart: W. Kohlhammer, 1973), 1:102: "The strongest argument against the tradition of the empty tomb is that Paul does not mention it and does not argue with it against the Corinthian deniers of the resurrection;"

words at the Last Supper shows that he knew the context of the tradition he delivered; but had the Corinthians not been abusing the Lord's table this knowledge would have remained lost to us. So one must not too rashly conclude from silence that Paul "knows nothing" of the empty tomb. Next, if Paul does accept the empty tomb, then we must ask: (1) does Paul *believe* Jesus's tomb was empty, and (2) does Paul *know* Jesus's tomb was empty? Again, as Grass is quick to point out, while (2) implies (1), (1) does not imply (2).[3] In other words, does Paul simply assume the empty tomb as a matter of course or does he have actual historical knowledge that the tomb of Jesus was empty? Thus, even if it could be proved that Paul believed in a physical resurrection of the body, that does not necessarily imply that he knew the empty tomb for a fact.

"He Was Buried"

Some exegetes have maintained that the statement of the formula "he was buried" implies, standing as it does between the death and the resurrection, that the tomb was empty.[4] But many critics deny this, holding that the burial does not

---

Karl Martin Fischer, *Das Ostergeschehen*, 2nd ed. (Göttingen: Vandenhoeck & Ruprecht, 1980), p. 58.

[3] Grass argues that even if Paul held that the old body would be raised transformed, that does not guarantee that Paul knew of Jesus's empty tomb. It would only show that he would have believed it to be so on dogmatic grounds (Grass, *Ostergeschehen*, p. 172). In more recent literature on the empty tomb, it seems to be conceded that point (1) is true, since Jewish anthropology could hardly permit a resurrection without an empty grave, but point (2) is then vigorously contested, since any implication of the empty tomb in Paul or the pre-Pauline formula may be written off as an inference forced precisely by that anthropology rather than regarded as indicative of historical knowledge that Jesus's tomb was empty. Sometimes these critics thus make a terminological distinction between the empty tomb (a dogmatic inference) and the open tomb (the actual discovery of the empty tomb). See Anton Vögtle and Rudolf Pesch, *Wie kam es zum Osterglauben?* (Düsseldorf: Patmos Verlag, 1975), p. 87; Lorenz Oberlinner, "Die Verkündigung der Auferweckung Jesu im geöffneten und leeren Grab," *ZNW* 73 (1982): 162, 168, 175; Rudolf Pesch, "Das 'leere Grab' und der Glaube an Jesu Auferstehung," *IKZ* 11 (1982): 13.

[4] James Orr, *The Resurrection of Jesus* (London: Hodder & Stoughton, 1909), p. 39; Archibald Robertson and Alfred Plummer, *First Epistle of Saint Paul to the Corinthians*, 2nd ed., ICC (Edinburgh: T & T Clark, 1967), p. 334; Ernst-Bernard Allo, *Première épître aux Corinthiens* (Paris: Librairie Lecoffre, 1934), p. 391; P. Gardner-Smith, *The Narratives of the Resurrection*, (London: Methuen, 1926), p. 11; C. F. D. Moule, "St. Paul and Dualism: the Pauline Conception of the Resurrection," *NTS* 12 (1965-66): 122; Neville Clark, *Interpreting the Resurrection* (London: SCM, 1967), p. 82; C. F. D. Moule, ed., *The Significance of the Message of the Resurrection for Faith in Jesus Christ*, SBT 8 (London: SCM, 1968), p. 8; C. K. Barrett, *A Commentary on the First Epistle to the Corinthians*, BNTC (London: Adam & Charles Black, 1968), p. 339; Franz Mussner, *Die Auferstehung Jesu*, BH 7 (München: Kösel Verlag, 1969), p. 134; J. A. T. Robinson, *The Human Face of God* (London: SCM, 1973), p. 133; Jacob Kremer, "Zur Diskussion über 'das leere Grab'," in *Resurrexit*, ed. Édouard Dhanis (Rome: Libreria Editrice Vaticana, 1974), pp. 143-144.

stand in relation to the resurrection, but to the death, and as such serves to underline and confirm the reality of the death. The close *Zusammenhang* of the death and burial is said to be evident in Rom. 6, where to be baptized into Christ's death is to be baptized into his burial. Grass maintains that for the burial to imply a physical resurrection the sentence would have to read ἀπέθανεν...καὶ ὅτι ἐγήγερται ἐκ τοῦ τάφου.[5] As it is, the burial does not imply that the grave was empty. Grass also points out that Paul fails to mention the empty tomb in the second half of I Cor. 15, an instructive omission since the empty tomb would have been a knock-down argument against those who denied the bodily resurrection.[6] It is also often urged that the empty tomb was no part of the early kerygma and is therefore not implied in the burial.

Now while I should not want to assert that the "he was buried" was included in the formula in order to prove the empty tomb, it seems to me that the empty tomb is implied in the sequence of events related in the formula. For in saying that Jesus died—was buried—was raised—appeared, one automatically implies that an empty grave has been left behind. The four-fold ὅτι and the chronological series of events weighs against subordinating the burial to the death. In baptism the burial looks *forward* with confidence to the rising again.[7] This seems to be the case in Rom. 6: "We were buried therefore with him by baptism into death, so that (ἵνα) as Christ was raised from the dead by the glory of the Father, we too might walk in newness of life" (Rom. 6:4). Even clearer is Col. 2:12: "...and you were buried with him in baptism, in which you were also raised with him through faith in the working of God, who raised him from the dead." And even if one denies the evidence of the four-fold ὅτι and the chronological sequence, the very fact that a dead-and-buried man was raised would itself seem to imply an empty grave. The force of Grass's assertion that the formula should read ἐγήγερται ἐκ τοῦ τάφου seems diminished by the fact that in I Cor. 15:12 Paul does write ἐκ

---

[5] Grass, *Ostergeschehen*, p. 146.
[6] Ibid., p. 147.
[7] Walther Künneth, *The Theology of the Resurrection*, trans. J. W. Leitch (London: SCM, 1965), p. 93; Karl Heinrich Rengstorff, *Die Auferstehung Jesu*, 4th rev. ed. (Witten: Luther-Verlag, 1970), p. 61; Ulrich Wilckens, *Auferstehung*, TT4 (Stuttgart and Berlin: Kreuz Verlag, 1970), p. 22; Raymond E. Brown, *The Virginal Conception and Bodily Resurrection of Jesus* (London: Geoffrey Chapman, 1973), p. 84.

νεκρῶν ἐγήγερται (cf. I Thess. 1:10; Rom. 10:9; Gal. 1:1; Mt. 27:64; 28:7).[8] In being raised from the dead, Christ is raised from the grave.

In fact the very verb ἐγήγερται seems to imply that the grave is left empty. The two verbs ἐγείρειν and ἀνιστάναι are used synonymously throughout the New Testament.[9] The passive and intransitive forms of the respective verbs implies God as the one who raises up. The primary meaning of ἐγείρειν is "to awaken" from sleep, a sense also possible of ἀνιστάναι. In both Old and New Testaments, sleep is a euphemism for death; no doctrine of "soul-sleep" is implied. The picture is thus of a dead person's waking up again to life. Both verbs also mean "to raise upright" or "to erect." This can only have reference to the body in the grave, which is raised up to new life.[10] The verb ἐγείρειν can also have the sense of "to draw out of," as out of a hole. Clearly these notions of resurrection would be unintelligible with regard to the spirit or soul alone. The spirit does not awaken, for it is not asleep, nor is the spirit prone that it needs to be raised or erected. The very words appear to imply resurrection of the body. It is the dead man in the tomb who awakens and is physically raised up to new life. As Brown reminds us, "It is not really accurate to claim that the New Testament references to the *resurrection* of Jesus are ambiguous as to whether they mean bodily resurrection—there was no other kind of resurrection."[11] Thus the grave must be empty.[12] Now the empty tomb does not necessarily imply that the new

---

[8] This phrase implies a bodily resurrection, according to Robertson and Plummer, *Corinthians*, p. 351; Birger A. Pearson, *The Pneumatikos-Psychikos Terminology in I Corinthians*, SBL Dissertation Series 12 (Missoula, Mont.: Scholars Press, 1973), p. 94; Kremer, "Grab," p. 144; Robert H. Gundry, Soma *in Biblical Theology* (Cambridge: Cambridge University Press, 1976), p. 177. Hoffmann explains, "Since the statements here also remain bound up with the concept of resurrection, they presuppose, like Christ's statements and the corresponding Jewish concept of resurrection, the old belief in Sheol, in the sojourn of the dead in the grave and in the underworld" (Paul Hoffmann, *Die Toten in Christus*, 3rd rev. ed., NTA 2 [Münster: Aschendorff, 1978], p. 184). Thus the phrase "raised *from the dead*" entails an emptying of the grave.

[9] On these verbs see *TWNT*, s.v. "ἀνίστημι, ἀνάστασις, ἐξανίστημι, ἐξανάστασις," by Albrecht Oepke; *TWNT*, s.v. "ἐγείρω, ἔγερσις, ἐξεγείρω, γρηγορέω, (ἀγρυπνέω)," by Albrecht Oepke; C. F. Evans, *Resurrection and the New Testament*, SBT 12 (London: SCM Press, 1970), pp. 21-26.

[10] There may be in I Enoch 22:13 a peculiar sense in which a soul may be said to be "raised" because in this work the souls of the dead are stored in sockets in the face of a great cliff until the end comes. At the resurrection the earth, Sheol, and hell give back what is confined to them (I Enoch 51:1). But the notion of store-houses for the soul from which they could be said to be raised is foreign to the New Testament.

[11] Brown, *Bodily Resurrection*, p. 70.

[12] See the excellent study by Karl Bornhäuser, *Die Gebeine der Toten*, BFCT 26 (Gütersloh: C. Bertelsmann, 1921). Some critics acknowledge the accuracy of Bornhäuser's exposition of resur-

life is a recommencement of the old, as it did for certain segments of Judaism; it could be that the body is radically changed, so that the resurrected body is almost utterly dissimilar to the old body. So the empty tomb does not settle the issue of the nature of the resurrection body. But nevertheless the very words ἐγείρειν and ἀνιστάναι imply that the body is resurrected and that the tomb is therefore left empty. And really, even today were we to be told that a man who died and was buried rose from the dead and appeared to his friends, *only* a theologian would think to ask, "But was his body still in the grave?" How much more is this true of first century Jews, who shared a much more physical conception of resurrection than we do![13]

---

rection in the Old Testament, but brush it aside with a word, that the New Testament knows nothing of such a conception. They ignore his clear statement that what is here most important is not what is said in the New Testament, but what is presupposed by the New Testament (Ibid., p. 6). On the question of the resurrection Jesus sided with the Pharisees and the Old Testament. Bornhäuser's thesis is that in the Old Testament the grave is the place where the corpse decays but the bones remain and rest until the resurrection, at which they are raised. The flesh of the body is thus unimportant, but the bones are to be preserved (I Sam. 31:11; II Sam. 21:10; II Kings 23:17). The Jews thus feared anything that might destroy the bones, like the sun, wild animals, or consuming fire. When a man dies, his body returns to the earth, while his spirit goes back to God, but the bones remain. Thus, the dead have a sort of double life: in the spirit and in the bones. The metaphor of sleep is used with regard to the bones, which sleep in the grave, while the spirit lives in Paradise. There is no *Auferweckung* of the soul, nor even of the flesh; it is much more, properly speaking, an *Auferstehung* and *Auferweckung* of the bones (Ibid., p. 26). But should the bones be destroyed, the Jews were confident that God could raise the dead even without the bones, as in the case of Jewish martyrs. The New Testament presupposes this same conception. Mt. 23:27; Jn. 5:28 show that Jesus regarded the tomb as the place where the bones are, which would be raised at the resurrection. Paul's terminology is thoroughly Pharisaic; it should never have come to be, states Bornhäuser, that in spite of the ἐτάφη, the "he was raised" should be understood as anything other than the resurrection from the grave (Ibid., p. 33). Phil. 1:23; II Cor. 5:8 show clearly that for Paul it is not the spirit that is asleep in death. When he says that those who are asleep will rise at the last trumpet (I Thess. 4:13-17), he means the *dead in the graves*. Thus, the grave would have to be empty after the resurrection. (See also *Hastings' Encyclopaedia of Religion and Ethics*, s.v. "Bones," by H. Wheeler Robinson; Joseph Bonsirven, *Le Judaisme palestinien au temps de Jésus Christ*, 2 vols. [Paris: Beauchesne, 1934], I: 484; Künneth, *Theology*, p. 94.)

[13] So true is Rengstorff's judgment:
"Absolutely nothing is gained from sentences like, 'We believe not in the empty tomb, but in the resurrected, living Lord.'[71] Such sentences construct an opposition that is foreign to the New Testament kerygma, and they are moreover defeated by logical considerations.

---

[71] So Grass, ...p. 8...and p. 185" (Rengstorff, *Auferstehung*, p. 62).

Comments Ellis: "It is very unlikely that the earliest Palestinian Christians could conceive of any distinction between resurrection and physical, 'grave-emptying' resurrection. To them an *anastasis* (resurrection) without an empty grave would have been about as meaningful as a square circle" (E. Earle Ellis, ed., *The Gospel of Luke*, NBC [London: Nelson, 1966], p. 273). See also Moule,

Grass's argument that had Paul believed in the empty tomb, then he would have mentioned it in the second half of I Cor. 15 seems to turn back upon Grass; for if Paul did not believe in the empty tomb, then why did he not mention the purely spiritual appearance of Christ to him alluded to I Cor. 15:8 as a knock-down argument for the immateriality of Christ's body? Grass can only reply that Paul did not appeal to his vision of Jesus to prove that the resurrection body would be heavenly and glorious because the meeting "eluded all description."[14] But could Paul not have said he saw a heavenly light and heard a voice? In fact the very ineffability of the experience would be a positive argument for immateriality, since a physical body is not beyond all description. Grass seems to misunderstand Paul's intention in discussing the resurrection body. Paul does not want to prove that it is physical, for that was presupposed by everyone and was perhaps what the Corinthians stuck at.[15] He wants to prove that the body is in some sense spiritual, and thus the Corinthians ought not to recoil from this doctrine. Hence, the mention of the empty tomb would be beside the point. There would thus be no reason to mention the empty tomb, but good reason to appeal to Paul's vision, which he does not do. Does this not suggest that Paul perhaps accepted both the empty tomb and the physical resurrection of Christ?

Finally, as to the absence of the empty tomb in the kerygma, the statement "he was buried" followed by the proclamation of the resurrection seems to indicate that the empty tomb was implied in the kerygma. The formula is a summary statement,[16] and it could very well be that Paul was familiar with the historical context of the simple statement in the formula, which would imply that he not only accepted the empty tomb but knew of it as well. The tomb is certainly alluded to in the preaching in Acts 2:24-32. The pointed contrast between David's death and burial and Jesus's not being held by death is the fact that whereas

---

Significance, p. 9; Joachim Gnilka, *Das Evangelium nach Markus*, 2 vols., EKKNT (Zürich: Benziger Verlag, 1979; Neukirchen-Vluyn, 1979), 2: 342.

[14] Grass, *Ostergeschehen*, p. 172.

[15] H. A. W. Meyer, *Handbuch über den ersten Brief an die Korinther*, 6th ed., rev. Georg Heinrici, KEKNT 5 (Göttingen: Vandenhoeck & Ruprecht's Verlag, 1881), p. 393; Johannes Weiss, *Der erste Korintherbrief*, 9th ed., KEKNT 5 (Göttingen: Vandenhoeck & Ruprecht, 1910), p. 344.

[16] The mention of the empty tomb would not pass well with the structure and rhythm of the formula in any case, since the subject of each sentence is Χριστός and the empty tomb is not something that Christ did.

David's tomb is with us to this day, God raised (ἀνέστησεν) Jesus up.[17] The empty tomb seems clearly in view here. The empty tomb also seems implicit in Paul's speech in Antioch of Pisidia, which follows point for point the outline of the formula in I Cor. 15:3-5: "...they took him down from the tree, and laid him in a tomb. But God raised him from the dead; and for many days he appeared to those who came up with him from Galilee to Jerusalem" (Acts 13:29-31). No first century Jew or pagan would have been so cerebral as to wonder if the tomb was empty or not. That the empty tomb is not more explicitly mentioned may be simply because it was regarded as *selbstverständlich*, given the resurrection and appearances of Jesus. Or again, it may be that the evidence of the appearances so overwhelmed the testimony of legally unqualified women to the empty grave that the latter was not used as evidence. But the gospel of Mark shows that the empty tomb was important to the early church, even if it was not appealed to as evidence in evangelistic preaching. So I think it apparent that the formula and Paul at least accept the empty tomb, even if it is not explicitly mentioned.[18]

"ON THE THIRD DAY"

A second possible reference to the empty tomb is the phrase "on the third day." Since no one actually saw the resurrection of Jesus, how could it be dated on the third day? Some critics argue that it was on this day that the women found the tomb empty, so the resurrection came to be dated on that day.[19] Thus, the phrase

---

[17] See Ernst Lichtenstein, "Der älteste christliche Glaubensformel," *ZKG* 63 (1950-51): 32; *Interpreter's Dictionary of the Bible*, s.v., "Resurrection," by J. A. T. Robinson; Ethelbert Stauffer, *Jesus and His Story*, trans. D. M. Barton (London: SCM, 1960), p.119; Vincent Taylor, *The Gospel according to St. Mark*, 2nd ed. (London: Macmillan, 1966), p. 606.

[18] So Lichtenstein, "Glaubensformel," p. 33; Wolfgang Nauck, "Die Bedeutung des leeren Grabes für den Glauben an den Auferstandenen," *ZNW* 47 (1956): 247-248; Jindrich Mánek, "The Apostle Paul and the Empty Tomb," *NT* 2 (1957): 277-278; *Interpreter's Dictionary of the Bible*, s.v. "Resurrection," by Robinson; Michael Perry, *The Easter Enigma*, with an Introduction by Austin Farrer (London: Faber & Faber, 1959), p. 92; Rengstorff, *Auferstehung*, p. 61; Künneth, *Theology*, pp. 92-93; Karl Lehmann, *Auferweckt am dritten Tag nach der Schrift*, QD 38 (Freiburg: Herder, 1968), p. 81; S. H. Hooke, *The Resurrection of Christ as History and Experience* (London: Darton, Longman & Todd, 1967), p. 114; Mussner, *Auferstehung*, p. 101; Wilckens, *Auferstehung*, p. 21; Berthold Klappert, "Einleitung," in *Diskussion um Kreuz und Auferstehung*, ed. idem. (Wuppertal: Aussaat Verlag, 1971), p. 16; Grant Osborne, "History and Theology in the Resurrection Narratives: a Redactional Study" (Ph.D. thesis, University of Aberdeen, 1974), p. 84.

[19] See Nauck, "Bedeutung," p. 263; Gerhard Koch, *Die Auferstehung Jesu Christi*, BHT (Tübingen: J. C. B. Mohr, 1959), p. 33; Hans Freiherr von Campenhausen, *Der Ablauf der Oster-*

"on the third day" not only presupposes that a resurrection leaves an empty grave behind but is a definite reference to the historical fact of Jesus's empty tomb. But, of course, there are many other ways to interpret this phrase: (1) The third day dates the first appearance of Jesus. (2) Because Christians assembled for worship on the first day of the week, the resurrection was assigned to this day. (3) Parallels in the history of religions influenced the dating of the resurrection on the third day. (4) The dating of the third day is lifted from Old Testament Scriptures. (5) The third day is a theological *Interpretament* indicating God's salvation, deliverance, and manifestation. Each of these needs to be examined in turn.

1. *The third day dates the first appearance of Jesus.*[20] In favor of this view is the proximity of the statement "raised on the third day in accordance with the Scriptures" with "he appeared to Cephas, then to the Twelve." Because Jesus appeared on the third day, the resurrection itself was naturally dated on that day. The phrase "according to the Scriptures" could indicate that the Christians, having believed Christ rose on the third day, sought out appropriate proof texts.

This understanding would be consistent with either a Jerusalem or Galilean appearance tradition, for whether the disciples remained in Jerusalem or fled to Galilee, they could have seen Jesus on the third day after his death. If it were proved, however, that the disciples returned slowly to Galilee and saw Christ only some time later, then this view would have to be rejected. A discussion of this question must be deferred until later.

Against this understanding of the third day it is sometimes urged that the Easter reports do not use the expression "on the third day" but prefer to speak of

---

ereignisse und das leere Grab, 3rd rev. ed., SHA (Heidelberg: Carl Winter, 1966), p. 12; Ellis, *Luke*, p. 273; Josef Blank, *Paulus und Jesus*, SANT 18 (München: Kösel Verlag, 1968), pp. 153-156; Gerhard Lohfink, "Die Auferstehung Jesu und die historische Kritik," *BiLeb* 9 (1968): 95; Ludger Schenke, *Auferstehungsverkündigung und leeres Grab* (Stuttgart: Katholisches Bibelwerk, 1968), p. 108; Gerhard Delling, "The Significance of the Resurrection of Jesus for Faith in Jesus Christ," in *Significance*, ed. Moule, p. 80; Jacob Kremer, *Das älteste Zeugnis von der Auferstehung Christi*, 3rd ed., SBS 17 (Stuttgart: Katholisches Bibelwerk, 1970), p. 4; Joachim Jeremias, *Neutestamentliche Theologie* (Gütersloh: Gerd Mohn, 1971), pp. 288-289; Kremer, "Grab," p. 142.

[20] J. W. Hunkin, "The Problem of the Resurrection Narratives," *ExpTim* 46 (1935): 153; Charles Masson, "Le tombeau vide: essai sur la formation d'une tradition," *RTPhil* 32 (1944): 170; Lichtensten, "Glaubensformel," p. 41; Ferdinand Hahn, *Christologische Hoheitstitel*, 3rd ed., FRLANT 83 (Göttingen: Vandenhoeck & Ruprecht, 1966), pp. 205-206; G. W. H. Lampe and D. M. MacKinnon, *The Resurrection*, ed. William Purcell (London: A. R. Mowbray, 1966), p. 42; Brown, *Bodily Resurrection*, p. 125.

"the first day of the week" (Mk. 16:2; Mt. 28:1; Lk. 24:1; Jn. 20:1, 19).[21] The passages in the gospels which do mention the third day may be grouped under four heads: (1) the predictions and occurrence of the resurrection: μετὰ τρεῖς ἡμέρας (Mk. 8:31; 9:31; 10:34; Mt. 27:63), τῇ τρίτῃ ἡμέραν (Mt. 16:21; 17:23; 20:18; Lk. 9:22; 24:7, 46; Acts 10:40); τῇ ἡμέρᾳ τῇ τρίτῃ (Lk. 18:33); τρίτην ταύτην ἡμέραν (Lk. 24:21); (2) the sign of Jonah: τρεῖς ἡμέρας καὶ τρεῖς νύκτας (Mt. 12:40); (3) the rebuilding of the Temple: ἐν τρισὶν ἡμέραις (Mk. 15:29, Mt. 27:40; Jn. 2:19); διὰ τριῶν ἡμερῶν (Mk. 14:58; Mt. 26:61); (4) Jesus's fulfillment in Jerusalem: τῇ τρίτῃ (Lk. 13:32). Scholars agree that because of the Jewish peculiarity of reckoning part of a day as a whole day, all these expressions come to the same thing.[22] But all the third day references are said to be in the Easter kerygma, not the Easter reports. Even Matthew, who in 27:63 mentions the third day in Jesus's prediction, does not use the phrase again in 28:1 but employs "the first day of the week." This shows, it is maintained, not only the independence of the Easter reports from the kerygma, but also that neither the empty tomb nor the appearances of Christ can be the *direct* cause of the "third day" motif."[23]

But why could they not be the root cause? All that has been proved by the above seems to be that the Easter reports and the Easter preaching are literarily distinct, but that fact cannot prove that they are not twin offshoots of an original event. The event could produce the report on the one hand; on the other hand it would set the believers a-searching in the Old Testament for fulfilled Scriptures. In this search they could find and adopt the language of the third day because, according to Jewish reckoning, the first day of the week was in fact the third day after Jesus's death. Scriptures in hand, they could thus proclaim "he was raised on the third day in accordance with the Scriptures." This language could then be

---

[21] Lehmann, *Auferweckt*, pp. 160-161, 337; Edward Lynn Bode, *The First Easter Morning*, AB 45 (Rome: Biblical Institute Press, 1970), pp. 117-119.
[22] Frederic Field, *Notes on the Translation of the New Testament* (Cambridge: Cambridge University Press, 1899). pp. 11-13; Gerhard Kittel, *Rabbinica: Paulus im Talmud* ARGU 1:3 (Leipzig: Hinrichs, 1920), pp. 31-38; Werner Georg Kümmel, *Verheissung und Erfüllung*, 3rd ed., ATANT 6 (Zürich: Zwingli Verlag, 1956), p. 61; Paul Billerbeck, *Kommentar zum Neuen Testament aus Talmud und Midrasch*, 6 vols., ed. Herrmann L. Strack (München: Beck, 1922-63), 1:649; TWNT, s.v. "ἡμέρα" by Gerhard von Rad and Gerhard Delling; Taylor, *Mark*, p. 378; Lehmann, *Auferweckt*, p. 163-166.
[23] Lehmann, *Auferweckt*, p. 161.

used by the evangelists outside the Easter reports or actually interwoven with them, as by Luke. Thus the same root event could produce two different descriptions of the day of the resurrection.

But was that event the first appearance of Jesus? Here one cannot exclude the empty tomb from playing a role, for the "third day" refers as much to it as to the appearances and "the first day of the week," which may be even more primitive, refers primarily to the empty tomb. If the first appearances occurred on the same day as the discovery of the empty tomb, then these two events together would naturally date the resurrection, and the "third day" language could reflect the LXX formulation, which is found in I Cor. 15:4 and was worked into the traditions underlying the gospels. So I think it unlikely that the date "on the third day" refers to the day of the first appearance alone.

2. *Because Christians assembled on the first day of the week, the resurrection was assigned to this day.*[24] Although this hypothesis once enjoyed adherents, it is now completely abandoned. Rordorf's study *Der Sonntag* has demonstrated to the satisfaction of New Testament critics that the expression "raised on the third day" has nothing to do with Christian Sunday worship.[25] More likely would be that because the resurrection was on the third day, Christians worshipped on that day. But even though the question of how Sunday came to be the Christian special day of worship is still debated, no theory is today propounded which would date the resurrection as a result of Sunday as a worship day.

3. *Parallels in the history of religions influenced the dating of the resurrection on the third day.*[26] In the hey-day of the *religionsgeschichtliche Schule*, all sorts of parallels in the history of religions were adduced in order to explain the resurrection on the third day; but today critics are more cautious. The myths of dying and rising gods in pagan religions are merely symbols for processes of nature and have no connection with a real historical individual like Jesus of Nazareth.[27] The three-day motif is found only in the Osiris and perhaps Adonis cults, and, in Grass's words, it is "completely unthinkable" that the early Christian community

---

[24] E. Schwartz, "Osterbetrachtungen," *ZNW* 7 (1906): 133; Carl Clemen, *Religionsgeschichtliche Erklärung des Neuen Testaments*, 2nd ed. (Giessen: Töpelmann, 1924), pp. 105-107.
[25] Willy Rordorf, *Der Sonntag*, ATANT 43 (Zürich: Zwingli Verlag, 1962), pp. 174-233; see also Grass, *Ostergeschehen*, pp. 131-133; Lehman, *Auferweckt*, pp. 185-191.
[26] Clemen, *Erklärung*, 96-105; Wilhelm Bousset, *Kyrios Christos*, 5th ed., FRLANT 4 (Göttingen: Vandenhoeck & Ruprecht, 1965). pp. 22-26.
[27] Künneth, *Theology*, pp. 50-63.

from which the formula stems could be influenced by such myths.[28] In fact there is hardly any trace of cults of dying and rising gods at all in first century Palestine.

It has also been suggested that the three-day motif reflects the Jewish belief that the soul did not depart decisively from the body until after three days.[29] But the belief was actually that the soul departed irrevocably on the fourth day, not the third; in which case the analogy with the resurrection is weaker. But the decisive consideration against this view is that the resurrection would not then be God's act of power and deliverance from death, for the soul had not yet decisively left the body but merely re-entered and resuscitated it. This would thus discredit the resurrection of Jesus. If this Jewish notion were in mind, the expression would have been "raised on the fourth day" after the soul had forever abandoned the body and all hope was gone (cf. the raising of Lazarus).

Some critics have thought that the third day reference is meant only to indicate, in Hebrew reckoning, "a short time" or "a while."[30] But when one considers the emphasis laid on this motif not only in the formula but especially in the gospels, then so indefinite a reference would not have the obvious significance which the early Christians assigned to this phrase. Few scholars are today so enthusiastic about the possibility of explaining New Testament motifs from *religionsgeschichtlichen* parallels, especially with regard to the resurrection; not only are the parallels often vague, but the genealogical tie between them and the New Testament is often missing.

---

[28] Grass, *Ostergeschehen*, pp. 133; cf. p. 134. See also the critique and literature in Lehmann, *Auferweckt*, pp. 193-200; Bode, *Easter*, pp. 110-111.

[29] Bousset, *Kyrios*, p. 25; Selby McCasland, "The Scriptural Basis Of 'On the Third Day'," *JBL* 48 (1929): 124-137; E. C. Hoskyns, *The Fourth Gospel*, 2nd ed., ed. F. N. Davey (London: Faber, 1967), pp. 199-200; Bruce M. Metzger, "A Suggestion Concerning of I Cor. XV.4b," *JTS* 8 (1958): 118-123. On the Jewish belief, see R. Mach, *Der Zaddik in Talmud und Midrasch* (Leiden: E. J. Brill, 1957), p. 174. For a critique, see Lehmann, *Auferweckt*, pp. 200-204; Bode, *Easter*, pp. 113-115.

[30] Maurice Goguel, *La foi à la résurrection de Jésus dans le christianisme primitif* (Paris: Leroux, 1939), pp. 164-165; Cecil J. Cadoux, *The Historic Mission of Jesus*, 2nd ed. (London: Lutterworth Press, 1941), pp. 286-288; J. B. Bauer, "Drei Tage," *Bib* 39 (1958): 354-358; Barnabas Lindars, *New Testament Apologetic: The Doctrinal Significance of Old Testament Quotations* (London: SCM, 1961), pp. 59-72; A. D. Nock, *Early Gentile Christianity and Its Hellenistic Background* (New York: Harper, 1964), p. 108; X. Léon Dufour, *Resurrection and the Message of Easter* (London: Geoffery Chapman, 1974), p. 9. For a critique, see Lehmann, *Auferweckt*, pp. 176-181; Bode, *Easter*, pp. 111-112.

4. *The dating of the third day is lifted from Old Testament Scriptures.*[31] Because the formula reads "on the third day in accordance with the Scriptures" many authors believe that the third day motif is drawn from the Old Testament, especially Hos. 6:2, which in the LXX reads τῇ ἡμέρᾳ τῇ τρίτῃ.[32] Although Metzger has asserted, with appeal to I Macc. 7:16-17 that the "according to the Scriptures" may refer to the resurrection, not the third day,[33] this view seems difficult to maintain in light, not only of the parallel in I Cor. 15:3, but especially of Lk. 24:45 where the third day seems definitely in mind.

Against taking the "on the third day" to refer to Hos. 6:2 it has been urged that no explicit quotation of the text is found in the New Testament, or indeed anywhere until Tertullian (*Adversus Judaeos* 13).[34] New Testament quotations of the Old Testament usually mention the prophet's name and are of the nature of promise-fulfillment. But nowhere do we find this for Hos. 6:2. Grass retorts that there is indirect evidence for Christian use of Hos. 6:2 in the Targum Hosea's dropping the reference to the number of days; the passage had to be altered because Christians had pre-empted the verse. Moreover, Jesus's own "predictions," written back into the gospel story by believers after the event, obviated the need to cite a Scripture reference.[35] But Grass's first point seems not only to be speculative, but actually contradicted by the fact that later Rabbis saw no difficulty in retaining the

---

[31] See especially *TWNT*, s.v. "ἡμέρα" by Gerhard Delling; F. Nötscher, "Zur Auferstehung nach drei Tagen," *Bib* 35 (1954): 313-319; Grass, *Ostergeschehen*, pp. 136-138; Jacques Dupont, "Ressuscité 'le troisième jour'," *Bib* 40 (1959): 742-761; Friedrich Mildenberger, "Auferstanden am dritten Tage nach der Schrift," *EvT* 23 (1963): 265-280; C. H. Dodd, *According to the Scriptures* (London: Collins, 1965), pp. 77, 103; Evans, *Resurrection*, pp. 48-50; Fischer, *Ostergeschehen*, pp. 72-73; Oberlinner, "Verkündigung," p. 177.

[32] Other Scriptures such as Jonah 1:17; II Kings 20:5 are so far removed from the idea of resurrection that they could not possibly have prompted belief that Jesus rose on the third day. Kirsopp Lake, after examining the various passages, admitted they were all improbable and confessed that the basis for the third day is unknown (Kirsopp Lake, *The Historical Evidence for the Resurrection of Jesus* [London: Williams and Norgate, 1907], pp. 29-33). According to Lehmann most critics choose Hos. 6:2 out of desperation and want of an alternative. Among those who see Hos. 6:2 behind I Cor. 15:4 are F. C. Burkitt, C. R. Browen, J. Weiss, M. Goguel, J. Finegan, G. Delling, H.-D. Wendland, J. G. S. S. Thompson, J. Dupont, C. H. Dodd, U. Wilckens, H. Grass, H. E. Tödt, H. Conzelmann, F. Mildenberger, G. Strecker, G. Schunack, P. Stuhlmacher, J. Bowman, J. W. Doeve, J. Wijngaards, W. Rudolph, B. Lindars, M. Black, T. Bowman (for particulars, see Lehmann, *Auferweckt*, pp. 228-229).

[33] Metzger, "Suggestion," p. 121; cf. Weiss, *Korintherbrief*, p. 348; Kremer, *Zeugnis*, p. 4; O'Collins, *Easter*, p. 15. For a critique, see Grass, *Ostergeschehen*, p. 135; Lehmann, *Auferweckt*, pp. 242-261; Bode, *Easter*, pp. 115-116.

[34] Georg Kittel, "Die Auferstehung Jesu," *DT* 4 (1937): 160; Bode, *Easter*, pp. 115-116.

[35] Grass, *Ostergeschehen*, pp. 137-138.

third day reference in Hosea.³⁶ No conclusion can be drawn from Targum Hosea's change in wording, for the distinctive characteristic of this Targum is its free haggadic handling of the text. And this still says nothing about New Testament practice of citing the prophet's name. As for the second point, Matthew's citation of Jonah (Mt. 12:40) seems to make this rather dubious. According to Bode, Matthew's citation is the decisive argument against Hos. 6:2, since it shows the latter was not the passage which Christians had in mind with regard to the three day motif.³⁷

But to my mind the greatest difficulty with the Hos. 6:2 understanding of "on the third day" is that it appears to necessitate that the disciples without the instigation of any historically corresponding event would find and adopt such a Scripture reference. For this understanding requires that no appearances occurred and no discovery of the empty tomb was made on the third day/first day of the week. Otherwise these events would constitute the basis for the date of the resurrection, not Hos. 6:2 alone. But if there were no such events, then it seems very unlikely that the disciples should land upon an obscure passage like Hos. 6:2 and apply it to Jesus's resurrection. It is much more likely that such events would prompt them to search the Scriptures for appropriate texts, which could then be interpreted in light of the resurrection (Jn. 2:22; 12:16; 20:8-9).³⁸ And insofar as the empty tomb tradition or appearance tradition proves accurate, the hypothesis in question is further undermined. For if the empty tomb was discovered on the first day of the week or Peter saw Jesus on the third day, then the view that "the third day" was derived *solely* from Scripture would seem untenable. At most one could say that the language of the LXX was applied to these events. The falsity of the gospel traditions concerning both the discovery of the empty tomb and the day of the first appearance is thus a *sine qua non* for the Hos. 6:2 understanding, and hence should either of these traditions prove accurate, the appeal to Hos. 6:2 as

---

³⁶ See Lehmann, *Auferweckt*, pp. 226-227.
³⁷ Bode, *Easter*, p. 116.
³⁸ As von Campenhausen urges, the detail "on the third day" must have a biblical counterpart to warrant its inclusion, but the Scripture passages are so vague that the third day must have been somehow already given before it could be discovered in the Old Testament (Von Campenhausen, *Ablauf*, pp. 11-12). So also Michael Ramsey, *The Resurrection of Christ* (London: Centenary Press, 1945), p. 25; C. F. D. Moule, *The Birth of the New Testament*, 2ⁿᵈ ed. rev. (London: Adam & Charles Black, 1966], pp. 84-85; Barrett, *First Epistle*, p. 340.

the basis (as opposed to the *language*) for the date of the resurrection must be rejected.

5. *The third day is a theological Interpretament indicating God's salvation, deliverance, and manifestation.*[39] This understanding is, I think, the only serious alternative to regarding the third day motif as based on the historical events of the resurrection, and it has been eloquently expounded by Lehmann and supported by Bode and McArthur as well. To begin with, there are nearly 30 passages in the LXX that use the phrase τῇ ἡμέρᾳ τῇ τρίτῃ to describe events that happened on the third day.[40] On the third day Abraham offered Isaac (Gen. 22:4; cf. Gen. 34:25; 40:20). On the third day Joseph released his brothers from prison (Gen. 42:18). After three days God made a covenant with His people and gave the law (Ex. 19:11, 16; cf. Lev. 8:18; Num. 7:24; 19:12, 19; Judg. 19:8; 20:30). On the third day David came to Ziklag to fight the Amalekites (I Sam. 30:1) and on the third day thereafter heard the news of Saul and Jonathan's death (II Sam. 1:2). On the third day the kingdom was divided (I Kings 12:24; cf. II Chron. 10:12). On the third day King Hezekiah went to the House of the Lord after which he was miraculously healed (II Kings 20:5, 8). On the third day Esther began her plan to save her people (Esther 5:1; cf. II Macc. 11:18). The only passage in the prophets mentioning the third day is Hos. 6:2. Thus, the third day is a theologically determined time at which God acts to bring about the new and better, a time of life, salvation, and victory. On the third day comes resolution of a difficulty through God's act. A second step is to consider the interpretation given to such passages in Jewish Midrash:

> 'And he put them all together into ward three days.' The Holy One, blessed be He, never leaves the righteous in distress more than three days.
> 'And Joseph said unto them the third day,' etc. (XLII, 18). Thus it is written, *After two days He will revive us, on the third day He will raise us up, that we may live in His presence* (Hosea VI, 2): on the third day of the tribal ancestors. (Midrash Rabbah, Genesis [Mikketz] 91:7.)

---

[39] Lehmann, *Auferweckt*, pp. 262-290; Bode, *Easter*, pp. 119-126; Harvey K. McArthur, "'On the Third Day'," *NTS* 18 (1971): 81-86, holds a related view but still casts his lot with Hos. 6:2; Reginald H. Fuller, *The Formation of the Resurrection Narratives* (London: SPCK, 1972), p. 27.
[40] Wengst observes that Lehmann actually produces 25 passages, not "nearly 30" and of these only nine can be truly said to have the theological significance that Lehmann sees in the third day (Gen. 22:4; Ex. 19:11, 16; Judg. 20:30; I Sam. 30:1; II Kings 20:5, 8; Esther 5:1; Hos. 6:2) (Klaus Wengst, *Christologische Formeln und Lieder des Urchristetums*, SNT 7 [Gütersloh: Gerd Mohn, 1972], p. 96).

Another explanation: 'Now it came to pass on the third day;' Israel are never left in dire distress more than three days. For so of Abraham it is written, *On the third day Abraham lifted up his eyes, and saw the place afar off* (ib. XXII, 4). Of Jacob's sons we read, *And he put them all together into ward three days* (ib. XLII, 17). Of Jonah it says, *And Jonah was in the belly of the fish three days and three nights* (Jonah II, 1). The dead also will come to life after three days, as it says, *On the third day He will raise us up that we may live in His presence* (Hos. VI, 2). This miracle also of Mordecai and Esther was performed after three days of their fasting, as it is written, 'Now it came to pass on the third day, that Esther put on her royal apparel'.... (Midrash Rabbah, Esther 9:2.)

'On the third day,' etc. (XXII, 4). It is written, *After two days He will revive us, on the third day He will raise us up, that we may live in His presence* (Hos. VI, 2). E.g. on the third day of the tribal ancestors: *And Joseph said unto them the third day: This do, and live* (Gen. XLII, 18); on the third day of Revelation: *And it came to pass on the third day, when it was morning* (Ex. XIX, 16); on the third day of the spies: *And hide yourselves there three days* (Josh. II, 16); on the third day of Jonah: *And Jonah was in the belly of the fish three days and three nights* (Jonah II, 1); on the third day of those returning from the exile: *And we abode there three days* (Ezra VIII, 32): on the third day of the resurrection: '*After two days He will revive us, on the third day He will raise us up*,' on the third day of Esther: *Now it came to pass on the third day, that Esther put on her royal apparel* (Est. V, 1)—i.e. she put on the royal apparel of her ancestor. For whose sake? The Rabbis say: For the sake of the third day, when Revelation took place. R. Levi maintained: In the merit of what Abraham did on the third day, as it says, 'On the third day,' etc. (Midrash Rabbah, Genesis [Vayera] 56.1.)

Another explanation: 'The Lord will open.' The Rabbis say: Great is the rainfall, for it is counted as equivalent to the Revival of the Dead. Whence this? For it says *And he shall come unto us as the rain, as the latter rain that watereth the earth* (Hos. VI, 3). What does scripture say immediately before this? *After two days He will revive us* (ib. 2). Therefore the Rabbis have inserted [the prayer for rain in the benediction of] the Revival of the Dead, because it is equal in importance to it. (Midrash Rabbah, Deuteronomy (Ki Thabo) 7.6.)

And why only a three day fast? Because the Holy One, blessed be He, does not leave the children of Israel in distress for more than three days. Thus, Scripture says, *On the third day Abraham lifted up his eyes and saw the place afar off* (Gen. 22:4); and it is said *He put them all together into ward three days* (Gen. 42:17); and it is said *And they went three days in the wilderness, and found no water* (Ex. 15:22); and again when Hezekiah was sick unto death, the word of the Lord came to Isaiah, saying: *Return, and say to Hezekiah: Behold, I will heal thee; unto the house of the Lord thou shalt go on the third day* (2 Kings 20:5). In like manner, Rahab the harlot said to the spies sent out by Joshua: You need suffer but three days, as is said *Get you to the mountain...and hide yourselves there three days...and afterward may ye go your way* (Josh. 2:16). And likewise of Jonah: *Jonah was in the belly of the fish three days and three nights* (Jonah 2:2), and then *The Lord spoke unto the fish, and it vomited out Jonah upon the dry land* (Jonah 2:11). The prophet Hosea also said: *After two days He will revive us, on the third day He will raise us up, and we shall live in His sight* (Hos. 6:2). (Midrash on Psalms, 22.5.)

From Jewish Midrash it is evident that the third day was the day when God delivered the righteous from distress or when events reached their climax. It is also evident that Hos. 6:2 was interpreted in terms of resurrection, albeit at the end of history. The mention of the offering of Isaac on the third day is thought to have had a special influence on Christian thought, as we shall see. The reference to the Israelites' three day trek to the sea is amplified by Samaritan sources (Marqua's Commentary on Exodus), Jewish sources (Midrash Rabbah, Exodus [Shemoth] 3.8), Philo (*De vita Mosis* 1.163), Josephus (*Antiquities of the Jews* 2.315), and Eusebius (*Praeparatio evangelica* 9.27). Further Jewish references to the significance of the number three and the third day may be found in Ginzberg's *Legends of the Jews*.[41] A third step in the argument is comparison of other Rabbinical literature concerning the third day with regard to the resurrection:

> He will give us life in the days of consolation which are coming; and in the day of the resurrection of the dead he will revive us so that we will live before him. (Targum Hosea 6.2.)
>
> R. Kattina said: Six thousand years shall the world exist, and one [thousandth, the seventh] it shall be desolate, as it is written, *And the Lord alone shall be exalted in that day*. Abaye said: It will be desolate two [thousand], as it is said, *After two days he will revive us; in the third day he will raise us up, and we shall live in his sight*. (B. Sanhedrin 97a; cf. B. Rosh Hashanah 31a.)
>
> Just as the resurrection from the dead brings life without end, so also one hopes that the descent of rain will bring life without end. So one understands why the two subjects appear in the same petition. R. Hiyabar Abba proved this by the verses (Hos. 6:2): *After two days he will revive us, on the third day he will raise us up, and we shall live before him. Come, let us press on to acquire the knowledge of God, which one will find in the morning*. (P. Berakoth 5.2.)
>
> That is different, replied the second questioner. Isaiah was concerned with the question of the resurrection of the dead...as it is said (Hos. 6:2): *After two days he will revive us; on the third day he will raise us up, and we shall live in his presence—*. (P. Sanhedrin 11.6.)
>
> All its inhabitants shall taste the taste of death for two days, when there will be no soul of man or beast upon the earth...On the third day He will renew them all and revive the dead, and He will establish it before Him, as it is said, "On the third day he will raise us up, and we shall live before him" (Hos. vi.2). (Pirkê de Rabbi Eliezer 51.73b-74a.)
>
> Even when, for their sins, God slays Israel in this world, there is healing for them in the world to come, as it is said, "Come, let us return unto the Lord, for it is He who has torn us, and He will bind us up; after two days He will revive us; on the third day He will raise us up" (Hos. vi.2). The two days are this world and the days of the Messiah; the third day is the world to come. (Tanna de-be Eliyyahu, p. 29.)

These passages make it evident that the rabbis were interpreting Hos. 6:2 in the sense of the eschatological resurrection. Now, according to Lehmann, when one brings together the testimonies of the Midrash Rabbah, the rabbinic writings, and the passages from the LXX, then it becomes highly probable that I Cor. 15:4 can

---

[41] Louis Ginzberg, *The Legends of the Jews*, 8 vols., trans. Paul Radin (Philadelphia: Jewish Publication Society of America, 1911), III: 79-80; V: 428; VI: 33, 129.

be illuminated by these texts and their theology. Of particular importance here is the sacrifice of Isaac, which grew to have a great meaning for Jewish theology.[42] In pre-Christian Judaism the sacrifice of Isaac was already brought into connection with the Passover. He became a symbol of submission and self-sacrifice to God. The offering of Isaac was conceived to have salvific worth. In the blood of the sacrifices, God saw and remembered the sacrifice of Isaac and so continued His blessing of Israel. This exegesis of Gen. 22 is thought to leave traces in Rom. 4:17, 25; 8:32 and Heb. 11:17-19. This last text particularly relates the resurrection of Jesus to the sacrifice of Isaac. When we consider the formula in I Cor. 15, with its Semitic background, then it is said to be much more probable that the expression "on the third day" reflects the influence of Jewish traditions that later came to be written in Talmud and Midrash than that it refers to Hos. 6:2 alone as a proof text. Thus, "on the third day" does not mark the discovery of the empty tomb or the first appearance, nor is it indeed any time indicator at all, but rather it is the day of God's deliverance and victory. It tells us that God did not leave the Righteous One in distress but raised him up and so ushered in a new eon.

Lehmann's case is well-documented and very persuasive; but second thoughts begin to arise when we inquire concerning the dates of the citations from Talmud and Midrash.[43] For all of them are hundreds of years later than the New Testament period. Midrash Rabbah, which forms the backbone of Lehmann's case, is a collection from the fourth to the sixth centuries. Pirkê de Rabbi Eliezer is a collection from the outgoing eighth century. The Midrash on Psalm 22 contains the opinions of the Amoraim, rabbinical teachers of the third to the fifth centuries. The Babylonian Talmud and the so-called Jerusalem Talmud are the fruit of the discussions and elaborations of these Amoraim on the Mishnah, which was redacted, arranged, and revised by Rabbi Judah ha-Nasi about the beginning of the third century. The Mishnah itself, despite its length, never once quotes Hos. 6:2; Gen. 22:4, 42:17; Jonah 2:1; or any other of the passages in question which mention the third day. The Targum on Hosea, says McArthur, is associated with

---

[42] See G. Vermes, *Scripture and Tradition in Judaism* (Leiden: E. J. Brill, 1961), pp. 193-227; R. LeDéaut, *La nuit pascale*, AB 22 (Rome: Pontifical Biblical Institute, 1963), pp. 198-207; J. E. Wood, "Isaac Typology in the New Testament," *NTS* 14 (1967-68): 583-589.

[43] Conzelmann dismisses Lehmann's case out of hand on this consideration alone (Hans Conzelmann, *Der erste Brief an die Korinther*, KEKNT 5 [Göttingen: Vandenhoeck & Ruprecht, 1969], p. 302). See also Wengst, *Formeln*, p. 96.

Jonathan b. Uzziel of the first century; but this ascription is quite uncertain and in any case tells us nothing concerning Hos. 6:2 in particular, since the Targum as a whole involves a confluence of early and late material. Thus all the citations concerning the significance of the third day and interpreting Hos. 6:2 in terms of an eschatological resurrection may well stem from literature centuries removed from the New Testament period.

Lehmann wants to believe that these citations embody traditions that go back orally prior to the Christian era. But if that is the case, then should not we expect to confront these motifs in Jewish literature contemporaneous with the New Testament times, namely, the Apocrypha and Pseudepigrapha? One would especially expect to confront the third day motif in the apocalyptic works. In fact, it is conspicuously absent. The book of I Enoch, which is quoted in Jude, had more influence on the New Testament writers than any other apocryphal or pseudepigraphic work and is a valuable source of information concerning Judaism from 200 BC to AD 100. In this work the eschatological resurrection is associated with the number seven, not three (91.15-16; 93). Similarly in IV Ezra, a first century compilation, the eschatological resurrection takes place after seven days (7.26-44). A related work from the second half of the first century and a good representative of Jewish thought contemporaneous with the New Testament, II Baruch gives no indication of the day of the resurrection at history's end (50-51). Neither does II Macc. 7.9-42; 12.43-45 or the Testament of the Twelve Patriarchs (Judah) 25:1, 4; (Zebulun) 10:2; (Benjamin) 10:6-18. All these works, which stem from intertestamental or New Testament times, have a doctrine of eschatological resurrection, but not one of them knows of the third day motif. Evidently the number seven was thought to have greater divine import than the number three (cf. Rev. 1:20; 6:1; 8:2; 15:1, 7). In II Macc. 5:14; 11:18 we find "three days" and "third day" mentioned in another context, but their meaning is wholly non-theological, indicating only "a short time" or "the day after tomorrow." It seems to be a significant weakness in Lehmann's position that he is unable to find any parallels in Jewish literature contemporaneous with the New Testament employing the third day motif or associating the resurrection with the third day. It appears that this interpretation is a peculiarity of later rabbinical exegesis of the Talmudic period.

Moreover, there is no indication that the New Testament writers were aware of such exegesis. Lehmann states that the conception of the offering of Isaac as a salvific event is characteristic of the New Testament. But this is not the question; the issue is whether the interpretation of the offering of Isaac *on the third day* plays a role in the New Testament. Here the evidence appears to be precisely to the contrary: Rom. 4:17, 25 not only have nothing to do with the offering of Isaac (it is to Gen. 15, not 22, that Paul turns for his doctrine of justification by faith), but refer to Jesus's resurrection without mentioning the third day; Rom. 8:32 makes no explicit mention of Isaac and no mention, implicit or explicit, of the resurrection, not to speak of the third day: Heb. 11:17-19 does not in fact explicitly use Isaac as a type of Christ but, more importantly, does not mention the third day. This last passage seems to be crucial, for in this passage, of all places, one would expect the mention of the third day theme in connection with the resurrection. But it does not appear. This can only suggest that the connection of the sacrifice of Isaac with a third day motif was not yet known. In the other passage in which the offering of Isaac is employed (Jas. 2:21-23), there is also no mention of the third day motif. (And James even goes on to use the illustration of Rahab the harlot and the spies, again without mentioning the three day theme, as did later Rabbinic exegesis.) Hence, the appeal to the offering of Isaac as evidence that the New Testament knows of the rabbinic exegesis concerning the theological significance of the third day is counter-productive.

Finally, Lahmann's interpretation seems to labor under the same difficulty as the appeal to Hos. 6:2 alone, namely, it requires that the traditions of the discovery of the empty tomb and the first appearances be false. For if these events did occur when it is said they did, then they could not but have had an effect on when the early believers thought that the resurrection had occurred. But if these traditions are false, the question then becomes whether the disciples would adopt the language of the third day. For suppose the first appearance of Christ was to Peter a week later as he was fishing in Galilee. Would the believers then say that Jesus was raised on the third day rather than, say, the seventh? Lehmann says yes; for the "third day" is not meant in any sense as a time indicator but is a purely theological concept. But were the disciples so subtle? Certainly Luke understands the third day as a time indicator, for he writes "But on the first day of the week....That very day...it is now the third day....the Christ should suffer and on the third day rise from the dead" (Lk. 24:1, 13, 21, 46). Lehmann and Bode's response is that Luke as a Gentile did not understand the theological significance of the third day, which would have been clear to his Jewish contemporaries, and so mistook it as a time indicator.[44] This cannot but make one feel rather uneasy about Lehmann's hypothesis, for it involves isolating Luke from all his Jewish contemporaries. And I suspect that this dichotomy between historical understanding and theological understanding is an import from the twentieth century. The Rabbis cited in the Talmud and Midrash no doubt believed both that the events in question really happened on the third day and that they were theologically significant, for they include in their lists of events that occurred on the third day not only events in which the third day was important theologically (as in the giving of the law) but also events in which the third day was not charged with theological significance (as in Rahab and the spies). There is no reason to think that the New Testament writers did not think Jesus actually rose on the third day; John, for example, certainly seems to take the three day figure as a time indicator by contrasting it with the 46 years it took to build the Temple (Jn. 2:20). But in this case, it is doubtful that they would have adopted the language of the third day unless the Easter events really did take place on the third day. At any rate, if the gospel traditions prove historical in their time indications, then it cannot be the case that the third day is only a theological *Interpretament* signifying God's deliverance and victory; rather, if the events occurred on the first day of the week, then the language of the "third day" was adopted because (1) the third day in the LXX was a day of climax and of God's deliverance, and (2) the first day of the week was in fact the third day subsequent to the crucifixion.

I think this is the most likely account of the matter. This means that the phrase "on the third day" in the formula of I Cor. 15 is a time indicator for the events of Easter, including the empty tomb, employing the language of the LXX concerning God's acts of deliverance and victory on the third day, perhaps with texts like Jonah 2:1 and Hos. 6:2 especially in mind. The phrase is, in Lichtenstein's words, a fusion of historical facts plus theological tradition.[45]

There seems to be little doubt, therefore, that Paul accepted the idea of an empty tomb as a matter of course. But did he know the empty tomb of Jesus? We know from Paul's own letters that Paul was in Jerusalem three years after his

---

[44] Lehmann, *Auferweckt*, p. 174; Bode, *Easter*, pp. 125-126.
[45] Lichtenstein, "Glaubensformel," p. 43.

conversion and that he stayed with Peter two weeks and also spoke with James (Gal. 1:18-19). We know that fourteen years later he was again in Jerusalem and that he ministered with Barnabas in Antioch (Gal. 2:1, 11). We know that he again was later travelling to Jerusalem with financial relief for the brethren there (Rom. 15:25; I Cor. 16:3; II Cor. 8-9). Furthermore, his letters testify to his correspondence with his various churches, and his personal references make it clear that he had a team of fellow workers like Titus, Timothy, Silas, Aristarchus, Justus, and others who kept him well-informed on the situation in the churches; he also received personal reports from other believers, such as Chloe's people (I Cor. 1:11). Paul knew well not only the aberrations of the churches (Gal.; I Cor. 15:29), but also the context of the traditions he delivered (I Cor. 11:23-26). Therefore, if the gospel accounts of the empty tomb embody old traditions concerning its discovery, it seems unthinkable that Paul would not know of it. If Mark's narrative contains an old tradition coming out of the Jerusalem community, then Paul would have had to be a recluse not to know of it. This point seems so elementary, but it is somehow usually overlooked by even those who hold that Mark embodies old traditions. If the tradition of the empty tomb is old, then it seems undoubtable that *somebody* would have told Paul about it.

But even apart from the Markan tradition, Paul must have known the empty tomb. Paul certainly believed that the grave was empty. Therefore Peter, with whom Paul spoke during those two weeks in Jerusalem, must have also believed the tomb was empty. Jerusalem was the fount of the tradition embodied in I Cor. 15:3-5. Therefore, the Christian community also, of which Peter was the leader, must have believed in the empty tomb. But that can only imply that the tomb was in fact empty. Not only would the disciples not believe in a resurrection if the corpse were still in the grave, but they could never have proclaimed the resurrection either under such circumstances.[46] But if the tomb was empty, then it is unthinkable that Paul, being in the city for two weeks six years later and after that often in contact with the Christian community there, should never hear a thing

---

[46] This presupposes that there was a tomb of Jesus, *i.e.*, that his body was not cast into a criminals' common graveyard. But the burial tradition of Jesus is one of the surest traditions concerning his death and resurrection which we have. And it ought to be questioned whether burial in a common plot would have necessarily meant loss of the body. Even after several weeks, a freshly dug grave could be identified fairly easily, and the Jewish authorities could have pointed to it to silence the disciples' preaching.

about the empty tomb. Indeed, is it too much to imagine that during his two week fact-finding visit Paul would want to visit the place where the Lord lay? Ordinary human feelings would suggest such a thing.[47] So I think that it is highly probable that Paul not only accepted the empty tomb, but that he also knew that the actual grave of Jesus was empty.

With regard then to the empty tomb, we have seen that the close connection in the formula between the "he was buried" and the "he was raised," as well as the very notion of resurrection itself, implies the belief that Jesus's body did not remain in the grave. Moreover, the phrase "on the third day" probably employs language of the LXX to date the events on the first day of the week, including the discovery of Jesus's empty tomb. Thus, not only is the empty tomb a necessary inference, but it was probably known to those who drafted the formula as a historical particular. Paul's personal contact with the early Jerusalem church precludes his not knowing that the tomb was empty. In this case, there seems to be good historical foundation for believing it was empty, especially if the traditions of Jesus's burial are trustworthy. Thus, Paul's evidence for the empty tomb, though not as extensive as that for the appearances, is quite important. From him we learn that *the earliest disciples not only inferred but probably also knew of Jesus's empty tomb as a historical fact through its discovery on the third day after the crucifixion, a conclusion strengthened in proportion to the evidence for his entombment.*

---

[47] Actually if Paul had been in Jerusalem prior to his trip to Damascus, as Acts reports, then he probably would have heard of the empty tomb then, not indeed, from the Christians, but from the Jewish authorities in whose employ he was. For even if the Christians in their enthusiasm had not checked to see if the tomb of Jesus was empty, the Jewish authorities could be guilty of no such oversight. So ironically Paul may have known of the empty tomb even before his conversion.

CHAPTER 4

THE NATURE OF THE RESURRECTION BODY

I CORINTHIANS 15:35-57

One final and gripping issue in I Cor. 15 now confronts us: the nature of the resurrection body as conceived by Paul. This will have important implications for the historicity of the gospel narratives, for Paul plainly holds that our resurrection bodies will be modeled after Christ's. What is true therefore of ours will be *ipso facto* true of his.[1] Paul's discussion of the nature of the resurrection body in I Cor. 15:35-57 arouses not only deep emotional feelings on the part of critics but also brings to the surface one's theological preconceptions, and few other passages of Scripture have been the subject of so much theologizing as this.[2]

---

[1] Paul's expression "first fruits" (I Cor. 15:20) means "a genuinely representative sample" (cf. Rom. 11:16) (J. A. T. Robinson, *The Human Face of God* [London: SCM, 1973], p. 134). It does no good to object with Bode that this is reasoning illicitly from doctrine to history (Edward Lynn Bode, *The First Easter Morning*, AB 45 [Rome: Biblical Institute Press, 1970], p. 99). For Paul explicitly affirms that our resurrection bodies will be like Christ's (I Cor. 15:20; Col. 1:18; Phil. 3:21; Rom. 6:5). Therefore, what is essentially true of ours is true of his. Because of Paul's temporal proximity to the events and his personal acquaintance with those involved, scholars are generally ready to take what Paul says or implies about Christ's resurrection body to be historically well-founded.

[2] Consider the heated reaction that Cullmann's book met with when he defended as biblical the resurrection of the dead against the immortality of the soul. Cullmann responded,

"The attacks provoked by my work would impress me more if they were based on exegetical arguments. Instead I am attacked with very general considerations of a philosophical, psychological, and above all sentimental kind. It has been said against me, 'I can accept the immortality of the soul, but not the resurrection of the body'..." (Oscar Cullmann, *Immortality of the Soul or Resurrection of the Dead* [London: Epworth Press, 1958], pp. 6-7).

Before we examine the passage more closely, therefore, a word needs to be said about Paul's anthropological terms σῶμα, σάρξ, and ψυχή.

Paul's Anthropological Terms

The most important term in the second half of I Cor. 15 is σῶμα.[3] During the nineteenth century under the influence of idealism, theologians interpreted the σῶμα as the form of a thing and the σάρξ as its substance.[4] In this way they could avoid the objectionable notion of a physical resurrection, for it was the form that was raised from the dead endowed with a new spiritual substance. Hence, in the old commentaries one finds that the σῶμα πνευματικόν was conceived to be a body made out of *himmlischer Lichtsubstanz*.[5] This understanding has now been all but abandoned; Gundry lists six considerations militating against taking σῶμα as form and σάρξ as substance:[6] (1) the influence upon the New Testament use of σάρξ by the Old Testament use of בשר for flesh as a whole body, as opposed to the Greek view of flesh as the soft part and primary substance of the body (Gal. 4:13-14; II Cor. 12:7; Rom. 2:28; I Cor. 6:16); (2) Paul's use of σῶμα to emphasize substance rather than form: (a) in the contrast between pummeling the body and beating the air (I Cor. 9:26-27), (b) in the contrast between body and shadow (Col. 2:17), and (c) in the contrast between bodily presence and communication by letter (II Cor. 10:10); (3) the use of μέλος in the plural as a synonym for σῶμα;

A good example of this sort of bias is Eduard Schweizer, "Die Leiblichkeit des Menschen: Leben—Tod—Auferstehung," in idem, *Beiträge zur Theologie des Neuen Testaments* (Zürich: Zwingli Verlag, 1970), pp. 177-181.

[3] The outstanding work on this concept, which I follow here, is Robert H. Gundry, Soma *in Biblical Theology* (Cambridge: Cambridge University Press, 1976). Other works include: Ernst Käsemann, *Leib und Leib Christi*, BHT 9 (Tübingen: Mohr, 1933); J. A. T. Robinson, *The Body* (London: SCM, 1952); *TWNT*, s.v. "σῶμα, σωματικός, σύσσωμος," by Eduard Schweizer and Friedrich Baumgärtel; Rudolf Bultmann, *Theologie des Neuen Testaments*, 7th ed., ed. Otto Merk (Tübingen: J. C. B. Mohr, 1961), pp. 193-203; Robert Jewett, *Paul's Anthropological Terms*, AGAJY 10 (Leiden: E. J. Brill, 1971), pp. 201-304; K.-A. Bauer, *Leiblichkeit—das Ende aller Werke Gottes*, SNT 4 (Gütersloh: Mohn, 1971).

[4] C. Holsten, *Zum Evangelium des Paulus und des Petrus* (Rostock: Stiller, 1868); Hermann Lüdemann, *Die Anthropologie des Apostels Paulus und ihre Stellung innerhalb seiner Heilslehre* (Kiel: Universitätsverlag, 1872); remarkably so also Hans Conzelmann, *Der erste Brief an die Korinther*, KEKNT 5 (Göttingen: Vandenhoeck & Ruprecht, 1969), p. 335. In fact, I have been amazed at how frequently I have encountered this viewpoint in discussions with contemporary German theologians.

[5] See Hans Lietzmann, *An die Korinther I, II*, 4th ed., rev. Werner Georg Kümmel, HNT 9 (Tübingen: J. C. B. Mohr, 1949), p. 194.

[6] Gundry, Soma, pp. 161-162.

(4) the implication of the exhortation to sanctity of the σῶμα that σῶμα entails substance as well as form (I Cor. 7:34); (5) the implication of the similar exhortation to sanctification of the σάρξ that σάρξ and σῶμα can interchange without reference to form or substance; (6) the same implication from the interchange of σῶμα, σάρξ, and μέλη as in Rom. 6-8 (except where σάρξ carries moral implications of sin) and in I Cor. 15:35-44. The view of σῶμα as merely form and σάρξ as its substance cannot be exegetically sustained; σῶμα *is* the body, form and substance.

This does not mean, however, that twentieth century theologians take σῶμα to mean the physical body. Rather under the influence of existentialism, particularly as adopted by Bultmann, they take σῶμα, when used theologically, as the whole person conceived abstractly in existentialist categories of self-understanding. Thus, σῶμα does not equal the physical body, but the person, and hence, a bodily resurrection means, not a resurrection of the physical body, but of the person. In this way the doctrine of physical resurrection is avoided as adroitly as it was in the days of philosophical idealism.

It is the burden of Gundry's study to show that this understanding is drastically wrong. Even if his exegesis suffers at times from over-kill,[7] Gundry succeeds admirably in carrying his main point: that σῶμα is never used in the New Testament to denote the whole person in isolation from his physical body but is much more used to denote the physical body itself or the man with special emphasis on the physical body.

Let us review the evidence for Paul's use of σῶμα in this way.[8] First, it is often alleged that because Paul uses σῶμα and personal pronouns interchangeably, σῶμα must refer to the person. But the presupposition of this allegation is that the pronoun, when used for σῶμα, *expands* the meaning of σῶμα rather than that σῶμα *restricts* the meaning of the pronoun. This presupposition is unjustified, for the σῶμα may limit the meaning of the pronoun as in "She slapped his face;" "She

---

[7] For example, in his attempts to find a rigid dualism in the Old Testament, he cannot explain the references to corpses as souls (Lev. 21:11; Num. 6:6), and he overdoes it when he maintains that Paul's "present in spirit" but "absent in body" (I Cor. 5:3-5) entails a literal presence of Paul's spirit, for this would technically imply the de-animation of Paul's body while his spirit was abroad (Gundry, Soma, pp. 122, 141)! Most of Gundry's texts do not support dualism, but merely aspectivalism; but they do prove an ubiquitous use of dualistic language. When it comes to texts that clearly contemplate the separation of soul or spirit and body at death, then Gundry's argument for dualism is strong and persuasive.

[8] Gundry, Soma, pp. 29-80.

slapped him." In fact, all the places where Paul interchanges σῶμα with personal pronouns are examples of this kind; the emphasis is on the physical. Hence, Rom. 6:12-14, 16a is strongly physical; note ἐν + σώματι, the parallel μέλη, the term ὅπλα, the references to sexual immorality (6:19; 7:1-3). Similarly II Cor. 4:10-12 is physically oriented: note the physical character of the persecution (I Cor. 1:8-10), the earthen vessel metaphor for the body (4:7), the contrast between the outer and inner man (4:16), the earthly tent which can be destroyed as a figure for the body (5:1), and the contrast between being at home in or away from the body (5:6, 8-9). And in Eph. 5:28-29 the physical orientation of the passage is apparent from the use of σάρξ (in a morally neutral sense) in a physical way parallel to the use of σῶμα. Thus the interchange of pronouns with σῶμα by no means implies that σῶμα refers to the "person" in isolation from the body.

Elsewhere Paul's use of σῶμα is equally physical. In I Cor. 7:4; Rom. 1:24 the orientation is sexual and physical. The same is true of I Cor. 6:12-20, a passage in which Bultmann's exegesis oscillates back and forth between physical and existential meanings for σῶμα. If the meaning were holistic, then marriage would also break union with Christ. The "one flesh" refers to physical union of two bodies in sexual intercourse. In Rom. 12:1 σῶμα stands for the physical life of man; it is contrasted with the mind (12:2) and is clearly physical in 12:4. I Cor. 9:26 refers to the physical side of man, as the context and the athletic metaphors show; I Cor. 13:3 can only mean the body, for the whole self or person cannot be burned. Phil. 1:20 refers to the physical presence in the world, as the phrase "to remain in the flesh" (1:24) makes clear. Rom. 8:11 refers to the body in which the Holy Spirit dwells.

There are several passages in which σῶμα appears to equal σάρξ in the morally evil sense (Rom. 6:6; 7:24; 8:10, 12-13). But in these cases the σῶμα is the instrument of σάρξ, not necessarily its equivalent; "body of death" and "body of sin" are not the flesh *per se* but the physical body enslaved and doomed to death by sin. The body of flesh in Col. 2:11 refers to Christ's physical body (cf. Col. 1:22; Rom. 7:4; 1 Pet. 2:24; 4:1).[9] The remaining passage in which σῶμα might

---

[9] This is, I think, the most difficult passage for Gundry. But even if the reference here is not to Christ's body, it is nonetheless apparent that body does not equal flesh in the passage, for then it would be unintelligible to speak of the "body of flesh." It may be that "body" is here a physical metaphor, as in "body of Christ," meaning the whole mass of sins. At any rate the use of "body" as "flesh" in the moral sense does not figure in I Cor. 15.

appear to equal σάρξ in a morally evil sense is Rom. 8:10. Now even if they were here synonymous, that does not win a holistic meaning for σῶμα, for σάρξ is the sinful proclivity *within* man's nature. But in fact the only way to equate the two is to make a radical break before v. 11, for there God is said to make alive the body, which He would never do to the evil flesh. But the carry-over of vocabulary precludes any such break. The dead bodies in v. 10 are the bodies to be made alive in the eschaton by Christ in v. 11 and therefore mean "mortal bodies" (cf. 6:12; 7:24). Thus σῶμα never means the morally evil σάρξ *simpliciter*. Paul's references to "bodily presence" (II Cor. 10:10) and "absent in body" (I Cor. 5:3; cf. Col. 2:5; I Thess. 2:17) refer to physical presence. Other passages are obviously physical: the wounds on Paul's body (Gal. 6:17), Abraham's impotent body (Rom. 4:19), the physical deeds in this world (Rom. 8:13), the transformation of the physical body (Phil. 3:21). Gundry's conclusion is worth quoting:

> The *soma* denotes the physical body, roughly synonymous with 'flesh' in the neutral sense. It forms that part of man in and through which he lives and acts in the world. It becomes the base of operations for sin in the unbeliever, for the Holy Spirit in the believer. Barring prior occurrence of the Parousia, the *soma* will die. That is the lingering effect of sin even in the believer. But it will also be resurrected. That is its ultimate end, a major proof of its worth and necessity to wholeness of human being, and the reason for its sanctification now.[10]

The importance of this conclusion cannot be overemphasized. Too long we have been told that for Paul σῶμα is the ego, the "I" of a man.[11] Like a dash of

---

[10] Gundry, Soma, p. 50.

[11] For example, Conzelmann writes,
"...σῶμα designates the 'I'...the 'I' in so far as it can be grasped by itself and others as the possible object of action through others and through itself. I am σῶμα in so far as I can stand over against myself, govern myself and risk myself. I am σῶμα in so far as I desire... σῶμα is thus the I as a subject which acts and an object which is acted upon, especially the I as one that acts upon itself" (Hans Conzelmann, *An Outline of the Theology of the New Testament* [New York: Harper & Row, 1968], pp. 176-177).

Cf. Bultmann, *Theologie*, pp. 196-198. This leads to the fallacy of Marxsen that because the σῶμα is the "I," the opposition between the present body and the resurrection body is really between the earthly "I" and the spiritual "I" (Willi Marxsen, *The Resurrection of Jesus of Nazareth*, trans. Margaret Kohl [London: SCM Press, 1970], pp. 69-70; cf. Erhardt Güttgemanns, *Der leidende Apostel und sein Herr*, FRLANT 90 [Göttingen: Vandenhoeck & Ruprecht, 1966], pp. 247-281). Logically this implies that death and resurrection is the death and resurrection of the ego, a viewpoint which is indistinguishable from the revivification and subsequent immortality of the soul. Robinson's error is somewhat different. He recognizes that σῶμα as the empirical ego (Bultmann) is strictly post-Cartesian and that σῶμα as the whole personality is unHebraic. He holds that σῶμα is the body created for God, *but* that it is not in the least constituted by its being physical. It fulfills its essence by being utterly subject to Spirit, not by being either material or immaterial. Its substance depends entirely on the nature of the medium through which the Spirit is manifesting

cold water, Gundry's study brings us back to the genuine anthropological consciousness of first century man. The notion of body as the "I" is a perversion of the biblical meaning of σῶμα: Robert Jewett asserts, "Bultmann has turned σῶμα into its virtual opposite: a symbol for that structure of individual existence which is essentially non-physical."[12] Hence, Gundry concludes, existentialist treatments of σῶμα, as much as idealist treatments, have been a positive impediment to accurate historical-critical exegesis of I Cor. 15 and have sacrificed theology to a philosophical fashion that is already passé.[13]

To say that σῶμα refers primarily to the physical body is not to say that the word cannot be used as *synecdoche* to refer to the whole man by reference to a part. "The *soma* may represent the whole person simply because the *soma* lives in union with the soul/spirit. But *soma* does not mean 'whole person,' because its use is designed to call attention to the physical object which is the body of the person rather than the whole personality."[14] Nor does this preclude metaphorical use of the word, as in the "body of Christ" for the church; for it is a physical metaphor: the church is not the "I" of Christ. When we turn to I Cor. 15 and inquire about the nature of the resurrection body, therefore, we shall be inquiring about a body, not about an ego, an "I," or a "person" abstractly conceived apart from the body.[15]

---

itself (Robinson, *Body*, p. 32). Nothing in Robinson's prior 31 pages justifies such a conclusion. Robinson never shows that σῶμα can be used in abstraction from the material component or aspect to describe a purely immaterial entity. He has only proved σῶμα is not the "prime matter" of which things are made. It is true that the body is fulfilled in its subjection to Spirit as a σῶμα πνευματικόν, but what is the proof that materiality is non-essential? Robinson never renders intelligible the notion of a literal, non-physical, immaterial body. The idea that σῶμα may have an immaterial substance or medium surreptitiously introduces the notion that σῶμα πνευματικόν is a body made out of spirit, which it is not (see p. 96-97).

[12] Jewett, *Terms*, p. 211.
[13] Gundry, Soma, p. 167.
[14] Ibid., p. 80.
[15] Even Weiss, who believes that σῶμα can stand for the whole personality, admits that in I Cor. 15 such a meaning is inadmissible (Johannes Weiss, *Der erste Korintherbrief*, 9th ed., KEKNT 5 [Göttingen: Vandenhoeck & Ruprecht, 1910], p. 372). See also John Gillman, "Transformation in I Cor. 15, 50-53," *ETL* 58 (1982): 328-329. Although Gillman, appealing to the reviews of Gundry's work by J. D. G. Dunn in *SJT* 31 (1978): 288-291 and Daniel J. Harrington in *Bib* 58 (1977): 136-138, considers himself in disagreement with Gundry's view, still he asserts that the σῶμα ψυχικόν is the totality of the created, corporeal person with particular attention to the mortal, physical body and the σῶμα πνευματικόν is the totality of the resurrected, heavenly, corporeal person animated by the Spirit. This is only a shade different from Gundry's view, however, and Gillman agrees that "...the believer has a body now and will have the same body, transformed, after death" (Ibid., p. 330). The point is that σῶμα does not refer to the "self" in abstraction from the physical body. As for the two reviews, only Dunn objects to Gundry's concept of σῶμα, but

I have already alluded to Paul's use of σάρξ, and it will not be necessary to say much here.[16] Theologians are familiar with σάρξ as the evil proclivity within man. This touches sensitive nerves in German theology because the Creed in German states that I believe in the resurrection of the *Fleisch*, not of the *body* as in the English translation.[17] Hence, many theologians are rightly anxious to disassociate themselves from any doctrine that the flesh as a morally evil principle will be resurrected. But they seem prone to overlook the fact that Paul often uses σάρξ in a non-moral sense simply to mean the physical flesh or body. In this morally neutral sense the resurrection of the flesh = resurrection of the body. Now in I Cor. 15 Paul is clearly speaking of σάρξ in a physical, morally neutral sense, for he speaks of the flesh of birds, animals, and fish, which would be absurd in any moral sense. Hence, Jewett draws attention to "the striking departure from the technical 'flesh' category and an appropriation of traditional Judaic use of σάρξ as interchangeable with σῶμα."[18] Understood in this physical sense, the doctrine of the resurrection of the flesh is therefore morally unobjectionable.

Finally, a brief word on the third term ψυχή:[19] Paul does not teach a consistent dualism of σῶμα – ψυχή, but often uses πνεῦμα and other terms to designate the immaterial element of man. In fact, in the adjectival form, (ψυχικός) has a meaning that does not connote immateriality at all, but rather the natural character of a thing in contradistinction to the supernatural character of God's Spirit. Thus in I Cor. 2:14-3:3 Paul differentiates three types of men: the ἄνθρωπός ψυχικός or natural man apart from God's Spirit; the ἄνθρωπός πνευματικός or spiritual man who is led and empowered by God's Spirit; and the ἄνθρωπός σαρκίνος or carnal man who, though possessing the Spirit of God (I Cor. 12:13), is nevertheless still

---

even he agrees that σῶμα designates man as embodied in the world. But he goes beyond the evidence and degenerates into self-contradiction when he asserts that it is a physical embodiment in this world and a spiritual embodiment in the next.

[16] See *TWNT*, s.v. "σάρξ, σαρκικός, σάρκινος," by Eduard Schweizer, Friedrich Baumgärtel, and Rudolf Meyer; Bultmann, *Theologie*, pp. 232-239; Alexander Sand, *Der Begriff "Fleisch" in den Paulinischen Hauptbriefen*, BU 2 (Regensburg: Friedrich Pustet, 1967); E. Brandenburger, *Fleisch und Geist* (Neukirchen-Vluyn: Neukirchner Verlag, 1968); Jewett, *Terms*, pp. 49-166.

[17] See Karl Bornhäuser, *Das Recht des Bekenntnisses zur Auferstehung des Fleisches* (Gütersloh: C. Bertelsmann, 1899).

[18] Jewett, *Terms*, p. 454.

[19] See Erwin Rohde, *Psyche*, 2 vols., 2nd ed. (Tübingen: Mohr, 1921); *TWNT*, s.v., "ψυχή, ψυχικός, ἀνάψυξις, αναψύχω, δίψυχος, ὀλιγόψυχος," by Georg Bertram, Albert Dihle, Edmond Jacob, Eduard Lohse, Eduard Schweizer, and Karl-Wolfgang Tröger; Bultmann, *Theologie*, pp. 204-211; Jewett, Terms, pp. 334-357; Gundry, Soma, pp. 83-86.

under the sway of the σάρξ or evil principle in human nature. This makes it evident that for Paul ψυχικός did not have the connotations which we today associate with "soul."

Three Analogies to the Resurrection

With these terms in mind we now turn to Paul's discussion in I Cor. 15:35-57. He begins by asking two polemical questions: How are the dead raised? With what kind of body do they come? (v. 35)[20] The structure of Paul's answer led Jeremias to suggest that in vs. 36-50 he first answers the second question and then in vs. 51-57 the first question.[21] But Morissette has shown that Paul is using here the traditional rabbinical schema of argument and that repetition and parallelism are typical in this style of argument.[22] The two questions probably amount to the same thing. Paul's opponents seemed to have been unable to accept the resurrection because the resurrection of a material body was either inconceivable or offensive to their Greek minds (cf. Bultmann's "resuscitation of a corpse"). Paul's answer steers a careful course between the crasser forms of the Pharisaic doctrine of resurrection, in which the raised will, for example, each beget a thousand children and eat the flesh of Leviathan, and the Platonistic doctrine of the immortality of the soul apart from the body. Paul will contend that the resurrection body will be radically different from this natural body, but that it will nevertheless be a body—he envisions no release of the soul from the prison house of the body. Paul's answer is that the resurrection body will be a marvelous transformation of our present body, making it suitable for existence in the age to come—a doctrine not unusual in the Judaism of Paul's day and remarkably similar to that of the contemporary II Baruch 50-51, which should be read in conjunction with Paul's argument.[23]

---

[20] Cf. Baruch's questions:
"'In what shape will those live who live in Thy day?
Or how will the splendour of those who (are) after that time continue?
Will they then resume this form of the present, ...
Or wilt Thou perchance change these things which have been in the world
As also the world?'" (II Baruch 49:2-3)

[21] Cf. Joachim Jeremias, "'Flesh and Blood Cannot Inherit the Kingdom of God' (I Cor. XV. 50)," *NTS* 2 (1955-56): 156-157.

[22] Rodolphe Morissette, "La condition de ressucité. I Corinthiens 15, 35-49: structure littéraire de la péricope," *Bib* 53 (1972): 209, 216-224.

[23] Paul's teaching is essentially the Jewish doctrine of glorified bodies, according to Weiss, *Korintherbrief*, p. 345; W. D. Davies, *Paul and Rabbinic Judaism*, 2nd ed. (London: SPCK, 1965),

In the first paragraph, vs. 36-41, Paul searches for analogies to the resurrection of the dead (v. 42). The first analogy is the analogy of the seed.[24] The point of the analogy is simply to draw attention to how different the plant is from the seed that is buried in the ground (cf. Mt. 13:31-32 for Jesus's use of a similar analogy in another context).[25] It is a good analogy for Paul's purposes, for the sowing of the seed and its death are reminiscent of the burial of the dead man (vs. 42-44). To criticize Paul's analogy from the standpoint of modern botany—saying, for example, that a seed does not really die—presses the analogy too far. Similarly some commentators criticize Paul's analogy because he lacked the modern botanical notion that a particular type of seed yields a particular type of plant; Paul thought God alone determined what plant should spring up from *any* seed that was sown (v. 38).[26] But this is quite unreasonable, as though Paul could think that a date-palm could conceivably spring from a grain of corn! He specifically says that God gives "each kind of seed its own body" (v. 38) which harks back to the Genesis account of the creation of σπέρμα κατὰ γένος (LXX Gen. 1:11, 12). In an agrarian culture, the Israelites certainly knew the difference between sowing wheat and tares and that thorns do not bring forth grapes or thistles figs. At any rate this loses the whole point of the analogy: that from the mere seed God produces a wonderfully different plant.

Paul then appeals to the analogy of different sorts of flesh again in order to prove that if we recognize differences even in the physical world then the resurrection body could also be different from our present body. Paul's analogy may have in mind the creation account, but I think the Jewish distinction between

---

pp. 305-308; Ulrich Wilckens, *Auferstehung*, TT4 (Stuttgart and Berlin: Kreuz Verlag, 1970), pp. 128-131; Joseph L. Smith, "Resurrection Faith Today," *TS* 30 (1969): 406. It is highly instructive that in Acts 23:6 Luke identifies Paul's doctrine of the resurrection with that of the Pharisees (cf. 24:14; 26:6, 21-23).

[24] On the dying of the seed, cf. Jn. 12:24. On the nakedness of the seed cf. later parallels in the rabbinical writings (Sanhedrin 90b; Tractate Kethubboth 111b; Pirkê de Rabbi Eliezer 33.17c); but these have to do with whether we shall have clothes at the resurrection. The analogy is that as the plant comes clothed from the naked seed, so shall we at the resurrection. Paul uses the analogy differently.

[25] H. A. W. Meyer, *Handbuch über den Ersten Brief an die Korinther*, 6th ed., rev. Georg Heinrici, KEKNT 5 (Göttingen: Vandenhoeck & Ruprecht's Verlag, 1881), pp. 442-443; Jeremias, "'Flesh and Blood,'" p. 156; Ronald J. Sider, "The Pauline Conception of the Resurrection Body in I Corinthians xv. 35-54," *NTS* 21 (1975): 431.

[26] Héring, *Première épître*, p. 145. Allo thinks that on the contrary Paul wants to say that the nature of the plant corresponds to that of the seed (Ernst-Bernard Allo, *Première épître aux Corinthiens* (Paris: Librairie Lecoffre, 1934), p. 422; cf. Sider, "Conception," p. 431).

clean and unclean food is closer (cf. Lev. 11; animals: 1-8; fish: 9-12; birds: 13-19; insects: 20-23; swarming things: 29-30).[27] So I do not think σάρξ here is precisely identical with σῶμα. Not only would that reduce Paul's argument to the rather banal assertion that men have different bodies from fish, but it would also entail the false statement that all animals have the same kind of body. Rather in the present connection σάρξ means essentially "meat" or "organic matter."[28] The old commentaries were therefore wrong in defining σάρξ *tout simple* as "substance," for inorganic matter would not be σάρξ; Paul would never speak of the flesh of a stone. To say that the resurrection body has therefore a different kind of flesh than the present body probably presses the analogy too far; all Paul wants to show is that as there are differences among mundane things, analogously the supernatural resurrection body could also differ from the present body.

The third analogy is that of terrestrial and celestial bodies (vs. 40-41). There can be no doubt from v. 41 that Paul means astronomical bodies, not angels.[29] Again the point of the analogy is the same: there are radical differences among bodies in the physical world, so why should not the body in the world to come differ from the present body? Paul's analogy is particularly apt in this case because as the heavenly bodies exceed terrestrial bodies in glory, so does the resurrection body the natural body (v. 43; cf. Phil. 3:21).[30] The δόξα of the heavenly bodies is their brightness, which varies; there is no trace here of *Lichtsubstanz*. When applied to the resurrection body, however, δόξα seems to be honor (v. 43). The analogy is also particularly apt because the σώματα ἐπίγεια bear a close analogy to the σῶμα ψυχικόν, which can be described as ἐκ γῆς χοϊκός (v. 47)

---

[27] See also the very interesting list in I Kings 4:33b: animals, birds, reptiles, and fish. On the different types of flesh, see Tractate Chullin 8.1, where the author explains that one cannot cook flesh in milk, unless it is the flesh of fish or of grasshoppers; fowl may be set on the table with cheese, but not eaten with it. See also Davies, *Paul*, p. 306.

[28] This is not to say, however, that Paul contemplates any formal dichotomy between form and substance that carries over to the other analogies, as the older commentaries held and as Conzelmann still asserts (Conzelmann, *Korinther*, pp. 334-336).

[29] So Heinrici *contra* Meyer ([Heinrici-] Meyer, *Ersten Brief*, p. 444).

[30] Cf. II Baruch 51:1-10 where the glory of the righteous seems to be a literal brightness like the stars'. For Paul, the glory of the righteous seems to mean majesty, honor, exaltation, *etc.*, not so much physical radiance, which is a mere analog. See Joseph Coppens, "La glorification céleste du Christ dans la théologie néotestamentaire et l'attente de Jésus," in *Resurrexit*, ed. Édouard Dhanis (Rome: Libreria Editrice Vaticana, 1974), pp. 37-40. This exposes a serious deficiency in the argument of Robinson, who infers from Phil. 3:21 that Paul visualized Christ's resurrection body as a luminous, heavenly body (James M. Robinson, "Jesus from Easter to Valentinus (or to the Apostles' Creed)," *JBL* 101 [1982]: 7).

and ἐπίγειος (II Cor. 5:1), and the σώματα ἐπουράνια resemble the σῶμα πνευματικόν, which is described as ἐξ οὐρανοῦ (v. 47; II Cor. 5:2) and ἐπουράνιος (v. 48). These descriptions make it evident that realms of reality, not substances, are being here contrasted: the present body is earthly, while the resurrection body will be heavenly.

Paul has thus prepared the way for his doctrine of the world to come by three analogies from the present world. All of them show how things can be radically different from other things of the same genus; similarly a σῶμα πνευματικόν will be seen to be radically different from a σῶμα ψυχικόν. Moreover, Paul's analogies form an ascending scale from plant to animal to terrestrial bodies to celestial bodies; the next type of body to be mentioned will be the most wonderful and exalted of all.

The σῶμα πνευματικόν

From vs. 42-50 Paul spells out his doctrine of the σῶμα πνευματικόν. The body that is to be differs from the present body in that it will be imperishable, glorious, powerful, and spiritual; whereas the present body is perishable, dishonorable, weak, and physical (vs. 42-44). These are the four essential differences between the present body and the resurrection body. What do they tell us about the nature of the resurrection body?

First, it is sown ἐν φθορᾷ, but it is raised ἐν ἀφθαρσίᾳ. These terms tell us clearly that Paul is not talking about egos, or "I's," but about bodies, for (1) the σπείρεται—ἐγείρεται has primary reference to the burial and raising up of a dead man's body, not the "person" in abstraction from the body; and (2) only the body can be described as perishable (II Cor. 4:16), for man's spirit survives death (II Cor. 5:1-5; cf. Rom. 8:10; Phil. 1:23).[31] Rather the disjunction under discussion concerns the radical change that will take place in our bodies: Paul teaches personal bodily immortality, not immortality of the soul alone (cf. vs. 53-54). Strange as this may sound to modern ears, the Christian teaching (or at least

---

[31] For this second reason I do not think we can agree with those commentators who suggest that the resurrection body is the culmination of a process already begun in a Christian's life (Cullmann, *Immortality*, pp. 36-37; Héring, *Première épître*, p. 148), for clearly our bodies are getting worse, not better, while our spirits survive death. Even in Rom. 6:1-11 Paul speaks of the resurrection as a future event.

Paul's) is not that our souls will live forever, but that we shall have bodies in the after-life.

Second, it is sown ἐν ἀτιμίᾳ, but it is raised ἐν δόξῃ. Our present bodies are wracked by sin, are bodies of death, groaning with the whole creation to be set free from sin and decay; we long, says Paul, for the redemption of our bodies (II Cor. 5:4; Rom 8:19-24). This body, dishonored through sin and death, will be transformed by Christ to be like his glorious body (Phil. 3:21). In a spiritual sense we already have an anticipation of this glory insofar as we are conformed inwardly to the image of Christ and are sanctified by his Spirit (II Cor. 3:18), but Paul teaches that the body will not simply fall away like a useless husk but will be transformed to partake of this glory also.

Third, it is sown ἐν ἀσθενείᾳ, but it will be raised ἐν δυνάμει. How well Paul knew of physical weakness! Afflicted with a bodily malediction which was offensive to others and a burden to those around him—his "thorn in the flesh" which he implored God three times to take away—Paul found in his weakness the power of Christ (Gal. 4:13-14; II Cor. 12:7-10). And on his poor body which had been stoned, beaten, and scourged for the sake of the gospel, Paul bore the marks of Christ, so much so that he dared to write "...in my flesh I complete what is lacking in Christ's afflictions..." (Col. 1:24). Just as Christ "was crucified in weakness, but lives by the power of God" (II Cor. 13:4), so Paul longed to know the power of the resurrection and looked forward to the day when he, too, would receive a powerful resurrection body (II Cor. 5:1-4; Phil. 3:10-11).

Fourth, it is sown a σῶμα ψυχικόν, but it is raised a σῶμα πνευματικόν. By a σῶμα ψυχικόν Paul clearly does not mean a body made out of ψυχή.[32] Rather just as Paul frequently uses σαρκικός to indicate, not the physical substance of a thing (cf. σάρκινος) but its orientation, its dominating principle, so ψυχικός also indicates, not a substance, but an orientation. In the New Testament ψυχικός always has a negative connotation (I Cor. 2:14; Jas. 3:15; Jude 19); that which is ψυχικός partakes of the character and direction of natural human nature. Hence, the emphasis in σῶμα ψυχικόν is not that the body is physical, but that it is natural. Accordingly, σῶμα ψυχικόν ought rightly to be translated "natural body;" it

---

[32] See Weiss, *Korintherbrief*, p. 372; Archibald Robertson and Alfred Plummer, *First Epistle of Saint Paul to the Corinthians*, 2nd ed. , ICC (Edinburgh: T & T Clarke, 1967), p. 372; Clavier, "Remarques," pp. 345-351; Jewett, *Terms*, p. 354.

means our ordinary human body. This is the body that will be sown. But it is raised a σῶμα πνευματικόν. And just as σῶμα ψυχικόν does not mean a body made out of ψυχή, neither does σῶμα πνευματικόν mean a body made out of πνεῦμα.³³ Virtually every modern commentator agrees on this point: Paul is not talking about a rarefied body made out of spirit or ether; he means a body under the lordship and direction of God's Spirit.³⁴ Thus, philological analysis leads, in

---

³³ Allo, *Première épître*, p. 425; (Kümmel-) Lietzmann, *Korinther I*, p. 195; C. F. D. Moule, "St. Paul and Dualism: the Pauline Conception of the Resurrection," *NTS* 12 (1965-66): 108; *TWNT*, s.v. "πνεῦμα, πνευματικός, πνέω, ἐκπνέω, θεόπνευστος," by Hermann Kleinknecht, Friedrich Baumgärtel, Werner Bieder, Eric Sjöberg, Edward Schweizer; D. E. H. Whitely, *The Theology of St. Paul* (Oxford: Basil Blackwell, 1970), p. 252; Gundry, Soma, pp. 165-166. According to Bornhäuser the opposite of a body made out of spirit would be a σῶμα σάρκινον, not a σῶμα ψυχικόν. Ψυχή and πνεῦμα are here determining factors, not substances (Bornhäuser, *Auferstehung*, pp. 22-23). Even Weiss, who asserts that Paul "obviously" imagines an ethereal, light, pure heavenly stuff of which all πνεύματα are made, above all God himself, admits that as the opposite of σῶμα ψυχικόν, σῶμα πνευματικόν cannot be formed out of spirit (Weiss, *Korintherbrief*, p. 373). He muses that the notion of a "spiritual body" is problematic because we cannot imagine an immaterial, bodiless body! I doubt that Paul could either. The same unintelligibility confronts Robertson and Plummer when they assert that in the resurrection body the πνεῦμα will be connected to an immaterial germ (whatever that is!) which enables it to develop according to a law beyond our comprehension; this, despite the fact that they recognize that the adjectival forms here mean "congenital with" or "formed to be an organ of" (Robertson and Plummer, *Corinthians*, p. 372). Conzelmann, though he employs the old form/substance distinction and thinks πνεῦμα is a substance, yet admits that the spiritual body is not one made out of spirit, but one determined by spirit (Conzelmann, *Korinther*, p. 336). Pamment, observing that for Paul πνεῦμα is that which determines a man's disposition or action so that a man who is living κατὰ πνεῦμα is πνευματικός, concludes that a σῶμα πνευματικόν "is a body enlivened by God's Spirit, no longer dedicated to self-indulgence but to God" (Margaret Pamment, "Raised a Spiritual Body: bodily resurrection according to Paul," *NB* 66 [1985]: 378). But she adds that the body must be transformed, presumably materially, by the Spirit so that it is no longer a body of flesh, but a body of glory. But this presumption is gratuitous and forces her to lapse back into the old form-substance dichotomy.
³⁴ The natural body is ψυχικόν insofar as the ψυχή is its life-principle and determinant. The ψυχή reigns over the natural body. But the resurrection body will be spiritual, not in the sense of an ethereal substance, which the opposition to ψυχικόν prohibits, but insofar as the πνεῦμα will be its life-principle and determinant. In the resurrection life, the body will be the organ for the πνεῦμα, and the ψυχή will have ceased to dominate. Instead all powers and activities of the body will be subordinated to the πνεῦμα. ([Heinrici-] Meyer, *Ersten Brief*, pp. 447-448). In the present body the Spirit "has been limited and hampered in its action; in the future body it will have complete freedom of action and consequently complete control, and man will at last be, what God created him to be, a being in which the higher self is supreme" (Robertson and Plummer, *Corinthians*, p. 372). According to Pearson, "...the πνεῦμα-ψυχή differentiation is basically a Jewish version of the νοῦς-ψυχή differentiation of common Hellenistic parlance" (Birger A. Pearson, *The Pneumatikos-Psychikos Terminology in I Corinthians*, SBL Dissertation Series 12 [Missoula, Mont.: Scholar's Press, 1973], p. 82). Hellenistic thought had distinguished the νοῦς and the ψυχή as the higher and lower elements of the soul respectively. In the Hellenistic-Jewish exegesis of Gen. 2:7, πνεῦμα was substituted for νοῦς as the higher element. Thus, no opposition was here contemplated between physical/non-physical, since both were elements of the soul. Rather, what is ψυχικός is lower and mortal, while what is πνευματικός is higher and heavenly. Paul's argument is that at the resurrection our bodies will be transformed from being ψυχικόν to

Clavier's words, to the conclusion that "...the 'spiritual body' is, in substance, the same body, this body of flesh, but controlled by the spirit, as is the body of Jesus Christ."[35] The contrast is not between physical body/non-physical body, but between naturally oriented body/spiritually oriented body.[36] They do not differ *qua* σῶμα; rather they differ *qua* orientation. Another way of putting the same thought is to say that they belong to two different spheres or realms of reality. The conceptual distinction between σῶμα ψυχικόν and σῶμα πνευματικόν seems to be reproduced in II Cor. 5 as the distinction between the ἐπίγειος οἰκία and οἰκία ἐν τοῖς οὐρανοῖς. Again the contrast is not of substance, but of proper sphere. Both are bodies, but one is oriented toward and belongs to the natural order, whereas the other is oriented toward and belongs to the heavenly order. Hence, I think it very unfortunate that Paul's carefully chosen term σῶμα πνευματικόν has been usually translated "spiritual body," for such a rendering tends to be very misleading, as Héring explains:

> This term is very well-chosen; for it gives us an indication of two qualities of the resurrection bodies which we have difficulty conceiving, but which Pauline theology invites us to consider: first, the supernatural life bestowed by the Holy Spirit and second, its perfect submission to the spirit, which will make it truly its temple. In French, however, the literal translation *spiritual body* risks creating worse misunderstandings. For most French readers, being more or less consciously Cartesians, yield to the tendency of identifying the spiritual with the non-extended and of course with the immaterial as well, which is the opposite of Pauline ideas and creates, moreover, *a contradictio in adjecto*; for what would be a body without either extension or matter?[37]

πνευματικόν. See Michael Ramsey, *The Resurrection of Christ* (London: Centenary Press, 1945), pp. 107-108; Gerald O'Collins, *The Easter Jesus*, 2nd ed. (London: Darton, Longman, & Todd, 1980), p. 113; Sider, "Conception," p. 435.

[35] Clavier, "Remarques," p. 361. Despite the philological evidence, Clavier goes for a substantival understanding of spiritual body on two grounds: (1) in the seed/plant analogy, the plant is not numerically identical with the seed, and (2) I Cor. 15:50. The first reason is astounding, for the plant certainly is numerically identical with the seed! Pressing the analogy this far supports the continuity of the resurrection body with this body. Clavier sadly misunderstands v. 50, as evident from his remark that Paul should have mentioned bones along with flesh and blood. See pp. 101-102.

[36] It is the same contrast that Paul draws between the natural man and the spiritual man in I Cor. 2:14-15, a passage which seems decisive for the understanding of Paul's contrast in I Cor. 15. Just as Paul obviously does not by "natural man" mean "material, tangible man" and by "spiritual man" "invisible, intangible man" so neither does he mean by "natural body" "material, extended, tangible body" and by "spiritual body" "invisible, intangible, unextended body."

[37] Héring, *Première épître*, p. 147.

Héring therefore suggests that it is better to translate σῶμα πνευματικόν as the opposite of natural body (σῶμα ψυχικόν), that is, as *supernatural* body.[38] Although this has the disadvantage of ignoring the connotation of πνευματικός as "Spirit-dominated," it avoids the inevitable misunderstandings engendered by "spiritual body." As Héring rightly comments, this latter term understood substantively is practically a self-contradiction. By the same token, "physical body" is really a tautology. Thus, natural body/supernatural body is a better rendering of Paul's meaning here.

The Two Adams

Having described the four differences between the present body and the resurrection body, Paul elaborates the doctrine of the two Adams.[39] He cites Gen. 2:7 LXX to prove that the first Adam became εἰς ψυχὴν ζῶσαν, and he adds to this that the last Adam became εἰς πνεῦμα ζῳοποιοῦν. By this last expression he does not mean that Christ turned into a disembodied spirit any more than he means by the first that Adam turned into a disembodied soul.[40] Rather the same

---

[38] It is interesting that the RSV and NEB translators also use *supernatural* to render πνευματικόν in the expressions πνευματικὸν βρῶμα καὶ πόμα in I Cor. 10:3-4: "all ate the same supernatural food and all drank the same supernatural drink." The manna and water in the desert were certainly not immaterial or unextended, rather they were from heaven (LXX Ps. 77:24) and thus belonging to the supernatural order.

[39] There has been much discussion of the relation between Paul's doctrine of the two Adams and Philo's theory of God's creation of the earthly and heavenly man (Philo *De opificio mundi* 134; idem, *Legum allegoriae* 1.41-43; idem, *De plantatione Noe* 44-45; idem, *De confusione linguarum* 62-64). In content Paul's thought is utterly diverse. Philo's theory concerns the Neoplatonic dichotomy between the realm of the universal and the particular. The heavenly man is a Platonic form or idea; the earthly man is an exemplification thereof. For Paul the distinction is historical, not philosophical. The first Adam is the historical father of the human race; the second Adam is Jesus the Messiah and redeemer of mankind. Philo has no soteriology and Paul no Platonism in mind. Cf. Jn. 3:34.

[40] *TWNT*, "πνεῦμα" by Kleinknecht, *et al*. I am astounded by the number of scholars who appeal to I Cor. 15:45; II Cor. 3:17-18; *etc.* to prove that Christ turned into the Spirit at the resurrection and so is now immaterial and invisible (*e.g.*, Robinson, "Easter to Valentinus," p. 13). Morissette shows from Jewish texts that "life-giving" means "to resurrect" and comments,

"The appellation 'Spirit,' for its part, is sometimes used by Paul to designate Christ.[129] Nonetheless, there is no formal identification whatever.[130] The identification is always *functional*: it serves to show what Christ means, 'now' *for* the faithful.[131] The statement of I Cor. 15.45b is no exception, as the verb ζῳοποιοῦν and the entire context indicate.

---

[129] Cf. II Cor. 3.17a, 18c; comp. Rom. 8.9-11. This affirmation is implied occasionally by Luke: comp. Lk. 12.12; 21.15; Acts 16.6, 7.

[130] Between II Cor. 3.17a ('the Lord is the Spirit') and 18c ('the Lord who is the Spirit'), Paul distinguishes in v. 17b 'where the Spirit of the Lord is, etc.'

entities are described as σῶμα ψυχικόν (v. 44), ψυχή ζῶσα (v. 45), τὸ ψυχικόν (v. 46) and as σῶμα πνευματικόν (v. 44), πνεῦμα ζῳοποιοῦν (v. 45), τὸ πνευματικόν (v. 46). It is because of the parallelism of his play on the words of Gen. 2:7 that Paul omits explicit reference to Christ's body in v. 45. Paul teaches in v. 45 that the natural body came into being at creation, while the supernatural body came into existence via the resurrection (cf. vs. 42-44a).[41] Similarly, we bear first the natural body, but we shall in the resurrection bear the supernatural body patterned after Jesus's (vs. 46, 49).

Now Paul calls the natural body χοϊκός and contrasts it with the heavenly body (vs. 47-49), which might lead us to think that the difference between the two is, after all, the stuff of which they are made. But while Paul does seem to associate the ψυχικός and the χοϊκός, he in no way implies that the heavenly body will be immaterial. That materiality is not the issue seems clear from v. 47:

ὁ πρῶτος ἄνθρωπος ἐκ γῆς χοϊκός
ὁ δεύτερος ἄνθρωπος ἐξ οὐρανοῦ

There is something conspicuously missing in this parallel between τὸ ψυχικὸν and τὸ πνευματικὸν (v. 46): the first Adam is *from* the earth, *made of* dust; the second Adam is *from* heaven, but *made of*—?[42] Clearly Paul recoils from saying the second Adam is made of heavenly substance. The contrast between the two Adams seems to be their origin, not their substance. This is reinforced by a comparison of these verses with II Cor. 5:1-3. Here the first man is called ἐκ γῆς χοϊκός; there the tent dwelling is described as ἐπίγειος (cf. I Cor. 15:40). Here the second man is ἐξ οὐρανοῦ; there what is variously characterized as the building, house, or dwelling is described as ἐξ οὐρανοῦ (cf. I Cor. 15:40). Again it seems evident that the contrast is one of origin, not substance. Thus, the doctrine of the two Adams seems to confirm the philological analysis above.

---

[131] The Apostle frequently attributes similar functions to Christ and the Spirit; W. D. Davies in *Paul and Rabbinic Judaism*, p. 177, has a good summary of these texts" (Rodolphe Morissette, "L'antithèse entre le 'psychique' et le 'pneumatique' en I Corinthiens, XV, 44 à 46," *RScR* 46 [1972]: 141).

[41] That the one verb ἐγένετο holds the sentence together cannot force the conclusion that the same act of creation is referred to, as is thought by Weiss, *Korintherbrief*, p. 473, for this violates the context.

[42] Or alternatively, the first Adam is made of the dust of the earth, the second Adam is from heaven. The first speaks of constitution, the second of origin. See also TWNT, s.v. "πνεῦμα" by Kleinknecht, *et al.*; Bultmann, *Theologie*, p. 249; S. H. Hooke, *The Resurrection of Christ as History and Experience* (London: Darton, Longman, & Todd, 1967), p. 146; Gundry, Soma, p. 166.

"Flesh and Blood Cannot Inherit The Kingdom of God"

Then comes a phrase that has caused great difficulties for interpreters: "I tell you this, brethren, flesh and blood cannot inherit the kingdom of God, nor does the perishable inherit the imperishable" (v. 50).[43] Does not this seem to clearly indicate that the resurrection body will be immaterial? Jeremias has tried to escape this conclusion by arguing that "flesh and blood" refers to those alive at the Parousia, while the "perishable" refers to the dead in Christ; Paul means that neither living nor dead as they are can inherit God's kingdom, but must be transformed (v. 51).[44] This however, seems unlikely, for it requires that v. 50 go with v. 51. But not only does v. 50 appear to be a summary statement of the foregoing paragraph, but v. 51 introduces a new paragraph and a new thought, as is indicated by the introductory words, "Lo! I tell you a mystery!" and by the fact that something new and previously unknown is about to be communicated.[45] Neither need one adopt the expedient of Bornhäuser that Paul means flesh and blood will

---

[43] According to Jeremias, the misunderstanding of this verse "has played a disastrous role in the New Testament theology of the last sixty years until the present day;" it has led to a spiritualizing of the resurrection so that only the πνεῦμα survives—"This is nearly commonplace in New Testament scholarship" (Jeremias, "'Flesh and Blood'" pp. 157-158). Typical is the disastrous exegesis of McLeman:

"If Paul had been able to read and accept the last chapter of the canonical Gospels, he would not have been so insistent that flesh and blood (*sarx kai haima*) cannot inherit the kingdom of God (I Cor. 15:50). The belief that the risen Jesus had flesh and bones (*sarka kai ostea*, Luke 24:39) stands in contrast to the view that we must be changed (*allagesometha*, I Cor. 15:51) and that the resurrection body is quite different from the body of flesh. 'Paul believes in the resurrection of the *body*, not of the flesh. The flesh is the power of death, which must be destroyed.'*

* O. Cullmann, *Immortality of the Soul or Resurrection of the Dead?* p. 46" (James McLeman, *Resurrection Then and Now* [London: Hodder & Stoughton, 1965], p. 202).

McLeman not only confuses flesh-and-blood with anatomical flesh, but both these with the ethical meaning of "flesh"! Haenchen also tries to play Paul off against the author of Acts, declaring, "For Paul Jesus was no longer 'flesh and blood'...after his resurrection—he and Peter had been allowed to see the transfigured Lord (I Cor. 9:1), and the idea that the risen Christ has eaten and drunk with the disciples would have rung like a blasphemy in Paul's ears" (Ernst Haenchen, *The Acts of the Apostles*, 14th ed.; trans. B. Noble, G. Shinn, R. McL. Wilson [Oxford: Basil Blackwell, 1971], p. 114). Precisely the opposite is true. Also stumbling at this verse are Robertson and Plummer, *Corinthians*, p. 369; Clavier, "Remarques," pp. 348-349; Hans Grass, *Ostergeschehen und Osterberichte*, 4th rev. ed. (Göttingen: Vandenhoeck & Ruprecht, 1963), p. 164; Raymond E. Brown, *The Virginal Conception and Bodily Resurrection of Jesus*, (London: Geoffrey Chapman, 1973), p. 87; James W. D. G. Dunn, *Jesus and the Spirit* (London: SCM, 1975), pp. 121, 391; Robinson, "Easter to Valentinus," pp. 11-12.

[44] Jeremias, "'Flesh and Blood,'" pp. 151-159.

[45] Sand, "Fleisch," pp. 152-153.

decay in the grave, but the bones will be raised.[46] This fails to reckon with the fact that v. 50 refers to the living at the Parousia as well as the dead and falsely assumes that Paul is here speaking of anatomy.

Rather, most commentators are agreed that "flesh and blood" is a typical Semitic expression denoting the frail human nature.[47] In other words it means pretty much the same thing as τὸ ψυχικόν, applied to human nature generally. It emphasizes our feeble mortality over against God; hence, the second half of v. 50 is Paul's elaboration in other words of exactly the same thought.[48] The fact that the verb is in the singular may also suggest that Paul is not talking of physical aspects of the body, but about a conceptual unity: "flesh and blood is not able to inherit...." Elsewhere Paul also employs the expression "flesh and blood" to mean simply "people" or "mortal creatures" (Gal. 1:16; Eph. 6:12). Therefore, Paul is not talking about anatomy here; rather he means that mortal human beings cannot enter into God's eternal kingdom; therefore, they must become imperishable (cf. v. 53). This imperishability does not imply immateriality or unextendedness; on the contrary, Paul's doctrine of the world to come is that our resurrection bodies will be part of, so to speak, a resurrected creation (Rom. 8:18-23). The universe will be delivered from sin and decay, not materiality, and our bodies will be part of that universe.[49]

The Transformation at the Parousia

In the following paragraph, Paul tells how this will be accomplished. When he says "We shall not all sleep, but we shall all be changed" (v. 51) it is not clear

---

[46] Karl Bornhäuser, *Die Gebeine der Toten*, BFCT 26 (Gütersloh: C. Bertelsmann, 1921), p. 37; Walther Künneth, *The Theology of the Resurrection*, trans. J. W. Leitch (London: SCM Press, 1965), p. 94.

[47] It is found in Mt. 16:17; Gal. 1:16; Eph. 6:12; Heb. 2:14; see also Sirach 14:18 and the references in Paul Billerbeck, *Kommentar zum Neuen Testament aus Talmud und Midrasch*, 6 vols., ed. Herrmann Strack (München: Beck, 1922-63), 1:730-731, 753. The Semitic word pair σάρξ καὶ αἷμα is first attested by Sirach 14:18; 17:31 and its equivalent occurs frequently in rabbinic texts, especially rabbinic parables. See K. G. Kuhn, "Πειρασμός—ἁμαρτία—σάρξ im Neuen Testament und die damit zusammenhängenden Vorstellungen," *ZTK* 49 (1952): 200-222; J. N. Sevenster, "Some Remarks on the γυμνός in II Cor. V.3," in *Studia Paulina*, ed. J. N. Sevenster and W. C. Unnik (Haarlem, Netherlands: Erven F. Bohn, 1953), p. 205; Moule, "Dualism," p. 109; *TWNT*, s.v. "σάρξ," by Schweizer, *et al.*; Bultmann, *Theologie*, pp. 234-235; Sand, "Fleisch," pp. 152-153, 295; Pearson, *Pneumatikos-Psychikos*, pp. 22, 25; O'Collins, *Easter*, p. 113; Gundry, *Soma*, p. 166; Sider, "Conception," pp. 436-437; Gillman, "Transformation," pp. 317-318.

[48] Weiss, *Korintherbrief*, p. 377; Conzelmann, *Korinther*, p. 346.

[49] Cullmann, *Immortality*, pp. 37-38; Gundry, *Soma*, p.47.

whether he means by "all" Christians in general or Christians alive at his time. In the first case he means that there will be Christians alive at Parousia, but that they and the dead alike will be changed. In the second case, he means some of us will not die, but all of us, whether dead or living, will be changed. The same ambiguity exists in I Thess. 4:15, 17. But in either case, two things are clear: (1) Paul held that the transformation would take place instantaneously at the moment of the resurrection (v. 52). In this he differs sharply from II Baruch 50-51 which holds that the resurrection yields the old bodies again which are transformed only after the judgment.[50] Paul's doctrine is that we are raised imperishable and glorified. (2) For Paul the resurrection is a *transformation*, not an *exchange*.[51] In the resurrection, the "ego" of a man does not trade bodies. Rather the natural body in the grave is miraculously raised and transformed into a supernatural body. The metaphor of the sowing and raising clearly points to this: "It is sown..., it is

---

[50] According to Baruch the old bodies are raised for the purpose of recognition, that the living may know that the dead have been raised. But for Paul, believers, like Christ, emerge glorified from the tomb (Kirsopp Lake, *The Historical Evidence for the Resurrection of Jesus* [London: Williams & Norgate 1907], pp. 24-27; Weiss, *Korintherbrief*, pp. 349, 379; Grass, *Ostergeschehen*, pp. 151).

[51] Robertson and Plummer, *Corinthians*, p. xxxvii; Brooke Foss Wescott, *The Gospel of the Resurrection* (London: Macmillan, 1906), p. 94; Héring, *Première épître*, p. 148; M. E. Dahl, *The Resurrection of the Body*, SBT 36 (London: SCM, 1962), pp. 27-33; Berthold Klappert, "Einleitung," in *Diskussion um Kreuz und Auferstehung*, ed. idem (Wuppertal: Aussaat Verlag, 1971), pp. 14-15; Whitely, *Theology*, p. 249; O'Collins, *Easter*, p. 44; Sider, "Conception", p. 435; Gillman, "Transformation," pp. 330-332; Joseph Plevnik, "The Taking Up of the Faithful and the Resurrection of the Dead in I Thessalonians 4:13-18," *CBQ* 46 (1984): 274-283; Pamment, "Raised a Spiritual Body," pp. 383-384; Ben Meyer, "Did Paul's View of the Resurrection of the Dead Undergo Development?" *TS* 47 (1986): 376-377; idem, "Paul and the Resurrection of the Dead," *TS* 48 (1987): 157-158. Grass is simply wrong when he characterizes the resurrection as a re-creation, not a transformation (Grass, *Ostergeschehen*, p. 154). He falsely appeals to v. 50; his statement that Paul has no interest in the emptying of the graves ignores the statements of I Thess. 4:16; I Cor. 15:42-44, 52. He attempts to strengthen his case by arguing that the relation of the old world to the new is one of annihilation to re-creation and that this is analogous to the relation of the old body to the new (Ibid., pp. 167-171). But Grass's texts are chiefly non-Pauline (Heb. 1:10-12; Mk. 13:31; Rev. 6:14; 20:11; 21:1; II Pet. 3:10). Paul's doctrine suggests a transformation of creation (Rom. 8:18-23; cf. I Cor. 7:31). And even the other passages leave mixed impressions. According to Paul it is this creation which will be delivered from its bondage to sin and decay.

According to Dahl, the widely accepted exegesis of what he calls "hetero-somatism" is due more to Western philosophy than the true biblical outlook. He emphasizes that the very word 'resurrection" implies the restoration of something lost, not the provision of something new, that the seed-plant analogy shows the organic unity of the beginning and end of the change, and that the "it" which is sown and raised in v. 43 haunts the "accepted exegesis" (Dahl, *Resurrection*, pp. 27-28, 33). Dahl's own view of somatic continuity (Ibid., pp. 93-94) presses existentialist views of σῶμα onto Paul, for he thinks σῶμα = whole personality; but in Dahl's favor it must be said that he regards a physical body as an integral aspect of the whole personality.

raised," Paul repeats four times. His statement that we shall *all* be changed includes the dead as well as the living, and the change concerns the change in the body (v. 35). When Paul says "the dead will be raised imperishable" (v. 52) and "the dead in Christ will rise first" (I Thess. 4:16), he can only mean the dead in the graves. His use of τοῦτο four times in vs. 50-55 emphasizes the continuity between the natural and supernatural body: *this* perishable, mortal body will put on imperishability and immortality. In fact, as we have seen, the very concept of resurrection involves an emptying of the grave, for in an exchange of bodies there is no raising at all.

The idea of an exchange of bodies seems to be a peculiarly modern notion. In the Old Testament it is clearly the resurrection of the body which is contemplated (Is. 26:19; Dan. 12:2; cf. Ez. 37:1-14). In Jewish literature on the resurrection contemporaneous with the New Testament, the resurrection is conceived of as the reuniting of the souls of the dead, which are in Sheol or hell or chambers, with the bodies, which are interred in the earth (I Enoch 51:1; II Baruch 30:2-5; cf. 21:23; 42:8; IV Ezra 7:26-44). Resurrection *means* the raising of the dead man in the grave. For the Jews the primary object of the resurrection was the remains of the dead, which they conceived to be the bones. According to their understanding, the flesh decayed, but the bones endured. It was the bones, therefore, that were the principal subject of the resurrection, and with this hope in mind, Jews carefully preserved the bones of the dead, collecting them into ossuaries after the flesh had decomposed.[52] Only in a case in which the bones were destroyed, as with the Jewish martyrs, did God's creating a resurrection body *ex nihilo* come into question (cf. I Enoch 61:5). Otherwise, the body in the grave was raised.[53] In the New Testament we seem to find the same emphasis on the raising of the dead in the graves. In Mt. 27:52-53, we find an old tradition in which resurrection "is conceived in terms of the bodies of the dead coming out of the tombs in which they were laid."[54] It is the same in Jn. 5:28-29: "...the hour is coming when all who are in the tombs will hear his voice and come forth...." We must remem-

---

[52] See E. M. Meyers, *Jewish Ossuaries: Reburial and Rebirth*, BO 24 (Rome: Biblical Institute Press, 1971).

[53] As Hengel notes, "In Jewish Palestine, there was only one conception of the resurrection: the bodily.... It was not possible to speak of the resurrection of a dead person without taking into account his corpse" (Martin Hengel, "Ist der Osterglaube noch zu retten?" *TQ* 153 [1973]: 225).

[54] Dunn, *Jesus*, p. 118.

ber, too, that Paul was a Pharisee and that Luke identifies his doctrine of the resurrection with that of the Pharisees. Paul's language is thoroughly Pharisaic, and it is unlikely that he should employ the same terminology with an entirely different meaning.[55] Paul, like Baruch and others, held to a resurrection and transformation of the dead in the graves. He could not be more explicit: "It is sown a natural body, it is raised a supernatural body" (I Cor. 15:44).

If this were not clear enough, Paul's doctrine of the new creation in Rom. 8 seems to drive the point home. He writes,

> But if Christ is in you, although your bodies are dead because of sin, your spirits are alive because of righteousness. If the Spirit of him who raised Jesus from the dead dwells in you, he who raised Christ Jesus from the dead will give life to your mortal bodies also through his Spirit which dwells in you (Rom. 8:10-11).

Note: it is *our mortal bodies* to which God will give life. Grass attempts to escape this conclusion by arguing that the verses have nothing to do with eschatological resurrection. It would be very odd, he says, if the present indwelling Spirit were the factor to transform our bodies at the resurrection.[56] This point certainly has weight; but nevertheless this does appear to be an eschatological passage.[57] The eschatological resurrection would seem to be in view in light of the future tense ("*will* give life") and the context of Christ's resurrection as the parallel to our being given life ("to your mortal bodies *also*"). The body's being dead in v. 10 is equivalent to its being mortal in v. 11 and is the curse of sin (cf. Rom. 5:12-21). But our spirits are alive through regeneration by God's Spirit. So our spirits are alive, but our bodies are mortal. Paul's answer to this predicament is that just as God raised Jesus from the dead, so he will give life to our mortal bodies also (cf. I Cor. 15:22, 54-57; II Cor. 5:4). The oddity noted by Grass finds something of a parallel in II Cor. 5:5; the point may be that the Spirit which will raise us from the dead has already in measure been given to us. But however we resolve the odd-

---

[55] Gundry emphasizes that Paul as a former Pharisee could not use such traditional language without intending to imply a physical resurrection (Gundry, Soma, pp. 176-177). Smith adds: "Paul's conception of the new body of the Christian is not as radically different from all Jewish ideas as Grass and others maintain. Certainly he did not retain the hope of a crassly material resurrection of the old body which was the content of the popular hope. But he does indicate that he believes the spiritual body will be produced by a transformation of the physical body (or what is left of it—according to Jewish ideas, the bones in the grave or the one indestructible bone)" (Smith, "Resurrection Faith," p. 406). Paul's outlook is "thoroughly Pharisaic," according to Davies, *Paul*, pp. 303-308; so also Sider, "Conception," p. 438.
[56] Grass, *Ostergeschehen*, p. 165.
[57] See Gundry, Soma, pp. 44-46.

ity, the decisive confirmation that the passage does concern eschatological resurrection seems to come seven verses later in Paul's discussion of the deliverance of creation from sin and decay. Here there seems no doubt that the passage is eschatological. Paul says that the creation waits with eager longing for the day when it will be delivered from its bondage to decay. He continues, "We know that the whole creation has been groaning in travail together until now; and not only the creation, but we ourselves, who have the first fruits of the Spirit, groan inwardly as we wait for adoption as sons, the redemption of our bodies" (Rom. 8:22-23). Here the Christian dilemma is poignantly expressed: the first fruits of the Spirit are our spirits which are alive. But they are united with mortal bodies. So we groan inwardly—for what?—for *the redemption of our bodies* (cf. II Cor. 5:2, 4). Thus, vs. 10-11 concern an eschatological event. Therefore, Rom. 8 attests to the fact that the resurrection is a change wrought on our mortal bodies. It is not an exchange of the mortal body for a new one; rather God will give life to our *mortal bodies*, and we thus await the *redemption* of our bodies. In saying that it is the mortal body that will be given resurrection life in the eschaton, Paul precludes any attempt to view the resurrection as an exchange, and not a transformation.[58]

Although this is perhaps difficult to conceive, an interesting analogy to the sort of transformation envisaged by Paul is Jesus's changing the water into wine at Cana (Jn. 2:1-11). Why did Jesus command the servants to fill the jars with water? Clearly it was the water that Jesus changed into wine, according to John. He

---

[58] Still more confirmation of this fact comes from Paul's discussion of the sanctity of the body (I Cor. 6:12-20). In this passage, he is talking about the physical body, as the crassly physical proverb in v. 13, the admonitions to sexual purity in vs. 15-18, and the comparison between the body and the temple in v. 19 show. In v. 13 Paul affirms that the body is meant for the Lord and the Lord for the body. Then in v. 14 he states that just as God raised Jesus, He will also raise us up. And in v. 15 he asserts that our bodies are members of Christ. In these verses, Paul affirms in strongest terms the value of our physical bodies. Our mortal bodies are members of Christ and are intended for the Lord. Hence, God will raise us up, *i.e.*, raise our bodies. In very physical terms, then, Paul affirms that there is numerical identity between the mortal and resurrection body. The only reason to doubt this conclusion would be v. 13, that God will destroy the body, and v. 17, that a man united to the Lord becomes one spirit with Him. But the destruction of the body may very well be part of the quotation from the Corinthians themselves, who scorned the significance of the body. In any case, the destruction probably refers to death, a circumstance that is then overcome in the resurrection (v. 14). As for v. 17, the unity in spirit which one has with God is not meant substantively, for this would contradict chapter 15, which affirms a resurrection of the σῶμα and personal immortality. Besides, the verse refers to our being one spirit with the Lord now; this is our Christian experience, not an eschatological expectation. That expectation is expressed in v. 14b: God will also raise us up by His power.

did not command jars full of water to be emptied so that he could fill them with wine created *ex nihilo*. The water was not poured out or discarded; rather it was transformed. Similarly, Paul's doctrine is that the old body is not cast aside; rather it is changed. This may be difficult to conceive, but it seems to be what Paul believed. Thus, for him resurrection implied an empty tomb. Scholars who appeal to Paul's doctrine of the resurrection body to show that the tomb might not be empty would therefore appear to be seriously mistaken.[59] Of course, God could create a new body (or wine) *ex nihilo*, but the question is not what God could do, but what God does do. Paul fervently believed that God would raise and transform our bodies at the Parousia.

The Personal Return of Jesus

Perhaps one of the most convincing arguments that Paul believed that Christ's resurrection body was physical is his earnest adherence to the hope of the personal return of Christ (I Thess. 4:16-17; II Thess. 1:7, 8, 10; 2:1, 8; I Cor. 15:23; Phil. 3:20-21; 4:5; Col. 3:4). Though some of these references taken alone could be interpreted in a spiritual way (Phil. 4:5; Col. 3:4), most of them refer to a literal event and thus serve as the yardstick for the interpretation of the others. Paul seems to have awaited the personal, visible return of Christ. This hope runs through the entire New Testament (Mt. 24-25; Mk. 13; Lk. 21:5-36; Jn. 14:1-3; 21:22-23; Acts 1:6-7; 17:31; I Tim. 6:14; II Tim. 4:1; Tit. 2:13; Heb. 10:37; Jas. 5:7, 9; I Pet. 1:13; II Pet. 3:4, 10; I Jn. 2:28; 3:2). The Parousia was conceived to be the personal return of Jesus, at which believers would be resurrected and transformed and taken by the Lord into his kingdom. Grass dismisses the "meeting the Lord in the air" (I Thess. 4:17) as so mythological that it may be understood as an expression of the wholly other nature of the eschatological mode of being.[60] But the point is, Paul really *believed* it and re-iterated it ("Now concerning the coming of our Lord Jesus Christ and our assembling to meet him..." II Thess. 2:1). This blessed hope was evidently no symbol for Paul, but an imminent future event which he hoped to see. But this would seem to be possible only if the risen and coming Christ has, at least in this dimension, a physical, extended body.

---

[59] Grass, *Ostergeschehen*, pp. 146-173; Gerhard Koch, *Die Auferstehung Jesu Christi*, BHT (Tübingen: J. C. B. Mohr, 1959), pp. 168, 171; Jacob Kremer, *Die Ostervangelien—Geschichten um Geschichte* (Stuttgart: Katholisches Bibelwerk, 1977), p. 49.

[60] Grass, *Ostergeschehen*, p. 151.

II CORINTHIANS 5:1-10

The Earthly Tent and the Heavenly Dwelling

But this at once raises the puzzling question: what happens to those Christians who die before the Parousia? In I Thess. 4 Paul assures us that they will be raised first. But are they simply extinguished until the day of resurrection? The clue to Paul's answer may be found in another important passage concerning our hope for the next life, II Cor. 5:1-10.[61] The earthly tent we live in is the present body, the σῶμα ψυχικόν (v. 1; cf. 4:7).[62] By way of contrast the building we have from God is the resurrection body, the σῶμα πνευματικόν. The contrast between the tent and the building is one of stability and permanence. The ἔχομεν does not imply that the resurrection body is already waiting in heaven for us; rather it expresses certainty of possession, as when one says that one has an inheritance in heaven.[63] Similarly the fact that the house is eternal (αἰώνιον) does not mean that it has existed from eternity past, but that it endures forever.[64] The phrase ἐν τοῖς οὐρανοῖς does not go with ἔχομεν but with the immediately preceding words as a description of the house.[65] The idea that our house or body exists already in heaven may be seen to be untenable by reflecting upon the fact that the resurrection body is a σῶμα πνευματικόν. The notion of an unanimated σῶμα πνευ-

---

[61] For a survey of the various interpretations of this passage, see Friedrich Gustav Lang, *2 Korinther 5, 1-10 in der neueren Forschung*, BGBE 16 (Tübingen: J. C. B. Mohr, 1973). In this passage Paul takes account of dying before the Parousia, according to H. A. W. Meyer, *Handbuch über den zweiten Brief an die Korinther*, 6th ed., rev. Georg Heinrici, KEKNT 6 (Göttingen: Vandenhoeck & Ruprecht's Verlag, 1883), p. 132; Grass, *Ostergeschehen*, p. 157; C. K. Barrett, *A Commentary on the Second Epistle to the Corinthians*, BNTC (London: Adam & Charles Black, 1973), p. 159.

[62] The figure of a tent for the body is common in Hellenistic literature. See Plato *Phaedrus* 81C; Philo *Quaestiones in Genesin* 1.28; *Corpus hermeticum* 8.15, and literature cited in Rudolf Bultmann, *Der Zweite Brief an die Korinther*, ed. Erich Dinkler, KEKNT (Göttingen: Vandenhoeck & Ruprecht, 1976), pp. 132-133. In the Old Testament it appears only in Is. 38:12; see also Wisdom 9:15. In the New Testament we find the metaphor in II Pet. 1:13; Heb. 8:9; cf. Jn.1:14.

[63] (Heinrici-) Meyer, *Zweiten Brief*, p. 134; Alfred Plummer, *Second Epistle of St Paul to the Corinthians*, ICC (Edinburgh: T & T Clark, 1915), pp. 143-144; Ernst-Bernard Allo, *Seconde épître aux Corinthiens* (Paris: Librairie Lecoffre, 1956), pp. 120-121, 138; P. E. Hughes, *Paul's Second Epistle to the Corinthians*, NLC (Edinburgh: Marshall, Morgan & Scott, 1962), p. 163; Fuller, *Formation*, p. 20; Barrett, *Second Epistle*, p. 151; Bultmann, *Korinther*, pp. 133-134; Paul Hoffmann, *Die Toten in Christus*, 3rd rev. ed., NTA 2 (Münster: Aschendorff, 1978), p. 270. This seems to be nearly fatal to Grass's attempt to show that the resurrection consists in the exchange of the present body for a heavenly one.

[64] Plummer, *Corinthians*, p. 144; Allo, *Seconde épître*, p. 121.

[65] Bultmann, *Korinther*, p. 133.

ματικόν, stored up in the closets of heaven until the Parousia, is a contradiction in terms, since πνεῦμα is the essence and source of life itself.

"Putting On" the Resurrection Body

Paul goes on to say that while we are here we groan and long to put on our heavenly dwelling (v. 2). The metaphor is mixed (cf. II Pet. 1:13-14): the word ἐπενδύσασθαι has reference to pulling on top-clothing, but Paul uses it of the house we shall receive from God.[66] We long to put on the heavenly dwelling so that we may not be found naked (v. 3). The nakedness is defined in v. 4: we sigh in this earthly tent, not to be unclothed and so be naked, but to be further clothed (ἐπενδύσασθαι) so that mortality is swallowed up by life (καταποθῇ τὸ θνητὸν ὑπὸ τῆς ζωῆς). The language is irresistibly reminiscent of I Cor. 15. There we saw that the mortal (τὸ θνητὸν) must put on (ενδύσασθαι) the immortal, and the perishable the imperishable (I Cor. 15:53). This had reference to the transformation of the old body at the Parousia. When this occurs, then death is swallowed

---

[66] This is a very rare verb both in the New Testament and in ancient Greek literature. It has the sense of pulling one garment on over another one. Taken in isolation this might be thought to indicate that the resurrection consists in drawing on the new body "over" the old, so that the old is annihilated and only the ego is continuous ([Kümmel-] Lietzmann, *Korinther II*, p. 119). This, however, is to press the metaphor too far. Paul is not trying to be technical, as is evident by his use of the ordinary ἐνδυσάμενοι in v. 3 (cf. I Cor. 15:54). He wants only to say that rather than lose the body in death, he would rather be changed directly at the Parousia, thus avoiding the necessity of "undressing." In this sense, the transformation of the bodies of those alive at the Parousia is analogous to putting on top-clothing, *viz.*, one need not undress first. For Paul the resurrection is not an exchange of the body, but a transformation of the body. Indeed, the "putting on" consists precisely in being transformed. This is hinted at in II Cor. 5:4, for the swallowing up of the mortal in life corresponds with God's giving life to the mortal body (Rom. 8:11). The mortal body is not left alone; rather it is "swallowed up," it is transformed, into a resurrection life. The first-fruits of the Spirit are given to us as a guarantee of this event (II Cor. 5:5; Rom 8:23). Note also the parallel between II Cor. 4:14 and I Cor. 6:14, where the resurrection of the mortal body is in view.

It is also pressing the metaphor too far to emphasize parallels in *Religionsgeschichte* concerning the reception of a heavenly robe by the righteous (I Enoch 62:15; II Enoch 22:8-10; I Baruch 5:2; Ascension of Isaiah 7:22; 8:26; 9, Odes of Solomon 11:11; 21:3; 25:8). It is not at all evident that the robes of glory given to the righteous are new bodies, rather than new clothes. Much closer to these parallels than Paul's doctrine of the resurrection body are the white robes of Rev. 4:4; 6:11; 7:9, 13, 14. Paul does not refer to the resurrection body as a garment, but as a building. The point Paul wishes to express is that he wants to possess the resurrection body without the necessity of dying so that there would be no interval of separation of soul from body. This would prevent the disquieting state of being found naked (Plummer, *Corinthians*, pp. 147-148; [Kümmel-] Lietzmann, *Korinther II*, p. 117; Sevenster, "Remarks," p. 207; Allo, *Seconde épître*, p. 123; Grass, *Ostergeschehen*, pp. 158-159; Cullmann, *Immortality*, pp. 52-53; Moule, "Dualism." pp. 118-119, 122; Hughes, *Epistle*, pp. 168-169, Barrett, *Second Epistle*, p. 156).

up in victory (κατεπόθη ὁ θάνατος εἰς νῖκος) (I Cor. 15:54). This makes it likely that the building from God in II Cor. 5:1 is not received immediately upon death, but at the Parousia.[67] This fact also seems clear from a comparison with Rom. 8.[68] There the groaning (στενάζω; cf. II Cor. 5:2) concerned our waiting for the eschatological redemption of our bodies (v. 23). God will then give life to our mortal bodies (ζῳοποιήσει τὰ θνητὰ σώματα ὑμῶν) (v. 11), a phrase reminiscent of II Cor. 5:4, ἵνα καταποθῇ τὸ θνητὸν ὑπὸ τῆς ζωῆς. The indwelling Holy Spirit, alternately designated as the first fruits of the Spirit (τὴν ἀπαρχὴν τοῦ πνεύματος) (Rom. 8:23) or the down payment of the Spirit (τὸν ἀρραβῶνα τοῦ πνεύματος) (II Cor. 5:5), is our guarantee of eschatological redemption (cf. II Cor.

---

[67] The evidence of I Thess. 4; I Cor. 15; and Rom. 8 seems to stand decisively against those who think the new body is received immediately after death ([Heinrici-] Meyer, *Zweiter Brief*, p. 122; Davies, *Paul*, pp. 311, 317-318; Whitely, *Theology*, p. 260; Bultmann, *Korinther*, pp. 135-139; Meyer, "Paul's View of the Resurrection," p. 379). As Allo says, it is unbelievable that had Paul changed his mind on the dead's receiving their resurrection bodies at the Parousia, he would not have told the Corinthians but continued to use precisely the same language (Allo, *Seconde épître*, p. 151). If a new body is received immediately, then there is no resurrection of the dead. But Paul in his later letters did not abandon the doctrine and hope of the resurrection. The whole point of II Cor. 4:7-5:10, which ought to be read as a unit, is that though our weak and beleaguered bodies are gradually failing, we have the hope of the resurrection. The "outer nature" (4:16) is not the old man of sin, but the earthen vessel (4:7), the body (4:10; 5:6, 8, 10), the mortal flesh (4:11), the earthly tent (5:1), the mortal (5:4). As God raised Jesus, he will also raise us (4:14; cf. I Cor. 6:14). This hope is that which is expressed in 5:1. It would be a desperate expedient to posit a third intermediate body between the present body and the resurrection body; this would contradict the permanence of the building we receive, too. If we receive a body immediately upon death, v. 8 becomes unintelligible. There would also be no reason for the fear of nakedness. This viewpoint seems to forget as well that the resurrection body will be a transformation of the physical body in the grave. "Final result: there is a total lack of persuasive evidence that Paul's teaching on the resurrection of the dead underwent significant development either between I Thess. 4 and I Cor. 15, or between 1 Cor. 15 and 2 Cor. 5" (Meyer, "Paul's View of the Resurrection," p. 382).

[68] Rom. 8 and II Cor. 4:7-5:10 on the resurrection serve to illuminate each other. That the subject matter is the same is evident from the clear parallels between them: our quickened spirits in mortal bodies (Rom. 8:10; II Cor. 4:7, 16); the present sufferings versus the incomparable glory to come (Rom. 8:18; II Cor. 4:17); the groaning while in the present body until the time of deliverance (Rom. 8:22-23; II Cor. 5:2, 4); the mortal body's being given life (Rom. 8:11; II Cor. 5:4); the first-fruits of the Spirit having been given as a preparation (Rom. 8:23; II Cor. 5:5); and the patient waiting for that which is not yet seen (Rom. 8:24-25; II Cor. 5:6-9). This is exceedingly important, for it shows, since Romans was written after II Corinthians, that Paul retained the doctrine of the resurrection and transformation of the body from I Cor. 15. We also see that while the continuity of the earthly and resurrection body is masked by purposely sharp contrast in II Cor. 5:1, the continuity is nevertheless there, for the mortal's being swallowed up in life in v. 4 can only refer to the mortal body's being given life (Rom. 8:11), since our inner spirits are already alive. It needs to be emphasized that in both these passages, the longed for deliverance is not from corporeality as such; it is from the sin and consequent decay that infects our bodies. Paul looks forward, not to release from the body, but to the redemption of the body.

1:22; Eph. 1:13-14). This makes it evident that the "putting on" of the heavenly body is an eschatological event.

The Intermediate State

In I Cor. 15 Paul did not speak of a state of nakedness; the mortal simply "put on" the immortal. But in II Cor. 5 he speaks of the fear of being unclothed and the preference to be further clothed, as by top-clothing, rather than undressing and then being re-clothed. It seems likely that Paul is speaking here of the loss of the earthly tent or body through death as being unclothed and hence naked. He would rather not quit the old body but simply be transformed at the Parousia without experiencing the nakedness of death. This nakedness is thus the nakedness of the individual's spirit or soul apart from the body.[69] This is confirmed in vs. 6-9 where Paul contrasts being at home in the body and being at home with the Lord as mutually exclusive conditions. Paul is saying that while we are in this body we sigh, not because we want to leave the body by death and exist as a disembodied soul, but because we, burdened by the mortal body subject to sin and death, want to have our heavenly body, but without the necessity of passing through the intermediate state.

Despite the unsettling prospect of such an intermediate state, Paul sounds a note of cheer (v. 6). While we are in this body we are away from the Lord, and even with the nakedness it is better to be away from the body and with the Lord (v. 8). Christ makes all the difference; for Paul the souls of the departed are not shut up in caves or caskets until the end time as in Jewish apocalyptic; rather they go to be with Jesus and enjoy a nearer and deeper fellowship with him until he

---

[69] On nakedness as a description of a disembodied soul, see Plato *Cratylus* 403B; idem *Gorgias* 523, 524; idem *Phaedo* 67D, E; 81C; idem *Republic* 9; 377B; *Corpus hermeticum* 1.26; cf. 9.18; Philo *De virtutibus* 76; idem *Legum allegoriae* 2.57, 59; Lucian *Hermotimus* 7. The normative view of first century Judaism was anthropological dualism, including the continued existence of the disembodied soul after death (Hoffmann, *Toten*, pp. 26-174; Gundry, *Soma*, pp. 87-93). See also Weiss, *Korintherbrief*, p. 370; Plummer, *Corinthians*, p. 147; Sevenster, "Remarks," pp. 202-214; Allo, *Seconde épître*, pp. 121-122; Grass, *Ostergeschehen*, p. 161; Cullmann, *Immortality*, p. 52; Jean Héring, *Le seconde épître de Saint Paul aux Corinthiens*, CNT 8 (Neuchatel, Switzerland: Delachaux & Nièstle, 1958), pp. 48-49; Hughes, *Epistle*, pp. 169-170; Barrett, *Second Epistle*, pp. 153-155. Hoffmann also finds confirmatory evidence for an intermediate state from the use of the terms ἡ ἀβυσσος (Rom. 10:7), ἐκ νεκρῶν (I Cor. 15:12, 20), and παράδεισος (II Cor. 12:1-4; cf. Lk. 23:43; Acts 2:7) (Hoffmann, *Toten*, pp. 177-186). But the decisive passage proving Paul's belief in such a state is Phil. 1:21-26 (Ibid., pp. 286-320).

comes again to claim his kingdom.[70] Hence, Paul could write, "For to me to live is Christ, and to die is gain" (Phil. 1:21). Paul's desire, despite his distaste for the nakedness of the soul, was "to depart and be with Christ, for that is far better" (Phil. 1:23).

From this it seems to follow that the intermediate state of believers is conscious, blissful communion with Jesus. Paul explicitly contradicts any notion that the soul "sleeps" or is unconscious until the Parousia.[71] When Jesus returns again to earth he brings with him the souls of the departed, and they are reunited with their resurrected, transformed bodies, whereupon those alive at the Parousia are similarly transformed, and together they all go to be with the Lord (I Thess. 4:14, 16-17). Paul's hope was to live to see the Parousia; nevertheless, his comfort was that should he die he would go to be with Jesus. While he was in the flesh, in the body, he meanwhile sought to honor his Lord in all that he did (Phil. 1:24-25; II Cor. 5:9).[72]

---

[70] Cf. II Baruch 30:2-5; IV Ezra 7:26-44; I Enoch 22:1-14. See also Hoffmann, *Toten*, pp. 286-320.

[71] Bornhäuser, *Auferstehung*, p. 44; Plummer, *Corinthians*, p. 150; Allo, *Seconde épître*, p. 132; C. F. Evans, *Resurrection and the New Testament*, SBT 12 (London: SCM Press, 1970), pp. 22-24; Whitely, *Theology*, pp. 262-269; Robert E. Bailey, "Is 'Sleep' the Proper Biblical Term for the Intermediate State?" *ZNW* 55 (1964): 161-167; Hoffmann, *Toten*, pp. 186-206.

[72] This interpretation of Paul's doctrine would appear to involve the following inconsistency: on the one hand, he wants to live to the Parousia so as to avoid the state of nakedness; on the other hand, he explicitly says it is better to die and be with Christ than to go on living in the flesh. Now even should there be an irreconcilable inconsistency here, that would not of itself falsify the foregoing interpretation, for to be caught between conflicting desires, especially with regard to life and death, is a common human experience. Alternative interpretations of II Cor. 5 seem to be less plausible exegetically. But is the inconsistency so irreconcilable? I think that if we look at the three states involved, we shall see that Paul's desires are not so contradictory. The body and soul could exist in three states: (1) the soul united with the present mortal body away from the Lord, (2) the disembodied soul with the Lord, and (3) the soul united with the resurrection body with the Lord. Paul desires (3) above all, and (2) in preference to (1). Thus, with regard to states, it is better, even with the nakedness, to be with the Lord than to be in the present body; but even better than being with the Lord as a disembodied soul is being with him united with a resurrection body, since then one avoids the nakedness. Paul's desires therefore seem to be consistent. But the problem arises for the apostle when one considers how one reaches these states. For in order to get (3) without going through the nakedness, one has to remain in (1)! So what is one to do? Does he stick it out in the present in hopes of attaining the best, or does he settle for second best rather than endure the present? In other words, to get the best state, one has to go on living in the worst state, hoping only that the Lord will soon return! What I am suggesting is that the tension which we see in Paul's desires is not the result of exegetical interpretation; rather it was a real dilemma which confronted Paul himself, such that whatever he chose to do would involve him in a sort of inconsistency.

Paul's doctrine of the nature of the resurrection body would now seem to be reasonably clear. When a Christian dies, his conscious spirit or soul goes to be with Christ until the Parousia, while his body lies in the grave. When Christ returns, in a single instant the remains of the natural body are transformed into a powerful, glorious, and imperishable supernatural body under the complete lordship and direction of the Spirit, and the soul of the departed is simultaneously reunited with the body, and the man is raised to everlasting life. Then those who are alive will be similarly transformed, the old body miraculously changed into the new without excess, and all believers will go to be with the Lord.

Paul's Understanding of the Resurrection Body

This doctrine proves very fruitful in illuminating Paul's conception of the resurrection body of Christ, for Christ is "the first fruits of those who have fallen asleep" (I Cor. 15:20) and "will change our lowly body to be like his glorious body" (Phil. 3:21). In no sense did Paul appear to have conceived Christ's resurrection body to be immaterial or unextended. The notion of an immaterial, unextended body seems to be a self-contradiction; the nearest thing to it would be a shade in Sheol, and this was certainly not Paul's conception of Christ's glorious resurrection body! The only phrases in Paul's discussion that could lend themselves to a "dematerializing" of Christ's body are "σῶμα πνευματικόν" and "flesh and blood cannot inherit the kingdom of God." But virtually all modern commentators seem to agree that these expressions have nothing to do with substantiality or anatomy, as we have seen. Rather the first speaks of the heavenly orientation of the resurrection body, while the second refers to the mortality and feebleness of the natural body in contrast to God.

So it is difficult to understand how theologians can persist in describing Christ's resurrection body in terms of an invisible, intangible spirit; there seems to be a great lacuna here between exegesis and theology. I can only agree with O'Collins when he asserts in this context, "Platonism may be hardier than we suspect."[73] With all the best will in the world, it is extremely difficult to see what is

---

[73] O'Collins, *Easter*, p. 94. He remarks that the position of some theologians "looks scarcely distinguishable from the immortality of Jesus's soul" (Ibid). Cullmann agrees: "I Cor. 15 has been sacrificed for the *Phaedo*" (Cullmann, *Immortality*, p. 8). In fact, the position of many theologians today could, according to the exposition given by Robinson, "Easter to Valentinus," pp. 1-17, rightly be described as neo-Gnostic (Cf. Valentinus *Treatise on the Resurrection* [NH 1, 48:30-

the difference between an immaterial, unextended, spiritual "body" and the immortality of the soul. And this again is certainly not Paul's doctrine!

We have also seen that Paul gives apparently no clue as to the nature of Christ's appearance to him, though he does make clear that it was an appearance and not a vision. From Paul's doctrine of the resurrection body it could theoretically have been as physical as any gospel appearance. In describing Paul's appearance as a heavenly vision, Luke portrays it as one of a kind; he considered the appearance to Paul to be different because it was a post-ascension encounter. Paul himself gives no hint that he considered the appearance to him in any way determinative for a doctrine of the resurrection body or in any sense normative for the other appearances. On the contrary, Paul also seemed to recognize that the appearance to him was unusual and was exercised to bring it up to the level of objectivity and reality of the other appearances. The upshot of all this is the startling conclusion that *Paul's doctrine of the nature of the resurrection body is potentially more physical than that of the gospels, and if Christ's resurrection body is to be conceived in any less than a physical way, that qualification must come from the side of the gospels, not of Paul.* With these results in hand, we are now prepared to go over to an investigation of the gospels.

49:25])! Gundry observes that Paul's understanding of σῶμα in relation to the resurrection is as scandalous to twentieth century minds as to the ancient Greeks and proto-Gnostics. "The scandal is difficult—impossible—to avoid" (Gundry, Soma, p. 168).

PART II

THE EVIDENCE OF THE GOSPELS

CHAPTER 5

THE BURIAL NARRATIVE

INTRODUCTORY REMARKS

In examining the historical value of the gospel accounts of the resurrection, we shall have to answer two distinct questions: (1) what are the traditions underlying the gospel accounts, and (2) what is the historical reliability of these traditions and accounts? It is not enough simply to show that some prior tradition underlies a particular appearance story, for this does not explicitly answer the question of historicity. The tradition may, in fact, be false. Merely rediscovering old traditions does not, therefore, go far enough; indeed, from the very nature of the case, we should expect that the bulk of what the gospels narrate is traditional, especially where John and the Synoptics or Paul and the gospels agree, rather than an elaborate story spun out of the imagination of the writer. So the isolation of tradition does not it itself carry the verdict of historicity for those traditions.

On the other hand, it is equally unwise to dismiss out of hand as unhistorical information supplied by the evangelist which was not part of the tradition before him. Again the fact alone that a piece of information is redactional does not in itself address the question of historicity. This is especially the case where the information could possibly stem from reminiscences of an eyewitness, as is claimed for the Johannine narratives (Jn. 19:35; 21:24). The redactional material, too, must be examined for historicity.

In assessing the historicity of a passage, we must resist the frequent tendency to regard traditions in the later gospels as *ipso facto* themselves late and simply developments of early traditions. Though it is universally acknowledged that a late gospel may contain early traditions, it seems to be an irresistible temptation for scholars to show the line of evolution of a tradition from Mark to Matthew and Luke to John, just as Strauss confidently showed the development from Matthew and Luke to Mark. Too often the criteria of "lateness" employed seem to be very subjective and merely to accord with the writer's view of what he considers to be truly "primitive." So caution must be exercised in pronouncing judgment on the evolution of a tradition.

In assessing the historicity of a tradition or account, we inevitably run up against the problem of the burden of proof. Although in historiography in general, one approaches a document with an attitude of non-commitment, such that all things being equal its testimony will be accepted rather than rejected, many biblical scholars maintain that this rule does not or at least no longer applies to gospel studies. According to James M. Robinson, the old quest of the historical Jesus came to an end because of a basic change in New Testament scholarship: the discovery of theology in the gospels.[1] No longer were the oldest sources of the gospels seen as objective, positivistic sources, but as devotional literature of the early church. During the twentieth century the basic reorientation of New Testament scholarship has been that "*all* the tradition about Jesus survived only in so far as it served some function in the life and worship of the primitive Church."[2] This in turn radically affects the *prima facie* credibility of the gospels: "The twentieth century presupposes the kerygmatic nature of the Gospels and feels really confident in asserting the historicity of its details only where their origin cannot be explained in terms of the life of the Church."[3] Thus, the normal historiographical approach to the trustworthiness of a document must be abandoned: according to Robinson, the burden of proof now rests on the person who sees an objective, factual source in the gospels. If some element of the gospels can be explained by the church's life, the burden of proof is to show why we need to posit an additional source in Jesus himself.

---

[1] James M. Robinson, *A New Quest of the Historical Jesus*, BT 25 (London: SCM Press, 1959), pp. 34-39. Cf. Norman Perrin, *What is Redaction Criticism?*, GBS/NT (Philadelphia: Fortress Press, 1969), pp. 1-24.
[2] Robinson, *Quest*, p. 37.
[3] Ibid., pp. 37-38. Cf. the judgment of Perrin: "...the nature of the synoptic tradition is such that the burden of proof will be upon the claim to authenticity" (Norman Perrin, *Rediscovering the Teaching of Jesus* [New York: Harper and Row, 1976], p. 39).

Robinson's conclusions, however, may be overdrawn. His underlying presupposition appears to be that history and theology are mutually exclusive categories, such that the discovery of theology in the gospels automatically expels historical accuracy at that point. This, however, appears to be a *non sequitur*.[4] An event like the piercing of Jesus's side could be both historical and regarded as theologically significant.[5] Since one cannot assume *a priori* that history is falsified because it is seen to be pregnant with theological significance, the only way to prove this would be empirically, by a historical examination of the gospels. But since this investigation precedes the presupposition in question, it must begin without assuming the basic unreliability of the gospels. Undoubtedly, Robinson would contend that this was done during the nineteenth century and that the results have established the incompatibility of history and theology in the gospels. But this conclusion may be far from certain. A. N. Sherwin-White, for example, has compared favorably the gospels with Roman history with regard to external confirmation of narrated events.[6] He recognizes that Roman history and the gospels are of a different genre, but, he insists, this need not affect the historicity of particular stories. In Acts, he asserts, the historicity is indisputable. Yet Acts is just as much propaganda as the gospels. Moreover, in the gospels whenever Jesus comes into the Jerusalem orbit, the external confirmation inevitably begins. Therefore, the historical trustworthiness of the accounts of the Galilean ministry, which by its nature is less susceptible to external confirmation, ought to be presumed. According to Sherwin-White's analysis, not only are the categories of theology and

---

[4] Moltmann observes that the understanding of the resurrection narratives as no longer statements "about something" but as "expressions of" personal and corporate faith came about through the alliance of form-critical research and dialectical theology, especially in its existential interpretation. But, he protests, "The Easter reports in the New Testament proclaim in the form of narrative, and narrate history in the form of proclamation. The modern alternative, reading them either as historical sources or as kerygmatic calls to decision, is foreign to them, as the modern distinction between factual truth and existential truth is also foreign to them" (Jürgen Moltmann, *Theology of Hope*, trans J. W. Leitch [London: SCM, 1967], p. 188).

[5] The spear thrust as a means of ensuring death is a proven custom (Quintillian *Declamationes majores* 6.9), and the "blood and water" (Jn. 19:35), which could have been either a serum in the pericardial sac plus blood from the heart or a hemorrhagic fluid in the pleural cavity between the ribs and the lungs, was apparently seen by John to hold theological significance (Raymond E. Brown, *The Gospel according to John*, Anch Bib 29A [Garden City, N. Y.: Doubleday & Co., 1970], pp. 935, 947-952). Another example where historical and theological interests combine is the soldiers' dividing of Jesus's garments, for they had this right (A. N. Sherwin-White, *Roman Society and Roman Law in the New Testament* [Oxford: Clarendon Press, 1963], p. 46), and John saw it as a fulfillment of prophecy (Jn. 19:24).

[6] Sherwin-White, *Roman Society*, pp. 186-189.

history not mutually exclusive, but the external confirmation of the gospels is of such a degree that their trustworthiness ought to be accepted even in cases where specific confirmation is lacking. It is therefore by no means to be taken for granted that the discovery of theology in the gospels has vitiated their historical credibility, so that they must now be presumed to be historically false until they are proved to be true. If Sherwin-White's analysis is correct, the exact opposite is true: they should be presumed to be historically true until they are proved false.

Robinson also seems to be guilty of misuse of one of the traditional criteria of authenticity: the dissimilarity criterion. As has frequently been pointed out, the criterion can logically be used only to *establish* the authenticity of a tradition, not to *disprove* it.[7] If a tradition can be explained in terms of the life of the church, that does not give grounds for assuming that it is inauthentic; it could be both historically authentic and significant for the church. The criterion can only be used properly in a positive role: if a tradition cannot be explained in terms of Judaism on the one hand or the church on the other, then it is probably historically authentic. Therefore, if one could explain a certain aspect of a resurrection narrative by an element present in later church life, by no means has one thereby proved that that element was in fact the foundation of the narrative. One has only opened the possibility; but he who would assert that this element was the sole foundation in abstraction from the historical events in the narrative bears as much the burden of proof as he who finds the foundation in the events themselves and the motive for their preservation partly in the element of later church life.

Now in this study I shall not assume Robinson's historiography, but neither shall I presume that an account is accurate if it has not been falsified. Rather any proffered hypothesis will have to bear the burden of proof. What we want to determine is which explanation provides the most plausible reconstruction of what happened. In many particular cases, there may be alternative explanations, none of which can be satisfactorily proved, and the question should be left open. With regard to a particular tradition or motif, we may simply not know whether it goes back to historical events or whether it originated in the life of the church. But

---

[7] See Morna Hooker, "Christology and Methodology," *NTS* 17 (1970-71): 480-487; idem, "On Using the Wrong Tool," *Theol* 75 (1972): 570-581; Robert H. Stein, "The Criteria for Authenticity," in *Gospel Perspectives I*, ed. R. T. France and David Wenham (Sheffield, England: JSOT Press, 1980), pp. 225-263.

there may be other important instances in which there is good reason to accept an incident as historical, and these can be positively affirmed.

All the gospels concord with the pattern of events recorded in the formula of I Cor. 15: that Jesus died, was buried, was raised, and appeared. We shall step into this sequence of events at the burial, since it constitutes the prelude to the resurrection.

TRADITIONAL MATERIAL

The burial narrative is generally recognized as a straightforward, traditional recounting of Jesus's interment, uncolored by theological motifs. Bultmann calls Mark's account "a historical report which makes no impression of being legendary, apart from the women who appear again as witnesses in v. 47 and vs. 44, 45, which Matthew and Luke probably did not yet read in their Mark."[8]

The burial pericope was undoubtedly part of the pre-Markan passion story and served as a transition by closing the passion and looking forward to the resurrection.[9] Although it is customary to see Matthew and Luke's differences from Mark as mere editorial changes, the sporadic and uneven nature of their verbal agreements with Mark, their omissions from Mark, and their numerous agreements with each other against Mark[10] suggest that while Matthew and Luke shared the same stream of tradition as Mark, the Markan narrative as we have it was not their (only) source, which they simply re-worked, but that their sources were generically similar to those underlying Mark.[11] At any rate, the narrative of John is ap-

---

[8] Rudolf Bultmann, *Die Geschichte der synoptischen Tradition*, 2nd ed., FRLANT 12 (Göttingen: Vandenhoeck & Ruprecht, 1970), p. 296. Taylor says that Bultmann's estimate is "a notable understatement"; "The narrative belongs to the best tradition" (Vincent Taylor, *The Gospel according to St. Mark*, 2nd ed. [London: Macmillan, 1966], p. 599). Cf. Gunther Bornkamm, *Jesus von Nazareth*, 8th ed. (Stuttgart: Kohlhammer, 1968), p. 154; Berthold Klappert, "Einleitung," in *Diskussion um Kreuz und Auferstehung*, ed. idem (Wuppertal: Aussaat Verlag, 1971), p. 12.

[9] So Édouard Dhanis, "L'ensevelissement de Jésus et la visite au tombeau dans l'évangile de saint Marc (Mc XV. 40-XVI.8)," *Greg* 39 (1958): 367-410; Rudolf Pesch, *Das Markusevangelium*, 2 vols., HTKNT 2 (Freiburg: Herder, 1977), 2:509, 511.

[10] See William R. Farmer, *Synopticon: The verbal agreement between the Greek Texts of Matthew, Mark and Luke contextually exhibited* (Cambridge: Cambridge University Press, 1969), pp. 81, 135, 225; Edward Lynn Bode, *The First Easter Morning*, AB 45 (Rome: Biblical Institute Press, 1970), pp. 8-10.

[11] Lohmeyer agrees that Matthew follows his own tradition in the burial story. His literary independence is clear from the imperfect active in the dependent clause of v. 60 instead of Mark's past perfect passive; also ἐν τῇ πέτρᾳ instead of ἐκ πέτρας. He also thinks Matthew is not dependent on Mark for the empty tomb account (Ernst Lohmeyer, *Das Evangelium des Matthäus*, 4th ed., ed. W. Schmauch, KEKNT [Göttingen: Vandenhoeck & Ruprecht, 1967], pp. 398-399, 404,

parently literarily independent of Mark[12] and serves to confirm the cardinal points of the burial pericope: that late on the day of Preparation Joseph of Arimathea asked for and received permission from Pilate to take the body of Jesus, that he did so, wrapping the body in linen, and that he laid the body in a tomb. This much, at least, would seem to be traditional.

THE TIME OF THE BURIAL

According to Mark, Joseph went to Pilate "when evening had come, since it was the day of Preparation, that is, the day before the Sabbath" (Mk. 15:42). It is typical for Mark to give two time indicators, the second qualifying and making more precise the first.[13] Thus, while "evening" alone might make one think that the Sabbath had begun, Mark adds that it was still the day of Preparation before the Sabbath. That Joseph is able to buy the linen shroud suggests that the Passover had not yet begun, which would imply that Mark and John agree chronologically that that year Passover (15 Nisan) fell on Saturday, so that the Passover coincided with the weekly Sabbath (Jn. 19:31: "that Sabbath was a high day").[14] This suggestion is reinforced by the tradition embodied in Mk. 14:2.

It is paradoxical that John, who describes the most elaborate burial, is also the evangelist who senses most keenly the urgency of the hour and shortness of time allowed for the burial. He records that the Jews asked Pilate to break the victims' legs to prevent the bodies from remaining on the cross on the sabbath and that because of the impending sabbath Jesus's body was placed in a tomb which was close at hand to the place where he was crucified (Jn. 19:31, 42). By contrast, the course of events in Mark is measured and steady; there is no sense of urgency: Joseph asks for Jesus's body, Pilate summons and questions the centurion, Joseph

---

408). Similarly Grundmann maintains Luke is not dependent on Mark for the burial story, as the tradition in 23:53b; Jn. 19:41 makes clear (Walter Grundmann, *Das Evangelium nach Lukas*, 8th ed., THKNT 3 [Berlin: Evangelische Verlagsanstalt, 1978], p. 436). According to Bode, it is rather difficult to explain all the additions of the later evangelists to the basic Markan narrative as stemming out of the tradition preserved by Mark. One is therefore justified in speaking of independent traditions within the framework of the empty tomb tradition (Bode, *Easter*, p. 18).

[12] So Brown, *John*, p. 958.
[13] See Bode, *Easter*, p. 11.
[14] So Taylor, *Mark*, p. 601; Josef Blinzler, "Die Grablegung Jesu in historischer Sicht," in *Resurrexit*, ed. Édouard Dhanis (Rome: Liberia Éditrice Vaticanal, 1974), p. 61; see also F. Godet, *Commentar zu dem Evangelium Lucas*, ed. E. R. Wunderlich (Hannover: Carl Meyer, 1872), pp. 464-466; Joachim Gnilka, *Das Evangelium nach Markus*, 2 vols., EKKNT (Zürich: Benziger Verlag, 1979; Neukirchen-Vluyn, 1979), 2: 333.

after receiving the body wraps it in a shroud, lays it in a tomb, and rolls a stone across the door. There is a sense of completeness and finality in that last act—there is no hint of a rushed and unfinished burial.[15] This is paradoxical because it is Mark who is usually associated with a hasty burial. But Mark has no leg-breaking due to the impending sabbath and mentions no necessity of choosing a tomb nearby because of the lateness of the hour; instead he relates Pilate's interview with the centurion, which would consume what one would think to be precious time.

Whence John's concern over the impending sabbath? According to Deut. 21:22-23 the body of a man executed by hanging could not be allowed to remain on the tree overnight because he was accursed by God and would therefore defile the land (cf. Mishnah Sanhedrin 6.6; B. Sanhedrin 46b Bar; Josephus *Antiquities of the Jews* 4.202). The Jews applied this principle to crucifixion as well (Josephus *Jewish War* 4.317). Hence, because the day was beginning to wane, the Jews asked Pilate to employ the *crurifragum*, a breaking of the victim's legs with a mallet, which hastened death because the victim could no longer brace himself on his legs in order to breathe but would dangle helplessly, his lung cavity collapsed, until he died shortly thereafter. The practice is attested as a Roman method of execution, and the Jewish leadership apparently sought its use to prevent the bodies from hanging on the crosses overnight. This, however, created another problem: for the Jews always buried the dead (II Sam. 2:12-14; Tobit 1:17-19; 2:3-7; 12:12-13; Sirach 7:33; 38:16), even the dead of their enemies (Josh. 8:29; 10:27; Josephus *Jewish War* 3.377). But although Jewish law would permit burial after nightfall (Josephus *Antiquities of the Jews* 4.264), it did not allow burial on a sabbath. Since according to Jewish reckoning each new day began in the evening, Jesus's body had to be disposed of before nightfall, that is, the breaking of the sabbath day. This seems to be in the back of John's mind when he reports that Jesus's body was laid in the tomb in the garden because of the day of Preparation and because the tomb was close at hand.

There is thus in John a sense of urgency that one would probably not infer from Mark alone. Indeed, Mark's phrase "when evening had come" (cf. Mt.

---

[15] So also Blinzler, "Grablegung," p. 62; Robert Mahoney, *Two Disciples at the Tomb*, TW 6 (Bern: Herbert Lang, 1974), p. 144. It is ironical that Taylor should state that there are two traditions of the burial: in Mark a hasty one and in John an elaborate one (Taylor, *Mark*, p. 602)!

27:57) might make one think that it was already night; but he no doubt means the final quarter of the day, since Jesus died at 3 p.m.[16] Luke's expression is interesting: "It was the day of Preparation and the sabbath was beginning" (Lk. 23:54). The word ἐπέφωσκεν literally means "dawning" and has either lost here all sense of illumination (as when we say, a new age has dawned)[17] or perhaps refers to the appearance of the first evening star which marks the beginning of the new day.[18] Luke's picturesque phrase thus describes the hour of dusk as the time of Jesus's burial. Hence, all the gospels agree that Jesus was interred in the late afternoon on Friday.

JOSEPH OF ARIMATHEA

The gospels all record the request of Joseph of Arimathea for the body of Jesus. Arimathea is probably Ramathaion-zophim, the home of Samuel (I Sam. 1:1; cf. Eusebius *Onomasticon* 32), just north of Jerusalem. Mark reports that he was a member of the council, which probably refers to the Sanhedrin itself. Matthew states that he owned the tomb in which Jesus was laid (Mt. 27:60), and this seems plausible, as one cannot deposit a body in just anybody's rock tomb that happens to be close at hand. This suggests that Joseph was born in Arimathea but now made his home in Jerusalem.

According to Mark, Joseph was looking for the kingdom of God (Mk. 15:43); Luke also uses the phrase and adds that he was a "good and righteous man," who had not consented to the purpose or the deed of his fellow councilmen (Lk. 23:50-51); Matthew and John independently record that he was a disciple of Jesus, but John adds "secretly, for fear of the Jews" (Jn. 19:38; Mt. 27:57); Matthew says further that he was a rich man. Although these details are often regarded as redactional or legendary embellishments of Joseph's person,[19] this conclusion could be

---

[16] M.-J. Lagrange, *Évangile selon saint Marc* (Paris: Librairie Lecoffre, 1966), p. 439; Taylor, *Mark*, p. 599; Blinzler, "Grablegung," p. 60.

[17] So Alfred Plummer, *The Gospel according to S. Luke*, 5th ed., ICC (Edinburgh: T&T Clark, 1964), pp. 542-543.

[18] K. H. Rengstorff, *Das Evangelium nach Lukas*, NTD (Göttingen: Vandenhoeck & Ruprecht, 1937), p. 266; Grundmann, *Lukas*, p. 437; I. Howard Marshall, *The Gospel of Luke*, NIGTC (Exeter: Paternoster Press, 1978), p. 881.

[19] Hans Grass, *Ostergeschehen und Osterberichte*, 4th rev. ed. (Göttingen: Vandenhoeck & Ruprecht, 1970), pp. 173-176. It is customary to see particularly Joseph's being a disciple as an evolutionary development. Against this it might be pointed out that such a development would be counter-productive for Christians, since burial by a Sanhedrin member would insure that no hoax was perpetrated by the disciples to produce a "discovery" of an empty tomb as alleged in early

hasty. That he was rich as Matthew says is already implied by Mark's εὐσχήμων (appearing only here in Mark, the word is from pre-Markan tradition and means "noble," "influential," or "wealthy") as well as by the type and location of the tomb he employed for the burial (see below). These suggest that Joseph really was a wealthy individual.

It is not clear whether Mark's description "looking for the kingdom of God" implies that Joseph was a disciple. The phrase might mean only that Joseph was a godly Jew who awaited the Messianic coming. On the other hand, these are precisely the words used to describe Jesus's gospel (Mk. 1:14, 15), and it is not evident that Mark held that a man could sincerely be looking for the kingdom of God and not believe in Jesus. And the actions of Joseph are certainly those taken by one who had some special care for Jesus.[20] His are no perfunctory duties discharged as a cold emissary of the Sanhedrin. Mark says he *dared* (τολμήσας) to go to Pilate and ask for the body. According to the Roman practice the bodies of crucified criminals would remain on the cross for days until decayed or devoured by birds or animals, but when relatives or friends requested the body, it was usually granted (Plutarch *Antonius* 2; Cicero *Orationes Philippicae* 2. 7. 17; Philo *Against Flaccus* 10. 83). But in cases of major offenses, the body was not given over. Since Joseph was neither a relative nor a friend of Jesus and since Jesus had been convicted of treason against the state, it took courage for Joseph to request the body. That Pilate gave it over reinforces the picture painted by the gospels that Pilate really believed that Jesus was innocent; at a feast time, too, he could be more lenient.[21]

As noted, one gets the impression from Mark that Joseph gives Jesus a proper and careful burial; most surprising of all, instead of throwing the body into a shallow grave in a dirt plot reserved for criminals,[22] Joseph lays the body in a rock

---

Jewish polemic (Mt. 28:13). The supposed pattern of Christianization of Joseph may be illusory, since the Gospel of Peter calls him only a "friend" of Pilate and the Lord.

[20] James Orr, *The Resurrection of Jesus* (London: Hodder & Stoughton, 1909), p. 96. "The act of embalming was his act of love, and the grave was his own new family tomb" (E. Earl Ellis, ed., *The Gospel of Luke*, NCB [London: Nelson, 1966], p. 270).

[21] So Blinzler, "Grablegung," p. 87; William L. Lane, *The Gospel according to Mark*, NLCNT (London: Marshall, Morgan & Scott, 1974), p. 579. On the Roman practice of giving over bodies, see Josef Blinzler, *Das Prozess Jesu* (Regensburg: Pustet, 1969), pp. 385-387.

[22] There were two sites for the burial of executed criminals outside the city, one for those stoned or burned and another for the decapitated or hanged (Tosephta Sanhedrin 9.8-8; Mishnah Sanhedrin 6.5-7). There the bodies could be buried in shallow earth graves.

tomb of the most expensive variety, a tomb that was probably his own. It has been suggested that Joseph laid Jesus there only because time was short and his tomb was close, and he intended to later transfer the body to the criminals' common graveyard.[23] But then one seems to be at a loss to explain what happened to the two thieves crucified with Jesus (Mk. 15:27, 32). Why were they not also deposited in the tomb with Jesus? The reason why time was short for Jesus's interment, according to John, was precisely because of the elaborate burial procedures (Jn. 19:40), procedures which would probably not be wasted on the two thieves. According to John, the Jews asked the Romans that the bodies be taken away after their legs were broken, but Joseph came to Pilate and asked that he might take Jesus's body. None of the gospels suggests that Joseph was acting as a delegate of the Sanhedrin; there was nothing in the law that required that the bodies be buried immediately, and the Jews may have been content to leave that to the Romans. That Joseph *dared* to go to Pilate and ask *specifically* for Jesus's body is difficult to understand if he was simply an emissary of the Sanhedrin, assigned to dispose of the bodies. If he was not acting as an emissary of the Sanhedrin but as a private citizen, then the thieves' bodies would naturally have been disposed of by the Romans, while Joseph took Jesus's body. On the other hand, if Joseph was a delegate of the Sanhedrin and a secret disciple as well, he may have directed that the thieves' bodies be taken down and immediately dumped into some common grave, while Joseph tended for Jesus's body properly, knowing that his own tomb was near and intending to lay Jesus there.

Thus, it seems possible that Joseph was a disciple or at least a sympathizer of Jesus; his daring to ask Pilate for a request lacking legal foundation, his proper burial of Jesus's body alone, and his laying the body in his own, expensive tomb are acts that go beyond the duties of a merely pious Jew. But perhaps most importantly, Matthew and John give independent testimony of the fact that Joseph was a disciple of Jesus. This suggests that Joseph's discipleship is not a redactional inference but has traditional roots. To regard this tradition as a legendary development may not take seriously enough the evidence of Mark that Joseph did act in a manner that befits a disciple more than a Sanhedrin member. John states that many even of the authorities believed in Jesus but were afraid to confess it (Jn. 12:42-43), and he describes Joseph in the same way. It is not even impossible

---

[23] So Blinzler, "Grablegung," p. 97.

that Joseph refrained from attending the meeting that condemned Jesus or that he abstained from the vote, as Luke indicates. Joseph's being a secret believer does not therefore seem to be implausible; John and Matthew's tradition could be accurate—one must be careful to avoid the inference that because a gospel is late, the traditions contained therein are also late. In any case, most scholars grant that Joseph was a genuine historical individual, since it would be unlikely, given the antipathy in the early church toward the Jewish leadership for their role in the execution of Jesus, that the early believers would invent a Sanhedrist who does what is right by Jesus in giving him an honorable burial.

THE GRANTING OF JESUS'S CORPSE

The story of Pilate's questioning the guard is sometimes held to be an apologetic motif directed against Jesus's merely apparent death, especially since Matthew and Luke do not record the incident. On the other hand, one cannot regard a narrative as unhistorical simply because it is apologetic; the question of apologetics concerns the intention of a passage, not its historicity.[24] An apologetic intention may sometimes tell us why an evangelist *includes* an incident, not why he *invents* an incident.

That Matthew and Luke are silent about this incident cannot be decisive either; they may have regarded it as superfluous, especially Matthew, as he has the guard at the tomb to prevent any hoax. Stylistically, it does not seem to be true that v. 43 goes with v. 46, as this leaves a gap in the story concerning Pilate's decision. In leaving out vs. 44-45 of Mark, Luke creates such a gap in Lk. 23:52-53, whereas Matthew fills the gap with Mt. 27:58b. These two verses contain Markan expressions (θαυμάζω, προσκαλέομαι, κεντυρίων, ἐπερωτάω), but γνοὺς ἀπὸ is a unique construction here, and δωρέομαι and πτῶμα are technical terms, together reflecting perhaps the official language of the governor's order: *donavit cadaver*. This would indicate traditional material. The story itself is plausible and does not seem to merit Bultmann's judgment as legendary.[25]

All the gospels indicate that Joseph then took down the body of Jesus and carried it away. This does not necessitate that Joseph himself ascended the ladder

---

[24] This is recognized by Gerald O'Collins, *The Easter Jesus*, 2nd ed. (London: Darton, Longman, & Todd, 1980), p. 24.
[25] So Grass, *Ostergeschehen*, p. 174; Lagrange, *Marc*, p. 441; Taylor, *Mark*, pp. 600-601; Blinzler, "Grablegung," p. 59.

and pulled out the nails. The Romans may have taken down the body for him; in any case Joseph no doubt had, as a man of authority, servants to help him. Interesting is that Mk. 16:6 states, "See the place where *they* laid him" (contrast Mt. 28:6). Joseph himself would probably not have touched the corpse, as he would then have been defiled and could not have eaten the Passover (Num. 19:11). Similarly, servants could have taken care of the buying of the linen shroud. According to John's account, Nicodemus assisted Joseph in the burial. Like Joseph, Nicodemus is in John one of those among the authorities who seem to be incipient believers in Jesus (Jn. 3:1-15; 7:50-52). John reintroduces him here in the same way as in ch. 7, which is characteristic of John (cf. 11:2; 12:1; 12:21; 21:2, 20). It might be thought that Nicodemus is an unhistorical figure because he does not appear in the Synoptics; but there are other individuals in John who do not appear in the Synoptics but seem to be nonetheless historical persons. There is no inherent impossibility in Nicodemus's aiding Joseph in the burial or even in his having come to faith in Christ, which may be in the background here.[26]

The Burial in the Tomb

The manner of Jesus's burial is a matter of great controversy. Though none of the gospels mentions it, the body would normally have been washed, as was customary (cf. Acts 9:7), rather than wrapped bloody and sweaty in fresh linen. The washing of a corpse prior to burial was considered so necessary that it was even allowed on the sabbath (Mishnah Shabbath 23.5; B Moed Qatan 28b). But it could have been that time did not permit the corpse to be washed. The synoptics state simply that the body was wrapped (Mk. 15:46: ἐνειλέω; Mt. 27:59, Lk. 23:53: ἐντυλίσσω) in a shroud (σινδών). John says that it was bound (δέω) in linen cloths (ὀθόνια) with the spices, that is, the myrrh and aloes brought by

---

[26] Schnackenburg thinks that John did not invent Nicodemus; but his being at the burial is John's addition (Rudolf Schnackenburg, *Das Johannesevangelium*, 3 vols., HTKNT 4 [Freiburg: Herder, 1976], 3: 347-348). Blinzler states there is no reason he could not have helped in the burial; and it is possible that he was a councilor and disciple of Jesus (Blinzler, "Grablegung," p. 77; so also John A. T. Robinson, *The Priority of John*, ed. J. F. Coakley [London: SCM, 1985], p. 287). Remarkably, Mahoney thinks that the Johannine tradition was that Nicodemus buried Jesus (Mahoney, *Disciples*, pp. 129-130). But his reasoning is rather contrived: for example, Joseph is not said to be bold in asking for the body, while in Jn. 7:50 Nicodemus boldly speaks out; or again that Joseph brings no spices (but these are not mentioned in the Synoptics either), while Nicodemus does; or again that Joseph is not said to be rich, but Nicodemus can afford to buy 100 pounds of spices.

Nicodemus, in the burial custom of the Jews.[27] Undoubtedly, John gives us to understand that Jesus was buried in the same typical fashion as Lazarus, who came out of the tomb with his hands and feet bound (δέω) with bandages (κειρία) and his face wrapped (περιδέομαι) with a cloth (σουδάριον) (Jn. 11:44). John reports that at Jesus's resurrection the σουδάριον was rolled up (ἐντυλίσσω) in a place by itself and not lying with the ὀθόνια (Jn. 20:7). Remarkably, Luke himself, who had spoken only of the σινδών, also says that Peter found the ὀθόνια lying in the tomb on Easter morning (Lk 24:12). This makes it evident that the Synoptics see no contradiction between speaking of the σινδών and a plurality of ὀθόνια. It may be that the σινδών signifies simply the material of which ὀθόνια were made. Or it could be that the ὀθόνια in which Joseph and Nicodemus bound the body refer to the κειρία which bound the hands and feet together; the σουδάριον may have been a jaw band that kept the dead man's mouth closed (cf. Mishnah Shabbath 23.5). The body thus bound could have been wrapped in a large sheet with the dry spices, which were probably fragrant resin and powdered sandalwood, whose scent served to offset the stench of decay.

An issue (which until recently was a matter of genuine debate) inevitably arises at this point, namely, the authenticity of the Turin Shroud. Although Grass was able in 1956 to brush aside the *Anhänger* of the Turin Shroud with a couple of sentences, scientific tests conducted on the shroud during the 1970's made the authenticity of the shroud a serious question.[28] The shroud, which belongs to the former royal family of Italy and is kept and periodically exhibited in the Cathedral

---

[27] Haenchen points out that since Jewish burial practices did not include embalming, the corpse could not have been wrapped like a mummy because the gases produced by its corruption would have then caused it to explode. Ironically, however, instead of concluding that John did not therefore intend us to understand that Jesus's body was wrapped like a mummy, Haenchen concludes that the evangelist was unfamiliar with the Jewish practice of burial (Ernst Haenchen, *Das Johannesevangelium*, ed. Ulrich Busse [Tübingen: J. C. B. Mohr, 1980], p. 556). For more on Jewish burial practices, see Gnilka, *Markus*, 2: 334-336.

[28] On the background of the shroud see Ian Wilson, *The Shroud of Turin* (Garden City, N. Y.: Doubleday & Co., 1978); P. M. Rinaldi, *The Man in the Shroud*, rev. ed. (London: Sidgwick & Jackson: 1974). On scientific investigation see S. F. Pellicori, "Spectral Properties of the Shroud of Turin," *Applied Optics* 19 (1978): 1913-1920; J. S. Accetta and J. S. Baumgart, "Infrared Reflectance Spectroscopy and Thermographic Investigations of the Shroud of Turin," *Applied Optics* 19 (1980): 1921-1929; R. Gilbert and M. Gilbert, "Ultraviolet-visible Reflectance and Fluorescence Spectra of the Shroud of Turin," *Applied Optics* 19 (1980): 1930-1936; John H. Heller and Allan D. Adler, "Blood on the Shroud of Turin," *Applied Optics* 19 (1980): 2742-2744; R. A. Morris, et al., "X-Ray Fluorescence Investigation of the Shroud of Turin," *X-Ray Spectrometry* 9 (1980): 40-47. For a report of the results of radio carbon dating of samples of the shroud, see Steven Dickman, "Shroud a good forgery," *Nature* 335 (20 October 1988), p. 633.

of San Giovanni Battista in Torino, is reputedly the burial shroud in which Joseph of Arimathea wrapped Jesus's corpse and laid it in his tomb. According to the gospel accounts, the graveclothes of Jesus were found lying in the empty tomb on Sunday morning (Lk. 24:12; Jn. 20:4-9), and if the shroud is genuine, they were presumably kept by the disciples and handed down through the church. Hence, if the shroud were authentic, it would shed dramatic light on the manner of Jesus's burial. One's initial reaction to the shroud is scepticism, since the medieval Catholic church fairly swarmed with such relics of Jesus's life, for example, the cords which bound Christ, nails or pieces of wood from the cross, the sponge lifted to his lips, and so forth. Given such a historical milieu, it is difficult, indeed, to regard the shroud as anything more than just another medieval forgery. Moreover, when the shroud was first exhibited in the thirteenth century it was denounced as a fraud by the local bishop, who claimed to know the identity of the artist who painted the image.

Despite this circumstantial evidence, however, scientific data concerning the shroud began to make the hypothesis of forgery seem unlikely. The most important evidence prior to radio-carbon dating, which appears to have been an *experimentum crucis* for the shroud, may be summarized under three heads:

(1) *The shroud has marks of authenticity.* Pollen samples taken from the shroud have been identified as pollen from seven types of plants that grow in Palestine, suggesting that the shroud was likely once in that area. Some of these identifications may be tenuous, however, since the pollens are extremely close to European varieties; moreover, no olive pollen has been identified, which is strange if the cloth stems from Jerusalem. Textile analysis of the cloth is inconclusive, but consistent with authenticity. The cloth is linen, normally used in Palestine for graveclothes, with traces of cotton of a Middle Eastern variety. The thread is handspun, rather than spun on a wheel, which also indicates an old age. The thread may have been bleached prior to wearing, which was also an ancient practice. The weave itself is of a pattern not unknown in the ancient world, through not as common as a simpler pattern. The most recent tests, including X-ray and ultraviolet radiation experiments, have shown that the blood on the shroud is real blood. The wounds on the body are extremely realistic. The flow of blood from the wound on the side passes around to the small of the back, appearing on the back image of the shroud, something that a forger would perhaps have over-

looked. The angle of the blood flow from the wrist wound is also appropriate for crucifixion. Ultraviolet fluorescence photographs reveal auras around the side wound and the blood on the wrists and one foot, which may be a serum which is squeezed out of clotting blood. The same photographs reveal that the body is covered not only with lash wounds apparently inflicted with a *flagrum*, a multi-thonged Roman whip tipped with metal or bone, but also with fine, diagonal scratch marks, especially on the legs.

(2) *A forger would probably not have produced such a shroud.* The Shroud of Turin is not unique, but a comparison of its image with those on other medieval forgeries is dramatic, to say the least. The ghostly image on the Turin Shroud is extremely realistic, while other shrouds display pictures of cartoon-like figures, typical of pre-Renaissance painting. It is bewildering to think that a medieval painter could have produced so anomalous an image as the man on the Turin Shroud. It has been suggested that the image was produced by laying the cloth over a heated statue or by a rubbing, but it seems improbable that the dorsal image would have been so produced, since a statue of the dead Christ would naturally be lying prone so that no sculpture of the back would be available. Nor would a medieval forger have known to place the nail wound in the wrist rather than in the hand. All medieval paintings show the wounds in the hands, but this position of the nail could not support the weight of the body, as was discovered by the French surgeon Pierre Barbet in 1931. The term χείρ includes the wrist and forearm as well as the hand, and victims were crucified by their wrists, a fact no medieval forger would know. When one thinks of the religious significance attached to the stigmata, it seems very puzzling that a forger would locate the wound in the wrist rather than the hand.

(3) *There are no known means of producing the image on the shroud.* The first photographs of the shroud, taken in 1898 by Secondo Pia, revealed it to be a negative photographic image, a remarkable fact when one considers that it would have to have been forged hundreds of years prior to the invention of photography. In 1973 researchers discovered that the image lies only on the topmost fibrils of the threads and that there is no trace of pigment. The most recent examinations in 1978 confirm this, but also found that the blood stains had penetrated the cloth, indicating that the blood had been absorbed into the cloth, while the man's image only colors the surface. Paint could not have produced such an image. This con-

clusion is reinforced by the evidence stemming from a fire that damaged the shroud in 1532. Both the heat of the fire as well as the water used to extinguish it would have discolored an image made by paint in the areas nearest the burn marks. But there is no trace of such an effect: the color of the image is constant right up to the burn areas. A Brazilwood solution rather than paint has been used by modern artists to produce an image remarkably like the shroud's, but this cannot duplicate what is perhaps the most amazing discovery concerning the shroud. Using a VP-8 Image Analyzer, an instrument used to study the relief of the surface of the moon and of Mars, scientists in 1978 discovered that the image contains three-dimensional data, so that the original body that produced the image can actually be recreated. No painting or ordinary photograph yields such three-dimensional data. It has been suggested that the image may have been reproduced by a forger's scorching the cloth by laying it over a heated statue. But in that case, the scorch should be deeper where the most contact is made, for example, the nose. But in fact this does not occur; each fibril is an identical shade, and certain areas are darker only because there are more colored fibrils there. Hence, there simply is no known mechanism by means of which a medieval forger could have produced the image on the shroud.

In the fall of 1988, however, the results of radiocarbon dating of pieces of the shroud, carried out at the University of Arizona, Oxford University, and the Swiss Federal Polytechnic Institute, revealed the shroud to have a mid-thirteenth century date. These were blind tests, performed by the technicians of each laboratory on previously dated samples of ancient Egyptian cloth and medieval cloth as well as the bits cut from a corner of the shroud. The results unanimously yielded a medieval date for the shroud. Unless future dating tests (none of which is planned at the time of this writing) contradict these results, they constitute decisive proof that the Turin Shroud is a forgery, just as the good bishop claimed. This discovery does not, it must be said, remove the mystery of the shroud; on the contrary, it deepens it, for now it remains to be explained how it is that so anomalous an object could have been produced by a medieval forger.

The fraudulency of the Turin Shroud makes little objective difference for the resurrection of Jesus, but chiefly deprives us of what would have been direct and dramatic evidence concerning the manner of Jesus's burial. Despite the shroud's inauthenticity, however, it does seem quite plausible that Jesus was in fact wrapped and buried in the manner envisioned by the creator of the shroud.

It has been suggested that the amount of spices brought by Nicodemus (about 75 modern pounds) reflects John's desire to make Jesus's burial a kingly one. But by the same token, it might also have been Joseph's or Nicodemus's, who knew that Jesus had been unjustly condemned by their own council and crucified as King of the Jews (Mk. 15:2, 9, 12, 13, 18, 26, 31, 32). When Gamaliel died in AD 50, his follower Onkelos burned 80 pounds of spices, referring to Jer. 34:5 and commenting, "Gamaliel was better than 100 kings" (B Ebel Rabbathi 8.6). Thus, it is not impossible that so great an amount should have been employed in Jesus's burial.[29]

Some have felt that the time between Jesus's death and the breaking of the sabbath was too short to permit so elaborate a burial, but Acts 5:7 may indicate that Ananias was wrapped (συστέλλω) and buried within a space of three hours. Though he did not, of course, need to be taken down from a cross like Jesus, neither did one on the other hand expect his death like Jesus's, so that the wrapping cloth could be purchased and a grave site determined in advance. At any rate, Jesus's burial itself may not have been so lengthy—the hands and feet had to be bound, perhaps the jaw tied, the dry spices packed around the body, and the whole wrapped up in the sheet.[30] John states that because Joseph's tomb was near and time was short, the body was laid there (knowing the sabbath was coming, Joseph may have intended this all along, not as an afterthought), and all the gospels agree that the sabbath was breaking when the job was finished. So the burial procedure carries the marks of authenticity and seems quite plausible.

Joseph laid the wrapped body in a rock-hewn tomb and rolled a stone against the door (Mk. 15:46). In this the other gospels agree.[31] Matthew, Luke, and John

---

[29] The Johannine figure is quite within the bounds of credibility as a rich man's last tribute, according to Robinson, *Priority of John*, p. 283. For the interesting suggestion that the Johannine measurement concerns volume, not weight, and so is not in excess of twenty liters, see T. C. de Kruijf, "'More than half a hundredweight' of Spices (John 19, 39 NEB). Abundance and Symbolism in the Gospel of John," *Bijdragen* 43 (1982): 234-239.

[30] After Gamaliel II (AD 90) it was customary to bury a corpse in linen; prior to that time burials could be more elaborate. See references in Paul Billerbeck, *Kommentar zum Neuen Testament aus Talmud und Midrasch*, 6 vols., ed. Herrmann L. Strack (München: Beck, 1922-63), 1: 1048.

[31] The allegation that Luke mistook a tomb hewn out of rock for a tomb built of hewn stones is refuted by the use of λαξευτός in LXX Deut. 4:49. Lake's contention that John's grave is a mausoleum with a stone lid seems equally foundationless (Kirsopp Lake, *The Historical Evidence for the Resurrection of Jesus* [London: Williams & Norgate, 1907], p. 134).

all agree that the tomb was new and unused (Mt. 27:60; Lk. 23:53; Jn. 19:41). Matthew states that it was Joseph's own. Both these details are very likely, as a body of a condemned criminal would defile the bodies of other family members resting in the tomb, and Joseph could not take liberties to deposit a criminal's body in any tomb he happened to find. The gospels give the impression that Joseph had a specific tomb in mind, not that it was a chance discovery. So there is good reason to believe that all the gospels presuppose that it was his own. Mark says that Joseph shut the door of the tomb with a stone which was very large (Mk. 15:46; 16:4); the other gospels all mention the stone either in connection with the burial (Mt. 27:60) or the empty tomb (Lk 24:4; Jn. 20:1), but supply no additional information about it. Prescriptions for rock tombs are laid down in Mishnah BB 6.8. The tomb was shut with a large stone (גולל), which was made fast with a small stone (דופק).

Archaeological discoveries have revealed three different types of rock tombs in use during Jesus's time: (1) *kokim* or tunnels perpendicular to the walls of the tomb, about six or seven feet deep, three in each of the three inner walls of the tomb, into which the body was inserted headfirst; (2) *acrosolia* or semi-circular niches 2½ feet above the floor and two to three feet deep containing either a flat shelf or a trough for the body; (3) bench tombs containing a bench that went around the three walls of the tomb on which the body could be laid.[32] These tombs could consist of two chambers: an antechamber at the back of which was a small rectangular door about two feet high, which led to an inner chamber where the bodies were placed. The tomb was sealed with a stone slab to keep out animals. In a very expensive tomb, a round disc-shaped stone about a yard in diameter could be rolled down a slanted groove to cover the entrance. Although it would be easy to close the tomb, it would take several men to roll the stone back up away from the door. Only a few tombs with such disc-shaped stones have been discovered in Palestine, but they all date from Jesus's era. It is evident from the gospels' descriptions of the empty tomb that it was either of the *acrosolia* or bench type of tomb with a roll-stone for the door: In Mk. 16:5 the women see the angel seated on the right side; in Jn. 20:12 the angels are sitting at the head and

---

[32] R. H. Smith, "The Tomb of Jesus," *BA* 30 (1967): 87-88; Brown, *John*, pp. 982-983. On *kokim* tombs see R. A. S. Macalister, "Jewish Rock Tombs," in P. Gardner-Smith, *The Narratives of the Resurrection* (London: Methuen, 1926), pp. 191-192. Because he only knows this type of tomb, Lake's conclusions concerning the burial are vitiated (Lake, *Evidence*, pp. 170-176).

the feet where the body had lain. In Mk. 16:6 the angel tells the women to "see the place where they laid him;" in Mt. 28:6 the angel invites them to "see the place where he lay." Both Lk. 24:12 and Jn. 20:5, 11 mention the necessity of stooping in order to enter or look through the low door of the tomb. Lk. 24:12 and Jn. 20:5-8 indicate that the graveclothes which had been around the body were visibly lying out. Mk. 15:46; 16:3, 4; Mt. 27:60; 28:2; Lk. 24:2 indicate the stone had been rolled back from the tomb's entrance; Jn. 20:1 says it had been taken away. These details preclude a *kokim* sort of tomb.

Thus, Joseph's tomb is described as being a bench or *acrosolia* tomb; these types of tombs were scarce in Jesus's day and were reserved for persons of high rank. But such tombs were in fact used in Jerusalem during this period, as the tombs of the Sanhedria attest. Near the Church of the Holy Sepulchre, the traditional site for Jesus's grave, *acrosolia* tombs from Jesus's time have been found.

John adds the further detail that the tomb was in a garden (Jn. 19:41). Some have considered this a Johannine addition to emphasize the kingly nature of Jesus's burial, since in II Kings 21 Manasseh and Amon were buried in the garden of Uzza and LXX Neh. 3:16 says David's tomb was in a garden. But the context of II Kings 21 seems to make this suggestion far-fetched, for in one breath the writer is describing the abominations, idolatry, and murderousness of Manasseh and Amon and in the next stating matter of factly that they died and were buried in the garden of their house—no regal burial seems in sight here! That leaves LXX Neh. 3:16 a distant and rather unlikely source for John's description of the burial site. In fact it seems quite plausible that the detail is historical.[33] The word κῆπος means "plantation" or "orchard," and a κῆπος could contain rock tombs. Significantly one of the four gates in the North Wall of the city was called the Garden Gate, and Josephus attests to gardens outside the North Wall (Josephus *Jewish War* 5. 57, 147, 410). The tombs of the Hasmonean high priests John Hyrcanus and Alexander Jannaeus were in this area (Josephus *Jewish War* 5.259), and so it may have been a prestigious place for burial. In AD 350 Cyril of Jerusalem said that the remains of a garden were still to be seen next to the Church of the Holy Sepulchre which Constantine had recently built over the traditional site of Jesus's tomb (Cyril *Catechesis* 14.5; *PG* 33.829B). The expensive bench or

---

[33] See C. K. Barrett, *The Gospel according to St. John* (London: SPCK, 1972), p. 465; Brown, *John*, p. 943.

acrosolia tomb with a roll-stone and the location of this tomb in some sort of orchard near the tombs of other notables is consonant with the description of Joseph as a wealthy member of the Sanhedrin. That he would give his tomb to Jesus bespeaks a devotion that exceeds that of a merely religious Jew.

THE WOMEN WITNESSES

Finally, Mark states that Mary Magdalene and Mary the mother of Joses saw where Jesus was laid (Mk. 15:47). John does not mention women in connection with the burial, but in Jn. 20:1 Mary Magdalene is mentioned as coming to the tomb, of which she evidently knew the location. Matthew says Mary Magdalene and the "other Mary," that is, the Mary of v. 56 "Mary the mother of James and Joseph," were sitting opposite the sepulchre during the interment (Mt. 27:61). Luke states that the women who had come with Jesus from Galilee (cf. 23:49) saw the tomb and how the body was laid and returned to the tomb Sunday morning—they included Mary Magdalene, Joanna, and Mary the mother of James as well as other unnamed women with them (Lk. 23:55; 24:1, 10). From the accord between Mark and John alone it seems clear that at least the name Mary Magdalene was traditionally connected with the tomb of Jesus.

In order to assess the value of the list of women witnesses, it is necessary to return to the crucifixion and the women there (Mk. 15:40-41). Mark names Mary Magdalene, Mary the mother of James the younger and of Joses, and Salome; there were also other Galilean women there who came with them to Jerusalem. These two verses are not an independent piece of tradition, since they only have sense in this context.[34] But neither do they seem to be editorially constructed out of the names in 15:47 and 16:1 because then the appellation "the younger" is inexplicable, as is the fusion of what would normally designate the wife of James and wife of Joses into one woman, the mother of James and Joses. This seems to imply that the names in 15:40 are part of the pre-Markan passion tradition.[35] The

---

[34] See Pesch, *Markusevangelium*, 2: 504. Pesch notes the "looking on" in v. 40 and the flashback in v. 41, the threefold use of the personal pronoun αὐτῷ in v. 41 with its antecedent Ἰησοῦς in v. 37, and the reference of v. 41 back to Mk. 10:32-34 and forward to the burial and empty tomb stories, thus binding them together with the crucifixion.

[35] Pesch also thinks the verses give indication of belonging to the pre-Markan passion story: the naming of persons known to the *Urgemeinde* (cf. 10:46, 14:3; 14:10, 43; 15:1, 2, 5, 7, 9, 11, 12, 15, 21, 44-45), the paraphrase of 10:32, and the words ἀπὸ μακρόθεν (14:54), θεωρέω (12:41;

list serves to name witnesses of the crucifixion from the *Urgemeinde* and introduces some important *dramatis personae* who have yet their greatest role to play.

It is quite intriguing that women are named as the witnesses of the crucifixion and burial and as the discoverers of the empty tomb, given not only their lack of legal status as witnesses, but also the low rung on the ladder of Jewish society which they occupied.[36] Although some scholars have attempted to avoid this oddity by asserting that the women are not juridical witnesses to historical facts, but rather witnesses, that is, proclaimers, of the gospel, such an escape is not very plausible. For even if this were the case, it is far from clear why the pre-Markan passion tradition would employ women as the primary proclaimers of the good news of Christ's resurrection rather than the male disciples (cf. I Cor. 15:5) if this had not been the case. And the careful listing of the different women who attended the crucifixion, the burial, and the discovery of the empty tomb suggests that it is their witness to the facts that is being recalled, not merely their proclamation of the Easter message. In any case, the dichotomy between their being a witness either to the historical facts or to the gospel is doubtless a twentieth century import which is foreign to these accounts: the women bore witness to the truth of the gospel by bearing witness to the events they experienced.

Why do women appear in the tradition as witnesses and not men? Probably not because of any supposed flight of the disciples to Galilee inferred from Mk. 14:50, a theory which von Campenhausen rightly dismisses as a fiction of the critics;[37] the story of the denial of Peter indicates that all the gospels held the disciples to be in Jerusalem. So there seems to be no reason why they could not have

---

15:47; 16:4), ἀναβαίνω (10:32-33), εἰς Ἱεροσόλυμα (10:32; 11:1, 11, 15, 27) (Pesch, *Markusevangelium*, 2: 504).

[36] As evident from such expressions as these: "Sooner let the words of the Law be burnt than delivered to women" (J Sotah 19a); "Happy is he whose children are male, and alas for him whose children are female" (B Kiddushin 82b). See also chapter 2 note 3.

[37] Hans Freiherr von Campenhausen, *Der Ablauf der Osterereignisse und das leere Grab*, 3rd rev. ed., SHA (Heidelberg: Carl Winter, 1966), pp. 44-49. Early critics of this theory included Orr, *Resurrection*, pp. 217-218; Johannes Weiss, *Der erste Korintherbrief*, 9th ed., KEKNT 5 (Göttingen: Vandenhoeck & Ruprecht, 1910), p. 350: "I cannot convince myself of the scholarly legend that the apostles fled to Galilee;" and Martin Albertz, "Zur Formgeschichte der Auferstehungsberichte," *ZNW* 21 (1922): 269: "a critic's legend." Kremer observes that the denial of Peter precludes any flight to Galilee (Kremer, *Osterbotschaft*, p. 19). Koch admits that the "scattering of the sheep" in no way implies a flight to Galilee (Gerhard Koch, *Die Auferstehung Jesu Christi*, BHT [Tübingen: J. C. B. Mohr, 1959], p. 41). This undermines Grass's theory that the women were made discoverers of the empty tomb because no disciples were available (Grass, *Ostergeschehen*, p. 182).

been used as witnesses just as easily as the women. That the male disciples were not cast in this role suggests that the tradition is historically credible; the reason why the unqualified women are named as witnesses is most likely because, like it or not, they *were* the witnesses, the disciples lying low in fear of reprisals by the Jewish authorities against themselves as followers of Jesus.

John confirms that there were women at the cross; he names Jesus's mother and his mother's sister, Mary the wife of Clopas, and Mary Magdalene (Jn. 19:25). Matthew names Mary Magdalene, Mary the mother of James and Joseph, and the mother of the sons of Zebedee (Mt. 27:56); Luke states that all Jesus's acquaintances and the women who had followed him from Galilee witnessed the crucifixion (Lk. 23:49). Pesch has argued that Mark actually names four women: Mary Magdalene, Mary of James (Lk. 24:10); Mary mother of Joses (Mk. 15:47), and Salome.[38] The first two Maries are identified with an article plus an addition and the others with a preceding genitive or nothing. In order to make Mary the mother of James and Joses, Mark would have written Μαρία ἡ μήτηρ + the two names. However, this exegesis seems rather artificial. To say the third and fourth women are identified by a genitive or nothing appears to be question-begging, since there is only one example of each. Against this theory is the fact that the mother of Joses would now lack a definite article (this being surrendered exclusively to Μαρία ἡ Ἰακώβου) and would be unnamed here as just "mother of Joses," but named in 15:47 as Mary. It is perfectly good grammar to take the definite article with the μήτηρ so that both sons' names are enclosed with their mother's: Μαρία ἡ Ἰακώβου τοῦ μικροῦ καὶ Ἰωσῆτος μήτηρ. Schottroff remarks that we probably have here a reliable, old tradition, since it would be unusual to identify a woman by her two sons (rather than her husband) unless they were prominent figures in the *Urgemeinde*.[39] Matthew agrees with Mark, except that he calls Joses by the variant Joseph and does not name Salome but apparently identifies her as the mother of the sons of Zebedee. Luke speaks of Μαρία ἡ Ἰακώβου which may reflect Mk. 16:1, where Joses is omitted; he adds Joanna to the list, whom he identifies as the wife of Herod's steward Chuza (Lk. 8:3). He states that there were other women as well, which could include Salome or per-

---

[38] Pesch, *Markusevangelium*, 2: 506-507.
[39] Luise Schottroff, "Maria Magdalena und die Frauen am Grabe Jesu," *EvT* 42 (1982): 8-9; see also Pesch, *Markusevangelium*, 2: 507; Lagrange, *Marc*, p. 439.

haps even someone like Susanna (Lk. 8:3). John's Mary the wife of Clopas could be the mother of James and Joses. If the wife of Clopas and Jesus's aunt are not two persons,⁴⁰ then James and Joses would be Jesus's cousins. But some have wanted to identify Mary the wife of Clopas with Matthew's mother of the sons of Zebedee. Thus, James and John the sons of Zebedee would be Jesus's cousins. This latter identification would be nice for those who wish to identify the Beloved Disciple with John, for then Jesus's bond with him and Jesus's giving of his mother to him would become more understandable. But this is, of course, speculative. Clopas could also be identified with Cleopas (Lk. 24:18; Κλεόπος is an abbreviated form of Κλεόπατρος and was equivalent to the Semitic Κλωπᾶς) of the Emmaus appearance, but then Lk. 24:22-23 make little sense, since Cleopas's own wife was among those who found the empty tomb. Because all the lists contain unnamed women, multiple cross-identifications are possible, but none provable. Mark says there were many other women at the cross besides the three he names, and it seems likely there was a group no smaller than five or six.⁴¹

In Mk. 15:47 Mark says that of the women at the cross, Mary Magdalene and Mary the mother of Joses saw where he was laid. The verse is obviously not independent; is it a redactional construction? This seems unlikely since the redactor would have to arbitrarily select out of the longer identification just the words Μαρία ἡ Ἰωσῆτος; the work of a redactor is more like Matthew's "the other Mary" upon the second mention. And why, too, was Salome omitted? More likely is that only two women of the larger group at the cross saw the burial; rather than repeat the long identification of Mary, the pre-Markan tradition names her by one son in 15:47 and the other in 16:1.⁴² Thus 15:47 and 16:1 seem to presuppose each other's existence; if one is traditional, so is the other.⁴³

In 16:1 Mary Magdalene, Mary the mother of James, and Salome go to the tomb. Many critics regard this verse as either a redactional construction or evidence that the empty tomb pericope was not part of the pre-Markan passion story, since the juxtaposition of 15:47 and 16:1 creates a useless duplication of names.

---

⁴⁰ As is held by Barrett, *John*, p. 458.
⁴¹ So Taylor, *Mark*, p. 652.
⁴² So Lagrange, *Marc*, p. 444; Grant Osborne, "History and Theology in the Resurrection Narratives: a Redactional Study" (Ph.D. thesis, University of Aberdeen, 1974), pp. 146-147.
⁴³ Against the view that 16:1 is a much later addition based on Mt., see the critique by Taylor, *Mark*, pp. 652-653; cf. Blinzler, "Grablegung," pp. 65-66.

Now I have already suggested that the two verses actually seem to presuppose each other. And if the pericope does belong to the passion story, can we be so certain that the list is a needless repetition? The fact that Salome's name is reintroduced suggests that whereas only two women saw the burial, three women of the original larger group at the cross rose early to go to the tomb. As Pesch explains, the different roles played by individuals known in the *Urgemeinde* are being here recalled.[44] This may be no useless duplication at all—rather the mention of the different witnesses to the crucifixion, burial, and empty tomb begins the pattern of I Cor. 15: Christ died—was buried—rose.... Just as the formula emphasizes the witnesses to the appearances of Jesus, so the pre-Markan passion story carefully lists the women witnesses, who were not apparently adduced in the evangelistic preaching but were nevertheless remembered in the life of the church, to each of the events preceding the appearances.[45] Luke's addition of Joanna to the list may reflect a local tradition that remembered her role, which was not so important to the Jerusalem congregation;[46] his use of the unparalleled ἡ Μαγδαληνὴ Μαρία suggests that he did have another source. So I see no compelling reason to consider the juxtaposition of the different lists in 15:47 and 16:1 as evidence for either redactional editing or independent traditions. All three lists were probably part of the pre-Markan tradition remembering the role of the women in those dark and crucial hours before the dawn of resurrection hope.

Traces of Other Burial Traditions

Grass has said that the historicity of the burial story can be denied only if an earlier burial tradition can be discovered and if the present story can be shown to contain improbabilities.[47] He adduces therefore what he considers to be three improbabilities in the burial account: (1) there was insufficient time for burial in the tomb, (2) the linen shroud could not have been purchased on a holiday, and (3) criminals were normally buried in a common grave. But if our analysis has been correct, none of these improbabilities need prove insuperable. Grass himself acknowledges that Mark's account is not impossible and that if it is reliable, then the site of Jesus's tomb would have been known to both Jews and Christians. But

---

[44] Pesch, *Markusevangelium*, 2: 508.
[45] Taylor, *Mark*, p. 651; Lane, *Mark*, p. 577; cf. Gnilka, *Markus*, 2: 339.
[46] Taylor, *Mark*, p. 652; Osborne, "Resurrection," p. 229.
[47] Grass, *Ostergeschehen*, p. 178.

Grass also claims to have found other traditions in Acts 13:29 and Jn. 19:31 for burial of the body by either the Jews or the Romans. This, however, seems doubtful. In Acts Luke tends to polemicize against the Jews, and the remark here probably represents no separate burial tradition.[48] In any case, this does not resolve the problem of the empty tomb, since Acts 13:29 speaks of a μνημεῖον and not a common criminals' grave. In John the Jews ask only that the victims' legs be broken and the bodies taken away, but before they are taken down, Joseph requests Jesus's body. It seems entirely possible that the Romans did bury the thieves' bodies; in any case there is no suggestion that Joseph did not personally take charge of Jesus's burial in the tomb. So there appears to be no evidence of any burial tradition apart from the burial by Joseph of Arimathea.

Grass's conclusion that all we are left with is an uncertain tradition of burial by Joseph with other possible traditions seeming to appear therefore seems overly timorous. Rather the burial story seems quite plausible in itself, and has several positive marks of historical credibility. This is an important conclusion, for as Grass acknowledges, if the burial story is historical, then it seems impossible that the grave of Jesus would have remained unknown to either the Jews or the Christians.[49] That consideration would seem to be relevant, in light of the disciples' proclamation of Jesus's resurrection in Jerusalem, in assessing the historical credibility of the empty tomb.

---

[48] Wilckens, *Die Missionsreden der Apostelgeschichte*, 3rd ed., WMANT (Neukirchen-Vluyn: Neukirchner Verlag, 1974), p. 135; Gnilka, *Markus*, 2: 336.
[49] Grass, *Ostergeschehen*, p. 179; so also Blinzler, "Grablegung," p. 64; Gnilka, *Markus*, 2: 346.

CHAPTER 6

THE EMPTY TOMB NARRATIVE

TRADITIONAL MATERIAL

When we turn to the empty tomb narrative, we again find evidence of traditional material in the agreement between John and the Synoptics. The various traditions apparently related that on the first day of the week women, or at least Mary Magdalene, came to the tomb early and found the stone taken away, that they saw an angelic appearance, that they informed the disciples, or at least Peter, who went, found the tomb empty with the graveclothes still lying in the grave, and returned home wondering, that the women saw a physical appearance of Jesus shortly thereafter, and that Jesus gave them certain instructions for the disciples. Not all the Synoptics record all these traditions; but John does, and at least one Synoptic confirms each incident; thus given John's independence from the Synoptics, these incidents would seem to be traditional.[1]

The story of the discovery of the empty tomb was in all likelihood the conclusion or at least part of the pre-Markan passion story.[2] About the only argument

---

[1] Neirynck has recently argued that John knew the Synoptics and formed chapter 20 on the basis of them. His strategy is to show that the appearance to the women and the disciples' investigation of the empty tomb are redactional creations of the evangelists; since John also narrates these events, he must have used the Synoptics (Frans Neirynck, "John and the Synoptics: The Empty Tomb Stories," *NTS* 30 [1984]: 161-187). But while Neirynck succeeds in showing the possibility that the events narrated by John and the Synoptics are the same, the evidence for redactional creation is sparse, indeed, and John's account evinces no direct dependence on the Synoptics. Shared tradition is therefore the more plausible explanation.

[2] Rudolph Pesch, *Das Markusevangelium*, 2 vols., HTKNT 2 (Freiburg: Herder, 1977), 2:519-520; idem, "Der Schluss der vormarkinische Passionsgeschichte und des Markusevangeliums," in

against this seems to be the juxtaposition of the lists in 15:47 and 16:1. At the very most, however, this could only warrant explaining one list or the other as an editorial addition; it would not serve to break off the empty tomb story from the passion narrative.[3] Pesch explains that the empty tomb story is no independent pericope but is bound up with the passion story and the immediate context.[4] The burial story looks forward with expectancy to the empty tomb: Joseph's laying the body in the tomb anticipates the angel's proclamation, "He is not here; see the place where they laid him;" the mention of the roll-stone anticipates the women's question in v. 3 and the open tomb in v. 4, and the women's witnessing the location of the tomb prepares for the visit on Sunday morning. The burial story and the empty tomb story are also bound together by verbal and syntactical similarities.[5] But especially significant are the data in 15:42-47 which are presupposed in 16:1-8: the "when the sabbath was past" (16:1) presupposes the burial on "the day of Preparation, that is the day before the sabbath" (15:42); the use of the personal pronoun αὐτόν for Jesus (16:1) has its antecedent in the naming of Jesus in the burial story (15:43); the visit to the tomb (16:2) presupposes the knowledge of the grave's location (15:47); the discussion between the women (16:3) presupposes the knowledge of the shutting of the tomb with the roll-stone (15:46); the entering of the tomb (16:5) presupposes the nature of the tomb (15:46); and the words of

---

M. Sabbe, *L'Evangile selon Marc* (Leuven: Gembloux, 1974), pp. 365-409. Taylor also finds that the burial and empty tomb stories were part of the pre-Markan passion story; his qualification that 16:1-8 cannot have been a part of that tradition is entirely arbitrary and cannot explain what happened to the original story and why (Vincent Taylor, *The Gospel according to St. Mark*, 2nd ed. [London: Macmillan, 1966], p. 659). See also Édouard Dhanis, "L'ensevelissement de Jésus et la visite au tombeau dans l'evangile de saint Marc, (MC XV.40-XVI.8)," *Greg* 39 (1958): 391-392, 396; Joachim Jeremias, "Die älteste Schicht der Osterüberlieferungen," in *Resurrexit*, ed. Édouard Dhanis (Rome: Libreria Éditice Vaticana, 1974), p. 186; Joachim Gnilka, *Das Evangelium nach Markus*, 2 vols., EKRNT (Zürich: Benziger Verlag, 1979; Neukirchner-Verlag, 1979), 2:348-350.

[3] Thus Wilckens argues that 16:1 is a later addition designed to protect the women against the charge of breaking the sabbath. Originally 16.2-6a was the close of the Passion story (Ulrich Wilckens, *Auferstehung*, TT4 [Stuttgart & Berlin: Kreuz Verlag, 1970], pp. 56-63). For a critique of Wilckens's hypothesis see Josef Blinzler, "Die Grablegung Jesu in historischer Sicht," in *Resurrexit*, pp. 65-66. Blinzler argues that all the lists are old and unchanged (Ibid., pp. 65-68).

[4] Pesch, *Markusevangelium*, 2:519-520.

[5] Verbal: the time indicators (15:42; 16:1, 2); the buying of linen and spices (15:46; 16:1); mention of laying the body in the tomb (15:46, 47; 16:6); alternate use of μνῆμα/μνημεῖον for the tomb (15:46; 16:2, 3, 5, 8); the closing of the grave with a stone (15:46; 16:3, 4); the women's seeing (15:47; 16:4), and the list of names (15:47; 16:1). Syntactical: time indicators in *genitivus absolutus* (15:42; 16:1); καὶ series broken by δέ (15:44; 16:6); four *participia conjuncta* (15:43, 44, 45, 46; 16:1, 4, 5, 8); introduction of the action of characters by a change of subject with the article + δέ in 15:44, 47; 16:6, but not in 15:46; 16:8.

the angel (16:6) presuppose Joseph's action (15:46). Moreover, the empty tomb narrative is tied to the wider context of the passion story: the list of names (16:1) remembers 15:40; the time indicator πρωΐ (16:2) harks back to the trial and crucifixion accounts (15:1, 25, 33, 34; cf. 14:17); on θεωρέω (16:4) compare 15:40; for the identification of Jesus as a Nazarene (16:6) see 10:47; 14:67 and as the crucified (16:6) see 15:13, 14, 15, 20, 24, 25, 27; the proclamation of the resurrection (16:6) fulfills the prophecy of 14:28, and the motif of fear (16:8) recalls 10:32.

But perhaps the most telling argument in favor of 16:1-8's belonging to the passion story is that it is unthinkable that the passion story could end in defeat and death with no mention of the empty tomb or resurrection. As Wilckens has urged, the passion story is incomplete without victory at the end.[6] Confirmation of the inclusion of 16:1-8 in the pre-Markan passion story would also seem to be the remarkable correspondence to the course of events described in I Cor. 15: died—was buried—rose—appeared; all these elements appear in the pre-Markan passion story, including a reference to Christ's appearance (v. 7). Thus, there seem to be very strong reasons for taking the empty tomb account as part of the pre-Markan passion story.

Like the burial story, the account of the discovery of the empty tomb is remarkably restrained. Bultmann states, "...Mark's presentation is extremely reserved, in so far as the resurrection and the appearance of the risen Lord are not recounted."[7] Nauck observes that many theological motifs that might be expected are lacking in the story: (1) the proof from prophecy, (2) the in-breaking of the new eon, (3) the ascension of Jesus's spirit or his descent into hell, (4) the nature of the risen body, and (5) the use of Christological titles.[8] Although kerygmatic speech appears in the mouth of the angel, the fact of the discovery of the empty

---

[6] Wilckens, *Auferstehung*, p. 61. The passion story could not have ended with the death and burial of Jesus without assurance of victory; the discovery of the empty tomb by the women was part of the passion story (Raymond E. Brown, *The Gospel according to John*, Anch Bib 29A [Garden City, N. Y.: Doubleday & Co., 1970], p. 978; Blinzler, "Grablegung," p. 76; Rudolf Schnackenburg, *Das Johannesevangelium*, 3 vols., HTKNT 4 (Freiburg: Herder, 1976], 3: 353).

[7] Rudolf Bultmann, *Die Geschichte der synoptischen Tradition*, 2nd ed., FRLANT 12 (Göttingen: Vandenhoeck & Ruprecht, 1970), p. 309.

[8] Wolfgang Nauck, "Die Bedeutung des leeren Grabes für den Glauben an den Auferstandenen," *ZNW* 47 (1956): 243-267. According to Kremer, every theological reflection on the meaning of the resurrection is lacking, so the tradition must come from a very early time. For its origin in Palestine (Jerusalem) counts not only the interest in the empty tomb itself, but also the names of the women and the Semitic τῇ μιᾷ τῶν σαββάτων (cf. πρώτῃ σαββάτου [16:9]; "after three days" [8:31; 9:31; 10:34]) (Jacob Kremer, "Zur Diskussion über 'das leere Grab,'" in *Resurrexit*, p. 153).

tomb is not kerygmatically colored. All these factors point to a very old tradition concerning the discovery of the empty tomb.[9]

THE ANOINTING MOTIF

Mark begins the story by relating that when the sabbath was past, the women bought spices to anoint the body. In the next sentence, he almost seems to begin anew: "And very early on the first day of the week, they went to the tomb..." (16:2). This new beginning suggests that there is in fact a gap here, namely, that after the sabbath, that is, Saturday evening, they went and bought the spices.[10] Then early the next day they went to the tomb. Luke is the only other evangelist to mention the spices, and he also states that they had been prepared prior to the visit on the first day of the week (Lk. 24:1). The insertion of 23:56b gives the impression that the women prepared the spices on Friday night, but this is probably unintentional, since in v. 54 the sabbath was already beginning and Luke says in v. 56b they did no work on the sabbath. So there was no time to buy and prepare spices on Friday night. Rather v. 56b is probably to be taken as a parenthetical remark, not the narration of a chronologically successive event. The preparation of v. 56a was probably understood by Luke as taking place Saturday night, since Mark is quite clear. But by inserting his parenthetical remark on the pious behavior of the women he generates an apparent contradiction.

The women's intention to anoint the body has caused no end of controversy. It is often assumed that the women were coming to finish the hurried job done by Joseph on Friday evening; John, who has a thorough burial, mentions no intention of anointing. It is frequently said that the "Eastern climate" would make it impossible to anoint a corpse after three days.[11] It is sometimes pointed out that it

---

[9] Karl Heinrich Rengstorff, *Die Auferstehung Jesu*, 4th rev. ed. (Witten: Luther-Verlag, 1960), pp. 60-61.
[10] C. E. B. Cranfield, *The Gospel according to Saint Mark*, CGTC (Cambridge: Cambridge University Press, 1963), p. 463; Taylor, *Mark*, p. 603; William L. Lane, *The Gospel according to Mark*, NLCNT (London: Marshall, Morgan & Scott, 1974), p. 585; Pesch, *Markusevangelium*, 2: 520.
[11] Maurice Goguel, *La foi à la résurrection de Jésus dans le christianisme primitif* (Paris: Leroux, 1939), p. 144; Ernst Lohmeyer, *Das Evangelium des Markus*, KEKNT 2 (Göttingen: Vandenhoeck & Ruprecht, 1937), p. 353; Bultmann, *Geschichte*, p. 309; Hans Freiherr von Campenhausen, *Der Ablauf der Osterereignisse und das leere Grab*, 3rd rev. ed., SHA (Heidelberg: Carl Winter, 1966), p. 24; Hans Grass, *Ostergeschehen und Osterberichte*, 4th rev. ed. (Göttingen: Vandenhoeck & Ruprecht, 1970), p. 20; Taylor, *Mark*, p. 604; Eduard Schweizer, *Das Evangelium nach Markus*, NTD 1 (Göttingen: Vandenhoeck & Ruprecht, 1967), p. 211; E. Gut-

would not have violated sabbath law to anoint a body on the sabbath, instead of waiting until Sunday (Mishnah Shabbat 23:5). Besides, the body had been already anointed in advance (Mk. 14:8). And why do the women think of the stone over the entrance only after they are underway? They should have realized the venture was futile.

But what in fact were the women about? There seems to be no indication that they were going to complete a task poorly done. Mark gives no hint of hurry or incompleteness in the burial. That Luke says that the women saw "how" the body was laid (Lk. 23:55) does not necessarily imply that the women saw a lack which they wished to remedy; it could mean merely that they saw that the corpse was laid in a tomb, not buried in the criminals' common plot, thus making possible a visit to anoint the body. The fact that John does not mention the intention of anointing proves little, since Matthew does not mention it either. So there seems to be no conclusive indication that the women were going to complete Jesus's burial.

In fact, what the women may have been doing was precisely that described in the Mishnah, namely the use of aromatic oils and perfumes that could be rubbed on or simply poured over the body.[12] Even the threat of decay would not necessarily prevent this simple act of devotion. That same devotion could have induced them to go to try together to open the tomb, despite the stone. (That Mark only mentions the stone here does not mean that they had not thought of it before; it serves a literary purpose here to prepare for v. 4.) The opening of tombs to allow late visitors to view the body or to check against apparent death was Jewish practice,[13] so the women's intention was not extraordinary. It is true that anointing could be done on the sabbath, but this was only for a person lying on the death bed in his home, not for a body already wrapped and entombed in a sealed grave outside the city. On the contrary, Blinzler points out that, odd as it may seem, it would have been against the Jewish law even to carry the *aromata* to the grave

---

wenger, "Zur Geschichtlichkeit der Auferstehung Jesu," *ZKT* 88 (1966): 273; Ludger Schenke, *Auferstehungsverkündigung und leeres Grab* (Stuttgart: Katholisches Bibelwerk, 1968), p. 31; I. Broer, "Zur heutigen Diskussion der Grabesgeschichte (Mc 16, 1-8)," *BiLeb* 10 (1969): 40-52; Walter Grundmann, *Das Evangelium nach Markus*, 7th rev. ed., THKNT 2 (Berlin: Evangelische Verlagsanstalt, 1977), p. 321; Karl Martin Fischer, *Das Ostergeschehen*, 2nd ed. (Göttingen: Vandenhoeck & Ruprecht, 1980), p. 61.

[12] Brown, *John*, p. 940; Blinzler, "Grablegung," p. 81; Lane, *Mark*, p. 585.

[13] Semachoth 8; Ebel Rabbathi 4.11. See further Lohmeyer, *Markus*, p. 351; Blinzler, "Grablegung," p. 81.

site, for this was "work" (Jer. 17:21-22; Shabbath 8:1)![14] Thus, Luke's comment that the women rested on the sabbath is probably a correct description.

Sometimes it is asserted that Matthew leaves out the anointing motif because he realized one could not anoint a corpse after three days in that climate.[15] But Mark himself cannot be presumed to be ignorant of this fact, if true, since he also lived in the Mediterranean climate.[16] In fact, moreover, Jerusalem, being 700 meters above sea level, can be quite cool in April; interesting is the entirely incidental detail mentioned by John that at night in Jerusalem at that time it was cold—so much so that the servants and officers of the Jews had made a fire and were standing around it warming themselves (Jn. 18:18). Add to this the facts that the body, interred Friday evening, had been in the tomb only a night, a day, and a night when the women came to anoint it early Sunday morning, that a rock-hewn tomb in a cliff side would stay naturally cool, and that the body may have already been packed around with aromatic spices, and one can see that the intention to anoint the body cannot in any way be ruled out.[17] The argument that the body had been anointed in advance seems actually a point in favor of the tradition of the women's intention to anoint the body, for after 14:8, Mark would probably not have invented such a superfluous and almost contradictory intention for the women.[18]

---

[14] Blinzler, "Grablegung," p. 83.
[15] Willi Marxsen, *The Resurrection of Jesus of Nazareth*, trans. Margaret Kohl (London: SCM Press, 1970), pp. 44-45; Wilckens, *Auferstehung*, p. 46; Grundmann, *Markus*, p. 445. Gardner-Smith believes Matthew did not wish to mention Joseph's failure to anoint the body, since he was a disciple (P. Gardner-Smith, *The Narratives of the Resurrection*, [London: Methuen, 1926], p. 37)! More realistic is Osborne's remark that Matthew omits the motif because his theological interest is on what happens at the tomb (Grant Osborne, "History and Theology in the Resurrection Narratives: a Redactional Study" [Ph.D. thesis, University of Aberdeen, 1974], p. 190).
[16] Gerhard Koch, *Die Auferstehung Jesu Christi*, BHT (Tübingen: J. C. B. Mohr, 1959), p. 29; Brown, *John*, p. 982. In fact, Lindemann asserts that Mark makes the women's visit so early in the morning precisely because of the problem of anointing a corpse in that climate (Andreas Lindemann, "Die Osterbotschaft des Markus. Zur theologischen Interpretation von Markus 16: 1-8," *NTS* 26 [1979-80]: 303).
[17] Dhanis, "Ensevelissement," p. 383; Paul Gaechter, "Die Engelerscheinungen in den Auferstehungsberichten," *ZKT* 89 (1967): 195; Edward Lynn Bode, *The First Easter Morning*, AB 45 (Rome: Biblical Institute Press, 1970), pp. 14, 16; Luise Schottroff, "Maria Magdalena und die Frauen am Grabe Jesu," *EvT* 42 (1982): 15-16.
[18] It might be said that 14:8 reveals knowledge that Jesus's body was not properly interred and anointed and seeks to remedy that lack. But such a hypothesis in no way contradicts the women's intention, since they were not in fact successful in their mission. In any case, the women's visit even without the anointing motif is perfectly coherent in light of the practice of visiting the graves of loved ones until the third day (Thomas R. W. Longstaff, "The Women at the Tomb: Matthew 28:1 Re-examined," *NTS* 27 [1980-81]: 277-282).

THE WOMEN'S DISCOVERY OF THE EMPTY TOMB

According to Mark, the women came to the tomb "very early on the first day of the week" "when the sun had risen" (16:2). Here is the Markan pattern again of using the second time indicator to specify the first. It indicates that the women came around dawn.[19] Luke says in fact that they came at "early dawn" (Lk. 24:1); Matthew says "after the sabbath, toward the dawn" (Mt. 28:1). The word ὀψέ can mean either "late" or "after," depending on whether it is being used adverbially or prepositionally, respectively. It has been suggested that Matthew means late Saturday evening, dawn being used as in Lk. 23:24;[20] but the mention of the night in Mt. 28:13 excludes this understanding. Rather he refers to dawn on Sunday morning. John says Mary came "early, while it was still dark" (Jn. 20:1). Some commentators like to see in the darkness a symbol of sin, despair, *etc.*, as in 13:30; but as Brown observes, if John had said "it was light" there would probably be no less number of commentators who would see this as a symbol of resurrection dawn, the light of life, or something else.[21] Safer is to take it as a straight time-indicator. To say it contradicts the Synoptics would appear to be somewhat pedantic; John does not imagine Mary feeling her way through the dark—the gospels all seem to agree that sometime around dawn the women visited the tomb.

Which women? Mark says the two Maries and Salome; Matthew mentions only the two Maries; Luke says the two Maries, Joanna, and other women; John mentions only Mary Magdalene. There seems to be no difficulty in imagining a handful of women going to the tomb. Even John records Mary's words as "we do not know where they have laid him" (Jn. 20:2). It is true that Semitic usage could

---

[19] Cranfield, *Mark*, p. 464; M. J. Lagrange, *Évangile selon saint Marc*, (Paris: Libraire Lecoffre, 1966), p. 444; thorough discussion in Bode, *Easter*, pp. 6-13. This rebuts the purported contradiction seen by Kremer, "Grab," p. 152. Cf. Hugh Anderson, *Jesus and Christian Origins* (New York: Oxford University Press, 1964), p. 238-240.

[20] C. K. Barrett, *The Gospel according to St. John* (London: SPCK, 1972), p. 562; Ernst Lohmeyer, *Das Evangelium des Matthäus*, 4th ed., ed. W. Schmauch, KEKNT (Göttingen: Vandenhoeck & Ruprecht, 1967), pp. 404-405; Kremer, *Osterbotschaft*, p. 36; Bode, *Easter*, pp. 12-13; Walter Grundmann, *Das Evangelium nach Matthäus*, 3rd ed., THKNT 1 (Berlin: Evangelische Verlagsanstalt, 1972), p. 568; Robert H. Gundry, *Matthew: A Commentary on his Literary and Theological Art* (Grand Rapids, Mich.: Wm. B. Eerdmans, 1982), pp. 585-586. This case serves as a good illustration of the fact that not every editorial change by an evangelist should be seen as charged with significance, for though Matthew uses ὀψέ and drops "when the sun had risen," v. 13 makes it clear that he still thinks of Sunday morning. To say that in v. 1 he writes "from his own standpoint" (Gundry) explains nothing at all, for the whole chapter, including the guard story, is written from his own standpoint.

[21] Raymond Brown, "Échange de vues," in *Resurrexit*, p. 204.

permit the first person plural to mean simply "I" (cf. Jn. 3:11, 32), but not only does this seem rather artificial in this context, but then we should expect the plural as well in v. 13.[22] In any case, this ignores the Synoptic tradition and makes only an isolated grammatical point. If we have represented in John and the Synoptics independent traditions that women visited the tomb, then the weight of probability falls in favor of Mary's "we" being the remnant of a tradition of more than one woman. John has perhaps focused on her for dramatic effect.

THE GUARD AT THE TOMB

Of the canonical gospels, only Matthew mentions the setting of a guard at the tomb (Mt. 27:62-66; 28:4, 11-15). The story serves an apologetic purpose: the refutation of the allegation that the disciples had themselves stolen Jesus's body and thus faked his resurrection. Behind the story as Matthew tells it seems to lie a tradition history of Jewish/Christian polemic, a developing pattern of assertion and counter-assertion:

Christian: "The Lord is risen!"
Jew: "No, his disciples stole away his body."
Christian: "The guard at the tomb would have prevented any such theft."
Jew: "No, his disciples stole away his body while the guard slept."
Christian: "The chief priests bribed the guard to say this."

Though only Matthew recounts the story of a guard at the tomb (John mentions a guard in connection with Jesus's arrest; cf. Mk. 14:44), the Gospel of Peter also tells the story of the guard at the tomb, and its account may well be independent of Matthew, since the verbal similarities are practically nil.[23]

---

[22] So Brown, *John*, p. 984. Mahoney's answer that v. 13 is singular because Mary is being addressed a personal question misses the point that the Semitic idiom means precisely "I" and would therefore be entirely appropriate (Robert Mahoney, *Two Disciples at the Tomb*, TW 6 [Bern: Herbert Lang, 1974], p. 216). Bode attempts to support the Semitic usage by other uses of οἴδαμεν in Jn. 3:2, 11; 9:31; 14:5; 21:24 (Bode, Easter, pp. 73-74), but most of these are in fact genuine plurals. Bernard, Hoskyns, Barrett, Schnackenburg, and Kremer agree that οἴδαμεν implies a plurality of women (J. H. Bernard, *Gospel according to St. John*, 2 vols., ICC [Edinburgh: T & T Clark, 1928], 2: 656; E. C. Hoskyns, *The Fourth Gospel*, 2nd ed., ed. F. N. Davey [London: Faber, 1967], p. 540; Barrett, *John*, p. 563; Schnackenburg, *Johannesevangelium* 3: 358; Jacob Kremer, *Die Osterevangelien—Geschichten um Geschichte* [Stuttgart: Katholisches Bibelwerk, 1977], p. 166).

[23] So B. A. Johnson, "The Empty Tomb in the Gospel of Peter Related to Mt. 28:1-7" (Ph.D. dissertation, Harvard University, 1966), p. 17. This does not commit one to Johnson's view that this was an appearance tradition.

According to Matthew, on Saturday, that is, on the sabbath, which Matthew calls the day after the day of Preparation, the chief priests and Pharisees ask Pilate for a guard to secure the tomb to prevent the disciples from stealing the body and thus "fulfilling" Jesus's prediction of rising on the third day. Pilate says, "You have a guard; make it as secure as you can." It is not clear if Pilate gave them a Roman guard or told them to use their own Temple guard. The Gospel of Peter uses a Roman guard, but this could be read into the tradition and may be designed to emphasize the strength of the guard. If Pilate rebuffed the Jews, then one wonders why this part of the story be told at all; on the other hand, if the Jews really did go to Pilate, then perhaps this detail was remembered. If Pilate gave them a guard it is strange that Matthew does not make this explicit, as does the Gospel of Peter, as this would strengthen his apologetic. It is intriguing to note that according to John both Jewish guards and Roman soldiers were involved in Jesus's arrest (Jn. 18:3, 12). Mark calls the party which arrested Jesus a crowd (ὄχλος) armed with swords and clubs, delegated by the Jewish hierarchy; but he later refers to the ὑπηρέται (14:65) which included Jewish military police. John also states that these Jewish guards were involved in the arrest, but he alone adds that a Roman cohort (σπεῖρα) and its commander (χιλίαρχος) participated actively in the seizure and binding of Jesus (18:12). This could provide some precedent for further involvement of Roman soldiers in the guard at the tomb. It need not be thought that the whole cohort (theoretically 1,000 men, but usually, in fact, about 600) were involved in the arrest; a detachment large enough to warrant the commander's presence may have been involved. Fear of insurrection during the Feast days could have prompted Roman involvement. The historicity of John's information, however, is disputed. On the one hand, there does not seem to be any convincing reason why John would create the Roman participation. Indeed, since he tends to exonerate the Romans at the expense of "the Jews," it seems likely that this information is traditional. On the other hand, such participation seems out of place, for the Jewish leaders had not yet framed a charge against Jesus to Pilate, and upon Jesus's arrest the guards take him, not to Pilate, but to the high priest. But Jn. 18:30 might be taken as an expression of surprise on the part of the chief priests, indicating that some prior understanding with the governor had existed on which he was now ambivalent. And the proceeding to the high priest's house could indicate that the Jewish leaders were directing the affair, the Romans merely supplying the muscle. We do not know. Arrangements could have been similar in the setting of the guard at the tomb. Matthew attributes its instigation to the "chief priests and Pharisees" (27:62; cf. Jn. 17:3), a traditional phrase for him, and calls the guard "soldiers" (στρατιῶται 28:12) rather than ὑπηρέται (cf. 26:58). However, even if John is accurate concerning the Roman involvement in the arrest, this really affords no ground for inference concerning the identity of the guard at the tomb. The instigation of the setting of the guard by the Jewish leaders also provides no firm clue. Matthew's use of στρατιῶται is significant, but it should be noted that 26:58 is the only place in the gospel where ὑπηρέται appears, and here it is Markan (Mk. 14:54) and may refer to servants as well as guards. But in 28:12 he is specifically referring, perhaps, to ὑπηρέται who are στρατιῶται. Pilate's words in 27:65 may mean the Jews have the governor's permission to use their armed soldiers at the tomb. The fact that the guards return to the chief priests seems to be evidence that a Jewish guard is intended; contrast the Gospel of Peter, where the Roman guard report to Pilate the events at the tomb. The mention of the governor in v. 14 might indicate a Roman guard, but then it would not be clear how the Jews could do anything to keep them out of trouble. The fact that Roman guards could be executed for sleeping on watch and taking a bribe could further point to a Jewish guard. In the Gospel of Peter the bribe and the sleeping story are eliminated; Pilate simply commands the Roman guard to keep silent. The story is perhaps more plausible if one assumes that the guard is Jewish; but Matthew may well be describing the setting of a Roman guard.

So the guard is set and the sepulchre sealed. It has been said that Matthew omits the anointing motif because of the guard and the sealing,[24] but this surmise holds little weight, for the women were clearly ignorant of such actions taken on the sabbath. Rather it could be that Matthew is following different traditions here, since v. 15 makes it evident that there is a tradition history behind Matthew's story.[25] Before the women arrive, an angel of the Lord rolls back the stone, and

---

[24] Kirsopp Lake, *The Historical Evidence for the Resurrection of Jesus* (London: Williams & Norgate, 1907), p. 61; Grundmann, *Matthäus*, p. 568; Blinzler, "Grablegung," p. 82; Gundry, *Matthew*, p. 586.
[25] Evidence of pre-Matthean tradition is also found in the many words which are *hapax legomena* for the New Testament: ἐπαύριον, παρασκευή, πλάνος/πλάνη, κουστωδία, ἀσφαλίζω, σφραγίζω. Also the expression "chief priests and Pharisees" (cf. 21:45) is unusual for Matthew and never appears in Mark or Luke but is common in John (7:32, 45; 9:47, 57; 18:3). Moreover, the expres-

the guard are paralyzed with fear. It is not said that the guard see the resurrection or even that this is the moment of the resurrection.[26] After the women leave, some of the guard go to the Jewish authorities, who bribe them to say that the disciples stole the body. This story has been spread among the Jews until this day, adds Matthew.

Matthew's account has been nearly universally rejected as an apologetic legend, though the reasons for this assessment are of unequal worth. For example, the fact that the story is an apologetic answering the allegation that the disciples stole the body does not therefore necessarily mean that it is unhistorical. Similarly, it counts for little to press the theological objection against the story, as is often done, that it overshoots the remaining witness of the New Testament that Jesus only appeared to his own but remained hidden to his enemies.[27] Some scholars seem to be disturbed at the thought that pagan guards might see the "Risen Christ."[28] But the account says nothing about any appearance of Jesus to

---

sion τῇ τρίτῃ ἡμέρᾳ indicates tradition here, for Matthew everywhere changes this expression to μετὰ τρεῖς ἡμέρας. For discussion see R. Kratz, *Auferweckung als Befreiung*, SBS 65 (Stuttgart: Katholisches Bibelwerk, 1973), pp. 72-73; I. Broer, *Die Urgemeinde und das Grab Jesu*, SANT 31 (München: Kösel Verlag, 1972), pp. 69-78; F. Neirynck, "Les Femmes au tombeau: Étude de la rédaction mathéenne," *NTS* 15 (1968-69): 168-190; A. H. McNeile, *The Gospel According to Matthew* (London: Macmillan, 1961), p. 428. On the independence of Matthew from Mark see E. Ruckstuhl and J. Pfammater, *Die Auferstehung Jesu Christi* (Lucerne and München: Rex, 1968).

[26] Contrast the Gospel of Peter 8:35-42:
"Now in the night in which the Lord's day dawned, when the soldiers, two by two in every watch, were keeping guard, there rang out a loud voice in heaven, and they saw the heavens opened and two men come down from there in a great brightness and draw nigh to the sepulchre. The stone which had been laid against the entrance to the sepulchre started of itself to roll and gave way to the side, and the sepulchre was opened, and both the young men entered in. When now those soldiers saw this, they awakened the centurion and the elders—for they also were there to assist at the watch. And whilst they were relating what they had seen, they saw again three men come out from the sepulchre, and the two of them sustaining the other, and a cross following them, and the heads of the two reaching to heaven, but that of him who was led of them by the hand overpassing the heavens. And they heard a voice out of the heavens crying, 'Thou hast preached to them that sleep,' and from the cross there was heard the answer, 'Yea'."

and the *Ascension of Isaiah* 3:16:
"Gabriel, the Angel of the Holy Spirit, and Michael, the chief of the holy Angels, on the third day will open the sepulchre: and the Beloved sitting on their shoulders will come forth."

[27] Grundmann, *Matthäus*, p. 565; John E. Alsup, *The Post-Resurrection Appearance Stories of the Gospel-Tradition*, CTM A5 (Stuttgart: Calwer Verlag, 1975), p. 117.

[28] Thus, Grass says that besides the particularities, the guard story is unbelievable because heathen guards would see the resurrection (Grass, *Ostergeschehen*, p. 25). Von Campenhausen also states that the story implies pagan guards would be witnesses of the resurrection and we cannot agree that this should be (Von Campenhausen, *Ablauf*, p. 29). Similarly O'Collins makes the as-

the guards at all. On the contrary, the angel expressly says, "He is not here; for he has risen;" but the tomb is opened presumably that the women might come and "see the place where he lay" (Mt. 28:6). And in any case, the New Testament witness is that Jesus did appear to sceptics, unbelievers, and even enemies (Thomas, James, and Paul). The idea that only the eye of faith could see the risen Jesus seems to be foreign to the gospels and to Paul, for they all appear to agree on the physical nature of Christ's resurrection body. It is also sometimes urged that the chief priests and Pharisees would not go to Pilate on the sabbath day. But such an inference is again not very weighty, since it is not said that they went *en masse*, but merely met there,[29] and each could come a Sabbath day's journey without transgressing the law. Moreover, it is not said that they entered the praetorium (cf. Jn. 18:28). In any case, the objection takes no account of possible hypocrisy on the part of men who could bind others with heavy burdens, but they themselves not lift a finger to help. Nor again does it seem conclusive to object to the story because it contains what are regarded as inherent absurdities, for example, that the guards would not know that it was the disciples who stole the body because they were asleep or that a Roman guard would never agree to spread a story for which they could be executed.[30] The first assumes that the Jewish au-

---

tounding assertion that had Annas and Caiaphas been with the disciples when Jesus appeared, they would not have seen anything (Gerald O'Collins, *The Easter Jesus*, 2nd ed. [London: Darton, Longman, & Todd, 1980], p. 59). This, despite what Grass repeatedly describes as the "massive realism" of the gospels! Cf. Koch, *Auferstehung*, pp. 59-60, 204, who is scandalized by the objectivity of the gospel appearances, which he vainly attempts to construe in wholly subjective categories.

[29] See Lohmeyer, *Matthäus*, p. 400.

[30] Lake, *Evidence*, p. 178; Marxsen, *Resurrection*, p. 46; Grundmann, *Matthäus*, p. 571. Orr thinks that the guard's accepting the bribe is not so far-fetched, since their fleeing was already a breach of duty (James Orr, *The Resurrection of Jesus*, [London: Hodder & Stoughton, 1909], p. 160). Similarly, Gundry points out that the guard had nothing to lose by cooperating with the Jewish leadership, since the emptiness of the tomb would have exposed their failure anyway. Ironically, then, our judgment of the likelihood of the guards' compliance depends upon our estimate of the historicity of the empty tomb. For if the women did find the tomb empty, one cannot object to the fact that it had been guarded on the basis that the guards would not agree to spread a story for which they could be executed, since the emptiness of the tomb itself showed their failure of duty (Gundry, *Matthew*, p. 585). Von Campenhausen brings forth other absurdities, such as the fact that the guard reported to the Jewish leaders rather than Pilate and that Christians, despite the guards' lie, knew everything (Von Campenhausen, *Ablauf*, p. 29). But the former could be construed as evidence that the guard was Jewish or, if Roman, perhaps on loan under Jewish direction (as in the arrest). If Orr is correct, going to the Jews was the Roman guards' best hope of survival. As for the latter allegation, it is not surprising that the conspiracy should come to light. In any case, the Jews' conversation with Pilate is probably an imaginative Christian reconstruction of

thorities could not have fabricated a stupid cover-up story; really this story seems to have been as good as any other. At any rate the inference that it was disciples of Jesus was not so far-fetched, for who else would steal the body? The second absurdity assumes that the guard was Roman, which is not obligatory. And even if the guard were Roman, perhaps the chief priests' promise to "satisfy the governor" meant telling him the truth about the guards' loyal service, if they would agree to lie to the people. The guard had already compromised themselves by failing to keep the tomb secure (were they to tell their commander that God had miraculously opened it?) and deserting their post. Complying with the Jewish authorities was about all they could do.[31]

Rather the more serious difficulties with the story are two: (1) it is not related in the pre-Markan passion story nor in the other gospels, and (2) it presupposes not only that Jesus predicted his resurrection in three days, but also that the Jewish authorities understood this clearly while the disciples remained in ignorance. With regard to the first, it is exceedingly odd that the other gospels know nothing of so major an event as the placing of a guard around the tomb. This suggests that the account is a late legend reflecting years of Jewish/Christian polemic. The designation of Jesus as an impostor is an earmark of Jewish polemic against Christianity (Justin *Dialogue with Trypho* 108; *Testament of the Twelve Patriarchs* (Levi) 16:3). But perhaps this polemical interest supplies the very reason why this event, even if historical, was not included in the pre-Markan passion story. For the pre-Markan passion story arose in the life of the *Urgemeinde* before the *Auseinandersetzung* with Judaism became serious and reflects the inner concerns of the Christian fellowship. Since the guard played virtually no role in the events of the discovery of the empty tomb—indeed the Matthean account does not ex-

---

what they inferred took place, which would explain the third day motif and kerygmatic language employed.

Perry regards the placement of a Jewish guard at the tomb by the Jews, without knowledge of Jesus's prediction as historically defensible (Michael Perry, *The Easter Enigma*, with an Introduction by Austin Farrer [London: Faber & Faber, 1959], pp. 98-99). Schottroff claims that it was then feared that the graves of executed political opponents of the Empire would become assembly points of partisan conspiratorial elements (Luise Schottroff, "Maria Magdalena und die Frauen am Grabe Jesu," *EvT* 42 [1982]: 6); in view of Jesus's following and the highly charged atmosphere in Jerusalem, such distrust could have provoked Pilate to agree to the setting of a guard. Staudinger suggests that the guard was placed *after* the discovery of the empty tomb and the story displaced by Matthew (Hugo Staudinger, "The Resurrection of Jesus Christ as Saving Event and as 'Object' of Historical Research," *SJT* [1983]: 324-325).

[31] So Paul Gaechter, *Das Matthäusevangelium* (Innsbruck: Tyrolia-Verlag, 1963), p. 959.

clude that the guard had already left before the women arrived—, the pre-Markan passion story might simply omit them. If the slander that the disciples stole the body was restricted to certain quarters ("the story has been spread among Jews [παρὰ Ἰουδαίοις] to this day"), then it cannot be ruled out that Luke or John might not have these traditions. And the evangelists often inexplicably omit what seem to be major incidents that must have been known to them (for example, Luke's great omission of Mk. 6:45-8:26), so that it is dangerous to use omission as a test for historicity.

As for the second objection, we must be careful not to exclude *a priori* the possibility that Jesus did predict his resurrection, since ruling this out in advance seems to betray a philosophical presupposition against the miraculous. And if philosophical presuppositions cannot exclude Jesus's prediction, neither can theological, for example, that this represents a sort of "triumphalism" that minimizes the extent of Jesus's sacrifice since he knew he would rise again. Theological conceptions of what is "appropriate" to Jesus's person and work cannot dictate to history what must have happened; rather theological conceptions may simply have to be changed in light of history. The only valid grounds for accepting or rejecting Jesus's predictions as historical must be empirical.

What, then, are the empirical grounds for thinking that Jesus did not predict his resurrection? It is sometimes asserted that Jesus's prediction of his resurrection is incompatible with the despair and hopelessness of the disciples. But this may reckon too lightly with the statements of the gospels that the disciples could not understand how a dying and rising Messiah could be possible (Mk. 8:32; 9:10). The concept was utterly foreign to Judaism and would have passed ill with the common conception of the Messiah as the triumphant King of Israel, though, Mark reflects restrospectively, Jesus told the disciples *plainly* that he was to suffer, be killed, and rise (Mk. 8:32). It is interesting that when Jesus tells Martha that Lazarus will rise again, her response is, "I know that he will rise again in the resurrection at the last day" (Jn. 11:24). The disciples may have had no expectation that Jesus's prophesied resurrection would be otherwise; in fact this is implied by their question concerning the eschatological coming of Elijah prior to the resurrection (Mk. 9:10-11). Even the presence of the third day motif would not necessarily obviate this misconception, for they could have understood this to mean the third day after the end of the world, even as contemporary Jewish thought sometimes posited the resurrection after seven days or seven weeks following history's end. Their problem was not that they could not literally understand the sentences spoken by Jesus, but that they could not make any sense out of them. As Luke comments, "...they did not grasp what was said" (Lk. 18:34). So that the disciples failed to comprehend the significance of the predictions may have actually been the case, and their despair after the crucifixion cannot decisively preclude the historicity of Jesus's predictions.

It may be asserted that the language of the predictions is *ex ecclesia* and that therefore they are written back into the life of Jesus. But, in fact, there seem to be no words in the predictions that Jesus himself could not have employed, especially if he conceived of himself in the role of the suffering servant described in Is. 50:6; 53:3-10. Even the phrase "the third day" could have meant only a short time,[32] or, if one agrees with Lehmann that the third day is a theological expression connoting the day of God's deliverance, victory, and taking control, there seems to be no reason why, if the early church could have used this expression, Jesus himself could not also have used it in the same sense in predicting his resurrection. But even if this phrase were added from the kerygma, that need not imply that Jesus could not have predicted his resurrection *simpliciter*. In the same way, the speech of the chief priests to Pilate is a Christian reconstruction, and the third day motif may reflect the kerygmatic motif in I Cor. 15:4. In fact it is possible that the Jewish authorities may have asked for a guard to be posted for an indeterminate period of time or the duration of the Feast. That the predictions of the resurrection have taken on kerygmatic coloring does not seem to prove that they were not made.

Perhaps the most serious difficulty with the guard story, however, is that if the disciples did not grasp the import of the resurrection predictions, then the Jewish authorities, who had much less contact with Jesus, would not have grasped them either. There seem to be four categories of resurrection predictions: the sign of Jonah sayings (Mt.12:40; 16:21; Mk. 8:11; Lk. 11:29-30), the destruction of the

---

[32] Barnabas Lindars, *New Testament Apologetic: the Doctrinal Significance of Old Testament Quotations* (London: SCM, 1961), pp. 59-72; O'Collins, *Easter*, p. 12. Hooke also reminds us that all of Jesus's eschatological sayings presuppose the resurrection, as do his statements at the Last Supper (S. H. Hooke, *The Resurrection of Christ as History and Experience* (London: Darton, Longman & Todd, 1967], p. 30; cf. Michael Ramsey, *The Resurrection of Christ* [London: Centenary Press, 1945], pp. 38-39).

Temple sayings (Mt. 26:61; 27:40; Mk. 14:58; 15:29; Jn 2:19-21), the Son of Man sayings (Mt. 16:21; 17:22; 20:19; Mk. 8:31; 9:30; 10:34; Lk. 9:22; 9:44; 18:33; 24:6-7) and the appearance in Galilee sayings (Mt. 26:32; 28:7, 10; Mk 14:28; 16:7). Although each group but the last includes the motif of resurrection on the third day, the citation of the Jewish leaders in Mt. 27:63: μετὰ τρεῖς ἡμέρας ἐγείρομαι most closely resembles Mk. 9:31; 10:34: μετὰ τρεῖς ἡμέρας ἀναστήσεται (Matthew always prefers ἐγείρω). The problem is, while the other sayings are represented as being given before the Pharisees, Saduccees, chief priests, and crowds, these predictions are made privately to the Twelve, who did not grasp their import. The sign of Jonah saying is the only resurrection prediction which Matthew represents as having been made in the presence of the Jewish leaders, and Matthew seems to have modified it to make it clearer. So how could the Jewish leaders have known Jesus's resurrection predictions, so as to place the guard to prevent a hoaxed resurrection on the third day?

Since the Jewish leaders' conversation with Pilate is a Christian reconstruction, however, the chief priests' relating Jesus's prediction in the language most intimately associated with the Twelve is not surprising and thus does not imply that historically they learned of the prediction in this version. In any case, as weighty as the present objection is, still it remains essentially an argument from silence, since we do not know with any certainty how the Jewish leaders learned of Jesus's prediction. It seems to assume that we have recorded in the gospels all instances on which Jesus spoke of his resurrection or that if this prediction was conveyed to the Jewish hierarchy surreptitiously we must know about it. If they did learn of Jesus's prediction, it is clear that, not sharing the disciples' belief in Jesus's person, they would not have had the same difficulties in understanding it literally. Theologically, it would have appeared rubbish to them, and of course they did not believe it, but they might still take precautions to prevent Jesus's hare-brained disciples from trying to pull off a literal fulfillment of their master's prophecy. It is even possible that the actions of the Jewish leadership were not motivated by any knowledge of resurrection prophecies at all but were simply an afterthought to prevent any possible trouble that could be caused at the tomb by the disciples during the Feast.

Nevertheless, taken together, these considerations, though not decisive, have a cumulative weight and give good empirical grounds for scepticism about the historicity of the guard story. But there are other considerations that seem to count positively in its favor. For example, if the story is an apologetic fiction designed to preclude the theft of the body by the disciples, then the story is not entirely successful, for there is an obvious time period during which the disciples could have stolen the body undetected, namely between six o'clock Friday night and sometime Saturday morning. Because the tomb is already empty when the angel opens it, it is possible that it was already empty when the guards sealed the stone. Matthew fails to say that the sepulchre was opened and checked before it was sealed, so that it is possible that the disciples had removed the body and replaced the stone Friday night after Joseph's departure. Of course, we would regard such a hypothesis as fanciful, but the point is that if the guard is a Christian invention aimed at refuting the Jewish allegation that the scheming disciples had stolen the body, then the writer has not done a very good job. For the way a truly apologetic legend handles this story, see the Gospel of Peter: the scribes, Pharisees, and elders go on *Friday* to Pilate, who gives them a *Roman* guard; together the soldiers, the scribes, and the elders proceed to the sepulchre, and *they* all roll the great stone across the entrance of the tomb, seal it *seven* times, and keep watch. On Sunday morning *Jesus himself* is seen coming out of the tomb with the two angels, and the witnesses include not only the soldiers and the elders, but also a crowd from Jerusalem and the countryside who had come to see the sepulchre! This is a failsafe apologetic: the Romans and the Jews are the ones responsible for the entombment of Jesus on the same day of his death, they remain there without interruption, and when the tomb is opened, it is not empty, but Jesus comes out before the eyes of a multitude of witnesses.[33] By contrast, in Matthew's story the guard is something of an afterthought; the fact that they were not thought of and posted until the next day could reflect the fact that only Friday night did the Jewish authorities learn that Joseph had, contrary to expectation, placed the body in a tomb, rather than allowing it to be discarded in a common grave. This could have motivated their unusual visit to Pilate the next day.

---

[33] David F. Wright, "Apologetic and Apocalyptic: The Miraculous in the Gospel of Peter," in *Gospel Perspectives*, vol. 6: *The Miracles of Jesus*, ed. David Wenham and Craig Blomberg (Sheffield, England: JSOT Press, 1986), p. 413, maintains that the Gospel of Peter is a theological, not a historical, apologetic. But the many advances over the Matthean account which I note in the text, *e.g.*, moving the placement of the guard from Saturday to Friday, are convincing evidence of a historical apologetic interest.

But perhaps the strongest consideration in favor of the historicity of the guard is the history of polemic presupposed in this story. The Jewish slander that the disciples stole the body was probably the reaction to the Christian proclamation that Jesus was risen.[34] This Jewish allegation is also mentioned in Justin *Dialogue with Trypho* 108. To counter this charge the Christians would need only point out that the guard at the tomb would have prevented such a theft and that they were immobilized with fear when the angel appeared. At this stage of the controversy there is no need to mention the bribing of the guard. This arises only when the Jewish polemic answers that the guard had fallen asleep, thus allowing the disciples to steal the body. The sleeping of the guard could only have been a Jewish development, as it would serve no purpose to the Christian polemic. The further Christian response was that the Jews bribed the guard to say this, and this is where the controversy stood at Matthew's time of writing.

But if this is a probable reconstruction of the history of the polemic, then the historicity of the guard becomes more plausible. In the first place, it seems unlikely that the Christians would invent a fiction like the guard, which a great many, especially their Jewish opponents, would realize never existed. Since the Jewish/Christian controversy no doubt originated in Jerusalem, it is hard to understand how Christians could have tried to refute their opponents' charge with a falsification which would have been plainly untrue, since the Jewish leaders never placed a guard and there were no guards about who claimed to have been stationed at the tomb. But secondly, it seems even more improbable that confronted with this palpable falsehood, their Jewish antagonists would, instead of exposing and denouncing it as such, proceed to create another fabrication, even stupider, that the fictional guard had fallen asleep while the disciples broke into the tomb and absconded with the body. If the guard had not existed, then the Jewish polemic would never have taken the course that it did. Rather the controversy would have stopped right there with the renunciation that any such guard had ever been set by the Jewish authorities. It would never have come to the point that the Christians had to invent a third lie, that the Jews had bribed the imaginary guard.

---

[34] The proclamation may have been in the words repeated twice in Mt. 27:64; 28:7: "He has risen from the dead." Contrary to Grass, *Ostergeschehen*, p. 23, this alone could evoke the response that the disciples stole the body, if the empty tomb were also a historical fact. The Jewish response need not presuppose that the Christians were using the empty tomb itself as an apologetic argument.

So although there are good reasons to doubt the existence of the guard at the tomb, there are also weighty considerations in its favor. It seems best to leave it an open question. Ironically, the value of Matthew's story for the credibility of the resurrection has nothing to do with the guard or with his intention of refuting the allegation that the disciples had stolen the body. The conspiracy theory so dear to eighteenth century Deism has been universally rejected on moral and psychological grounds, so that the guard story as such is really quite superfluous. Guard or no guard, no critic today would defend the view that the disciples robbed the tomb and faked the resurrection. Rather the real value of Matthew's story seems to be the incidental information that Jewish polemic never denied that the tomb was empty but instead tried to explain it away. Thus, the early opponents of the Christians apparently bear witness themselves to the fact of the empty tomb.

THE ANGELIC VISION

Arriving at the tomb, the women find the stone rolled away. According to the Synoptics, the women actually enter the tomb and see an angelic vision. John, however, says Mary Magdalene runs to find Peter and the Beloved Disciple, and only after they come and go from the tomb does she see the angels. Mark's young man is probably intended to be an angel, as is evident from his white robe and the women's reaction.[35]

With regard to the historicity of the angelic appearance, the philosophical presuppositions of many critics tend to guide their exegesis.[36] Since modern man, as

---

[35] On νεανίσκος as an angel, cf. II Macc. 3:26, 33; Lk. 24:4; Gospel of Peter 9; Josephus *Antiquities of the Jews* 5.277. The white robe is traditional for angels (cf. Rev. 9:13; 10:1). In Mark, fear and awe is the typical response to the divine. The other gospels understood Mark's figure as an angel.

[36] For example, Grass asserts, "The legendary character is already simply given in that an angel appears here bodily, instructs the women, and confers upon them an assignment" (Grass, *Ostergeschehen*, p. 20). Koch writes, "When angels come up in the tomb story, then this is a thorn in the side to those who are asking about history, who are interested in what happened. They see therein the proof that history cannot be the subject; when angels appear and speak, then the historical character of the story is done for" (Koch, *Auferstehung*, p. 164). So also M. Dibelius, *Die Formgeschichte des Evangeliums*, 3rd ed. (Tübingen: Mohr, 1959), p. 191; Schenke, *Grab*, p. 71; C. F. Evans, *Resurrection and the New Testament*, SBT 12 (London: SCM Press, 1970), pp. 76-77; Alsup, *Stories*, p. 106; Fischer, *Ostergeschehen*, p. 59; Lorenz Oberlinner, "Die Verkündigung der Auferweckung Jesu im geöffneten und leeren Grab," ZNW 73 (1982): 178. Dunn vigorously protests the facility with which contemporary critics dismiss the historicity of the women's angelic vision:

a child of the Enlightenment, does not believe in the existence of angels, they dismiss the account as legendary and even non-traditional. But at least the exclusion of the narrative from the pre-Markan passion story seems arbitrary, since the earliest Christians certainly believed in the reality of angels and demons, even if we do not, and would not hesitate to relate an account such as is embodied in vs. 5-8.[37] And John confirms that there was a tradition of the women's seeing angels at the tomb, a conclusion strengthened by the fact that he keeps the angels in his account even though their role is oddly superfluous.[38] The unity of the entire account with the pre-Markan passion story has already been explained.

Are there any reasons other than *a priori* philosophical conceptions to regard the account as legendary? About the only grounds would be that the language of the angel is kerygmatic, for example, the Ἰησοῦν...τὸν Ναζαρηνὸν τὸν ἐσταυρωμένον and ἠγέρθη. But the fact that the Christians gave back the message of the angel in language colored by the vocabulary of preaching cannot force the conclusion that the women encountered no angel at all. We ought not to expect the *ipssisima verba* of the angel; in fact Luke leaves out the above words entirely and has instead "Why do you seek the living among the dead?" (Lk. 24:5). And the following words of the angel are not kerygmatic: "He is not here; see the

---

"If we once grant that the women discovered the tomb of Jesus empty..., then we must also allow the possibility, even probability that they had one (or more?) visionary experiences at or near the tomb.[133] It will simply not do to dismiss the claim that the women saw angels as legendary. The status of what they saw may of course be disputed on psychological grounds. That is one thing. But the claim to have seen an angel or had a vision can hardly be disputed on historical grounds simply because post-Enlightenment man no longer believes in angels! Visionary experiences are too common in the history of religions for the account here to be dismissed on that score.[134]

[133] ....

[134] Cf. [P. G. S.] Hopwood [*The Religious Experience of the Primitive Church*, T & T Clark, 1936,] p. 130..." (James W. D. G. Dunn, *Jesus and the Spirit* [London: SCM, 1975], p. 127).
Defending the historicity of the appearance of the angel is Gaechter, "Engelerscheinungen," pp. 191-202.

[37] Osborne, "Resurrection", p. 154. It is highly unlikely that the pre-Markan tradition lacked the angel, for the climax of the story comes with his words in vs. 5-6 and without him the tomb is ambiguous in its meaning (Ulrich Wilckens, "Die Perikope vom leeren Grabe Jesu in der nachmarkinischen Traditionsgeschichte," in *Festschrift für Friedrich Smend* [Berlin: Merseburger, 1963], p. 32; Schenke, *Grab*, pp. 69-71; Alsup, *Stories*, pp. 92-93; Kremer, *Osterevangelien*, pp. 45-47).

[38] Rudolf Bultmann, *Das Evangelium des Johannes*, 19th ed., KEKNT (Göttingen: Vandenhoeck & Ruprecht, 1968), p. 529; Mahoney, *Disciples*, p. 216; Schnackenburg, *Johannesevangelium*, 3: 373.

place where they laid him" (Mk. 16:6).[39] John mentions no message by the angels at all. So at the most the kerygmatic flavoring given to the angel's words merely shows that the story was told in the language of the believers.

Bode objects that if the angel belongs to the historical nucleus of the story, then this is opposed to the women's silence, the rejection of the angel's message by Luke, and the tradition that the apostles were commissioned directly by the Lord.[40] This, however, does not seem necessarily to follow: the women's silence was not permanent or we should not have any story at all; Luke does not reject the angel's message "He has risen," but merely omits the command to go to Galilee, since he will not report Galilean appearances; the angel in no way commissioned the disciples but merely told them to go to Galilee—Jesus is the one who commissions them to world mission.

Many scholars think that the angel is a purely literary device to signal a divine message.[41] But this does not seem to be the case in John; there is just no reason to believe that the Synoptic evangelists regarded the angel as exclusively literary and not literal. Why not both? Bode and Kremer believe the angelic messages would then not differ. But this seems clearly not to be true, as the different rendering of Jesus's words in the Synoptics shows. And really, apart from Luke's change of the Galilean prediction, the angelic messages are quite similar in the Synoptics. Thus, apart from *a priori* presuppositions, the reasons for regarding the angel as unhistorical do not appear to be compelling.

---

[39] It has been suggested that this reflects liturgical language from Christian worship services at the tomb, but such a conjecture is foundationless and has been widely rejected. See Bode, *Easter*, pp. 170-171; Kremer, *Osterevangelien*, p. 44.

[40] Bode, *Easter*, pp. 166-167. Bode also thinks that the omission of the angel gives a better insight into the tomb tradition. Not really; this only leaves one with a Johannine type account (leaving out vs. 11-14a). The key question is whether the disciples saw Jesus in Jerusalem.

[41] Ibid.; Kremer, "Grab," pp. 148-150; Raymond E. Brown, *The Virginal Conception and Bodily Resurrection of Jesus* (London: Geoffrey Chapman, 1973), pp. 122-123. Kremer's attempt to associate the angel with apocalyptic literature applies much better to Matthew than to Mark, whose angel is really quite modest. (Kremer's argument actually appears to be question-begging since it assumes that the other biblical instances of angels are also unhistorical; this judgment conceals a philosophical presupposition just below the surface.)

CHAPTER 6

THE FORETOLD APPEARANCE AND THE WOMEN'S REACTION

Many scholars wish to see v. 7 as a Markan interpolation into the pre-Markan tradition.[42] But the evidence for this seems inconclusive.[43] The fundamental reason for taking 16:7 as an insertion is the belief that 14:28 is an insertion to which 16:7 refers. But what is the evidence that 14:28 is an interpolation? The basic argument seems to be that vs. 27 and 29 read smoothly without it.[44] This, however, seems to be the weakest of reasons for suspecting an insertion (especially since the verses read just as smoothly when v. 28 is left in), for the fact that a sentence can be dropped out of a context without destroying its flow may be entirely coincidental and no indication that the sentence was not originally part of that context.

In fact there seem to be positive reasons for believing 14:28 is not an insertion. Jeremias points out that it continues the image of the shepherd in v. 27; προαγαγεῖν is a technical term of shepherding (cf. Jn. 10:4, 27). The emphasis of Jesus's words lies not on v. 27, but on v. 28: the sheep will not only be scattered but reassembled.[45] Pesch explains that through the use of the *passivum divinum*, the death and resurrection through God are counter-balanced: God strikes the shep-

---

[42] Gardner-Smith, *Resurrection*, p. 136; Bultmann, *Geschichte*, p. 309; Wilhelm Michaelis, *Die Erscheinungen des Auferstandenen* (Basel: Heinrich Majer, 1944, pp. 19-20; Willi Marxsen, *Der Evangelist Markus* (Göttingen: Vandenhoeck & Ruprecht, 1956), pp. 51, 75-76; Grass, *Ostergeschehen*, pp. 21, 120; E. Gutwenger, "Auferstehung und Auferstehungsleib Jesu," *ZKT* 91 (1969): 274; Schenke, *Grab*, pp. 43-47; Evans, *Resurrection*, p. 78; Bode, *Easter*, pp. 35-37; Kremer, "Grab, " p. 151; Reginald H. Fuller, *The Formation of the Resurrection Narratives* (London: SPCK, 1972), p. 53, 60-61; Brown, *Bodily Resurrection*, p. 123.

[43] For example, Schenke's troop of objections against v. 7: (1) it introduces a thought independent of v. 6; (2) ἠγέρθη is not mentioned further; (3) 14:28 is an insertion; (4) v. 7 does not correspond with the women's reaction; (5) v. 7 introduces the apostles and switches to direct speech (Schenke, *Grab*, pp. 43-47). Except for (3) these hardly merit refutation. Verse 7 introduces a thought no more independent of v. 6 than v. 6b of v. 6a. There is no need to mention further the resurrection; having been raised, Jesus is going before the disciples to Galilee. Given Mark's theology, the women's reaction is typical. The introduction of the apostles says nothing for v. 7's being an insertion, nor does direct or indirect speech. By contrast Lindemann defends 16:7 and 14:28 as being traditional, though his argument seems to assume that 16:8 is traditional, which is dubious (Lindemann, "Osterbotschaft des Markus," pp. 307-308, 313). See also Pheme Perkins, *Resurrection: New Testament Witness and Contemporary Reflection* (Garden City, N. Y.: Doubleday & Co., 1984), pp. 120-121.

[44] It is sometimes urged that the Fayum Gospel Fragment, a third century compilation from the gospels which omits v. 28, testifies to a tradition lacking this verse (Grundmann, *Markus*, p. 395). But as a compilation the fragment by its very nature omits material and is no evidence for the absence of v. 28 in the passion tradition. See Lagrange, *Marc*, p. 383; Lane, *Mark*, p. 510; Pesch, *Markusevangelium*, 2: 381.

[45] Joachim Jeremias, *Neutestamentliche Theologie* (Gütersloh: Gerd Mohn, 1971), p. 282.

herd but raises him up. In contrast to the scattering of the disciples is Jesus's reassembling them in Galilee.[46] Pesch also sees a point of contact between Zech. 13:7 and Hos. 6:1-2, which was presupposed by I Cor. 15:4, in the word πατάσσω (נכה). Alone v. 28 is also not an independently intelligible *logion*.[47] And it is not just 14:28 and 16:7 that presuppose each other; it is death *and* resurrection of Christ that is predicted, so that 14:27 and 16:6 belong together as well. It is futile to object that in 14:29 Peter only takes offense at v. 27, not v. 28, for it is to be expected that he objects only to Jesus's telling him they will fall away and not to Jesus's promise to go before them (cf. the same pattern in 8:31-32). On this logic one would have to leave out not only the prediction of the resurrection, but also the striking of the shepherd, since Peter jumps over that as well. There do not seem to be, therefore, very good reasons to regard 14:28 as a redactional insertion, but good reasons to see it as firmly in place.[48]

This means that 16:7 also appears to be in place in the pre-Markan tradition of the passion story. The content of the verse reveals the knowledge of a resurrection appearance of Christ to the disciples in Galilee. Luke, who narrates no Galilean appearances, gives back the angel's words to recall verbatim the prediction made in Galilee that Jesus would be crucified and on the third day rise, but he mentions no coming appearance. It has been asserted that Mk. 16:7 precludes any appearances of Jesus in Jerusalem, but it must be said that Matthew, who repeats the verse, did not think so, and John confirms Matthew's tradition that there was an appearance to the women at or near the tomb. Mark does not say that the disciples were to go or did go immediately to Galilee—Moule makes the attractive suggestion that Mk. 16:7 means "when you return, you will find me there ahead of you."[49] Thus, there could have been Jerusalem appearances prior to their return to Galilee. (This seems especially possible if this is a genuine prediction and not only a retelling after the fact.) In any case, Mark may simply have chosen not

---

[46] Pesch, *Markusevangelium*, 2: 381-382.
[47] These considerations serve to rebut Grundmann, *Markus*, p. 394.
[48] If there is an insertion, it is all of vs. 27-31; cf. Lk. 22:31-34; Jn. 13:36-38 (Lagrange, *Marc*, p. 383; Lane, *Mark*, p. 510).
[49] C. F. D. Moule, "The Post-Resurrection Appearances in Light of Festival Pilgrimages," *NTS* 4 (1957-58): 59. The verb προαγαγεῖν should be taken to mean to go somewhere earlier than someone (Cranfield, *Mark*, p. 429; Lane, *Mark*, p. 510). Cf. Ramsey, *Resurrection*, p. 70. According to Wescott, the prediction of seeing Jesus in Galilee no more excludes Jerusalem appearances than Jn. 20:17 excludes any further earthly appearances (B. F. Wescott, *The Revelation of the Risen Lord*, 2nd ed. [London: Macmillan, 1884], p. 193).

to relate the Jerusalem appearances, perhaps because he regarded the Galilean appearances as for some reason more epochal or theologically significant. Perhaps Mark skips over the Jerusalem appearances because for him Jerusalem was the place of Jesus's rejection and enemies, whereas Galilee was the place where he was believed. There seems to be no basis, however, for the view that Mark has here the Parousia in mind.[50]

Mk. 16:8 has caused a great deal of consternation, not only because it seems to be a very odd note on which to end a book, but also because all the other gospels agree that the women did report to the disciples.[51] But the reaction of fear and awe in the presence of the divine is a typical Markan characteristic.[52] The silence of the women was surely meant just to be temporary,[53] otherwise the account itself could not be part of the pre-Markan passion story.

---

[50] The suggestion of Lohmeyer and Marxsen (Lohmeyer, *Markus*, pp. 355-356; Marxsen, *Markus*, pp. 33-77; also Perrin, *Resurrection*, pp. 27-37) has been rejected pretty much across the board by critics. (1) There is no more reason for Galilee's being the site of the Parousia rather than the site of resurrection appearances; (2) Mark and Matthew both refer in the same terms to a Galilean appearance; (3) ὄψεσθε is not a technical term used for the Parousia. For a critique, see Grass, *Ostergeschehen*, pp. 123-126; Von Campenhausen, *Ablauf*, p. 38; Koch, *Auferstehung*, p. 36; T. A. Burkill, *Mysterious Revelation* (Ithaca, N. Y.: Cornell University Press, 1963), pp. 252-257; Cranfield, *Mark*, p. 468; Ulrich Wilckens, "Der Ursprung der Überlieferung der Erscheinungen des Auferstandenen," in *Dogma und Denkstrukturen*, ed. W. Joest and W. Pannenberg (Göttingen: Vandenhoeck & Ruprecht, 1963), pp. 78-80; Taylor, *Mark*, p. 608; Schweizer, *Markus*, p. 212; Bode, *Easter*, pp. 33-34; Makota Yamauchi, "The Easter Texts of the New Testament: Their Tradition, Redaction and Theology" (Ph. D. thesis, University of Edinburgh, 1972), pp. 154-160.

[51] Although Mark's ending is to say the least abrupt, it has been shown that it is not unprecedented to end a sentence or even a book with the word γάρ. (See texts in R. H. Lightfoot, *The Gospel Message of St. Mark* [Oxford: Clarendon Press, 1950], pp. 80-97, 106-116.) And some critics think the ending is appropriate to Mark, given his use of fear and silence in response to the divine. He has narrated the passion, the burial, and the empty tomb and has foreshadowed the appearances, which is all he needs to do. It is difficult to understand how the ending could have been lost so soon after Mark wrote the gospel that no copies survived to give manuscript attestation of the original conclusion. If the original autograph were immediately damaged somehow, Mark could have resupplied the original ending. Or did he die suddenly in the meantime? For literature on the subject see Taylor, *Mark*, p. 609; also outstanding discussions by Kurt Aland, "Der Schluss des Markus evangeliums," in *L'Évangile*, pp. 435-470; idem, "Der wiedergefundene Markusschluss: Eine methodologische Bemerkung zur Textkritischen Arbeit," *ZTK* 67 (1970): 3-13; idem, "Bemerkungen zum Schluss des Markusevangeliums," in E. E. Ellis and A. Wilcox, ed., *Neotestamentica et Semitica* (Edinburgh: T & T Clark, 1969), pp. 157-180.

[52] See helpful chart and discussion in Bode, *Easter*, pp. 37-39.

[53] So C. F. D. Moule, "St. Mark xvi.8 once more," *NTS* 2 (1955-56): 58-59; Dhanis, "Ensevelissement," p. 389; Cranfield, *Mark*, p. 469; Lagrange, *Marc*, p. 448; I. Howard Marshall, *The Gospel of Luke*, NIGTC (Exeter: Paternoster Press, 1978), p. 887. See the helpful discussion of the women's silence in Bode, *Easter*, pp. 39-44. He distinguishes five possible interpretations: (1) The silence explains why the legend of the empty tomb remained so long unknown. (2) The silence is an instance of Mark's Messianic secret motif. (3) The silence was temporary. (4) The silence served the apologetic purpose of separating the apostles from the empty tomb. (5) The

The Disciples' Inspection of the Tomb

According to Luke the disciples do not believe the women's report (Lk. 24:11). But Luke and John agree that Peter and at least one other disciple rise and run to the tomb to investigate (Lk. 24:12, 24; Jn. 20:2-10). Although Lk. 24:12 was regarded by Wescott and Hort as a Western noninterpolation, its presence in the later discovered p[75] has convinced an increasing number of scholars of its authenticity. There seem to be no good reasons for denying that it was originally part of the Gospel of Luke.[54] This is of exceeding significance, for it proves that there

---

silence is the paradoxical human reaction to divine commands as understood by Mark. But (1) is now widely rejected as implausible, since the empty tomb story is a pre-Markan tradition. (2) is inappropriate in the post-resurrection period when Jesus may be proclaimed as the Messiah. As for (4), there is no evidence that the silence was designed to separate the apostles from the tomb. Mark does not hold that the disciples had fled back to Galilee independently of the women. So there is no implication that the disciples saw Jesus without having heard of the empty tomb. It seems pointless to speak of "apologetics" when Mark does not even imply that the disciples went to Galilee and saw Jesus without hearing the women's message, much less draw some apologetic conclusion as a result of this. In fact there were also traditions that the disciples did visit the tomb after the women told them of their discovery, but Mark breaks off his story before that point. As for (5) this solution seems entirely too subtle, drawing the conclusion that because people talked when Jesus told them not to, therefore, the women, having been told to talk, did not. It also runs aground of 5:19-20. Therefore (3) is most probable. The fear and silence are Markan motifs of divine encounter and were not meant to imply an enduring silence.

[54] Mahoney has tried to argue against the authenticity of the verse (Mahoney, *Disciples*, pp. 41-69). He admits that the verse is attested by a fine text of antiquity and omitted only by a capricious, if old, text. But he presses his case against it by internal criticism: (A) Grammatico-verbal evidence indicates a link between John and Luke: (1) Peter is at the beginning of the verse. (2) Peter runs to the tomb. (3) Both mention μνημεῖον. (4) Both use the aorist participle παρακύψας. (5) Both use the historical present βλέπει. (6) Both have the same object of βλέπει: ὀθόνια. (7) The phrase, found elsewhere only in LXX Num. 24:25, ἀπῆλθεν πρὸς ἑαυτὸν shows contact between the verses. But these only seem to prove that Luke and John share a similar tradition. In fact, as Mahoney acknowledges, Lk. 24:12 has characteristics of Lukan authorship as well: the pleonastic use of ἀναστάς (nine times in Luke, 19 times in Acts); θαυμάζων (12 times in Luke, five times in Acts); τὸ γεγονός (four times in Luke, three times in Acts). Mahoney wants to lay great weight on the historical present βλέπει. But this is not enough, for Luke has ten historical presents in verbs of saying, in addition to historical presents in 8:49; 16:23; 24:36. The historical present in 24:12, 36 could be traditional (See also Kremer, *Osterevangelien*, pp. 108-109, for a brief rebuttal of Mahoney's points). (B) Context: (1) Lk. 24:12 could be removed without disturbing the narrative. (2) It is awkward after ἠπίστουν αὐταῖς. (3) It is superfluous in light of 24:24. (4) The oldest tradition is of the first appearance to Peter, not of his visiting the tomb. These reasons seem weak: Lk. 24:12 may be an independent piece of tradition inserted by Luke, which would explain (1) and (2). In fact, it is not rendered superfluous, but rather is presupposed, by 24:24. In this sense (1) is false. And of course, Peter's role in seeing Jesus is not mutually exclusive with his visit to the tomb, which was less important. (C) Other Western Non-interpolations: Mahoney passes over 24:51-52 and 21:19b-20 to argue that 24:3, 6 and 24:36, 40 are non-Lukan. But it is illegitimate for him to pass over the first pair of verses, for if they are authentic, then credibility is lent to 24:12 as well. The reasons for dropping the verses disputed by Mahoney are not compelling. What especially weakens his case is the fact that in light of 24:24, a later scribe who knew John would definitely have made Peter go with someone else (F. Godet, *Commentar zu*

was tradition not only that the disciples were in Jerusalem (contra the flight to Galilee hypothesis), but also that they knew of the empty tomb. That Luke and John share generically the same tradition is evident not only from the close similarity of Lk. 24:12 to John's account, but also from the fact that Jn. 20:1 most nearly resembles Luke in the number, selection, and order of the elements narrated than any other gospel.[55] Most recent works agree that the visit of the disciples to the tomb is traditional.

The Beloved Disciple

Lk. 24:24 makes it clear that Peter did not go to the tomb alone; John names his companion as the Beloved Disciple. This would suggest that John intends this disciple to be a historical person, and his identification could be correct.[56] The authority of the Beloved Disciple stands behind the gospel as the witness to the accuracy of what is written therein (Jn. 21:24; the verse no doubt applies to the gospel as a whole, not just the epilogue, for the whole gospel enjoys the authentication of this revered disciple, not merely a single chapter[57]), and the identification of his role in the disciples' visit to the empty tomb could be the reminiscence of an eyewitness. So although only Peter was named in the tradition, accompanied by an anonymous disciple(s), the author of the fourth gospel claimed to know who this unnamed disciple was and identifies him.

Whether this identification is correct or not, what seems clear is that the Beloved Disciple was thought to be a real historical person who went with Peter to the empty tomb and whose memories stand behind the fourth gospel as their authentication. Attempts to reduce him to a mere symbol are so speculative that

---

dem Evangelium Lucas, ed. E. R. Wunderlich [Hannover: Carl Meyer, 1872], p. 470; Grundmann, *Lukas*, pp. 439-440). Mahoney's response is faltering: (1) the Beloved Disciple is left out as Johannine, while the unnamed companions are mentioned in 24:24, and (2) in this way the faith of the Beloved Disciple is left out. But the point is surely that a scribe would make disciples go to the tomb precisely because of those mentioned in v. 24 and in John. One could easily leave out the Beloved Disciple's cognomen and even faith without having Peter go to the tomb alone. Mahoney's failure to argue convincingly against the authenticity of Lk. 24:12 ought to leave little doubt that it is genuine.

[55] See Mahoney, *Disciples*, p. 209.
[56] See Brown, *John*, pp. 1119-1120; idem, *The Community of the Beloved Disciple* (New York: Paulist Press, 1979), pp. 22-23.
[57] Leon Morris, *The Gospel according to John*, NICNT (Grand Rapids, Mich.: Wm. B. Eerdmans, 1971), p. 10.

they produce no conviction.[58] Agreement cannot seem to be reached by commentators as to just what he is intended to symbolize.[59] If John wanted him to be a symbol of something else, then he would surely have made the meaning of the symbol clearer; otherwise it seems pointless. Moreover, the fact that a person is used as a symbol does not imply that the individual must be unhistorical. Peter is certainly a historical person, the same Peter that we find in the Synoptics, and it would seem very strange to have him accompanied by a purely symbolic figure who was not also a historical individual. In Jn. 21:20-24 the Beloved Disciple is clearly a historical person widely known in the Christian church as an original disciple who would live to see the Parousia and whose witness underlies the gospel. He was either still alive or had just recently died—that he had been long dead seems excluded by the urgency which correcting the false impression of v. 23 would necessitate. If he was still alive, then his being an unhistorical symbol in chap. 20 seems excluded. By the same token, had he recently died, then, even if his disciples had written chap. 21, they could not have mistakenly identified the symbol of chaps. 1-20 with their historical master, since they knew who he was and what relationship he had had with Jesus and whether he had in fact lain at the Lord's breast, visited the tomb, and so forth. They would also know what was meant by the symbol in 1-20 and not make the impossible identification of the symbolic Beloved Disciple with their own master of whom Jesus had said, "If it is my will that he remain until I come...." If, on the other hand, the role of the Beloved Disciple in the gospel is a redactional retrojection by these disciples of their master, it still follows that he is a historical individual, not a pure symbol. Schnackenburg agrees that the Beloved Disciple is a historical person who, as an eyewitness to some of the later events of the gospel, stands as an authority behind John.[60] But he thinks that the Beloved Disciple is idealized by his followers into

---

[58] Bultmann's view, which has generated no following, is that the Beloved Disciple is Jewish Christianity, which arrives first, while Peter is Gentile Christianity, which comes later. But in Jn. 13 the Beloved Disciple is Gentile Christianity, while Peter is Jewish Christianity. And in Jn. 19 Jesus's mother represents Jewish Christianity while the Beloved Disciple is Gentile Christianity (Bultmann, *Johannes*, pp. 369-370). According to Kragerud, Peter is the Church Office, while the Beloved Disciple is the Paraclete, or spiritual aspect of the church (Alv Kragerud, *Der Lieblingsjünger im Johannesevangelium* [Oslo: Osloer Universitätsverlag, 1959], pp. 53-82).

[59] For a survey of the broad field of alternatives, see Kragerud, *Lieblingsjünger*, pp. 46-51; Thorwald Lorenzen, *Der Lieblingsjünger im Johannesevangelium*, SBS 55 (Stuttgart: Katholisches Bibelwerk, 1971), pp. 74-82.

[60] Schnackenburg, *Johannesevangelium*, 3: 368, 452-456. So also Barnabas Lindars, ed., *The Gospel of John*, NCB (London: Oliphants, 1972), p. 602. Wilckens dismisses the historical aspect

the model Christian and serves to show the reactions of faith of the perfect believer. The evidence for this seems, however, slim. One may theologize on his lying close to Jesus's breast at the supper, but there is nothing here in reality that could not describe a historical situation. The same holds true of Jesus's giving over his mother to this disciple in 19:26-27. In 21:7 he exclaims to Peter, "It is the Lord!" but even he did not recognize Jesus until after the miraculous sign. Most importantly, in 20:8-9, although perhaps he alone comes to faith, he shares in the shortcoming of the other disciples that they did not believe in the resurrection of Jesus on the basis of Scripture alone. The point of v. 9, which rings at first so odd after v. 8, is the same point emphasized elsewhere in John, that the disciples were lacking in insight into the Scriptures until after the resurrection (cf. 2:22; 12:16).[61] Far from being the perfect Christian of post-Easter faith, the Beloved Disciple also shared in the disciples' ignorance of the Scripture and therefore did not have any inkling of the resurrection until that moment in the tomb when he saw and believed. In the same way that Thomas should have believed on the basis of the testimony of the disciples but instead saw and believed (v. 29), so the disciples should have believed on the basis of the testimony of Scripture, but instead they saw and believed. The ideal believer of perfect faith would have believed on the basis of Scripture alone. But the Beloved Disciple, like Thomas, saw and believed, for as yet they did not know the Scripture, that he must rise from the dead (v. 9). So even if the Beloved Disciple was revered by his pupils, and no doubt he was, they do not seem to have idealized him into the perfect believer and placed him in the narratives as a model. What then is the role of the Beloved Disciple? Quite simply, it seems to be that of a historical witness: "This is the disciple who is bearing testimony to these things, and who has written these things, and we know that his testimony is true" (Jn. 21:24; cf. 19:35). The Be-

---

of the Beloved Disciple and regards him as a symbolic representative of the true, perfectly believing disciple (Wilckens, *Auferstehung*, p. 151).

[61] So Bultmann, *Johannes*, pp. 530-531; Bode writes,

"Verse nine means that if they had understood the scripture they would not have had to visit the tomb, because from the scripture they would have understood that Jesus...was certainly going to rise from the dead. If he was to rise, then his body would no longer...have remained in the tomb. Thus there would have not been a need to check an empty tomb..." (Bode, *Easter*, p. 81).

Similarly Kremer states that v. 9 means "...they really should have already believed in the resurrection before the inspection of the open grave" (Kremer, *Osterevangelien*, p. 169).

loved Disciple was there as one of the *dramatis personae*, it is claimed, and thus the gospel is trustworthy.

If the Beloved Disciple in chap. 20 is, then, conceived as a historical witness of the events related, is his presence an unhistorical, redactional addition? I have suggested that he may be the unnamed companion of Peter in the tradition received by Luke and John. But Schnackenburg thinks that few words need to be said to prove that he is an unhistorical addition: in vs. 2, 3, he is easily set aside; the competitive race to the tomb is redactional; v. 8 is in style and content from the evangelist; and v. 9 refers in reality to Mary and Peter.[62] But these considerations do not seem to prove that the Beloved Disciple was not historically present, but only that he was not mentioned in the tradition. That could have been proved from Lk. 24:12 alone. What I am suggesting is that the reminiscences of the Beloved Disciple are employed by the evangelist to supplement and fill out his tradition. Thus the first three considerations ought not to surprise us. Indeed, the third consideration supports the fact that the Beloved Disciple's role here was not added later to the gospel by any supposed editor who tacked on chap. 21. That ὄν ἐφίλει instead of ὄν ἠγάπα is used in v. 2 also seems to indicate that the evangelist himself wrote these words and not a later redactor. In fact, the unity and continuity of vs. 2-10 seem to preclude that the evangelist wrote only of Peter and Mary's visit and that the Beloved Disciple was artfully inserted by a later editor. Lk. 24:24 reveals that Peter did not go to the tomb alone, so one cannot exclude that the Beloved Disciple went with him. As for v. 9, it refers to the disciples in v. 10 (Mary is not even mentioned after v. 2) and is not part of the pre-Johannine tradition, being, as I have indicated, typical for John. Thus, the evangelist, who knew the Beloved Disciple and wrote on the basis of his memories, includes his part in these events. To say that the evangelist simply invented the figure of the Beloved Disciple makes 21:24 a deliberate fabrication, ignores the close affinities between chaps. 1-20 and 21, makes it difficult to explain how then the person of the Beloved Disciple should come to exist and why he is inserted in the narratives, and renders unintelligible the widespread concern over his death. The evangelist and the gospel certainly stem out of the same circle that appended chap. 21 and adds its signature in 21:24c. Therefore, it seems to me that the role of the Beloved Disciple in 20:2-10 can only be that of a historical participant

---

[62] Schnackenburg, *Johannesevangelium*, 3: 359-360.

whose memories fill out the tradition received. Of the alternatives, this seems to be the most plausible explanation.[63]

The Rivalry Between Peter and the Beloved Disciple

Upon hearing Mary's startling news, Peter and the Beloved Disciple run toward the tomb; the latter reaches the tomb first but, hesitating outside, does not enter; Peter, however, apparently charges into the tomb without hesitation. Although it is often said that we see reflected here, as elsewhere in the gospel, some sort of rivalry between Peter and the Beloved Disciple in the early Johannine community, the grounds for this assertion ought perhaps to be re-examined.[64] In the fourth gospel, the two are close friends, and the situations in which they are described could be quite historical.[65] (This is particularly so if the Beloved Disci-

---

[63] I find it implausible to believe either that the Beloved Disciple should have told his students that he was there when he was not or that the entire Johannine community should assert that their master had taken part in certain historical events when they knew he had not. See excellent comments by Brown, *John*, pp. 1127-1129; idem, *Community*, p. 31.

[64] Note, as Brown and Schnackenburg agree, that those who hold to the rivalry hypothesis cannot also hold that the Beloved Disciple is purely symbolic (Raymond E. Brown, Karl P. Donfried, John Reumann, *Saint Pierre dans le Nouveau Testament*, Ld 79 [Paris: Les éditions du Cerf, 1974], p. 165).

[65] So Brown, *John*, pp. 1006-1007. But Brown still wants to believe the Beloved Disciple reaches the tomb first because he "loves more." More recently, Brown seems to have succumbed to the conventional wisdom in seeing the Beloved Disciple set over against Peter in the fourth gospel. He believes that Johannine Christians regarded themselves as closer to Jesus and more perceptive than Christians of the apostolic churches, as evidenced by the one-upmanship of the Beloved Disciple over Peter. Brown substantiates his view by pointing out that while the other disciples scattered at the crucifixion (16:32), the Beloved Disciple remains at the foot of the cross (19:26-27), that while Peter denied Jesus (18:17, 25) and needs rehabilitation (21:15-17), the Beloved Disciple does not, that while Peter does not see the significance of the graveclothes, the Beloved Disciple does (20:8-10), and that while Peter does not recognize the Lord, the Beloved Disciple does (Brown, *Community*, pp. 34, 178). But 16:32 refers to all the disciples, including the Beloved Disciple, and 18:15 says that Peter and another disciple in fact followed Jesus. The Beloved Disciple's being at the cross is historically credible, and no contrast with Peter is implied. Similarly, Peter's denial is historically credible and no contrast to the Beloved Disciple is implied. The scene in 21:15-17 is best understood as a commissioning, not a rehabilitation, and actually exalts Peter to a position not enjoyed by the Beloved Disciple. It is not clear from John's narrative that Peter does not also perceive the significance of the graveclothes, and more importantly, the Beloved Disciple shares in Peter's obtuseness in not believing simply on the basis of Scripture. Finally, the appearance story, like the empty tomb investigation, is told from the perspective of the Beloved Disciple so that we have no way of knowing whether Peter recognized Jesus when the Beloved Disciple did. It is very interesting that even more recently Brown seems to have undercut this supposed one-upmanship by contending that John 21 is designed to recommend Peter to Johannine readers! The three-fold question and answer gives assurance that Peter is a genuine disciple and that Jesus has given him pastoral authority, a role which is not given to the Beloved Disciple. In fact, Brown feels constrained to comment that the Beloved Disciple is not of less dig-

ple was John the son of Zebedee; there is no evidence that any church group saw a competitive relationship for prominence or leadership between Peter and John or played one off against the other.) Running to the tomb is the natural thing to do (cf. Jn. 20:2a) and is traditional (Lk. 24:12). That the Beloved Disciple should outrun Peter seems unremarkable, especially if he is younger; to hesitate before the open door of a tomb where a man had recently been buried would be the natural reaction of any of us. But true to his character, Peter brashly enters without hesitation. Those who see a rivalry here suggest that the Beloved Disciple thus wins the race to the tomb, but Peter evens the score by entering first.[66] It has even been suggested that Peter is not really earning any points here; the evangelist is just allowing him to catch up so that the Beloved Disciple can give him another drubbing by coming to faith first![67] Mahoney thinks that the arrival at the tomb must be contrived because, what with the later gospels' increasing desire to verify the empty tomb, the disciples would otherwise have been made to enter directly.[68] But Mahoney's view is predicated on the position that Lk. 24:12 is not in Luke and the disciples' visit is a late Johannine redaction. If this is not true, one cannot *ohne weiteres* ascribe the origin of the story of the visit to increasing interest in verifying the tomb. The tradition could be quite old. Therefore, the historicity of the hesitation at the entrance cannot be automatically precluded because of a supposedly increasing interest in verifying the empty tomb, for the only evidence for the increasing interest is the tradition itself. John's fuller story could well be the result of historical reminiscence. It does not seem implausible that Peter's companion should stop at the door, stoop, and peer into the dark tomb, but that Peter should charge right in past him.

Entering the tomb and seeing the graveclothes, the Beloved Disciple, writes John, saw and believed, or came to faith.[69] It is not clear whether John intends us

---

nity than Peter, even though he did not die a martyr's death like Peter (Raymond E. Brown, *The Epistles of John*, Anch Bib 30 [Garden City, N. Y.: Doubleday & Co., 1982], p. 111)! I cannot help but suspect that the supposed rivalry of Peter and the Beloved Disciple is a construct of the critic's mind.

[66] For example, Kremer, *Osterbotschaft*, pp. 90-91; cf. Pierre Benoit, *The Passion and Resurrection of Jesus Christ*, trans. B. Weatherhead (New York: Herder & Herder, 1969; London: Darton, Longman & Todd, 1969), p. 252; Lorenzen, *Lieblingsjünger*, p. 32.

[67] Kragerud, *Lieblingsjünger*, p. 30. By contrast Marxsen thinks the race is designed to bring out the primacy of Peter (Marxsen, *Resurrection*, p. 58)!

[68] Mahoney, *Disciples*, p. 246.

[69] Given Johannine usage, "saw and believed" indicates religious faith in the true sense of the word, not some mundane belief, *e.g.*, that Mary was right, the tomb was empty (Brown, *John*, pp.

to understand that Peter also came to faith in that moment. Bultmann believes that the fourth gospel intends to convey the impression that Peter also believed; otherwise the opposition between the two would have been mentioned.[70] If the rivalry hypothesis were correct, this consideration would have a good deal of force. Since John does not play off Peter's disbelief against the Beloved Disciple's faith, the presumption of a rivalry ought to be called into question. Far from suggesting a rivalry, the remark that the Beloved Disciple saw and believed sounds like the personal reminiscence of a man who was there and upon whose heart the truth at that moment first began to dawn.

In the other stories in which Peter and the Beloved Disciple appear, the grounds for seeing a competition between them seem equally dubious. In Jn. 13 the Beloved Disciple at Peter's prompting asks Jesus the betrayer's identity. The situation seems thoroughly realistic, and there is no suggestion that the Beloved Disciple is some sort of mediator between Jesus and Peter. Similarly, in Jn. 21:7 that the Beloved Disciple says to Peter, "It is the Lord" seems quite plausible and in no way suggests that the Beloved Disciple is more attuned to Jesus than Peter. Peter's jumping into the sea is in character for him; it seems fanciful to see this as the evangelist's attempt to "even the score" again between the two. And in Jn. 21:20-23 there seems to be no competition in view at all; indeed, the point is to show that the Beloved Disciple will die just like Peter. We have here an attempt to correct a misimpression that the Beloved Disciple was to live to the Parousia. The hypothesis that the Beloved Disciple and Peter are being played off against each other in the gospel has difficulty explaining why the Beloved Disciple is introduced alone in 19:26-27, 35 and Peter alone in 21:9-19. Is it so implausible that the Beloved Disciple and Peter were in fact companions and close friends and

---

1005-1006; Bode, *Easter*, p. 79). Kremer's assertion that if one accepts this information as historical, then the fact that the Beloved Disciple believed earlier than Peter stands in "*krassem Widerspruch*" to the conviction of the New Testament that Jesus appeared first to Simon (Kremer, *Osterevangelien*, p. 177) is groundless, since John does not say Jesus appeared first to the Beloved Disciple, which would be necessary to generate a contradiction. Besides, what is the evidence for this conviction of the New Testament of a first appearance to Peter? According to Matthew and John, Jesus appeared first to the women. Paul and Luke do not mention them probably because they are not legal witnesses. And Luke does not even say unequivocally that Jesus appeared to Peter before the Emmaus disciples. The inner faith of the Beloved Disciple, which is remembered here, does not seem to contradict the New Testament data.

[70] Bultmann, *Johannes*, p. 530; so also Marxsen, *Resurrection*, p. 58.

so naturally appear together in certain narratives, just as Peter and the sons of Zebedee do in the Synoptics?

The Graveclothes

According to the tradition, the disciples found only the graveclothes lying in the tomb. John adds a fact that had perhaps left a personal impression on his source: the face cloth was rolled up in a place by itself. If this was a jaw band, then perhaps it was lying still in its oval shape. There are two theories as to why John puts so much emphasis on the graveclothes: (1) The clothes were still in their wrapped-up shape, and the body had passed through them, leaving them like an unbroken, though collapsed, cocoon. (2) The presence of the graveclothes indicated that the body had not been stolen, since robbers would not have bothered to unwrap the body. Since John believed that Jesus after the resurrection could materialize and de-materialize at will (20:19, 26), it is quite possible that he conceived the resurrection body as passing through the enveloping graveclothes, in contrast to Lazarus, who stumbled from the grave bound hand and foot.[71] But there is no evidence that the Jews wrapped their dead like mummies, and if the burial were in a shroud, then the jaw band should have been found *inside* the shroud, not in a place by itself. It is sometimes alleged that the chief problem with theory (1) is that the unbelief of Peter is then difficult to explain, since an unbroken cocoon would have been obvious to all. But, contrary to received opinion, it is not clear that Peter did not also come to faith while in the tomb. The narrative, like that in Jn. 21, is written from the perspective of the Beloved Disciple and so leaves Peter's reaction out of account, concentrating instead on the Beloved Disciple's reaction. But, as Thiede points out, the construction of v. 8 with its repetition of καὶ and the plural verb in v. 9 could indicate by implication that Peter also saw and believed.[72] It might be said that in Lk. 24:12 Peter merely returns home wondering at what had happened. But we must not be hasty here: for Luke uses θαυμάζω to indicate wonder, not in the sense of "to be puzzled," but in the sense "to marvel at," "to be amazed at" (1:63; 2:18, 33; 11:14; 24:41; Acts 3:12; 4:13). In Luke we have the same course of events that we read in John: the

---

[71] Barrett, *John*, p. 563.
[72] Carsten P. Thiede, *Simon Peter* (Exeter: Paternoster, 1986), p. 89. Critics are divided on whether John implies that Peter came to faith; see Schnackenburg, *Johannesevangelium*, 3:369.

stooping and seeing the graveclothes, the reaction of wonder or faith, and the departure home. It might be thought that Peter's going home is anti-climactic and not indicative of his having come to faith; but John sees no inconsistency with the Beloved Disciple's doing precisely this. Given Luke's vocabulary, Peter may return marveling at what had happened (cf. Lk. 1:18, 20). This could help to explain the abruptness of v. 34; for if Peter had already told the others of what he thought had happened, then the appearance to him confirmed to them that the Lord was risen indeed, as he had said. Perhaps the strongest argument against Peter's coming to faith along with the Beloved Disciple is that in John, Mary continues to believe that someone had stolen Jesus's body. While we might imagine the Beloved Disciple's keeping his thoughts to himself, pondering them in his heart, we can hardly think that if the truth of Jesus's resurrection had dawned on both him and Peter that the two would keep it from Mary. On the other hand, Mary rather disappears from John's narrative after v. 2, and one could hold that she arrived again at the tomb much later, after the two disciples had departed or, again, that John has interrupted the appearance to Mary story by inserting vs. 2-10, thereby creating this apparent difficulty. All of this is, of course, extremely conjectural and no sure conclusion is possible; my only point is that the widely accepted view that Peter did not come to faith in the resurrection while inspecting the tomb is not incontestable.[73]

In any event theory (1) still has the first consideration mentioned above against it, so that theory (2) seems preferable. It is more likely that the graveclothes were lying neatly on the bench, so that the Beloved Disciple, upon seeing them, realized the body had not been taken from the tomb; but this could only mean—! Whether Peter also grasped this clue is, as I say, uncertain.

Objections to the Story's Historicity

It might be urged against the historicity of the disciples' visit to the tomb that the disciples had fled Friday night to Galilee and so were not present in Jerusalem. But not only does Mk. 14:50 not seem to contemplate this, but it is implausible to think that the disciples, fleeing from the garden, would return to where

---

[73] In a recent review of this issue, Byrne argues that the evangelist does not highlight Peter's faith because it is the faith of the Beloved Disciple that is to have center stage. Therefore, Peter's coming to faith is left an open question (Brendan Byrne, "The Faith of the Beloved Disciple and the Community in John 20," *JSNT* 23 [1985]: 93).

they were staying, grab their things, and keep on going all the way back to Galilee. And scholars who do support such a flight must also prove that the denial of Peter is unhistorical, since it presupposes the presence of the disciples in Jerusalem. But there seems insufficient reason to regard this tradition, attested in all four gospels, as unhistorical.[74] In its favor is the fact that it seems improbable that the early Christians should invent a tale concerning the apostasy of the man who was their leader.

Sometimes it is said that the disciples could not have been in Jerusalem, since they are not mentioned in the trial, execution, or burial stories. But an obvious and, I think, plausible answer to this is that the disciples were hiding "for fear of the Jews," just as the gospels indicate. There is no reason why the passion story would want to portray the church's leaders as cowering in seclusion while only the women dared to venture about openly, were this not historical; the disciples could have been made to flee to Galilee while the women stayed behind. This would even have had the apologetic advantage of making the appearances unexpected by keeping the empty tomb unknown to the disciples. But, no, the pre-Markan passion story says, "But go, tell his disciples and Peter that he is going before you to Galilee; there you will see him..." (Mk. 16:7). So the disciples were probably in Jerusalem, but lying low.

Besides this, it is not in fact true that the disciples are missing entirely from the scene. All the gospels record the denial of Peter while the trial of Jesus was proceeding; John adds that there was another disciple with him, perhaps the Beloved Disciple (Jn. 18:15). According to Luke, at the execution of Jesus, "All his acquaintances...stood at a distance and saw these things" (Lk. 23:49). It would have been quite dangerous for the disciples to have observed the crucifixion at close hand, for it was forbidden to weep for crucified victims on pain of being crucified oneself; even women and children could be crucified for such displays of sympathy.[75] Hence, the disciples perhaps viewed the crucifixion from the city

---

[74] So Brown, *John*, pp. 840-841; 983. Von Campenhausen, *Ablauf*, p. 44, also maintains the presence of disciples in Jerusalem. His view that Peter, inspired by the empty tomb, led the disciples back to Galilee to see Jesus assumes that the empty tomb awakened resurrection faith and is predicated on a doubtful interpretation of Lk. 22:31, which says nothing about Peter's convincing the others to believe that Jesus was risen. Kremer regards Peter's visit to the tomb as historical, since he was in Jerusalem, as the denial story shows (Kremer, "Grab," p. 158).

[75] See Schottroff, "Frauen am Grabe Jesu," pp. 5-6.

wall opposite Golgotha, known today as Suk es-Zeit.[76] John says that the Beloved Disciple was at the cross with Jesus's mother and bore witness to what happened there (Jn. 19:26-27, 35). Attempts to interpret the Beloved Disciple as a symbol here or to lend a purely theological meaning to the passage seem to have been fruitless. Though Mahoney admits that no consensus has been reached as to what is meant theologically by John here, he staunchly insists that it cannot be historical because the disciples fled[77]—which appears to be a *petitio principii*. Mahoney thinks the mother is an anti-docetic reminder and that the story shows the break with Jesus's earthly life as he discharges his responsibility to his mother. But surely the crucifixion is reminder enough of Jesus's humanity! Besides, Docetists did not necessarily deny that the man Jesus was born and died, only that the divine Son himself became incarnate as Jesus. They gladly held the divine Christ inspired the man Jesus from his baptism to his crucifixion. In that case, Mary's presence says nothing against Docetism. Moreover, the break with Jesus's early life seems to be more in view in the appearance to Mary Magdalene (Jn. 20:17). But the discharging of his responsibility toward his mother is just the sort of merciful act that we could expect from Jesus. Again, the source of this incident could be the memory of the Beloved Disciple himself. So it is not true that the disciples are completely absent during the low point in the course of events prior to the resurrection. There are therefore a number of traditions that the disciples were in Jerusalem during the weekend; that at least two of them visited the tomb ought not, therefore, to be excluded.

It is often asserted by scholars that the story of the disciples' visit to the tomb is an apologetic development designed to shore up the weak witness of the women.[78] Not only does there not seem to be any proof for this, but against it stand the traditions that the disciples were in Jerusalem. For if the women did find the tomb empty on Sunday morning, as most critics today are willing to ad-

---

[76] Thiede, *Simon Peter*, p. 87.
[77] Mahoney, *Disciples*, p. 100.
[78] Lake, *Evidence*, p. 189; Marxsen, *Resurrection*, p. 59; Wilckens, *Auferstehung*, p. 67; Fuller, *Formation*, p. 136. Gardner-Smith states that John wanted the men to be the first to inspect the empty tomb, so that he puts the angels out of place, leaving them nothing to do (Gardner-Smith, *Resurrection*, p. 36). This does not follow at all, for the angels could have told Mary after the departure of the disciples that Jesus is risen, he is going to Galilee, *etc.*; then would follow Jesus's appearance, as in Matthew. According to Benoit, *Resurrection*, pp. 256, 259, the tradition of Peter's visit to the tomb is old and reliable. Brown argues that because in the original story the tomb did not produce faith, the story was not invented for apologetic purposes (Brown, *John*, p. 1002).

mit, and reported this to the disciples, then it seems implausible that the disciples would sit idly by, not caring to check out the women's news. That one or two of them should run back to the tomb with the women, even if only to satisfy their doubts that the women were mistaken, seems very likely.

CHAPTER 7

THE APPEARANCE NARRATIVES

THE APPEARANCE TO THE WOMEN

Traditional Material

As we turn from the empty tomb to the resurrection appearances of Christ, we find that the first appearance is to the women who visited the tomb (Mt. 28:9-10; Jn. 20:11-18). It is likely that we have here traditional material concerning the same appearance: the gospels agree that women (of whom John focuses on Mary Magdalene) visited the tomb, that shortly thereafter Jesus appeared to them and gave them a charge to convey to the disciples, and that they carried out his instructions. Especially significant is that the action of the women in grasping Jesus's feet (Mt. 28:9) seems to be presupposed in Jesus's words to Mary, "Do not hold me" (Jn. 20:17). A remarkable verbal similarity between the two passages is the use of "brothers" for "disciples" (Mt. 28:10: τοῖς ἀδελφοῖς μου; Jn. 20:17: πρὸς τοὺς ἀδελφούς). That the disciples are in view here and not Jesus's earthly brothers is evident from the fact that the women carry the message to the eleven. Against the suggestion that this represents later Christian usage and is only coincidental here stands the fact that these two verses are unique in all the resurrection stories in using "brothers" for the disciples—the evangelists always speak of the disciples or the apostles or the Eleven or the Twelve. Matthew frequently uses "brethren" for "disciples" in his gospel (see especially 12:46-50; 23:8; see also 5:22, 23, 24, 47; 7:3, 4, 5; 18:15, 21, 35; 25:40), but it is striking that the only other verse where "brethren" appears in John sharply distinguishes between the original disciples and the Christian brethren who are later believers ("The saying spread abroad among the *brethren* that this *disciple* was not to die" [Jn. 21:23a]). John never uses ἀδελφός for the disciples but reserves the term for blood relations or in 21:23 for later Christians. Thus it seems unlikely that the use of "brothers" in 20:17 is a Johannine redaction reflecting later Christian usage, for this has not infected his gospel at any other point; quite the contrary, the terms are kept distinct.

As for Matthew, matters of vocabulary and style cannot determine whether redaction or tradition is responsible for vs. 9-10. Assuming that John is independent of Matthew's gospel, it is most plausible that John and Matthew share a tradition. Though one might seek to explain the individual similarities of the passages in other ways, the cumulative weight of the parallels suggests that neither passage is purely redactional, but that they both remember the same event.

Some Points of Comparison

In Matthew the appearance to the women is related right after the story of the empty tomb in Mk. 16:1-8. Were it not for the fact that Matthew writes, "So they departed quickly from the tomb with fear and great joy, and ran to tell his disciples" (Mt. 28:8), one would be tempted to think Jesus's appearance occurred at this point to halt the stunned and fleeing women of Mk. 16:8 and to reiterate the instructions which they had disobeyed to go tell the disciples. Some think vs. 8-9 reflect an appearance story in a lost ending to Mark in which the appearance did serve to overturn the women's silence in Mk. 16:8. But then it seems difficult to understand why Matthew should abandon this motif in favor of what seems to be a somewhat redundant appearance. In John the appearance also occurs after an angelic vision at the tomb, but Mary is standing and crying, not running to the disciples, since she has not yet heard that Jesus is risen. Interestingly in John, Jesus also essentially repeats the angels' words, though the words are different in Matthew and John.

John's dramatic scene in which Mary confronts and recognizes Jesus is one of the most tender and lovely stories of the gospels. In Matthew, there is no difficulty recognizing Jesus, but in John we find a motif that also appears in two other resurrection stories (the Emmaus and Lake of Tiberias appearances) that Jesus is not at first recognized. Though in the Tiberias appearance, the difficulty of recognition could theoretically be due to distance, it is idle to contend that the Emmaus disciples do not recognize Jesus on the road because they do not look him full in the face as they walk side by side or that Mary mistakes Jesus for the gardener because she cannot see through her tears. Nor does it seem legitimate to appeal to Paul's doctrine of the spiritual body as grounds for non-recognition, since the change envisioned by Paul was apparently not one that changed the facial appearance but the perishable nature of the body. Rather the cause of the non-recognition seems to have been supernatural: "But their eyes were kept from recognizing him...And their eyes were opened and they recognized him" (Lk. 24:16, 31). When Jesus speaks her name, then Mary's eyes are similarly opened and she immediately recognizes him (cf. Jn. 10:3).

Jesus's words μή μου ἅπου in the present imperative are a command to halt either an action about to be done or an action being done. Comparison with Matthew's account makes it probable that Mary has fallen at Jesus's feet to hold and kiss them,[1] and that Jesus's command means, "Do not cling to me."[2] The verbs used in Mt. 28:9 and Jn. 20:17 can be used interchangeably, as in Mt. 8:15; Mk. 1:31. The message Jesus gives Mary to convey is not that he will go before them to Galilee, but that he is ascending. The difficulty here is that the ascension of Jesus seems to be placed before the appearance to the Twelve rather than afterwards as in Luke. And why would it be improper for Mary to touch Jesus before the ascension, but not improper for Thomas afterwards? Brown has argued that the concept of ascension is different for John than for Luke.[3] For John it means glorification, but for Luke it is simply the cessation of appearances. The reason Jesus puts Mary off is that she had misunderstood Jn. 14:18-19; 16:22 in terms of a permanent earthly presence of Jesus with the disciples instead of in terms of the presence of the Holy Spirit. Brown thinks that this interpretation would remove

---

[1] So Rudolf Schnackenburg, *Das Johannesevangelium*, 3 vols., HTKNT 4 (Freiburg: Herder, 1976), 3:376; Jacob Kremer, *Die Osterevangelien—Geschichten um Geschichte* (Stuttgart: Katholisches Bibelwerk, 1977), p. 172. On kissing the feet see Tractate Kethubboth 63a.

[2] Raymond E. Brown, *The Gospel according to John*, Anch Bib 29A (Garden City, N. Y.: Doubleday & Co., 1970), p. 992; Reginald H. Fuller, *The Formation of the Resurrection Narratives* (London: SPCK, 1972), p. 138; Grant Osborne, "History and Theology in the Resurrection Narratives: a Redactional Study" (Ph.D. thesis, University of Aberdeen, 1974), p. 287; M. McGhee, "A Less Theological Reading of John 20:17," *JBL* 105 (1986): 299-302.

[3] Brown, *John*, pp. 1012-1014.

the discrepancy between John and Luke concerning the time of the ascension, since the same event is not in view.

But the problem with Brown's view is that it implies that Mary sees an appearance of Jesus in his unglorified state. This seems wrong—Mary's words are the same as the disciples': "I have seen the Lord." Brown tries to escape this conclusion by arguing that the time lag is accidental and unimportant; for John the resurrection is the glorification. But this reply seems unconvincing, for how could Jesus then possibly say, "I have not yet ascended to the Father?" John forces the time lag upon us; Brown cannot escape it. When Jesus met Mary he had not yet ascended. It is more plausible that John did not equate the resurrection-glorification of Jesus, which was one event, with the ascension, which was another event. Perhaps he means, "Do not cling to me, to keep me here, since I have not ascended to the Father yet; but tell my brethren I will ascend, *etc.*" When Mary sees Jesus he is thus raised and glorified, but since his ascension is a future event, she need not worry about hanging on to him.[4] The difficulty with this interpretation is that the present tense would seem to indicate the contrary, that Jesus is in the process of ascending and Mary must not halt him as he is underway. But the present tense can mean "I am about to ascend to my Father," which would eliminate the difficulty. For John, as much as for Luke, the ascension may have simply closed the series of appearances.

Traditions Behind John 20:1-18

The traditions in Jn. 20:1-18 are notoriously difficult to separate. The narrative is so smooth and continuous as it now stands that it is virtually impossible to pick out specific verses as marking the borders of different traditions. Most of the criteria used by scholars to spot the traditions seem somewhat contrived. Brown, for example, points to the following "difficulties": (1) Mary comes to the tomb alone, but speaks as "we"; (2) she says the body is stolen but does not look into the tomb until v. 11; (3) there is a duplication in the description of Peter and the Beloved Disciple: (a) two "to" phrases in v. 2, (b) literally "Peter went out...and they were coming" in v. 3, (c) repetition of what is seen in vs. 5, 6, (d) the contrast between vs. 8, 9; (4) the faith of the Beloved Disciple has no effect on the others; (5) it is

---

[4] So C. F. D. Moule, "The Individualism of the Fourth Gospel," *NT* 5 (1962) :175; James D. G. Dunn, *Baptism in the Holy Spirit* (London: SCM, 1970), pp. 176-177.

not clear how or why Mary got back to the tomb in v. 11; (6) she sees angels instead of the burial clothes in v. 12; (7) her conversation with the angels does not advance the story; and (8) she turns to Jesus twice.[5]

But while (1) shows a trace of tradition, it gives no clue of separate traditions combined here. The inference mentioned in (2) would be quite natural, and vs. 1 and 11 could not have once been contiguous, since then there would be no reason for the weeping before she looks into the tomb (cf. v. 13). Point (3) again shows no separation of traditions, but only that the evangelist has perhaps filled out his tradition with personal information. In any case, (3a) is perfectly acceptable grammar; (3b) is no duplication when the words substituted by ellipsis points are restored: "and the other disciple"; (3c) is not a simple duplication, since v. 7 goes with v. 6; and (3d) shows no separation of tradition, since v. 9 is the evangelist's own comment. As for (4), the Beloved Disciple's keeping these things in his heart until he had thought them through or further events clarified matters, rather than perhaps raising false hope by vocalizing them, seems perfectly plausible. With regard to (5), it is naturally assumed that she ran back with or after the disciples whom she fetched. Point (6) has little weight—of course, she would notice two angels suddenly sitting in the tomb rather than the burial clothes which had already been seen! Again, (7) indicates traditional material but says nothing about separate traditions. Point (8) seems rather trivial, since the first turning would otherwise have to belong to a separate tradition in vs. 11-14, which only increases the difficulties, since this looks more like an empty tomb than an appearance story.

Hartmann reconstructs a text which he thinks lay before the evangelist which leaves vs. 1-11a pretty much intact except that the Beloved Disciple is not included, skips over vs. 11b-14a, and continues again from v. 14b.[6] His reasons for excerpting 11b-14a, which he thinks were not added by the evangelist, but a redactor, include: (1) Mary is weeping before she looks inside, leaving the stooping unmotivated; (2) the dialogue is artificial and fits better with Jesus's words; and (3) the singular of v. 13 contrasts with the plural of v. 2. But (1) cannot preclude that Mary should want to look into the tomb a second time; one must not expect

---

[5] Brown, *John*, p. 995; cf. Schnackenburg, *Johannesevangelium*, 3:355-356. Robinson complains that Brown's so-called inconsistencies are merely infelicities or repetitions in the telling (J. A. T. Robinson, *The Priority of John*, ed. J. F. Coakley [London: SCM, 1985], p. 290).

[6] Gert Hartmann, "Die Vorlage der Osterberichte in Joh 20," *ZNW* 55 (1964): 197-220.

her to act like a passionless robot. As for (2), Jesus's words could be a repetition of the angels', not vice versa. And (3) could be accounted for as a rewriting of the evangelist's hand rather than of a later redactor's. The fact that angels appear in the synoptic tradition also strongly suggests that the angelic appearance is traditional. Why else should a later redactor wish to insert it? The fact is that the Johannine chapter is so well-written that, were it not for the Synoptics, we should have little grounds for positing multiple traditions.

Given the Synoptics, however, it is evident that there were separate traditions which are reflected in John. First, there is a tradition of the women's visit to the empty tomb, combined with an angelic vision. Second, there is the tradition of Peter and another disciple's visit to the tomb. And third, there is a tradition that Jesus appeared near the tomb to the women. That these traditions were separate is evident from the fact that not all the gospels include them. Interestingly, John alone attests all three of these traditions. Because these traditions are separate, the chronological order is difficult to reconstruct. Logically, one would expect (1) the women find the empty grave; (2) they report this to Peter and the disciples who return (with them) to the grave site; and, finally, (3) the women see Jesus after the disciples' departure. Actually, this is not so far from what the gospels relate. Mark tells only (1); Luke relates (1) and (2); Matthew has (1) and (3); and John recounts (1), (2), and (3). Because Matthew has appended the appearance tradition, which was originally separate and *selbstständig*, directly to the Markan tomb story, it gives the illusion that the appearance occurred before the women reached the disciples, which Luke and John tell us is not so. The appearance did not occur until the disciples and women had all returned to the tomb. As for the angelic appearance, this was part of the tradition of the discovery of the empty tomb. Interestingly, the verses regarded by Hartmann as a redactional addition (Jn. 20:11b-14a) would fit well with Jn. 20:1: she saw the stone ἠρμένον ἐκ τοῦ μνημείου. παρέκυψεν εἰς τὸ μνημεῖον.... She sees the angels and answers their question; ταῦτα εἰποῦσα ἐστράφη εἰς τὰ ὀπίσω τρέχει οὖν καὶ ἔρχεται πρὸς Σίμωνα Πέτρον.... That would leave vs. 11a and 14b in juxtaposition: ὡς οὖν ἔκλαιεν θεωρεῖ τὸν Ἰησοῦν.... Of course, this is speculative, and it could be that Jn. 20:1 conceals all of Mk. 16:1-8 and that Jn. 20:11-14 is in place. We should not be surprised that John's angels or Jesus do not command the disciples to go to Galilee, for John intends only to narrate Jerusalem appearances. Thus, they ask about weeping or speak of the imminent ascension. The resurrection narratives are, from a historical point of view, most uncertain when it comes to the words that are spoken, and so it is here.[7]

Objections to the Historicity of the Appearance

The appearance of Jesus to the women is often dismissed as an unhistorical legend, but this conclusion may be hasty. For example, it is sometimes asserted that the Christophany is a legendary product of the angelophany.[8] Now while this is an interesting possibility, there just seems to be no evidence for it; against it stands the fact that the tradition of the Christophany is almost entirely dissimilar to the angelophany. If they are genealogically related one would expect some traces of the former in the latter. And it would be a bit strange that Matthew and John should relate both traditions, unsuspecting that they are in reality the same incident. Again, it is sometimes asserted that the Christophany represents an apologetic attempt to reinforce the message of the angel.[9] But this seems to be question-begging, since the only evidence for such an interest is the tradition itself. And really, to add an appearance to *women* hardly seems to be rigorous apologetics. Sometimes it is asserted that the Christophany is designed to unite the originally separate empty tomb and appearance traditions.[10] But it seems to

---

[7] So Gerald O'Collins, *The Easter Jesus*, 2nd ed. (London: Darton, Longman & Todd, 1980), pp. 26-27, though one cannot agree with all his reasoning.

[8] Gardner-Smith, *The Narratives of the Resurrection*, (London: Methuen, 1926), p. 46; Fuller, *Formation*, p. 138. Interestingly, Michaelis has argued just the opposite, that the Christophany is primitive and the angelophany is a legendary copy! (Wilhelm Michaelis, *Die Erscheinungen des Auferstandenen* [Basel: Heinrich Maier, 1944], pp. 17-21). See also James W. D. G. Dunn, *Jesus and the Spirit* (London: SCM, 1975), p. 126.

[9] Ulrich Wilckens, *Auferstehung*, TT4 (Stuttgart and Berlin: Kreuz Verlag, 1970), p. 68; John E. Alsup, *The Post-Resurrection Appearance Stories of the Gospel-Tradition*, CTM A5 (Stuttgart: Calwer Verlag, 1975), p. 106.

[10] Hans Grass, *Ostergeschehen und Osterberichte*, 4th rev. ed. (Göttingen: Vandenhoeck & Ruprecht, 1970), pp. 27, 120; C. F. Evans, *Resurrection and the New Testament*, SBT 12 (London: SCM Press, 1970), p. 83. Wilckens asserts that Mk. 16:7 represents the first attempt to combine originally separate empty tomb and appearance traditions (Wilckens, "History," p. 71; so also X. Léon Dufour, *Resurrection and the Message of Easter* [London: Geoffery Chapman, 1974], p. 133). But we have seen that v. 7 was part of the pre-Markan passion story; certainly it has not been proved that it was not. But now the distinction between the two traditions collapses, since the earliest tradition which we possess mentioned them both (as is also implied in I Cor. 15). Schnackenburg dismisses the appearance to the women as unhistorical because Luke does not know it; John's interest is not historical but theological, and the story is a prelude to the next appearance (Schnackenburg, *Johannesevangelium*, 3: 380). But Luke is not the yardstick of historicity (and he may have known it but not mentioned it because women are weak witnesses and Luke-Acts is very concerned to adduce the witnesses to the Christian faith); there is no reason to think

me that this view involves a fundamental misunderstanding. The appearance traditions were, of course, originally separate, as the different appearance stories of the gospels show, and probably none of them a part of the pre-Markan passion story. There was no running account of all the appearances, just separate stories. Different evangelists knew or chose different stories. This is one reason why the course of events is so difficult to reconstruct. One story was of the appearance of Jesus to the women near the tomb. Matthew and John knew or chose this story. To say this story represents the attempt to fuse the tomb with appearances already assumes the story is not true—a *petitio principii*. To say there was a desire to unite appearances with the tomb is question-begging since the only evidence for such an interest is the story itself; that Luke shows no such concern seems to be evidence against the existence of such an interest. In any case, we have already seen that the pre-Pauline appearance tradition cited in I Cor. 15:3-5 implies the empty tomb and that the pre-Markan empty tomb tradition mentions, even if it does not narrate, a resurrection appearance. It seems that the story of the appearance to the women was simply one of several independent traditions concerning Jesus's appearances.

THE APPEARANCE TO EMMAUS DISCIPLES

Chronologically, the next appearances mentioned in the gospels are those to the Emmaus disciples and to Peter later the same day (Lk. 24:13-35). The story of the walk to Emmaus is another of the gospels' most beautiful stories, a literary masterpiece. The main purposes of the story are to show that the resurrection is the fulfillment of Old Testament prophecies and that Jesus was recognized by witnesses; liturgical motifs are secondary. If we regard the appearance of Jesus to Mary and the women as historical, then it is evident that the two travellers to

---

that John did not regard the appearance to Mary as historical as her visit to the tomb. In no sense is it a prelude to the next appearance; Brown remarks that the appearance to the Twelve could come as it is wholly apart from the appearance to Mary (Brown, *John*, p. 1027-1028). Bode objects to the historicity of the appearance to the women on three grounds: (1) it only repeats the angel's message; (2) it is strange that women should be the first to see Jesus when they are not official witnesses; (3) there would be no value to the report of women (Edward Lynn Bode, *The First Easter Morning*, AB 45 [Rome: Biblical Institute Press, 1970], p. 56). Remarkably, (2) and (3) are very good reasons to accept the appearance's historicity, since these would be reasons against such a story's evolving without foundation in fact. As for (1), it may be that Matthew lacked the words, so he just used the angel's again. On the other hand, Grundmann protests this is not just a duplication, but the accent of importance (Walter Grundmann, *Das Evangelium nach Matthäus*, 3rd ed., THMT 1 [Berlin: Evangelische Verlagsanstalt, 1972], p. 370).

Emmaus, if they are also historical, left Jerusalem after Peter and the other disciples returned from the empty tomb (Lk. 24:22-24) and before the women came with their report that he was risen (Mt. 28:11; Jn. 20:18). Luke himself is either unaware of or does not choose to employ the appearance of Jesus to the women. The exact location of Emmaus is disputed.[11] Only one of the travellers is named, Cleopas, the other being perhaps his wife. As they walk along, Jesus joins them and during the course of their journey explains to them the Old Testament basis for the suffering and resurrection of the Messiah. When the travellers prevail upon Jesus, whom they still have not recognized, to stay the night at Emmaus, Jesus breaks bread with them, during which they recognize him. He vanishes. The excited pair return at once to Jerusalem to the disciples. Before they can relate their story, the disciples exclaim, "The Lord has risen, indeed, and has appeared to Simon!" Then the two from Emmaus share their experience.

Traditional Material

Considerations of vocabulary and style suggest that in the Emmaus story Luke is following traditional material, though freely giving it back often in his own words.[12] There is nothing in v. 13 that evinces a redactional hand, except perhaps for the phrase "that very day;" there are here no indications of a Lukan theological interest, for despite Luke's theological concentration on Jerusalem, Emmaus is definitely *not* Jerusalem. Two Lukan words ὁμιλεῖν and συμβαίνω in v. 14 show Luke's own wording, but the discourse motif was probably in his source, since the word ἔιπεν, which occurs frequently in the discourse with πρὸς αὐτούς occurs in v. 19 with αὐτοῖς. The latter usage occurs 65 out of 82 times in Lukan source material, which points to a pre-redactional discourse motif. In the same verse Ναζαρηνοῦ is non-Lukan, as are ἀνόητοι and βραδεῖς in v. 25. In v. 28 Luke appears to return more closely to his tradition: the combination of ἐγγίζειν with πορεύειν (or cognate) found in v. 15 appears again in v. 28, as does the εἰς κώμην of v. 13. The καὶ αὐτός used from v. 15 recurringly without the antecedent is found in vs. 28, 31. Other non-Lukan terms are προσποιέω with the comparative adverb πορρώτερον (*hapax legomenon* for the New Testament),

---

[11] See literature in Kremer, *Osterevangelien*, p. 116; I. Howard Marshall, *The Gospel of Luke*, NIGTC (Exeter: Paternoster Press, 1978), pp. 892-893.
[12] B. Rigaux, *Dieu l'a ressuscité*, SBFA 4 (Gembloux: Duculot, 1973), pp. 226-229; Alsup, *Stories*, pp. 190-194; Osborne, "Resurrection," pp. 232-235.

παραβιάζεσθαι (here and once in Acts for the entire New Testament), πρὸς ἑσπέραν ἐστὶν (here and twice in Acts for the New Testament), and perhaps εἰσῆλθεν τοῦ μεῖναι σὺν αὐτοῖς and διανοίγειν. The story is therefore not a Lukan creation, but came to Luke at least in the major points of the outline through his source. These were probably the encounter on the road, perhaps some sort of discourse, and finally the recognition at the meal and Jesus's disappearance.[13]

Eucharistic Motifs

It is frequently alleged that the recognition by the meal is a eucharistic motif of the early church.[14] The words of v. 30: "he took the break and blessed, and broke it, and gave it to them" (λαβὼν τὸν ἄρτον εὐλόγησεν καὶ κλάσας ἐπεδίδου αὐτοῖς) certainly echo the words of 22:19 "he took bread, and when he had given thanks he broke it and gave it to them" (λαβὼν ἄρτον εὐχαριστήσας ἔκλασεν καὶ ἔδωκεν αὐτοῖς). But there are not *verbatim* parallels except the general participle λαβών. Significant is perhaps the fact that the important verb εὐχαριστέω (also found in the old tradition of I Cor. 11:24) is lacking in v. 30, though Matthew and Mark use εὐλογέω in the Last Supper (Mt. 26:26; Mk. 14:22). It may be that v. 30 is the typical formula for the breaking of bread at an ordinary Jewish meal. While it would be unusual for the guest to assume the role of head of the house in breaking the bread, it may be that Jesus did this during his earthly ministry as well.

At any rate, the meal motif is quite subordinate in the story and serves the major theme of recognition, as the eating in 24:41-43 serves the theme of corporeal-

---

[13] Paul Winter, "The Treatment of his Sources by the Third Evangelist in Luke XXI-XXIV," *ST* 8 (1954): 138-172.

[14] Gardner-Smith, *Resurrection*, p. 69; Eduard Lohse, *Die Auferstehung Jesu Christi in Zeugnis des Lukasevangeliums*, BS 31 (Neukirchen-Vluyn: Neukirchnerverlag, 1961), p. 30; Hugh Anderson, *Jesus and Christian Origins* (New York: Oxford University Press, 1964), p. 229; Pierre Benoit, *The Passion and Resurrection of Jesus Christ*, trans. B. Weatherhead (New York: Herder & Herder, 1969), pp. 279-282; H.-D. Betz, "Ursprung and Wesen christlichen Glaubens nach der Emmauslegende (Lk. 24, 13-32)," *ZNW* 66 (1969): 12. More recent scholarship tends, on the contrary, to view the meal motif in the framework of Jesus's table fellowship with his disciples during his ministry. See, *e.g.*, Pheme Perkins, *Resurrection: New Testament Witness and Contemporary Reflection* (Garden City, N. Y.: Doubleday & Co., 1984), p. 162; B. P. Robinson, "The Place of the Emmaus Story in Luke-Acts," *NTS* 30 (1984): 481-497.

ity.¹⁵ A problem in regarding this as a eucharistic motif is that the points of contact with the words of institution and the fellowship of the believers is altogether lacking.¹⁶ The moment one would expect a reference to meal fellowship with his disciples, the principal character disappears and the other two hurry back to Jerusalem. The structure of the story is that when Jesus is incognito he appears, but when he is recognized, he disappears—the very opposite of the eucharistic presence! Attempts to find a "trigger" for the recognition of Jesus in the breaking of the bread because the Emmaus disciples were at the Last Supper are without foundation. Luke gives no suggestion that any earthly memory of the pair or any sign to them "triggered" their recognition of Jesus—it was purely a divine act, and the meal framework seems to be of secondary importance, perhaps even incidental.

Objections to the Historicity of the Appearance

It has been said that the Emmaus story is a pure example of the literary genre of legend: God walks with men unrecognized in human form, reveals himself, and disappears.¹⁷ However, little solid evidence seems to have been brought forth in support of this classification.¹⁸ We shall return to this question later when we discuss the *Gattung* of the Hellenistic disappearance legends and the gospel appearance stories.

---

¹⁵ Berger has argued that the eating with the disciples is not meant to evoke the eucharist but to serve as a link to the pre-resurrection Jesus, who shared meals with the disciples, thus showing the continuity between the earthly and risen Christ (Klaus Berger, *Die Auferstehung der Propheten und die Erhöhung des Menschensohnes*, SUNT, 13 [Göttingen: Vandenhoeck & Ruprecht, 1976], p. 162).
¹⁶ Alsup, *Stories*, p. 197; cf. J. Roloff, *Das Kerygma und der irdische Jesu* (Göttingen: Vandenhoeck & Ruprecht, 1970), p. 257. Plummer also notes that the imperfect is never used of the eucharist as it is in v. 30; bread is not of eucharistic significance either, being the common word for food (Alfred Plummer, *The Gospel according to S. Luke*, 5ᵗʰ ed., ICC [Edinburgh: T & T Clark, 1964], pp. 556-557). See also Paul Billerbeck, *Kommentar zum Neuen Testament aus Talmud und Midrasch*, 6 vols., ed. Herrmann L. Strack (München: Beck, 1922-63), 1: 685-687.
¹⁷ M. Dibelius, *Die Formgeschichte des Evangeliums*, 3ʳᵈ ed. (Tübingen: Mohr, 1959), p. 190-193; Rudolf Bultmann, *Die Geschichte der synoptischen Tradition*, 2ⁿᵈ ed., FRLANT 12 (Göttingen: Vandenhoeck & Ruprecht, 1970), p. 310; Betz, "Ursprung," p. 8; Walter Grundmann, *Das Evangelium nach Lukas*, 8ᵗʰ ed., THKNT 3 (Berlin: Evangelische Verlagsanstalt, 1978), p. 443; Perrin, *Resurrection*, p. 66.
¹⁸ Kremer remarks that the resemblances of the Emmaus story to visits of the gods are tangential; even the recognition scene is not the main point (Kremer, *Osterevangelien*, p. 128; so also Perkins, *Resurrection*, p. 159).

THE APPEARANCE TO PETER

When the Emmaus disciples arrive back in Jerusalem, they are greeted by the words ὄντως ἠγέρθη ὁ κύριος καὶ ὤφθη Σίμωνι (Lk. 24:34). The language seems to be kerygmatic and recalls the formula of I Cor. 15. It is a mark of Luke's integrity as a historian that although he either lacked an accompanying story for this incident or had one he could not use, he did not invent or distort one to insert here.[19] Rather he is content with this shout of joy. According to 24:12 Peter had returned home after visiting the empty tomb, and 24:24 indicates that he reported back to the group of disciples. Sometime after the Emmaus disciples had left, Jesus appeared to Peter when he was alone.

We have no other certain information concerning this appearance. It has been argued that the appearance to Peter is hidden in other gospel stories. (This assumes that Luke and, implicitly, John as well have incorrectly placed the appearance to Peter in Jerusalem.) Lk. 5 and Jn. 21 are the most likely candidates to contain an appearance to Peter. The stories are very similar and Luke's pre-Easter account has certain difficulties: the context is different than Mk. 1:16-20; Mt. 4:1-2; the other fishermen presumably remain on the shore, but when the catch is made, they are there; Peter's falling to his knees and "Depart from me" would be more appropriate on land; and the transition to the call of the disciples is awkward.[20]

Now even if this indicates that Luke has displaced an Easter story, it remains a story of an appearance to the *disciples*; there is no warrant for either dissolving them or excluding their participation in the experience. Luke has focused on Peter for dramatic effect, but the presence of others with him in the boat is already implicit in the plural verb of v. 4 as well as in vs. 6, 7. Lk. 24:34; I Cor. 15:4 show the appearance to Peter alone was not confused with appearances to multiple disciples. But, in fact, Luke's difficulties may not warrant regarding the story as a displaced appearance story: it is the call of the disciples that is in a different

---

[19] Dodd remarks that Luke refused, despite his literary skill, to create a whole story out of a bare statement of the appearance to Peter (C. H. Dodd, "The Appearances of the Risen Christ: A study in form-criticism of the Gospels," in idem, *More New Testament Studies* [Manchester: Manchester University Press, 1968], p. 126). This ought to give us serious pause before one concludes that Luke has constructed a false sequence of Jerusalem appearances out of theological motives.

[20] Brown, *John*, pp. 1089-1090; see also Raymond E. Brown, Karl P. Donfried, John Reumann, *Saint Pierre dans le Nouveau Testament*, LD 79 (Paris: Les éditions du Cerf, 1974), pp. 141-147, 154-158.

context, regardless of the catch story's being part of it; the other fishermen's sudden helping in the catch says nothing in favor of this being a displaced appearance story and only supports the tradition that others were involved; and in view of the disciples' astonishment, Jesus's words are not so awkward. Peter's personal reaction could take place in his fishing boat; but more importantly it contradicts his reaction in Jn. 21. Rather than begging Jesus to depart, he there rushes eagerly to meet him. Peter's confession of sinfulness is said to reflect his absolution by Jesus in Jn. 21 for his three-fold denial. But is it true that Jn. 21:15-17 is Jesus's absolution? While the three-fold commissioning probably reflects the three-fold denial (Jn. 21:17), this sequence is exactly that: a commissioning, not a rehabilitation.[21] There is no confession of sin, no word of forgiveness—this does not appear to be an absolution scene. The absolution may have already taken place when Jesus appeared to Peter alone in Jerusalem; now he commissions him as shepherd. This would explain why Peter is so eager to see Jesus that he plunges into the sea to meet him and does not beg Jesus to depart—he is already a forgiven man, reconciled to his Lord. So not only do Lk. 5 and Jn. 21 seem to portray incompatible reactions; even Jn. 21 alone does not necessarily furnish evidence of a first appearance of Jesus to Peter.

But if this is true, then much of the motivation is gone to discern also evidence of an appearance to Peter in Matthew's addition about Peter's walking on the water (Mt. 14:28-33) or his great confession (Mt. 16:16-19). For the miraculous catch and the walking on the water are incompatible elements; but with these set aside, there is little information left. The great confession, even if a post-Easter retrojection, has little to suggest an appearance scene. Once one strips away the conflicting external circumstances of these scenes we know little more than what Luke himself tells us: that having previously denied Jesus, Peter after leaving the empty tomb and going home, saw Jesus. With that we must be content.

---

[21] So Rudolf Bultmann, *Das Evangelium des Johannes*, 19th ed., KEKNT (Göttingen: Vandenhoeck & Ruprecht, 1968), p. 551; he argues this is not a story of a restoration after the denial, since there is no repentance and no absolution, but a variant of the commissioning of Peter to lead the church (cf. Mt. 16:17-19; Lk. 22:32).

Chapter 7

The Appearance to the Twelve

Traditional Material

Luke and John agree that on the evening of the day on which the empty tomb was discovered (Luke has apparently moved the time indicator to v. 13 in order to replace it with a transitional phrase), Jesus stood in the midst of the Twelve and greeted them and displayed his wounds to them. Both Luke and John include teaching on the disciples' mission and the Holy Spirit (Lk. 24:36-49, Jn. 20:19-23). This probably represents the core of the tradition which lay before Luke and John. Although many scholars, by comparing Luke and John to Matthew's Galilean appearance, contend that the location of the appearance is purely redactional, the fact that the time indicator was probably part of the tradition[22] seems necessarily to imply that the location of the appearance in Jerusalem was traditional, since the disciples could not have reached Galilee by this time and all the gospel traditions agree that the disciples remained in Jerusalem over the weekend. John adds the detail that the disciples were hiding behind closed doors for fear of the Jews, which seems historically credible. This detail accentuates the miraculousness of Jesus's sudden appearance in their midst. According to the best texts, both Luke and John record Jesus's greeting, Εἰρήνη ὑμῖν, which for John might have theological significance (Jn. 14:27), but is probably for Luke a customary greeting.

Luke records that the disciples are startled and frightened and suppose that they are seeing a spirit (πτοηθέντες δὲ καὶ ἔμφοβοι γενόμενοι ἐδόκουν πνεῦμα θεωρεῖν), language which some scholars have compared with Mk. 6:49-50: οἱ δε ἰδόντες αὐτὸν...ἔδοξαν ὅτι φάντασμά ἐστιν, καὶ ἀνέκραξαν· πάντες γὰρ αὐτὸν εἶδον καὶ ἐταράχθησαν. The similarity caused some copyists to insert the words from Mk. 6:50, "It is I; have no fear!" into the text of Luke after Jesus's greeting. But the verbal similarities are minimal, and one cannot even say that Luke has transported the language of the Markan incident to this appearance, much less assert that similar traditions of the same root event are here in view. The one event evokes the thought of the other, but one cannot say that they are genealogically related. Alsup, who tries to show that the passages are related, can

---

[22] Schnackenburg, *Johannesevangelium*, 3: 382, points out that John's time indicator is unusual for the evangelist: a *vorangestellte* participle of the genitive absolute. On Luke's tradition, see Marshall, *Luke*, p. 901.

only find the following similarities (and only *after* leaving out the "water motif" and the "crucifixion scar motif"!): (1) Jesus comes to the disciples; (2) the disciples are struck with fear, thinking they are viewing a spirit apparition; (3) Jesus dispels their fears by assuring them that it is he himself.[23] Not only are these similarities so general as to be of little help in showing a genealogical relationship between the two narratives, but the second element, which is the real point of comparison, is lacking in John. One must also ignore the traditional items that Luke and John share that are incompatible with the walking on the water story, such as the displaying of the wounds. And Alsup does not seem to be exaggerating when he admits that the incongruities of content and location nevertheless constitute "a very thorny problem."[24] The similarities between Luke and John's accounts are so striking that it seems fruitless to try to construct another tradition used in addition by Luke.

In the Lukan version, doubt plays a major role in the story.[25] But this needs to be carefully qualified. The doubt does not concern the identity of the appearing person but his corporeality. Both vs. 37, 39 clearly show that the disciples think they are seeing a ghost, that is, a nonphysical apparition. This is why Jesus invites the disciples to handle him and why he eats the fish before them. This does not therefore seem to be in any sense a recognition scene. Jesus does not appear incognito, nor are the disciples' eyes opened. It is simply a matter of proving that Jesus is bodily raised from the dead.

The doubts of the disciples stand in a certain tension with v. 34, since it appears there that the disciples believed Jesus was risen and had appeared to Peter.[26] This might be taken to prove that this appearance was in reality the first. But even if Jesus did appear first to Peter, given the suddenness and the unexpectedness of Jesus's encounter with the Twelve, it is little wonder that they thought

---

[23] Alsup, *Stories*, p. 170.
[24] Ibid.
[25] It is frequently maintained that the doubt motif increases in inverse proportion to the age of the gospels, perhaps as an apologetic attempt to free the disciples of the charge of gullibility (Hans Freiherr von Campenhausen, *Der Ablauf der Osterereignisse und das Leere Grab*, 3rd rev. ed., SHA [Heidelberg: Carl Winter, 1966], pp. 39-40; Wilckens, *Auferstehung*, p. 74; Grundmann, *Matthäus*, p. 576). But this fails to reckon with the fact that the doubt motif is traditional and is found in all the gospels which narrate an appearance. So it seems idle to speak of the motif's development. Later use of the motif in apocryphal literature is an apologetic taking its cue from what was found in the gospels.
[26] Bultmann, *Johannes*, p. 534; Grass, *Ostergeschehen*, p. 39; Brown, *John*, pp. 1027-1028.

they were seeing a ghost. Since v. 34 is kerygmatic language, moreover, one need not assume that all the disciples had heartily embraced Peter's experience as real.

The Purpose of the Physical Demonstrations

Jesus's displaying of his wounds serves to show the disciples the continuity between the earthly and risen Jesus: "See my hands and my feet, that it is I myself" (Lk. 24:39); the body that was crucified and buried is the body that is raised. The wounds play the same role in John (Jn. 20:20, 25, 27). John mentions hands and side because of his record of the spear thrust (Jn. 19:34), whereas Luke mentions hands and feet. The dual purpose of the physicalism of Luke and John is the demonstration of *corporeality* and *continuity* on the part of the risen Jesus.[27] Interesting is the fact that βρώσιμον and ἰχθύς are unique here in the New Testament and indicate that Jesus's eating before the disciples is not a Lukan redaction, but part of the tradition received by Luke. The presence of fish cannot count as evidence for an original Galilean setting of the story, since fish was available in Jerusalem (Neh. 3:3; 13:16). Certainly no eucharistic overtones should be read into this demonstration by eating: the bread is missing, as are any of the traditional actions except λαβών; Jesus receives the food, not the disciples; Jesus alone eats; and the purpose is the rather mundane proof that Jesus is corporeal.[28]

---

[27] Perhaps a word should be said here about Berger's view that the question involved in the demonstrations is neither Docetism nor corporeality, but identity, *i.e.*, whether it is Jesus who is appearing or a demonic spirit impersonating Jesus. Citing a series of texts from Midrash and Targum, Berger shows that the Rabbis often took the eating and drinking of heavenly beings to be illusory, not real. Berger thinks that for Luke a πνεῦμα = a demon; therefore, the point of the eating is to prove Jesus is not an impersonating demon. Berger believes the key text in all this is *Lib. Ant.* 53.3, which states that if a voice calls twice, it is a *spiritus pessimus*, but if three times, it is God (Berger, *Auferstehung*, pp. 159, 458-459). But however Rabbinic exegesis may have taken them, it is nevertheless clear that in the Old Testament itself, the appearances of heavenly visitors were not visionary, but real events. Berger vitiates his own case when he supplies many references showing that both angels and demons were thought to be able to take on human form and become just like men. In this state, the heavenly being could take in food and drink (Ibid., pp. 159, 458). Therefore, eating would be useless to dispel the hypothesis of an impersonating demon. Besides this, the equation of spirits and demons for Luke is not true, as Acts 23:9 shows, a verse which Berger is reduced to interpreting disjunctively: an angel or a demon has spoken to him! In Lk. 24:37 the idea that the issue is an impersonating demon seems an extravagant hypothesis. Berger's key text, on God's calling, appears to be utterly irrelevant to the Lukan story. The point of the demonstration of eating seems to be only to prove that Jesus had been raised bodily from the dead.

[28] So also Grass, *Ostergeschehen*, pp. 42, 89; Fuller, *Formation*, p. 115. Pointing to Gen. 19:1; Tobit 12:19, Ellis asserts that eating does not serve to prove materiality (E. Earl Ellis, ed., *The Gospel of Luke*, NCB [London: Nelson, 1966], p. 279). But this is certainly mistaken; Genesis does not speak of a vision, but an actual bodily appearance of divine beings. Eating would be a

Theological Themes

Luke and John then conclude with theological themes. Luke emphasizes again the fulfillment of Old Testament prophecies in Jesus's dying and rising on the third day, Jesus charges the disciples to witness to the truths of the gospel, and he gives the promise of the Holy Spirit. John mentions the sending out, the reception of the Holy Spirit, and the forgiveness of sins. In Matthew's commissioning, he speaks of Jesus's authority, the sending out of the disciples to evangelize, baptize, and teach, and Jesus's promise of his abiding presence. An investigation of the discourses of the risen Jesus exceeds the limits of our inquiry, but the obvious similarities of these commissionings show that they are not purely redactional, but that "...common traditions underlie these accounts, the basic nucleus being that Jesus commanded his disciples to spread the good news widely and offer forgiveness of sins and that he promised them divine power for their tasks."[29]

It is very often asserted that Luke envisions in his gospel that the ascension of Jesus occurred on Easter, a viewpoint which he later changed in Acts. But this seems to be a very wooden reading of the gospel. Luke obviously presents in vs. 44-53 a foreshortened or telescoped account of the post-resurrection events, for by the time Jesus led the disciples out to Bethany it would be the middle of the night, and Luke certainly does not imagine an ascension by moonlight.[30] Rather he summarizes the teaching given by Jesus during the 40 day period of Acts 1:3,

---

failsafe demonstration of corporeality, for after a vision had passed, the food would remain uneaten; but after a real appearance, the food would be gone, having been consumed. Evans states that in Tobit the eating and drinking is visionary, but Luke intends it to be real (Evans, *Resurrection*, p. 63).

[29] Marshall, *Luke*, pp. 903-904. Cf. Dunn, *Jesus*, pp. 129-130, who provides five reasons to believe commissioning was involved in the first appearances: (1) Some word of command is integral to the most primitive narratives. (2) Paul assumes the earlier apostles were also commissioned through appearances. (3) The appearance to Peter stems from a kerygmatic formula, and the impulse to use it as kerygma goes back to Peter. (4) The acknowledged leaders of the early church owed their leadership to their having seen an appearance. (5) The decision to return to Jerusalem from Galilee was due to the disciples' commission to preach. See also G. R. Beasley-Murray, *Baptism in the New Testament* (rep. ed.: Grand Rapids, Michigan: Wm. B. Eerdmans, 1981), pp. 79-88.

[30] A point well made by James Orr, *The Resurrection of Jesus* (London: Hodder & Stoughton, 1909), pp. 192-193. An ascension in the dark is "incredible" according to Plummer; there is a break at v. 44. Vs. 44-49 are a condensation of what Jesus taught between the resurrection and ascension (Plummer, *Luke*, pp. 561-564). See also Gardner-Smith, *Resurrection*, p. 16; Grass, *Ostergeschehen*, pp. 45, 48; Kremer, *Osterevangelien*, p. 146, Marshall, *Luke*, p. 904. This bridges the "unüberbrückbare Spannung" between the gospel and Acts seen by Grundmann, *Lukas*, p. 450.

ending with the ascension. The continuity and unity of Luke's double-work seems to preclude that he has radically altered his chronology in Acts.

Matthew's Mountaintop Appearance

Matthew also relates an appearance to the Eleven which occurs in Galilee (Mt. 28:16-20). The difficulty is knowing whether this is meant to be the same appearance that is related in Luke and John. The appearance takes place on a mountain in Galilee, but it is usually urged that the mountain is a Matthean redaction, a mountain's being the place of revelation (Mt. 5:1; 14:23; 15:29; 17:1; 24:3).[31] There are practically no similarities to the accounts of Luke and John, but the οἱ δὲ ἐδίστασαν could reflect the tradition found in Lk. 24:38, 41 and the doubting Thomas story. And the verb προσελθών (Mt. 28:18) might be thought to resemble the ἦλθεν in Jn. 20:19. The structure of the appearance is that of Luke and John's: first the appearance, then the commissioning.

But while these considerations have weight, they afford no decisive conclusion. If Matthew is describing the same event, then it seems very odd that his appearance should have so little in common with Luke and John. The common traditional elements, "that day," Jesus's unexpected standing in their midst, the "Peace be with you," and the showing of the wounds to prove corporeality and continuity are all lacking. The similar structure could be the result of appending separate commissioning traditions onto an appearance story, since it was, after all, the disciples who were commissioned by the risen Jesus. This may have been done by all three evangelists, using whatever appearance story to the disciples they had. The Matthean story lacks especially the ἔστη ἐν μέσῳ or ἔστη εἰς τὸ μέσον of the encounter; προσέρχομαι is not a synonym of this; indeed, it is a Mattheanism.[32]

---

[31] Werner Schmauch, *Orte der Offenbarung und der Offenbarungsort im Neuen Testament* (Göttingen: Vandenhoeck & Ruprecht, 1956), pp. 67-80. Wilckens even asserts that in Matthew Jesus appears on the same mountain on which he gave the sermon! (Wilckens, *Auferstehung*, pp. 70-71). Cf. Grundmann, *Matthäus*, p. 576; Makota Yamauchi, *The Easter Texts of the New Testament: Their Tradition, Redaction and Theology* (Ph.D. thesis, University of Edinburgh, 1972), p. 199; Kremer, *Osterevangelien*, p. 82. Though it has also been contended that the Matthean appearance is an enthronement scene, a comparison with such texts as Phil. 2:6-11; I Tim. 3:16; Heb. 1:5-9 show that many elements there fail here and elements here are lacking there. The account in Matthew lacks the three acts of the ritual: the exaltation, presentation, and enthronement (Grundmann, *Matthäus*, p. 574; Kremer, *Osterevangelien*, p. 89).

[32] See Robert H. Gundry, *Matthew: A Commentary on his Theological and Literary Art* (Grand Rapids, Mich.: Wm. B. Eerdmans, 1982), p. 594.

The doubt motif is not used here as in Luke or John to show how Jesus dispels the disciples' doubts. It is forcing conclusions to reason that because in the other gospels Jesus overcomes doubt by corporeal demonstrations, therefore in Matthew the doubt *must* also be overcome, but this time by Jesus's words.[33] No, Matthew's doubt seems to remain unresolved. Though one could say this motif is only a distant echo (or rudimentary progenitor) of the doubt in Luke and John, it is also possible that it is unrelated to their traditions. Significantly, perhaps, the words are not even the same: John uses ἄπιστος to describe Thomas (Jn. 20:27: cf. ἀπιστούντων [Lk. 24:41]); Luke speaks of διαλογισμοί (Lk. 24:38) or considerations, questionings mounting in the disciples' minds. But Matthew uses the verb διστάζω, to hesitate or doubt, a word which appears only two times in the New Testament, here and in Mt. 14:31. Interestingly, this is in Matthew's account of Peter's walking on the water with Jesus. When Peter begins to sink, Jesus asks, why did you doubt (ἐδίστασας)? When they are in the boat again, the disciples worship (προσεκύνησαν) Jesus, an act also found in Matthew's appearance story with exactly the same form of the verb. In Luke the disciples are not said to worship (προσκυνέω) Jesus until Lk. 24:52; in John this verb is used in reference to Jesus only in 9:38. The appearance of this verb in the Matthean appearance story suggests again that Matthew is not drawing on the same tradition as Luke and John. In fact that the pair διστάζω and προσκυνέω appear in the peculiarly Matthean story of Peter's walking on the water and in his appearance story could suggest that Matthew's appearance story is purely redactional. But προσκυνέω is a common verb (60 times in the New Testament) so that its appearance with διστάζω does not count for much. More importantly, in Mt. 14:31 the worship follows the doubt after Jesus overcomes it, but in Mt. 28:17 the doubt follows the worship and is not overcome! This would seem very curious, indeed, from Matthew's own hand. So even if the language is Matthean, the appearance story does not seem to have been constructed out of the air. Neither, on the other hand, does it show clear ties with Luke and John. It could be that Matthew is relating another appearance to the disciples in Galilee; Jn. 21 mentions a Galilean appearance and Acts 1:3 refers to multiple appearances.

And it must be said that only a selective survey of the mountain texts in the gospels could lead one to conclude that the appearance on the mountain is a

---

[33] Yamauchi, *Easter*, p. 200; cf. I. P. Ellis, "But Some Doubted," *NTS* 14 (1968): 579-580.

Matthean redaction concerning a place of divine revelation. For *all* the gospels narrate revelatory events as occurring on a mountain (Mk. 3:13-19; 9:2; 13:3; 14:26-28; Lk. 6:12-16; 9:28; Jn. 6:3; Acts 1:12). So the emphasis is not uniquely Matthean. In fact it is John who places the Feeding of the 5,000 on a mountain, not Matthew. And the Mount of Transfiguration originates with Mark. But more than that, revelation also takes place *off* the mountain (Mt. 1:20; 2:13; 3:1, 16-17; 4:17; 8:23-27; 9:6; 11:25-30; 13; 17:9-13; 18; 20:1-16; 22; 26:26-29). If we have the Sermon on the Mount and the Olivet Discourse, then we also have the Parables of the Kingdom and a great deal of other teaching given in the streets and on the seashore, every bit as much revelation as that given on the mountain, which appears to enjoy no privileged position in Matthew. Furthermore, positively anti-revelatory events can take place on the mountain (Mt. 4:8; also Mk. 5:5; Lk. 4:29). And finally, ordinary, mundane events also occur on the mountain (Mt. 3:14; 14:23; also Mk. 5:11; 6:46; Lk. 8:32; 21:37; 22:39; Jn. 6:15; 8:1). In this connection certain events' occurring on a mountain may be merely incidental, like the Olivet Discourse. It is the testimony of all the gospels that Jesus often went apart into the seclusion of the mountains, to be alone with God. Thus, it should not seem odd that some of the events of the gospels take place on a mountain. Sometimes great acts of God are done on the mountain; other times the same acts are done on level ground (Mt. 8:1-4; 15:29-31; also Lk. 9:37-43). From this mélange one would be hard-pressed to construct a "theology of the mountain" for Matthew.[34] Noteworthy, too, in this connection is the fact that τάσσω in v. 16 is not a Matthean word, suggesting that the reference to the mountain may be traditional. The fact is, there *are* hills in Galilee, where Jesus often went apart; there

---

[34] Having said this, I see that an entire dissertation has been written on this topic by Terence L. Donaldson, *Jesus on the Mountain*, JSNT Supplement Series 8 (Sheffield, England: JSOT Press, 1985)! Of Matthew's eleven mountain references, Donaldson finds six of these theologically significant, of which four are unique to Matthew. He argues that the mountain is not a place of revelation, but a place where God renews His presence with His people in constituting the true Messianic community. Doubtless more and different theological constructs will be read by scholars into Matthew's ambivalent data. It is interesting that according to Donaldson, each of the Matthean mountain settings is rooted in tradition: "Nowhere...has Matthew created a mountain setting *ex nihilo* in order to further his redactional purposes" (Ibid., p. 172). With regard specifically to Mt. 28, Donaldson argues for tradition on the basis of (i) the phrase "to which Jesus appointed them" is non-Matthean and out of context, (ii) Acts 1:12 supplies evidence of a tradition of a mountain top appearance, and (iii) later Gnostic and non-canonical material employ a mountain as the scene of post-resurrection discourse (Ibid., p. 173). Cf. J. D. Kingsbury, "The Composition and Christology of Mt. 28: 16-20, " *JBL* 93 (1974): 580-583.

seems little reason to think that Matthew's location of the appearance of Jesus is theological and not geographical.

The designation of this mountain as the one to which Jesus directed the disciples comes as a surprise, since Matthew does not report that Jesus in his appearance to the women gave specific instructions. It has been said that Matthew is forced to add the phrase because, having decided to set the appearance on the mount of revelation, he has to manufacture some means of getting the disciples there.[35] This view depends, however, on the dubious Matthean "mountain theology." If Jesus did appear to the Twelve in Jerusalem as Luke and John state, then he could have given further instructions for a rendezvous with the disciples in Galilee. It is not impossible that this was related to the appearance to the 500 brethren. All this is, of course, quite speculative; but one cannot rule out that Luke and John narrate one event and Matthew quite another.

THE APPEARANCE TO THOMAS

The next appearance recorded in the gospels occurred eight days later in Jerusalem to the assembled Twelve (Jn. 20:24-29). Thomas, says John, was not with the Twelve when they saw the Lord, and he refused to believe unless he could physically touch the wounds of Jesus himself. So eight days later, the doors being shut, Jesus stands among them and meets Thomas's challenge. Thomas exclaims, "My Lord and my God!" Jesus then blesses those who have not seen and yet believe. The story is often explained as John's elaboration of the doubt motif, which he left out of the appearance to the Twelve in order to make it a special point here. Much of the story can be constructed out of the prior appearances: v. 25 < v. 18, 20; v. 26 < v. 19. The eight day figure means one week later and seems to contradict the traditions that the disciples went back to Galilee. It is thought to reflect

---

[35] Brown, *John*, p. 1093. Oddly enough, Brown, who holds to an original Galilean appearance reflected in Jn. 21, just takes it for granted that the eleven disciples would somehow all come together on the shore of the Lake of Galilee. But if that gathering requires no explanation, why should the other? Could not Matthew have said that the disciples went to the mountain to pray and there Jesus appeared to them unexpectedly? Osborne argues more plausibly than Brown that since the mountain is connected with a non-Matthean phrase (τάσσω), the location may well be traditional and that since Matthew never mentions this command, he would not have made it up. Therefore, it was probably in his source (Osborne, "Resurrection," p. 200). Osborne therefore regards the Matthean appearance tradition as distinct from the appearance in the upper room (Ibid., pp. 392-393). Lohmeyer thinks Jesus was waiting on the mountain, otherwise his appearing would have been described (Ernst Lohmeyer, *Das Evangelium des Matthäus*, 4th ed. W. Schmauch, KEKNT [Göttingen: Vandenhoeck & Ruprecht, 1967], p. 415).

later Christian Sunday worship. The final blessing is also thought to reflect a later time when the first generation of believers were passing away.

On the other hand, the story is not simply a dramatization of the doubt motif, for it is not merely the story of how Thomas's doubts were overcome. The story also contains a Christological statement which constitutes the climax of the gospel. And the lesson at the end deals with the relation between faith and first-hand experience. Moreover, the story cannot be produced simply by reiterating phrases of the foregoing appearance, as the difference between v. 20 and vs. 25b, 27 shows. Actually, despite its similarity to the appearance to the Twelve, there are even some words that are not typically Johannine: τύπος (only in v. 25 in John), ἧλος (only here in the New Testament), δάκτυλος (only in vs. 25, 27 in John [and fragment in chap. 8]), ἔσω (only in v. 26 in John), ἄπιστος (only in v. 27 in John), πιστός (only in v. 27 in John).[36]

There seems to be no evidence, moreover, that the eight day interval is designed to land the appearance on the Christian Lord's Day. Brown points out that the earliest Christian worship gatherings were not on Sunday at all, but on Saturday night after the close of the Jewish sabbath, when the Christians would meet at their homes to break bread. "Thus it would seem that the earliest Christian celebrations on 'the first day of the week' were not on the day of Sunday, but late in the evening on the vigil of Sunday."[37] Saturday evening could still be reckoned in the Jewish manner to be after eight days; but there is no sign here of worship or of bread-breaking.

If we take the Galilean appearance traditions seriously, one must ask what the disciples are doing in Jerusalem a week after the discovery of the empty tomb. An answer may be at hand in the consecutive Jewish feasts of Passover and Unleavened Bread (Deut. 16:3), for these feasts lasted eight days. Since Passover fell on Saturday, according to John, that means the feast lasted until the next Saturday. If the disciples stayed in Jerusalem for the duration of the feast, then that

---

[36] In fact Bultmann, pointing to John's rare use of δώδεκα and the fact that the reader already knows Thomas, thinks the Thomas story could be traditional (Bultmann, *Johannes*, p. 537). On the basis of Johannine stylistic criteria, Osborne also concludes that the story is traditional (Osborne, "Resurrection," p. 301). Schnackenburg, *Johannesevangelium*, 3:394-395, asserts that the Thomas story has the same structure as the Nathanael story (Jn. 2:43-51), but a reading of this passage makes it evident that the similarities are superficial. The Nathanael story has Nathanael coming to Jesus, Jesus praising Nathanael, and no blessing after the confession, all of which are contrary to the Thomas story.

[37] Brown, *John*, p. 1093.

would explain why they would still be in the city eight days later.[38] (Interestingly, the Gospel of Peter has the disciples remain in Jerusalem until the eighth day of the feast before returning to Galilee.) Thus, the eight day figure could reflect historical circumstances and not ecclesiastical practice. The disciples may have assembled often during the week, anticipating the appointed meeting with Jesus later in Galilee, and this assembly could have been the last prior to departure. Thomas may have been an outsider in all this. His scepticism fits his character as John portrays him, a man who is not afraid to bluntly contradict Jesus (Jn. 14:5) and who has a touch of cynicism (Jn. 11:16). His full commitment was secured only by Jesus's unexpected and personally directed appearance.

The appearance to Thomas serves to handle the problem of believers temporally or geographically removed from the original appearances, but this need not imply either that the incident is unhistorical or that it is late, since such a problem would arise almost immediately in the church. Grass points out, "The contemporaries of the apostles were fundamentally in no different position than later generations or ourselves. Christ was proclaimed to them as crucified and risen, ...and they believed in him without having seen him before he died or after his death (in Easter visions)."[39] Because only John tells the story, one would be inclined to think that it is not based on tradition, but rather on the reminiscences of the Beloved Disciple to the Johannine community.

THE APPEARANCE BY THE LAKE OF TIBERIAS

The Relationship Between Chapters 20 and 21

The final appearance mentioned in Jn. 21 takes place in Galilee. In order to analyze this appearance, one must first determine as far as is possible the relationship between chaps. 1-20 and 21. On the one hand, there are strong reasons to believe that the evangelist closed the gospel with 20:30-31 and did not intend to write another chapter, for (1) 20:28 brings the gospel to its theological and Christological climax; (2) 20:29 blesses those who believe without seeing, thus making

---

[38] Swete, *Appearances*, p. 52; M.-J. Lagrange, *Évangile selon saint Jean* (Paris: Librairie Victor Lecoffre, 1925), p. 517; C. F. D. Moule, "The Post-Resurrection Appearances in Light of Festival Pilgrimmages," *NTS* 4 (1957-58): 59; Barnabas Lindars, ed., *The Gospel of John*, NCB (London: Oliphants, 1972), p. 609.

[39] Hans Grass, *Christliche Glaubenslehre*, 2 vols. (Stuttgart: W. Kohlhammer, 1973), 1:107.

further appearances somewhat inappropriate; (3) 20:30 leaves the scene of the narrative and makes the transition to the closing; (4) 20:31 summarizes the intent of the gospel and concludes it suitably; and (5) the material in chap. 21 tends to be anticlimactic after the commissioning of 20:21-23.[40]

On the other hand, there is unanimous textual evidence that John always had chap. 21. The gospel apparently never circulated with only chaps. 1-20. So either the author or someone else added the chapter before publishing the gospel. Analysis of the choice of words, the grammatical style, characteristic manner of expression, and theological outlook makes it practically certain that chap. 21 has the same author as chaps. 1-20:[41] (1) Choice of words: the researches of Schweizer, Jeremias, Menoud, Ruckstuhl, and Solanges have demonstrated on the basis of grammar and vocabulary the linguistic unity of chaps. 1-21.[42] Morgenthaler's statistical approach found 75 characteristic Johannine words, 37 of which appear in chap. 21, a normal distribution when compared with the distribution in chaps. 1-20.[43] Expressed as a percentage of total words in the chapter, the favored words in chap. 21 constitute 25.6% of the words, compared, for example, with a 25.8% ratio for chap. 20; this despite the fact that chap. 21 contains many atypical words inherently required by the fishing story. This homogeneity of chap. 21 with the rest of the gospel seems decisive for authorship, for while an imitator might be able to pick up certain Johannine characteristics of style, perhaps exaggerating them, it would be virtually impossible for him to achieve just the right ratio that is homogeneous with the remainder of the gospel. (2) Grammatical style: the results are similar to the above. The 23 instances of historical

---

[40] But see Paul S. Minear, "The Original Functions of John 21," *JBL* 102 (1983): 85-98, who argues that (i) a strong case can be made for the fact that the last verses of chap. 20 close that chapter alone, (ii) chap. 21 is necessary to close the story of Peter and the Beloved Disciple, (iii) chap. 21 clarifies the relation between the evangelist and the Beloved Disciple, (iv) there are several incidental links between chap. 21 and the earlier chapters, and (v) the closing verses of chaps. 20 and 21 are quite similar.
[41] See Robert Mahoney, *Two Disciples at the Tomb*, TW 6 (Bern: Herbert Lang, 1974), pp. 18-36.
[42] Eduard Schweizer, *Ego Eimi*, 2nd ed., FRLANT 56 (Göttingen: Vandenhoeck & Ruprecht, 1965), pp. 82-112; Joachim Jeremias, "Johanneische Literarkritik," *TB* 20 (1941): 33-46; Philippe Menoud, *L'Évangile de Jean d'après les recherches récentes*, 2nd ed. (Paris: Delachaux & Niestle, 1947), pp. 12-36; Eugen Ruckstuhl, *Die literarische Einheit des Johannesevangeliums*, SF 3 (Freiburg, Switzerland: Paulusverlag, 1951); B. de Solanges, *Jean et les Synoptiques* (Leiden: E. J. Brill, 1979), pp. 191-235.
[43] Robert Morgenthaler, *Statistik des neutestamentlichen Wortschatzes* (Zürich and Frankfurt: Gotthelf, 1958), pp. 49-55, 57-65, 181-187.

present preclude a Lukan redaction, as is sometimes suggested. A time lag or tradition could account for the three grammatical anomalies of chap. 21: ἀπό as causal instead of διά + accusative (v. 6), ἀπό as partitive instead of ἐκ (v. 10), and the absence of a ἵνα clause, used 147 times in the gospel (but note, only once in chap. 20 at the very end, v. 31). (3) Characteristic manner of expression: the editorial work of vs. 1, 14 is not atypical for the evangelist. The μετὰ ταῦτα and θαλάσσης τῆς Τιβεριάδος in v. 1 are Johannine (cf. 6:1) as is the enumeration of the event and the expression "raised from the dead" in v. 14 (cf. 4:54; 2:22). φανερόω in v. 1 (nine times in John) cannot, in light of Jn. 14:22, be said to be un-Johannine merely because it is only here used of a resurrection appearance. The explanatory notes in vs. 19a, 20b are common in the gospel. The use and repetition of different words with the same meaning in vs. 15-17 is Johannine. The misunderstanding motif in v. 23 is a Johannine characteristic. While an imitator would perhaps be able to pick these up, they are nevertheless in harmony with common authorship of chaps. 1-21. (4) Theological outlook: though this is the most subjective of the criteria, the outlook is nonetheless the same as the gospel's—the same Jesus and the same fellowship of love continue. Two differences, the mention of the Parousia and the leadership role of Peter, are not without parallel in the gospel (5:27-29; 6:39, 44, 54; 14:3; 1:42; 13:36-38) and could again reflect a time lag between the composition of the gospel and chap. 21. That chap. 21 was written after, and not before, the gospel is evident from the fact that it serves as an epilogue to complete some lines of thought not ended in the gospel.[44] Thus, the evidence appears to indicate conclusively that the author of chaps. 1-20 is also the author of chap. 21.

It next needs to be asked who added chap. 21 to the gospel. It has been argued that had the author later decided to incorporate this material, he could have worked it into the text where it belongs, whereas a redactor would tack it onto the end. Now it is interesting that this argument implies that the author either was himself or was in contact with an eyewitness, because it ascribes to him knowledge of when the events originally occurred. If he did not have eyewitness information, then he would know no better than the redactor where the tradition "belonged." The only way to avoid this would be to hold that chaps. 20-21 were

---

[44] So Brown, *John*, p. 1079. Cf. Schnackenburg, *Johannesevangelium*, 3:408-409, though one cannot concur with all his assertions.

originally a unified tradition out of which the evangelist separated chap. 21, and the later redactor did not know how to put it together again. The argument also assumes that the events are in fact not in chronological order as they stand. If the disciples did return to Galilee after seeing Jesus in Jerusalem, then the appearance is where it belongs. But assuming that the event is out of order, is it true that the author could have or would have worked it back into the text? Where could it be inserted? The appearance to Mary at the tomb had to come first, so it could not have belonged there. But neither could it be inserted before the appearance to the Eleven, because that would destroy the doubting Thomas episode. To narrate it after the appearance to Thomas would be somewhat superfluous and anticlimactic—so the author simply left the material out. Later he could have added it as an epilogue.

But if the author wanted to add the material that he had left out, it is argued, then he surely would have moved 20:30-31 to the very end.[45] But so would a redactor! The verses are so obviously a concluding comment on the gospel as a whole that it would take no literary genius whatsoever to insert the material of chap. 21 after 20:29 and put 20:30-31 on the end of the whole. It seems difficult to understand how scholars can believe that a later redactor could so skillfully insert the figure of the Beloved Disciple back into the text of the gospel but be unable to detach vs. 30-31 to keep them at the end of the entire gospel. But if the author did add the epilogue later, why would he leave vs. 30-31 where they are? Perhaps the bond between vs. 29 and 30 is stronger than has been perceived. Verse 29 could give the misimpression to readers that the author means to depreciate faith based on sight, that faith without signs is a superior faith.[46] Thus, vs. 30-31 serve to dispel any such misunderstanding: these signs are written so that you may believe. The "those" of v. 29 are the "you" of v. 31. The author tells us

---

[45] C. K. Barrett, *The Gospel according to St. John* (London: SPCK, 1972), p. 577; Brown, *John*, p. 1080; Mahoney, *Disciples*, p. 38; Schnackenburg, *Johannesevangelium* 3: 416.

[46] Despite the close connection of vs. 29-30, some commentators still cannot avoid this misimpression; for example, Bultmann, *Johannes*, p. 539; Schnackenburg, *Johannesevangelium*, 3: 393. It is illegitimate to appeal to Jn. 4:48 for support, for Jesus is here testing the man's faith (cf. Mt. 15:22-28). Jesus would not perform a sign merely so that the people might have "bread and circuses," but he did urge seekers after truth to believe in him on the evidence of signs (Jn. 10:38; 14:11). Brown remarks that the idea that Thomas's faith is not praiseworthy because it is based on sensible perception and is thus radically opposed to faith reflects Bultmann's personal theology rather than the evangelist's thought (Brown, *John*, p. 1050). No discrediting of an eyewitness's faith is intended, for this is foreign, not only to John, but the whole New Testament, states Grass, *Ostergeschehen*, p. 72.

that we are blessed when we believe on the basis of the signs done in the presence of the disciples and written in the gospel, without having seen them ourselves. Thus the author would not want to break the unity of the gospel by inserting chap. 21 between vs. 29 and 30—better to append the material as an epilogue.

The author might have been persuaded by his fellows to add it because of the valuable material it contains; it also serves to draw together some threads in the gospel and was made perhaps more urgent because of the necessity of quashing the false rumor that was being circulated. Even if the Beloved Disciple had died recently, there is no indication that the author of the gospel had died (unless the Beloved Disciple were the author), so that it would be very odd that the author of the chapter would be unaware that someone else was appending this chapter, which he had written subsequent to the gospel, onto chaps. 1-20. But whoever added chap. 21, it is highly significant that the same individual probably authored both chaps. 1-20 and 21, for it shows that he was aware of both Jerusalem and Galilean appearances and that these were attested by the authority of the disciple whom Jesus loved.

Traditions Behind John 21:1-14

The chapter as a whole falls into two halves at vs. 14, which closes the appearance story, and 15, which begins the section dealing with Peter. But v. 14 is an editorial remark, as v. 15a makes evident. It is less likely that v. 15a should be redactional because of its specific time indication; Johannine style is vaguer, as in v. 1: "after this." In fact, the prominence of Peter in vs. 2, 3, 7 almost requires continuity with the remainder of the chapter to bring the theme to a resolution. The fact that fish are present in vs. 1-14 whereas sheep are used in vs. 15-17 cannot count decisively against this, since one does not tend for fish as one does for sheep; the first would be hopeless as a symbol for pastoral care. Hence, the two scenes ought to be regarded as a unity.[47]

As for vs. 1-14, these are usually regarded as a combination of two traditions: a miraculous catch of fish and an appearance of Jesus to the disciples during a meal.[48] The internal evidence usually adduced for such a separation includes: (1) in v. 5 Jesus appears to have no fish, but in v. 9 he has fish prepared. (2) In v. 10

---

[47] So Brown, *John*, pp. 1083-1084.
[48] Barrett, *John*, p. 578; Brown, *John*, pp. 1084-1085; Alsup, *Stories*, pp. 201-202.

he asks that fish be brought, but in vs. 12-13 it is not clear that they are eaten. (3) In v. 7 the miraculous catch causes them to recognize Jesus, but in v. 12 they are still puzzled. (4) In v. 11 Peter goes ἀνέβη, but in v. 9 the disciples are already ashore. (5) In v. 5 προσφάγιον, in vs. 6, 8, 11 ἰχθύς, and in vs. 9, 10, 13 ὀψάριον is used for "fish."

These indicators seem, however, inconclusive: (1) It is not said in v. 5 that Jesus does not have any fish nor is it implied. (2) Nor is it either said or implied that the fish of v. 10 were not eaten. (3) It states in v. 12 that the disciples *knew* it was the Lord, which could actually presuppose the recognition in v. 7; compare 1:19; 8:25 for the motif that this question was no longer necessary. (4) The ἀνέβη means aboard the boat, for a fisherman secures the ends of the net in the boat while allowing the fish to remain in the water (cf. v. 8). Peter pulled the net up onto the beach to get some of the fish. (5) The word προσφάγιον is not comparable to the other two words, but indicates a staple food, which was usually fish. Jesus's question used the typical words addressed to a hunter or fisherman: "Got anything?" The variation of the other two words may be no more significant than the variation between ἀρνία and πρόβατα. These are not sure guides to separating the traditions, for critics often combine the two words in one story. Bultmann thought the original story was vs. 2-3, 4a, 5-6, 8b-9a, 10-11a, 12.[49] Pesch thinks the miraculous catch story was vs. 2, 3, 4a, 6, 11; the appearance story was 5b, 7, 8, 9, 12, 13.[50] Fortna believes the catch story was 2, 3, 4a, (5?), 6, 7b, 8b, 10, 11, (12?), 14.[51] Brown and Schnackenburg, while holding to dual traditions behind vs. 1-14, have given up on trying to reconstruct precisely the original stories.[52] Taken in isolation the Johannine story is actually quite logical and well-told and gives no grounds for assuming the existence of two underlying stories that have become so intricately interwoven that modern scholars cannot separate them with any degree of certainty.[53]

The chief basis for suspecting an independent, underlying story of a miraculous catch of fish is the very similar story in Lk. 5. The significant similarities

---

[49] Bultmann, *Johannes*, pp. 544-545.
[50] Rudolph Pesch, *Der reiche Fischfang* (Düsseldorf: Patmos Verlag, 1969), pp. 42-52.
[51] R. T. Fortna, *The Gospel of Signs* (Cambridge: Cambridge University Press, 1970), pp. 87-98.
[52] Brown, *John*, p. 1085; Schnackenburg, *Johannesevangelium*, 3: 412.
[53] Against the existence of separate traditions in vs. 1-14, see Lindars, *John*, p. 623; Osborne, "Resurrection," pp. 307-308.

between the two stories are: the disciples have fished all night and caught nothing, Jesus tells them to put out the net for a catch, they do so and catch a miraculously great quantity of fish, the effect on the net is mentioned, Jesus is called Lord, missionary activity is symbolized, following Jesus is mentioned. But the missionary activity ("fishers of men") and the "following Jesus" probably come from Mk. 1:16-20; the "following motif" is very far removed from the appearance in John (v. 19), and calling Jesus "Lord" occurs in numerous contexts; so these are doubtful parallels. The differences between the stories seem to be equally significant: in John Jesus is on the shore, but in Luke he sets out to sea with the disciples; in John the disciples are alone, but in Luke two boats are involved, as well as other fishermen; in John Jesus asks a question, but in Luke he does not ask anything; in John he tells them to cast the net on the right side, but in Luke merely to let down the nets; in John they cannot haul in the net, but in Luke they do; in John the net does not break, but in Luke they are breaking; in John the boat does not sink, but in Luke the boats begin to sink; in John Peter rushes to Jesus, but in Luke he begs Jesus to leave.

Equally important, the verbal similarities between the two stories are largely incidental, such as arise from the content matter: fish, nets, and so forth. Some of the vocabulary (boat, nets) could come from Mk. 1:16-20, as well as the *dramatis personae* (on "Simon Peter" cf. Mt. 4:18).[54] Significantly, the un-Johannine grammatical peculiarities we noted before do not occur in the Lukan account. Even the expressions for the fruitless night's work and casting the net are different in the two accounts.[55]

---

[54] Fitzmeyer lays great emphasis on the name "Simon Peter" which occurs in Luke only in 5:8 and is found in a similar context in Jn. 21:7. Luke does employ the expression "Simon called/named Peter" in 6:14; Acts 10:5, 18, 32; 11:13, but Fitzmeyer does not take this as counter-evidence, since Luke is consistent in calling him Simon before 6:14, when Jesus names him Peter (Joseph A. Fitzmeyer, *The Gospel according to Luke (I-IX)*, Anch Bib 28 [New York: Doubleday & Co., 1981], pp. 549, 560-561, 564). But Fitzmeyer's argument seems fanciful, since prior to 6:14 Simon is mentioned *only once* (4:38) apart from the miraculous catch story, where he is called Simon Peter. Moreover, 6:14 is not the occasion upon which Jesus bestows the surname "Peter," but a retrospective comment, so that 6:14 is itself an instance of Luke's using the double name prior to its bestowal. The double name is found in Mt. 4:18 in the call of the disciples and could well be the source of the name in Lk. 5, especially if Luke used Matthew, as is argued by Gundry, *Matthew*, pp. 599-609.

[55] J. N. Sanders's conclusion, "It is fairly clear from the limited amount of common material that one narrative cannot be an edited version of the other" (J. N. Sanders, *The Gospel according to St. John*, ed. B. A. Mastin, BNTC [London: Adam & Charles Black, 1968], pp. 449-450) can be strengthened: neither do they appear to be edited versions of an independent story differently ap-

One must ask if it is not possible that we have here two similar, but distinct events. Against this it might be said that it would be impossible for Peter to go through the same situation and not recognize that it was Jesus. But this seems to forget that v. 7 is probably a redactional addition, so that in the traditional story, Peter did, upon catching the multitude of fish, recognize that it was Jesus on the shore. In the tradition 7b may have been something like "when Simon Peter knew/saw that it was the Lord...." It is not so odd that they would not recognize Jesus until this moment of disclosure. Jesus's calling them παιδία in v. 5 was not pastoral but colloquial. His question was, "Haven't caught anything, have you, boys?"[56] When the stranger said to cast the net on the right side of the boat (the side of good luck), they may have sensed something peculiar was going on but obeyed to see what would happen. When the nets were suddenly crammed with fish, their suspicions were confirmed. If he was there, the Beloved Disciple may have immediately cried out, "It is the Lord!" upon which word Peter girded himself, flung himself into the sea, and swam to Jesus. It may be that the Beloved Disciple was the first to realize that it was the Lord or it may be that Peter realized it simultaneously, but because the story is told from the standpoint of the Beloved Disciple, whom the evangelist inserts here, Peter appears to have a delayed reaction. Precisely because the event had happened in a similar way before, it was the means of their recognizing that it was Jesus. The fact that this time the nets do not break almost seems to make this a consciously contrapuntal event which presupposes the previous incident, in order to show perhaps that their mission to be fishers of men will not fail. At any rate, even if the miraculous catch stories of Lk. 5 and Jn. 21 derive from the same story, many, if not most, critics agree that it is Luke who has taken and displaced a post-resurrection story, rather than that John has appropriated a story from the life of Jesus.[57] As Brown urges, the most compelling argument that this was a post-resurrection story is that there is no reason a Christian preacher would turn an incident from the life of Jesus into a post-Easter occurrence. All the other examples of displacement spotted by New Tes-

---

propriated by the two evangelists. See also Stephen S. Smalley, "The Sign in John XXI," *NTS* 20 (1974): 275-288; Marshall, *Luke, p.* 200; Osborne, "Resurrection," p. 310.
[56] See J. H. Bernard, *Gospel according to St. John*, 2 vols., ICC (Edinburgh: T & T Clark, 1928), 2: 696; Brown, *John*, p. 1070.
[57] Bultmann, *Johannes*, p. 546; Wilckens, *Auferstehung*, p. 83; Lindars, *John*, p. 623; Grundmann, *Lukas*, p. 127; Brown, *John*, pp. 1089-1092; Fitzmeyer, *Luke*, p. 561.

tament scholars are in the other direction, from the post-resurrection period back into the life of Jesus. Moreover, there is a perfectly good reason why Luke would not use the incident as a post-resurrection appearance, namely, its occurrence in Galilee. Because he centers his attention on the Jerusalem tradition, Luke would have a motive for placing the event in the pre-Easter period. Really Lk. 5 has so many similarities to Mk 1:16-20 and so many dissimilarities to Jn. 21 that one could only say that Luke has spiced up the Markan story with the miraculous catch motif, but not that he has transferred the event itself. One could maintain, of course, that Luke is using some early variant of the same story that we have in Jn. 21, but then the hypothesis becomes unfalsifiable. There seems to be no reason to suppose any more than that the incident did occur as we have it in John, but that Luke borrowed the motif of the miraculous catch from the tradition. Thus, Luke 5 could be an extracted motif from a tradition, rather than Jn. 21 a composition—and a very intricate interweaving at that—of two. The un-Johannine elements in the chapter do not belong exclusively to either the miraculous catch or the meal (insofar as one might separate them). For example, v. 6 has un-Johannine traces, but also ἑλκύω, which is a Johannine style criterion. Verse 10 also has un-Johannine features, but is usually regarded as redactional; it plays no role in the miraculous catch story. There is an unusual expression in v. 4 for daybreak, but this verse could be connected with either story. So it seems impossible to discern separate traditions on the basis of grammar and style.

The Appearance's Claim to Chronological Primacy

In Jn. 21 we are told that "after this" Jesus revealed himself to seven disciples by the Sea of Tiberias. They do not recognize him, but when at his command they catch a miraculous quantity of fish, they recognize that it is the Lord. Proceeding to shore they find a meal of bread and fish waiting for them, which they then consume. It is very often observed that the story sounds very much like a first appearance of Jesus: the fishing in Galilee seems terribly incongruous with the commissioning and the breathing of the Holy Spirit by Jesus in chap. 20; the disciples do not recognize Jesus; the appearance seems utterly unexpected; the rehabilitation of Peter smacks of a first time appearance.[58] Also the fact that the appearance is in Galilee accords with the Markan account of the appearance to Peter and the disciples. It is sometimes said that the Gospel of Peter supports this appearance's being first, since it has the disciples returning forlorn to Galilee, picking up their nets, and going fishing; here the fragment breaks off.[59]

All these facts must be acknowledged. But as Schnackenburg points out, those who regard the story of Jn. 21 as a fusion of two separate stories cannot argue for this appearance's being first on the basis of its unexpectedness, since this is the result of the redactional intertwining of the original traditions.[60] In this case, the original traditions could have concerned a Galilean appearance which was not first. If, however, we agree that we do have here a unified tradition, must this appearance be the first? The evidence seems inconclusive. While this appearance, taken in isolation, does seem to be a first appearance, this is true of just about *all* the appearances: the appearance to Mary seems to be a first appearance, so does the appearance to the Twelve. This makes one sceptical that this appearance is unique in its "firstness." The return to Galilee may have been commanded by Jesus himself with a view toward meeting at an appointed time and place (Mt. 18:16); in the meantime the disciples exercise their old livelihood. It is interesting that the names in v. 2 include some non-fishermen. If the list is not wholly unreliable, then it seems odd that non-fishermen should be fishing here. Why did they not return to their trades as well? That the disciples are together requires more explanation than that they simply went back to their old way of life. But if Jesus had arranged to meet them in Galilee after their return from the feast, then the disciples might probably stay together, and when Peter announced, "I am going fishing," some of the non-fishermen among the disciples might participate.

Because the fourth evangelist did not intend to include events subsequent to chap. 20, the bestowing of the Holy Spirit in 20:22 is, I suspect, either not a per-

---

[58] Kirsopp Lake, *The Historical Evidence for the Resurrection of Jesus* (London: Williams & Norgate, 1907), pp. 137-162; Bultmann, *Johannes*, p. 543; Grass, *Ostergeschehen*, p. 76; Barrett, *John*, pp. 579, 582; Brown, *John*, pp. 1070, 1083, 1086-1092; Fuller, *Formation*, p. 149.

[59] Gospel of Peter 14:58-60 reads:
"Now it was the last day of unleavened bread and many went away and repaired to their homes, since the feast was at an end. But we, the twelve disciples of the Lord, wept and mourned, and each one, very grieved for what had come to pass, went to his own home. But I, Simon Peter, and my brother Andrew took our nets and went to the sea. And there was with us Levi, the son of Alphaeus, whom the Lord...."

[60] Schnackenburg, *Johannesevangelium*, 3: 414. This consideration presses hard against Brown.

formative utterance, but a command, or a telescoped account of future events analogous to Luke's telescoped account of the ascension. If the first, then Jesus's breathing on them is a symbolic portrayal of bestowal recalling the language of Gen. 2:7 (cf. Ez. 37:9); obviously Jesus's breath was not literally the Holy Spirit. It is interesting that he first breathes on them and then commands to receive (these acts could not, of course, be done simultaneously), which is the opposite of what we should expect, had this actually been the moment of bestowal. It may be that this act is a prefiguring of the giving of the Holy Spirit, analogous in function to the statement of Lk. 24:49 "I send the promise of my Father upon you," which was apparently not a performative utterance either. Passages concerning Jesus's *sending* the Holy Spirit and the Spirit's *coming* seem to imply strongly that so long as Jesus was physically present with the disciples, the Spirit would not yet come (Jn. 14:16-17, 22-23, 25-26; 15:26-27; 16:5-7, 13), and in John's conception Jesus's presence with the disciples after his resurrection was definitely physical. This suggests Jn. 20:22 is a command concerning the Spirit's coming. On the other hand, it may be that John has telescoped his account here to place the giving of the Spirit at this appearance,[61] just as Luke gives the impression in the gospel that the ascension was on Easter Sunday. In either case, it is then understandable how the disciples could return to Galilee to fish until they were to meet Jesus.

The view under discussion could conceivably also help to explain why the disciples did not recognize Jesus. Not expecting to see him prior to the appointed time, they did not recognize the figure on the shore 100 yards away (the length of an American football field). But when the miraculous catch occurred, the realization broke in upon them: "It is the Lord!" On the other hand, John mentions the 100 yards, not to emphasize how far from shore the disciples were, but how close. It could be that, like the Emmaus disciples, their eyes were simply supernaturally held from recognizing Jesus until the miraculous moment of disclosure. In any case, in v. 12 the disciples *knew* it was the Lord; there is no recognition during the meal itself. On John's comment that none dared to ask him, compare Jn. 4:27: "They marveled, ...but none said, 'What do you wish?'" We need to remember that these appearances must have been a wondrous mystery to the disciples, as were the Old Testament epiphanies to the prophets (cf. Jn. 12:41), and they were

---

[61] This would be more probable if the promise of the Spirit is not part of the appearance story tradition, but a theological element appended to it.

no doubt still gripped with awe and perhaps a holy trembling as their risen master stood before them and spoke with them.

As for the rehabilitation of Peter, I have already suggested that this may be a misinterpretation of Peter's pastoral commissioning as chief shepherd. If there was a rehabilitation of Peter, it probably took place in Jerusalem after Peter had returned from the tomb and was alone. As indicated before, the Galilean tradition in Mark does not necessarily preclude appearances first in Jerusalem. The Gospel of Peter's placing the fishing appearance first is of little historical worth, for it knows the gospels and may have placed this appearance first precisely for the very same reasons that have persuaded some scholars to regard it as a first appearance. The fragment is too short to determine if the appearance there is based on the tradition in Jn. 21. So it seems doubtful that the appearance in Jn. 21 must be a first appearance of Jesus to the disciples.

Allegorical Exegesis

The story itself has proved to be fertile ground for allegorizing exegesis. While the miraculous catch probably symbolizes the successful mission of the fishers of men, it seems doubtful whether the imagery extends beyond this. According to Grass, however, the whole story is full of symbolism: the futile night's work is the disciples' fruitlessness without Jesus; the net is the mission; that it is unbroken shows the church can handle the influx of members; the 153 fish are something, but what they are, Grass does not know.[62] Barrett says the fishing incident is the mission, and the fish are the converts;[63] this, however, is difficult in light of Jesus's command to eat the fish, which would make the meal a cannibalistic feast! Wilckens believes the fact that Peter pulls the net ashore symbolizes his special leadership in the church.[64] Schnackenburg thinks the seven disciples symbolize the whole church. In his view, there is no missionary motif in the fishing; rather the net symbolizes the universal church.[65] Kremer says the fishing is not a return to the old life, but is the apostolic labor of being fishers of men. Peter's nakedness is a symbol of his sin. The seven disciples and 153 fish are also symbols. But when it comes to the night in v. 3, Kremer, despite his symbolic

---

[62] Grass, *Ostergeschehen*, p. 78.
[63] Barrett, *John*, p. 580.
[64] Wilckens, *Auferstehung*, p. 83.
[65] Schnackenburg, *Johannesevangellum*, 3: 420, 427.

interpretation of the night in 13:30, here asserts that night is simply the best time to fish![66] One could go on and on.

But Christian interpreters throughout the ages seem to have really outdone themselves in the interpretation of the 153 fish.[67] Jerome reported that Greek naturalists had determined 153 different kinds of fish; accordingly, the number is a symbol of the universality of the church. Unfortunately, Jerome's source (Oppian *Halieutica*) does not in fact list 153, but 157, and says that there are countless more; according to Pliny (Pliny *Natural History* 9.43) there are 104 varieties of fish. Augustine observed that 153 is the sum of the numbers from 1 to 17; it symbolizes the fullness of the church. But such mathematical juggling seems somewhat far-fetched and the very plurality of the various mathematical solutions (for example, 153 dots could be arranged in an equilateral triangle with 17 dots on each side, and $17 = 10 + 7$, both of which are numbers of perfection) show that these peculiarities are coincidental. Cyril of Alexandria proposed an allegorical solution: $100 =$ the fullness of the Gentiles; $50 =$ the remnant of Israel; and $3 =$ the Trinity. But it goes without saying that this reads later ecclesiological interests back into John. Gematria is proposed by some modern authors; for example in Ez. 47:10, which is the passage on which Jerome made his comment concerning the different varieties of fish, the numerical value of the Hebrew consonants of (En-)gedi is 17 and of (En-)eglaim is 153. But again, this is probably fortuitous, since it was later churchmen, not John, who pointed to Ez. 47 as the key to the number of Jn. 21. Brown remarks that all these solutions encounter the same difficulty: there is no reason to believe that such a complicated interpretation of the number would have been intelligible to John's readers.[68] Because the symbolism is not evident, it probably did not prompt the invention of the number. It is probably meant to emphasize the eyewitness character of the incident, perhaps in association with the Beloved Disciple as in Jn. 19:35. Later the number came to be interpreted symbolically.

---

[66] Kremer *Osterevangelien*, pp. 205-210.
[67] See the fine discussion in Brown, *John*, pp. 1074-1076.
[68] Ibid., p. 1075.

Eucharistic Motif

Many exegetes have also wanted to interpret the meal of bread and fish in vs. 9-13 in terms of the eucharist. John writes in v. 13: ἔρχεται Ἰησοῦς καὶ λαμβάνει τὸν ἄρτον καὶ δίδωσιν αὐτοῖς, καὶ τὸ ὀψάριον ὁμοίως. In his account of the feeding of the 5,000 John writes: ἔλαβεν οὖν τοὺς ἄρτους ὁ Ἰησοῦς καὶ εὐχαριστήσας διέδωκεν τοῖς ἀνακειμένοις, ὁμοίως καὶ ἐκ τῶν ὀψαρίων ὅσον ἤθελον (Jn. 6:11). The language is similar at several points; but again the key word εὐχαριστέω is lacking in the Jn. 21 meal. It seems difficult to understand how this element can be absent if this incident is supposed to symbolize the eucharist. Moreover, the evidence we have indicates that fish was not used in early Christian eucharistic meals;[69] the use of bread and fish instead of bread and wine seems a strong argument against the story's containing a eucharistic motif from the early church, since the eating of fish would not have been invented by later ecclesiastical redactors. Those who think that v. 12b contains remnants of a recognition scene during the eucharist (though v. 12b as it now stands seems definitely not that) similar to the recognition scene in the Emmaus story, fail to reckon with the fact that here the purported recognition takes place before the taking and distribution of the elements in v. 13. This seems to be a substantial weakness in attempts to interpret the incident as teaching that Jesus will be met and recognized in the eating of the eucharist.

Actually, the so-called "meal motif" in the resurrection appearances seems to have been greatly overblown by commentators; of all the appearances only two have a meal associated with them (Lk. 24:41-43 is definitely not a meal). The early Christian believers did not apparently lay so great an emphasis on Jesus's post-resurrection presence in the eucharist that this colored the accounts of the resurrection appearances. For them Jesus was a living reality, always present with them in their daily lives (Mt. 28:20; cf. Rom. 8:10), not just in a sacramental meal. At the most one could say that in the two appearances in which Jesus shares a meal with the disciples, some eucharistic language has been taken over in narrating the events,[70] but the lack of the key words indicates that eucharistic interests were not the source of these stories. If one accepts the Pauline and gospel testimony that Jesus rose physically from the grave, there need be no inherent im-

---

[69] C. Vogel, "Le repas sacré au poisson chez les chrétiens," *RScRel* 40 (1966): 1-26.
[70] See Brown, *John*, pp. 247-248, 1099.

plausibility in Jesus's eating with his disciples after his resurrection. Perhaps one of the chief reasons for many scholars' interpreting these incidents in terms of symbols of the eucharistic presence of Jesus is that the physical realism which would be entailed in a historical understanding of the incidents is offensive to them. But again, the biblical accounts cannot be forced into the mold of modern sensibilities, for that would be contrary to sound historical methodology.

The Beloved Disciple Once More

In John 21 the Beloved Disciple again plays a key role. He is the same disciple who in chapter 13 lay against Jesus's breast at the Last Supper (v. 20), and he is known to the evangelist as the disciple of whom Jesus said, "If it is my will that he remain until I come..." (v. 22). He is well-known among Christian brethren, and the Parousia was expected to come before his death (v. 23). Most incredibly, he is finally declared to be witnessing to these things and to have written these things (v. 24). The most straightforward interpretation of this verse is that, contrary to any impression gained from v. 23, he is still alive and is, in fact, the evangelist himself. This holds true whether the writer is referring to himself in the third person or whether v. 24 is a comment of his associates or followers. This would mean that the accounts of at least the events where the Beloved Disciple is mentioned are written by an eyewitness. We should thus possess stories written by an eyewitness relating the crucifixion of Jesus, the visit to the empty tomb, and the resurrection appearance on the Sea of Tiberias.

Leon Morris has collected confirmatory internal evidence for the authorship of the fourth gospel by the Beloved Disciple.[71] (1) Palestinian knowledge: the author writes of Elijah and the Messianic expectation (1:21), the low status of women (4:27), the importance of various religious schools (7:15), the hostility

---

[71] Morris, *John*, pp. 10-28. Barrett's critique of the evidence for an eyewitness reduces largely to a "'t is—'t ain't" dispute with a Morris-like opponent (Barrett, *John*, pp. 119-123). In light of the cumulative nature of Morris's argument, this sort of refutation loses conviction after a while. For an impressive piece of work by a great scholar of the last century on the external evidence for the authenticity of John's gospel, see J. B. Lightfoot, *Essays on the Work Entitled Supernatural Religion* (London: Macmillan, 1889). He argues that Eusebius's silence respecting early witnesses to the fourth gospel is evidence in favor of its authenticity, for Eusebius's intention is to support only the disputed books, which was superfluous in the case of John (Ibid., pp. 38-51). He argues extensively for the testimony of Polycarp and Papias to the authenticity of John (Ibid., pp. 91-211). Finally, he examines other external evidence for the authenticity of the fourth gospel from Melito of Sardis, the churches of Gaul, *etc.*

between Jews and Samaritans (4:9), the contempt of the Pharisees for the common people (7:47), the unlawfulness against carrying one's bed on the sabbath (5:10), the priority of circumcision over the sabbath (7:22), and gives accurate topographical references. (2) Style of thought and writing: the parallels in ideas and expressions between the gospel and the Dead Sea scrolls confirm that it is a Palestinian document. The parallels to the rabbinical writings reinforce this judgment. (3) Eyewitness touches: many incidental comments indicate observations of an eyewitness, such as the time of day (1:39; 4:6), the time of a feast (2:13, 23), incidental place names (*e.g.*, Cana), eyewitness reminiscences (1:35-51; 13:1-20), persons not mentioned in the Synoptics (Nicodemus, Lazarus, and others), relationships such as Malchus's being related to a servant of the high priest (18:10, 26), or Annas's being the father-in-law of Caiaphas (18:13). (4) Eyewitness claims: 1:14 would be very unnatural if it meant believers in general, especially since the verb means simply physical seeing; similarly 19:35 is a self-reference by the author (cf. Josephus *Jewish War* 3.202). (5) Dogmatic controversies: the theological disputes are young, for example, the use and abuse of the sabbath (ch. 5) and whether the Messiah would bring deliverance from the Romans (6:15; 11:47-50). (6) Personal knowledge of the inner circle of disciples: the author portrays circumstances and thoughts only known to the Twelve (2:11, 16, 17, 21-22; 4:27, 33; 6:19, 60-61; 11:13, 54; 16:7; 18:2; 20:25; 21:3, 7). Taken together these considerations have a cumulative weight, supporting v. 24's claim that the evangelist is the Beloved Disciple. Against the objection that no one would call himself by this title, Morris reminds us that by assuming this title the author is able to avoid using his proper name; his anonymity actually shows modesty.[72] Since the title was doubtlessly given him by others (the Johannine community[73]) and he was widely known in this way, the author could simply use it, too, without having to use his own name.

Perhaps the greatest objection to eyewitness authorship is, however, the evangelist's use of sources.[74] The extent of the evangelist's use of sources is not clear,

---

[72] Morris, *John*, p. 12.
[73] Brown, *Community*, pp. 22-23.
[74] Brown, *John*, pp. C-CI; Schnackenburg, *Johannesevangelium*, 3: 458; Brown, *Community*, p. 178. But see the critique of source theories by Donald A. Carson, "Current Source Criticism of the Fourth Gospel: Some Methodological Questions," *JBL* (1978): 411-429. Carson examines the theories of Bultmann, Becker, Schnackenburg, Nicol, Fortna, Teeple, and Temple and pleads for a probing agnosticism.

however; more importantly, the objection rests on the assumption that an eyewitness would not use sources, which he could fill out with his own memories. Whether one makes or rejects this assumption will largely determine whether he regards the evangelist as the Beloved Disciple or not. If, in order to allow the use of sources by the evangelist, we differentiate between the Beloved Disciple and the evangelist, then in order to give due weight to the considerations adduced by Morris, we must interpret 21:24 as stating that the Beloved Disciple is bearing witness in the written gospel and that he caused these things to be written. In this case, the Beloved Disciple is the authority and personal source behind the fourth gospel, though not himself its author. As Brown remarks, this is the minimal interpretation that can be given to v. 24.[75] This would allow for use of sources by the evangelist, perhaps a pupil of the Beloved Disciple, but at the same time account for the evidence of an eyewitness noted by Morris and the personal reminiscences that seem to be reflected in the Johannine resurrection narratives. Whether the Beloved Disciple was still alive or had recently died would not materially affect this picture.

If, then, the Beloved Disciple is either the author of the gospel or the personal source standing behind the gospel, who is this man revered as the Beloved Disciple? To put the conclusion first, there seems little doubt that he was John the son of Zebedee.[76] Since he is present in 21:7, that means that of the seven disciples

---

[75] Brown, *John*, p. 1127; cf. XCIV-CI; 1119-1129. According to Brown, the Beloved Disciple was the personal source of the evangelist, who was a Johannine disciple. The Beloved Disciple was a historical figure who stood in an intimate relationship with his community, and the information about him is probably accurate. After the Beloved Disciple's death, a redactor added chap. 21 from ancient material he had. Both the evangelist and the redactor claim the witness of the Beloved Disciple, and this claim could not be false, for he had just died. The anonymity of the Beloved Disciple is literary and symbolic; the people in the community knew who he was: probably John the son of Zebedee. (But see note 78.) One would want to adjust Brown's view mainly in that the evangelist and the redactor were probably the same person.

[76] Objections to this identification do not seem to be too weighty. It may be urged that John was a Galilean, yet there is little mention of Galilee in the gospel. But the centering on Jerusalem could be the result of theology, not ignorance. Again, that John is called illiterate and ignorant in Acts 4:13 cannot preclude his being the Beloved Disciple, since the terms mean merely "unschooled." In any case, he could still be the personal source behind the gospel. It is true that two scenes where John was present, the Transfiguration and Gethsemane, are not mentioned in the gospel, but there may be traces of these in 12:23, 27-28. That the sons of Zebedee do appear finally in 21:2 cannot affect these conclusions, since anonymity is preserved by the use of two unnamed disciples; since this chapter came later as an appendix, perhaps even after the Beloved Disciple's death, the mention of them here does not violate the intent of the Beloved Disciple to remain anonymous in the gospel. Objections that the intended identification of John with the Beloved Disciple was wrong are not any more significant. It is unfounded to think that John is trying

mentioned in 21:2, he must be one of the two unnamed disciples or one of the sons of Zebedee. His presence at the last supper makes it evident that he was one of the Twelve, for John gives us to believe that only the Twelve were present, even if he does not say so explicitly (cf. Lk. 22:14, 30). We have seen the Beloved Disciple's close association with Peter; in the Synoptics, Peter, James, and John form a trio that were closely bound to Jesus and to each other. Since James was martyred early, that leaves John as the Beloved Disciple. According to Brown, "The close association with Peter posited on the description of the BD would fit no other NT figure as well as it fits John son of Zebedee."[77]

Probably the most significant confirmation of this identification is that neither John nor James is ever mentioned in the gospel until the reference to the sons of Zebedee in 21:2. So important a disciple as John could fail to be mentioned only if he were hidden behind the anonymity of the title "the Beloved Disciple." Though other persons in the gospel are carefully distinguished (6:71; 11:16; 13:2, 26; 14:22; 20:24; 21:2), John the Baptist is referred to only as "John." This may reflect the fact that John the Beloved Disciple could not be confused by the author with John the Baptist, since he either knew or was the former. Other candidates for the Beloved Disciple such as Lazarus or John Mark have little to commend them; according to Barrett, we may say with some assurance that "...the author of the gospel, whoever he may have been, described as the disciple whom Jesus loved, John, the son of Zebedee and one of the Twelve."[78] The fact that John stands behind the resurrection accounts of the fourth gospel is, of course, tremen-

---

to reconcile through the Beloved Disciple the two traditions that Judas was and was not unmasked as the betrayer at the Last Supper, especially since John probably is independent of the Synoptics. It is not impossible that John should be at the foot of the cross with Mary, nor does this contradict the flight of the disciples, which was general and temporary. That Mary is named with Jesus's brothers in Acts 1:14 cannot overturn the historicity of Jn. 19, since the disciples are mentioned in the preceding verse and Mary would naturally be listed with her sons; besides Acts 1:14 is itself questioned historically by some critics, as noted earlier. The visit of Peter and John to the tomb cannot be dismissed merely on account of Mk. 16:8, as explained already. In none of the cases where the Beloved Disciple appears do we have substantial grounds for doubting that John the son of Zebedee could have historically played the role described.

[77] Brown, *John*, pp. XCVI-XCVII.
[78] Barrett, *John*, p. 117; so also Brown, *John*, p. 1046. Brown now believes that the Beloved Disciple should not be identified with John because the fourth gospel, by setting the Beloved Disciple over against Peter, gives the impression that the Beloved Disciple was an outsider to the circle of best known disciples (Brown, *Community*, p. 34). But this argument is based on the fiction of a "one upmanship" of the Beloved Disciple over Peter in the gospel. Moreover, the confirmation of the Beloved Disciple's identity with John deriving from the fourth gospel's silence about John remains, Brown admits, a mystery.

dously significant for their historical credibility, for although Grass shrugs this off (to prove the author was a witness would not increase the credibility of the accounts, but only decrease the credibility of the witness), his conclusion is shaped by the conviction that the accounts are hopelessly legendary, a conclusion which we have seen to be unwarranted.[79]

THE ASCENSION

The Lake of Tiberias appearance is the last of the resurrection appearances as such in the gospels. Luke does refer to the ascension of Jesus in his gospel,[80] and this might be called a resurrection appearance. But an investigation of the ascension is a study all of its own and would not substantially affect the results of our discussion; therefore, we shall not cross the line to include it in this study.[81]

But it should be observed that the oft-repeated claim that Luke is the only evangelist to mention the ascension because the gross materialism of his resurrection appearances demanded that he somehow get Jesus off the scene and that he therefore invented the ascension is surely wrong.[82] In point of fact *all* the gospels

---

[79] Grass, *Ostergeschehen*, p. 73. An example of Grass's reasoning: the miraculous catch stories of Luke and John probably belong to the same tradition; Luke has dislocated a post-resurrection appearance narrative. Nevertheless, it is still a legend. Why? "This story was also an Easter legend, for the fact that the miraculous catch of fish really took place neither in the Easter days nor at the call of the first disciples needs no proof" (Grass, *Ostergeschehen*, p. 81).

[80] See Marshall, *Luke*, pp. 907-909.

[81] The standard work on the ascension is Gerhard Lohfink, *Die Himmelfahrt Jesu*, SANT 26 (München: Kösel Verlag, 1971); but see also Ferdinand Hahn, "Die Himmelfahrt Jesu, Ein Gesprach mit Gerhard Lohfink," *Bib* 55 (1974): 418-426; also Osborne, "Resurrection," pp. 253-265.

[82] Typical is Wilckens's assertion that the entire New Testament knows of no ascension of Jesus other than the resurrection. The resurrection and exaltation go together (Rom. 8:34; Eph. 1:19; Col. 1:18; Heb. 1:3; 13:20). Thus when Jesus appears, he appears out of heaven. Luke needs an ascension to get rid of Jesus's earthly sojourn; if the resurrection was not understood as the exaltation, then a second act was necessary (Wilckens, *Auferstehung*, pp. 91-98; so also Gunther Bornkamm, *Jesus von Nazareth*, 8th ed. [Stuttgart: Kohlhammer, 1968], p. 162; Grass, *Glaubenslehre*, 1: 100; Perrin, *Resurrection*, p. 72). This frequently repeated reasoning seems to rest on the false assumption of a dichotomy between resurrection and exaltation. For the evangelists as well as Paul, the resurrection entailed the exaltation of Jesus. When he appears, he appears in his exalted state. Hence, statements concerning Jesus's death and exaltation in no way intend to preclude his appearances on earth. Those who envision a dichotomy here seem to presuppose (once again) that tangible corporeality is incompatible with exaltedness, a conviction not shared by the New Testament. O'Collins points out that resurrection, along with translation, is a sub-category of exaltation, and thus the death-exaltation texts of the New Testament are not contrary to, but merely more general than, the death-resurrection texts (O'Collins, *Easter*, pp. 50-53). It would be implausible to suppose that the death-exaltation texts envisaged, not the resurrection, but the translation of Jesus (see chapter 11).

are "grossly materialistic" in their presentation of Jesus's resurrection appearances, as we shall see; hence, Luke's ascension narrative is not to be accounted for merely on the basis of his physicalism.

It ought to be noted that for Luke the ascension does not seem to be the glorification of Jesus; when Jesus appears to the disciples after his resurrection he is already glorified (Lk. 24:26). The ascension is simply the decisive end of the appearances of Jesus. I have suggested that we ought to reconsider whether John may not have the same sort of conception of the ascension as Luke: that the resurrection and glorification are the same, but that the ascension is a decisive end to Jesus's physical presence here; the alternative seems to be that Jesus appeared to Mary in an unglorified state.[83] However this may be, for Luke there could be no more physical appearances of Christ after the ascension, not because Christ was then changed, but simply because he had left decisively the earthly world.

---

[83] Coppens argues that for John Jesus enters his glory at his death (Joseph Coppens, "La glorification céleste du Christ dans la théologie néotestamentaire et l'attente de Jésus," in *Resurrexit*, ed. Édouard Dhanis [Rome: Libreria Éditrice Vaticana, 1974], pp. 33-36). But if this is so, then in view of Jesus's statement, "I have not yet ascended," the conclusion that the ascension is for John virtually the same as for Luke is almost irresistible.

CHAPTER 8

THREE ISSUES RAISED BY THE GOSPEL NARRATIVES

THE LOCALITY OF THE APPEARANCES

One of the most disputed questions concerning the resurrection appearances in general is their geographical location. Most scholars would probably incline toward the Galilean appearance tradition, largely on the authority of Mark. Since the flight of the disciples hypothesis is unrealistic, the most convincing presentation of this view would probably be that after the discovery and inspection of the empty tomb, the disciples returned, perhaps still unbelieving, to Galilee, where they then saw Jesus.

But this theory is forced to ride rough-shod over so many traditions that Jesus did appear in Jerusalem that it seems difficult to embrace with firm conviction. It is not true that Mark necessarily precludes Jerusalem appearances; both Matthew and John accept Jerusalem and Galilee appearances and perhaps so does Paul's formula; Luke, given his 40 days telescoped to one, does not necessarily preclude Galilean appearances. Therefore, we need to ask seriously whether these traditions are so irreconcilable after all.

Contrary to frequent assertion, it is not *impossible* to construct a series of appearances in Jerusalem and then in Galilee. It is *possible* that the appearances took place in the following way: after the disciples had investigated the tomb and departed, the women (or Mary) lingered outside the tomb, whereupon they saw Jesus. The Emmaus disciples, having heard only the report of the disciples that the body was missing, departed forlorn back to Emmaus; Jesus joined them, and they recognized him during the evening bread breaking. They hurried to return to Jerusalem; meanwhile, Jesus appeared to Peter. When the Emmaus disciples reached Jerusalem that evening, the disciples and they exchanged the stories of what had happened. Some were perhaps sceptical; Thomas was not with the group. Jesus then suddenly stood among them, which must have terrified the disciples, who thought they were seeing a ghost; Jesus, however, reassured them of his corporeality and continuity with the Jesus they knew. The disciples remained in Jerusalem for the remainder of the Feast of Unleavened Bread, after which they were to return to Galilee where a rendezvous with Jesus had been set. Thomas was stiff-necked, however, and refused to believe; therefore, just prior to the disciples' return to Galilee, Jesus appeared once more to Thomas and the disciples, which climaxes the gospel of John. The disciples returned to Galilee as arranged and, while waiting for the rendezvous with Jesus, engaged in the old livelihood of some of them, namely, fishing. During this fishing expedition, Jesus unexpectedly appeared to them on the beach; the disciples, though having no inkling that Jesus should appear to them before the pre-arranged time and place, recognized him in the miraculous draught of fish. Some time later the disciples and perhaps others with them assembled on the hillside where Jesus had arranged to meet them, and he appeared to them there, as Matthew relates. This need not have been the last appearance; Luke says Jesus continued to appear to the disciples during the time between Passover and Pentecost, and Paul specifically names appearances to the 500 brethren, to James, and to all the apostles. It is possible that the disciples returned to Jerusalem for Pentecost and that this last mentioned appearance took place there, prior to the feast itself and the outpouring of the Holy Spirit. One would thus have a sequence of appearances in Jerusalem-Galilee-Jerusalem.

Now, I am not asserting that this is in fact the way it must have happened; but it is not impossible.[1] The conclusion that "It is impossible to harmonize the ac-

---

[1] C. F. D. Moule, "The Post-Resurrection Appearances in Light of Festival Pilgrimages," *NTS* 4 (1957-58): 58-59; idem, *The Significance of the Message of the Resurrection for Faith in Jesus Christ*, SBT 8 (London: SCM, 1968), p. 5. Anderson retorts that Moule's solution "leaves unexplained the thorny problem of Mark's and Matthew's 'addiction' to Galilee, or Luke's or John's 'addiction' to Jerusalem" (Hugh Anderson, *Jesus and Christian Origins* [New York: Oxford University Press, 1964], p. 196). Luke's centering on Jerusalem is, however, widely acknowledged to be the result of his scheme of salvation history moving toward a climax in Jerusalem. Similarly, John may concentrate on Jerusalem because this was where the Messianic events reached their fulfillment. And John does have a Galilean appearance in the epilogue. It contradicts the facts to

counts of the resurrection appearances" has come too quickly from scholars' pens.[2] Though one is loath to try to harmonize all the accounts, this being speculative and tenuous, the fact remains that negative judgments of the historical worth of the accounts on this basis alone do not seem to be warranted. One is not forced to accept either the Jerusalem or Galilee tradition and therefore to suppress the other; both traditions are well-attested and both could be accurate.

A *GATTUNG* FOR THE APPEARANCE STORIES

Dodd's Form Critical Analysis

Is there a particular *Gattung* or form that characterizes the resurrection appearances across the board? C. H. Dodd in his influential essay, "The Appearances of the Risen Christ," attempted to discover the common form of the various appearance stories.[3] He differentiated between concise and circumstantial narratives, the latter being stories filled with picturesque details, the former being brief accounts worn down to the bare essentials. Examples of circumstantial narratives include the walk to Emmaus and the appearance by the Sea of Tiberius; examples of the concise form include Mt. 28:9-10, 16-20; Jn. 20:19-21. Dodd believed that five elements common to the concise narratives could be discerned: (1) the situation is that the disciples are bereft of the Lord, (2) the Lord appears, (3) he gives a greeting, (4) the disciples recognize him, (5) he gives a word of command. The circumstantial narratives are characterized by unnecessary details of the storyteller's art.

---

speak of any "addiction" by Matthew to Galilee. Mark's mentioning only Galilee could be explained in a number of ways—as I have suggested in the text—and cannot justify our ignoring the Jerusalem tradition. The objections of C. F. Evans, *Resurrection and the New Testament*, SBT 12 (London: SCM Press, 1970), pp. 112-113, to Moule's thesis are implicitly answered in the text; similarly, the objections of Karl Martin Fischer, *Das Ostergeschehen*, 2nd ed. (Göttingen: Vandenhoeck & Ruprecht, 1980), pp. 45-55. Supporting Moule is Grant Osborne, "History and Theology in the Resurrection Narratives: a Redactional Study" (Ph.D. thesis, University of Aberdeen, 1974), pp. 351-353.

[2] See the surprising list of citations in John Wenham, *Easter Enigma* (Exeter, England: Paternoster Press, 1984), pp. 9-10, 140, whose own failing is that he tends to take his often unnecessarily elaborate speculations, not as mere possibilities, but as actual facts.

[3] C. H. Dodd, "The Appearances of the Risen Christ: A study in form-criticism of the Gospels," in idem, *More New Testament Studies* (Manchester: Manchester University Press, 1968), pp. 102-115.

But Dodd's *schema* faces a fundamental dilemma: either the formal characteristics he adduces as common to the accounts seem to be so general as to be of little worth or, when they are made more specific, they are no longer common characteristics of all the accounts. For example, the characteristics (1) and (2) are actually tautologous, for *any* appearance of Jesus in whatever form must presume that he is not present and that he then appears. These elements then seem to be of little value in discovering a common form to the appearance accounts. But when we come to the remaining three, these simply do not seem to hold for all the appearance narratives. In Mt. 28:9-10 we have (3) and (5), but (4) is missing (unless it is so generalized as to become trivial). In Mt. 28:16-20, (5) is present, but (3) and (4) are lacking. In Lk. 24:36-42 we find (3), but (4) and (5) are lacking. This is not a recognition scene in the proper sense of the word, as in the Emmaus and Mary Magdalene appearances, for the disciples do not doubt the *identity* of the apparition, but rather his corporeality and continuity with the Jesus who was laid in the grave. The word of command is included in the appearance only if we add on vs. 44-49; but then the distinction between a circumstantial and concise narrative becomes pretty thin, for the content of these verses is very similar to the discussion on the Emmaus road. There we have a basic story expanded with theological motifs; but here we have precisely the same thing. It seems somewhat arbitrary to call the first circumstantial and the second concise. In Jn. 20:11-18, we have (4) and (5), but (3) is lacking (Jesus's question cannot be called a greeting in comparison with "Peace be with you," or "Hail"). Here, too, one must seriously question the distinction between circumstantial and concise accounts, for this story shows as much the storyteller's art as the Emmaus appearance. It certainly includes unnecessary details. Dodd's classification of this story as concise because it "follows the familiar pattern"[4] seems a good illustration of the danger of the misunderstanding that can result from pressing forms onto the accounts. In Jn. 20:19-23 we have (3) and (5), but not (4); as in the Lukan account it is not the identity of the apparition that is doubted. The appearance to Thomas has only (3), but Dodd does not regard this as an independent story, but an addendum to the foregoing appearance. Dodd regards Mk. 16:14-15 as an independent tradition; but it has only (5) and lacks (3) and (4). Death by a thousand qualifications seems to have already begun when Dodd asserts that these are lacking but are neverthe-

---

[4] Ibid., p. 113.

less implied. In fact, not one of the supposed concise narratives has all three of the elements that delineate the form of the concise narratives, and there are other elements that are just as common as these three. These characteristics thus do not seem to constitute formal earmarks of the resurrection accounts; the only common form is that Jesus is absent and then appears, which is of no help in identifying a literary form.

The inadequacy of Dodd's *schema* seems to become especially evident when it is applied to the Markan account of Jesus's walking on the water, for according to Dodd this story has four of the five formal characteristics of a resurrection narrative, but it nevertheless is not one and is firmly welded in its context.[5] Dodd's schema seems, therefore, a Procrustean bed into which the gospel accounts ought not to be coerced.

Hellenistic Gattung

It is often alleged that the gospel appearance stories have been shaped by Hellenistic myths concerning the appearances of quasi-divine heroes.[6] John Alsup has given considerable analysis to the question of whether a story *Gattung* existed concurrent with the gospels that told of divine appearance in human form or an appearance of the dead in a way comparable to the gospel stories and whether a formal and essential relationship can be drawn between them.[7] Very often the gospel appearances, especially the Emmaus road appearance, are compared to the Hellenistic stories.[8] Most often adduced as a parallel are Philostratus's tales of

---

[5] Ibid., p. 121.
[6] For example, Ingo Broer, "Der Herr ist wahrhaft auferstanden (Lk. 24, 34)," in *Auferstehung Jesu—Auferstehung der Christen*, QD 105, ed. Lorenz Oberlinner (Freiburg: Herder, 1986), pp. 56-57.
[7] John Alsup, *The Post-Resurrection Appearance Stories of the Gospel Tradition*, CTM A5 (Stuttgart: Calwer Verlag, 1975), pp. 214-265.
[8] Typical is Wilckens's statement:
"The appearance stories of the gospels obviously belong to an entirely different realm of tradition: not to the Jewish-Christian *urgemeindlichen* or to the realm of the Pauline mission, but rather to that of the Hellenistic communities of the Palestinian-Syrian area bordering in the north. Here the old Palestinian tradition about Jesus was taken up and—as in Jerusalem—made the center of the traditions of the community, granted, under the simultaneous transformation of the frame of conception. Out of Jesus, the eschatological, omnipotent Rabbi, came Jesus, the epiphanal Son of God, the unique θεῖος ἀνήρ and σωτήρ. The conception of the appearance stories handed down in the gospels is shaped by this Hellenistic Christology, as is especially to be seen in particular features of the Emmaus pericope (Lk. 24, 12ff.), for which there are, as is well-known, striking Hellenistic parallels.[87]....only in the total context of this general transformation process in the his-

Apollonius of Tyana; particularly of interest is the story of his disappearance from his trial before Domitian and his reappearance to Damis and Demetrius in the grotto of Dicaerchia (Philostratus *Vita Apollonii* 7.41-8.13). Prior to the trial Apollonius tells the two to go to the sea by the island of Calypso, "for there you shall see me appear to you." When Damis asks, "Alive?" Apollonius answers, "As I myself believe, alive, but as you will believe, risen from the dead." Three days later the two are in Dicaerchia to see Apollonius. At the trial Apollonius proclaims that even if his body is taken, no one could touch his soul, and adds, "Nay, you cannot even take my body," quoting Homer: "For thou shalt not slay me, since I tell thee I am not mortal." Thereupon Apollonius vanishes. Meanwhile Damis and Demetrius walk along the shore, despairing that Apollonius would not come. As they sit in the grotto, Damis asks whether they will ever see him again, whereupon Apollonius suddenly appears and answers, "Ye shall see him; nay, ye have already seen him." Demetrius asks, "Alive?" and Apollonius in response extends his hand and invites them to take hold of it. They then embrace him with joy and ask about his trial. When Apollonius informs them that he had made his defense that day, Demetrius is amazed that he could make so long a journey to the grotto in one day. As they walk back to town together, they talk along the way, "and he told them exactly how he vanished from the seat of judgment."

Another frequently mentioned analogy is the *apotheosis* of Romulus as related by Plutarch (Plutarch *Lives* 1.27.7-8). Amidst natural disorders of the weather, Romulus is said to have been "caught up into heaven" and to have become a "benevolent god," instead of a good king. Some, however, suspect that Romulus's disappearance was the result of his murder by the patricians. Later a patrician friend of Romulus swears by the sacred emblems that he saw Romulus coming to meet him on the road, fair and stately and arrayed in bright armor. He asked Romulus why he had left the patricians prey to these unjust accusations, to which

---

tory of the Jewish Christian Jesus tradition in the Hellenistic communities of Palestine and Syria can the gospel appearance stories be suitably understood in terms of the history of religions.

[87] R. Bultmann, *Geschichte der synoptischen Tradition*³ (1957) 310, note 1" (Ulrich Wilckens, *Auferstehung*, TT4 [Stuttgart and Berlin: Kreuz Verlag, 1970], p. 94).
So also Norman Perrin, *The Resurrection according to Matthew, Mark, and Luke* (Philadelphia: Fortress, 1977), p. 66.

Romulus answered that he had to return to heaven, but that if the Romans practice self-restraint and valor they will attain the heights of power. Because of the noble character of the witness and his oath, this account was accepted.

A similar story is the *apotheosis* of Aristeas of Proconnesus (Herodotus *Persian Wars* 4.14.1-2; 15.1-2). Aristeas had entered a textile shop, where he died. The owner closes the shop to inform relatives of the misfortune. But a man of Cyzicus reports that he saw Aristeas and spoke with him on the way to Cyzicus. When the shop is opened, the body is not to be found. Seven years later, Aristeas reappears in Proconnesus. He is said to have appeared again 240 years later to the Metapontines of Italy, whom he tells that he had once visited their country in the form of a crow.

A not dissimilar story is told of Cleomedes of Astypaleia (Pausanias *Descriptions of Greece* 6.9.6-8). Having killed a man in an Olympic boxing match, Cleomedes returns to Astypaleia without the prize. In anger he pulls down the pillar supporting the roof of a schoolhouse containing sixty children. When the parents want to stone him, he takes refuge in the sanctuary of Athena. He climbs into a chest and shuts the lid; when, however, the chest is broken open, no one is found. The oracle at Delphi proclaims him the last of the heroes, and from that time he has been honored among the Astypalaeans.

Plutarch relates one more similar story: the disappearance of Alcmene (Plutarch *Lives* 1.28.6-8). It is said that her body disappeared on the way to the burial, and a stone was found on the bier instead. Plutarch's comment on all these "fables" is that we ought not to accept the idea that the body can be taken into heaven, but that only the soul survives.

Another story of death, ascension, and appearance from Hellenistic literature is that concerning Peregrinus Proteus as related with a measure of ridicule by Lucian of Samosata (Lucian *Passing of Peregrinus* 36-40). Peregrinus leaps into a fire and disappears. Lucian made up the story that out of the flames a vulture flew, crying that he was done with earth and was flying to Olympus. Later Lucian hears an elderly man telling how he had just seen Peregrinus wearing a white robe and an olive garland; the old man swore that he had even seen the vulture, which Lucian had invented, flying up out of the flames.

Lucian records another story, the appearance of a deceased woman Demainete to her husband (Lucian *Passing of Peregrinus* 3.27). Her husband had burned all her personal effects with her on the funeral pyre. Seven days after her death, as he was reading Plato on the soul, she came and sat down beside him, as real as life. He embraced her, but she reprimanded him for not burning one of her sandals, which was under a chest. A dog in the room then barked, and she vanished. The sandal, however, was found under the chest and then burned.

In analyzing the individual stories, one notes that the greatest difficulty in comparing the Apollonius story with the gospel appearance stories is that Apollonius was not really dead. Nevertheless, the parallels to the Emmaus story in particular are striking. One might be tempted to think that the two stories share a common *Gattung*, but as Alsup points out, it "is very probable in the light of chronological and biographical factors that this was not the case, but that Philostratus in one sense or another is dependent upon the gospel accounts (especially Luke) and maybe directly upon the Emmaus story."[9] Philostratus's work was designed to provide a non-Christian alternative to Jesus, and given the fact that his story resembles the Emmaus incident not so much in its broad form but in its particularities, the most likely explanation for the similarities is direct dependence. On the other hand, in the Romulus story the key motifs are the disappearance of the hero and his encounter with a person later on. The stories of Aristeas, Cleomedes, and Alcmene show that the key element in this type of story is the disappearance, not the appearance. Similarly in the Peregrinus story, the original account was only of his disappearance in the flames. The Demainete story does not fit into this *Gattung*; Alsup wants to regard it as a visionary dream story, but the vividness of the story and its similarity to accounts in the case studies of parapsychology concerning veridical visions of recently deceased individuals make one wonder if there could not be an actual historical incident in back of the story.

Now when one relates the *Gattung* of the θεῖος ἀνήρ disappearance stories to the resurrection appearance narratives of the gospels, decisive differences at once appear. The θεῖος ἀνήρ *Gattung* is a Greek story designed to answer the question: where has the hero gone? The reappearance only goes to show that the θεῖος ἀνήρ has not died, but only disappeared, as Alsup explains,

> The 'appearance' or its substitute gave the solution to a particular problem: the θεῖος ἀνήρ did not die, but has *disappeared*, he has been *translated* from this to another sphere, he lives on in a higher form of existence... Moreover this is a necessity from the view-

---

[9] Alsup, *Stories*, p. 232.

point of the *Gattung* because a θεῖος ἀνήρ cannot die like others, but...must be exalted on high. This story *Gattung* is a Greek type and has its origins in the heroic epics of the Homeric period and was developed further in the transition from small literary units to larger ones—as in the background of ancient novels in general. Where similarities in these stories thoroughly overlap with those of the gospel accounts—as in the case of Apollonius—dependence of a direct nature, the latter upon the former, is probable....[10]

Hence, in the gospel accounts, the motif of disappearing occurs only once, in the Emmaus story, and there it does not have the same dimensions as in the θεῖος ἀνήρ stories, for it is unrelated to the question where the hero has gone. Moreover, the resurrection appearances are radically unlike the reappearance of the θεῖος ἀνήρ, for their purpose is not to show that Jesus did not really die and lives on, but rather that he has been raised from the dead. Thus, although the two types of appearance stories show some similarities, as one would expect from the nature of the subject matter, such as a figure's being seen, conversing with people, a message's being given, and so forth, in *essence* the two types of story are distinct and not genealogically related.[11]

Jewish Gattung

Alsup argues instead that the *Gattung* for the resurrection appearance stories actually comes from Jewish theophany stores.[12] He considers first the anthropomorphic theophanies of the Old Testament. In Gen. 18, God appears to Abraham at Mamre. Abraham sees three men and, unaware that the Lord is among them, offers them a meal. The promise of an heir is given. As two of the men go on to Sodom, Abraham remains before the Lord and speaks with him. In Ex. 3, the angel of the Lord appears to Moses in the burning bush. God speaks to Moses out of the bush with words that are familiar to any Bible reader. In Judges 3, the angel of the Lord appears to Gideon and tells him to go into battle, for the Lord is with him. After Gideon brings an offering, the angel causes it to be consumed with fire, and then he disappears. Gideon now knows that he has seen the angel of the Lord face to face. In Judges 13, the angel of the Lord appears to Manoah's wife and promises her a child. Manoah asks that the man of God might appear to

---

[10] Ibid., p. 238.
[11] Cf. a similar conclusion concerning the miracle stories of the gospels and miracle-working "divine men" by Barry L. Blackburn, "'Miracle Working ΘΕΙΟΙ ΑΝΔΡΕΣ' in Hellenism (and Hellenistic Judaism)," in *Gospel Perspectives*, vol. 6: *The Miracles of Jesus*, ed. David Wenham and Craig Blomberg (Sheffield, England: JSOT Press, 1986), pp. 185-218.
[12] Alsup, *Stories*, pp. 239-265.

them again. The angel appears again to the woman, who fetches her husband, who then speaks with the angel about his identity. The angel refuses Manoah's offer of a meal and urges that an offering be given instead. As the flames consume the offering, the angel ascends out of sight in the flames. Manoah knew that it had been the angel of the Lord. In I Sam. 3. the boy Samuel hears the voice of one calling his name. Upon Eli's instructions, he responds, "Speak, Lord." The Lord comes and speaks with him as man to man.

Alsup next turns to anthropomorphic theophanies in intertestamental literature. In Tobit 5 and 12, Tobias goes to Media accompanied by Azarius, who is really the angel Raphael in disguise. In Media they free Sarah from demonic oppression with the heart, liver, and gall of a fish. Upon their return, Tobias cures his father's blindness with leftover fish gall. When the time comes for Azarius to be rewarded, he reveals his identity as the angel Raphael and, after exhorting them, disappears. In the Testament of Abraham, the angel Michael goes to inform Abraham of his coming death. Abraham does not know who he is. As they walk together, a tree tells Abraham that his companion is holy. In a tearful scene, the angel is unable to communicate his message. But God tells Isaac in a dream of his father's coming death. Sarah recognizes Michael as one of the three who had visited them at Mamre. Abraham admits that he also recognized him, as he washed his feet. Michael confirms Isaac's dream and at Abraham's request takes Abraham to see heaven before he dies and his soul is separated from his body.

In analyzing these texts, Alsup admits both that they have nothing to do with death and resurrection and that the gospel narratives never refer in any way to these texts.[13] Moreover, the above examples differ considerably among themselves in context and particular message.[14] Nevertheless, he maintains that they share a unity of form and intention. They are all immediate, personal encounters between the Lord and persons singled out for an appearance, and the appearances focus on God's chosen people. Furthermore, Alsup contends that in terminology, motifs, structural elements, and conceptual scope the gospel appearance stories are a deliberate reflection of the Old Testament theophany. The subject matter is the same: a personal encounter where the resolution of non-recognition is important, where the human partner receives a promise and commission, and where the

---

[13] Ibid., p. 251.
[14] Ibid., p. 263.

human participants experience fear, doubt, and awe at the presence of the one who appears. In order to express that Jesus appeared, that he reunited the disciples out of apparent tragedy, and that he commissioned them, the early Christians utilized the form of Old Testament anthropomorphic theophanies.

It seems puzzling, however, why Alsup should regard the theophany stories as the source of the *Gattung* for the resurrection appearance stories, since the similarities seem to be no greater than those of the θεῖος ἀνήρ stories. The chief motif that is present in some of them is the non-recognition of the divine visitant. But even this is not essential, and as I indicated in the discussion of Dodd's form proposal, this so-called recognition motif in the gospel stories seems to have been blown out of proportion by some New Testament scholars. In fact only three of the resurrection appearance stories contain this motif. It cannot be emphasized enough that in the appearance to the Twelve, there seems to be no problem of recognizing Jesus, as is evident from the fact that there is no moment of disclosure; rather the disciples' doubts concern Jesus's corporeality.[15] (Compare Acts 12:15 where Peter is mistaken for an angel; there seems to be no problem of recognizing Peter, since the angel is identified as his, but the doubt concerns his bodily presence.) Most of the resurrection stories contain no recognition motif comparable to that contained in some of the Jewish theophany stories. This makes it difficult to believe that the gospel appearance stories are borrowing a *Gattung* from the Old Testament theophanies; at most one could say that one feature of some theophany stories was taken over by some gospel appearance accounts.

But more than that: even in the three instances where Jesus is not recognized, the situation is unlike the theophany stories. For in the theophany stories, the situation is essentially the Lord or an angel's appearing incognito among men; he is *disguised*. But in the gospel stories, there is no indication that Jesus appears disguised in another form; he is not incognito; rather the eyes of the beholder seem to be supernaturally held from recognizing him. This is at least the case in the Emmaus appearance. At the Lord's discretion, the scales fall from the eyes, and he is recognized. Actually, in the Jewish theophany stories, one cannot speak of a re-cognition at all (except in the Testament of Abraham, where Gen. 18 is being deliberately recalled), for the human participant did not know the divine

---

[15] Jacob Kremer, *Die Osterevangelien—Geschichten um Geschichte* (Stuttgart: Katholisches Bibelwerk, 1977), p. 139.

being previously in order to recognize him. In the theophanies it is a matter of penetrating an intentional disguise; in the gospels those who knew Jesus best did not recognize him, though he was not disguised. The Jewish motif is really a disguise motif, God incognito; in the three instances in the gospels where the recognition motif occurs, the theme is not the divine person's assuming a disguise in order to sojourn unnoticed among men, for Jesus was already in human form before his death, resurrection, and appearances.

This last fact alone seems, moreover, to make the anthropomorphic theophanies a dubious source of the *Gattung* of the resurrection appearance stories, for the only significant element common to all the anthropomorphic theophanies is that they are anthropomorphic (even the disguise motif is not always present). But the fact that the Lord or his angel appears in human form cannot be assumed to be the source of Jesus's so appearing since Jesus already was a man. A radical difference between the theophanies and the resurrection appearances seems to lie in the fact that in a theophany a heavenly being assumes a human form in order to appear, but in a resurrection appearance, a human being appears as risen from the dead. Certainly the concept of Jesus's resurrection appearances could never have been deduced from the Old Testament anthropomorphic theophanies. But, it is alleged, the disciples turned to the *Gattung* to express what they had experienced. But why should they do this? For if, on the one hand, they experienced heavenly visions of Jesus after his death, then a much closer *Gattung* lay in the Jewish concept of translation (Gen. 5:24; 2 Kings 2:11-18; Testament of Job 40), in which case neither resurrection nor anthropomorphic appearances comes into view. But if, on the other hand, they experienced bodily appearances of Christ, then any borrowing of anthropomorphism from the theophanies would be superfluous. For given that the disciples believed that Jesus had risen from the dead and that these were therefore *resurrection* appearances, they could only be physical encounters, for that is what a resurrection implies, a physical raising of the man in the tomb. The appearances are anthropomorphic because Jesus is an ἄνθρωπος who was raised. The Jewish theophanies do not even seem to come into view. But if one takes away this parallel, then what significant resemblance is left between the theophanies and the resurrection appearances? The elements of personal encounter, divine promise or commission, and reactions of fear, doubt, and awe seem to be so generalized as to be of little help in determining genealogical relationship.

The fact is that there are no across the board features common to all the anthropomorphic theophanies and to the resurrection appearances, except the most general considerations, for example, a divine person appears to human persons; and these are insufficient to show that the one is using a *Gattung* borrowed from the other. There is thus no evidence, it seems, to believe that the disciples were using the theophany *Gattung* to formulate their experience. Therefore, it seems misleading to speak of the resurrection appearance stories' using the *Gattung* of Old Testament anthropomorphic theophanies. The uniqueness of the resurrection appearance stories ought to be recognized.[16]

---

[16] Klaus Berger has also sought to find in Judaism, not indeed a detailed *Gattung* for all the resurrection appearances, but various *Gattungen* and motifs which he believes are taken up in the resurrection narratives. The empty tomb narrative follows a *Gattung* of "the futile search for the body" of some exalted person (Klaus Berger, *Die Auferstehung der Propheten und die Erhöhung des Menschensohnes*, SUNT 13 [Göttingen: Vandenhoeck & Ruprecht, 1976], pp. 117-122). Berger traces the *Gattung* back to II Kings 2:17 and finds it in 4 Macc. 17:2-6; Test. Job 18; 40:9, 13-14 and apocryphal stories of the absence of the bodies of Zechariah, the thief in Paradise, and Mary. The appearance stories conform to a *Gattung* of "Who are you?...I am..." in divine calls and appearances, which stresses the identity of the calling or appearing one (Ibid., pp. 154-200). Doubt is often an element in such stories and serves to evoke a sign of identity. In this regard, Berger places great stock in the motif of God's calling three times, for the third call makes certain that it is God (Lib. Ant. 53:4; I Sam. 3:1-18). He thinks that the demonstrations in the appearance stories are signs of identity to prove that Jesus is not an impersonating demon. The "third time" motif plays a direct role in the arrangement of the appearance stories. They are arranged so as to increase in number of witnesses; the women are placed first because they are poorer witnesses; the last appearance is the most important.

Berger has produced a prodigious tome, choking with documentation, but one cannot help but feel that here is the *religionsgeschichtliche Methode* gone out of control. Berger mixes his material without discretion from sources whether Jewish or Christian, early or late. Most of his texts are from late Christian sources, which he reads back into the New Testament narratives. He does not discriminate between the subject matter in the texts, whether it concerns a translation to heaven, a divine calling, an epiphany, a resurrection appearance, and so forth. All are thrown into the potpourri, and any and all parallels are drawn, while genealogical ties are simply assumed.

With regard to the empty tomb, the *Gattung* discerned by Berger has to do with a person's being translated directly to heaven, not with his resurrection. But since the disciples believed Jesus had been raised from the dead, the emptiness of his grave was automatically entailed. Thus, the question is whether the empty tomb is a legendary product of this assumption; there is no need to appeal to the translation *Gattung* at all. In fact, in its details the empty tomb story does not truly correspond to the "futile search for the body" *Gattung*, for while the sons of the prophets were actually *searching* for Elijah's missing body, the women knew the location of Jesus's body, having observed the burial, and were coming to anoint it, not to find it.

Actually, the real value of Berger's work seems to be that it confirms that the appearances of Jesus were physical in nature. For had the disciples seen only heavenly visions of Jesus, then even in the presence of the empty tomb, they would probably not have concluded that he had been raised from the dead, a notion which ran contrary to Jewish concepts of the resurrection; rather they would have concluded that God had translated and exalted him to heaven, whence he appeared to them, and therefore his body was not to be found. That they proclaimed, contrary to

CHAPTER 8

THE NATURE OF THE RESURRECTION BODY

Finally, we need to examine the nature of the resurrection body of Jesus as conceived by the evangelists. Many contemporary theologians try to play off the "massive realism" of the gospels against Paul's purely spiritual conception of the resurrection body.[17] Because Paul's letters ante-date the gospels, the gospel ac-

---

Jewish notions, the resurrection of Jesus, and not his translation, on the analogy of Enoch or Elijah, thus seems strong evidence for the physical appearances of Jesus to them.

With regard to the appearance *Gattung*, Berger has attempted to use parallels from stories of God's calling to discern a *Gattung* for stories of Jesus's appearing. But he rather forces his texts to come up with his results. For example, in Samuel's call, he is summoned, not three times, but four times. In Jos. As. 14, Asenath is only called twice; but Berger says the second time her name is repeated two times, so all together she is called three times! (If one applied this rule to Samuel's call, then he was called six times!) This makes it doubtful if there really is a motif here that the third call = God's voice. At any rate, this seems pretty far removed from the gospels. None of the gospel appearances have the form "Who are you?...I am..." Only the appearance to Paul has this element involved. That doubt is a common element in stories of divine calls and appearances is not surprising, but Berger seems mistaken when he asserts that the disciples' doubts concerned the *identity* of the one appearing to them. Rather they doubted the *reality* of what they saw. This does not at all seem historically improbable. In any case, the "third time" motif plays no role in overcoming those doubts. Berger's attempts to see this motif in the arrangement of the resurrection narratives seems fanciful. They do not, in fact, form bunches of threes as Berger asserts. He arrives at this only by arbitrarily counting or not counting the angelophany. Thus, if one counts it in Matthew one gets three "appearances"; but if one counts it in Luke or John one gets four. Similarly, Berger wants to see the "third time" motif in Jn. 21:14; but then one must discount the appearance to Mary. Berger even sees two sets of three in the list of I Cor. 15:5-8! But Paul's list of appearances is probably chronologically arranged, as we have seen, which suggests that any increase in number of witnesses is purely incidental. That the women are placed first in the gospels probably has nothing to do with their status as witnesses, but with their discovery of the empty tomb. That the last appearance is the most important probably has more to do with ending the gospel on a climax than with a "third time" motif; and in John the second appearance would seem to be the most important. At any rate, the number of appearances seems to have absolutely nothing to do with the third time=God's voice, which was supposed to be the basis of the motif. Nor has a genealogical tie to the gospels been shown for any of this. Berger himself admits, "Certainly one cannot say that a report must therefore be unhistorical, if the concept in it shows parallels in the history of traditions. In the end one can find parallels to everything" (Ibid., pp. 234-235).

[17] Typical is the reasoning of Scroggs:

"The New Testament church does not agree about the nature of Christ's resurrected body. Material in Luke and John perhaps suggest this body to be corporeal in nature.[43] Paul, on the other hand, clearly argues that the body is a spiritual body. If any historical memory resides in the accounts of Paul's conversion in Acts, he must not have understood the appearance of Christ to have been a corporeal appearance. Most critics identify this conversion with the event referred to in I Cor. 15:8: 'Last of all, as to one untimely born, he appeared also to me.' The arguments in verses 47-50 of this chapter for the identity between Christ's body and the spiritual body of the resurrection indicate that for the Apostle his Lord rose from the dead in a spiritual body. Most importantly, Paul has equated the appearance of Christ to him with the appearances to the other apostles. The resurrected Christ, as he was manifested to the church is thus a spiritual body...."

counts of the physical resurrection are regarded as late legends, their physicalism usually being explained as an anti-docetic device. The physicalism of the gospels' portrayal of the resurrection body accounts, I think, more than any other single factor, for critical scepticism concerning the historicity of the gospel narratives of the resurrection of Jesus.[18]

---

[43] Luke 24:39-43; John 20:26-38. There are, of course, contradictory elements in the stories which imply the body is more than physical" (Robin Scroggs, *The Last Adam* (Oxford: Basil Blackwell, 1966), pp. 92-93).
What Scroggs calls contradictory elements are integral parts of the overall portrayal of Jesus's glorified body. We have already seen that Paul did not seem to equate the mode of the appearances to the disciples with the one to him, nor did he mean by "spiritual body" an immaterial, intangible, unextended entity. Paul and the gospels seem to be in complete accord. For the most brilliant, if misguided, attempt to drive a wedge between Paul and the gospels on the nature of the resurrection body, see Hans Grass, *Ostergeschehen und Osterberichte*, 4th rev. ed. (Göttingen: Vandenhoeck & Ruprecht, 1963), pp. 138-186. See also Gerald O'Collins, *The Easter Jesus*, 2nd ed. (London: Darton, Longman, & Todd, 1980), p. 84; James W. D. G. Dunn, *Jesus and the Spirit* (London: SCM, 1975), pp. 115-122; Kremer, *Osterevangelien*, p. 153; Walter Grundmann, *Das Evangelium nach Lukas*, 8th ed., THKNT 3 (Berlin: Evangelische Verlagsanstalt, 1978), p. 451; *TRE*, s.v. "Auferstehung II. Auferstehung Jesu Christi II/l. Neues Testament," by Paul Hoffmann, pp. 490-497; Fischer, *Ostergeschehen*, pp. 78-81; James M. Robinson, "Jesus from Easter to Valentinus (or to the Apostles' Creed)," *JBL* 101 (1982): 6-17. Perhaps a word should be said in particular about Dunn's hypothesis of a three stage development of the doctrine of the resurrection body. The first stage was the original disciples' understanding that God had raised Jesus physically from the tomb. The second stage was Paul's "dematerialization" of the body to a σῶμα πνευματικόν. The third stage was Luke and to a certain extent John's heightening and underscoring the original belief. We have seen, however, that Dunn's second stage is probably an imaginative reconstruction based on an incorrect exegesis of Paul's doctrine. Indeed, Dunn's sole proof that Paul, contrary to both Hebraic and Hellenistic-Gnostic thought of his time, made a "neat distinction" between σῶμα and σάρξ such that materiality was associated only with the latter, is I Cor. 15:50 (Dunn, *Jesus*, pp. 120-121)! Dunn's third stage is based on a purported materializing tendency in Luke. Although Dunn thinks this tendency is easy to demonstrate, his texts do not seem to support the weight he lends them. To see such a tendency in Lk. 9:32; Acts 2:3 seems fanciful. Luke's angelophanies are no more physical than those of the other gospels (cf. Lk. 24:23). Nor does Luke's supposedly crude conception of the Spirit (Acts 2:4, 33; 8:17-18; 10:44-46; 19:6)—a moot point indeed—go to prove any materializing tendency. Dunn's only substantial text is Lk. 3:22, but this loses much of its force in light of Mt. 3:16. Both Matthew and Luke want perhaps simply to make it clear that the Spirit actually came as a dove, not merely in the manner of a dove. However all this may be, when it comes to the resurrection narratives, Dunn forgets that Luke and John's physicalism is probably *traditional*, not redactional. Therefore, it does not seem to be a purposeful attempt to heighten the physical nature of Jesus's resurrection body, but stems out of the old, original belief. As Dunn himself admits in another place, "In view of the other evidence, it is likely that Luke's materialistic view of Jesus' resurrection body is prompted as much by the primitive traditions of which he became aware as by his own interests..." (Dunn, *Jesus*, p. 390). Dunn at least has the perspicuity, in contrast to Robinson, to discern the first stage.

[18] This is especially true for Grass. He asserts, "Above all, [the Easter reports] have throughout a strong legendary character. For a Jesus who, after his resurrection, interacts in this way with his disciples is a figure of legend, of a legend of which it must be asked whether it does justice to the mystery of what Jesus's resurrection means" (Hans Grass, *Christliche Glaubenslehre*, 2 vols. [Stuttgart: W. Kohlmanner, 1973], 1:101-102). The result of this anti-physicalism for his exegesis is clearly illustrated in his treatment of the historicity of the appearance to the women: the legen-

But we have seen that such reasoning rests on a fundamental and drastic misinterpretation of Paul's doctrine. The idea that Paul conceived of the resurrection body of Christ as an immaterial, intangible, unextended entity is without foundation. It is therefore futile to try to play Paul's doctrine off against the gospels'. One cannot but suspect that the reason for much scholarly scepticism concerning the historicity of the gospel appearance narratives is that, as Bultmann openly stated, this is offensive to "modern man," and so Paul has been made an unwilling accomplice in critics' attempt to find reasons to support a conclusion already dictated by *a priori* philosophical assumptions.[19] But Paul will not allow himself to

---

dary character of Mt. 28:9-10 is proved above all by its *"massiven Realismus,"* for the women grasp Jesus's feet; he has flesh and bones (Grass, *Ostegeschehen*, p. 28). Again, the legendary character of Acts 1 is shown by the realism entailed in the 40 days of Jesus's physical presence with the disciples (Ibid., pp. 48-49). According to Alsup, "...no other work has been so widely used or of such singular importance for the interpretation of the gospel accounts...as Grass'..." (Alsup, *Stories*, p. 32). Alsup protests that Grass's "insistence that the heavenly type [of appearance] stands behind the other is predicated upon the impossibility of the material realism of that latter form as an acceptable answer to the 'what happened' question.... Grass superimposes this criterion over the gospel appearance accounts and judges them by their conformity or divergence from it" (Ibid., p. 34). Others have imitated Grass's approach. Koch, for example, protests that in having the women grab Jesus's feet, the Jerusalem tradition is in danger, *"das Ereignis der Erscheinung zu verdinglichen"* (Gerhard Koch, *Die Auferstehung Jesus Christ*, BHT [Tübingen: J. C. B. Mohr, 1959], p. 48). Similarly, Fuller claims this appearance is legendary and begins the materialization process (Reginald H. Fuller, *The Formation of the Resurrection Narratives* [London: SPCK, 1972], p. 79). Anderson warns that we must not dwell upon the physical aspect of Easter or else we run the peril of reducing it to something like a "nature miracle" (Anderson, *Origins*, p. 200). Brown asserts indignantly that speculation about whether the risen Jesus could have been photographed "does not show any appreciation for the transformation involved in the resurrection" (Raymond E. Brown, *The Virginal Conception and Bodily Resurrection of Jesus* [London: Geoffrey Chapman, 1973], p. 91). Schweizer claims that as "modern men" we cannot be obliged to believe in the crass corporeality of the gospel resurrection appearances; instead we believe what the gospels intend thereby, which in Schweizer's analysis reduces to the moralistic maxim that we must live within the boundaries of this earthly life alone and enjoy music, art, love, and poetry (Eduard Schweizer, "Die Leiblichkeit des Menschen: Leben—Tod—Auferstehung," in idem, *Beiträge zur Theologie des Neuen Testaments* [Zürich: Zwingli Verlag, 1970], pp. 177-180)! Thus, because the offense of the physical resurrection and appearances, Christianity is virtually reduced to Epicureanism. Alsup remarks,

"...the contemporary spectrum of research on the gospel resurrection appearances displays a proclivity to the last century (and to Celsus of the second century) in large measure under the influence of Grass' approach. In a sense the gospel stories appear to be something of an embarrassment; their 'realism' is offensive" (Alsup, *Stories*, p. 54).

[19] See Rudolf Bultmann, "New Testament and Mythology," in *Kerygma and Myth*, 2 vols., ed. H. W. Bartsch, trans. R. H. Fuller (London: SPCK, 1953), 1:39-40; see also idem, "Bultmann Replies to his Critics," in *Kerygma and Myth*, 1:197, which especially illustrates Bultmann's *a priori* assumption of history and the universe as a closed system. According to Niebuhr, Bultmann retained uncriticized the nineteenth century idea of nature and history as a closed system, which forced him to insist that the resurrection is only the wonder of faith (Richard R. Niebuhr, *Resurrection and Historical Reason* [New York: Charles Scribner's Sons, 1957], pp. 60-61). In the

be put to this use; careful exegesis of Pauline doctrine supports a physical resurrection body. The ground thus seems to be cut from beneath those who object to the historicity of the appearance traditions solely on the basis of the "massive realism" of the gospel appearances.

But more than that: if Paul's doctrine of the resurrection body conforms to that of the gospels, then ought not the historicity of physical appearances of Jesus to be accepted precisely for the same reason that the "spirituality" of the appearances was accepted, namely, the earliness and closeness of Paul's information to the original events? The fact is, as we shall see, that every gospel appearance of the resurrected Jesus seems to be a physical appearance, a fact made more remarkable when one remembers that these traditions were originally independent, and they thus seem to be in complete harmony with Paul's doctrine of the resurrection body.

Anti-Docetic Apologetic

Though it is constantly repeated that the physicalism of the gospels is an anti-docetic apologetic,[20] scarcely a single piece of evidence ever seems to be produced in favor of this assertion. Perhaps Talbert's is the best attempt to prove this viewpoint.[21] His main contention is that Luke's witness motif is constructed to

---

same vein as Bultmann, Pesch asserts that the central task of dogmatic theology today is to show how Jesus can be the central figure of God's revelation without presupposing "a 'theistic-supernaturalistic model of revelation and mediation,' which is no longer acceptable to our thought" (Rudolf Pesch, "Zur Entstehung des Glaubens an die Auferstehung Jesu," *TQ* 153 [1973]: 277). "The talk of the resurrection of Jesus is then an expression of the believing confession to the eschatological meaning of Jesus, his mission and authority, his divine legitimation in face of his death" (Ibid., p. 226). According to Carl Braaten, the resurrection is denied today not on historical/exegetical grounds; rather theology, derouted by philosophical existentialism, has determined the results. Historicism and existentialism have a "stranglehold" on the process of forming theological statements, the end product being theologians like Ogden and Fuchs who use theology to jettison all the historical events of the Christian faith, including Jesus himself (William Hordern, gen. ed., *New Directions in Theology Today*, 7 vols. (London: Lutterworth Press, 1968), vol. 2: *History and Hermeneutics*, by Carl E. Braaten, pp. 80-86).

[20] Kirsopp Lake, *The Historical Evidence for the Resurrection of Jesus* (London: Williams & Norgate, 1907), pp. 221-224; Grass, *Ostergeschehen*, p. 71; James McLeman, *Resurrection Then and Now* (London: Hodder & Stoughton, 1965), p. 203; S. H. Hooke, *The Resurrection of Christ as History and Experience* (London: Darton, Longman, & Todd, 1967), p. 146; Charles H. Talbert, "An Anti-Gnostic Tendency in Lucan Christology," *NTS* 14 (1967-68): 259-271; Ernst Haenchen, *The Acts of the Apostles*, 14th ed., trans. B. Noble, G. Shinn, R. McL. Wilson (Oxford: Basil Blackwell, 1971), p. 115; Joachim Jeremias, *Neutestamentliche Theologie* (Gütersloh: Gerd Mohn, 1971), p. 287.

[21] Charles H. Talbert, *Luke and the Gnostics* (Nashville: Abingdon Press, 1966), pp. 17-32.

guarantee the reality of Jesus's death and burial and the materiality of his resurrection, appearances, and ascension. This motif is a response to Gnostics who denied the materiality of the passion and resurrection. Talbert argues that because the witness terminology in Acts is equally characteristic of Aramaic/less-Aramaic sections, kerygmatic/non-kerygmatic sections, and Pauline/Petrine speeches, it is entirely Lukan in origin and not part of the primitive kerygma. In the gospel, Luke has an equally strong emphasis on witness. Why is this so? The reason is that Luke wants to guarantee the total career of Jesus. But, Talbert proceeds, he especially wants to guarantee the passion and above all the resurrection. Hence, he has witnesses at the crucifixion, burial, empty tomb, appearances, and ascension of Jesus. Now Luke picks these events because (except for the crucifixion) he wants to emphasize their materiality. Talbert's proof of this final assertion is that Luke mentions Jesus's body in 23:55; 24:23, has proofs of corporeality in 24:36-43, and refers to Jesus's eating with the disciples in Acts 1:4; cf. 10:41. He concludes, "This means that the entire witness motif is constructed to guarantee especially the materiality of these events as the valid content of the church's proclamation."[22] Talbert thus regards Luke's emphasis on materiality as an antidocetic device.

But these seem to be rather weighty conclusions to rest on such support. We have already seen in chapter 1 that the appeal to witnesses was in fact characteristic of the primitive preaching of the church. That Luke also adopts this motif as his own does not undercut its authenticity. Now certainly Luke uses this motif to construct an apologetic for the career of Jesus—indeed, he says as much (Lk. 1:1-4)—and the resurrection constitutes the pinnacle of this career. But does this mean that Luke therefore wants to prove the materiality of the events of the passion and resurrection? Is it not rather their historicity? His mentioning of the body with regard to the empty tomb does seem to show that he wants to underline the emptiness of the tomb: the women saw the body laid in the tomb, but when they returned the body was gone. But this is already forcefully stated in Mark. Again, Luke does want to emphasize the corporeality of the risen Jesus in the physical demonstrations. But these, too, are largely traditional elements in the story, not Lukan inventions. Luke's emphasis is clear, but this is no proof that the physicality is an unhistorical, anti-docetical fiction. The same is true of the Acts

---

[22] Ibid., p. 31.

sermons, which in fact do not usually emphasize the corporeality of the appearances. Luke certainly wants to present a historical apologetic for the reality of the resurrection, but that in no way seems to warrant the sweeping conclusion that Luke constructed the entire witness motif to prove the materiality of the events of Easter. Nor does it seem to be proved that Luke invented the physical appearances to combat Gnosticism.

More recently, Robinson has argued that the trajectory which led to second century Gnosticism was already present in the first century and that the gospel appearance stories are shaped by an anti-Gnostic, materializing tendency which has almost completely obscured the original visionary experiences of the disciples.[23] Robinson holds that the resurrection appearances were experiences of a blinding light, including the visualization of a luminous, heavenly body such as Stephen is reported to have seen. This primitive stage of luminous, bodily appearances is identifiable from (i) vestiges in the non-luminous gospel appearance stories and in the misplaced appearances, (ii) Paul and John's identification of the risen Christ with the Spirit (I Cor. 15:44; II Cor. 3:17-18; Rev. 1:17-18; 2:7, 8, 11, 17, 29, etc.), and (iii) the outcome of these trajectories in second century Gnosticism. With regard to (i) Robinson appeals to the luminous attendants at the empty tomb, Jesus's passing through closed doors in Docetic style, the non-recognition motif, and the transfiguration. Concerning (ii), Robinson appeals to Paul's Damascus road experience and John's vision in Rev. 1:13-16 (the only resurrection appearances in the New Testament described in any detail) to prove that the only accounts we have by eyewitnesses of appearances concerned luminous visions; therefore, the original experiences were of that sort. Both Paul and John do not think of a materially risen Christ, for they identify Him with the Spirit. Finally, as to (iii) Robinson argues that because the Gnostics distained corporeality, they abandoned the heavenly body motif in the appearances, retaining only pure luminosity. Now, according to Robinson, what we find in Luke and John is an apologetic against this Gnostic spiritualizing away the resurrection. By construing the resurrection as the raising of the same fleshly body, the evangelists sought to counteract the Gnostic attempt to cast the appearances as disembodied, radiant manifestations of the Spirit. Luke's statement that the disciples did not see a ghost is precisely an attempt to break the identification of Christ and the Spirit.

---

[23] Robinson, "Easter to Valentinus," pp. 6-17.

John has a similar apologetic, but in 20:29 moves back in the Gnostic direction because the appearances to the Twelve and Thomas were "a bit too materialistic" even for him! Thus, just as we today reject the view that Jesus rose in disembodied radiance, so we ought to reject the view that he rose in physical corporeality.

But our study thus far makes it clear that Robinson's ingenious reconstruction is multiply flawed. His grounds for postulating the primitive stage of appearances of a luminous body seem very weak. Concerning (i): angels are typically described in terms of dazzling light, so that there is no reason to see any vestige here. Jesus does not in fact pass through the doors but simply appears in the room. There is no suggestion that non-recognition is due to luminosity. Though Paul did not recognize the one who called him, there is no indication that he saw a bodily form at all. By contrast, in the transfiguration, there is no problem with recognition. Finally, we have seen that most critics reject the typically suggested identifications of supposedly misplaced appearance stories. Concerning (ii): Robinson does not understand the difference between a resurrection appearance and a vision. What Stephen and John describe are pure visions; Paul's experience could still be characterized by the apostle as an appearance, in contrast to his later experiences, because it had extra-mental aspects perceptible to standers-by. There is no evidence that the original experiences of the disciples were visionary in character. Finally, we have seen that the idea that Paul and John think that Christ is numerically identical with the Spirit rests on sloppy exegesis. Concerning (iii): O'Collins rightly objects that "What Robinson calls a trajectory looks more like a scholarly retrojection, or reading later documents too far back into earlier history."[24] There is no basis for thinking that New Testament writers were opposed by persons who espoused luminous appearances lacking a bodily shape. In fact, Robinson appears to be lapsing back into 19th century exegesis's identifying *soma* with form and its substance with light or glory. He thinks the Gnostic bias against *soma* meant a bias against bodily form and that Paul's affirmation of a resurrection *soma* meant affirmation of a bodily form, all of which is mistaken and, therefore, outmoded exegesis. But what Paul affirmed and Gnostics objected to was *real* corporeality, not just the form thereof, so that proto-Gnostics could quite happily affirm the view which Robinson ascribes to Paul and John. Indeed, an examination of Gnostic resurrection appearance texts reveals that the Gnostics

---

[24] Gerald O'Collins, "Luminous Appearances of the Risen Christ," *CBQ* 46 (1984): 248.

did affirm such a view; for contrary to Robinson, the Gnostic resurrection appearances were not visions of bodiless radiance, but were usually visions of a luminous human body (Apocryphon of John [NHL 3.1]; Sophia of Jesus Christ [NHL 3.4]; cf. Letter of Peter to Philip [NHL 6.2])[25] or, in other words, precisely the view which Robinson ascribes to primitive Christianity! In fact even the luminosity is absent in some Gnostic resurrection appearance stories (Acts of Peter and the Twelve Apostles [NHL 6.1]).[26] Moreover, even if the proto-Gnostics were denying the bodily form of the luminous appearances, an anti-Gnostic apologetic would merely have to affirm that; the materialism of the gospel narratives remains unexplained. The fact is that the gospels' portrayal of Jesus's glorified body is quite balanced, and critics like Robinson are forced to interpret this balance of materiality and glorification as some sort of inconsistency.

Actually, there are positive reasons to think that the physicalism of the gospels is not an anti-docetic apologetic: (1) As we have seen, for a Jew the very term "resurrection" entailed a physical resurrection of the dead man in the tomb. The notion of a "spiritual resurrection" was not merely unknown; it was a contradiction in terms. Therefore, in saying that Jesus was raised and appeared, the early believers must have understood this in physical terms. It was Docetism which was the response to this physicalism, not the other way around.[27] The physical

---

[25] Text in James M. Robinson, ed., *The Nag Hammadi Library* (Leiden: E. J. Brill, 1977), pp. 99, 207-208, 395.
[26] Text in ibid., p. 269.
[27] As Robinson says, in the Gnostic view, bodily existence is "deficient, stupefied with fatigue, passion, drunkenness, sleepiness, a prison from which the soul is liberated by its ecstatic trip at conversion and by the sloughing off the mortal coil at death" (Robinson, "Easter to Valentinus," p. 11). Hence, Ellis very plausibly contends that Luke did not materialize the appearances; rather the Gnostics had de-materialized them (E. Earl Ellis, ed., *The Gospel of Luke*, NCB [London: Nelson, 1966], p. 275). Similarly Dunn argues on the basis of the old traditions in Mt. 27:52-53; Jn. 5:28-29; Acts 2:26-27, 31; 13:35-37 and the empty tomb tradition that "...the first believers took up the straightforward resuscitation of the corpse view of Jesus' resurrection...—that his body had indeed quite literally been raised from the dead.... There is no reason to suppose that this physical understanding of Jesus's resurrection was ever abandoned by the Jerusalem centered believers" (Dunn, *Jesus*, pp. 119-120). He thinks that Luke was merely reasserting the original views of the church against Hellenistic tendencies. See also Karl Bornhäuser, *Das Recht des Bekenntnisses zur Auferstehung des Fleisches* (Gütersloh: C. Bertelsmann, 1899), pp. 47-61, who points out that the letters of Clement and Ignatius prove early wide acceptance of the physical resurrection of Jesus in first century churches, even where Paul himself had taught. Künneth argues convincingly that it is extremely difficult to see how the gospel accounts of the bodily resurrection could have arisen in opposition to the original apostolic preaching and to the teaching of Paul. The authority of the apostles was extraordinarily strong, and it is inconceivable that there should have arisen in opposition to their authoritative witness a consistent tradition of physical resurrection, if that had no basis in the message of the eye-witnesses. It is more probable that Paul and the original apostles held

resurrection is thus primitive and prior, Docetism being the later reaction of theological and philosophical reflection. (2) Moreover, had purely "spiritual appearances" been original, then it is difficult to see how physical appearances could have developed. For (a) the offense of Docetism would then be removed, since the Christians, too, believed in purely spiritual appearances, and (b) the doctrine of physical appearances would have been counter-productive as an apologetic, both to Jews and to pagans; to Jews because they did not accept an individual resurrection within history and to pagans because their belief in the immortality of the soul could not accommodate the crudity of physical resurrection. The church would therefore have retained its purely spiritual appearances. (3) Besides, Docetism was mainly aimed at denying the reality of the incarnation of Christ (I Jn. 4:2-3; II Jn. 7), not the physical resurrection.[28] Docetists were not so interested in denying the physical resurrection as in denying that the divine Son perished on the cross; hence, some held that the Spirit deserted the human Jesus at the crucifixion, leaving the human Jesus to die and be physically raised (Irenaeus *Against Heresies* 1.26.1). An anti-docetic apologetic aimed at proving a physical resurrection therefore misses the point entirely. (4) The demonstrations of corporeality and continuity in the gospels, as well as the other physical appearances, do not seem to have been redactional additions of Luke or John (it is thus incorrect to speak, for example, of "Luke's apologetic against Gnosticism"), but were part of the traditions received by the evangelists. Docetism, however, was a later theological development, attested in John's letters. Therefore, the gospel accounts of the physical resurrection tend to antedate the rise and threat of Docetism. Moreover, not even all later Gnostics denied the physical resurrection (cf. Gospel of Philip, Letter of James, and Epistle of Rheginus). It is interesting that in the ending added to Mark there is actually a switch away from material proofs of the resurrection to verbal rebuke by Jesus for the disciples' unbelief. (5) The demonstrations themselves do not evince the rigorousness of an apologetic against Docetism. In both Luke and John it is not said that either the disciples or Thomas actually accepted Jesus's invitation to touch him and prove that he was not a spirit. Contrast the statements of Ignatius that the disciples did physically touch

---

the same view as is expressed in the gospel accounts (Walther Künneth, *The Theology of the Resurrection*, trans. J. W. Leitch [London: SCM Press, 1965], pp. 92-93).

[28] See Wilckens, *Auferstehung*, p. 76; I. Howard Marshall, *The Gospel of Luke*, NIGTC (Exeter: Paternoster Press, 1978), pp. 900-901.

Jesus (Ignatius *Ad Smyrnaeans* 3.2; cf. *Epistula Apostolorum* 11-12). As Schnackenburg has said, if an anti-docetic apology were involved in the gospel accounts, more would have to have been done than Jesus's merely *showing* the wounds.[29] (6) The incidental, off-hand character of the physicality of Jesus's resurrection appearances in most of the accounts shows that the physicalism was a natural assumption or presupposition of the accounts, not an apologetic point consciously being made. For example, the women's grasping Jesus's feet is not a polemical point, but just their response of worship.[30] Similarly, Jesus says, "Do not hold me," though Mary is not explicitly said to have done so; this is no conscious effort to prove a physical resurrection. The appearances on the mountain and by the Sea of Tiberias just naturally presuppose a physical Jesus; no points are trying to be scored against Docetism. Together these considerations strongly suggest that the physical appearances were not an apologetic to Docetism, but always part of the church's tradition; there seems to be no good historical reason to doubt that Jesus did, in fact, show his disciples that he had been physically raised from the dead.[31]

---

[29] Rudolf Schnackenburg, *Das Johannesevangelium*, 3 vols., HTKNT 4 (Freiburg: Herder, 1976), 3: 383. He argues that this not only goes for the appearance to the Twelve, but for the Thomas appearance as well. The point of the Thomas story is the believing without seeing, not an antidocetic apology. It is not even said whether Thomas touched Jesus or not (Ibid., p. 391). This latter point shows that corporeality was a natural presupposition, not an intentional apologetic. Clearly the author's concern is with Thomas's confession, not with the touching (Ibid., p. 396).

[30] It is not, therefore, an attempt to prove corporeality, according to Ernst Lohmeyer, *Das Evangelium des Matthäus*, 4th ed., ed. W. Schmauch, KEKNT (Göttingen: Vandenhoeck & Ruprecht, 1967), pp. 407-408.

[31] Again, the theological objection that this would involve "an overwhelming of the senses to faith in the Risen One" (Koch, *Auferstehung*, p. 48), so that the disciples' faith would no longer be true faith, holds no weight. For theological conceptions cannot change historical events; *a priori* constructs of what can and cannot have happened will be broken by the facts themselves. Besides, the objection contains a fundamental misunderstanding of faith, which has plagued post-Bultmannian theology. Bultmann construed faith in epistemological categories, opposing it to knowledge based on proof. Historical evidence is, therefore, not merely irrelevant to faith, but actually inimical to faith. Because faith cannot be based on evidence, the decision to believe necessarily involves risk and uncertainty. The result of this interpretation of faith may be seen in Willi Marxsen, *The Jesus of Nazareth*, trans. Margaret Kohl (London: SCM Press, 1970), pp. 143-183. He tells us that Jesus wanted a daring faith. A verifiable resurrection, on the other hand, would have given Jesus his legitimation. Who he was would be a matter of certainty. It would no longer be a venture for the witnesses to enter the life of faith. Indeed, it would have been a counsel of wisdom; it would have been simply stupid not to do what Jesus said. So typically Bultmannian is Marxsen's dichotomy: "It may have been that those first witnesses experienced Jesus' legitimation and then no longer needed to believe" (Ibid., p. 151; cf. the similar remark of Kasper: "...if one understands the 'appearances' as exorbitant miracles that simply 'cut down' the disciples, then that would amount to the grotesque assertion that the first witnesses of the faith were

CHAPTER 8

The Balance of the Gospel Portrayal

And it must be said that despite the disdain of some theologians for the gospels' conception of the nature of the resurrection body, it is nonetheless true that like Paul the gospels steer a careful course between gross materialism and the immortality of the soul.

A Physical Resurrection

On the one hand, every gospel appearance of Jesus that is narrated is a physical appearance.[32] Mark does not narrate an appearance, but the discovery of the empty tomb could only suggest to his readers that the predicted appearance in Galilee would be physical. Mark seems to imply the corporeality and continuity of the resurrection body in the angel's words, "You seek Jesus of Nazareth, who was crucified. He has risen, he is not here; see the place where they laid him"

---

themselves dispensed from having faith" [Walter Kasper, "Der Glaube an die Auferstehung Jesu vor dem. Forum historischer Kritik," *TQ* 153 (1973): 239]). But to believe on the basis of preaching, according to Marxsen, well, that is *really* believing, since preaching offers no legitimation. Were we today able to show through historical-critical investigation that the resurrection occurred, then faith would not be a venture for us; we should be merely stupid not to accept Jesus's challenge. But as it is, we have no such proof. Jesus is dead. Doing what he asks is "contrary to all human reasoning" (Ibid., p. 183). But his offer continues—*die Sache Jesu geht weiter*—reliance on God, freedom to love, losing oneself for one's neighbor and discovering that as salvation. Van Daalen puts it succinctly: faith is a leap in the dark. "That such a leap in the dark is a risk worth taking can only be found out by actually doing it" (D. H. Van Daalen, *The Real Resurrection* [London: Collins, 1972], p. 74).

This catastrophic misunderstanding springs from the error of taking faith as an epistemological category, a way of knowing. It ignores the fact that in biblical usage, faith is not merely *assensus*, but *fiducia*. Because faith is a whole-souled trust or commitment, it cannot in any way be opposed to either knowledge or evidence. On the contrary, Paul and the gospels invite us to believe on the basis of the evidence. Precisely because the evidence shows that Jesus is risen, I can place my trust in him. No biblical writer could construct a dichotomy such that if one saw the risen Jesus, then one no longer needed to believe. Now Marxsen is right in one thing: if Jesus did appear to the disciples, as the gospels say he did, then they would have been stupid not to place their faith in him; and equally so, if the weight of the evidence indicates that Jesus rose from the dead, then we are stupid if we do not believe in him. But the stupidest thing of all is to believe in preaching which is without legitimation and contrary to all human reasoning. As O'Collins urges, most people refuse to agree that it is better to be committed than to be rational (O'Collins, *Easter*, p. 33). If Jesus is dead, then so be it. But let us have none of this mushy-minded theologizing about *die Sache Jesu* or faith in the preaching of the cross. As Wilckens emphasizes, neither Marxsen nor Bultmann can pretend to represent biblical Christianity (Wilckens, *Auferstehung*, pp. 157-158), and only theologians are apt to be impressed with their theological salvage operations. The layman knows better, and he is fully justified if he follows his common sense in refusing to take a leap into the dark in believing that a dead man can be of life-determining significance for him today.

[32] Grass, *Ostergeschehen*, p. 92.

(Mk. 16:6b). Even the displaying of the wounds of crucifixion does not seem to be a more powerful statement of the continuity of the risen Jesus with the Jesus who was crucified and buried than this. The resurrection is bodily; Mark knows nothing of the annihilation of the old body. The appearance in Galilee would therefore probably have been understood as bodily.

In Matthew's appearance to the women, their act of grasping Jesus's feet shows that a physical appearance is in view here. In the Galilean appearance on the mountain, some critics have wanted to see a vision from heaven, like Paul's Damascus road experience, but this seems to be an attempt to read this into the story.[33] Matthew himself certainly considered the appearance to be physical, as the appearance to the women and Jesus's commissioning the disciples show. Even in the appearance itself, there are signs of physicality: the disciples' worshipping Jesus recalls the act of the women in v. 9 and does not suit a heavenly appearance well; and Jesus's coming toward the disciples (προσελθών) seems to weigh decisively in favor of a physical appearance.

Luke's Emmaus story is obviously physical and is acknowledged as such by those who think the story is shaped by the Hellenistic tales of gods visiting men; also the broken bread shows Jesus's physicality. Luke's version of the appearance to the Twelve stresses Jesus's corporeality: "See my hands and my feet, that it is I myself; handle me and, see; for a spirit has not flesh and bones as you see that I have" (Lk. 24:39). It is noteworthy that the word for handling (ψηλαφήσατέ) here is the same verb employed in I Jn. 1:1.

John's account of the appearance to Mary presupposes a physical body, for whether Mary had grasped his feet or not, Jesus's command, "Do not hold me" presupposes that she could have. In John's version of the appearance to the Twelve the mention of the crucifixion scars shows that the appearance is physical. The reality of the physical resurrection is the point of the demonstration in the Thomas story. Barrett comments, Thomas "would be satisfied neither with a substituted body which was not the body of the Lord who died on the cross, nor with a spiritual body or apparition;" even if Thomas did not touch Jesus, Barrett continues, John was convinced that Jesus's resurrection body could be handled.[34]

---

[33] For example, O'Collins's description of this appearance: the "...disciples become aware of a presence. Some recognize at once their risen Lord..." (O'Collins, *Easter*, p. 85). Cf. Fuller, *Formation*, p. 82; Dunn, *Jesus*, p. 124; Perrin, *Resurrection*, p. 72.

[34] C. K. Barrett, *The Gospel according to St. John* (London: SPCK, 1972), p. 572.

Finally, the appearance by the Sea of Tiberias was corporeal, as evident from the fact that the disciples ate a meal prepared by Jesus and took food from his hands.

So in every case, the gospels present bodily appearances of the risen Jesus. Their unanimity in this conviction is very impressive, especially in view of the various independent strands of tradition represented; they confirm Paul's doctrine that the resurrection preserves the continuity with and corporeality of the earthly body.

A Supernatural Resurrection

On the other hand, the gospels insist that Jesus's resurrection is not simply the resuscitation of a corpse. Lazarus would die again some day, but Jesus rose to everlasting life (Mt. 28:18-20; Lk. 24:26; Jn. 20:17). And his resurrection body was possessed of powers that no normal human body possesses. Thus, in Matthew when the angel opens the tomb, Jesus does not come forth; rather he is already gone. Similarly in Luke, when the Emmaus disciples recognize him at bread-breaking, he disappears. The same afternoon Jesus appears to Peter, miles away in Jerusalem. When the Emmaus disciples arrive back in Jerusalem that evening, Jesus suddenly appears in their midst. John says the doors were shut, but Jesus stood among them. A week later Jesus did the same thing. Very often commentators make the error of stating that Jesus came through the closed doors,[35] but neither John nor Luke says this. Rather Jesus simply appeared in the room: contrast the pagan myths of gods entering rooms like fog through the keyhole![36] According to the gospels, Jesus in his resurrection body had the ability to appear and vanish at will, without regard to spatial distances.

Many scholars have stumbled at Luke's "a spirit has not flesh and bones as you see that I have," claiming that this is in direct contradiction to Paul.[37] In fact, Paul speaks of "flesh and blood," not "flesh and bones." Is the difference significant?

---

[35] Barrett, *John*, 1st ed., pp. 471, 472, 476 (note the qualifying phrase, however, added in the second edition: "or, perhaps, to cause his body to materialize where he wills" [Ibid., 2nd ed., p. 567; cf. pp. 568, 572]); Marxsen, *Resurrection*, pp. 61-62; Wilckens, *Auferstehung*, p. 91; Schweizer, "Leiblichkeit," p. 178.

[36] Homer *Odyssey* 6.19-20; *Homeric Hymns* 3.145. See comments by Berthold Klappert, "Einleitung," in *Diskussion um Kreuz und Auferstehung*, ed. idem (Wuppertal: Aussaat Verlag, 1971), p. 21.

[37] For example, Grass, *Ostergeschehen*, p. 40; Schweizer, "Leiblichkeit," p. 177; Brown, *Bodily Resurrection*, p. 87; Robinson, "Easter to Valentinus," pp. 11-12.

I think it is. "Flesh and blood," as we have seen, is a Semitic expression for mortal human nature and has nothing, strictly speaking, to do with anatomy; Paul is not, therefore, necessarily opposed to Luke. But furthermore, neither is "flesh and bones" meant to be an anatomical description. Rather, proceeding from the Jewish idea that it is the bones that are preserved and raised, the expression probably connotes the physical reality of Jesus's resurrection.[38] Though it implies corporeality, its primary emphasis is not on the constituents of the body. Thus, neither Paul nor Luke is talking about anatomy, and both agree on the physicality and supernaturalness of Jesus's resurrection body.

Some critics have also scoffed at Luke's 40 days of Jesus's appearing to the disciples, wondering if he was hiding in a cave between appearances. This seems to show a lack of understanding of the biblical conception of reality; as Rengstorff explains, in the biblical conception this physical universe does not exhaust reality.[39] There is also the unseen world, which, though invisible, is no less real than the visible. The unseen world is just as much a part of reality as the visible world which men inhabit. This "universe next door" is closed to human eyes, but spiritual beings of that world can become visible and active in this. One is reminded of the story of Elisha and the servant who feared the might of the Syrians. "He said, 'Fear not, for those who are with us are more than those who are with them.' Then Elisha prayed and said, 'Lord, I pray these, open his eyes that he may see.'

---

[38] Michaelis writes,
"When according to Luke a spirit has neither flesh nor bones, and the Risen One is no spirit, that is not to say that the Risen One does not have, to use the Pauline terminology, a '*pneumatic* (glorified, heavenly) *soma*,' but rather a '*psychical* (natural, earthly) *soma*.' By flesh and bones in the Lukan statement is much more...expressed what Paul expresses by the concept of '*soma*' (body, corporeality). By pointing to flesh and bones, the *pneumatic* character of the *soma* is not disputed; rather the reality of the *somatic* is attested. Luke also stands under the presupposition—as follows, moreover, from all of the indications he gives (cf. 24:13ff; Acts 1:3)—that in the appearances it can only be a matter of meeting the Risen One in his glorified corporeality" (Wilhelm Michaelis, *Die Erscheinungen des Auferstandenen* [Basel: Heinrich Majer, 1944], p. 96).
On the Jewish emphasis on the bones, see Genesis Rabbah 28:3; Leviticus Rabbah 18:1; Ecclesiastes Rabbah 12:5. Further see Evans, *Resurrection*, p. 108; Grundmann, *Lukas*, p. 451. According to Lucian *Vera historia* 2.12, the Blessed are intangible and without flesh and bone, but one can only determine their incorporeality by trying to touch them. See further *TWNT*, s.v. "σάρξ." On Paul and Luke's unity on the resurrection see Borgen, "Paul to Luke," pp. 179-181.

[39] Karl Heinrich Rengstorff, *Die Auferstehung Jesu*, 4th rev. ed. (Witten: Luther Verlag, 1960), p. 56. This may help to answer the query concerning the whereabouts of Jesus's body now, a question posed by John B. Cobb, "Wolfhart Pannenberg's 'Jesus: God and Man,'" *JR* 49 (1969): 197; G. N. Lampe and D. M. MacKinnon, *The Resurrection*, ed. William Purcell (London: A. R. Mowbray, 1966), p. 54.

So the Lord opened the eyes of the young man, and he saw; and, behold, the mountain was full of horses and chariots of fire round about Elisha" (II Kings 6:16-18). The opening of the eyes reminds one of the Emmaus appearance, although in that case the disciples' eyes were held from recognizing Jesus, not from seeing him. But in the biblical conception of reality the invisible realm is as real as the visible. Jesus did not necessarily "hide out" in this world between appearances but may have moved in and out of the visible and unseen realms of reality.

Christ's resurrection appearances were appearances in the visible realm out of the invisible. We can only speculate as to the nature of this invisible realm, which is in the biblical view inhabited by beings such as angels and demons. It could be that the resurrection body is analogous to the bodies of angelic beings, who can materialize and dematerialize in the physical universe. Interesting in this regard is Jesus's answer to the Sadducees' conundrum designed to show the absurdity of physical resurrection: "For when they rise from the dead, they neither marry nor are given in marriage, but are like angels in heaven" (Mk. 12:25). The saying could mean that the resurrection body will be of the same nature as the body of an angel.[40] This would certainly accord with the Pauline description, for in the Bible angels are everywhere presented as appearing with imperishable, glorious, powerful, and supernatural bodies. This description seems very similar to Luke's version of Jesus's answer: "But those who are accounted worthy to attain to that age and to the resurrection from the dead neither marry nor are given in marriage, for they cannot die anymore, because they are equal to angels and are sons of God, being sons of the resurrection" (Lk. 20:3-36). On the other hand, the saying does not concern the bodies of the raised *per se*, but rather their marital status. The saying in Mark could mean only that the raised are unmarried like the angels. Luke's version does seem to imply, however, that because the raised are imperishable like the angels, there is no further need for marriage, since procreation is unnecessary. Luke's version thus draws a closer parallel between resurrection bodies and angelic bodies than is explicit in Mark. In II Baruch the raised are explicitly compared to angels:

---

[40] See H. A. W. Meyer, *Handbuch über den ersten Brief an die Korinther*, 6th ed., rev. Georg Heinrici, KEKNT 5 (Göttingen: Vandenhoeck & Ruprecht's Verlag, 1881), p. 448; Wolfhart Pannenberg, "Ist Jesus wirklich auferstanden?" in *Ist Jesus wirklich auferstanden? Geistliche Woche für Südwestdeutschland der Evang. Akademie Mannheim von 16. bis 23. Februar 1964* (Karlsruhe: Evangelische Akademie Mannheim, 1964), p. 26.

> ...they shall...be transformed...into the splendour of angels
> For they shall behold the world which is now invisible to them,
> And time shall no longer age them.
> For in the heights of that world shall they dwell,
> And they shall be made like unto the angels,
> And be made equal to the stars,
> And they shall be changed into every form they desire,
> From beauty into loveliness,
> And from light into the splendour of glory
> (II Baruch 51:5, 8-10).[41]

I do not mean to suggest that the gospels draw an explicit comparison between Christ's resurrection body and the bodies of angels; but the description of Jesus's resurrection body reminds one of angelic bodies, and the latter are a useful analogue to make the former more understandable.

The gospels therefore present, like Paul, a balanced view of the nature of Jesus's resurrection body. On the one hand, Jesus has a body—he is not a disembodied soul. For the gospels and Paul alike, the incarnation is an enduring state, not limited to the 30 some years of Jesus's earthly life. On the other hand, Jesus's body is a supernatural body. We must keep firmly in mind that for the evangelists, as well as for Paul, Jesus rises glorified from the grave. In his resurrection body Jesus can materialize and dematerialize in and out of the physical universe. The gospels and Paul agree that the appearances of Jesus ceased and that physically he has left this universe for an indeterminate time. During his physical absence he is present through the Holy Spirit who functions in his stead. But someday he will personally return to judge mankind and establish his reign over all creation.

---

[41] On stars' being equated with angels, see Job 38:7; Dan. 8:10; Rev. 1:20. Cf. Dan. 12:2; 1 QH 11:10-14; Pss. Sol. 3:16.

PART III

ASSESSING THE EVIDENCE

CHAPTER 9

THE EVIDENCE FOR THE EMPTY TOMB

The principal historical basis for belief in the resurrection of Jesus consists in the evidence for the empty tomb, for the appearances of Jesus to the various witnesses, and for the origin of the Christian Way in the disciples' coming to believe in Jesus's resurrection. If the evidence for these facts is strong and cannot be plausibly accounted for by alternative explanations, then the resurrection of Jesus from the dead would seem to be the historical hypothesis that most suitably fits the facts of the case. Marxsen has protested that the resurrection is merely the apostles' inference from or interpretation of the facts, an interpretation not binding on us today, since no one actually witnessed the resurrection. But this objection only seems to revive the old arguments against induction, which would land us in nearly absolute scepticism.[1] In fact, if one were to find empty the grave of a friend who had recently died and thereafter on repeated occasions one encountered him again, talked with him, and ate with him, then, as Bode dryly remarks, the "interpretation" that he had been raised from the dead would not seem to be

---

[1] Willi Marxsen, *The Resurrection of Jesus of Nazareth*, trans. Margaret Kohl (London: SCM Press, 1970), p. 114; cf. S. H. Hooke, *The Resurrection of Christ as History and Experience* (London: Darton, Longman, & Todd, 1967), p. 149. Notice that Marxsen does *not* object to the interpretation of the resurrection because it infers a supernatural cause instead of a natural one, but simply because it is an *inference*. On this basis if one were to hear shots from a neighbor's house, see a man with a gun fleeing from the house, and find one's neighbor lying dead on the living room floor, and were fingerprint and ballistics tests to determine that the murder weapon was carried by the fleeing man, then on Marxsen's principles one could still not say the man killed the neighbor, since this is an *inference*. But such evidence is allowed in any court of law.

either unwarranted or merely subjective.² The question is, is the historical credibility of Jesus's resurrection sufficiently high to warrant our belief?

In order to answer that question, we need to address the historical evidence for the empty tomb, the resurrection appearances of Christ, and the origin of the Christian Way. First, let us direct our attention to the evidence for the empty tomb.

The Historical Fact of the Empty Tomb

On the basis of our study in Parts I and II, we can summarize the evidence in support of the empty tomb under ten headings:

1. *The historical credibility of the burial story supports the empty tomb.* If the burial story is basically reliable, then the inference that Jesus's tomb was found empty lies very close at hand. For if the burial story is fundamentally accurate, the burial site of Jesus would have been known to Jew and Christian alike. But in that case, it would surely have been impossible for the resurrection faith to survive in the face of a tomb containing the corpse of Jesus. The disciples could not have adhered to the resurrection; scarcely any one else would have believed them, even if they had; and their Jewish opponents could have exposed the whole affair as a poor joke by pointing to the occupied tomb or perhaps even displaying the body of Jesus, as the medieval Jewish polemic portrays them doing (*Toledot Yeshu*). Hence, it would seem to be infeasible to affirm the historicity of the burial story and yet deny the historicity of the empty tomb.

And, in fact, the burial story is widely recognized as a historically credible narrative:

(a) *Paul's testimony provides early evidence for the historicity of Jesus's burial.* We saw that in I Cor. 15:4 the pre-Pauline formula received and delivered by the apostle refers in its second line to the fact of Jesus's burial. The four-fold ὅτι, the chronological succession of the events, and particularly the remarkable concordance between the formula and the preaching of Acts 13 and the narratives of the gospels concerning the order of events (death—burial—resurrection—appearances) make it highly probable that the formula's mention of the burial is not meant merely to underscore the death but refers to the same event related in

---

² Edward Lynn Bode, *The First Easter Morning*, AB 45 (Rome: Biblical Institute Press, 1970), p. 165.

the gospels, that is, the laying of Jesus in the tomb. If this is so, then it seems very difficult to regard Jesus's burial in the tomb as unhistorical, for (i) given the age of the formula (AD 30-36), there was not sufficient time for legend concerning the burial to accrue; (ii) the women witnesses (see below) to the burial were known in the *Urgemeinde* in which the formula was probably drafted, and their testimony stands behind it; (iii) Paul himself knew the context of the traditions he delivered (*e.g.*, I Cor. 11:23-26), which makes it probable that he, too, knew the burial story behind the formula. His two week visit to Jerusalem in AD 36 seems to make this conclusion firm, so that his word confirms the reliability of Jesus's burial in the tomb.

(b) *The burial story was part of the pre-Markan passion story and is therefore very old.* It is universally acknowledged that the burial account is part of the pre-Markan passion story, the narrative of the crucifixion and burial being a continuous unity. This gives good reason to accept the burial as historical, on grounds similar to those listed above: (i) the time was insufficient for a purely legendary burial of Jesus to arise; (ii) the presence of eyewitnesses who would know better would probably preclude such; and (iii) the age of the story seems to insure that Paul must have known it, for with his intercourse with Jerusalem he could not but know at least the content of the pre-Markan passion story. This would confirm that his mention of the burial in I Cor. 15:4 refers to the same burial that is mentioned in the gospels. The age of the formula on the one hand and the age of the pre-Markan passion story on the other seem to insure the historicity of the burial story in its fundamental elements. Their age also probably affords us the authority of the apostle Paul for the reliability of this tradition.

(c) *The story itself is simple and in its basic elements lacks theological reflection or apologetic development.* Most scholars would concur with Bultmann's judgment in this regard. According to Bornkamm, "The report of Jesus's burial is kept concise and matter of fact, without any bias [*Tendenz*]."[3] We appear to have here a primitive tradition recounting Joseph's begging the body of Jesus and his laying it, wrapped in linen, in a tomb, a tradition which has not been significantly overlaid with either theology or apologetics. This seems to be confirmation that the story is basically a factual report of what happened.

---

[3] Günther Bornkamm, *Jesus von Nazareth*, 10th rev. ed., UT 19 (Stuttgart: W. Kohlhammer, 1975), p. 148.

(d) *The person of Joseph of Arimathea is probably historical.* Even the most sceptical scholars, such as Broer and Pesch, agree that it is unlikely that Joseph, as a member of the Sanhedrin, could have been a Christian invention. To this may be added the fact that the gospels' descriptions of Joseph receive unintentional confirmation from incidental details; for example, his being rich from the type and location of the tomb. His being at least a sympathizer of Jesus is not only independently attested by Matthew and John, but seems likely in view of Mark's description of his treatment of Jesus's body as opposed to those of the thieves.

(e) *Joseph's laying the body in his tomb is probably historical.* The consistent descriptions of the tomb as an *acrosolia* or bench tomb and the archaeological discoveries that such tombs were used by notables during Jesus's day makes it likely that Jesus was placed in such a tomb. The incidental details that it was new and belonged to Joseph we have seen to be quite probable, since Joseph could not lay the body of a criminal in just any tomb, especially as this would defile the bodies of any family members also reposing there. The dovetailing of all these incidental details gives the narrative an aura of credibility.

(f) *Jesus was probably buried late on the day of Preparation.* If the foregoing is probable, then the time of Jesus's interment, given what we know from extrabiblical sources about Jewish regulations concerning the handling of executed criminals and burial procedures, must have been Friday before the evening star appeared. The body could not have been allowed to remain on the cross overnight without defiling the land, and since the sabbath was impending the body had to be buried before nightfall. With help, Joseph should have been able to complete a simple burial prior to the breaking of the sabbath, as the gospels describe.

(g) *The observation of the burial by women is probably historical.* The women are used as witnesses of the crucifixion, burial, and empty tomb. Unless they actually were the witnesses, it seems inexplicable why they should be used and not the disciples themselves (see below). Moreover, their roles in the burial and empty tomb stories seem to be mutually confirmatory. If their role in any one of these events is historical, their role in the others becomes likely as well. For example, if they witnessed the crucifixion, they would probably have remained for the burial, in which case the grave site would have been known, making the fact of the empty tomb likely, as explained above. If they witnessed the burial, they were no doubt present at the crucifixion, since they would not suddenly show up at the entombment. And again, then the grave site would have been known, making likely the fact of the empty tomb. Finally, if they discovered the empty tomb, they must have been at the burial so as to know its location. But then they were probably at the crucifixion as well. So if any of the lists of witnesses seems reliable, the others probably are, too. That the role of the women is historical is made likely by these traditional lists of names, for it is difficult to see how the names of people known in the early Christian fellowship could be associated with such events unless this were in fact the case.

(h) *No other burial tradition exists.* If the burial of Jesus in the tomb by Joseph of Arimathea is legendary, then it is very strange that conflicting traditions nowhere appear, even in Jewish polemic. That no remnant of the true story or even a conflicting false one should remain is hard to explain unless the gospel account is substantially the true account.

(i) *The graves of Jewish holy men were carefully preserved.* During Jesus's time there was an extraordinary interest in the graves of Jewish martyrs and holy men and these were scrupulously cared for and honored.[4] This suggests that the grave of Jesus would have also been noted so that it, too, might become such a holy site. The disciples had no inkling of any pre-eschatological resurrection, and they would probably therefore not have allowed the burial site of the teacher to go unnoted. This interest makes very plausible the women's lingering to watch the burial and their subsequent intention to anoint Jesus's body with spices and perfumes (Lk. 23:55-56).

Taken together these nine considerations make the historical credibility of the burial account quite high, a fact recognized by most New Testament scholars. According to Trilling, "The particulars show at least that there was a *strong interest* to be able to specify as precisely as possible the whereabouts of Jesus's corpse and the witnesses for the particular facts. It appears unfounded to doubt the fact of Jesus's honorable burial—even historically considered."[5] But in that case, the

---

[4] Joachim Jeremias, *Heiligengräber in Jesu Umwelt* (Göttingen: Vandenhoeck & Ruprecht, 1958). The discovery in 1973 of the bones of a victim of crucifixion named Johohanan in an ossuary within a rock tomb shows that the corpse of someone executed by crucifixion was cared for and attended to later (V. Tzaferis, "Jewish Tombs at and near Giv'at ha-Mivtar," *IsrEJ* 20 [1970]: 18-32; J. Naveh, "The Ossuary Inscriptions from Giv'at haMivtar," *IsrEJ* 20 [1970]: 33-37; N. Haas, "Anthropological Observations on the Skeletal Remains from Giv'at ha-Mivtar," *IsrEJ* 20 [1970]: 38-59).

[5] Wolfgang Trilling, *Fragen zur Geschichtlichkeit Jesu* (Düsseldorf: Patmos Verlag, 1966), p. 157.

conclusion that the tomb was found empty lies close at hand. Even if the disciples left for Galilee and did not return to Jerusalem preaching the resurrection until some time later, the prospect of a closed tomb would have silenced them effectively.

Against this first consideration in support of the empty tomb, Fischer lodges two objections: (i) The argument presupposes that the Christian concept of resurrection was like the Jewish concept, that *this* flesh and *these* bones are constitutive for the resurrection body. But Paul precludes any such understanding in his doctrine of the resurrection body. Fischer's point is apparently that the Christian concept of resurrection would permit the disciples' affirmation of Jesus's resurrection even given common knowledge of the place where his body still lay interred. (ii) The argument presupposes that Christians appealed to the empty tomb in their proclamation, which is false.[6]

But as for (i), we have seen at length that it is futile to try to drive a wedge between Paul and the gospels concerning the nature of the resurrection. Paul held that the mortal body had to be raised and transformed into the resurrection body: it is sown a natural body, it is raised a supernatural body (I Cor. 15:44). The idea that a person can be raised from the dead while his corpse remained in the grave would have been nonsense to early Christian believers. Objection (ii) is puzzling, since this first consideration says nothing about the place of the empty tomb in the kerygma. Even if Christians did not appeal to the empty tomb, the fact remains that given the reliability of the burial account, Jesus's tomb would have been known and so must have been empty in order for resurrection faith to flourish. Whether the Christian preachers drew this inference themselves or used it apologetically is simply irrelevant. Hence, this first consideration seems to me strong evidence for the historical fact of the empty tomb.

2. *Paul's testimony implies the fact of the empty tomb.* I think there can be little doubt that Paul accepted not only the burial but also the empty tomb of Jesus, as is evident (i) from the sequence in I Cor. 15:3-5 "died—was buried—was raised", (ii) from the concept of resurrection itself, (iii) from his Pharisaic background and language, (iv) from the expression "on the third day," (v) from the phrase "from the dead," (vi) from his doctrine of resurrection and transformation

---

[6] Karl Martin Fischer, *Das Ostergeschehen*, 2nd ed. (Göttingen: Vandenhoeck & Ruprecht, 1980), pp. 63-64.

of the body, and (vii) from his belief in the personal return of Christ. It seems nearly certain, then, that Paul believed in the empty tomb.

Vögtle and Pesch, Oberlinner, and others are willing to concede this much, but they protest that this does not allow the inference that the tomb was actually empty.[7] But the question surely presses, how is it historically conceivable for the apostle Paul to have believed in the empty tomb of Jesus if in fact the tomb were not empty? Paul was in Jerusalem six years after the events themselves. The tomb must have been empty by then. But more than that, Peter, James, and the other Christians in Jerusalem with whom Paul spoke must have also believed that the tomb was empty and had been empty from the moment of the resurrection. Were this not so, then Pauline theology would have taken an entirely different route, trying to explain how resurrection could still be possible, though the body remained in the grave. But neither Christian theology nor apologetics ever had to face such a problem. It seems unintelligible how Pauline theology could have taken the direction that it did had the tomb not been empty from the start.

But furthermore, we have observed that the "he was raised" in the formula corresponds to the empty tomb pericope in the gospels, the ἐγήγερται mirroring the ἠγέρθη. This makes it likely that the empty tomb tradition stands behind the third element of the formula, just as the burial tradition stands behind the second. Two conclusions follow. First, the tradition that the tomb was found empty must in all probability be reliable. For time would have been insufficient for an empty tomb legend to accrue by the date of the drafting of the formula, and the presence of witnesses in the *Urgemeinde* would have also tended to prevent it. Second, Paul no doubt knew the tradition of the empty tomb summarized in the formula and thus lends his testimony to its reliability. If the discovery of the empty tomb is not historical, then it seems virtually inexplicable how both Paul and the early formula could accept it.

Finally, we have seen that the expression "on the third day" is most probably a time indicator, perhaps in language fraught with connotations of God's victory, for the events of Easter, including the discovery of the empty tomb. Included in the formula and preached by Paul, this phrase provides very early evidence for the

---

[7] Anton Vögtle and Rudolf Pesch, *Wie kam es zum Osterglauben?* (Düsseldorf: Patmos Verlag, 1975), p. 87; Lorenz Oberlinner, "Die Verkündigung der Auferweckung Jesu im geöffneten und leeren Grab," *ZNW* 73 (1982): 168.

empty tomb, such that the same two conclusions follow here as in the foregoing paragraph. In sum, the testimony of Paul strongly implies the historicity of the empty tomb.

Again Fischer objects to this second consideration by raising two contentions: (i) Paul could not have understood the "he was buried" as implying an empty tomb because he would have then somewhere referred to the empty tomb tradition, and (ii) all kerygmatic traditions lack the empty tomb.[8] But with regard to (i), an argument from silence cannot overcome the positive evidence that Paul did believe in the empty tomb. The objection seems to forget the accidental nature of the epistles and presupposes a completeness on their part that is simply not to be expected. Similarly with regard to (ii), the information from I Cor. 15:3-5 and the sermons in Acts suggest that the empty tomb was implicit in the kerygma, even if it was not explicitly proclaimed. What was proclaimed was Christ and what he *did*, namely, rose and appeared, not the empty grave left behind. And even if it was not used in preaching, the presence in the pre-Markan passion story of the narrative of the discovery of the empty tomb reveals that the latter was valued and preserved in the inner life of the *Urgemeinde*. Hence, such objections, based as they are on silence, carry very little weight. The evidence suggests that both Paul and the formula he transmitted reflect knowledge of the historical fact of Jesus's empty tomb.

3. *The presence of the empty tomb pericope in the pre-Markan passion story supports its historical credibility.* We have seen that the empty tomb story was part of, perhaps the close of, the pre-Markan passion story. This is evident from the fact that (i) the empty tomb pericope is bound up with the immediate context of the burial account and the passion story, (ii) verbal and syntactical similarities bind the empty tomb story to the burial narrative; (iii) the passion story would probably not have been circulated without victory at its end, and (iv) the correspondence between the events of the passion and the formula of I Cor. 15:3-5 confirms the inclusion of the empty tomb account in the pre-Markan passion story. From the nature of the events themselves, such a conclusion makes good sense: there was no continuous, running account of the appearances because the appearances themselves were unexpected, sporadic, and to different people at

---

[8] Fischer, *Ostergeschehen*, p. 58.

various locations and occasions, whereas the empty tomb story related a fact which was, so to speak, "common property" of the *Urgemeinde*.

According to Pesch,[9] geographical references, personal names, and the use of Galilee as a horizon all point to Jerusalem as the fount of the pre-Markan passion story. As to its age, Pesch argues that Paul's Last Supper tradition (I Cor. 11:23-25) presupposes the pre-Markan passion account: therefore, the latter must have originated in the first years of existence of the Jerusalem *Urgemeinde*. Confirmation of this is found in the fact that the pre-Markan passion story speaks of the "high priest" without using his name (14:53, 54, 60, 61, 63). This implies (nearly necessitates, according to Pesch) that Caiaphas was still the high priest when the pre-Markan passion story was being told, since then there would be no need to mention his name. Since Caiaphas was high priest from A.D. 18-37, the *terminus ante quem* for the origin of the tradition is A.D. 37.

Now if this is the case, then it seems futile to attempt to construe the empty tomb account as an unhistorical legend. It seems astounding that Pesch himself can try to convince us that the pre-Markan empty tomb story is an unhistorical fusion of three *Gattungen* from the history of religions: door-opening miracles, epiphany stories, and stories of seeking but not finding persons who have been translated to heaven.[10] Make no mistake: given the age (even if not as old as

---

[9] Rudolf Pesch, *Das Markusevangelium*, 2 vols., HTKNT 2 (Freiburg: Herder, 1977), 2:21; cf. 2:364-377.

[10] Ibid., 2:522-536. Cf. Rudolf Pesch, "Zur Entstehung des Glaubens an die Auferstehung Jesu," *TQ* 153 (1973): 201-228; idem, "Stellungnahme zu den Diskussionsbeiträgen," *TQ* 153 (1973): 270-283. Pesch thinks the account of the stone's being rolled away is the product of door-opening miracle stories. When it is pointed out that no such door-opening is narrated in Mark, Pesch gives away his case by asserting that it is a "latent" door-opening miracle! The angelic appearance he attributes to epiphany stories, though without showing the parallels. Finally he appeals to a *Gattung* for seeking, but not finding someone for the search for Jesus's body, adducing several largely irrelevant texts (*e.g.*, II Kings 2:16-18; Ps. 37:36; Ez. 26:21) plus a spate of post-Christian or Christian-influenced sources (Gospel of Nicodemus 16:6; Testament of Job 39-40) and even question-begging texts from the New Testament itself. He uncritically accepts Lehmann and MacArthur's analysis of the third day motif, which he confuses with Mark's phrase "on the first day of the week." His assertion that eyewitnesses in the *Urmeinde* cannot prevent legend since many legends are attested about the disciples seems to be a *petitio principii*. He does not come to grips with his own early dating and does not show how legend could develop in so short a span in the presence of those who knew better. In connection with Pesch's exegesis, Stuhlmacher has given a timely warning concerning the danger of New Testament exegesis's returning to the fleshpots of the old *religionsgeschichtliche* school:

"Next comes...the *religionsgeschichtliche* method, markedly speculative in its constructions, which Pesch in connection with U. Wilckens and above all Kl. Berger makes use of. In Gnostic research the attempt to infer from a few ambiguous Hellenistic, Jewish, and New Testament passages on the one hand and from many clear, but second to fifth

Pesch argues) and the vicinity of origin of the pre-Markan passion story, it seems very unlikely that the account could, at its core, be an unhistorical legend.

4. *The use of "the first day of the week" instead of "on the third day" points to the primitiveness of the tradition.* The tradition of the discovery of the empty tomb must, it seems, be very old and very primitive because it lacks altogether the third day motif prominent in the kerygma, which is itself extremely old, as evident by its appearance in I Cor. 15:4. If the empty tomb narrative were a late and legendary account, then, as Bode points out, it could hardly have avoided being cast in the prominent, ancient, and accepted third day motif.[11] This strongly implies that the empty tomb tradition antedates the third day motif itself. Again, the proximity of the tradition to the events themselves seems to make it idle to regard the empty tomb story as a legend. It seems quite probable that on the first day of the week the tomb was indeed found empty.

5. *The nature of the narrative itself is theologically unadorned and non-apologetic.* The resurrection is not described, and we have noted the lack of later theological motifs that a late legend might be expected to incorporate. Comparison of Mark's account with those in later apocryphal gospels like the Gospel of Peter underlines the simplicity of the Markan story. This suggests the account

---

century Gnostic texts on the other a foundational model of pre-Christian thought and then with the help of this model (*e.g.*, of the redeemed redeemer) to interpret the New Testament has shown itself to be useless, and we are just now freeing ourselves from this constructional method of interpretation. But now the terrifying impression arises that one wants to repeat the same error with Jewish texts. The reconstruction of that Jewish model of interpretation which is so important for Pesch...is by all appearances only possible with the help in part of late, post-New Testament and clearly Christian-influenced texts. The extra-New Testament texts adduced by Pesch are in any case predominantly from the second to fifth century. But instead...of drawing attention to this difficulty, Pesch simply presupposes that this model of interpretation already lies behind Mk. 6:14ff and Rev. 11:3ff...and was already available as an *Interpretament* for Jesus's disciples. I regard this chain of hypothetical conclusions as extremely problematical historically and again much too weakly grounded methodologically to be able to be made valid as a main critical argument...." (Peter Stuhlmacher, "'Kritischer müssten mir die Historisch-Kritischen Sein!'" *TQ* 153 [1973]: 246).

[11] Bode, *Easter*, p. 161; Brown agrees: "...the basic time indication of the finding of the tomb was fixed in Christian memory before the possible symbolism in the three-day reckoning had yet been perceived" (Raymond E. Brown, *The Gospel according to John*, Anch Bib 29A [Garden City, N. Y.: Doubleday & Co., 1970], p. 980). The fact that τῇ μιᾷ τῶν σαββάτων is probably a Semitism (C. K. Barrett, *The Gospel according to St. John* [London: SPCK, 1972], p. 562; Bode, *Easter*, p. 6; Jacob Kremer, "Zur Diskussion über 'das leere Grab'," in *Resurrexit*, ed. Édouard Dhanis [Rome: Libreria Éditrice Vaticana, 1974], p. 152, contra J. H. Moulton, *A Grammar of New Testament Greek*, vol. 1: *Prolegomena*, 3rd ed. [Edinburgh: T & T Clark, 1980], pp. 95-96) also points to the early origin of the phrase.

is primitive and factual, even if dramatization should occur in the role of the angel. Very often contemporary theologians urge that the empty tomb is not a historical proof for the resurrection because for the disciples it was in itself ambiguous (*mehrdeutig*) and not a proof.[12] But that is precisely one reason why the empty tomb story is today so credible: because it was not an apologetic device of early Christians; it was, as Wilckens nicely puts it, "a trophy of God's victory."[13] The very fact that they saw in it no certain proof helps to insure that the narrative is substantially uncolored by apologetic motifs and in its primitive form.

This analysis seems to undermine the two objections of Oberlinner to the historicity of the Markan account: (i) the presence of an angel precludes historicity, and (ii) why and by whom was the tomb opened? If the account is meant to be taken historically, says Oberlinner, then the answer must be either that the women opened it or that it was miraculously opened by God. But if one says, "God," then why should He do that? The answer can only be: as a proof of the resurrection. But this is wrong, since the angel must proclaim the resurrection and he is a later addition. The empty tomb in itself is susceptible to many explanations.[14] But with regard to (i), even if one concedes that the angel is unhistorical (itself a moot point), it simply does not follow that the entire account is therefore unhistorical. The reasoning in (ii), unless I misunderstand Oberlinner, strikes me as very confused. Suppose we say that God miraculously opened the tomb to permit the women's entry. How does it follow that the empty tomb in and of itself is proof of the resurrection? And even if it were, the fact that Christians felt the need to add the angel only indicates that they did not regard it as proof, so that we today can be confident that the narrative is not an apologetic fiction. What so many scholars do not seem to grasp is that precisely because the empty tomb was ambiguous and not a proof for the early Christians, the narrative of its discovery can be regarded as credible by later generations of researchers.

Michael Goulder, on the other hand, claims that the Markan narrative is thoroughly theologically determined, being a Christian midrash.[15] He attempts to

---

[12] For example, Hans Grass, *Christliche Glaubenslehre*, 2 vols. (Stuttgart: W. Kohlhammer, 1973), 1:103; Kremer, "Grab," p. 139, 158; Vögtle and Pesch, *Osterglauben*, p. 88; Pesch, "'leere Grab'," p. 12; Oberlinner, "Verkündigung der Auferweckung," p. 172.
[13] Ulrich Wilckens, *Auferstehung*, TT4 (Stuttgart and Berlin: Kreuz Verlag, 1970), p. 64.
[14] Oberlinner, "Verkündigung der Auferweckung," pp. 178-180.
[15] Michael Goulder, "The Empty Tomb," *Theol* 79 (1976): 206-214.

show the presence of Old Testament motifs in the narrative, for example, Josh. 10:16-27. But Goulder's procedure is no better than the old *religionsgeschichtliche Methode* which finds parallels scattered everywhere without showing any genealogical link between them. It is ironic that Goulder's article in *Theology* is followed by a piece entitled "The Use of Evidence in New Testament Studies," in which the author complains that too many scholars think it sufficient to show that the evidence *can* be interpreted in accordance with their hypothesis rather than that their interpretation is *required* by the evidence.[16] This is certainly Goulder's failing, and following his method would bring chaos to historical studies. Against his view of the empty tomb story stands the fact that the most significant elements of the Joshua story are conspicuously missing from the Markan story: the guard at the tomb (this is, of course, Matthean, which complicates Goulder's thesis by requiring that the other evangelists, too, are writing midrash), reflection on Jesus as the King, description of Jesus coming out of the tomb, and declaration of Jesus's conquering his enemies. Minor similarities such as the rock-hewn tomb with a roll-stone door and the taking down of the bodies before nightfall are established Jewish practice. For other details of the Markan story, Goulder searches hither and yon: the stone and its sealing come from the lion's den in Dan. 6:17, Joseph of Arimathea from Joseph of Gen. 50, Mary as a witness from Miriam in Exod. 15:21 in connection with Ps. 38:11-14, Salome from Solomon, and so forth. After a while, such a methodology suffers self-refutation by *reductio ad absurdum*. The fact is that the Markan narrative appears to transmit a primitive tradition with little or no theological reflection, and this counts in favor of its historical reliability.

6. *The discovery of the empty tomb by women is highly probable.* Given the low status of women in Jewish society and their lack of qualification to serve as legal witnesses, the most plausible explanation, in light of the gospels' conviction that the disciples were in Jerusalem over the weekend, why women and not the male disciples were made discoverers of the empty tomb is that the women were in fact the ones who made this discovery. This conclusion receives confirmation from the fact that there seems to be no reason why the later Christian church should wish to humiliate its leaders by having them hiding in cowardice in Jerusalem, while the women boldly carry out their last devotions to Jesus's body, unless this were in fact the truth. Their motive of anointing the body by pouring oils

---

[16] J. M. Ross, "The Use of Evidence in New Testament Studies," *Theol* 19 (1976): 214-221.

over it is entirely plausible in light of contemporary custom; indeed, its apparent conflict with Mk. 14:8 makes it unlikely that Mark invented this intention. Furthermore, the listing of the women's names again weighs against unhistorical legend at the story's core, for these persons were known in the *Urgemeinde* and so could not be easily associated with a false account.

Oberlinner objects to this consideration because the women are not being used as witnesses to the empty tomb, but merely to relay the angel's message. Since they were at the crucifixion, they are the most obvious candidates for the job.[17] But why have the message relayed at all? Why not given directly to the disciples? Why not have the male disciples at the cross as well? The careful recounting of the women at the cross, then at the burial, then at the empty tomb shows that their role as historical witnesses of those events is being recalled. Vögtle and Pesch, on the other hand, object that this sixth consideration presupposes the accuracy of the burial story. The fact that the male disciples do not discover the empty tomb is just one more proof that the tomb was not found empty![18] But I fail to see how the present consideration presupposes the credibility of the burial account (itself a pretty safe presupposition in any case). For on the objectors' view, the empty tomb story is a legend and therefore unrelated to whether the burial account is accurate or not. Suppose Jesus was buried in the common plot for criminals. Why do we have a legend arise about women discovering his empty tomb, rather than one describing the male disciples' making this discovery? Vögtle and Pesch offer nothing to explain this anomaly. The most plausible explanation of the women's role is surely that they were in fact the ones who discovered Jesus's tomb empty.

7. *The investigation of the empty tomb by Peter and John is historically probable.* Behind the fourth gospel stands, it seems, John the son of Zebedee, whose reminiscences fill out the traditions employed. The visit of the disciples to the empty tomb is apparently therefore attested, not only in tradition, but by John himself. His testimony has therefore the same first hand character as Paul's letters and ought to be accorded equal weight. We thus possess testimony for the investigation of the empty tomb that cannot be easily disregarded. Entirely apart from that, however, the historicity of the disciples' visit is also made likely by the plausibility of the denial of Peter tradition, for if he were in Jerusalem, then hav-

---

[17] Oberlinner, "Verkündigung der Auferweckung," p. 177.
[18] Vögtle and Pesch, *Osterglauben*, p. 94.

ing heard the women's report he would quite likely check it out. Fischer's objection that in the oldest traditions there is no trace of the disciples' remaining in Jerusalem and that only later traditions attempt to connect them to the empty tomb[19] is, as we have seen, simply false. The inherent implausibility of and absence of any evidence for the disciples' flight to Galilee render it highly likely that they were in Jerusalem, which fact makes the visit to the tomb also very plausible.

8. *It would have been virtually impossible for the disciples to proclaim the resurrection in Jerusalem had the tomb not been empty.* The empty tomb is a *sine qua non* of the resurrection. The notion that Jesus rose from the dead with a new body while his old body lay in the grave is a purely modern conception. Jewish mentality would never have accepted a division of two bodies, one in the tomb and one in the risen life.[20] Even if the disciples failed to check the empty tomb, the Jewish authorities could have been guilty of no such oversight. Moreover, even if the burial story were false and Jesus had been buried in the criminal's graveyard, it is not at all obvious that the Jewish authorities could not have relocated a recently dug dirt grave, even after several weeks. When therefore the disciples began to preach the resurrection in Jerusalem, and people responded, and the religious authorities stood helplessly by, the tomb must have been empty.[21] The fact that the Christian fellowship, founded on belief in Jesus's resurrection, could come into existence and flourish in the very city where he was executed and buried seems powerful evidence for the historicity of the empty tomb.

---

[19] Fischer, *Ostergeschehen*, p. 50.

[20] Bode, *Easter*, pp. 162-163. Pesch maintains that Mk. 6:14 proves that it was possible to speak of a resurrection without an empty tomb. People who believed that Jesus was John the Baptist raised from the dead did not go to John's grave for verification or falsification (Pesch, "Entstehung," pp. 206, 208). But as Schelkle observes, since Jesus was thirty years old at the time and a contemporary of John, the saying in Mk. 6:14 did not mean John had come back to life, but that Jesus was working miracles in his power. No one really seriously asserted the resurrection of the Baptist (Karl Herrmann Schelkle, "Schöpfung des Glaubens," *TQ* 153 (1973): 243). Hengel suggests that the saying concerns, not literal resurrection, but personal identity. In Jewish Haggada, this concern led to all sorts of identifications, such as Pinchas = Elijah; Shem = Melchizedek; Melchizedek = Michael; Aachan = Zimri, etc. It is not a question of literal resurrection (Martin Hengel, "Ist der Osterglaube noch zu retten?" *TQ* 153 [1973]: 258-259).

[21] This conclusion is not altered by any uncertainty as to when the disciples began to preach, as Pesch alleges (Pesch, "Entstehung," p. 207). The point is, when the disciples returned from Galilee to Jerusalem, preaching the resurrection, the tomb by that time had to be empty, whenever that was.

In response to this consideration, Oberlinner objects once more that the empty tomb is *mehrdeutig*. The disciples would not have checked to see if Jesus's grave was empty, even if they believed on the presupposition of Jewish anthropology that it was, since they had already come to faith in the resurrection and the empty tomb had played no role in bringing them to faith. Nor would their opponents have bothered to check this fact because an empty grave, should it be found, would merely have led them to other sorts of explanation.[22] But again, this reasoning strikes me as very confused. Even if we concede, for the sake of argument, that the story of the empty tomb's discovery and investigation by the disciples prior to the appearances is false and that the disciples were, subsequent to the appearances, so wanting in interest in Jesus's tomb that none of them sought to visit it again, how could the Jewish authorities be so apathetic? Oberlinner's answer makes no sense at all: the Jewish leaders' motivation in investigating Jesus's grave was not to *verify* his resurrection, but to *falsify* it. Their hope would have been to find it occupied. If it were found empty, then other explanations for this could be devised; but the discovery of Jesus's occupied grave would decisively silence his followers. Hence, they had every reason to check his gravesite.[23] Given that fact, the proclamation in Jerusalem by the disciples of Jesus's resurrection and the flourishing of the *Urgemeinde* can have occurred only if the tomb of Jesus were empty or unknown. But there is ample evidence that the site of Jesus's body was known—the historicity of Joseph of Arimathea alone suffices for this—; therefore, since the disciples did so proclaim Jesus's resurrection, the tomb must have been empty.

9. *The Jewish polemic presupposes the empty tomb.* From information unintentionally furnished by Matthew, we know that the Jewish opponents of the Christian Way did not deny that Jesus's tomb was empty. Instead they charged that the disciples had stolen Jesus's body. From here the controversy over the guard at the tomb sprang up. The entire polemic presupposes that the tomb was empty. The proclamation "He is risen from the dead" (Mt. 27:64) prompted their

---

[22] Oberlinner, "Verkündigung der Auferweckung," pp. 169-175.

[23] Vögtle and Pesch assert that the Christian proclamation would have struck the Jewish leaders as such *barer Unsinn* that they would have had no reason to take seriously so unconventional a message (Vögtle and Pesch, *Osterglauben*, p. 91). But this misunderstands the point: of course, the Jewish leaders did not take seriously the content of the disciples' message, *i.e.* its truth, but they certainly took seriously schism or heresy within Jewish religion; after all, they had had Jesus crucified!

Jewish opponents to respond, "His disciples...stole him away" (Mt. 28:13). Why? The most probable answer is that they could not deny the fact of the empty tomb and had to come up with an alternative explanation. So they said the disciples stole the body, and from there it all began. Even the gardener hypothesis is an attempt to explain away the empty tomb. The fact that the Jewish polemic never denied that Jesus's tomb was empty but only tried to explain it away is persuasive evidence that the tomb was in fact empty.

Fischer objects to this consideration that because the Jewish polemic is post-AD 70, it was impossible for anyone to check out the truth of the guard story or the empty tomb. Matthew's account shows only that the Jews knew the story of the empty tomb.[24] But Fischer fails to reckon with the fact that there is an obvious tradition history behind the debate into which Matthew enters and the fact that pre-Matthean tradition is evident in the story itself, as we have seen. And in any case, even on Fischer's hypothesis, it remains inexplicable why Jews in the post-70 period, first encountering the legend of the empty tomb, would respond, not by denouncing the fiction, but by agreeing with it and trying to explain it away!

Mahoney's objection, that the Matthean narrative presupposes only the preaching of the resurrection, and that the Jews, who would naturally assume that a physical resurrection was meant, argued as they did only because it would have been "colorless" to say the tomb was unknown or lost, fails to perceive the true force of the argument.[25] The point is that the Jews did not respond to the preaching of the resurrection by pointing to the tomb of Jesus or exhibiting his corpse but entangled themselves in a hopeless series of absurdities trying to explain away the empty tomb. The fact that the enemies of Christianity felt obliged to explain away the empty tomb by the theft hypothesis shows not only that the tomb was known (confirmation of the burial story), but that it was empty.[26]

---

[24] Fischer, *Ostergeschehen*, pp. 63-64.
[25] Robert Mahoney, *Two Disciples at the Tomb*, TW6 (Bern: Herbert Lang, 1974), p. 159. His further objection that this admission by the Jews is only found in a Christian document also misses the point; the course of the argument in the polemic presupposes the empty tomb. The Christians were doing their best to refute the charge of theft, an allegation which tacitly presupposes the tomb was empty.
[26] Oddly enough, Mahoney contradicts himself when he later asserts that it was more promising for the Jews to make fools of the disciples through the gardener-misplaced-the-body theory than to make them clever hoaxers through the theft hypothesis. So it was not apparently the fear of being "colorless" that induced the Jewish authorities to resort to the desperate expedient of the theft hypothesis.

10. *The fact that Jesus's tomb was not venerated as a shrine indicates that the tomb was empty.* We saw earlier that it was customary in Judaism that the tomb of a prophet or holy man be preserved or venerated as a shrine. But it is important to understand why this was so. It was because the remains of the prophet lay in the tomb and thus imparted to the site its religious value. But, of course, if the body were not there, then the grave would lose its significance as a shrine. Now in the case of Jesus's tomb, we find, in Dunn's words, "absolutely no trace" of any veneration of Jesus's burial place.[27] It was apparently not regarded as a shrine nor remembered as a holy site. In light of the disciples' peculiar reverence for Jesus, the reason for this absence of veneration for his burial place is most probably due to the fact that Jesus's body was not in the tomb—his grave was empty.

Taken together these ten considerations seem to furnish good evidence that the tomb of Jesus was actually found empty on Sunday morning by a small group of his women followers. As a plain historical fact this seems to be amply attested. As Van Daalen has remarked, it is extremely difficult to object to the fact of the empty tomb on historical grounds; most objectors do so on the basis of theological or philosophical considerations.[28] But these cannot, of course, change empirical facts. And interestingly, New Testament scholars seem to be increasingly recognizing this: according to Kremer, "By far, most exegetes hold firmly...to the reliability of the biblical statements about the empty tomb," and he lists 28 prominent scholars in support.[29]

---

[27] James W. D. G. Dunn, *Jesus and the Spirit* (London: SCM, 1975), p. 120.
[28] D. H. Van Daalen, *The Real Resurrection* (London: Collins, 1970), p. 41; so also Gerald O'Collins, *The Easter Jesus*, 2nd ed. (London: Darton, Longman, & Todd, 1980), p. 91. The historian Michael Grant concludes,

"Even if the historian chooses to regard the youthful apparition as extra-historical, he cannot justifiably deny the empty tomb. True, this discovery, as so often, is differently described by the various Gospels—as critical pagans early pointed out. But if we apply the same sort of criteria that we would apply to any other ancient literary sources, then the evidence is firm and plausible enough to necessitate the conclusion that the tomb was indeed found empty" (Michael Grant, *Jesus: an Historian's Review of the Gospels* [New York: Charles Scribner's Sons, 1977], p. 176).

[29] Jacob Kremer, *Die Osterevangelien—Geschichten um Geschichte* (Stuttgart: Katholisches Bibelwerk, 1977), pp. 49-50. He furnishes this list, to which his own name may be added: Blank, Blinzler, Bode, von Campenhausen, Delorme, Dhanis, Grundmann, Hengel, Lehmann, Léon-Dufour, Lichtenstein, Mánek, Martini, Mussner, Nauck, Rengstorff, Ruckstuhl, Schenke, Schmitt, K. Schubert, Schwank, Schweizer, Seidensticker, Strobel, Stuhlmacher, Trilling, Vögtle, Wilckens. He should also have mentioned Benoit, Brown, Clark, Dunn, Ellis, Gundry, Hooke, Jeremias, Klappert, Ladd, Lane, Marshall, Moule, Perry, J. A. T. Robinson, Schnackenburg, and

Chapter 9

Explaining the Historical Fact

But if the tomb of Jesus was found empty on the first day of the week, the question must be, how did this situation come to be?[30] Although the empty tomb may have proved at first ambiguous and puzzling to the disciples, today we know that most alternative explanations for the empty tomb are more incredible than the resurrection itself (for example, the disciples' stealing the body, the gardener's moving the corpse, Jesus's not being dead, the women's going to the wrong tomb, and so forth).[31] Only either misinformation or theological presuppositions could

---

Vermes. Schnackenburg concurs with Kremer's judgment: "...most exegetes accept the historicity of the empty tomb, so that this question is not the decisive point in the discussion about the resurrection" (Rudolf Schnackenburg, personal letter, September 21, 1979). Contrast Perrin's judgment: "Scholars are coming increasingly to the conclusion that the empty tomb tradition is an interpretation of the event—a way of saying 'Jesus is risen!'—rather than a description of an aspect of the event itself" (Norman Perrin, *The Resurrection according to Matthew, Mark, and Luke* [Philadelphia: Fortress, 1977], p. 80). In this and some other key points, Perrin seemed remarkably out of touch with recent discussion on the resurrection.

[30] This question occasions consternation among some theologians. Koch pronounces, "It is not a legitimate question to ask how the grave became empty because it isolates the grave and wants to provide objective insight into its emptiness" (Gerhard Koch, *Die Auferstehung Jesu Christi*, BHT [Tübingen: J. C. B. Mohr, 1959], p. 171). Wilckens says, "How the grave of Jesus became empty is a question that cannot be...answered in a historical way;" but then he turns around and persuasively refutes all naturalistic efforts to explain it (Wilckens, *Auferstehung*, pp. 152-153). The problem here is not historical but theological. Such scholars recoil from the New Testament's understanding of the resurrection as a historical event which is every bit as objective as the crucifixion; instead they substitute the notions of "an eschatological event" (Wilckens) or "a meta-historical event" (Fuller), phrases which are in reality nonsensical. An eschatological event is either an event that has yet to occur, which is not true of Jesus's resurrection, or an event pregnant with divine significance, in which case there is no problem in verifying or falsifying it, since it has occurred. A meta-historical event is a self-contradiction, since an event is that which happens and so is part of history. Robinson scores Fuller's opinion that this "meta-historical event" left only a negative mark on history: "Yet the negative mark, by which he evidently means not simply that there was nothing to show for it but that there was *nothing* to show for it (i.e. an empty tomb) *is* 'within history' and must therefore be patient of historical inquiry" (J. A. T. Robinson, *The Human Face of God* [London: SCM Press, 1973], p. 136).

[31] See William Lane Craig, *The Historical Argument for the Resurrection of Jesus during the Deist Controversy*, Texts and Studies in Religion 23 (Toronto: Edwin Mellen, 1985). The point is well-illustrated by M. E. Thrall's recent attempt to defend the wrong tomb/subjective vision hypothesis (M. E. Thrall, "Resurrection Traditions and Christian Apologetics," *Thomist* 43 [1979]: 197-216). She suggests that the women went to a tomb mistakenly thought to be Jesus's and found it empty, which in turn triggered hallucinations in the disciples' minds, which Thrall interprets as external projections of Jungian archetypal ideas. She presents the hypothesis simply as a possible counter-explanation to the resurrection, with little evidence of a positive nature in favor of it, but she does try to rebut the traditional objections to her theory. For example, the Jews did not disinter the corpse perhaps because it would have been a threat to public order or because by the time the disciples began to preach, decay would have rendered the corpse unrecognizable. The guard story reflects Jewish/Christian controversy outside Palestine after AD 70. Thus, the historical component of belief in the resurrection is ambiguous. Unfortunately, Thrall never answers what was perhaps one of the chief implausibilities of the wrong tomb theory: that having observed

move Pesch to declare that the empty tomb permits "all possible explanations," as shown by the Jewish polemic and later anti-Christian rationalism.[32] This is simply not true; the old rationalistic explanations have thoroughly failed to provide plausible historical explanations that fit the facts without bruising them.

To my knowledge, the only natural explanation of the empty tomb that deserves any consideration is the suggestion that some third party stole the body.[33] The famous Nazareth inscription seems to imply that tomb-robbery was a widespread problem in first century Palestine. It could be that some unknown zealot group broke into the tomb and absconded with the body. Now there is no positive proof for this hypothesis, and to that extent it is a mere assertion. But it remains at least a possibility and should therefore be taken into account.

The hypothesis does not seem, however, to be very plausible: (1) We know of no third party who would have any motive for stealing the body. Robbers would have no reason to break into the tomb, since nothing of value was interred with the body, nor would they cart away the dead man's body. Political zealots would simply have nothing to gain by removing the corpse and hiding it. Their mention in this connection is puzzling, since their cause seems unrelated to and would in no way be furthered by the disappearance of Jesus's body. Enemies or persons bitterly disappointed in Jesus might conceivably desecrate the grave, but again it

---

the burial with a view toward returning, the women should together mistake another tomb for Jesus's and, having made the mistake, should not subsequently discover their error. Thrall says nothing concerning the extensive evidence we have reviewed for the fact that the site of the burial was well-known. Her view entails, for example, that Joseph of Arimathea was an unhistorical figure, since he could have identified the correct site of his own tomb. But apart from its inherent implausibility, the denial of Joseph's historicity does not answer the problem of how those who buried Jesus should be subsequently unable to identify his grave. After all, the Jewish authorities did not need to disinter the corpse to refute the resurrection; they had only to point to the correct tomb. But the Jewish polemic shows they did not even do that. Even if Matthew's guard is a later apologetic legend, the tradition history of the controversy shows that the Jews did not deny the empty tomb of Jesus. Disinterment would no doubt have been a last, drastic measure, but it is not evident that the Jewish authorities would not have attempted it had earlier efforts to refute the women's error failed—but the evidence is that no such efforts were ever made. Thrall's attempt to defend the wrong tomb hypothesis will probably generate as little following as did Kirsopp Lake's original attempt. On her view of the appearances, see note 11 of chap. 10.

[32] Pesch, *Markusevangelium*, 2:536; so also Kremer, "Grab," p. 139. Contemporary scholarship seems to have a woeful ignorance of the historical debate over the resurrection, a fact made evident from Wilckens's bibliography from the "history of the research": it consists of Thomas Woolston, Peter Annet, H. S. Reimarus, and D. F. Strauss (Wilckens, *Auferstehung*, pp. 171-172)!

[33] J. A. T. Robinson, *Can We Trust the New Testament?* (London and Oxford: Mowbrays, 1977), p. 124; David Whittaker, "What Happened to the Body of Jesus? a Speculation," *ExpTim* 81 (1970): 307-310. Whittaker supposes the thieves to have been ordinary vandals. This hypothesis takes for granted that there was no guard at the tomb.

would be just pointless to carry off the corpse and hide it. (2) Apparently no one but Joseph and those with him and the women knew exactly where the tomb was. Joseph probably surprised the Jewish authorities by placing the body in his tomb instead of having it buried in criminal's graveyard. Hence, it is difficult to see how some third party could take the body, not having been present at the burial. (3) A related problem is the time factor. Since it is probable that the women found the tomb empty Sunday morning, this means that would-be thieves would have had to hatch their conspiracy, steal the body, and dispose of it sometime between Friday night and Sunday morning. Given the tumultuous confusion at Jesus's public trial and execution—and during Passover time no less—this sort of dering-do strains one's credulity. (4) The fact of the graveclothes in the tomb, which so struck John, does seem to preclude theft of the body. This fact is vouched for by the witness of the Beloved Disciple and by the tradition embodied in Lk. 24:12. (5) Conspiracies such as this almost inevitably come to light eventually, either through discovery or disclosure or at least rumor. It seems hard to believe that when the disciples began to preach that Jesus had been raised from the dead, the malefactors could have kept their secret long. The Jewish authorities would certainly have been glad to have any such information. But we find no trace of this whatever in any of the traditions. (6) Finally, perhaps the most serious objection to this hypothesis is that it seeks to explain only half of the evidence, namely, the empty tomb, in isolation from the appearances. A second hypothesis to explain the appearances will have to be conjoined with it. But if explanatory scope is a criterion for preferring one hypothesis to another, then the resurrection as an overarching explanation for the empty tomb and appearances is to be preferred to separate hypotheses for the same facts. As John Cobb confesses, once one gives up the presupposition that dead men do not rise, how can one deny that the simplest explanation of the facts is that Jesus did indeed rise from the dead?[34]

---

[34] John B. Cobb, "Wolfhart Pannenberg's 'Jesus: God and Man'," *JR* 49 (1969): 198.

CHAPTER 10

THE EVIDENCE FOR THE RESURRECTION APPEARANCES

Turning from the empty tomb to the appearances, we need to inquire what evidence there is that Jesus appeared alive after his death to his disciples.

THE HISTORICAL FACT OF THE APPEARANCES

Here the evidence may be summarized under four heads:

1. *The testimony of Paul shows that the disciples saw "appearances of Jesus."* The age alone of the formula cited in I Cor. 15, which probably reaches back to within the first five years after the crucifixion, seems to preclude regarding the appearances in the list as legendary. No less important is Paul's own early, personal contact with Peter and James and his acquaintance with some of the 500 brethren. It is nothing short of astounding that we should have here information from a man who spoke both with Jesus's brother and chief disciple, each of whom claimed to have seen Jesus alive from the dead and who went to his death because of that conviction. The appearance to the 500 brethren, which in itself sounds unbelievable because of the number involved, is nonetheless probably historical, not only because of Paul's personal acquaintance with them, but also because most of them were still alive to be questioned. The reason we hear so little of the appearance may well be because it may have taken place in Galilee. And, of course, the appearance to Paul himself, which changed his whole life to the point that he also went to his death for faith in the risen Jesus, is historically certain. We may try to explain these appearances as hallucinations if we choose, but we cannot deny that they occurred. As Norman Perrin remarks, "The more we study the tradition with regard to the appearances, the firmer the rock begins to appear upon which they

are based."[1] Paul's list makes it evident that on separate occasions different individuals and groups saw "appearances of Jesus" alive from the dead. This fact is virtually undeniable.

2. *The gospel accounts of the resurrection appearances are fundamentally reliable historically.* Though it may be impossible to prove that any single appearance narrative is historically accurate, there are nevertheless good grounds for holding to the historicity of the appearance accounts in general, as Trilling explains:

> From the list in I Cor. 15 the particular reports of the gospels are now to be interpreted. Here may be of help what we said about Jesus's miracles. It is impossible to 'prove' historically a particular miracle. But the totality of the miracle reports permits no reasonable doubt that Jesus in fact performed 'miracles.' That holds analogously for the appearance reports. It is not possible to secure historically the particular event. But the totality of the appearance reports permits no reasonable doubt that Jesus in fact bore witness to himself in such a way.[2]

Indeed, I think that the evidence for the reports in general is such that we may affirm that the appearance traditions of the gospels, far from being basically legendary, are substantially credible from a historical standpoint. Three basic considerations support this conclusion.

(a) *There was insufficient time for legend to accrue significantly.* Ever since Strauss broached his theory that the gospel accounts of Jesus's life and resurrection are the products of legendary development, the unanswered difficulty for this conception has been that the temporal and geographical distance between the events and the accounts seems to be simply insufficient to allow for the extent of development postulated. Julius Müller's critique of Strauss has yet to be answered:

> Most decidedly must a considerable interval of time be required for such a complete transformation of a whole history by popular tradition, when the series of legends are

---

[1] Norman Perrin, *The Resurrection according to Matthew, Mark, and Luke* (Philadelphia: Fortress, 1977), p. 80.

[2] Wolfgang Trilling, *Fragen zur Geschichtlichkeit Jesu* (Düsseldorf: Patmos Verlag, 1966), p. 153. With regard to Jesus's miracles, Trilling has written, "We are convinced and hold it for historically certain that Jesus did in fact perform miracles.... The miracle reports occupy so much space in the gospels that it is impossible that they could all have been subsequently invented or transferred to Jesus" (Ibid., p. 153). According to Trilling, the fact that miracles in general belong to the historical Jesus is widely recognized and no longer disputed. He refers here, not to the interpretation of miracles as supernatural events, but to the historical facticity of the gospel miracles attributed to Jesus. So also Hans Grass, *Christliche Glaubenslehre*, 2 vols. (Stuttgart: W. Kohlhammer, 1973), p. 84.

formed in the same territory where the heroes actually lived and wrought. Here one cannot imagine how such a series of legends could arise in an historical age, obtain universal respect, and supplant the historical recollection of the true character and connexion of their heroes' lives in the minds of the community, if eye-witnesses were still at hand, who could be questioned respecting the truth of the recorded marvels. Hence, legendary fiction, as it likes not the clear present time, but prefers the mysterious gloom of grey antiquity, is wont to seek a remoteness of age, along with that of space, and to remove its boldest and more rare and wonderful creations into a very remote and unknown land.[3]

Roman historian A. N. Sherwin-White has urged the same consideration. He remarks that in classical historiography the sources are usually biased and removed at least one or two generations or even centuries from the events they narrate; but historians still reconstruct with confidence what happened.[4] In the gospels, by contrast, the tempo is "unbelievable" for the accrual of legend; more generations are needed.[5] The writings of Herodotus enable us to test the tempo of myth-

---

[3] Julius Müller, *The Theory of Myths, in its Application to the Gospel History, Examined and Confuted* (London: John Chapman, 1844), p. 26. Müller further argues that one cannot ascribe to the apostles such carelessness that they should not have remarked the formation and general diffusion of unhistorical legends about Jesus among the communities of Palestine, or if they remarked them, that they should not have opposed them vigorously. Moreover, were the stories without historical foundation, the enemies of Christianity would surely have seized upon this fact. Luke's use of eyewitnesses in particular (Lk. 1:4) ensures that he at least is not copying down myths, thinking it is history (Ibid., pp. 29-33). Compare the argument of August Tholuck, who in his critique of Strauss also laid great weight on Luke's proximity to the events in question and ability as a historian (A. Tholuck, *The Credibility of the Evangelical History* [London: John Chapman, 1844]). He argues that the author of Luke-Acts was a companion of Paul and that several lines of evidence point to a date for Acts of AD 63-64, which puts the gospel even earlier (Ibid., pp. 5-8). We are thus placed in the time of eyewitnesses to the recorded events. Tholuck then argues on the basis of the details in Acts for Luke's competence as a historian (Ibid., pp. 8-23). This means not only that Luke's narratives are historically credible, but the narratives of the other gospels as well, since they generally concur. Athanase Coquerel also scored Strauss for allowing insufficient time for the accrual of legend. Comparing the gospel stories to the myths about Charlemagne, he maintains that it takes ages for myths to form; the legends Strauss seeks are actually the apocryphal gospels (Athanase Coquerel, *Reply to Dr. Strauss's Book*, 'The Life of Jesus' [n.p.; n.d.], pp. 37-45). All these considerations press with almost equal force today.

[4] A. N. Sherwin-White, *Roman Society and Roman Law in the New Testament* (Oxford: Clarendon Press, 1963), pp. 188-191.

[5] Ibid., p. 189. This consideration becomes especially forceful if one follows critics such as Guthrie, Reicke, and Robinson in a pre-70 dating of Luke-Acts (Donald Guthrie, *New Testament Introduction*, 3rd ed. rev. [London: Inter-Varsity Press, 1970], pp. 340-345; Bo Reicke, "Synoptic Prophecies on the Destruction of Jerusalem," in *Studies in New Testament and Early Christian Literature*, ed. D. E. Aune [Leiden: E. J. Brill, 1972], pp. 121-134; John A. T. Robinson, *Redating the New Testament* [London: SCM Press, 1976], pp. 13-30, 86-117). Robinson has sharply criticized the current consensus of scholars concerning the dating of New Testament materials, charging that the post-70 dating is largely the result of the tyranny of unexamined presuppositions and almost willful blindness on the part of the critics. It would be unfortunate were we to reject Robinson's case out of hand simply because of some of his more extreme positions (*e.g.*, all the New Testament materials are pre-70), for the case for a pre-70 dating for at least Mark and Luke-Acts is very persuasive.

Though most scholars regard John Mark as the author of Mark, Feine-Behm-Kümmel maintain that an early origin of the gospel (40-60) is "improbable" because "the development of the evangelical tradition is already far advanced, and in Mk. 13 at least the threatening nearness of the Jewish war can probably be perceived" (Paul Feine and Johannes Behm, *Introduction to the New Testament*, 14th rev. ed., ed. Werner Kümmel, trans. A. J. Mattill, Jr. [Nashville: Abingdon Press, 1966], pp. 70-71). An approximate date of around 70 must serve as the time of Mark's composition. Since Luke is dependent on Mark, a date of Luke before 70 is also untenable. But the decisive factor is that Luke looks back on the fall of Jerusalem in his gospel, as evident in Jesus's "predictions" of that event. Hence, Luke was probably composed between 70 and 90.

The force of these arguments depends, however, largely upon certain presuppositions. (1) The first reason mitigating against an early date for Mark, the "advanced evangelical tradition," presupposes that such tradition did not reflect the historical Jesus's teaching. But such tradition may not be "advanced," but substantially authentic (R. N. Longenecker, *The Christology of Early Jewish Christianity* [London: SCM Press, 1970]; M. Hengel, *The Son of God: The Origin of Christology and the History of Jewish-Hellenistic Religion* [London: SCM Press, 1976]; C. F. D. Moule, *The Origin of Christology* [Cambridge; Cambridge University Press, 1977]; Royce Gorden Gruenler, *New Approaches to Jesus and the Gospels* [Grand Rapids, Mich.: Baker, 1985]). In fact, the argument cuts both ways: one could argue that since Mark is early, the tradition is not so advanced. And there do seem to be good reasons to think that Mark is early. First, there is a sort of *prima facie* justification for assigning to Mark a date as early as is permissible. For there is strong tradition that John Mark was dependent in part upon Peter's preaching for his information. Now it seems *prima facie* incredible in this case that Mark would wait *thirty to forty years* to write down his gospel. Can it be plausibly supposed that he would wait decades before he composed his brief gospel, a tract that would be simply invaluable in sharing with fledgling churches as the ministers of the gospel went about preaching and teaching? But second, if Luke-Acts was written before 70 and if Luke used Mark, then this *prima facie* early date for Mark is confirmed. The date of Luke-Acts will be briefly discussed below. (2) The second argument against an early date for both gospels is the same: historical information regarding Jerusalem's fall in 70. This argument, however, rests on the presupposition that Jesus did not have prophetic powers. As Guthrie points out, if Jesus did have predictive powers, then the main prop in the Markan dating falls away and with it the principal basis for a post-70 dating of the other synoptics (Guthrie, *Introduction*, p. 46). But secondly, even on a purely naturalistic account of the matter, the predictions cannot be taken as decisive proof of post-70 composition. Reicke argues that the prophecies actually have nothing to do with the destruction of Jerusalem in AD 70. Lk. 19:43-44 is a familiar line of prophecy that could have been uttered at any time. As for Lk. 21:20-24, it could be based on Old Testament passages; it concerns an apocalyptic event, not the destruction of Jerusalem in 70; and it shows no knowledge of the Christians' exodus from the city in 66. Prophecies of the destruction of the Temple (Mk. 13:2) were common prior to 70. Reicke then turns the tables and argues that the prophecies are actually evidence for a pre-70 dating of the synoptics. When the evangelists wrote, they had no knowledge of the event in AD 70. Had Luke, for example, been looking back on the destruction of Jerusalem, his portrait of the Romans would have been different. In Luke's writings, the Romans were never enemies, but in Jesus's prediction, the destruction of the city is by her enemies. After 70, addressing Theophilus as "honored sir" would have been impossible. So Luke's gospel must have a pre-70 date (Reicke, "Prophecies," pp. 121-134). Robinson argues that the fact that the disciples' question about the Temple in Mk. 13:2 is never really answered suggests the discourse was not written retrospectively, nor could the injunction to flee to the mountains be after the fact, since in 66 the Christians fled to Pella, which is actually below sea level. The siege of the city predicted in Luke bears as much resemblance to the capture of Jerusalem in 586 BC as in AD 70; indeed, the peculiarities of the latter noted by Josephus are missing from the prediction. On these grounds alone, Robinson asserts, the burden of proof ought to be on the scholar who sees the prophecies as having a post-70 date (Robinson, *Redating*, pp. 15-19, 26-30).

Hence, the evidence against an early date for Mark and Luke-Acts is not only insufficient, but perhaps even counter-productive.

What evidence is there for a pre-70 date for Luke-Acts and hence for Mark? Several lines of evidence point to a date for Luke-Acts prior to 64 (Guthrie, *Introduction*, pp. 340-345). (1) There is an absence of reference to events which happened between 60 and 70. Though Luke centers more attention in his gospel on Jerusalem than the other synoptics, the fall of Jerusalem is nowhere mentioned in Acts, which seems amazing when one reflects what a cataclysmic event this must have been for both Jews and Christians alike. A second event conspicuously absent is the Neronian persecution of the church. It may be said that Luke cut his narrative short for apologetic purposes to allow Paul unhindered freedom to preach the gospel in Rome; but, as Robinson remarks, such an apologetic would have appeared less than cogent "by glossing over in silence the common knowledge that he and Peter and 'a vast multitude' of other Christians in the city had within a few years been mercilessly butchered" (Robinson, *Redating*, p. 89). A third unrecorded event is the martyrdom of Jesus's brother and leader of the Jerusalem church James. Although Luke records the martyrdom of Stephen and James the son of Zebedee, he does not mention this important martyr, who died by stoning illegally instigated by the high priest Ananus during the interregnum after the death of Festus in 61 (Josephus *Antiquities of the Jews* 20.9). Robinson comments, "No incident could have served Luke's apologetic purpose better, that it was the Jews not the Romans who were the real enemies of the gospel" (Ibid.). (2) There is no mention of the death of the apostle Paul. Since Paul was probably martyred about 64, it is very strange that Acts would break off with Paul still a prisoner in Rome, but enjoying a good degree of freedom, if, in fact, he had been slain earlier for the gospel. It is usually asserted that Paul's martyrdom is foreshadowed in Acts 20:25; 27:24, but these references are far from clear. His seeing the Ephesians no more could reflect his plans to open new mission fields and not to return to Ephesus (Rom. 15:28) and his standing before the emperor his expectation in Rome. We have no clear "prophecy" of his martyrdom in Rome; quite the contrary, on this logic we should have expected the death of Paul in Jerusalem, as it is clearly fore-shadowed in 21:13. Other explanations of Acts' breaking off where it does seem highly contrived. Harnack's judgment remains sound: it is "hopeless" to think "that we can explain why the narrative breaks off as it does, otherwise than by assuming that the trial had actually not yet reached its close. It is no use to struggle against this conclusion" (Adolf von Harnack, *The Date of Acts and the Synoptic Gospels* [New York: Putnam; 1911], pp. 96-97). (3) The subject matter is primitive. The burning issue in Acts is the Jewish-Gentile controversy, which ceased to be a problem after 70. Also concern with food requirements and the Jerusalem council points to a date before 70, since after the city's destruction these were of secondary importance. (4) The theology is primitive. Titles for Jesus as "the Christ," "the Servant of God," and "the Son of Man" indicate primitive traditions, as do descriptions of Christians as "disciples," the Jewish nation as λαός and Sunday as "the first day of the week." These could be deliberate archaisms, but the more natural explanation is that the author is early enough to be in contact with the primitive climate of the early church. (5) The attitude of the state toward the church is still beneficent. Guthrie observes, "Luke is at pains to demonstrate the impartiality of the imperial officials regarding Christianity. In no case is it the Roman officials who persecute the church" (Guthrie, *Introduction*, p. 344). Such a characterization would be possible prior to the Neronian persecution in 64, but thereafter it would have been a cruel and palpable falsehood. (6) There is no substantial knowledge of Paul's writings in Acts. The author of Acts shows no familiarity with Paul's letters, a fact that favors a date as early as possible for Acts. The later one dates Acts the more difficult is this fact to explain. These six convergent lines of evidence suggest strongly that Acts was written before 64 and Luke therefore sometime before that (late 50's or early 60's). Mark therefore was written even earlier; Robinson suggests a first edition in Rome in 45 (Robinson, *Redating*, p. 114).

In an important analysis of Robinson's viewpoint, E. E. Ellis finds the arguments for a pre-70 date for many of the New Testament books quite strong but points out that most scholars today give more weight to the results of 19th-early 20th century literary criticism than to external correla-

making, and the tests suggest that *even two generations are too short a span to allow the mythical tendency to prevail over the hard historic core of oral tradition.*[6] Müller challenged scholars of his day to show where in 30 years a great series of legends, the most prominent elements of which are fictitious, have anywhere gathered around an important historical individual and become firmly fixed in general belief;[7] the challenge was never met. Dibelius sought an analogy in the *Apophthegmata Patrum*,[8] but the tradition in this case took a century to form, not thirty or forty years; such a temporal gap for the gospel traditions would land us in the period when the apocryphal gospels were beginning to originate.

(b) *The controlling presence of living eyewitnesses would retard significant accrual of legend.* Related to the temporal and geographical proximity of the gospels to the events they narrate is the controlling presence of living eyewitnesses who knew what did and did not happen. Taylor has twitted sceptical New Testament scholars for their neglect of this factor, observing that if these critics were right, then the disciples "must have all been translated into heaven immedi-

---

tions with historical facts, as championed by Robinson (E. Earle Ellis, "Dating the New Testament," *NTS* 26 [1980]: 487-502). But Ellis contends that at least three axioms of such literary criticism are doubtful: (1) that Christian theology underwent a unilinear or dialectical development which allows New Testament books to be progressively dated; (2) that authorship of New Testament books was an individual affair, such that authenticity may be tested by matters of vocabulary and style elsewhere; and (3) that Jewish Palestine was a Semitic island in a Hellenistic sea, so that New Testament documents reflecting Hellenistic ideas could not have belonged to the earliest form of Christianity but reflect a later state of development. The first and third axioms are particularly relevant to the gospels' dating. The first is questionable because, as Hengel and Moule have shown, New Testament Christology was in full bloom within two decades after Jesus's resurrection. Hence, purportedly "advanced" Christology cannot serve as an indication for a late date of a book in which it appears. The third axiom has been shown to be simply false. Greek language and thought pervaded Palestine, even in daily life, so that any dating based on a dichotomy between Palestinian/Hellenistic milieu cannot stand. According to Ellis, "...the literary criticism of New Testament literature accepted by most scholars today, and the New Testament chronology based upon it, has underpinnings that are tenuous and that in some cases can be shown to be historically false" (Ibid., p. 501). Therefore, the weight must fall on the sort of considerations adduced by Robinson, which, as we have seen, incline toward a pre-70 dating for at least some of the gospels.

If this line of reasoning is sound, then it becomes very difficult to regard the gospel accounts as unhistorical, since there simply was not sufficient time for unbridled legend to accrue. Indeed, one cannot but suspect that it is this very implication that causes many scholars to resist the force of this reasoning and to opt for a later date.

[6] Sherwin-White, *Roman Society*, p. 190.
[7] Müller, *Theory*, p. 29.
[8] Martin Dibelius, "Zur Formgeschichte der Evangelien," *Tru* 1 (1929): 173. Contra, see A. H. McNeile, *An Introduction to the Study of the Study of the New Testament* (London: Oxford University Press, 1953), p. 54.

ately after the Resurrection."⁹ The witnesses listed by Paul in I Cor. 15 continued to live and move in the early community and would exercise a control on the appearance traditions. As Plummer observes, those who had seen Christ after the resurrection would soon become "marked men."¹⁰ Similarly, if persons like Mary Magdalene and the women did not see Jesus, then it is difficult to see how the tradition could arise and continue that they did, in opposition to the better knowledge of first generation believers.

(c) *The authoritative control of the apostles would have helped to keep legendary tendencies in check.* Since the apostles were the guardians of the Jesus tradition, it would have been difficult for fictitious appearance stories incompatible with the apostles' own experience to arise and flourish so long as they were alive, or for the true story to be supplanted by a false. Künneth's judgment is worth repeating:

> It is extremely difficult to see how the gospel accounts of the resurrection could arise in opposition to the original apostolic preaching and that of Paul.... The authority of the apostolic eyewitnesses was extraordinarily strong. It would be inconceivable how there should have arisen in opposition to the authoritative witness of the original apostles a harmonious tradition telling of an event that has no basis in the message of the eyewitnesses.¹¹

Fabrication of stories on the part of Christians, he believes, would have been "sharply contradicted by the apostles or their pupils."¹² Discrepancies in secondary details could exist, and the theology of the evangelists could affect the traditions, but the basic traditions themselves could not have been legendary so long as the disciples were in charge of the deposit of Christian tradition and directing the

---

⁹ Vincent Taylor, *The Formation of the Gospel Tradition*, 2nd ed. (London: Macmillan & Co., 1935), p. 41; cf. A. M. Hunter, *The Work and Words of Jesus* (Philadelphia: Westminster Press, 1950), p. 14.

¹⁰ Archibald Robertson and Alfred Plummer, *First Epistle of St. Paul to the Corinthians*, 2nd ed., ICC (Edinburgh: T & T Clarke, 1967), p. 337. The fact that living witnesses had memories of their experiences vitiates the view that all that existed at first was a list of names and that stories grew up later. This view also leaves us at a loss to explain the lack of stories for certain appearances in the list. The brevity of the mention of the appearances in I Cor. 15 is no argument against equally early stories, since the passion is also mentioned just as briefly (Wilhelm Michaelis, *Die Erscheinungen des Auferstandenen* [Basel: Heinrich Majer, 1944], p. 10; C. H. Dodd, "The Appearances of the Risen Christ: A study in form-criticism of the Gospels," in idem, *More New Testament Studies* [Manchester: Manchester University Press, 1968], pp. 127, 133; John Alsup, *The Post-Resurrection Appearance Stories of the Gospel Tradition*, CTM A5 [Stuttgart: Calwer Verlag, 1975], p. 68).

¹¹ Walther Künneth, *The Theology of the Resurrection*, trans. J. W. Leitch (London: SCM, 1965), pp. 92-93.

¹² Ibid., p. 93.

Christian community. The accounts which are unhistorical in substance did not arise until the second century, and even then they were universally rejected by the early church.

These three factors—the insufficient temporal and geographical distance between the events and the accounts, the controlling presence of eyewitnesses, and the authoritative control of the apostolic leaders—seem to insure that the traditions underlying the gospel appearance narratives are not unhistorical legends and that therefore the appearance stories of the gospels are substantially accurate accounts of what took place.

3. *Particular resurrection appearances have specific marks of historical credibility.* In addition to the general consideration above, several of the resurrection appearances have good grounds in themselves for affirming their historicity. By way of brief review:

(a) *The appearance to the women.* The fact that women are chosen for the first appearance and not the male disciples lends credibility to this incident. It would seem purposeless to make unqualified women the first witnesses of the risen Jesus, were this not the case. In fact Paul's formula and Luke may well omit them because of their lack of legal status. So why have such a story at all? Any conceivable purpose for such an appearance would have been better served by, say, an appearance to Peter at the tomb. That Christ appears first to the women therefore speaks in favor of its historicity.

(b) *The appearance to Peter.* Although we have no account of this incident, the historicity of this appearance is granted by nearly all New Testament scholars. It is attested in the very old formula quoted by Paul and in what is probably an old tradition cited by Luke. Moreover, Paul had personal contact with Peter during his visit in AD 36, and in citing the formula vouchsafes its accuracy in this regard.

(c) *The appearance to the Twelve.* The reference to this appearance in the pre-Pauline formula, as well as Paul's personal contact with the disciples, prevent it from being a late legend, and Luke and John hand on traditions of this event. Behind the Johannine account stands the witness of the Beloved Disciple, one of the Twelve, which serves as a guarantee of the fundamental accuracy of the traditions of the event. In light of Luke and John's agreement, it is probable that the appearance occurred in Jerusalem on Sunday.

(d) *The Lake of Tiberias appearance.* The activity of the disciples in fishing subsequent to Christ's resurrection and commissioning of them is unusual and bespeaks a primitive and probably accurate tradition of an appearance on the Lake. Moreover, the witness of the Beloved Disciple also stands behind this appearance and vouches for the traditions contained therein.

(e) *The appearance in Galilee.* The tradition of an appearance of Jesus to the disciples in Galilee is referred to in the pre-Markan passion story via Jesus's and the angel's predictions. Since Mark's source arose in the *Urgemeinde* quite early, it seems that this preserves the memory of an actual incident.

(f) *The appearance to the 500 brethren.* Perhaps the most unlikely of the appearances, this incident must, it seems, have taken place, for Paul had first hand contact with some of these people and in effect appeals to them as eyewitnesses for the resurrection of Jesus. The appearance probably occurred in Galilee under open air, prior to the disciples' return to Jerusalem.

(g) *The appearance to James.* Given James's antipathy to Jesus during his lifetime and his leadership of the church thereafter, it seems very plausible that his turnabout was due to a resurrection appearance of Jesus to him. Paul's personal contact with James in Jerusalem in AD 36 and his naming James in the list of witnesses makes this a firm conclusion.

(h) *The appearance to Paul.* We have in Paul's letters first-hand information concerning the appearance of Jesus to him, an event that revolutionized the life of this learned Pharisee. There can be no reasonable doubt that this event occurred, and most scholars are willing to recognize the fundamental historical credibility of the Acts account.

Hence, in addition to the evidence for the general historical credibility of the gospel appearance stories, these individual accounts have in themselves positive marks of historical reliability. From these we may infer with good probability that the disciples witnessed appearances of Jesus first in Jerusalem and then in Galilee, that these appearances were witnessed by both groups and individuals, and that they occurred under varying conditions (near the tomb, in the upper room, on the Lake of Tiberias, at an outdoor assembly). The nature of these appearances is considered more closely in the next point.

4. *The resurrection appearances were physical, bodily appearances.* There is a widespread consensus among New Testament scholars that the disciples did see

"appearances of Jesus" after his death, and a considerable number interpret these appearances in terms of the bodily resurrection and appearances of Jesus. But at the same time, a great many critics, while affirming the "bodily resurrection" of Christ, hold that because the body was spiritual, this concept entails in no sense physicality. The appearances of the risen Christ are construed as heavenly visions involving no extra-mental component. Sometimes they are described as "objective visions" in order to differentiate them from mere hallucinations, or subjective visions. For in the appearances, Jesus is actually seen in his spiritual resurrection body. Hence, according to this widespread viewpoint, the resurrection appearances of Jesus were bodily but not physical. If, then, one wishes to assert the contrary viewpoint, one is forced, it seems, to employ what at first sight appears to be the rather redundant expression "physical, bodily appearances." Were one to speak merely biblically, it would be enough, as we have seen, to affirm the bodily appearances of Christ, since for the New Testament writers this term would seem to entail materiality and extension, but in light of modern interpretations of Pauline terms, the more cumbrous expression becomes unavoidable to denote unequivocally the corporeal resurrection of Christ. What grounds are there, then, for affirming physical, bodily resurrection appearances of Jesus?

(a) *Paul implies that the appearances were extra-mental events.* Those who adhere to the viewpoint described above usually discern a sharp division between Paul and the evangelists concerning the nature of Christ's resurrection body. Seeking to align themselves with what they perceive to be Paul's position, they reason as follows:

1. Paul's information is at least *prima facie* more reliable than the gospels.
   a. For he stands in closer temporal and personal proximity to the original events.
2. Paul's information, in contrast to the gospels, indicates that Jesus possessed a purely spiritual resurrection body.
   a. First argument:
      i. Paul equated the appearance of Jesus to him with the appearances of Jesus to the disciples.
      ii. The appearance of Jesus to Paul was a nonphysical appearance.
      iii. Therefore, the appearances of Jesus to the disciples were nonphysical appearances.

b. Second argument:
      i. Paul equated Jesus's resurrection body with our future resurrection bodies.
      ii. Our future resurrection bodies will be spiritual bodies.
      iii. Therefore, Jesus's resurrection body was a spiritual body.
   3. Therefore, Jesus possessed a purely spiritual resurrection body.

By now it is clear that such reasoning is unsupported by an exegesis of Paul's teaching. Step 1 represents the usually unspoken presupposition of the argument,[13] a presupposition which in light of the foregoing discussion is moot. Even granting that presupposition, however, we have seen that neither of the two supporting arguments for step 2 can be exegetically sustained.

With regard to the first supporting argument, point (i) seems doubtful indeed. About the only evidence that is adduced in its favor is that Paul adds his name to the list of appearances in I Cor. 15. But does it follow from this that the other appearances were also heavenly visions like that to Paul? This inference seems unwarranted, for (a) Paul is not concerned here with the *how* of the appearances, but with *who* appeared, and (b) in placing himself in the list, he is not trying to put the appearances to the others in a plane with his own, but precisely *vice versa*. As for point (ii), we have seen that while the appearance to Paul was semi-visionary in nature, it cannot be properly conceived of as a simple vision, for the experience involved extra-mental accompaniments, namely, the light and the voice, perceptible to Paul's companions. We have seen that attempts to attribute these phenomena to Luke's hand are unconvincing. That these were traditional is supported by the fact that (a) Luke would have the opposite tendency, to reduce post-ascension experiences of Christ to pure visions, such as Stephen's, and (b) it seems unlikely that he would invent the inconsistencies in the three accounts concerning these phenomena. According to Luke, the appearance to Paul was semi-visionary and unique because it was a post-ascension encounter, and nothing in Paul's letters would seem to indicate that the apostle himself thought otherwise. But if this is the case, then the first argument cannot provide adequate grounds for the conclusion that the appearances of Jesus to the disciples were non-physical appearances.

---

[13] As Trilling explains, "Due to the great age of the Pauline text and its terseness, it is today always accorded greater historical credibility over against the texts of the gospels" (Trilling, *Geschichtlichkeit Jesu*, p. 151).

The second supporting argument also seems to falter exegetically. While point (i) is certainly true, point (ii) contains an inherent ambiguity. For if by "spiritual body," one understands a body which is intangible, unextended, or immaterial, then it seems false to assert that Paul taught that we shall have that kind of resurrection body. We have seen that by σῶμα Paul meant, not the "I" or the self, but the body and that it is this body that will be raised. The transformation to a σῶμα πνευματικόν does not rescue it from materiality, but from mortality. A σῶμα which is unextended and intangible would likely have been a contradiction in terms for the apostle. The resurrection body will be an immortal, powerful, glorious, supernatural body suitable for inhabiting a renewed creation. All commentators agree that Paul did not teach immortality of the soul alone, but this assertion seems intelligible only if he did teach the tangible, physical, bodily resurrection. Accordingly, this argument for the immateriality of the resurrection appearances seems to backfire on its proponent.

The exegetical evidence does not, therefore, seem to support the bifurcation between Paul and the evangelists with regard to the resurrection appearances. More than that, however, there are positive grounds to believe that Paul implies extra-mental appearances of Jesus: (i) Paul and, indeed, the whole New Testament distinguishes between an appearance and a vision of Jesus. We have seen that while visions continued in the church, the resurrection appearances were unrepeatable and confined to a brief initial period. A vision, whether subjective or objective (in the mind of the early church this would have meant a hallucination or a vision caused by God), was wholly in the mind, while a resurrection appearance seemed to involve something's actually happening in the external world. Now if this is the case, then Paul, in listing the resurrection appearances in I Cor. 15, does imply unintentionally something about the nature of these experiences, namely, that they were extra-mental events, not visions. Because Paul's own experience, though semi-visionary in character, nevertheless included extra-mental phenomena, he can add himself to the list in good conscience. More than that, however: since Paul evidently believed in a physical resurrection body, if our exegesis has been correct, then in stating that "he was raised, and he appeared," he probably means appeared physically and bodily, just as he was raised physically and bodily. Paul thus seems to imply, if he does not say, that the appearances were physical, bodily appearances. At the very least, he implies that they were extra-mental events. (ii) A second indication of Paul's belief in this regard may be seen by a consideration of the reverse side of the coin. If originally there had been no physical, bodily appearances, but only visions, then the development of Paul's teaching on the resurrection becomes difficult to explain. He could not have taught that we shall have resurrection bodies patterned after Christ's, for Christ apparently had no resurrection σῶμα. Indeed, as we shall see, it seems doubtful that such visionary experiences would have led Paul to speak of resurrection at all. Mere visions of Jesus after his death, in other words, do not seem to be sufficient to explain the direction and development of Paul's doctrine of the resurrection body—which seems to imply once again that the original appearances were extra-mental phenomena.

Now if Paul implies that the resurrection appearances of Christ were extra-mental events, then in view of his temporal and personal proximity to the people involved, his testimony ought to be regarded as credible. If only by implication, Paul's testimony and teaching alone would incline us to interpret the resurrection appearances as events in the external world.

(b) *The gospels confirm that the appearances were physical and bodily.* Although the physicalism of the gospels is often alleged to be an anti-docetic apologetic, we have seen that the grounds for this assertion seem to be weak and that there are positive considerations mitigating against it. Indeed, Paul's doctrine seems to show early belief in a physical resurrection body of Christ which cannot be written off to an anti-docetic apologetic, since that would have been counter-productive against his Corinthian opponents. We have also seen that the physicalism of the gospel appearance stories cannot be convincingly attributed to the shaping of the traditions by a literary form of Old Testament theophanies. More than that, however, there are positive reasons to affirm the historical credibility of the gospel narratives in this regard: (i) Every resurrection appearance narrated in the gospels is a physical, bodily appearance. The unanimity of the gospels on this score seems very impressive when one remembers that the appearance pericopes were originally more or less separate, independent stories, which the different evangelists collected and arranged. All the separate traditions agree that Jesus appeared physically and bodily alive to the various witnesses. There is no trace of nonphysical visions in the traditions, a remarkable fact if all the appearances were really visionary. It seems incredible to think that a series of heavenly visions could become so thoroughly corrupted or recast as to produce a uniform tradition of physical appearances. The fact that *all* the gospel narratives agree on the physical, bodily nature of the appearances and that no trace of visionary "appearances" is to be found seems to weigh strongly in favor of the gospels' historical credibility in this matter. (ii) The decisive point, however, seems to be that we have already seen that the gospel resurrection narratives in general, and some in particular, are fundamentally historically reliable. The physicalism of the appearance stories is so prominent, though often inadvertent, a feature of these narratives that it could not fall through the net of this general consideration. The implication of this would seem to be that time would have been too short for legends of Jesus's physical appearances to have expunged the historical memory of what had actually happened, that the presence of living eyewitnesses to the appearances would have served as a control against false accounts of the events, and that the authoritative control of the apostles over the appearance traditions would have helped to keep legendary tendencies in check. If the appearances had originally been mere visions, then these factors would probably have prevented their wholesale perversion into the gospel appearance narratives. It seems inexplicable how a sequence of visions could be so thoroughly materialized into the unanimous physicalism of the gospel appearance stories in so short a time, in the very presence of the witnesses to those appearances themselves, and under the eyes of the apostles responsible for preventing such corruption.

Hence, the evidence of the gospels goes to confirm the intimation acquired from Paul. Incredible as it may seem, the evidence for the physical, bodily appearances of Christ after his death is quite strong and cannot, it seems, be plausibly rejected on historical grounds.

Explaining the Historical Fact

In sum, it seems probable that the disciples did, in fact, witness physical, bodily appearances of Jesus alive after his death. How is this remarkable fact to be accounted for?

Subjective Visions

Sometimes the appearances, the occurrence of which cannot plausibly be denied, are regarded as subjective visions.[14] Peter, burdened with guilt for having denied Jesus, found release only in a hallucination of the exalted Lord; he then persuaded the others that Jesus was risen. But such a hypothesis faces what seem to be insuperable difficulties:

1. *The theory cannot make sufficient allowance for points (2), (3), and (4) above.* It cannot explain how subjective visions could, in such temporal and geographical proximity to the events in question, be transformed into the gospel appearance stories; nor why the influence of eyewitnesses to what had really occurred should be nonexistent; nor how such accounts could arise in opposition to the apostolic tradition. The theory cannot account for the massive realism of the gospel accounts, since the first visions were supposedly "spiritual." And it must ignore the evidence for the historicity of particular appearance stories, such as the Lake of Tiberias appearance or the appearance to the Twelve, for these traditions described physical appearances.

2. *The number and various circumstances of the appearances attested to by Paul alone makes the subjective vision hypothesis unlikely.* The appearances in the list are historically credible, but that a series of hallucinations should so multiply itself to different individuals and groups at different times and places seems unlikely. The chain reaction hypothesis fails because neither James nor Paul stood in the chain. There is no basis in the records for postulating a psychological crisis for Paul resulting in hallucination; on the contrary, he hated the Christian heresy. He himself writes confidently that he was blameless under the law (Phil.

---

[14] See, for example, Emmanuel Hisrch, *Jesus Christus der Herr* (Göttingen: Vandenhoeck & Ruprecht, 1926), p. 39; Rudolf Bultmann, *Offenbarung und Heilsgeschehen*, BET 7 (München: Albert Lempp, 1941), pp. 66-68; James McLeman, *Resurrection Then and Now* (London: Hodder & Stoughton, 1965), pp. 170-190; Howard M. Teeple, "The Historical Beginnings of the Resurrection Faith," in *Studies in New Testament and Early Christian Literature*, ed. D. E. Aune (Leiden: E. J. Brill, 1972), pp. 107-120. For a crushing critique of the theory that the subjective visions were products of the Easter faith, see Hans Grass, *Ostergeschehen und Osterberichte*, 4th rev. ed. (Göttingen: Vandenhoeck & Ruprecht, 1963), pp. 233-243. Grass argues convincingly that there are no objective historical factors which would create an Easter faith prior to the resurrection appearances, neither Jesus's predictions, nor reflection on Old Testament texts, nor the personality of Jesus, nor messianic beliefs; nor can subjective facts such as religious enthusiasm or guilt complex account for the appearances. See also J. A. T. Robinson, *The Human Face of God*, (London: SCM Press, 1973), p. 131.

3:6), and there was no reason he should turn to the schismatic Nazarenes to alleviate any inner struggles with the Law which he experienced.

3. *The evidence suggests that the disciples were in no frame of mind to hallucinate.* In no way did they anticipate any revivification of Jesus. Subjective visions require either artificial stimulus through medicines or a psychological state that did not seem to be present in the disciples. As Grass has stressed, the great weakness of the subjective vision theory is that it cannot really take seriously either Jesus's death nor the crisis it caused for the disciples. For the change in the disciples must be explained by the theory on the basis of factors already present in the disciples; but these factors seem to be absent in their case.

4. *The early Christians differentiated between mere visions and resurrection appearances.* Paul and the gospels are one that the appearances involved an additional aspect lacking in a subjective vision and that the appearances were therefore not visions. This seems fatal for the hallucination theory.

5. *Subjective visions would not have led to the doctrine of the resurrection of Jesus.* I shall develop this point in the following chapter. But in passing, it may be noted that because subjective visions are purely projections of the individual's mind, they can contain nothing new. But in the doctrine of Jesus's resurrection, there are two elements that are radically different from the popular Jewish belief of Jesus's day. The disciples would not, therefore, have projected hallucinations of Jesus risen from the grave.

6. Finally, the hypothesis confronts the same problem as the old theft hypothesis for the empty tomb: *it fails to account for the full scope of the evidence.* In order to explain the empty tomb one will have to conjoin another hypothesis with the subjective vision theory. But the simpler explanation is that Jesus rose from the dead; this one hypothesis accounts for all the evidence.

On the basis of these six considerations, then, it seems clear that the evidence for Jesus's resurrection appearances cannot be plausibly explained on the model of hallucinations.

Veridical Visions

A second possible explanation for the resurrection appearances comes from the casebooks of parapsychology: the appearances were veridical visions of the departed Jesus. This theory, which is probably the most provocative and stimulating alternative to the resurrection, is masterfully expounded by Michael Perry.[15] Perry, an archdeacon in the Church of England, avows that it is his intent to render the resurrection more credible; but a discerning reader will perceive that Perry is the heir of H. E. G. Paulus and the natural explanation school of nineteenth century theological rationalism. The real significance to Perry's theory is that it provides a fashionably modern, naturalistic alternative to God's raising Jesus from the dead. After arguing convincingly against the subjective vision theory, Perry maintains that the appearances could have been veridical visions of the dead. A veridical vision is a hallucination generated by an individual's mind when he receives an external extra-sensory stimulus (a telepathic message). Perry relates intriguing accounts of persons who have seen other individuals, who in reality were dead, or dying, miles away. Such appearances are experienced only by loved ones or close friends of the person seen. Unlike subjective visions, no special emotional mood is required to experience a veridical vision. Also unlike subjective visions, they are vivid in detail, and the hallucination may even be seen to move physical objects. Perry's theory is that Jesus died and rose in a "spiritual body," but because the disciples were Jewish and could only conceive of a physical resurrection, Jesus telepathically caused them to project an image of his body so that they could grasp the truth, as a mere apparition would not have convinced them. Thus, belief in a physical resurrection arose.

Ironically, the most unconvincing aspects of Perry's hypothesis are his appeals to supernaturalism. For example, to explain the empty tomb, he has God annihilate the body, a somewhat pointless exercise, since it has no connection with Jesus's new "spiritual body." His notion of Jesus's "spiritual body" seems to be predicated on what we have seen to be a misunderstanding of Paul's σῶμα πνευματικόν. And as A. B. Bruce long ago protested against Keim's "telegram theory" of objective visions,[16] Perry's view makes God and Jesus himself responsible for the disastrous misunderstanding of the physical resurrection on the part of the Christian church. One can only shudder when Perry intones: God deceived the

---

[15] Michael Perry, *The Easter Enigma*, with an Introduction by Austin Farrer (London: Faber & Faber, 1959), pp. 141-195; Robinson has adopted Perry's view (Robinson, *Face*, p. 130; idem, *Can We Trust the New Testament?* [London and Oxford: Mowbrays, 1977], p. 126).

[16] A. B. Bruce, *Apologetics; or, Christianity Defensively Stated*, ITL 3 (Edinburgh: T & T Clark, 1892), pp. 392-393; so also James Orr, *The Resurrection of Jesus* (London: Hodder & Stoughton, 1909), pp. 229-230.

disciples so that from evil, good might come.[17] Hence, as a supernatural explanation, the hypothesis seems singularly unconvincing; the supernatural aspect is an artificial *deus ex machina*. Better is the purely naturalistic explanation that the disciples saw veridical visions of a dead person; extraordinary, but nothing unique or momentous. The disciples, however, interpreted these as a resurrection of Jesus.

But as a purely naturalistic explanation, the hypothesis seems in the end to be untenable:

1. *There is no comparable case to Jesus's resurrection appearances.* As Perry admits, in order to find parallels to the appearance stories one must ransack the literature of parapsychology and build up a composite picture of striking aspects from many different cases. The fact is, no single parapsychological case is fully analogous to a resurrection appearance. Perry asserts that the appearances must have been veridical visions because such visions square with the character and result of the appearances. But this overlooks the fact that real resurrection appearances explain the data even better.

2. *The number of occasions on which Jesus was seen over so lengthy a duration of time is unparalleled in the casebooks.* Usually veridical visions are singular, occurring at a person's death to a loved one far away. But Jesus's appearances were repeated over an extended period of time. Perry is unable to explain the repetition and temporal duration of the appearances.

3. *Veridical visions are non-physical and leave no physical effects.* The resurrection appearances seem to have been unmistakably physical, as we have seen. But a veridical vision only appears to be physical. As a mental projection, it cannot be grasped by the feet or handled or eat food or prepare a meal. Hence, Mt. 28:9-10, in which the women are said to touch Jesus, is the only appearance Perry rejects as unhistorical. But this conclusion seems to be forced by his theory, not historical-critical considerations. It is implausible to think the disciples could have taken a vision for reality when it left no effect on reality. We have seen, in fact, that ancient Judaism distinguished precisely on this basis between an angelic vision and an actual angelic appearance: if the food seen to be eaten by the angel was left undisturbed, then the angel was just a vision; but if the food had been consumed, then the angel had actually appeared. Thus, the disciples could not

---

[17] Perry, *Enigma*, p. 214.

have mistaken a veridical vision for an appearance of Jesus, for the basis for distinguishing between a vision and an appearance was their physical reality. In any case, we have seen the physicalism of the gospels to be well-grounded historically; this would preclude the appearances' being mere veridical visions.

4. *Veridical visions of dead persons only occur to individuals who are unaware of the death of the person in question.* The casebooks show that persons experiencing veridical visions are unaware of the death of the person seen. By contrast, the disciples not only knew that Jesus was dead, but they were shattered by his death. Therefore, naturalistic veridical visions would not seem to have been possible. This consideration seems decisive against paranormal explanations of the appearances.

5. *The hypothesis fails to account for all the evidence.* Multiple hypotheses are necessary to explain the New Testament data: the empty tomb must be explained by some unrelated theory, since one cannot appeal to God's annihilating the body; the appearance to the 500 brethren must be regarded as a subjective vision, according to Perry, because too many people were involved for this to have been a veridical vision; and Paul's hallucination must also be a subjective vision brought on by a guilt complex, in Perry's view (presumably because he lacked intimate contact with Jesus). Thus, multiple hypotheses, against each of which weighty objections may be lodged, are necessary to explain the data which the one overarching hypothesis that Jesus rose from the dead can account for. We can only concur with Grass's conclusion: "...one will have to say that none of the psychological and historical attempts at explanation of the belief in the resurrection on the part of the disciples has up to now led to a convincing result."[18]

---

[18] Grass, *Ostergeschehen*, p. 234.

CHAPTER 11

THE ORIGIN OF THE CHRISTIAN WAY

THE FACT OF BELIEF IN THE RESURRECTION

Whatever they may think of the historical resurrection, even the most sceptical scholars admit that at least the *belief* that Jesus rose from the dead lay at the very heart of the earliest Christian faith. Bultmann acknowledges that historical criticism can establish that the first disciples believed in the resurrection.[1] According to Bornkamm,

> The last datum within history's reach is the Easter faith of the first disciples. The New Testament does not keep back how important the message and experience are which ground it. This faith is not the peculiar experience of a few enthusiasts or a peculiar theological opinion of a few apostles, who in the course of time had the luck to prevail and mark an epoch. No, wherever there were primitive Christian witnesses and fellowships and however much their message and theology varied, they are all one in the belief and confession to the Risen One.[2]

Gerhard Koch concurs, "It is everywhere clear that the event of Easter is the central point of the New Testament message. Resurrection by God and appearing before his disciples constitute the basis of the New Testament proclamation of Christ, without which there would be virtually no witness to Christ."[3] When Paul

---

[1] Rudolf Bultmann, "New Testament and Mythology," in *Kerygma and Myth*, 2 vols., ed. H. W. Bartsch, trans. R. H. Fuller (London: SPCK, 1953), 1:42. Similarly, Marxsen declares, "Historically one can only establish (but that with certainty!) that after Jesus's death people claimed to have had an experience which they characterized as seeing Jesus—and reflection upon this experience led these people to the interpretation: Jesus has been raised" (Willi Marxsen, *Die Auferstehung Jesu als historisches und theologisches Problem*, 2nd ed. [Gütersloh: G. Mohn, 1965], p. 19).

[2] Günther Bornkamm, *Jesus von Nazareth*, 10th rev. ed., UT 19 (Stuttgart: W. Kohlhammer, 1975), p. 159.

[3] Gerhard Koch, *Die Auferstehung Jesu Christi*, BHT (Tübingen: J. C. B. Mohr, 1959), p. 25.

wrote to the Corinthian fellowship, "If Christ has not been raised, then our preaching is in vain and your faith is in vain" (I Cor. 15:14), he spoke not for himself alone. The entire New Testament testifies to the fact that the resurrection of Jesus stood at the center of the church's faith and preaching.

In fact, they pinned nearly everything on it. The resurrection was the *sine qua non* for their belief in Jesus as Messiah and in his death as the basis for forgiveness of sins. It is difficult to exaggerate what a devastating effect the crucifixion must have had on the disciples. They had left everything for him, and now he was dead. They had no conception of a dying, much less a rising, Messiah, for Messiah would reign forever (cf. Jn. 12:34). Without prior belief in the resurrection, belief in Jesus as Messiah would have been impossible in view of his death. But the resurrection turned catastrophe into victory. Because God raised Jesus from the dead, he could be proclaimed as Messiah after all (Acts 2:32, 36). The resurrection was God's decisive vindication of the person of Christ. This is not to say that belief in Jesus's resurrection generated belief in his Messiahship, but merely to point out that it was a necessary condition without which that belief could not have been possible in view of his execution. Similarly for the significance of the cross—it was his resurrection that enabled Jesus's shameful death to be interpreted in salvific terms. An early formula asserted that Jesus "was put to death for our trespasses and raised for our justification" (Rom. 4:25). Without the resurrection, Jesus's death could only have meant humiliation and accursedness, but in view of the resurrection it could be seen to be the event by which forgiveness of sins was obtained. Hence, belief in Jesus's resurrection was an essential condition of salvation; an early confession affirms: "If you confess with your lips that Jesus is Lord and believe in your heart that God raised him from the dead, you will be saved" (Rom. 10:9). Apart from belief in the resurrection, there could be no salvation or forgiveness of sins, for without the resurrection the cross would have no meaning. Hence, Paul could write, "If Christ has not been raised, then your faith is futile and you are still in your sins" (I Cor. 15:17).

It seems clear that without a prior belief in the resurrection of Jesus, the Christian Way could never have come into being. The disciples would no doubt have remained defeated men. Even had they continued to remember Jesus as their beloved teacher, it would have remained impossible in view of his execution for belief in his Messiahship, much less deity, or in his salvific work on the cross to develop so quickly as it did. According to Grass, the life and impact of Jesus was in itself not enough to account for the disciples' faith, since the crucifixion put this into question. If Jesus's death had been the last word, it would have meant the end of any impact created by his person during his life. Perhaps his words would have been remembered, like Socrates's, but they would not have possessed the meaning which the *Urgemeinde* attributed to them.[4] The origin of the Christian Way therefore hinges on the belief of the early disciples that God had raised Jesus from the dead.

EXPLAINING THE BELIEF IN THE RESURRECTION

But the question now becomes: What was the cause of that belief? Though Bultmann protests against any further historical probing behind the faith of the first disciples, yet, as R. H. Fuller points out, even the most sceptical critic must posit some mysterious X to get the movement going.[5] But the question is, what was that X?

If one denies that the historical event of the resurrection was that mysterious X, then one must, it seems, have recourse to antecedent Judaism in order to discover the facts which led to the disciples' belief and proclamation that Jesus was risen from the dead.[6] The Jewish doctrine of resurrection is attested three times in the Old Testament (Ez. 37; Is. 26:19; Dan. 12:2) and flowered during the intertestamental period (II Macc. 7:9-42; 12:43-45; I Enoch 5:7; 22:1-14; 51:1; 61:5;

---

[4] Hans Grass, *Christliche Glaubenslehre*, 2 vols. (Stuttgart: W. Kohlhammer, 1973), 1:99, 105.

[5] Reginald H. Fuller, *The Formation of the Resurrection Narratives* (London: SPCK, 1972), p. 2. Similarly, Pheme Perkins, noting the "anomalous character" of resurrection language in application to a single individual, concludes, "Consequently, even the historian is pressed to ask what sort of events may have led to the use of such language" (Pheme Perkins, *Resurrection: New Testament Witness and Contemporary Reflection* [Garden City, N. Y.: Doubleday & Co., 1984], p. 138).

[6] The only other alternatives would seem to be Greek or Christian influences. But it is now widely recognized that belief in Jesus's resurrection cannot be traced to pagan factors (see Walther Künneth, *The Theology of the Resurrection*, trans. J. W. Leitch [London: SCM, 1965], pp. 50-63), nor can it be ascribed to the influence of the Church since it is itself the cause of the Church's coming into being. On the Jewish doctrine of resurrection, see S. H. Hooke, *The Resurrection of Christ as History and Experience* (London: Darton, Longman, & Todd, 1967). pp. 2-18; Franz Mussner, *Die Auferstehung Jesu*, BH7 (München: Kösel Verlag, 1969), pp. 39-49; Ulrich Wilckens, *Auferstehung*, TT4 (Stuttgart and Berlin: Kreuz Verlag, 1970), pp. 109-144; C. F. Evans, *Resurrection and the New Testament*, SBT 12 (London: SCM Press, 1970, pp. 14-17, 27-40; G. W. E. Nickelsburg, Jr., *Resurrection, Immortality, and Eternal Life in Intertestamental Judaism*, HTS 26 (Cambridge, Mass.: Harvard University Press, 1972); H. C. C. Cavallin, *Life After Death* (Lund: Gleerup, 1974).

90:33; 91:9-10; 100:4-5; Testament of the Twelve Patriarchs [Judah] 25:1, 4; [Zebulun] 10:2; [Benjamin] 10:16-18; II Baruch 30:2-5; 50:1; IV Ezra 7:26-44). It was probably not the result of Iranian influences, but rather the logical outworking of Yahweh's power over death and the future (Ps. 16:10; 49:16; Is. 25:8; 49:16). The deaths of the Jewish martyrs provided a powerful stimulus to the development of this doctrine. During Jesus's day the belief in bodily resurrection had become a widespread hope, being championed by the Pharisees, with whom Jesus sided on this score against the Sadducees (Mt. 22:23-33; cf. Acts 23:8). Thus, the concept of bodily resurrection from the dead was part of Jewish religious mentality.

But the Jewish conception of resurrection differed from the belief in Jesus's resurrection in at least two fundamental respects:

1. *Jewish belief always concerned an eschatological resurrection, not a resurrection within history.* The content of the Jewish conception always concerned a resurrection of the dead after the end of human history. There were, to be sure, instances in the Old Testament of resuscitations of the dead; but these dealt with a return to the earthly life, and those so resuscitated would eventually die again. The resurrection to glory and immortality did not occur until after God had terminated world history. According to Jeremias,

> Ancient Judaism did not know of an anticipated resurrection as an event of history. Nowhere does one find in the literature anything comparable to the resurrection of Jesus. Certainly resurrections of the dead were known, but these always concerned resuscitations, the return to the earthly life. In no place in the late Judaic literature does it concern a resurrection to δόξα as an event of history.[7]

It seems quite probable that the traditional Jewish conception was the prepossession of Jesus's own disciples (Mk. 9:9-13; Jn. 11:24). The notion that a genuine resurrection could occur prior to God's eschatological action would have been foreign to them. Confronted, therefore, with Jesus's crucifixion and death, the disciples would most probably have looked forward to the resurrection at the final day and perhaps carefully honored their Master's tomb as a shrine, where his bones might rest until the resurrection. But it is improbable that they would have conceived the idea that he was already raised.

---

[7] Joachim Jeremias, "Die älteste Schicht der Osterüberlieferungen," in *Resurrexit*, ed. Édouard Dhanis (Rome: Libreria Éditrice Vaticana, 1974), p. 194.

2. *Jewish belief always concerned a general resurrection of the people, not the resurrection of an isolated individual.* Whether it was the righteous, or all of Israel, or all mankind righteous and wicked alike, the resurrection in Jewish thinking always had reference to the general resurrection of the dead. Moreover, the thought was simply unknown that the people's resurrection in some way hinged on Messiah's resurrection. In this respect, the Jewish conception stands opposed to the disciples' belief in Jesus's resurrection, as Wilckens explains:

> For nowhere do the Jewish texts speak of the resurrection of an individual which already occurs before the resurrection of the righteous in the end time and is differentiated and separate from it; nowhere does the participation of the righteous in the salvation at the end time depend on their belonging to the Messiah, who was raised in advance as the 'First of those raised by God'[I Cor. 15:20].[8]

Once again, it seems probable that in light of Jewish religious mentality, the disciples after the death and burial of Jesus could only have waited with eager longing for that day when Jesus and all the righteous of Israel would be raised by God to glory. The disciples' belief in Jesus's resurrection cannot therefore, it seems, be plausibly explained in terms of the beliefs of antecedent Judaism. The mysterious X is still missing. According to Moule, we have here a belief which nothing in terms of previous historical factors can account for.[9] He points out that we have a situation in which (i) a large number of people all shared tenaciously a conviction organically connected with their way of life, (ii) this conviction cannot be derived from the Old Testament or Pharisaism, and (iii) this conviction persisted until they were squeezed out of the synagogue for this belief. The origin of this belief is therefore most plausibly accounted for in terms of Jesus's historical resurrection:

---

[8] Wilckens, *Auferstehung*, p. 131. Wilckens concludes that there was in the Jewish tradition no widespread preparation for the Christian proclamation of the resurrection—only the 'narrow bridge' of the expectation that Elijah would come before the end, be killed, and rise from the dead. Hence, the Christian proclamation cannot be feasibly explained as an extension of Jewish tradition (Ibid., pp. 143-144).

Even Wilckens's suggestion—shared by Berger and Pesch—that there was an expectation of the resurrection of an eschatological prophet is dubious; see the remarks by Stuhlmacher in note 10 of chapter 9. It is most instructive that Pesch, under the weight of the critique received by Berger's work, has now admitted that this position is no longer tenable and has proposed *"ein neuer Versuch"* to explain the origin of the disciples' faith in Jesus's resurrection (Rudolph Pesch, "Zur Entstehung des Glaubens an die Auferstehung Jesu: Ein neuer Versuch," *FZPT* 30 [1983]: 84; for a list of literature criticizing his earlier *Versuch*, see page 53-54). But this new try is even more superficially supported than the old; see my comments below.

[9] C. F. D. Moule and Don Cupitt, "The Resurrection: A Disagreement," *Theol* 75 (1972): 507-519.

> If the coming into existence of the Nazarenes, a phenomenon undeniably attested by the New Testament, rips a great hole in history, a hole the size and shape of the Resurrection, what does the secular historian propose to stop it up with? ...the birth and rapid rise of the Christian Church...*remain an unsolved enigma for any historian who refuses to take seriously the only explanation offered by the Church itself.*[10]

Left to themselves in the aftermath of their Master's crucifixion, the disciples would probably not have conceived the queer notion that he had been raised from the dead. But, it might be argued, perhaps the disciples were led to that conclusion by certain events following Jesus's crucifixion and burial.[11] For example, it has recently been suggested that the disciples experienced visions of the eschatological Son of Man, which they interpreted in terms of the Jewish anticipation of the resurrection of the dead; the story of the empty tomb is a late legend which arose as a consequence of their belief that Jesus had been raised.[12] Now I have

---

[10] C. F. D. Moule, *The Phenomenon of the New Testament*, SBT 2/1 (London: SCM, 1967), pp. 3, 13.

[11] Michael Grant, *Jesus: an Historian's Review of the Gospels* (New York: Charles Scribner's Sons, 1977), p. 176; M. E. Thrall, "Resurrection Traditions and Christian Apologetics," *Thomist* 43 (1979): 197-216. Thrall argues that after the women went to the wrong tomb, the disciples, unconsciously stimulated by belief that the tomb was empty, projected visions of Jesus risen from the dead. Though the disciples were not consciously prepared emotionally to hallucinate, she admits, nevertheless different forces were at work in their unconscious which were much more favorable to the production of visions. Appealing to Jung's theory of archetypal ideas of man's collective unconscious, Thrall suggests the death of Jesus activated the archetypal ideas of death and immortality and caused the resultant images to be projected and externalized as visions. As the source of myth and religion, these archetypes have a numinous quality that would set them apart from typical visions. The disciples' seeing Jesus's death as one archetype could cause its correlate to be projected as a hallucination, leading to belief in Jesus's resurrection. Thrall's theory is, however, so incredible that it nearly takes one's breath away. Fundamentally, it needs to be said that Jung's theory of the collective unconscious and archetypal ideas is the one aspect of his thought which is empirically unverifiable and so has not commended itself to modern psychology. Yet Thrall treats this essentially non-scientific theory as true. Moreover, one must have serious doubts as to whether she is not misusing Jung's theory when she talks vaguely of "activating" the archetypes and "external projection" of archetypes as visions. More specifically, however, her attempt to portray the resurrection appearances as projections of the disciples' unconscious cannot be sustained, since, as we have seen, it was precisely in this sphere that their religio-cultural beliefs which precluded such events were ingrained. It is of no help to appeal to archetypal ideas in a collective unconscious, for, as Thrall admits, Jung did not posit an archetype which distinguished resurrection from immortality in general. But, she insists, the activated archetypal idea of immortality had to attach itself to some conscious idea to become perceptible, and the Jewish belief in resurrection was the ready candidate. Here, I think, we see the decisive failure of Thrall's hypothesis. For, as I explain in the text, the Jewish category of translation would be the most appropriate candidate, not resurrection, since the latter would run contrary to the disciples' Jewish mentality. Hence, such visions, even if they could occur, would not have led to belief in the resurrection of Jesus.

[12] See Pesch, "Neuer Versuch," pp. 87-98; *TRE*, s.v. "Auferstehung II. Auferstehung Jesu Christi II/1. Neues Testament," by Paul Hoffmann, pp. 496-497. I am amazed at how superficially supported Pesch's "new try" is. He presupposes that the appearances were purely visionary experi-

argued that such a scenario contradicts the evidence; but putting that aside, could such experiences have been the cause of the disciples' belief in the resurrection?

In order to answer this question, we need to return to our discussion of hallucinations in the previous chapter. As projections of the mind, hallucinations can contain nothing new, nothing that is not already in the mind. But we have seen that Jesus's resurrection involved at least two aspects not part of the Jewish frame of thought: it was a resurrection within history, and it was the resurrection of an isolated individual. What this seems to imply, therefore, is that even if the disciples, for whatever reason, projected hallucinatory visions of Jesus, they would not have projected him as literally risen from the grave. Rather, given first century Judaism's beliefs concerning immortality, they would have projected visions of him in glory, in Paradise or Abraham's bosom. There the souls of the righteous dead went to await the final resurrection. So if the disciples were to experience visions, they would have projected them on the Jewish model of the after-life.

But in that case, it needs to be seriously questioned whether the disciples would have arrived at the doctrine of Jesus's resurrection.[13] Even given the prior discovery of the empty tomb, they would probably have inferred that Jesus had been translated directly into heaven on the model of Enoch and Elijah (Gen. 5:24; II Kings 2:11-18). The Testament of Job 40 shows that translation was a category applicable to recently deceased persons as well as living. It should be emphasized that for Jewish mentality a translation and a resurrection are entirely diverse. A translation is the direct assumption of an individual into heaven, while a resurrection is the physical and bodily raising up of the dead man in the tomb to eschato-

---

ences perceptible only to the eye of faith and assumes the correctness of his analysis of the empty tomb story as a legendary fusion of three *Gattungen* from the history of religions. He makes no attempt to explain what would have induced such visions. His attempt to show that the appearances were visions of the Son of Man is astounding: *e.g.*, Paul's vision was revelatory and the tradition of the Son of Man in apocalyptic is revelatory, so Paul probably saw Jesus as the Son of Man (a clear *non sequitur!*); the *Gospel of the Hebrews* states that Jesus appeared to James as the Son of Man; the use of "Lord" in the appearances to Mary and the Emmaus disciples refers to the Son of Man; the Transfiguration is the most impressive proof that the disciples saw visions of the Son of Man. Despite Pesch, I can find *no* evidence whatsoever that the appearances were Son of Man visions like that in Dan. 7.

[13] As Brown insists, the contention that the Jewish mind had to express Jesus's victory over death by resurrection language is simply inaccurate, for we know of several other models current in Judaism which might have been employed. On the contrary, since there was no expectation of an isolated resurrection within history, the choice of the category of resurrection must be explained (Raymond E. Brown, *The Virginal Conception and Bodily Resurrection of Jesus* [London: Geoffrey Chapman, 1973], p. 76).

logical life. Therefore, even if the disciples did see hallucinatory visions of Jesus in glory after finding his tomb empty, it seems unlikely that they would have concluded that he had been raised from the dead, a notion that ran contrary to Jewish concepts of the resurrection; rather they would most likely have concluded that God had translated him into heaven, whence he appeared to them, and that therefore his tomb was empty. This objection presses particularly hard against those who want to construe the appearances as visions of the apocalyptic Son of Man.[14] As Dunn explains,

> Quite apart from such other matters as the empty tomb, the degree of independence of several at least of the appearance experiences (Peter, James and Paul), and the divine significance so quickly attributed by monotheistic Jews to one of their fellows,[146] it remains an indisputable fact that the earliest believers (including the initial doubters), no less than Paul, were absolutely convinced that they had seen Jesus risen from the dead. And yet why should they assume that what they saw was *Jesus*?—why not an angel? And why did they conclude that it was Jesus *risen from the dead*?—why not simply a vision of the dead man?—why not visions 'fleshed out' with the apparatus of apocalyptic expectation, coming on clouds of glory and the like...? Why draw the astonishing conclusion that the *eschatological* resurrection had already taken place in the case of a single individual quite separate from and prior to the general resurrection?[147] There must have been something very compelling about the appearances for such an extravagant, not to say ridiculous and outrageous conclusion to be drawn.
>
> [146] C. F. D. Moule, *The Phenomenon of the New Testament*, SCM Press 1967, especially ch. 2.
> [147] Note the lack of satisfactory parallels in the history of religions which would explain the rise of Easter faith....[15]

It is intriguing to observe that some scholars, perhaps feeling the weight of these considerations, have actually taken to arguing that in fact a death-exaltation model was primitive and that the death-resurrection model was subsequently deduced or developed therefrom. The empty tomb story is interpreted as an *En-*

---

[14] Pesch tries neatly to avoid this problem by claiming that Jesus did prophesy his resurrection and that the disciples took these visions to be the fulfillment of his prediction. Hence, the origin of their belief in his resurrection. But the difficulty with this move is that the acceptance of Jesus's predictions as authentic is wholly arbitrary and hence rejected even by those who agree with the remainder of Pesch's hypothesis (Werner Georg Kümmel, "Das Urchristentum," *TRu* 50 [1985]: 156). For if one takes the resurrection predictions to be an authentic part of the historical Jesus, what reason remains for rejection other equally attested aspects of the gospel tradition, *e.g.*, the gospel appearance stories or the empty tomb?
[15] James W. D. G. Dunn, *Jesus and the Spirit* (London: SCM, 1975), p. 132. What Dunn does not see is that these considerations press with equal force against not only subjective visions, but also so-called objective visions, for the latter would only have led the disciples to infer that Jesus had been translated into glory, in accordance with Jewish models. Only real, bodily appearances could have led the disciples to proclaim, contrary to Jewish modes of thinking, the resurrection of Jesus from the dead.

trückungsgeschichte (translation story) and the appearances are understood as visions of Christ in heavenly glory, exalted to eternal life in the *Entzogenheit bei Gott* (removed-ness with God).[16] But this hypothesis of last resort simply cannot be sustained. Had what amounts to a death-translation scheme been primitive, then the development of the disciples' belief in and proclamation of Jesus's resurrection becomes unintelligible. Besides that, there seems to be no evidence that a death-exaltation model which did not include the literal resurrection was primitive—on the contrary, as O'Collins explains:

> Was the more inclusive concept (exaltation) the primary one from which the claim about Christ's resurrection evolved? The New Testament fails to support an affirmative answer.... The resurrection claim was not derived from the less specific assertion that God had exalted Jesus in his death....we fail to find that death-exaltation texts occur early in the New Testament, while the pattern of death-resurrection (or death-resurrection-exaltation) surfaces only later. In fact, if a pattern does exist, it is rather the opposite. The theme of 'exaltation' emerges as a comment on and subsequent interpretation of the resurrection. The death-resurrection model...appears in such earlier works as 1 Corinthians and Romans, and that in passages where Paul draws on traditional creedal formulations. The earliest examples of the death-exaltation pattern come in Mark and in what is probably one of Paul's last letters, Philippians (when in 2:8ff. he quotes a hymn to Christ).[17]

The fact that the disciples proclaimed, not the translation of Jesus, in accord with a common Jewish category perfectly suited to explain their experience, but—contrary to fundamental Jewish modes of thought—the resurrection of Jesus, strongly suggests that the origin of the disciples' belief in Jesus's resurrection cannot be accounted for as their inference from an experience of visions of Christ. It therefore seems unavailing to try to rescue the vision hypothesis by positing a primitive death-exaltation model to account for the disciples' interpretation of their visionary experiences of Jesus. Had the disciples projected visions of Jesus, these would have been in accord with typical Jewish thought forms and would probably not have led to the inference of his resurrection, but rather of his translation. The fact that the disciples proclaimed, not the translation of Jesus, in accord

---

[16] See the original piece by E. Bickermann, "Das leere Grab," *ZNW* 23 (1924): 281-292, which is being cited anew in recent discussion; see also Lloyd Geering, *Resurrection: A Symbol of Hope* (London: Hodder & Stoughton, 1971), pp. 146-148; and, more recently, *TRE*, s.v. "Auferstehung," p. 499; Karl Martin Fischer, *Das Ostergeschehen*, 2nd ed. (Göttingen: Vandenhoeck & Ruprecht, 1980), pp. 80, 97-105; Pesch, "Neuer Versuch," pp. 88-89.

[17] Gerald O'Collins, *The Easter Jesus*, 2nd ed. (London: Darton, Longman & Todd, 1980), pp. 50-51. Even the hymn cannot be regarded as more primitive than I Cor. 15:3-5 and may even reflect Gnostic influence. Cf. the late texts adduced by Fischer to support the primitiveness of the translation model: Hebrews, John's Christology, and a very dubious reference to Lk. 23:39-43.

with a common Jewish category perfectly suited to explain their experience, but—contrary to fundamental Jewish modes of thought—the resurrection of Jesus, strongly suggests that the origin of the disciples' belief in Jesus's resurrection cannot be accounted for as their inference from an experience of visions of Christ.

Thus, according to the strictest use of the dissimilarity criterion, we ought to conclude to the basis in historical fact for the origin of the disciples' belief in the resurrection of Jesus, for it cannot be adequately explained from the side of Judaism nor from the side of the church, since it is itself the foundation of the church. The origin of the belief in Jesus's resurrection and, hence, of the Christian Way itself cannot therefore, it seems, be plausibly accounted for apart from the historical fact of the bodily resurrection and appearances of Jesus.

Conclusion

The most reasonable historical explanation for the facts of the empty tomb, the resurrection appearances, and the origin of the Christian Way would therefore seem to be that Jesus rose from the dead. Now it has become part of conventional theological wisdom that such is a conclusion that must not be drawn. But why not? If it is the case that the evidence can only be plausibly explained by the historical fact of the resurrection of Jesus, why are we debarred from that conclusion?

Certain theologians have objected to such an inference on the grounds that though the resurrection occurred in space and time and left a historical margin accessible to research, the resurrection itself is not verifiable because the historian cannot consider causes outside history.[18] The objection, however, seems to confuse the *event* of the resurrection with the *cause* of the resurrection. The event of the resurrection occurs within human history, but the cause of the resurrection is outside human history. Thus, even given the historiographical presuppositions of such theologians, the resurrection (= Jesus's rising transformed from the dead) would seem to be susceptible to historical proof. The hypothesis of the resurrec-

---

[18] Berthold Klappert, "Einleitung," in *Diskussion um Kreuz und Auferstehung*, ed. idem (Wuppertal: Aussaat Verlag, 1971), pp. 18, 50-51; Wolfgang Trilling, *Fragen zur Geschichtlichkeit Jesu* (Düsseldorf: Patmos Verlag, 1966), pp. 141-142; Künneth, *Theology*, p. 31; Makota Yamauchi, "The Easter Texts of the New Testament: Their Tradition, Redaction, and Theology" (Ph.D. Thesis, University of Edinburgh, 1972), pp. 23-30; Herbert Burhenn, "Pannenberg's Argument for the Historicity of the Resurrection," *JAAR* 40 (1972): 375-376.

tion is both verifiable and falsifiable: verifiable through proving the historicity of the empty tomb, the appearances, and the origin of the Christian Way; falsifiable by either disproving the above or providing naturalistic explanations of them. In fact, I should go so far as to say that there is not a single event in the resurrection narratives that is not *in principle* historically verifiable or falsifiable.

The real problem comes when we inquire concerning the *cause* of the resurrection. According to above methodology, the historian *qua* historian could conclude that the best explanation of the facts is that "Jesus rose from the dead;" but he could not conclude, "God raised Jesus from the dead." But what I wish to suggest for the reader's consideration is that the historian "in his off-hours," to paraphrase Bertrand Russell, that is, the historian as a human being, may indeed rightly infer from the evidence that God has acted here in history. The situation is somewhat analogous to the scientist and *creatio ex nihilo*. The astrophysicist pushes back to an event for which there are no empirical antecedents, the beginning of the universe; similarly the historian discovers an event for which there is no historically antecedent cause, the resurrection of Jesus. *Qua* scientist or historian, he may halt his inquiry, lacking data; but I submit that as human beings searching for meaning and significance for man and the universe, we must go farther. This is especially so for the resurrection, given the context in which it occurred: the life, teachings, and claims of Jesus and the effect on those who followed him.[19] They saw in it the key to human life and salvation (Rom. 10:9). We should be foolish to ignore their claims.

But furthermore, the methodological principle that prohibits any historian from adducing a supernatural cause for an event in history seems to be either arbitrary

---

[19] As Grass explains, Jesus cannot be regarded as a mere prophet or rabbi:
"He proclaimed and acted as one who had authority [*Vollmacht*], an authority which surpasses or even annuls the very statements of the Old Testament law with his 'But I say to you,' an authority which takes the part of sinner and outcast because that is God's way, an authority which links the dawn of the Kingdom of God with his person and calls men to his imitation. Those who followed him saw him as Messiah and commissioned by God and believed the word: 'Whoever confesses me before men, him will I also confess before my Father in heaven' (Mt. 10:32)" (Grass, *Glaubenslehre*, 1:91).
In the context of these claims, Jesus's resurrection takes on a religious significance of great importance, for as Pannenberg explains, "The resurrection can only be understood as the divine vindication of the man whom the Jews had rejected as a blasphemer" (Wolfhart Pannenberg, "Jesu Geschichte und unsere Geschichte," in *Glaube und Wirklichkeit* [München: Chr. Kaiser, 1975], pp. 93-94; cf. idem, *Jesus: God and Man*, trans. L. L. Wilckens and D. A. Priebe [London: SCM, 1968], p. 67).

or based on bad science or philosophy.[20] For as long as the existence of God is even possible, an event's being caused by God cannot be ruled out. To be sure, the historian ought first, as a methodological principle, to seek natural causes; but when no natural cause can be found that plausibly accounts for the data and a supernatural hypothesis presents itself as part of the historical context in which the event occurred, then the rational alternative would seem to be to choose the supernatural explanation. Naturalism has had nearly 2,000 years to explain the resurrection of Jesus and has failed to do so. The rational man can hardly now be blamed if he infers that at the tomb of Jesus on that early Easter morning a divine miracle has occurred.

---

[20] See my discussion of the problem of miracles in the companion volume to this study, viz., William Lane Craig, *The Historical Argument for the Resurrection of Jesus during the Deist Controversy*, Texts and Studies in Religion 23 (Toronto: Edwin Mellen Press, 1985), pp.477-518.

APPENDIX A

FROM EASTER TO VALENTINUS AND THE APOSTLES' CREED ONCE MORE: A CRITICAL EXAMINATION OF JAMES ROBINSON'S PROPOSED RESURRECTION APPEARANCE TRAJECTORIES[1]

INTRODUCTION

Several years ago in his SBL Presidential Address, James Robinson sought to delineate three related sets of parallel trajectories stretching from a common origin in primitive Christianity to their termini in second-century Gnosticism and in credally orthodox Christianity, both of these later viewpoints being divergent (mis)interpretations of the beliefs and experiences of the earliest Christians.[2] Trajectory 1 represents the development beginning with the traditions concerning the first disciples' experiences of Jesus' post-resurrection appearances and ending with, on the one hand, the orthodox interpretation of these as physical, corporeal manifestations of the resurrected Christ, and, on the other hand, the Gnostic interpretation of these as visions of disembodied radiance. Trajectory 2 charts the emergence of the orthodox doctrine of the final resurrection of believers in each individual's fleshly body, on the one hand, and of the Gnostic doctrine of spiritual and mystical resurrection attained already in baptism, on the other, from the original apocalyptic expectation of a resurrection of believers at the end of time in a luminous, heavenly body comparable to Christ's. Finally, Trajectory 3 concerns

---

[1] This paper originally appeared in the *Journal for the Study of the New Testament* 52 (1993): 19-39.
[2] J. M. Robinson, "Jesus from Easter to Valentinus (or to the Apostles' Creed)," *JBL* 101 (1982): 5-37.

the evolution of the sayings attributed to Jesus to, on the one hand, the orthodox incarnation of Jesus' sayings within the pre-Easter biography of Jesus in the canonical Gospels and, on the other hand, the mystification of Jesus' sayings by means of hermeneutically loaded dialogues of the risen Christ with his Gnostic disciples. Robinson emphasizes that neither the orthodox nor the Gnostic position represents the original Christian position, though both are consistent and serious efforts to interpret it.[3] Although both positions should be heeded as worthy segments of the heritage of transmission and interpretation of Christian beliefs, nevertheless, neither can be literally espoused by serious critical thinkers of today.[4]

The existence of Trajectory 1 is logically foundational for Robinson's construction of the other two, and so in this paper I wish to focus our critical attention on his case for the existence of this first trajectory. According to Robinson, the primitive resurrection appearances were visualizations of the resurrected Christ as a luminous, heavenly body. But due to their aversion to bodily existence, Gnostics disembodied Christ's appearances so as to retain the original luminous visualization while abandoning any corporeality associated with that radiance. In reaction, the emerging orthodoxy emphasized the corporeality of the resurrection appearances by construing them in terms of the resurrection of the flesh, so that in the canonical Gospels Christ's appearances are not only corporeal, but material as well.

Robinson's proposed reconstruction is probably quite appealing to many, since he is claiming, in effect, that the received view in German theology of the resurrection body and appearances of Christ was, in fact, the view of the primitive church itself, and it is rather reassuring to believe that one is holding steadfastly to the faith of the *Urgemeinde* in the face of extremist corruptions thereof. But does a dispassionate weighing of the evidence really support Robinson's proposal? In order to answer that question, let us turn to an examination of his arguments.

EXAMINATION OF ROBINSON'S PROPOSED TRAJECTORIES

In support of his claim that the primitive traditions of Jesus' post-resurrection appearances related luminous, bodily visualizations which were subsequently construed in opposite directions by orthodoxy and Gnosticism, Robinson adduces

---
[3] Ibid., p. 37.
[4] Ibid.

four lines of evidence: (1) the only two NT eyewitnesses of a resurrection appearance both authenticate visualizations of luminous appearances; (2) vestiges of luminous appearances remain in the non-luminous resurrection appearance stories and in the misplaced appearance stories; (3) the only two eyewitnesses of a resurrection appearance both identify the resurrected Christ with the Spirit; and (4) the outcome of these trajectories may be seen in second-century Gnosticism.

In support of (1), Robinson appeals to the experiences of (a) the apostle Paul and (b) John of Patmos. (a) On the basis of Paul's reference to Christ's "glorious body" in Phil. 3:21 (cf. I Cor. 15:43), Robinson concludes, "Thus, it is clear that Paul visualized the resurrected Christ as a heavenly body, luminous."[5] The Acts accounts of Paul's Damascus Road encounter (Acts 9:1-19; 22:4-16; 26:9-18) seem to reflect accurately Paul's own visualization of his experience. (b) In Rev. 1:13-16 we have another resurrection appearance narrated, although it is usually overlooked because it lies outside the Gospels. Like Paul, John of Patmos experienced an "uninhibited luminous visualization of the resurrection".[6] Since these are the only two resurrection appearances recorded by eyewitnesses and both were of the luminous kind, we may conclude "that the original visualizations of resurrection appearances had been luminous, the experiencing of a blinding light, a heavenly body such as Luke reports Stephen saw (Acts 7:55-56)".[7]

In support of (2), Robinson sees vestiges of the original luminous, non-human visualizations in the following: (a) the angelic attendants at the empty tomb of Jesus are described as clothed in "white" (Mk. 16:5), in "dazzling apparel" (Lk. 24:4), having an appearance "like lightning and...raiment white as snow" (Mt. 28:2-3). Says Robinson, "In the canonical Gospels this luminous apparition of the attendant is all that is left of the luminous visualization of the resurrected Christ..."[8] (b) In "quite docetic style" Jesus passes through locked doors (Jn. 20:19, 26; cf. Lk. 24:36) and disappears abruptly (Lk. 24:31, 51; Acts 1:9). (c) The non-recognition motif of some resurrection appearance stories (Jn. 20:14-15; 21:4; Lk. 24:16, 31) may derive ultimately from the luminous visualization, as is evident from Paul's question, "Who are you, Lord?" in his Damascus Road ex-

---

[5] Ibid., p. 7.
[6] Ibid., p. 10.
[7] Ibid.
[8] Ibid., p. 14.

perience (Acts 9:5; 22:8; 26:15). It is understandable that one would not recognize a blinding light, but the lack of recognition and then sudden recognition of Jesus is no longer intelligible in the canonical Gospels' all-too-human visualizations. Thus, this motif may be a vestige from the more primitive luminous, non-human visualizations. (d) Christ's resurrection appearance to Peter seems to be described in II Pet. 1:16-17 using the motif of luminosity. Although these verses probably refer to Jesus' transfiguration, the Markan account of that event (Mk. 9:2-8) is probably a misplaced resurrection narrative. "Mark has 'historicized' what was originally the resurrection appearance to Peter, tying it down to an unambiguous bodiliness by putting it well before the crucifixion, in spite of its luminousness..."[9] Robinson conjectures that the reason Mark narrates no resurrection appearances is "perhaps because those available were so luminous as to seem disembodied".[10]

In support of (3) Robinson argues that in the two instances where the NT contains an eyewitness report of a resurrection appearance, the identification of that appearance as the Spirit seems near at hand. (a) Paul calls the resurrection body "spiritual" (I Cor. 15:44), identifies the last Adam as "a life-giving Spirit" (I Cor. 15:45) and calls Christ "the Spirit" (II Cor. 3:17-18). (b) John of Patmos describes his experience as "in the Spirit" (Rev. 1:10) and, although the revelation is from the resurrected Christ, John repeatedly exhorts his readers to hear "what the Spirit says to the churches" (Rev. 2:7, 11, 17, 29; 3:6, 13, 22). In fact, says Robinson, it is precisely "this identification of the luminously resurrected Christ as the Spirit" that Luke rejects when he denies that what the disciples saw was a ghost.[11]

Finally, in support of (4), Robinson cites a number of second-century Gnostic texts which, he claims, show that the resurrection appearances were being construed as visions of disembodied radiance. It was in reaction to this tendency that the non-luminous resurrection appearance stories in Matthew, Luke and John were composed. Thus, just as the trajectory from Easter to Valentinus involved increasing spiritualization, so the trajectory from Easter to the Apostles' Creed involved increasing materialization.

---

[9] Ibid., p. 9.
[10] Ibid., p. 10.
[11] Ibid., p. 13.

Examination of Argument (1)

Robinson's first argument, that the only two NT witnesses of a resurrection appearance both authenticate visualizations of luminous appearances, implicitly presupposes that we do not have the voice of an eyewitness behind the resurrection appearance stories in the Gospel of John. But whatever his identity, the person known in Johannine circles as the Beloved Disciple is explicitly stated to be an eyewitness whose testimony stands behind the events narrated in the Gospel (Jn. 21:24). Although in the past some scholars have regarded the Beloved Disciple as a pure symbol lacking any historical referent, the leading contemporary commentators, such as Brown and Schnackenburg, agree that the Beloved Disciple was a historical person whose testimony, as an eyewitness to some of the events recorded in the latter part of the Gospel of John, including the resurrection appearances, stands authoritatively behind them.[12] And, of course, the appearances related in that Gospel are physical and bodily.

Moreover, Robinson's point seems to serve a purpose more polemical than historical, since it ignores altogether the genuinely relevant question of whether the appearance traditions embodied in the Gospels are historically credible in favor of the less relevant question of whether the accounts are first-hand, eyewitness reports. It would be far too facile to dismiss as unhistorical the narratives of, for example, the post-resurrection appearance to the Twelve simply because they were not written by an eyewitness. Hence, even if Robinson's first point were correct, it is far from clear how much force it really has.

But is it in fact correct? Consider first (a) Paul's testimony concerning his Damascus Road experience. Because Paul elsewhere characterizes Christ's resurrection body as "glorious", are we justified in inferring that it is luminous? In I Cor. 15:40-41 Paul uses "glory" as a synonym for luminosity, for the differing glory of the sun, moon and stars is their varying brightness. Significantly, the difference between the glory of terrestrial versus celestial bodies is used as an analogy between the present body and the resurrection body. But did Paul think that

---

[12] Raymond E. Brown, *The Gospel according to John*, AB, 29A (Garden City, N. Y.: Doubleday, 1970), pp. 1119-1120; idem, *The Community of the Beloved Disciple* (New York: Paulist Press, 1979), pp. 22-23; R. Schnackenburg, *Das Johannesevangelium*, 3 vols., HTKNT, 4 (Freiburg: Herder, 1976), III, pp. 368, 452-456; so also B. Lindars (ed.), *The Gospel of John*, NCB (London: Oliphants, 1972), p. 602.

whereas our earthly body is dull, our resurrection body will be literally luminous? Is that the difference he means to express between them in saying that the resurrection body is glorious? There are reasons to doubt it, for in contrasting the earthly body with the resurrection body, the antithesis he draws in I Cor. 15:43 is not between their relative luminescence, but between their relative *honor*. The present body is dishonorable, no doubt due to sin and its consequences (*e.g.*, mortality), whereas the resurrection body is glorious (cf. the contrast between the lowly state of the earthly body and the exalted state of Christ's resurrection body in Phil. 3:21). This suggests that the glory of the resurrection body has to do with majesty, exaltation, honor and so forth, rather than its becoming luminous.[13] Indeed, if it were not for the Acts narrative of Paul's experience on the Damascus Road, it seems extremely doubtful that anyone could have taken Paul's "glorious" to mean that the resurrection body would be shining. Paul himself gives no indication of the nature of Christ's appearance to him.[14] From all we know from his hand, the appearance to Paul could have been as physical as the resurrection appearances in the Gospels.[15] In fact, it has even been argued that Luke has dematerialized the appearance to Paul because it was in Luke's scheme a post-ascension encounter and so could not involve Christ's material presence, since Christ had ascended![16] Be that as it may, I think it is evident that Paul does not provide eyewitness testimony to a luminous resurrection appearance of Christ.

---

[13] See the study by J. Coppens, "La glorification céleste du Christ dans la théologie néotestamentaire et l'attente de Jésus," in E. Dhanis (ed.), *Resurrexit* (Rome: Libreria Editrice Vaticana, 1974), pp. 37-40.

[14] Sometimes appeal is made to II Cor. 4:6, which is thought to refer to the blinding light on the Damascus Road. But in fact the verse does not seem to be connected to Paul's conversion experience: the light is the light of the gospel (4:4) and is compared to God's act of creation (cf. Gen. 1:3). There appears to be no reason to think that it refers to the Damascus Road experience.

[15] All Paul tells us is that Jesus appeared (ὤφθη) to him (I Cor. 15:8), that he saw (ἑώρακα) Jesus (I Cor. 9:1), and that God revealed (ἀποκαλύψαι) his Son to him (Gal. 1:16). Dunn argues that Paul's use of ἐν ἐμοί in Gal. 1:16 instead of the simple dative shows that he is describing "a personal subjective experience" (J. D. G. Dunn, *Jesus and the Spirit* [London: SCM Press, 1975], pp. 105-106), but Dunn concedes that it is his *conversion* that Paul describes as a subjective experience; Paul "is not talking about the visionary side of his conversion experience as such". Hoffmann agrees that ἐν ἐμοί says nothing about the nature of Paul's experience, but he appeals to ἀποκαλύψαι as evidence of the appearance's being visionary and eschatological (P. Hoffmann, "Auferstehung II. Auferstehung Jesu Christi II/1. Neues Testament," *TRE* [1979]: 492-497). But apart from other difficulties, Hoffmann's argument rests on the unproven presupposition that in the mind of the biblical writers one cannot have an apocalyptic-eschatological experience of a physically real entity.

[16] See P. Borgen, "From Paul to Luke," *CBQ* 31 (1969): 180; cf. C. F. Evans, *Resurrection and the New Testament*, SBT, 12 (London: SCM Press, 1970), pp. 55-56; X. Léon-Dufour,

Still, most critics are prepared to accept the general historicity of the Acts account, and Robinson might appeal to that as grounds for regarding the original resurrection appearances as visualizations of a luminous body. But now a number of difficulties arise.

1. If one is willing to accept the substantial historicity of Luke-Acts with regard to the appearance to Paul, then one must re-open the question of the historical credibility of Luke-Acts with respect to the appearances to the disciples. Why are we willing to accept the one but not the other, apart from an aversion to the physical realism of the Gospel appearances?[17]

2. On what grounds do we assume that Paul's Damascus Road experience involved the visualization of a bodily shape? As the narrative presents it the experience was of a non-corporeal radiance and auditory phenomena, which were also, with some inconsistency, experienced by Paul's traveling companions. In other words, the narrative presents *prima facie* precisely the sort of unembodied luminous experience which Robinson wishes to locate on the Gnostic trajectory. Paul's experience thus provides no clear basis for the claim that visualizations of a luminous bodily form were primitive.

3. On what basis are we to assume that Paul's experience on the Damascus Road was normative for the experiences of the disciples, so that its form can be imposed on them and used as a yardstick for assessing historicity? It is sometimes said that in placing himself in the list of witnesses to the resurrection appearances in I Cor. 15:3-8, Paul implies that all of these experiences were of the same sort. But surely Paul's concern here is with *who* appeared, not with *how* he appeared; moreover, in placing himself in the list, Paul is not trying to put the others' experiences on a plane with his own, but, if anything, is rather trying to level up his own experience to the objectivity and reality of the others'.[18] Luke

---

"L'apparition du Ressucité à Paul," in Dhanis (ed.), *Resurrexit*, p. 294; C. W. Hedrick, "Paul's Conversion/Call: A Comparative Analysis of the Three Reports in Acts," *JBL* 100 (1981): 430-431.

[17] See the remarks of J. E. Alsup, *The Post-Resurrection Appearance Stories of the Gospel-Tradition* (Stuttgart: Calwer Verlag, 1975), pp. 32, 34, 54.

[18] For good statements of this point, see B. F. Westcott, *The Gospel of the Resurrection* (London: Macmillan, 1906), pp. 93-94; J. Orr, *The Resurrection of Jesus* (London: Hodder & Stoughton, 1909), p. 39; P. Gardner-Smith, *The Narratives of the Resurrection* (London: Methuen, 1926), pp. 21-22; J. A. T. Robinson, "Resurrection in the New Testament," *IDB*. Dunn even hypothesizes that Paul's placing himself in the list could be a case of special pleading—interpreting a less distinctive religious experience as a resurrection appearance in order to boost his claim to apos-

presents Paul's experience as *sui generis*, and, far from contradicting this, Paul also seemed aware of its unusualness (I Cor. 15:8) and was anxious to class himself with the apostles as a recipient of an authentic resurrection appearance. If we are to use Paul's experience as a criterion for the historicity of other appearance narratives, then Robinson owes us substantial reasons for such a methodology.

4. Robinson's argument seems to rest upon a fundamental presupposition that luminosity and physicality are mutually exclusive categories, such that if the visualized bodily shape were luminous, it could not also be material and tangible. Without such an assumption I cannot see that the demonstration that the original visualizations of Jesus were characterized by luminosity does anything logically to prove that they did not also involve the perception of a physical object. Unfortunately, Robinson's presupposition is obviously false. Paul himself, as we have seen, referred to the brightness of the sun, moon, and stars, which he no doubt took to be physical objects; even more relevantly, he mentions the brightness of Moses' face as it shone with splendor (II Cor. 3:7, 12). The decisive counter-example to Robinson's principle is his own example of the transfiguration, in which Jesus' face and garments shone, but for all that did not become immaterial or intangible. Robinson simply assumes that the luminosity of some appearing entity is evidence of that entity's non-physicality. Indeed, that conclusion seems to be implicit in Robinson's use of the very term "visualization", which he never defines, but which seems to carry with it connotations of subjectivity and non-physicality. After all, one would hardly speak of the disciples' "visualizing" the pre-Easter Jesus; why, then, apply this term to the post-resurrection appearances, unless one is already assuming their purely intra-mental reality? The vocabulary associated with the resurrection appearances in the NT is fully consistent with their physicality and objectivity.[19] Hence, the demonstration that the original resurrection appearances involved luminosity does nothing to demonstrate that the physicality of those appearances is a later corruption on the trajectory from Easter to the Apostles' Creed. It seems to me, then, that on the basis of Paul's experience, we are not entitled to conclude either that the original resurrection appear-

---

tolic authority (Dunn, *Jesus and the Spirit*, p. 99)! Dunn rejects the hypothesis in the end because the pillar apostles accepted Paul's claim without serious dispute (*Jesus and the Spirit*, p. 108).

[19] See H. Grass, *Ostergeschehen und Osterberichte*, 4th ed (Göttingen: Vandenhoeck & Ruprecht, 1970), pp. 186-189.

ances were characterized by luminosity or that, even if they were, they were therefore non-physical in character.

What, then, can we conclude about John of Patmos's experience of the exalted Christ? It is rather surprising that Robinson should categorize this as a resurrection appearance. The reason it is "overlooked" by all students of the resurrection is not because it occurs outside the Gospels, but because it is quite clearly a vision rather than a resurrection appearance.[20] Although the resurrection appearances took place within a community that enjoyed visions, revelations and ecstatic experiences (I Cor. 12-13; II Cor. 12:1-5; Gal. 2:1; Acts 16:9), that community nevertheless drew a distinction between visions of Christ and the resurrection appearances of Christ: the appearances were restricted to a small circle designated as witnesses, and even to them Jesus did not continually reappear but appeared only at the beginning of their new life. Thus, for example, although Paul considers Christ's appearance to him to have been "last of all" (I Cor. 15:8), nevertheless, he continued to experience "visions and revelations of the Lord" (II Cor. 12:1; cf. Acts 22:17). Similarly, the revelation of Christ to John on Patmos is clearly a vision of the exalted Christ, replete with allegorical imagery, not a resurrection appearance of Christ. In the same way, the visions of Christ seen by Stephen, Ananias, and Paul (Acts 7:55-56; 9:10; 22:17) are not regarded by Luke as resurrection appearances of Christ, but as veridical, divinely induced visions of Christ. Thus, Robinson's appeal to John's experience as an eyewitness account of a resurrection appearance is spurious.

Nor is this all, however; for the question at once arises as to what distinguishing feature served to mark off an experience as a resurrection appearance of Jesus rather than as a merely veridical vision of Jesus? So far as I can tell, the answer of the NT to that question is that only an appearance involved extra-mental realities, whereas a vision, even if veridical, was purely intra-mental.[21] But if that is the case, then Robinson's construction collapses, since the hypothesized trajectories did not then grow out of visualizations of Christ lacking any extra-mental referent, experiences which would have been indistinguishable from simple visions.

---

[20] On the difference between a resurrection appearance and a vision see the discussion by Grass, *Ostergeschehen*, pp. 189-207. It should be noted that this distinction is conceptual in nature, not primarily linguistic.
[21] See the discussion in note 29, chapter 2.

It is therefore incumbent upon Robinson, at the expense of his construction, to provide us with a more plausible explanation of the basis upon which the early church distinguished between resurrection appearances and visions of Christ.

I thus find Robinson's first argument based on the testimony of Paul and John rather unconvincing. We have not seen any compelling reasons to think that the original resurrection appearances were uniformly characterized by luminosity or that if they were, this fact implies non-physicality. On the contrary, the distinction drawn by the NT church between a resurrection appearance and a veridical vision suggests that the appearances were conceived to be physical events in the external world.

EXAMINATION OF ARGUMENT (2)

Let us then turn to point (2) concerning the vestiges of luminosity in the canonical Gospel appearance stories. With the collapse of point (1), Robinson faces here a very difficult methodological problem: how does one prove that elements of luminosity in the narratives are truly a *vestige* rather than simply a *feature* of the stories? In other words, in the absence of a prior proof that the original resurrection appearances were uniformly luminous in character, the elements of luminosity in the Gospel stories cannot themselves be taken as evidence of some more primitive stage. With that in mind, let us consider Robinson's examples.

a. The Angelic Attendants at the Tomb

Robinson is not clear whether the primitive tradition underlying these stories attributed luminosity to the angels or whether this feature of the story is a relic of a luminosity originally attributed to the risen Christ but, under the pressure of opposing Gnosticism, now transferred to the angelic attendants. If the luminescence is truly a vestige of a luminous resurrection appearance, then it would seem that the latter would have to be the case. But the difficulty in proving such a supposed transference is that divine beings are typically portrayed as radiant or clothed in white robes (Ezek. 10; Dan. 7:9; 10:5-6; Lk. 2:9; Acts 1:10; II Cor. 11:14; Rev. 4:4; 10:1; 1 En. 22:8). So why should it be thought that the angel's being dressed in white or dazzling in appearance is a vestige of a radiance originally attributed to the risen Christ? Robinson himself seems to recognize the frailty of such an inference, for he asserts, "The apologetic that apparently caused the resurrected

Christ's luminosity to fade into the solidity of a physical body did not affect the luminosity of the accompanying figure(s)."[22] In this statement he seems to allow that the radiance of the angel(s) is primitive and that only the original luminescence of Christ has disappeared. But in that case, how is the angelic radiance a *vestige* of a luminous resurrection appearance? Once one allows it to be primitive and distinct, then it becomes question-begging to assume that it is all that remains of a doubly ascribed luminescence in the original tradition.

b. The Docetic Elements in the Narratives

Contrary to what Robinson states, Jesus is never said to pass through locked doors in the appearance narratives. He simply appeared miraculously in the closed room, even as he miraculously vanished during bread-breaking in Emmaus. The physical demonstrations of showing his wounds and eating before the disciples indicate that Jesus is conceived to appear physically. His appearances are no more docetic than are similar angelic appearances, which may also begin and end abruptly. In fact, it is instructive to note that the rabbis distinguished between a mere vision of an angel and an extra-mental appearance of an angel precisely on the basis of whether food seen to be consumed by the angelic visitant remains or is gone after the angel disappears.[23] The mode of his coming or going is irrelevant to his physical reality.

c. The Non-recognition Motif as a Vestige of Luminous Appearances

This is an ingenious and more interesting argument. Two questions arise in assessing its force. Does luminosity serve to obscure the identity of the individual appearing? And does the non-recognition motif serve some theological purpose in the resurrection narratives or is it a useless, vestigial feature in those accounts? In favor of an affirmative answer to the first question Robinson appeals to Paul's question, "Who are you, Lord?" in the Acts narrative of his Damascus Road experience. But the force of this example is diminished by two facts. (1) The Acts account does not say that Paul saw any bodily form whatsoever in the blinding

---

[22] Robinson, "Easter to Valentinus," p. 15.
[23] See various texts cited in K. Berger, *Die Auferstehung der Propheten und die Erhöhung des Menschensohnes*, SUNT, 13 (Göttingen: Vandenhoeck & Ruprecht, 1976), pp. 159, 458.

light that surrounded him. Hearing the voice, he asks for the identity of the speaker. Thus, the incident is not portrayed as a recognition scene.[24] (2) Since Paul had apparently never known the earthly Jesus, it is not clear that he could be expected to recognize him (as opposed to, say, an angel), even if he saw him in the light. Since they had lived with Jesus, the disciples' case would thus be different. Moreover, a forceful counter-example to Robinson's claim that luminescence conceals identity is again his own example of the transfiguration of Jesus. The disciples had no difficulty recognizing Jesus and distinguishing him from Elijah and Moses. This counter-example presses all the more strongly against Robinson if one takes this pericope to be a misplaced resurrection appearance story. Hence, I think it is far from clear that the luminosity of an appearing individual masks his identity. As to the second question, is the non-recognition motif really so unintelligible and useless that it is probably vestigial? I am not so sure. Could it not, for example, serve to underline the difference between the earthly Jesus and the numinous, risen Lord, to say to the disciples that their former way of relating to Jesus was now at an end and a new relationship had begun? That seems to be the point of Jesus' cryptic remark to Mary, "Do not cling to me, for I have not yet ascended to the Father..." (Jn. 20:17). So while the non-recognition motif is puzzling, it is not evident that it should be regarded as a relic of some earlier stage in the tradition.

d. The Account of the Transfiguration

It is remarkable that Robinson is prepared to accept II Pet. 1:16-17 as a factual description of the appearance to Peter, while rejecting the Gospel accounts of the resurrection appearances. One can only take this double standard to result from Robinson's apologetic zeal. As to the claim that the transfiguration represents a misplaced resurrection appearance story, while we may agree that Mark does think of it as a proleptic display of Christ's coming glory, perhaps even rendering a narration of a resurrection appearance in fulfillment of the angel's prediction (16:7) therefore superfluous, nevertheless the narrative is so firmly embedded in

---

[24] This conclusion is not affected by any inference from Paul's letters that he saw a bodily form in the light, for the question concerning the speaker's identity occurs in the Acts account only, and in that account there is no suggestion of a bodily form.

its context that it is unlikely to be a misplaced appearance story.²⁵ More importantly, we have seen that this story actually serves to undercut rather than support Robinson's construction, for it shows that luminosity is not incompatible with physicality and does not serve to obscure the identity of the glorified individual. Hence, it seems to me that Robinson has failed to demonstrate that the elements of luminosity in the canonical Gospels are truly vestiges or that their presence supports his proposed trajectories.

EXAMINATION OF ARGUMENT (3)

Turning to point (3), we need to ask whether Paul and John of Patmos really believed, as Robinson apparently claims, that Jesus and the Holy Spirit are numerically identical, that in rising from the dead Jesus was somehow transformed into the Holy Spirit. Consider first the case of Paul. When Paul speaks of a σῶμα πνευματικόν, we must not overlook the obvious fact that he is talking about a σῶμα, not an incorporeal spirit. Although σῶμα is often taken to be a synonym for the whole person, it is evident that in I Corinthians 15 it is used to refer to the physical body and is roughly synonymous with "flesh" in a morally neutral sense.²⁶ Modern commentators agree that by a "spiritual body" Paul does not mean a body made out of spirit, but a body under the domination of and oriented toward the Spirit.²⁷ Now when Paul says that the last Adam became a life-giving Spirit, he does not mean that Jesus turned into the Holy Spirit (thereby negating his somatic reality) any more than when Paul says the first Adam became a living soul, he means that Adam turned into a disembodied ψυχή.²⁸ Rather, he describes

---

[25] For a discussion of suggested misplaced appearance stories, see C. H. Dodd, "The Appearances of the Risen Christ: A Study in Form-Criticism of the Gospels," in *More New Testament Studies* (Manchester: Manchester University Press, 1968), pp. 119-122; R. H. Fuller, *The Formation of the Resurrection Narratives* (London: SPCK, 1972), pp. 160-167; Alsup, *Post-Resurrection Appearance Stories*, pp. 139-144.

[26] See J. Weiss, *Der erste Korintherbrief*, KEK, 5 (Göttingen: Vandenhoeck & Ruprecht, 1910), p. 372. The most important work on this subject is certainly R. H. Gundry, *Soma in Biblical Theology* (Cambridge: Cambridge University Press, 1976); see his summary statement on p. 50. See also J. Gillman, "Transformation in I Cor 15:50-53," *ETL* 58 (1982): 328-339.

[27] See pp. 96-99.

[28] Kleinknecht et. al., "πνεῦμα," *TWNT*. I am astounded by the number of scholars who appeal to I Cor. 15:45, II Cor. 3:17-18, *etc.*, to prove that Christ turned into the Spirit at the resurrection and so is now immaterial and invisible (*e.g.*, Robinson, "Easter to Valentinus," p. 13). Morissette shows from Jewish texts that "life-giving" means "to resurrect" and comments, "The appellation 'Spirit', for its part, is sometimes used by Paul to designate Christ. (Cf. II Cor. 3:17a, 18c; comp.

the same two entities respectively as σῶμα ψυχικόν (15:44), ψυχὴν ζῶσαν (15:45), τὸ ψυχικόν (15:46) and as σῶμα πνευματικόν (15:44), πνεῦμα ζῳοποιοῦν (15:45), τὸ πνευματικόν (15:46). It is because of his desire to construct a parallelism on the words of Gen. 2:7 that Paul abbreviates his reference to Christ's spiritual body in 15:45. As for II Cor. 3:17-18, there is no good reason to think that Paul is claiming more than an identity of *function* between the risen Lord and the Holy Spirit.[29] Given his teaching on the resurrection σῶμα and his personal belief in the bodily return of Christ (I Thess. 4:16-17; II Thess. 1:7-8, 10; 2:1, 8; I Cor. 15:23; Phil. 3:20-21; 4:5; Col. 3:4), it seems to me exegetically fanciful to suppose that Paul thought the risen Christ was numerically identical with the Holy Spirit.

The evidence for the case of John is even less compelling for Robinson's thesis. John's being in the Spirit refers only to the mode of his vision of Christ. That Christ himself commands the churches to give heed to the Spirit affords no inference that Christ has turned into an unembodied Spirit, especially when one contemplates John's vision of Christ's millennial reign and personal presence in the new heavens and new earth (Rev. 20-21). Hence, I must confess that I find Robinson's third point to be the weakest of the four.

EXAMINATION OF ARGUMENT (4)

Finally, in support of point (4) Robinson cites a number of second-century Gnostic texts in order to show that the Gnostics held the resurrection appearances to be visualizations of pure radiance without any bodily form. Here two questions

---

Rom. 8:9-11. This affirmation is implied occasionally by Luke: Comp. Lk. 12:12; 21:15; Acts 16:6, 7.) Nonetheless, there is no formal identification whatever. (Between II Cor. 3:17a ['the Lord is the Spirit'] and 18c ['the Lord who is the Spirit'] Paul distinguishes in v. 17b 'where the Spirit of the lord is, *etc.*') The identification is always *functional*: it serves to show what Christ means 'now' *for* the faithful. (The Apostle frequently attributes similar functions to Christ and the Spirit; W. D. Davies in *Paul and Rabbinic Judaism*, p. 177, has a good summary of these texts.) The statement of I Cor. 15:45b is no exception, as the verb ζῳοποιοῦν...and the entire context indicate." (Rodolphe Morissette, "L'antithèse entre le 'psychique' et le 'pneumatique' en I Corinthiens, XV, 44 à 46," *RScR* 46 [1972]: 141.)

[29] See the remarks of Dunn (*Jesus and the Spirit*, pp. 318-326), particularly the following: "Of course he is speaking primarily in existential rather than in ontological terms. Jesus still has a personal existence; there is, we may say, more to the risen Jesus than life-giving Spirit (cf., *e.g.*, Rom. 1:3f.; 8:34; I Cor. 15:24-28). But so far as the religious experience of Christians is concerned Jesus and the Spirit are no different. The risen Jesus may not be experienced independently of the Spirit, and any religious experience which is not in character and effect an experience of Jesus Paul would not regard as a manifestation of the life-giving Spirit" (pp. 322-323).

present themselves. (a) Are the second-century Gnostic beliefs the issue of a process of reinterpretation of primitive traditions of visualizations of a luminous bodily form? And (b) did the second-century Gnostics hold that the resurrection appearances of Christ were visions of pure, unembodied radiance? With respect to (a), it seems clear that apart from his first three points, Robinson's fourth point alone does nothing to prove the existence of an earlier, developing trajectory, but only shows us what second-century Gnostics believed. What Robinson must show is that the second-century Gnostic position is the terminus of a process whereby primitive visualizations of a radiant bodily shape were transformed into visualizations of unembodied radiance. Not only has he failed to shoulder that burden of proof, but, it seems to me, such a hypothetical development is quite improbable. There is simply no evidence that the New Testament writers were opposed by persons who espoused luminous resurrection appearances lacking a bodily shape. In fact, Robinson appears to be lapsing back into nineteenth-century German exegesis's identification of σῶμα with the *form* of the body and light or glory as its *substance*. Under the influence of idealism, theologians like Holsten and Lüdemann held that the σῶμα is the form of the earthly body and the σάρξ its substance.[30] This enabled one to maintain that in the resurrection the σῶμα or bodily form was retained but was endowed with a new spiritual substance. In this way one could affirm a bodily resurrection without affirming its physicality. Hence, in the older commentaries such as Hans Lietzmann's commentary on the Corinthian correspondence, one finds the σῶμα πνευματικόν to be conceived as a body made out of *himmlischer Lichtsubstanz*.[31] Although Gundry states that this interpretation has now been almost universally abandoned,[32] Robinson seems to be presupposing such an understanding. For he thinks that the Gnostic aversion to the σῶμα meant an aversion to bodily *form* and that Paul's affirmation of a resurrection σῶμα meant an affirmation of bodily *form*. But what Paul affirmed and the Gnostics objected to was real, physical, material corporeal-

---

[30] C. Holsten, *Zum Evangelium des Paulus und des Petrus* (Rostock: Stiller, 1868); H. Lüdemann, *Die Anthropologie des Apostel Paulus und ihre Stellung innerhalb seiner Heilslehre* (Kiel: Universitätsverlag, 1872).

[31] H. Lietzmann, *An die Korinther I, II*, 4th ed., rev. W. G. Kümmel; HNT, 9 (Tübingen: J. C. B. Mohr, 1949), p. 194.

[32] Gundry, *Soma in Biblical Theology*, pp. 161-162, where he lists six factors contributing to this consensus.

ity, not just the form thereof. Proto-Gnostics could have affirmed quite happily the allegedly primitive visualizations of an intangible, immaterial, luminous bodily form.

In fact—and this leads me to my second point (b)—an examination of Robinson's texts reveals that this is precisely what the Gnostics often *did* affirm. For, contrary to Robinson, the Gnostic resurrection appearance texts do not speak of a bodiless radiance, but usually refer to visions of a luminous human bodily form. The only text which suggests a bodiless radiance is found in the *Letter of Peter to Philip* and even that text is not unequivocal, stating, "Then a great light appeared so that the mountain shone from the sight of him who had appeared" (134:10-13).[33] For the rest, bodily appearances are clearly described. For example, in the *Apocryphon of John* we find a sort of trinitarian vision described in which the same human being appears successively as a youth, an old man, and a servant, all enveloped in light (1:30-2:9).[34] In the *Pistis Sophia* 1.4 we read of a post-ascension appearance of Jesus in radiant bodily form: "As they were saying these things and were weeping to one another, on the ninth hour of the following day the heavens opened, and they saw Jesus coming down, giving light exceedingly, and there was no measure to the light in which he was."[35] In the *Sophia of Jesus Christ* we read,

> After he rose from the dead, his twelve disciples and seven women followed him and went to Galilee on the mountain that is called 'Place of Harvest Time and Joy'...The Savior appeared not in his first form, but in the invisible spirit. And his form was like a great angel of light. And his likeness I must not describe. No mortal flesh can endure it, but only pure and perfect flesh like that which he taught us about on the mountain called 'Of the Olives' in Galilee. And he said, 'Peace to you! My peace I give to you!' And they all wondered and were afraid.
> The Savior laughed and said to them, 'What are you thinking about? Why are you perplexed?' (90:14-92:2).[36]

In fact in some of the Gnostic resurrection appearance stories the element of luminosity is completely lacking. For example, in *Acts of Peter and the Twelve Apostles* Peter is confronted by a pearl merchant named Lithargoel, who is described in the following way:

---

[33] Text from J. M. Robinson (ed.), *The Nag Hammadi Library* (Leiden: Brill, 1977), p. 395.
[34] Ibid., p. 99.
[35] Text in C. Schmidt (ed.), *Pistis Sophia*, trans. V. MacDermot; NHS, 9 (Leiden: Brill, 1978), p. 15.
[36] Robinson, *Nag Hammadi Library*, pp. 207-208.

> A man came out wearing a cloth bound around his waist, and a gold belt girded it. Also a napkin was tied over his chest, extending over his shoulders and covering his head and arms.
> I was staring at the man, because he was beautiful in his form and stature. There were four parts of his body which I saw: the tops of his feet, and a part of his chest, and the palm of his hand, and his visage (2:10-24).[37]

Lithargoel later changes into the dress of a physician, and a recognition scene follows in which Lithargoel reveals his true identity as the risen Christ:

> He answered and said, 'It is I! Recognize me, Peter.' He loosed his garment, which clothed him—the one into which he had changed himself because of us—revealing to us in truth that it was he.
> We prostrated ourselves on the ground and worshipped him. We comprised eleven disciples. He stretched forth his hand and caused us to stand (9:13-23).[38]

This story is especially interesting, since it adopts the recognition motif from the canonical appearance stories and yet without any use of the luminosity motif. Another non-luminous resurrection appearance is related in the *Apocryphon of James*:

> Now when the twelve disciples were all sitting together and recalling what the Savior had said to each one of them...lo, the Savior appeared, after he had departed from us, and we had waited for him. And after five hundred and fifty days since he had risen from the dead, we said to him, 'Have you departed and removed yourself from us?'
> But Jesus, said, 'No, but I shall go to the place from whence I came. If you wish to come with me, come!' ...And having called [James and Peter] he drew them aside and bade the rest occupy themselves with that which they were about (2:7-39).[39]

In this text it is only with Jesus' ascension into heaven that the fleshly body is stripped away; similarly in the *Pistis Sophia* 1:1-6 Jesus is said to have spent eleven years with his disciples after his resurrection prior to his ascension in radiant glory (and even in his post-ascension appearance he, at the disciples' request, retracts his radiance so as to appear in a non-luminescent condition). This is instructive because it shows that the resurrection of the physical body and physical appearances were not objectionable to Gnostics, since further transformation could always be deferred until the ascension. In fact, some Gnostic texts are quite content to preserve the flesh throughout resurrection and glorification, insisting only that in the resurrection the body comes to possess a higher, incorruptible

---

[37] Ibid., p. 266.
[38] Ibid., p. 269.
[39] Ibid., p. 30.

flesh (*Treat. Res.* 47:2-12).[40] Thus in *Gos. Phil.* 57:18-19 we read, "It is necessary to rise in the flesh, since everything exists in it."[41] With regard to Jesus' resurrection the same text states, "The Lord rose from the dead. He became as he used to be, but now his body was perfect. He did indeed possess flesh, but this flesh is true flesh. Our flesh is not true, but we possess only an image of the true" (68:31-37).[42] With such a conception of the resurrection body we can readily understand why Gnostic writings show no compunction about relating bodily and even physical resurrection appearances. Thus, it seems that the view which Robinson wants to pass off as "the original Christian position" is in danger of being even more Gnostic than that of the Gnostics!

It therefore seems to me that Robinson's construction of a trajectory from Easter to Valentinus collapses. The Gnostics did not take as their point of departure visualizations of a radiant bodily form and then disembody them to arrive at visions of pure radiance. Rather, they departed from the primitive conception of physical, bodily resurrection appearances and sometimes dematerialized them in order to arrive at visualizations of a radiant bodily form.[43]

By the same token, it does not seem that Robinson has provided sufficient evidence to support his constructed parallel trajectory from Easter to the Apostles' Creed. We have seen no convincing reasons to think that the original resurrection appearances were visualizations of an immaterial and intangible refulgent bodily form. Indeed, had this been the case, then it is difficult to understand why the trajectory should have advanced to the Apostles' Creed's affirmation of the resurrection of the flesh, for faced with the supposed Gnostic denial of bodily form in the radiance, all that would have been necessary was to reaffirm the bodily form or shape of the resplendent glory, not to materialize it by means of crass physical demonstrations of displaying wounds and eating fish. And those who like Robinson are wont to speak of Luke or John's "apologetic against Gnosticism" need to recall that the physicalism of the stories belongs to the traditional material re-

---

[40] Ibid., p. 52. For a list of similar Gnostic affirmations of the resurrection of the flesh or body, see the comment on this passage by M. L. Peel, *The Epistle to Rheginos* (Philadelphia: Westminster Press, 1969).
[41] Robinson, *Nag Hammadi Library*, p. 135.
[42] Ibid., p. 141.
[43] See the remarks of E. E. Ellis, *The Gospel of Luke*, NCB, (London: Nelson, 1966), p. 175; Dunn, *Jesus and the Spirit*, pp. 119-120; K. Bornhäuser, *Das Recht des Bekenntnisses zur Auferstehung des Fleisches* (Gütersloh: Bertelsmann, 1899), pp. 47-61; W. Künneth, *The Theology of the Resurrection*, trans. J. W. Leitch (London: SCM Press, 1965), pp. 92-93.

ceived by these authors, not their redaction of it. There are, in fact, substantive reasons for thinking that the physicalism of the resurrection appearance stories is not a counter-response motivated by Gnostic opponents.[44] Therefore, I see no reason to think that Robinson's hypothesized trajectory from Easter to the Apostles' Creed is any firmer a span than the bridge he has built from Easter to Valentinus.

Conclusion

In summary, none of Robinson's four points supplies sufficient evidence for the existence of twin trajectories taking as their common point of departure primitive first-century visualizations of the resurrected Christ as a luminous bodily form and finding their respective termini in second-century Gnosticism's supposed reinterpretation of these experiences as visions of unembodied luminosity, on the one hand, and in the affirmation of the Apostle's Creed of the resurrection of the flesh, on the other. Robinson has invested an enormous amount of time and industry in the study of the Nag Hammadi documents, and he is understandably anxious that these texts should prove fruitful in the interpretation of the New Testament. But the results of this examination suggests that their value is not to be found in their relevance to the post-resurrection appearances of the Gospel tradition.

---

[44] See pp. 243-245.

APPENDIX B

JOHN DOMINIC CROSSAN ON THE RESURRECTION OF JESUS[1]

INTRODUCTION

As the views of the chairman of the Society of Biblical Literature's Historical Jesus Section, the opinions of John Dominic Crossan on the historicity of the resurrection of Jesus demand attention, and as the views of the co-chairman of the highly publicized Jesus Seminar they cannot in any case be ignored. According to Crossan, after the crucifixion Jesus' corpse was probably laid in a shallow grave, barely covered with dirt, and subsequently eaten by wild dogs; the story of Jesus' entombment and resurrection was the result of "wishful thinking". In this essay, I wish to evaluate critically Crossan's reconstruction of the events of Easter as well as his interaction with evidence allegedly supporting the fact of Jesus' resurrection.

Immediately we encounter a difficulty. Crossan presents no specific evidence, much less probative evidence, for his hypothesis concerning the fate of Jesus' corpse. Rather, the above scenario represents his hunch as to what happened to the body of Jesus based on customary burial procedures.[2] Since he does not ac-

---

[1] This paper originally appeared in *The Resurrection: An Interdisciplinary Symposium on the Resurrection of Jesus*, ed. Stephen Davis, Daniel Kendall, and Gerald O'Collins (Oxford: Oxford University Press, 1997), pp. 249-271.

[2] John Dominic Crossan, *Who Killed Jesus? Exposing the Roots of Anti-Semitism in the Gospel Story of the Death of Jesus* (San Francisco: HarperSan Francisco, 1994), ch. 6; idem, *The Historical Jesus: The Life of a Mediterranean Jewish Peasant* (San Francisco/Edinburgh: HarperSan Francisco/T. & T. Clark, 1991), pp. 392-393; idem, *The Cross that Spoke: The Origins of the Passion Narrative* (San Francisco: Harper & Row, 1988), pp. 21, 235-240; idem, *Four Other Gospels* (Minneapolis: Winston, 1985), pp. 153-164.

cept the historicity of the discovery of the empty tomb (not to speak of the resurrection), Crossan surmises that Jesus' corpse was laid in the graveyard normally reserved for executed criminals, but he offers no specific evidence for this surmise. Instead, he seeks to undercut the credibility of the Gospel accounts of Jesus' burial and resurrection by means of a general analysis of the Gospel texts and traditions. Unfortunately, his tradition-historical analysis is so bizarre and so contrived that the overwhelming majority of New Testament critics find it wholly implausible.[3] For this reason it is difficult to engage Crossan in a conversation concerning the historicity of the resurrection of Jesus, since the presuppositions from which he works are so at odds with the consensus of New Testament criticism concerning the development of the Gospels in general. Discussion of specific points of evidence is rendered difficult because that evidence is being viewed by Crossan through a significantly different lens.

Crossan's theory of the formation of the passion and resurrection narratives in the Gospels is founded on his claim that the *Gospel of Peter* has embedded within it the most primitive Gospel of all, the so-called Cross Gospel, which Crossan identifies as the story of Jesus' crucifixion, entombment, and resurrection. The author of the Gospel of Mark had no other source for Jesus' passion and resurrection than the Cross Gospel, but he invented additional details of the passion and burial based on Old Testament passages—what Crossan calls "historicized prophecy". For the resurrection narratives virtually nothing was available from the Old Testament, but out of his theological conviction that Jesus' passion was to be followed immediately by his coming again in glory, without any intermediate manifestation of the resurrection, Mark retrojected the Cross Gospel's resurrection appearance back into his Gospel in the form of Jesus' transfiguration. But canonical Mark was not the original form of this Gospel. Crossan accepts Morton Smith's claim that canonical Mark is based on an earlier "Secret Gospel of Mark", which Crossan believes ended with the centurion's confession in 15:39 (itself a

---

[3] In a blistering critique Howard Clark Kee hails Crossan's procedure as "a triumph of circular reasoning" (Kee, "A Century of Quests of the Culturally Compatible Jesus," *Theology Today*, 52 [1995]: 22; cf. p. 24). Slightly more charitably, N. T. Wright says that Crossan's *Historical Jesus* "is a book to treasure for its learning, its thoroughness, its brilliant handling of multiple and complex issues, its amazing inventiveness, and above all its sheer readability.... It is all the more frustrating, therefore, to have to conclude that the book is almost entirely wrong" (Wright, *Jesus and the Victory of God* [Minneapolis: Fortress, 1996], p. 44). Similarly, Ben Meyer praises the book for its readability, rapid pace, and useful information, but concludes: "As historical-Jesus research, it is unsalvageable" (Meyer, critical notice of *The Historical Jesus*, CBQ 55 [1993], p. 576).

retrojection of the guard at the tomb's confession in the Cross Gospel). Canonical Mark, in addition to cleaning up the potentially offensive texts in secret Mark, also created 15:40-16:8. The other canonical Gospels are based on both the Cross Gospel and canonical Mark (see *Figure 1*).

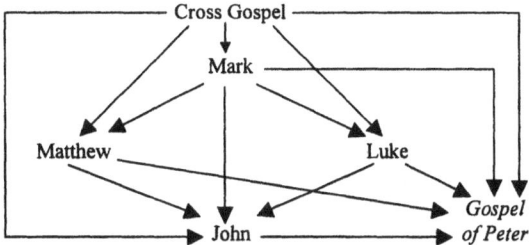

Figure 1: Crossan's diagram of the tradition history behind the Gospels (*Cross that Spoke*, 18). The diagram needs to be supplemented by Crossan's subsequently embraced "Secret Mark" hypothesis. Reproduced by permission of the author.

On the basis of this analysis, Crossan identifies several strata of tradition behind the passion and resurrection narratives and, in reconstructing the historical Jesus, adopts the methodological principle of refusing to allow as historically authentic any passage not attested by multiple, independent sources, even if that passage is found in the first stratum of tradition. This ensures agnosticism concerning Jesus' burial and resurrection, since, on Crossan's analysis, we lack multiple, independent accounts of the exact sequence of what happened at the end of Jesus' life. Given this idiosyncratic approach to the Gospels, it is small wonder Crossan comes to conclusions so radically diverse from those of the majority of critics, who deny the existence of the hypothesized Cross Gospel, reject any dependence of canonical Mark on a secret Mark, hold that the Gospel traditions concerning the burial and empty tomb of Jesus are rooted in history rather than in the Old Testament, regard the *Gospel of Peter*, even if it contains some independent tradition, as a composition basically compiled from the canonical Gospels, and maintain that multiple attestation is not a necessary condition of judging a passage to be authentic.[4] It would be a hopeless undertaking to try to provide in

---

[4] On the purported Secret Gospel of Mark as a pastiche of elements drawn from the canonical Gospels, see F. F. Bruce, *The 'Secret' Gospel of Mark* (London: Athlone, 1974); for a critique of Crossan's hypothesis that canonical Mark revises secret Mark, see Robert H. Gundry, *Mark: A Commentary on his Apology for the Cross* (Grand Rapids, Mich.: Eerdmans, 1993), pp. 613-623;

the limited space available a critical analysis of Crossan's presuppositions; but I think that it is important at least to mention them because so doing will serve both to facilitate our understanding of Crossan's peculiar perspective as well as to underline the fact that much of Crossan's scepticism *vis-à-vis* the resurrection of Jesus is predicated upon presuppositions which most critics would regard as extremely dubious.[5]

EVIDENCE FOR THE RESURRECTION OF JESUS

In my previous work, I have found it convenient to consider the evidence pertinent to the alleged resurrection of Jesus under three main headings: (A) the empty tomb, (B) the post-mortem appearances of Jesus, and (C) the origin of the disciples' belief in Jesus' resurrection. In the following I shall consider the evidence under each head only in so far as Crossan interacts with it, with a view to assessing the success of his proposed reconstruction.

The Empty Tomb

Crossan recognizes that if the story of Jesus' burial is fundamentally reliable, then the inference that Jesus' tomb was found empty lies very close at hand. For if the burial story is basically accurate, the site of Jesus' tomb would have been known to Jew and Christian alike. But in that case, it would have been impossible for resurrection faith to survive in the face of a tomb containing the corpse of Jesus. The disciples could not have adhered to the resurrection; scarcely any one else would have believed them, even if they had; and their Jewish opponents

---

on the Gospel of Peter being a late compilation containing no primitive Cross Gospel, see Raymond E. Brown, "The Gospel of Peter and Canonical Gospel Priority," *NTS* 33 (1987): 321-343, which is expanded in appendix I, "The Gospel of Peter—A Noncanonical Passion Narrative," of Brown's magisterial *The Death of the Messiah: A Commentary on the Passion Narratives in the Four Gospels*, Anchor Bible Reference Library, 2 vols. (New York: Doubleday, 1994); on the illegitimacy of making multiple attestation a necessary condition of authenticity, see C. F. D. Moule, *The Phenomenon of the New Testament* (London: SCM, 1967), p. 71.

[5] The extremity of Crossan's scepticism is perhaps best illustrated by his remark that he firmly believes that Jesus was crucified under Pontius Pilate, because his crucifixion is attested by Josephus (AD 93-94) and Tacitus (AD 110/120), two "early and independent non-Christian witnesses" (*Historical Jesus*, p. 372)! This is quite amazing. We have on the one hand a NT chock full of early and independent references to Jesus' crucifixion, including Paul's citation of the very early tradition in I Cor. 15:3, and on the other hand a doctored reference a half-century later in Josephus and a reference no doubt dependent on Christian tradition by Tacitus, and Crossan accepts the crucifixion on the basis of the latter! This evinces a prejudice against the NT documents which can only be described as historically irresponsible.

could have exposed the whole affair by pointing to the occupied tomb, or perhaps even displaying the body of Jesus, as the medieval Jewish polemic portrays them doing (*Tolĕdot Yeshu*). Hence, as Crossan recognizes, it would seem to be unfeasible to affirm the historicity of the burial story and yet deny the historicity of the empty tomb.

But the burial story is widely recognized as a historically credible narrative. In I Corinthians 15:3-5 the tradition received and delivered by Paul refers in its second line to the fact of Jesus' burial. The grammatically unnecessary fourfold ὅτι, the chronological succession of the events, and particularly the remarkable concordance between this tradition and both the preaching of Acts and the Gospel narratives with respect to the order of events (death, burial, resurrection, appearances) make it highly probable that the tradition's mention of the burial is not meant merely to underscore the death, but refers to the same event related in the Gospels—that is, the laying of Jesus in the tomb. If this is so, then it seems very difficult to regard Jesus' burial in the tomb as unhistorical, given the age of the tradition (AD 30-6), for there was not sufficient time for legend concerning the burial to significantly accrue. Remarkably, Crossan overlooks entirely this early tradition concerning Jesus' burial.

Moreover, it is generally acknowledged that the burial account is part of Mark's source material for the story of Jesus' passion. Even Crossan's hypothesized Cross Gospel includes Jesus' being sealed in a tomb, not buried in the criminals' graveyard (*Gospel of Peter* 8:30-33). Apart from his methodological requirement of multiple attestation, Crossan provides no reason why this putatively pre-Marcan source is not to be trusted in this regard. In any case the burial *is* multiply attested, as we have seen, since the tradition delivered by Paul also refers to it. Thus, on Crossan's own principles, we have good reason to accept the burial as historical. The age of Paul's tradition and the age of the pre-Marcan passion story support the fundamental historical credibility of the burial story.

Furthermore, the burial story itself is simple, and in its basic elements lacks theological reflection or apologetic development. Most scholars would concur with Bultmann's judgement to this effect.[6] Crossan, on the other hand, thinks that

---

[6] Rudolf Bultmann, *The History of the Synoptic Tradition*, trans. John Marsh, 2nd ed. (Oxford: Blackwell, 1963), p. 274.

the burial story is a fictitious account manufactured out of Deuteronomy 21:22-23 and Joshua 10:26-27. Now since the supposed Cross Gospel contains no burial story at all—Crossan attributes *Gospel of Peter* 6:23-24 (Joseph's entombment of Jesus) to a later stratum based on the canonical Gospels—it must be Mark's account that is supposed to be manufactured out of these Old Testament texts in conjunction with the Cross Gospel. Wholly apart from the question of whether early Christians felt free just to invent incidents without any historical basis, two problems with Crossan's hypothesis arise.

First, such an approach to the Gospels is in danger of repeating with Jewish texts the same error committed by the old *Religionsgeschichtliche Schule* with pagan texts. That nineteenth-century movement sought to find parallels to Christian beliefs in pagan religions, and some scholars sought to explain Christian beliefs, including the resurrection of Jesus, as the product of pagan influences. The movement collapsed, however, largely because no genealogical link could be shown between the pagan beliefs and Christian beliefs. Crossan's Jewish parallels are similarly devoid of significance unless a causal connection to incidents narrated in the Gospels can be shown. In the case at issue, it is very doubtful that this can be done, since one only notices the parallels if one reads the relevant texts in the light of and with full knowledge of the Gospel narratives. The parallels are too distant to think that a first-century Christian with knowledge only that Jesus was crucified would find such texts relevant to Jesus' fate.[7]

Second, the dissimilarities between the burial story and Joshua 10:26-27 suggest that Mark's account is not based on the latter. Joshua speaks of a cave, whereas Mark makes a point of the manmade, rock-hewn sepulchre in which Jesus is laid (cf. Isa. 11:16); Joshua has a guard at the cave, whereas Mark has no guard; Mark has Joseph of Arimathea, the scene with Pilate, and the linen shroud, no parallels to which occur in Joshua. Details like the stone over the entrance and burial before nightfall are features which belong to the attested historical Jewish milieu, and so provide no genealogical clue. Crossan thinks that the Cross Gospel simply took it for granted that the Jews buried Jesus, but that the Joshua passage provided the buried body, the great rolled stone, and the posted guards for the

---

[7] In his most recent book Crossan seems to concede this point, remarking, "The burial stories are not history remembered, but neither are they prophecy historicized. What prophecies were present to be historicized?" (Crossan, *Who Killed Jesus?*, p. 188). Rather, the burial story is Mark's free invention designed to shift the responsibility for Jesus' burial from his enemies to his friends.

Cross Gospel's guard at the tomb story. But surely the buried body is already provided by the fact of the crucifixion coupled with Jewish customs with respect to burial of the dead; the stone is an archaeologically confirmed feature of tombs of notable persons in first-century Palestine; and the guard is more plausibly derived from Matthew than Joshua, particularly in light of the *Gospel of Peter*'s heightening of the guard story by identifying it clearly as a Roman guard (complete with the name of the commander), having it posted on Friday rather than on Saturday, so that the tomb is never left unguarded, and emphasizing that the soldiers did not fall asleep, but were constantly on watch.[8] We appear to have in Mark a primitive tradition recounting Joseph's begging the body of Jesus and his laying it, wrapped in linen, in a tomb, a tradition which has not been significantly overlaid with either theology or apologetics.

With respect to Joseph of Arimathea in particular, even sceptical scholars agree that it is unlikely that Joseph, as a member of the Sanhedrin, was a Christian invention. Again Crossan disagrees, asserting that Mark invented Joseph of Arimathea to take Jesus' burial from his enemies to his friends, and so winds up with "an impossible creation: one with access to power but still on the side of Jesus".[9] Unfortunately, Crossan gives no evidence for his assertion that such was Mark's intent, nor an explanation as to why a person such as Joseph is impossible. Since

---

[8] Crossan provides one argument in support of the priority of the Gospel of Peter's guard story: it is less likely that the Gospel of Peter would preserve Matthew's three-day motif but drop its connection with Jesus' prophecy of his resurrection than that Matthew would connect the three-day motif already present in Peter with prophecy. Crossan argues that the reason why the Jewish elders in Peter ask that the tomb be guarded for three days is that by then Jesus would be "really and irrevocably a corpse so that the disciples cannot resuscitate Jesus and remove him," leading the people to infer that Jesus was risen from the dead (Crossan, *Who Killed Jesus?*, pp. 177-181). This is an enormously implausible explanation of the three-day motif in Peter. (i) It ignores the fact that the three-day motif was already normative in primitive Christian belief (I Cor. 15:4) and is there associated with OT prophecy. (ii) There is no reason to think that the elders were concerned (in line with the Jewish belief that the soul of the deceased lingered about the grave until the fourth day) with Jesus' resuscitation; on the contrary, their concern is that "his disciples come and steal him away" (Gospel of Peter 8:30), a threat which, as Crossan notes, is not limited to three days' time. Therefore, the three-day motif in Peter, even if primitive, cannot be understood in isolation from the normative Christian belief that Jesus was raised on the third day. But in that case there is no reason to think that the same explanation should not suffice for Peter's retention of that motif in the likelihood that Peter is late and derivative. He gives his own free account of the guard in any case, and, for all we know, may have included Jesus' prophecies of his resurrection on the third day earlier in his Gospel, so that the motif plays implicitly the same role as in Matthew. Crossan's argument for Petrine priority is therefore without weight.

[9] Crossan, *Who Killed Jesus?*, p. 172.

neither the Cross Gospel nor Mark say clearly that Jesus was buried by his enemies or that Joseph was a friend of Jesus, it is dubious that Mark's intent was to shift the burial from Jesus' enemies to his friends. Even more simply, if Mark was so inventive, why should he create a figure like Joseph rather than just have the disciples bury Jesus? If he wanted more historical verisimilitude, he could have had Jesus buried by his family. Or why not just stick with burial by his enemies? As for Joseph himself, Raymond Brown judges that Joseph's being responsible for burying Jesus is "very probable", since a Christian fictional creation of a Jewish Sanhedrist who does what is right for Jesus is "almost inexplicable", given the hostility toward the Jewish leaders responsible for Jesus' death in early Christian writings.[10] In particular, it is unlikely that Mark invented Joseph in view of his statements in 14:55, 64 and 15:1 that the whole Sanhedrin voted for Jesus' condemnation. Brown notes that the thesis of Joseph's invention is rendered even more implausible in light of his identification with Arimathea, a town of no importance and having no scriptural symbolism. To this may be added the fact that the later descriptions of Joseph receive unintentional confirmation from incidental details in the Marcan narrative: for example, his being rich, from the type and location of the tomb. His being at least a sympathizer of Jesus is not only independently attested by Matthew and John, but seems likely in view of Mark's description of his special treatment of Jesus' body as opposed to those of the thieves. I see no reason to agree with Crossan that it is "impossible" that a Sanhedrist could have been a sympathizer of Jesus.

On the other hand, if the burial of Jesus in the tomb by Joseph of Arimathea is legendary, then it is very strange that conflicting traditions nowhere appear, even in Jewish polemic. That no remnant of the true story or even a conflicting false one should remain is hard to explain unless the account is substantially the true account. Crossan attempts to find other burial traditions in the *Epistula Apostolorum* (a Coptic document from the second century) and Lactantius *Divine Institutes* 4.19 (from the early fourth century). That Crossan thinks that these late, derivative, and sometimes fanciful sources are more trustworthy purveyors of historical tradition than the New Testament documents is a comment on his methodology. In any case, these sources do not in fact offer alternatives to the account. The *Epistula Apostolorum* 9 (20) speaks of Jesus' body being taken down from the

---

[10] Brown, *Death of the Messiah*, vol. ii, p. 1240.

cross along with those of the thieves, but then singles him out as being buried in a place called "skull", where Mary, Martha, and Mary Magdalene went to anoint him. The summary nature of the passage no more excludes burial by Joseph of Arimathea than does the Apostles' Creed. The same is true of Lactantius' summary, in which he says in reference to the Jews, "they took his body down from the cross, and enclosing it safely in a tomb, they surrounded it with a military guard" (4.19). The desire to polemicize against the Jews leads Lactantius to include Joseph under the general rubric "the Jews". The same motive governs Acts 13:27-29, to which Crossan also appeals. Finally, John 19:31 has only to do with a request, not with actual burial. That Crossan has to appeal to passages such as the above only serves to underline how strained is the attempt to find competing burial traditions.

It is thus not without reason that the majority of New Testament critics today agree, in the words of Wolfgang Trilling, that "it appears unfounded to doubt the fact of Jesus' honorable burial even historically considered."[11] But in that case., the conclusion that the tomb was found empty lies close at hand.

Consider now the empty tomb narrative itself, as we find it in Mark. It has frequently been observed how theologically unadorned and non-apologetic in nature this account is. The resurrection is not described, and later theological motifs that a late legend might be expected to incorporate are wholly lacking. Comparison of Mark's account with those in the apocryphal gospels like the *Gospel of Peter* underlines the simplicity of the Marcan story. The *Gospel of Peter* inserts between Jesus' being sealed in the tomb and the visit of Mary Magdalene early Sunday morning an account of the resurrection itself. In this account, the tomb is surrounded not only by Roman guards but also by the Jewish Pharisees and elders, as well as by a multitude from the surrounding countryside. Suddenly, in the night, there rings out a loud voice in heaven, and two men descend from heaven to the tomb. The stone over the door rolls back by itself, and they go into the tomb. Then three men come out of the tomb, two of them holding up the third man. The heads of the two men reach up into the clouds, but the head of the third man reaches up beyond the clouds. Then a cross comes out of the tomb, and a

---

[11] Wolfgang Trilling, *Fragen zur Geschichtlichkeit Jesu* (Düsseldorf: Patmos Verlag, 1966), p. 157; see also Raymond E. Brown, "The Burial of Jesus (Mark 15:42-47)," *CBQ* 50 (1988): 233-245.

voice from heaven asks, "Have you preached to them that sleep?" And the cross answers, "Yes." In contrast to the Marcan account, this narrative is brightly coloured by theological and apologetic motifs that display its unhistorical character.

Crossan agrees that the above account found in the Cross Gospel (= *Gospel of Peter* 9:35-10:42) is theologically determined, but he thinks that Mark's account is, too. For Mark's closely linking Jesus' passion and parousia leads him to suppress the Cross Gospel's colourful account of the resurrection (and, presumably, the guard) so that his simple narrative results. For Mark, "The resurrection was simply the departure of Jesus pending a now imminent return in glory."[12] The retrojected appearance from the Cross Gospel became the transfiguration, which functions as a foretaste of Jesus' parousia, not his resurrection.

Crossan's hypothesis hinges crucially on the widely rejected idea that Mark's Gospel envisions no resurrection appearances, but only Jesus' parousia (Mark 13:26; 14:62). Now clearly, Jesus' predictions of his glorious return do not preclude resurrection appearances after he rises from the dead, as he predicted he would (Mark 8:31; 9:9, 31; 10:34). And in 14:28; 16:7 Mark gives us clearly to understand that such resurrection appearances will take place. Jesus' going before the disciples to Galilee and the restricted circle of the witnesses make it clear that Mark is not envisioning Jesus' second coming in Galilee (not to mention the problem that Mark knows that such did not occur).[13] Crossan cannot retreat to the position that these verses were not part of the original, secret Mark, for the issue is the simplicity of Mark 16:1-8, which was supposedly added by canonical Mark. If canonical Mark contemplates resurrection appearances, then no reason remains for him not to give a resurrection narrative akin to the *Gospel of Peter's*. As for the transfiguration, most critics regard this narrative as so firmly embedded in its context that it is not plausibly thought of as a retrojected resurrection narrative. Crossan confesses that the parallels between Mark's transfiguration narrative and the *Gospel of Peter's* resurrection story (for example, the height of the heads

---

[12] Crossan, *Historical Jesus*, p. 296.

[13] Perhaps Crossan would attempt to elude the force of these considerations by holding that Mark does envisage resurrection appearances, but implies that they never occurred due to the women's failure to convey the angel's message to the disciples. This strange interpretation is unavailing, however, since Mark's audience is led to infer that these predictions, like all the rest of Jesus' prophecies in the Gospel, will be fulfilled, despite the women's stunned silence. Moreover, Crossan's hypothesis hinges on his assumption that Mark is writing to a community that has experienced persecution and defeat, and so needs to see the disciples' failures, an assumption which needs to be re-examined in light of Gundry's commentary.

reaching to heaven becomes the high mountain) are "not very persuasive" in themselves, but blames this on Mark's having "incompletely recast" the narrative.[14] But this explanation serves only to lend an air of unfalsifiability to his hypothesis. In any case, Mark 16:1-8 lacks any theological reflection on Jesus' glorious return, as well as other theological motifs, like his descent into hell, victory over his enemies, and so forth, which bespeaks its primitiveness.

Furthermore, the discovery of the empty tomb by women is highly probable. Given the relatively lower status of women in Jewish society and their lack of qualification to serve as legal witnesses, the most plausible explanation, in light of the Gospels' conviction that the disciples were in Jerusalem over the Easter weekend, of why women and not the male disciples were made discoverers of the empty tomb is that the women were in fact the ones who made this discovery.

At this point Crossan's speculations really go off the rails. The Secret Gospel of Mark, he says, lent itself to an erotic interpretation which the author of canonical Mark wished to avoid. But rather than simply remove the offending text, Mark dismembered it and scattered its parts throughout his Gospel. For example, the angelic figure of the young man in the tomb (Mark 16:5) derives from the young man in secret Mark who comes to Jesus for instruction in the mystery of the Kingdom of God. More relevant to the present point, the three women who discover the empty tomb (Mark 16:1) are the dismembered residue of secret Mark 2r:14-16, which followed canonical Mark 10:46a and reads: "And the sister of the young man whom Jesus loved and his mother and Salome were there, and Jesus did not receive them." Thus, the women's role in the empty tomb narrative does not undergird its historical credibility.

In an extensive discussion of Crossan's hypothesis, Robert Gundry has shown that the supposedly dismembered elements do not intrude unnaturally in canonical Mark, as Crossan claims, leaving the theory without any positive evidentiary support.[15] Moreover, one might ask, why in the world would Mark scatter these various figures and motifs throughout his Gospel, rather than just delete them if he found them potentially offensive? Crossan's ingenious answer is that Mark did this so that if someone should come upon a copy of secret Mark with the offend-

---

[14] Crossan, *Four Other Gospels*, p. 173; cf. idem, *Who Killed Jesus?*, p. 202.
[15] Gundry, *Mark*, pp. 613-621.

ing passages, then orthodox Christians could claim in response that the passages were just a pastiche assembled from disparate elements in the original Mark! Now this answer is just scholarly silliness. Not only does it ascribe to Mark prescience of redaction criticism, but, more importantly, it tends to render Crossan's hypothesis unfalsifiable, since evidence ostensibly disconfirmatory of the theory is reinterpreted in terms of the theory itself to be actually confirmatory—compare Freudian psychology, which takes someone's claim not to have experienced Oedipal desires as evidence that that person is, in line with the theory, suppressing such experiences. To critics who assert that the Secret Gospel of Mark passages are not primitive, but look like amalgamations drawn from other Gospel stories, it is said, "Aha! That's just what Mark wanted you to think!" In any case, the answer will not work, because some elements of the pastiche are drawn from John's Gospel (the Beloved Disciple, the raising of Lazarus), which secret Mark is supposed to antedate. With respect to the women at the tomb, Crossan's hypothesis still fails to explain why Mark would insert them here, rather than elsewhere in the Gospel, when he could have made male disciples (perhaps even the young man!) discover the empty tomb.

In his most recent book, Crossan does provide an explanation of why the women are assigned the role they play in the empty tomb story: Mark invents their role here to show that the female followers of Jesus, like the men, fail him. They do so in two ways: first, they fail him by coming to the tomb to anoint him, thus evincing their failure to believe his prediction of his resurrection, in contrast to the unnamed woman in 14:3-9, who, says Crossan, "believes Jesus and knows that, if she does not anoint him for burial now, she will never be able to do it later" because he will have risen; and second, the women fail him by fleeing from the tomb, so that the angel's message is never delivered or received. Thus, on Crossan's view, the role of the women is not to bear witness to the empty tomb, but to serve as female illustrations of failure, and so their presence in the narrative is not surprising.

It seems to me that this is a serious misinterpretation of the empty tomb story. I see no evidence for Crossan's assertion that "Male and female followers of Jesus are important for Mark, and the inner three from each group are especially important for him."[16] Mark does not show a great deal of interest in women, and none

---

[16] Crossan, *Who Killed Jesus?*, p. 184.

whatsoever in female followers of Jesus up until their introduction in 15:40-41, and it is fatuous to speak of obscure figures like Salome and the two Marys as an inner trio comparable to that of Peter, James, and John. There is no reason to think that Mark is exercised to provide peculiarly feminine examples of failure. Moreover, the role of the women in the stories of the cross, burial, and empty tomb is not to serve as illustrations of failure. Mark does not give us to understand that the anonymous woman of 14:3 consciously believed in Jesus' resurrection and so wanted to anoint him now before it was too late; that sort of prescience is reserved for Jesus, and it is he who interprets the woman's action in light of his impending death. As for the women at the tomb, Gundry rightly points out that

> The women cannot be faulted for having failed to believe the predictions of Jesus that he would rise. They had never heard those predictions, and neither here nor in 14:3-9 has Mark hinted at their knowing the remark of Jesus that the pouring of perfume on his head had amounted to an anticipatory preparation of his body for burial. Besides, differences in diction and substance make doubtful that Mark wished his audience to draw any sort of comparison between 14:3-9 and 16:1-8.... At no point does Mark signal that he is comparing the women's intention unfavourably with the woman's act.[17]

As for their failure to report to the disciples, the emphasis here lies not on their failure but on the overwhelming awesomeness of the resurrection, which induces trembling, astonishment, and stupefaction in them. Thus the role of the women as the principal witnesses to the crucifixion, burial, and empty tomb of Jesus cannot be plausibly reinterpreted along the lines of Crossan's hypothesis.

According to the Gospels, the male disciples of Jesus did go to the tomb later to confirm the women's report. Crossan says—without argument—that Peter's visit to the tomb is Luke's creation (from which he seems to infer non-historicity). But the visit of Peter and another unnamed disciple to the empty tomb is attested by both Luke and John (Luke 24:12, 24; John 20:3); and, as I have tried to show elsewhere, the hypothesis of Lucan creation and Johannine copying in this case is less plausible than the hypothesis of independent sources.[18] The story is thus multiply attested, and so cannot be written off even on the basis of Crossan's own strict standard of historicity. Moreover, the historicity of the disciples' visit is

---

[17] Gundry, *Mark*, p. 998.
[18] William L. Craig, "The Disciples' Inspection of the Empty Tomb (Lk. 24:12-24; Jn. 20:2-10)," in A. Denaux (ed.), *John and the Synoptics*, BETL 101 (Leuven: Leuven University Press, 1992), pp. 614-619.

also made likely by the plausibility of the denial of Peter tradition (Mark 14:66-72), for if he were in Jerusalem, then, having heard the women's report, he would quite likely check it out. Crossan, on the other hand, embraces without argument the hypothesis of the flight of the disciples, who knew nothing more than the fact of the crucifixion, back to Galilee, a hypothesis which most scholars today would regard, in von Campenhausen's words, as "a fiction of the critics".[19] The inherent implausibility of, and absence of any evidence for, the disciples' flight to Galilee render it highly likely that they were in Jerusalem, which reinforces the plausibility of their inspecting the empty tomb.

Further evidence could be adduced in support of the fact of empty tomb, but Crossan does not interact with it. What is clear from his limited interaction with the evidence is that Crossan is forced again and again to adopt extremist positions which the wide majority of scholars would reject, thus bearing out the truth of D. H. Van Daalen's comment that it is extremely difficult to object to the fact of the empty tomb on historical grounds; most objectors do so on the basis of theological or philosophical considerations.[20]

The Post-mortem Appearances

Turning from the empty tomb to the second category of evidence pertinent to Jesus' alleged resurrection—namely, his post-mortem appearances—we want to see how Crossan handles the evidence that Jesus appeared alive after his death to his disciples.

As we all know, Paul's citation of the traditional formula in I Corinthians 15:3-5 closes with references to various post-mortem appearances of Jesus to both individuals and groups. The age alone of the traditions in I Corinthians 15, which probably reach back to within the first five years after the crucifixion, seems to preclude regarding the appearances of the list as legendary. Crossan himself states that it would take five to ten years just to discover the Old Testament motifs necessary to invent the passion story alone.[21] Yet the tradition delivered by Paul

---

[19] Hans F. von Campenhausen, *Der Ablauf der Osterereignisse and das leere Grab*, 3rd ed. (Heidelberg: Carl Winter, 1966), p. 449. Intriguingly, the Jesus Seminar also endorses this hypothesis (R. W. Funk, R. W. Hoover, and the Jesus Seminar, *The Five Gospels: The Search for the Authentic Words of Jesus* [New York: Macmillan, 1993], p. 468).

[20] D. H. Van Daalen, *The Real Resurrection* (London: Collins, 1970), p. 41.

[21] Crossan, *Jesus*, p. 145; cf. idem, "The Historical Jesus in Earliest Christianity," in Robert Ludwig and Jeffrey Carlson (eds.), *Jesus and Faith: A Conversation with John Dominic Crossan*

antedates even the lower limit assigned by Crossan and already knows not only the Old Testament warrant for the passion, but also the resurrection with its scriptural warrant. Incredibly, Crossan scarcely touches on I Corinthians 15:1-11, and he adopts the old interpretation of von Harnack that the list of witnesses reflects rival factions looking to Cephas and James as their respective leaders.[22] Of the resurrection appearances, Crossan says, "None...was an illusion, hallucination, vision, or apparition. Each was a symbolic assertion of Jesus' continued presence *to the general community, to leadership groups*, or to specific and even competing *individual leaders*."[23] The interpretation of the list as reflecting competitive leadership has been rejected by virtually all contemporary commentators, not only because there is no evidence of first generation factions centered on Peter and James, but also because the chronological ordering of the list as well as the great age of the tradition Paul hands on precludes such an interpretation. Virtually every contemporary New Testament scholar thus agrees that the original disciples had apparitional experiences of Jesus alive after his death. As for Crossan's claim that belief in the resurrection was a purely symbolic assertion, I shall have more to say when we examine the origin of the disciples' belief in the resurrection.

The fact that the disciples experienced appearances of Jesus is also independently attested in the Gospels. Though it may be impossible to prove that any single appearance narrative is historically accurate, there are nevertheless good grounds for holding to the credibility of the Gospels' claim that that the disciples did experience post-mortem appearances of Jesus, given their breadth of tradition in the Gospel records. Trilling compares in this respect the appearance stories to the Gospel miracle accounts:

> From the list in I Cor. 15 the particular reports of the gospels are now to be interpreted. Here may be of help what we said about miracles. It is impossible to "prove" historically a particular miracle. But the totality of the miracle reports permit no reasonable doubt that Jesus in fact performed "miracles." That holds analogously for the appearance reports. It is not possible to secure historically the particular event. But the totality of the

---

(Maryknoll, N. Y.: Orbis, 1994), p. 16—and this is said to be the case even when "You know, first of all, exactly what you are looking for".

[22] Crossan, *Historical Jesus*, pp. 397-398; idem, *Who Killed Jesus?*, p. 203. It is noteworthy that the Jesus Seminar adopts Crossan's interpretation to explain away the denial of Peter tradition (Funk and Hoover, *Five Gospels*, p. 119).

[23] Crossan, *Historical Jesus*, p. 407; emphasis original.

appearance reports permits no reasonable doubt that Jesus in fact bore witness to himself in such a way.[24]

From these reports we may infer with good probability that both groups and individuals under varying conditions witnessed post-mortem appearances of Jesus.

All Crossan has to contribute on this head is to carry over to the Gospels his unfounded inference from I Corinthians 15:5-8 that the resurrection appearances "have nothing whatsoever to do with ecstatic experiences or entranced revelations", but with "questions of authority" and leadership.[25] According to Crossan, "Followers of Jesus also sought to be brokers of the kingdom, contrary to Jesus' own teaching.... [T]he last chapters of the Gospels...are carefully constructed stories which try, for the most part, to establish who's in charge by naming those to whom he appeared."[26] Wholly apart from the illegitimacy of this inference in I Corinthians 15, it is unclear how all the Gospel appearance stories, such as those to the women, can be forced into this mould,[27] or how the disciples' abandoning Jesus' vision of the brokerless kingdom is consistent with Crossan's claim that the reason why Jesus' death did not spell the end of the disciples' faith was because that faith was not lodged in Jesus but in the brokerless kingdom.

As one reflects on this second category of evidence concerning the post-mortem appearances of Jesus, what is most striking about Crossan's treatment is his relative silence on this important issue.[28] When he does speak to it, it is only to adopt once again outmoded, long-refuted positions. Especially astonishing is his assertion that the disciples did not have *any* post-mortem, apparitional experi-

---

[24] Trilling, *Fragen zur Geschichtlichkeit Jesu*, p. 153. Trilling notes that the fact that miracles in general belong to the historical Jesus is widely recognized and no longer disputed.

[25] Crossan, *Who Killed Jesus?*, p. 208; cf. p. 210.

[26] John Dominic Crossan, "The Historical Jesus: An Interview with John Dominic Crossan," *Christian Century*, 108/37 (18 Dec. 1991): 1203.

[27] I consider it extremely dubious whether even the most frequently cited instance of questions of authority being played out—*viz.*, the supposed competition between Peter and the Beloved Disciple in John 20—is not a scholarly fiction.

[28] Crossan does try to play off Paul's assertion that "flesh and blood cannot enter the kingdom of God" (I Cor. 15:50) against a physical resurrection (Crossan, *Historical Jesus*, pp. 404-405). But such an opposition is spurious. "Flesh and blood" is a typical Semitic word-pair connoting frail, mortal human nature (cf. Gal. 1:16; Eph. 6:12), so v. 51b expresses in parallel form the same idea: "neither does the perishable inherit the imperishable". Paul is not talking about anatomy. The resurrection body will be an immortal, powerful, glorious, Spirit-directed body suitable for inhabiting a renewed creation. A *soma* which is unextended and intangible would probably have been a contradiction in terms for the apostle. All commentators agree that Paul did not teach the immortality of the soul alone; but his affirmation of the resurrection of the body becomes vacuous and indistinguishable from such a doctrine unless it is understood to mean the tangible, physical resurrection.

ences of Jesus at all, a position which is not defended by any other contemporary scholar in my acquaintance.

Origin of the Disciples' Belief in Jesus' Resurrection

Finally, let us turn to the third category of evidence concerning the alleged resurrection of Jesus: the very origin of the disciples' belief that Jesus had been raised from the dead. Whatever they may think of the historical resurrection, even sceptical scholars admit that at least the belief that Jesus rose from the dead lay at the very heart of the earliest Christian faith. Without prior belief in the resurrection, belief in Jesus as Messiah would have been impossible in view of his death. Without the resurrection, Jesus' death could only have meant humiliation and accursedness by God, but in view of the resurrection it could be seen to be the event by which forgiveness of sins was obtained. The origin of the Christian Way thus hinges on the disciples' belief that God had raised Jesus from the dead.

Crossan's position on this issue is ambiguous. On the one hand, he seems to agree with the undeniable fact that the earliest disciples proclaimed the resurrection of Jesus and that that doctrine was crucial to the origin of the Christian faith. On the other hand, he reinterprets the belief in Jesus' resurrection to be the symbolic assertion of Jesus' continued presence. He writes, "That *is* the resurrection, the continuing presence in a continuing community of the past Jesus in a radically new and transcendental [*sic*] mode of present and future existence";[29] the problem the disciples faced was "how to *express* that phenomenon". Crossan thinks that in order to express their sense of Jesus' ongoing, invisible presence with them, Christians appropriated the language of resurrection from the dead. He explains:

> Those who had originally experienced divine power through his vision and example still continued to do so after his death. Jesus' followers, who initially fled from the danger of the crucifixion, talked eventually of not just continued affection, but of resurrection. They tried to express what they meant by telling, e.g., of the journey to Emmaus. They were disappointed and in dejected sorrow. Jesus joined them unrecognized and explained that Hebrew scripture 'should have prepared them for his fate.' Later they recognize him by the meal, as of old. Then they go back to Jerusalem in high spirits. The symbolism is obvious, as is the metaphoric condensation of the first years of Christian thought and practice into one parabolic afternoon.[30]

---

[29] Crossan, *Historical Jesus*, p. 404.
[30] Ibid., p. xii.

Thus, on Crossan's view, in a literal sense the first disciples did not really believe in the resurrection of Jesus.

Crossan's view thus raises two questions: (i) When the earliest Christians said that Jesus was raised from the dead, did they mean it literally or not? (ii) Can the origin of their belief be explained as a result of their reflection on Hebrew Scripture?

With respect to (i), I think there can be no doubt that the earliest Christians asserted a literal resurrection of Jesus. Paul's earnest declarations in I Corinthians 15:12-23, 29-32 about the essentiality of Jesus' being raised from the dead, and especially his linking it with our own resurrection from the dead (which cannot be interpreted in terms of continuing presence), show how literally and seriously this event was taken. So also do Paul's disquisitions about the nature of the resurrection body in answer to the questions "How are the dead raised? With what kind of body do they come?" (I Cor. 15:35). The sermons in the book of Acts also present Jesus' resurrection as a literal event, which could only present gratuitous obstacles to their hearers if no such event were being asserted (Acts 17:31-32). The empty tomb tradition would be superfluous and pointless were not a literal event in view, since mere continuing spiritual presence does not require an empty tomb. Moreover, the earliest Christians were perfectly capable of expressing the idea of Jesus' spiritual presence with them without recourse to the misleading language of resurrection from the dead (cf. I Cor. 5:3; Col. 2:5). Indeed, in the notion of the Holy Spirit of Christ the Christians had the perfect vehicle for expressing in a theologically rich way the idea of Jesus' continuing, numinous presence with and in them (Rom. 8:9-11). But they were not content to assert merely the presence of Christ through the Spirit with them; they also believed in Jesus' resurrection from the dead, the harbinger of their own resurrection (Rom. 8:11, 23).

As for (ii), it is now widely agreed that the disciples' belief in Jesus' resurrection cannot be plausibly explained as the result of their reflection on the Old Testament. For as Crossan himself admits,[31] the Old Testament furnishes very little that could be construed in terms of Christ's resurrection, much less prompt such a belief in the absence of any experiences of appearances or an empty tomb. When Crossan says that the Hebrew Scripture should have prepared the disciples for Jesus' fate, what that refers to is his death; but there is almost nothing there to pre-

---

[31] Crossan, *Four Other Gospels*, p. 174.

pare them for his resurrection. For this reason most critics concur that Old Testament proof-texts of the resurrection could be found only after the fact of the disciples' coming to believe that Jesus was risen, not before.

In his more recent book *Jesus*, Crossan takes an even more radical line: the primitive Christians did not even express their sense of Jesus' continuing presence in terms of his resurrection, but held simply to belief in Jesus' passion and second coming. "Where, then did all the emphasis on resurrection come from? In a word, from Paul.... For Paul...bodily resurrection is the only way that continuing presence can be expressed."[32] Crossan considerably complicates this remarkable hypothesis by positing at least four different Christian groups responding to the historical Jesus by the 50s: Thomas Christianity (an ascetic group behind the *Gospel of Thomas*, for whom Jesus' death and resurrection held no interest), Pauline Christianity (which focused on Jesus' historical execution and held to his bodily resurrection as the first-fruits of the general resurrection), Q Christianity (a pre-Easter community behind the Q document, which had no interest in the death and resurrection of Jesus, but saw him as living according to Wisdom and empowering others to do so), and Exegetical Christianity (a scholarly group which searched the Scriptures to invent the passion story and concentrated on passion-parousia, not passion-resurrection).[33] Even if we concede the existence of such groups, however, it is not at all clear how the belief in resurrection is supposed to have originated. Belief in Jesus' continuing presence sounds most characteristic of the Q community, as Crossan describes it:

---

[32] Crossan, *Jesus*, pp. 163, 165.
[33] Crossan, *Historical Jesus*, p. 12. Wright observes that this "mind-blowing reconstruction" lies at the heart of Crossan's work, for without it his use of the sources makes no sense; nor does his highly idiosyncratic interpretation of the passion and resurrection narratives. "Yet," says Wright, "it is, arguably, the most threadbare part of his whole rich tapestry" (*Jesus and the Victory of God*, p. 63). Specifically, to imagine that Paul's Corinthian opponents were a recognized group identified with the Gospel of Thomas strains credibility beyond the breaking-point. To separate Paul from Exegetical Christianity is extraordinary, given Paul's own earnest search of the Scriptures. In order to postulate the existence of Q Christianity, Crossan has to distinguish an early Q from a later Q in order to separate out the apocalyptic elements in Q so as to render it purely sapiential; but he has no non-question-begging criteria for such a division. There is in any case no reason to suppose that Q (the extent of which is literally unknowable) represents the beliefs of a group within Christianity. So-called Exegetical Christianity is a simple fiction, since the examples Crossan gives of it are notable precisely for how unlike the writings of the evangelists and Paul they are.

> To believe that the Wisdom of God appeared performanically [*sic*] in Jesus' life meant, for them, to live likewise. That faith was there before he died and continued not so much despite, but because of it. He had warned them to expect refusal and even persecution, to live the life of Wisdom spurned. I wonder if anyone ever told them that they had lost their faith on Good Friday and had it restored by visions on Easter Sunday?[34]

But obviously belief in Jesus' resurrection did not originate in such a group, since the ongoing validity of Wisdom did not require such a metaphor; nor is it in evidence in Crossan's Q. Obviously it did not originate among Thomas Christians, since they were ostensibly Paul's opponents in Corinth, and resurrection plays no role in the *Gospel of Thomas*. Crossan admits that Exegetical Christianity did not invent the resurrection, since there were no Old Testament proof-texts available for that event, and this group conceived the passion to be followed by the parousia rather than the resurrection. So it could only have come from Pauline Christianity. But how is this hypothesis consistent with the view that the resurrection is just the symbolic assertion of the continuing presence of Jesus? Crossan admits that Paul wrote to Corinth to defend "the possibility and actuality of bodily resurrection" and that Paul held Jesus' resurrection to be the first-fruits of the general eschatological resurrection of the dead. Crossan wants to maintain both that "resurrection is the only possible way to articulate the presence of Jesus for Paul, but it is also inextricably linked to the imminent general resurrection at the end of the world".[35] If we are to bring consistency into Crossan's view, he must hold that Paul believed in the literal, bodily resurrection of Jesus because he believed that Jesus was present and that Jesus could only be present if he had been raised. Now if Pauline Christianity is supposed to have originated with Paul, this means that none of the original followers of Jesus believed in or even used the language of resurrection symbolically prior to Paul. But in light of the early tradition received and delivered by Paul in I Corinthians 15:3-5 alone, not to mention Paul's declaration that this is the *kerygma* proclaimed by all the apostles (I Cor. 15:11), such a view is simply impossible, for the normative belief in Jesus' resurrection antedated Paul. Moreover, the claim that Paul was at a loss to express the notion of Jesus' continuing presence other than through the language of resurrection is incredible, since it was Paul himself who wrote so eloquently of Christ's presence in the believer through his indwelling Holy Spirit. Paul could have held

---

[34] Crossan, *Historical Jesus*, p. 15
[35] Ibid., pp. 7, 8.

Jesus to be present in spirit or, as divine, present even as God is present. If we try to rescue Crossan's hypothesis by holding that Paul did not originate "Pauline" Christianity, but merely represented it, having inherited the belief in Jesus' resurrection from what we might more accurately call resurrection Christianity before him, then the origin of this group's belief is left unexplained by anything Crossan says. Apart from the event of the resurrection itself, it remains mysterious how the Christian belief in Jesus' resurrection from the dead, and the movement founded on that belief, should have come into being at all.

Conclusion

In conclusion, I think that it is evident that Crossan has not been able to render plausible his reconstruction of the events of Easter, including Jesus' burial, empty tomb, post-mortem appearances, and the origin of the disciples' belief in Jesus' resurrection. His entire approach is predicated upon idiosyncratic presuppositions concerning sources and methodology which would not be accepted by any other major New Testament critic. Like an inverted pyramid, Crossan's whole reconstruction balances on the putative existence of the Cross Gospel, in the absence of which the whole structure collapses.

More specifically, we saw with respect to the burial story that, even if we concede the existence of the primitive Cross Gospel, the burial account meets Crossan's demand of multiple attestation, and is therefore to be accepted as *prima facie* historical. Crossan was unable to make a plausible case for regarding Mark's account as historicized prophecy; nor could he render doubtful the historicity of Joseph of Arimathea's role in the burial.

With respect to the empty tomb, Crossan's attempt to construe Mark's account as a distillation of the account of the resurrection in the *Gospel of Peter* forces him to adopt a number of untenable hypotheses, such as Mark's envisioning no resurrection appearances prior to the parousia and the transfiguration story's being a recast version of the resurrection appearance related in *Peter*. Crossan is also forced to embrace without evidence the fanciful hypothesis of the flight of the disciples to Galilee. The *reductio ad absurdum* of his position, however, is his treatment of the role of the women in the empty tomb account, the explanation of which forces Crossan to what can only be described as desperate lengths.

With respect to the post-mortem appearances, Crossan's treatment is surprisingly brief and superficial. Again we see the desperation, as Crossan denies without argument that the disciples experienced any post-mortem appearances of Jesus, despite the multiple attestation enjoyed by the appearances, and embraces without evidence the long-refuted interpretation of the appearances as solely authority-conferring constructs of the early Church.

Finally, with respect to the origin of the disciples' belief in Jesus' resurrection, Crossan's developing views seem to be self-contradictory, at first ascribing to the disciples a purely symbolic use of resurrection language, but later attributing to Pauline Christianity the original application of the notion of resurrection to Jesus' fate. The first hypothesis is merely enormously implausible; the second is absurd. None of Crossan's hypothetical Christian communities, even if they existed, can be plausibly thought to have originated the idea of Jesus' resurrection.

Crossan has announced that his next project will be a book dealing with the events following Jesus' death. It is greatly to be hoped that his more studied reconstruction will be more substantial, more plausible, and more consistent than what he has heretofore produced.

APPENDIX C

VISIONS OF JESUS: A CRITICAL ASSESSMENT OF GERD LÜDEMANN'S
HALLUCINATION HYPOTHESIS

INTRODUCTION

Gerd Lüdemann has become one of the most prominent and sharpest critics of the historicity of the resurrection of Jesus. After igniting a firestorm of controversy in his native Germany, Lüdemann's writings have leapt the Atlantic to spark debate in this country as well. His conclusions are important not just for New Testament scholarship, but for dogmatic theology as well. As one who has previously defended the historical credibility of the event of Jesus's resurrection,[1] I propose in this paper to assess critically Lüdemann's historical reconstruction of the events of Easter.

Before we begin, it is perhaps worth mentioning that there are a number of dogmatic issues on which we do agree, which deserve to be highlighted. First, I agree, in Lüdemann's words, that "The resurrection of Jesus is the central point of the Christian religion."[2] Second, I agree that if someone asks "What really happened?", it is not enough to be told to "just believe."[3] Third, I agree that the historian's task is very much like that of the trial lawyer: to examine the witnesses in

---

[1] William Lane Craig, *The Historical Argument for the Resurrection of Jesus during the Deist Controversy*, Texts and Studies in Religion 23 (Lewiston, N. Y.: Edwin Mellen, 1985); idem, *Assessing the New Testament Evidence for the Historicity of the Resurrection of Jesus*, Studies in the Bible and Early Christianity 16 (Lewiston, N. Y.: Edwin Mellen, 1989).

[2] Gerd Lüdemann, *What Really Happened to Jesus?*, trans. John Bowden (Louisville, Kent.: Westminster John Knox Press, 1995), p. 1.

[3] Ibid., p. 3.

order to reconstruct the most probable course of events.[4] Fourth, I agree that if someone does not believe in the literal resurrection of Jesus, he should have the honesty to say that Jesus just rotted away—and that he should not be persecuted for having had the courage to say it.[5] Fifth, I agree that if someone does not believe in the literal resurrection of Jesus, then he should have the honesty to say that he is not a Christian—just as Lüdemann has done.[6] Finally, sixth, I agree that if someone does believe in Jesus's literal resurrection, he should admit that he believes in a miraculous intervention of God in the natural world.[7]

Despite these areas of agreement, however, we obviously have wide-ranging differences, too. I maintain that any adequate historical hypothesis about the resurrection must explain four facts: Jesus's honorable burial, the discovery of his empty tomb, his post-mortem appearances, and the origin of the disciples' belief in his resurrection. I shall first summarize some of the evidence for each of these facts and then examine Lüdemann's treatment of them.

THE INDUCTIVE EVIDENCE

The Burial

Fact #1: *After his crucifixion Jesus was buried by Joseph of Arimathea in the tomb.* My statement of this fact represents the core of the burial narrative. I do not include secondary details, such as Joseph's Christian commitments. Such circumstantial details are inessential to the historicity of Jesus's honorable burial. The fact of Jesus's honorable burial is highly significant because it implies that the location of Jesus's tomb was known in Jerusalem. In that case, it is extremely difficult to see how the disciples could have proclaimed Jesus's resurrection in Jerusalem if the tomb had not been empty.

---

[4] Gerd Lüdemann, "Zwischen Karfreitag und Ostern," in *Osterglaube ohne Auferstehung?*, ed. Hansjürgen Verweyen, Quaestiones Disputatae 155 (Freiburg: Herder, 1995), p. 21; cf. idem, *What Really Happened?*, p. 6.
[5] Lüdemann, "Zwischen Karfreitag und Ostern," p. 27; cf. idem, "Für die Jünger war sie wichtig," *Evangelische Zeitung*, February 2, 1994; idem *What Really Happened?*, p.v.
[6] Gerd Lüdemann, *The Great Deception* (Amherst: Prometheus Books, 1999); idem, *Jesus after 2000 Years* (London: SCM Press, 2000).
[7] Lüdemann does not exactly put it this way; he says that anyone who holds to a supernatural or miraculous element behind the events of Easter should openly admit that he is a fundamentalist (Lüdemann, "Zwischen Karfreitag und Ostern," p. 7). See also Gerd Lüdemann, *The Resurrection of Jesus*, trans. John Bowden (Minneapolis: Fortress Press, 1994), p. 180.

We may summarize some of the evidence for Fact #1 as follows:

1. Jesus's burial is attested in the very old tradition quoted by Paul in I Cor. 15:3-5.
2. The burial is part of very old source material used by Mark in writing his gospel.
3. As a member of the Sanhedrin, which condemned Jesus, Joseph of Arimathea is unlikely to be a Christian invention.
4. The burial story itself lacks any traces of legendary development.
5. No other competing burial story exists.

With respect to the first supporting line of evidence, we know that in the second line of the pre-Pauline formula in I Cor. 15:3-5 Jesus's burial is mentioned. Lüdemann recognizes this early evidence for the burial but questions whether the burial referred to is the same event as the burial by Joseph of Arimathea.[8] A comparison of the four-line formula transmitted by Paul with the Gospel narratives on the one hand and the sermons in the Acts of the Apostles on the other makes the answer clear:

I Cor 15:3-5	Acts 13:28-31	Mk 15:37-16:7
Christ died...	Though they could charge him with nothing deserving death, yet they asked Pilate to have him killed.	And Jesus uttered a loud cry and breathed his last.
he was buried...	They took him down from the tree and laid him in a tomb	And he [Joseph] bought a linen shroud, and taking him down, wrapped him in the linen shroud and laid him in a tomb.
he was raised...	But God raised him from the dead...	"He has risen, he is not here; see the place where they laid him."
he appeared...	...and for many days he appeared to those who came up with him from Galilee to Jerusalem, who are now his witnesses to the people.	"But go, tell his disciples and Peter that he is going before you to Galilee; there you will see him."

---

[8] Lüdemann, *Resurrection of Jesus*, p. 45.

This remarkable correspondence of independent traditions reveals that the four-line formula is a summary in outline form of the basic events of Jesus's passion and resurrection, including his burial in the tomb. Lüdemann holds that this early formula dates from just two years after the crucifixion.[9] It thus represents fantastically early evidence for Jesus's honorable burial.

With respect to the second supporting line of evidence, I take it for granted that Mark is working with a pre-Markan passion narrative, and I claim that the burial account was part of that passion narrative. This latter claim is relatively uncontroversial, I think, since the burial is an essential part of the story line, common to all the Gospels, bringing the passion narrative toward its conclusion. Even if we do not postulate a full-blown pre-Markan passion narrative, we must, in light of the independence of John's Gospel from the Synoptics, recognize a pre-Markan burial tradition of Jesus's entombment by Joseph of Arimathea.[10] And even among the Synoptics, the sporadic and uneven nature of Luke and Matthew's verbal agreements with Mark, their omissions from Mark, and their numerous agreements with each other against Mark suggest that Mark's narrative was not their only source, but that they had additional sources for the burial and empty tomb accounts.[11] This multiplicity of independent sources is important because, as Marcus Borg explains, "if a tradition appears in an early source *and* in another independent source, then not only is it early, but it is also unlikely to have been made up."[12] It is remarkable that in the case of the burial we have some of the

---

[9] Ibid., p. 38.
[10] See further William Lane Craig, "The Disciples' Inspection of the Empty Tomb (Luke 24:12-24; John 20:1-10)," in *John and the Synoptics*, ed. A. Denaux, Bibliotheca Ephemeridum Theologicarum Lovaniensium 101 (Louvain: University Press, 1992), pp. 614-619.
[11] Their differences from Mark are therefore not plausibly attributed to mere editorial changes. For examples of the uneven verbal agreements with Mark, see Mk. 15:46 "a tomb which had been hewn out of rock" and Mt. 17:60 "tomb which he had hewn in the rock;" of omissions see Pilate's interrogation of the centurion in Mk. 15:44-45; and of agreements against Mark see Mt. 27:58; Lk. 23:52 "This man went in to Pilate and asked for the body of Jesus." See further Ernst Lohmeyer, *Das Evangelium des Matthäus*, 4th ed., ed. W. Schmauch, Kritisch-exegetischer Kommentar über das Neue Testament (Göttingen: Vandenhoeck & Ruprecht, 1967), pp. 398-399, 404, 408; Walter Grundman, *Das Evangelium nach Lukas*, 8th ed., Theologischer Handkommentar zum Neuen Testament 3 (Berlin: Evangelische Verlagsanstalt, 1978), p. 436.
[12] Marcus J. Borg and N. T. Wright, *The Meaning of Jesus* (San Francisco: Harper Collins, 1999), p. 12. Borg observes that most cases of multiple attestation in the New Testament are double; the cases of triple or more attestation are relatively few. It is all the more striking, then, that the honorable burial of Jesus is multiply attested in Paul's formula, Mark's passion source, the sermons in Acts, Matthew and Luke's sources, and John.

earliest sources behind the New Testament (*e.g.,* the pre-Pauline formula and the pre-Markan passion story) as well as a number of others.

The third point concerns the enigmatic figure Joseph of Arimathea, who suddenly appears to provide an honorable burial for Jesus, in contrast to the two criminals crucified with him. The late Raymond Brown stated this point forcefully in his magisterial *The Death of the Messiah:*

> That the burial was done by Joseph of Arimathea is very probable, since a Christian fictional creation from nothing of a Jewish Sanhedrist who does what is right is almost inexplicable, granted the hostility in early Christian writings toward the Jewish authorities responsible for the death of Jesus.... While high probability is not certitude, there is nothing in the basic pre-Gospel account of Jesus's burial by Joseph that could not plausibly be deemed historical.[13]

Given his status as a Sanhedrist—all of whom, Mark reports, voted to condemn Jesus—, Joseph is the last person one would expect to care properly for Jesus. Moreover, his association with Arimathea, an obscure town with no theological or historical significance, further lends historical credibility to the figure of Joseph. In a sense, this third line of evidence for the burial is an example of the application of the criterion of dissimilarity. For given the hostility in the early Church toward the Jewish leaders, who had, in Christian eyes, engineered a judicial murder of Jesus, the figure of Joseph is startlingly dissimilar to the prevailing attitude in the Church toward the Sanhedrin. Therefore, Joseph is unlikely to have been a fictional creation of the early Church.

The fourth line of evidence concerns the lack of any traces of legendary development in the burial story as transmitted by Mark. The burial narrative is this-worldly, perfunctory, and lacking in theological reflection. The stark simplicity of the Markan account is in contrast with what one might expect to find in late, legendary accounts (such as in the Gospel of Peter). Given the early age of the pre-Markan passion story, it is implausible to see Mark's account as an unhistorical legend, nor does it evince any signs of being such.

Finally, the fifth supporting line of evidence for the burial account is that no other competing burial story exists. If the Markan account is at its core a legendary fiction, then it is odd that we find no trace of alternative, competing legendary accounts, not to speak of traces of what really happened to the corpse. One

---

[13] Raymond E. Brown, *The Death of the Messiah,* 2 vols. (Garden City, N. Y.: Doubleday, 1994), 2: 1240-1241.

might profitably contrast here the competing myths/legends about what happened to the bodies of such pagan figures as Osiris and Empedocles. In the absence of any check by historical facts, alternative legendary accounts can arise simultaneously and independently. If the burial narrative is purely legendary, why is there no competing account of Jesus's burial, say, by some faithful disciple(s) of Jesus or by his family or by Romans at the direction of a sympathetic Pilate? Whence the unanimity of the tradition in the absence of a historical core? Feeling the force of this question, Lüdemann thinks to discern a separate tradition of burial by the Jews in Jn. 19:31-37; Acts 13:29.[14] But as Broer points out, these cannot be the same because in the one Romans are asked to dispatch the bodies and in the others the Jews are said to have done so.[15] More fundamentally, the ascription in Acts of the burial to the Jews is part of a wider tendency by Luke to polemicize against the Jewish authorities and which leads him to ascribe even Jesus's *crucifixion* to the Jews (Acts 2:23; 2:36; 4:10)![16]

Together these mutually reinforcing lines of evidence provide a strong *prima facie* case for accepting the historicity of Jesus's burial by Joseph of Arimathea in the tomb. For these and other reasons, the majority of New Testament critics concur with the late John A. T. Robinson that the honorable burial of Jesus is "one of the earliest and best-attested facts about Jesus."[17]

Notice that anti-miraculous historiographical principles do not even come into play in assessing the historicity of the burial account, for it is as down to earth as the crucifixion account. Any historian *qua* historian can ask the question, "What was done with Jesus's corpse?" just as straightforwardly as he can ask, "How did Jesus of Nazareth die?" If, then, Lüdemann will deny the force of the cumulative evidence for Jesus's honorable burial, he needs to have at least equally compelling evidence to the contrary.

---

[14] Lüdemann, "Zwischen Karfreitag und Ostern," p. 22.

[15] Ingo Broer, "Die Glaube an die Auferstehung Jesu und das geschichtliche Verständnis des Glaubens in der Neuzeit," in *Osterglaube ohne Auferstehung?*, p. 61. Broer observes that only a few scholars would support Lüdemann's interpretation of these passages as indicative of distinct burial traditions.

[16] See S. G. Wilson, "The Jews and the Death of Jesus in Acts," in *Anti-Judaism in Early Christianity*, vol. 1: *Paul and the Gospels*, ed. Peter Richardson, Studies in Christianity and Judaism 2 (Waterloo, Ontario: Wilfrid Laurier Press, 1986), p. 157; cf. Lloyd Gaston, "Anti-Judaism and the Passion Narrative in Luke and Acts," in *Anti-Judaism in Early Christianity*, vol. 1: *Paul and the Gospels*, p. 129.

[17] John A. T. Robinson, *The Human Face of God* (Philadelphia: Westminster, 1973), p. 131.

In response to this evidence, Lüdemann admits that it would be "going too far" to deny that Joseph of Arimathea is historical,[18] but, he says, "We can no longer know where Joseph (or Jews unknown to us) put the body."[19] His main reason for denying Joseph's laying Jesus in the tomb is that the later gospels tend to exalt Joseph, calling him "a good and just man" (Lk. 23:50) or even "a disciple" (Jn. 19:38). But even if the later gospel writers exhibit this tendency, that does not seem to be a good reason for denying the historical fact reported in the pre-Markan source of Joseph's interment of Jesus in the tomb. Indeed, if anything, it serves principally to underscore point (4) above, the primitiveness of the pre-Markan account. In fact, if Lüdemann is willing to grant Joseph's historicity, then how can we deny his role in the burial, since the principal proof of his historicity is precisely that a fictional burial account would not link Jesus's honorable burial with a Sanhedrist? It is precisely his link with Jesus's burial that makes Joseph's historicity plausible. Thus, the tendency of later gospel writers to exaggerate Joseph's devotion to Jesus has not led most scholars to deny the fundamental reliability of the burial story.

The Empty Tomb

Fact #2: *On the Sunday following the crucifixion Jesus's tomb was found empty by a group of his women followers.* Among the reasons which have led most scholars to this conclusion are the following:

1. The empty tomb story is part of the very old source material used by Mark.
2. The old tradition cited by Paul in I Corinthians implies the fact of the empty tomb.
3. The story is simple and lacks signs of legendary embellishment.
4. The fact that women's testimony was worthless in first century Palestine counts in favor of the women's role in discovering the empty tomb.
5. The earliest Jewish allegation that the disciples had stolen Jesus's body shows that the body was in fact missing from the tomb.

The first supporting line of evidence refers once more to the pre-Markan passion narrative and claims that the empty tomb account was included in that narra-

---

[18] Lüdemann, *Resurrection of Jesus*, p. 207.
[19] Ibid., p. 45.

tive. This precludes the story's being a late-developing legend. Lüdemann, however, lists four reasons why Mark 16:1-8 is in his opinion "worthless" as an argument for the historicity of the empty tomb.[20] (1) Such an argument assumes that the burial site was known, which is seriously in doubt. (2) The argument assumes contrary to v. 8 that the women did say something. (3) The passage, does not, strictly speaking, tell of the discovery of the empty tomb but rather proclaims the resurrection at the empty tomb. And (4) How will one avoid Kirsopp Lake's inference that the women went to the wrong tomb? These objections are not so weighty as Lüdemann seems to think. First, we have seen good reason to accept the historicity of Jesus's honorable burial by Joseph of Arimathea, so that unless Lüdemann can provide some reason for assessing negatively the women's presence at the crucifixion and burial—which he has not, to my knowledge, done—there is no reason to think that the women could not have come to the burial site on Sunday morning. The women's silence and terror reflect a Markan motif of stunned human reaction to the presence of the divine[21] and is not intended in any case to be taken as an enduring silence; otherwise Mark would have no story to tell! Lüdemann's third objection makes a fatuous distinction, since proclamation of Jesus's resurrection at his empty tomb entails an empty tomb. The angel's proclamation actually draws attention to the emptiness of the tomb: "He is risen; he is not here! Behold—the place where they laid him!" (Mk. 16:6) As for Lake's theory, one of the reasons it generated almost no following is that it succumbs to the obvious objection that the Jewish authorities would have been only too glad to point out the women's mistake once the disciples began to preach the resurrection. So it is difficult to see how on the basis of such misgivings Lüdemann's verdict can be justified that the empty tomb narrative in Mark is historically worthless.

With respect to the second supporting line of evidence, Lüdemann hopes to avert the implication of the empty tomb by denying that the burial is an autonomous event.[22] But the Greek text belies this claim. For each line is prefixed by a

---

[20] Gerd Lüdemann, "Die Auferstehung Jesu," in *Fand die Auferstehung wirklich statt?*, ed. Alexander Bommarius (Düsseldorf: Parega Verlag, 1995), p. 21.
[21] See Edward Lynn Bode, *The First Easter Morning*, Analecta Biblica 45 (Rome: Biblical Institute Press, 1970), pp. 37-39.
[22] Lüdemann, "Die Auferstehung Jesu," pp. 18-19; idem, "Zwischen Karfreitag und Ostern," p. 22. He also suggests, inconsistently it seems, that the four-fold ὅτι is indicative of disparate traditions.

grammatically unnecessary ὅτι which serves to distinguish and order serially the separate events. It is fanciful to think that either the ex-Pharisee Paul or the early Jerusalem fellowship from which the formula sprang could have asserted that Christ "was buried and he was raised" and yet think that his corpse still lay in the tomb.[23] Moreover, a comparison once more of the four-line formula with the Gospel narratives on the one hand and the sermons in Acts on the other reveals that the third line is a summary of the empty tomb narrative, the "he has been raised" mirroring the "he is risen!"

The third supporting line of evidence has reference once more to the Markan empty tomb narrative. Like the burial account, it is remarkably straightforward and unembellished by theological or apologetic motifs likely to characterize a later legendary account. The resurrection itself is not witnessed or described, and there is no reflection on Jesus's triumph over sin and death, no use of Christological titles, no quotation of fulfilled prophecy, no description of the Risen Lord. Even if we excise the angelic figure as, say, a purely literary figure which provides the interpretation of the vacant tomb, then we have a narrative that is all the more stark and unadorned (cf. John 20:1-2). This suggests that the story is not at its core a legend. To appreciate how restrained Mark's narrative is, one has only to read the account in the Gospel of Peter, which describes Jesus's triumphant egress from the tomb, accompanied by angelic visitants, followed by a talking cross, heralded by a voice from heaven, and all witnessed by a Roman guard, the Jewish leaders, and a multitude of spectators!

The fourth supporting line of evidence is essentially an appeal to the criterion of embarrassment, again one of the important criteria of authenticity. Given the second-class status of women in first century Palestine and their inability to serve as witnesses in a Jewish court, it is amazing that they should appear here as the discoverers and chief witnesses to the fact of Jesus's empty tomb, for so unreliable a witness was an embarrassment to the Christian proclamation. Any later, legendary account would surely have made male disciples discover the empty tomb. Indeed, critics often see the story of Peter's inspection of the empty tomb

---

[23] Lüdemann, "Zwischen Karfreitag und Ostern," p. 24, cites Jub. 23:31 as evidence of a non-corporeal conception of resurrection in Judaism; but this verse, which states that the bones of the dead rest in the earth whereas their spirits are with God, is simply an expression of the dualism typical of Hellenistic Judaism and actually supports the idea that it is the bones which are the proper object of the resurrection.

(along with another disciple) as just such a legendary progression. The fact that it is women, whose testimony was worthless, rather than men who are said in the earliest narrative to be the discoverers of the empty tomb is best explained by the fact that the tradition here is reliable.[24]

Finally, we have the evidence of the earliest Jewish polemic against the resurrection, referred to in Matthew's guard story, as evidence for the empty tomb. Lüdemann grants that the Jewish polemic does show Jewish belief in the empty tomb; but he dismisses this evidence because, he asserts, the Jews came to think that the tomb was empty only through Christian tradition. We can rule out the suggestion that they knew of the empty tomb as a historical fact, he asserts, because Jesus did not have a regular burial and so no one knew what had happened to the corpse.[25] But wholly apart from the fact that we have good reasons to accept the honorable burial of Jesus, the point remains that even if the burial account were a legend and no one knew what had happened to Jesus's corpse, when the disciples began to proclaim in Jerusalem "He is risen from the dead!" (Mt. 27:64), their Jewish antagonists would not have invented for the Christians the empty tomb by saying that the body had been stolen. Lüdemann has to explain why, if no one knew where the body had been laid, the Jewish opponents of the Christians would have alleged that the body had been stolen. As for the assertion that Jews knew only of the Christian tradition of the empty tomb, this claim fails to reckon with the tradition history lying behind Matthew's story. That the story is not a Matthean creation out of whole cloth is evident by the many non-Matthean linguistic traits in the narrative.[26] Behind the story evidently lies a developing pattern of assertion and counter-assertion:

Christian: "He is risen from the dead!"

Jew: "No, his disciples stole away his body."

Christian: "The guard at the tomb would have prevented any such theft."

---

[24] Schwager reports that in contrast to the legend hypothesis it has become customary to assess positively the women's role at the crucifixion and on Easter morning (Raymund Schwager, "Die heutige Theologie and das leere Grab Jesu," *Zeitschrift für Katholische Theologie* 115 [1993]: 436).

[25] Lüdemann, *Resurrection of Jesus*, p. 124.

[26] See discussion in my "The Guard at the Tomb," *New Testament Studies* 30 (1984): 279-280.

Jew: "No, the guard fell asleep."

Christian: "The chief priests bribed the guard to say this."

This pattern probably goes right back to controversies in Jerusalem following the disciples' proclamation of the resurrection, for as John Meier observes, "The earliest fights about the person of Jesus that raged between ordinary Jews and Christian Jews after Easter centered on the Christian claims that a crucified criminal was the Messiah, that God had raised him from the dead...."[27] The non-Matthean vocabulary and evident tradition history behind the dispute makes this assumption plausible. But if Jerusalem is the fount of this on-going dispute, then the question presses why the Jewish opponents of the Christian Way, confronted with spurious claims about an empty tomb, would, instead of denouncing such a fiction, have claimed instead that the disciples had stolen the body out of a tomb which did not exist and no one could point to.

So we have a pretty strong *prima facie* case for accepting the fundamental reliability of the account of the empty tomb. Hence, in the words of Jacob Kremer, "By far most exegetes hold firmly to the reliability of the biblical statements concerning the empty tomb."[28] Lüdemann, however, regards the story as "an apologetic legend."[29] But so far as I can see, he offers no positive evidence for this assertion. Indeed, it is difficult to see how this hypothesis can be sustained, given the multiple, independent attestation enjoyed by the empty tomb narrative. Rather Lüdemann's scepticism is based upon four assumptions, each of which strikes me as very dubious. (1) He assumes that the only primary source we have for the empty tomb is Mark's gospel.[30] But this is almost certainly wrong. At least Matthew and John have independent sources about the empty tomb, it is also mentioned in the sermons in the Acts of the Apostles (2:29; 13:36), and it is implied by Paul (I Cor. 15:4). According to Klaus Berger, "The reports about the empty tomb are related by all four gospels (and other writings of early Christianity) in a

---

[27] John P. Meier, *A Marginal Jew*, 3 vols., vol. 2: *Mentor, Message, and Miracles*, Anchor Bible Reference Library (New York: Doubleday, 1994), p. 150.

[28] Jacob Kremer, *Die Osterevangelien—Geschichten um Geschichte* (Stuttgart: Katholisches Bibelwerk, 1977), pp. 49-50; cf. his more recent judgment that "most exegetes tend to ascribe to the tomb narratives a historical core, in whatever way this may be more precisely delineated (*Lexikon für Theologie und Kirche* [1993], s.v. "Auferstehung Christi I. Im Neuen Testament," by Jacob Kremer).

[29] Lüdemann, *Resurrection of Jesus*, p. 118.

[30] Lüdemann, "Auferstehung Jesu," p. 21.

form independent of one another....we have a great abundance of reports, which have been separately handed down."[31] (2) Lüdemann assumes that when Jesus was arrested, the disciples fled back to Galilee;[32] that is why women appear as the discovers of the empty tomb. But the flight of the disciples is rightly dismissed by the historian Hans von Campenhausen as a scholarly fiction.[33] Not only is there no evidence for this assumption, itself inherently implausible, but Lüdemann's *own theory* contradicts this assumption, since it is crucial for his theory that at least Peter remained in Jerusalem, where he denied Jesus. In any case, if the story of the women's discovery of the empty tomb is a pure legend, then why could we not have a purely legendary account of the discovery of the empty tomb by male disciples? (3) Lüdemann assumes that the Jewish authorities, who he takes to have disposed of Jesus's corpse, suffered a sort of collective amnesia about what they did with the body of Jesus. Even if Joseph (or the Jewish authorities) only gave Jesus a dishonorable burial, why did they not point to his burial place as the easiest answer to the disciples' proclamation of the resurrection? Lüdemann admits, "Jews showed an interest in where Jesus's corpse had been put, and of course a proclamation of Jesus as the Risen One...provoked questions about his body from opponents or unbelievers."[34] So why, when the disciples began to preach the resurrection of Jesus, did the Jewish authorities not say where they had put Jesus's body? Lüdemann's answer: they forgot![35] Again, this is less than convincing. (4) Finally, Lüdemann assumes that belief in the empty tomb arose as an inference from the belief that Jesus was risen from the dead.[36] While Lüdemann is quite right, I think, to recognize, in contrast to scholars who hold that belief in the resurrection of Jesus did not for first century Jews or Christians imply anything's happening to the corpse, still his suggestion cannot be the whole story because it leaves unexplained the inference that Jesus's corpse, contrary to custom, had been laid *in a tomb*. Belief in the resurrection would, indeed, imply that

---

[31] Klaus Berger, "Ostern fällt nicht aus! Zum Streit um das 'kritischste Buch über die Auferstehung'," *Idea Spektrum* 3 (1994): 21-22. Cf. idem, "Die Auferstehung Jesu Christi," in *Fand die Auferstehung wirklich statt?*, p. 48.
[32] Lüdemann, "Auferstehung Jesu," p. 19.
[33] Hans Freiherr von Campenhausen. *Der Ablauf der Osterereignisse und das leere Grab*, 3rd rev. ed., Sitzungsberichte der Heidelberger Akademie der Wissenschaften (Heidelberg: Carl Winter, 1966).
[34] Lüdemann, *Resurrection of Jesus*, p. 116.
[35] Lüdemann, "Zwischen Karfreitag und Ostern," p. 23.
[36] Lüdemann, *Resurrection of Jesus*, p. 121.

the corpse would no longer be around, but it would not, without further ado, lead one to infer that there was an empty tomb to show for it. Thus, Lüdemann still has not explained belief in the empty tomb.

In sum, we have good grounds for believing that Jesus's tomb was found to be empty by a group of his women followers.

The Post-Mortem Appearances

Fact #3: *On multiple occasions and under various circumstances, different individuals and groups of people experienced appearances of Jesus alive from the dead.* This is a fact which is almost universally acknowledged among New Testament scholars, for the following reasons:

1. The list of eyewitnesses to Jesus's resurrection appearances which is quoted by Paul in I Cor. 15:5-7 guarantees that such appearances occurred.
2. The appearance traditions in the gospels provide multiple, independent attestation of such appearances.

With respect to the first supporting line of evidence, it is universally accepted on the basis of the early date of Paul's tradition as well as the apostle's personal acquaintance with many of the people listed that the disciples did experience post-mortem appearances of Christ. Among the witnesses of the resurrection appearances were Peter, the immediate circle of the disciples known as "the Twelve," a gathering of 500 Christian believers (many of whom Paul evidently knew, since he was aware that some had died by the time of his writing), Jesus's younger brother James, and a wider group of apostles. "Finally," says Paul, "as to one untimely born, he appeared also to me" (I Cor. 15:8).

The second supporting line of evidence appeals again to the criterion of multiple attestation. The Gospels independently attest to post-mortem appearances of Jesus, even to some of the same appearances found in Paul's list. Wolfgang Trilling explains,

> From the list in I Cor. 15 the particular reports of the Gospels are now to be interpreted. Here may be of help what we said about Jesus's miracles. It is impossible to 'prove' historically a particular miracle. But the totality of the miracle reports permits no reasonable doubt that Jesus in fact performed 'miracles.' That holds analogously for the appearance reports. It is not possible to secure historically the particular event. But the totality of the

appearance reports permits no reasonable doubt that Jesus in fact bore witness to himself in such a way.[37]

The appearance to Peter is independently attested by Paul and Luke (I Cor. 15:5; Lk. 24:34), the appearance to the Twelve by Paul, Luke, and John (I Cor. 15:5; Lk. 24:36-43; Jn. 20:19-20), the appearance to the women disciples by Matthew and John (Mt. 28:9-10; Jn. 20:11-17), and appearances to the disciples in Galilee by Mark, Matthew, and John (Mk. 16:7; Mt. 28:16-17; Jn. 21). Taken sequentially, the appearances follow the pattern of Jerusalem—Galilee—Jerusalem, matching the festival pilgrimages of the disciples as they returned to Galilee following the Passover/Feast of Unleavened Bread and traveled again to Jerusalem two months later for Pentecost.

Lüdemann himself concludes, "It may be taken as historically certain that Peter and the disciples had experiences after Jesus's death in which Jesus appeared to them as the risen Christ."[38] Thus, we are in basic agreement that following Jesus's crucifixion various individuals and groups of people experienced appearances of Christ alive from the dead. The real bone of contention will be how these experiences are best to be explained.

Origin of the Christian Way

Fact #4: *The original disciples believed that Jesus was risen from the dead despite almost every predisposition to the contrary.* Three aspects of the disciples' disposition following Jesus's crucifixion put a question mark behind the faith and hope they had placed in Jesus:

1. Jesus was dead, and Jews had no anticipation of a dying, much less rising, Messiah.

2. According to Jewish law, Jesus's execution as a criminal showed him out to be a heretic, a man literally under the curse of God.

3. Jewish beliefs about the afterlife precluded anyone's rising from the dead before the general, eschatological resurrection of the dead.

---

[37] Wolfgang Trilling, *Fragen zur Geschichtlichkeit Jesu* (Düsseldorf: Patmos Verlag, 1966), p. 153. With respect to Jesus's miracles, Trilling had written: "We are convinced and hold it for historically certain that Jesus did in fact perform miracles.... The miracle reports occupy so much space in the Gospels that it is impossible that they could all have been subsequently invented or transferred to Jesus" (Ibid., p. 153). The fact that miracle-working belongs to the historical Jesus is no longer disputed.
[38] Lüdemann, *What Really Happened?*, p. 80.

It is important to appreciate, with respect to the first aspect of their situation, that in Jewish expectation Messiah would conquer Israel's enemies and restore the throne of David, not be shamefully executed by them. Jesus's ignominious execution at the hands of Rome was as decisive a disproof as anything could be to a first century Jew that Jesus was not Israel's awaited Messiah, but another failed pretender. Failed Messianic movements were nothing new in Judaism, and they left their followers with basically two alternatives: either go home or else find a new Messiah. These were no doubt hard choices, but nevertheless they were the choices one had. After surveying such failed Messianic movements before and after Jesus, N. T. Wright remarks,

> So far as we know, all the followers of these first-century Messianic movements were fanatically committed to the cause. They, if anybody, might be expected to suffer from this blessed twentieth century disease called 'cognitive dissonance' when their expectations failed to materialize. But in no case, right across the century before Jesus and the century after him, do we hear of any Jewish group saying that their executed leader had been raised from the dead and he really was the Messiah after all.[39]

Wright raises the interesting question, if the disciples did not want simply to go home, then why did they not pick someone else, like James, to be the Messiah? As Jesus's younger brother, he would have been the natural choice. But although James eventually did emerge as the most powerful leader in the Jerusalem church, he was never called the Messiah. When Josephus refers to him, he calls him merely "the brother of the so-called Messiah" (*Antiquities of the Jews* 20.200). Based on the typical experience of failed Messianic movements, it is to be expected that the disciples should have either gone home or fastened upon someone else—but we know that they did not, which needs explaining.

As for the second point, Old Testament law dictated that anyone executed by hanging on a tree was under God's curse (Deut. 21:23), and Jews applied this verdict to those executed by crucifixion as well. Thus, seen through the eyes of a first century Jewish follower of Jesus, the crucifixion meant much more than the death of one's beloved Master, akin to the death of Socrates. Rather it was a catastrophe; for it meant that far from being God's Anointed, Jesus of Nazareth had actually been accursed by God. The disciples had been following a man whom God had rejected in the most unequivocal terms.

---

[39] N. T. Wright, video-taped lecture presented at Asbury Theological Seminary, November, 1999.

APPENDIX C

Finally, Jewish hope in the resurrection of the dead was invariably a corporate and eschatological hope. The resurrection of all the righteous dead would take place after God had brought the world as we know it to an end. Surveying the Jewish literature, Joachim Jeremias concluded,

> Ancient Judaism did not know of an anticipated resurrection as an event of history. Nowhere does one find in the literature anything comparable to the resurrection of Jesus. Certainly resurrections of the dead were known, but these always concerned resuscitations, the return to the earthly life. In no place in the later Judaic literature does it concern a resurrection to δόξα as an event of history.[40]

Even if the disciples' faith in Jesus had somehow managed to survive the crucifixion, they would at most have looked forward to their reunion with him at the final resurrection and would perhaps have preserved his tomb as a shrine, where Jesus's bones might rest until the eschatological resurrection. That was the Jewish hope.

But we know that that did not happen. Despite their having most every predisposition to the contrary, it is an indisputable fact that the earliest disciples suddenly and sincerely came to believe that God had raised Jesus of Nazareth from the dead. Lüdemann himself declares that historical analysis leads to the "abrupt origination of the Easter faith of the disciples."[41] Any responsible historian wanting to give an account of the origins of Christianity must explain the origin of this belief on the part of those who had known and followed Jesus. Most everyone will agree with Luke Johnson when he writes, "Some sort of powerful transformative experience is required to generate the sort of movement earliest Christianity was and the sort of literature the New Testament is."[42] The question is: how do we best explain that experience—by the resurrection of Jesus or by hallucinations on the part of the disciples?

In summary, then, there are four facts which any adequate historical hypothesis concerning Jesus's fate must account for: his honorable burial, the discovery of his empty tomb, his post-mortem appearances, and the origin of the disciples' belief in his resurrection.

---

[40] Joachim Jeremias, "Die älteste Schicht der Osterüberlieferungen," in *Resurrexit*, ed. Édouard Dhanis (Rome: Libreria Editrice Vaticana, 1974), p. 194.
[41] Lüdemann, "Zwischen Karfreitag und Ostern," p. 27.
[42] Luke Timothy Johnson, *The Real Jesus* (San Francisco: Harper San Francisco, 1996), p. 136.

The Best Explanation

What hypothesis best explains the historical data concerning the fate of Jesus? In his book *Justifying Historical Descriptions*, historian C. B. McCullagh lists six criteria which historians use in testing historical descriptions: *explanatory scope, explanatory power, plausibility,* ad hoc-*ness, accord with accepted beliefs,* and *superiority to rival hypotheses.*[43] Now we have before us two competing hypotheses, which I shall call the Resurrection Hypothesis and the Hallucination Hypothesis respectively.[44]

The Hallucination Hypothesis

According to Lüdemann, Peter, having denied Christ, was so consumed with guilt that he found psychological release in projecting a vision of Jesus, which led him to believe that Jesus was risen from the dead.

> Under the impression of Jesus's proclamation and death, there finally awoke in Peter the 'And yet...' of faith. Thereby the crucified Jesus showed himself to be the living Jesus, so that Peter could once again apply to himself—and this time with profound clarity— God's word of forgiveness present in Jesus's work.[45]

Peter's experience was infectious in the early Christian community, and soon others, too, who did not share Peter's trauma, also saw hallucinations of the Risen Lord. When Jewish opponents objected and asked where the body was, "it could immediately be reported that the women had found the tomb empty and later that Jesus had even appeared to the women at the tomb."[46] Much later, the legend of the discovery of Jesus's empty tomb arose. Meanwhile, Saul of Tarsus struggled

---

[43] C. Behan McCullagh, *Justifying Historical Descriptions* (Cambridge: Cambridge University Press, 1984), p. 19.

[44] I am not using the word "hallucination" pejoratively; rather a hallucination is a non-veridical vision. It is an appearance to its percipient which has no extra-mental correlate and is a projection of the percipient's own brain. It is therefore purely subjective and corresponds to no reality. That is what Lüdemann takes the resurrection appearances to be. A vision, he explains, is the visual appearing of persons, things, or scenes which have no external reality (Lüdemann, "Auferstehung Jesu," p. 22). He says that visions and hallucinations belong to the same realm, viz., "what we ourselves bring forth, what ultimately has no basis in objective reality" (Ibid., p. 23). They are the product of "imagination and fantasy" (idem, "Zwischen Karfreitag und Ostern," p. 28). I suspect that any preference on Lüdemann's part for the terminology of "visions" rather than "hallucinations" merely reflects a desire to make the hypothesis more palatable to religious sensibility. For a subjective vision just is a hallucination; if not, then some explanation is owed us of what the difference is between a subjective vision and a hallucination.

[45] Lüdemann, "Auferstehung Jesu," p. 25.

[46] Lüdemann, *Resurrection of Jesus*, pp. 174-175.

inwardly with guilt as he labored under the yoke of the Law, and his zeal in persecuting Christians was a manifestation of a secret inner attraction to the Christian message. According to Lüdemann, "...if one had been able to analyze Paul prior to his Damascus vision, the analysis would probably have shown a strong inclination to Christ in his subconscious; indeed, the assumption that he was unconsciously Christian is then no longer so far-fetched."[47] On the Damascus road the pent-up struggle erupted in a hallucination of Jesus, resulting in Paul's wholesale conversion to the faith he once persecuted. "The guilt complex which had arisen with the persecution was resolved through the certainty of being in Christ."[48]

Let us examine how this hypothesis fares as an explanation of the facts when assessed by McCullagh's six criteria.

Criterion 1: *Explanatory Scope*. This is the central failing of the Hallucination Hypothesis. Offered only as a way of explaining the post-mortem appearances of Jesus, its explanatory scope is too narrow because it offers nothing by way of explanation of the empty tomb. In order to explain the empty tomb, one must conjoin some independent hypothesis to the Hallucination Hypothesis. Now, of course, Lüdemann denies the fact of the empty tomb. But that is a matter of establishing one's inductive data base, and we saw in our discussion there that Lüdemann's handling of the evidence for the burial and empty tomb was less than convincing. In a sense, his denial of the burial and empty tomb of Jesus is born out of necessity; for once we admit these facts, then the inadequate explanatory scope of the Hallucination Hypothesis becomes patent, and the theory is in deep trouble. For that reason Lüdemann finds himself in the awkward position of denying so banal a fact as Jesus's honorable burial, recognized by most scholars as historical.

Criterion 2: *Explanatory Power*. Here we grant for the sake of argument that Peter did experience a hallucination of Jesus after his death due to the psychological factors postulated by Lüdemann. The question then becomes whether this explanation has sufficient power to account for the post-mortem appearances and the origin of the disciples' belief in Jesus's resurrection. There two reasons to think that these facts are not well-explained by the Hallucination Hypothesis.

---

[47] Ibid., p. 26.
[48] Ibid., pp. 26-27.

First, with respect to the appearances, the *diversity of the appearances* is not well-explained by means of such visions. The appearances were experienced many different times, by different individuals, by groups, at various locales and under various circumstances, and by not only believers, but also by unbelievers like James the brother of Jesus and the Pharisee Saul of Tarsus.

This diversity is very difficult to explain by recourse to hallucinations. For hallucinations require a special psychological state on the part of the percipient. But since a guilt complex *ex hypothesi* obtained only for Peter and Paul, the diversity of the post-mortem appearances must be explained as a sort of contagion, a chain reaction. But Lüdemann is unable to provide any example of this.[49] It is important to keep in mind that it is the diversity that is at issue here, not merely individual incidents. Even if one could compile from the casebooks an amalgam consisting of stories of hallucinations over a period of time (like the visions in Medjugorje), mass hallucinations (as at Lourdes), hallucinations to various individuals, and so forth, the fact remains that there is no single instance in the casebooks exhibiting the diversity involved in the post-mortem appearances of Jesus. It is only by compiling unrelated cases that anything analogous might be constructed.

One might mention three specific cases which are not well-explained by the Hallucination Hypothesis:

---

[49] But see Michael Goulder, "The Baseless Fabric of a Vision," in *Resurrection Reconsidered*, ed. G. D'Costa (Oxford: One World, 1996), pp. 48-61, who catalogues a number of interesting cases of mass delusions in order to explain how Peter's hallucinatory experience could have been multiplied in a series of secondary visions. But it is a striking feature of Goulder's catalogue that *none* of his cases of collective behavior, such as sightings of Big Foot or of UFO's, is an instance of hallucinations or subjective visions at all. No one attempts to explain Big Foot sightings by saying that people were having subjective visions of Big Foot. Rather they saw a dark form moving in the distant bushes or found large footprints in the snow or mud or in other cases simply concocted a story. Or again, UFO sightings turn out for the most part to be weather balloons, ball lightning, optical illusions, or lies, not hallucinations. Hallucinations require a very special psycho-biological preparation and are usually associated with mental illness or substance abuse. The sorts of collective behavior to which Goulder appeals are not hallucinatory experiences. But in the case of the post-mortem appearances of Jesus it is universally acknowledged that the disciples did see appearances of the Risen Lord. To be sure, there may well have also been in the early church false claims to an appearance of the Lord analogous to the mass behavior described by Goulder; but no one thinks that the Twelve, for example, had merely mistaken a distant shape for Christ or concocted the story of his appearance and then were prepared to go to tortuous deaths in attestation to its truth. Thus, the resurrection appearances remain unparalleled by Goulder's cases.

- *James*: Jesus's brother did not believe that his elder sibling was the Messiah or even anybody special during his lifetime (Mk. 3:21, 31-35; 6:3; Jn. 7:1-10). But unexpectedly we find Jesus's brothers among those gathered in the upper room in Christian worship following the resurrection appearances (Acts 1:14), and in time James emerges as a leader in the Jerusalem church (Acts 12:17; Gal. 1:19). We learn from Josephus that James was eventually martyred for his faith in Jesus Christ during a lapse in the civil government in the mid-60s. This remarkable transformation is in all probability due to the fact, recorded by Paul, that "then he appeared to James" (I Cor. 15:7). Lüdemann himself goes so far as to say that it is "certain" that James experienced a resurrection appearance of Jesus,[50] but he is strangely mute when it comes to explaining how his theory accounts for that experience. The Hallucination Hypothesis has weak explanatory power with respect to this appearance, since James, as an unbeliever and no part of the Christian community, was unlikely to experience a "secondary vision" of the Risen Jesus.

- *The 500 brethren*: Most of these people were still alive in AD 55 when Paul wrote I Corinthians and could be questioned about the experience. Lüdemann explains this appearance as a legendary reference to the event of Pentecost, which he represents as an experience of "mass ecstasy."[51] But such an explanation is weak, not only because the eyewitnesses were still around, but because the event of Pentecost was fundamentally different from a resurrection appearance. As Hans Kessler in his critique of Lüdemann's suggestion writes,

> Equating this appearance with the event of Pentecost is more than questionable, especially since in Acts 2.1-13 all the characteristics of an Easter narrative are missing (above all the appearing of Christ), and, conversely, in the early Easter texts the Spirit plays no role.[52]

It would be highly implausible that an event like Pentecost (which is presumably supposed to have been more or less accurately preserved in Christian tradition as found in Acts 2) to have evolved into a resurrection

---

[50] Gerd Lüdemann, *Resurrection of Jesus*, p. 109.
[51] Ibid., p. 107.
[52] Hans Kessler, *Sucht den Lebenden nicht bei den Toten*, new ed. (Würzburg: Echter, 1995), p. 425.

appearance, given that the event had none of the basic elements of an appearance, especially Christ's appearing! And again, the point deserves underlining that while collective hallucinations do rarely occur, it is the diversity of all these different sorts of appearances that taxes the explanatory strength of the Hallucination Hypothesis.

- *The women*: That women were the first recipients of a post-mortem appearance of Jesus is both multiply attested and established by the criterion of embarrassment. For this reason, as Kremer reports, there is an increasing tendency in recent research to regard this appearance as "anchored in history."[53] Lüdemann himself calls it "historically certain"—though his theory forces him gratuitously to deny its primacy.[54] Nowhere in the New Testament, however, not even in I Cor. 15:5, is it said that Peter was the first to see a resurrection appearance of Christ, despite the widespread assumption of his chronological priority. Rather the women have priority. They are doubtless omitted from the list in I Cor. 15:5-7 because naming them as witnesses would have been worse than worthless in a patriarchal culture. But this is fatal to Lüdemann's hypothesis, since then the women's experience cannot be regarded as a "secondary vision" prompted by Peter's experience. Since they did not share Peter's guilt, having remained singularly faithful to Jesus to the end, they lacked the special psychological conditions leading to hallucinations of Jesus. Thus, Lüdemann's hypothesis has no explanatory power with respect to this appearance.

In sum, the Hallucination Hypothesis does not have strong explanatory power with respect to the diversity of the resurrection appearances.

Secondly, the Hallucination Hypothesis has weak explanatory power with respect to *the origin of the disciples' belief* in Jesus's resurrection. Subjective visions, or hallucinations, have no extra-mental correlate but are projections of the percipient's own brain. So if, as an eruption of a guilty conscience, Paul or Peter were to have projected visions of Jesus alive, they would have envisioned him in Paradise, where the righteous dead awaited the eschatological resurrection. But

---

[53] *Lexikon für Theologie and Kirche* (1993), s.v. "Auferstehung Christi I. Im Neuen Testament," by Jacob Kremer.
[54] Lüdemann, *What Really Happened to Jesus?*, p. 66.

such exalted visions of Christ leave unexplained their belief in his resurrection. The inference "He is risen from the dead," so natural to our ears, would have been wholly unnatural to a first century Jew. In Jewish thinking there was already a category perfectly suited to describe Peter's postulated experience: Jesus had been assumed into heaven. An assumption is a wholly different category from a resurrection. To infer from heavenly visions of Jesus that he had been resurrected ran counter to Jewish thinking in two fundamental respects, *viz.*, its individuality and historical embeddedness, whereas Jesus's assumption into heaven would have been the natural conclusion. So far as I know, Lüdemann nowhere addresses the question of why hallucinations, had they occurred, would have led to the conclusion that Jesus had been raised from the dead.

Thus, the hallucination theory has weak explanatory power both in that it cannot account for the diversity of the appearances and in that it cannot account for the origin of the disciples' belief in Jesus's resurrection.

Criterion 3: *Plausibility.* There are at least two respects in which Lüdemann's Hallucination Hypothesis is implausible.

First, there is little plausibility in Lüdemann's psychoanalysis of Peter and Paul. Here two points may be made:

(a) There are *insufficient data* to do a psychoanalysis of Peter and Paul. All we have from Paul is a few autobiographical passages in his letters, and the information about Peter's psyche is, by Lüdemann's own admission, "incomparably worse."[55] We do not have in the New Testament any narrative at all of Peter's experience of seeing Jesus, but merely a pair of epigrammatic references: "then he appeared to Cephas" (I Cor. 15:5); "The Lord is risen, indeed, and has appeared to Simon" (Lk. 24:34). Lüdemann's whole theory is based on imaginative conjectures about Peter's psychological state, of which we know almost nothing. Psychoanalysis is notoriously difficult even with a patient seated in front of oneself on the couch, but it is virtually impossible with historical figures. That is why the genre of psycho-biography is rejected by historians. Martin Hengel rightly concludes, "Lüdemann...does not recognize these limits on the historian. Here he gets into the realm of psychological explanations, for which no verification is

---

[55] Lüdemann, *Resurrection of Jesus*, p. 89.

really possible.... the sources are far too limited for such psychologizing analyses."[56]

(b) The evidence we do have suggests that *Lüdemann's psychoanalysis of Peter and Paul is mistaken.* In the first place, Lüdemann's imaginative reconstruction of Peter's emotional state following his denials and Jesus's crucifixion fails to diagnose correctly the true problem Peter faced. It was not so much that he had failed his Lord as that his Lord had failed him! Lüdemann thus fails to enter into the mindset of a first century Jew who had been following a failed Messianic pretender. As Grass has emphasized in his trenchant critique of the subjective vision hypothesis, one of the greatest weaknesses of that theory is that it cannot really take seriously what a catastrophe the crucifixion was for the disciples' faith in Jesus.[57] Ignoring the disaster of the cross, Lüdemann imagines without a shred of evidence a self-preoccupied Peter wrestling with his own guilt and shame rather than struggling with dashed Messianic expectations. And lest it be said that such shattered expectations led to Peter's hallucinating Jesus alive from the dead, let me simply remind us that no such hope existed in Israel, either with respect to the Messiah or to the final resurrection. Linking these concepts is the result, not the cause, of the disciples' experience.

As for Paul, the evidence that we have indicates that Paul did not struggle with a guilt complex under the Jewish law. Nearly forty years ago, Krister Stendahl pointed out that Western readers have the tendency to interpret Paul in light of Martin Luther's struggles with guilt and sin. But Paul the Pharisee experienced no such struggles. Stendahl writes,

> Contrast Paul, a very happy and successful Jew, one who can...say..., 'As to the righteousness under the law, (I was) blameless' (Philip. 3:6). That *is* what he says. He experiences no troubles, no problems, no qualms of conscience. He is a star pupil, the student to get the thousand dollar graduate scholarship in Gamaliel's Seminary.... Nowhere in Paul's writings is there any indication...that psychologically Paul had some problem of conscience....[58]

---

[56] Martin Hengel and Anna Maria Schwemer, *Paul between Damascus and Antioch*, trans. John Bowden (Louisville: Westminster/John Knox Press, 1997), p. 342; cf. pp. 40-41. See also Martin Hengel, *The Pre-Christian Paul*, in collaboration with Roland Deines (London: SCM, 1991), p. 79.
[57] Grass, *Ostergeschehen und Osterberichte*, pp. 233-243.
[58] Krister Stendahl, "Paul among Jews and Gentiles," in *Paul among Jews and Gentiles* (Philadelphia: Fortress, 1976), pp. 12-13; cf. idem, "The Apostle Paul and the Introspective Conscience of the West," in *Paul among Jews and Gentiles*, p. 80.

Lüdemann claims that in Rom. 7:7-25 Paul's guilt-ridden, pre-Christian experience under the Law is disclosed to us.[59] But here it has to be said that the autobiographical interpretation of Rom. 7:7-25 in terms of Paul's pre-Christian versus Christian experience is overwhelmingly rejected by contemporary Pauline interpreters and commentators.[60] Paul's use of the first person singular pronoun and past tense verbs are not indicators of autobiographical reflection; rather the "I" is the representative self assumed by Paul (cf. Rom. 3:7; I Cor. 6:15; 10:29-30; 13:1-3; Gal. 2:18-19), and the past tense verbs link his disquisition with the aforedescribed history of sin in the world (Rom. 5:12-14). To postulate a pre- and post-conversion divide is to create a false dichotomy in this chapter, for the switch to the present tense in v. 14 is not accompanied by a change in the attitude of the speaker (cf. v. 25). Therefore, in Kessler's words, "almost all expositors" of Rom. 7 since the late 1920s have abandoned the autobiographical interpretation adopted by Lüdemann.[61] When we turn to genuinely autobiographical passages in Paul's letters on his pre-Christian experience (Phil. 3:4-14), then, as I say, we find a quite different picture.

Lüdemann's procedure at this point is classic. In response to the objection that Paul's own testimony indicates that he was satisfied as a Jew and felt no conflict with guilt, Lüdemann rejoins that Paul's conflict was *unconscious*.[62] This typical Freudian move renders Lüdemann's psychoanalysis non-falsifiable, since any evidence against it is just re-interpreted in terms of the theory itself. The hypothesis thereby reveals itself to be sterile.

Thus, both for its want of data as well as for its misconstrual of Peter and Paul's experience, Lüdemann's attempt at psycho-biography has little plausibility.

Second, there is also little plausibility in Lüdemann's claim that the resurrection appearances were merely visionary experiences. Again, two points may be made:

(a) Lüdemann's claim rests on the implausible presupposition that *Paul's experience on the Damascus road is paradigmatic for all the other post-mortem appearances*. Lüdemann admits that his construal of the post-mortem appearances as hallucinatory visions depends on the presupposition that what Paul experienced on

---

[59] Lüdemann, *Resurrection of Jesus*, p. 80.
[60] Lüdemann himself observes that this interpretation is "given up almost everywhere" (Ibid.).
[61] Kessler, *Sucht den Lebenden*, p. 423.
[62] Lüdemann, "Zwischen Karfreitag und Ostern," p. 39.

the Damascus road was the *same* as what the all the other disciples experienced.[63] Lüdemann's hypothesis is thus like a pyramid balancing on its point, for if this presupposition is false, there is no reason to think that the disciples' experiences were visionary, and the whole theory topples. But there is no warrant for that presupposition. John Dominic Crossan correctly observes,

> Paul needs in I Cor. 15 to equate his own experience with that of the preceding apostles. To equate, that is, its *validity* and *legitimacy*, but not necessarily its mode or manner. Jesus was revealed to all of them, but Paul's own entranced revelation should not be presumed to be the model for all others.[64]

Surprisingly, Lüdemann himself concedes that Paul in I Cor. 15 is "not concerned to give a precise account of...*what* his resurrection appearances were like.... The only important thing for Paul...was *that* they had taken place."[65] But once we recognize that Paul's concern in I Cor. 15:3-8 is with the fact of Christ's appearance, not with its mode, and realize Paul's strong motivation in his historical context for adding his name to the list of witnesses, then no reason at all remains to think that Paul's testimony implies that all the post-mortem appearances were like Paul's post-ascension encounter. But once that presupposition is gone, there is simply no reason to reduce all these experiences to visionary ones.

(b) The New Testament consistently differentiates between a vision of Christ and a resurrection appearance of Christ. Paul was familiar with "visions and revelations of the Lord" (I Cor. 12:1). Yet Paul, like the rest of the New Testament, did not equate such visions of Christ with resurrection appearances. The appearances were to a limited circle of witnesses at the birth of the Christian movement and soon ceased, Paul's untimely experience being "last of all" (I Cor. 15:8). Yet visions of the exalted Lord continued to be experienced throughout the Church. The question then presses: what essential difference exists between a vision of Christ and a resurrection appearance of Christ? The answer of the New Testament seems clear: a resurrection appearance was an extra-mental event, whereas a vision was merely in the mind of the percipient. To say that some phenomenon was visionary is not to say that it was illusory. Biblical scholars have found it

---

[63] Lüdemann, *Resurrection of Jesus*, p. 30: "Anyone who does not share the presupposition made here will not be able to make anything of what follows."
[64] John Dominic Crossan, *Jesus: A Revolutionary Biography* (San Francisco: Harper SanFrancisco, 1994), p. 169.
[65] Lüdemann, *What Really Happened?*, p. 10.

necessary to distinguish between what are sometimes called "objective visions" and "subjective visions." An objective, or, less misleadingly, veridical vision is a vision caused by God. A subjective or non-veridical vision is a product of the percipient's imagination. A veridical version involves the seeing of an objective reality without the normal processes of sense perception. A non-veridical vision has no extra-mental correlate and is therefore hallucinatory. Now visions of the exalted Christ such as Stephen's (Acts 7:55-56), Paul's (Acts 22:17-21), or John's (Rev. 1:10-18) were not regarded as hallucinatory; but neither did they count as resurrection appearances of Christ. Why not?—because appearances of Jesus, in contrast to veridical visions of Jesus, involved an extra-mental reality which anyone present could experience. Even Paul's experience on the Damascus road, which was semi-visionary in nature, could count as a real appearance because the light and the voice were experienced by Paul's traveling companions (though they were not experienced by them as a revelation of Christ). As I say, this seems to be the consistent answer throughout the New Testament to the question of what the difference was between a vision and an appearance of Jesus. And this answer is thoroughly Jewish in character: the rabbis similarly distinguished between an angelic vision and an angelic appearance based on whether, for example, food seen to be consumed by the angel was actually gone after the appearance had ceased.

Now if this is correct, it is devastating for the claim that the post-mortem appearances of Christ were visionary experiences. For then the distinction running throughout the New Testament between a vision of Christ and a resurrection appearance of Christ becomes inexplicable. Lüdemann admits that most exegetes recognize this distinction, but since he finds himself at a loss to explain it, he simply has to deny it.

Thus, Lüdemann's claim that the resurrection appearances of Jesus were visionary events is doubly implausible, both in its presupposition that all the appearances conformed to the model of Paul's experience and in its failure to render intelligible the New Testament distinction between an appearance and a vision of Jesus. Not only that, but we have also seen that his psychoanalysis of Peter and Paul has in various respects little plausibility. Thus, the Hallucination Hypothesis does not fare well when assessed by the third criterion.

Criterion 4: *Accord with Accepted Beliefs.* According to this criterion, that hypothesis is best which forces us to abandon the fewest of generally accepted beliefs. But Lüdemann's hypothesis, if accepted, would compel us to abandon a number of beliefs which are generally accepted by New Testament scholars; for example, the beliefs that:

1. Jesus received an honorable burial (by Joseph of Arimathea).
2. Jesus's tomb was discovered empty by some of his women followers.
3. Psychoanalysis of historical figures is infeasible.
4. Paul was basically content with his life under the Jewish Law.
5. The appearance to the 500 brethren was distinct from the event at Pentecost.
6. The New Testament makes a distinction between a vision of Christ and a resurrection appearance of Christ.

All of the above statements are generally accepted conclusions of New Testament scholars; yet in order to adopt Lüdemann's hypothesis we should have to reject all of them. This weighs against at least Lüdemann's version of the Hallucination Hypothesis.

Criterion 5: Ad hoc-*ness*. A theory becomes increasingly *ad hoc*, or contrived, in proportion to the number of additional assumptions it requires us to adopt. Lüdemann's Hallucination Hypothesis involves several such additional assumptions:

(a) The disciples fled back to Galilee on the night of Jesus's arrest. Lüdemann needs this assumption in order to separate the disciples from the gravesite of Jesus. Otherwise it becomes difficult to explain why they did not investigate the tomb. But this assumption has not a shred of evidence in its favor and is on the face of it implausible in the extreme.

(b) Peter was so obsessed with guilt that he projected a hallucination of Jesus. The records tell us nothing about the state of Peter's mind following his denial of Jesus. We have no reason to think that Peter's primary concern in the face of Jesus's execution was with his failure to stand by Jesus rather than with the shattering of Jesus's Messianic claims.

(c) The remaining disciples became so carried away that they also hallucinated visions of Jesus. We have no evidence that the other disciples, who presumably lacked Peter's guilt complex, were emotionally prepared to hallucinate visions of Jesus alive. We are simply asked to assume this.

(d) Paul had an unconscious struggle with the Jewish Law and a secret attraction to Christianity. Since the conflict is said to have been unconscious and the struggle secret, this assumption defies support by evidence. It is completely *ad hoc*.

These are just some of the additional assumptions that one must adopt if one is to embrace Lüdemann's Hallucination Hypothesis. Thus, his theory has a certain air of contrivance about it.

Criterion 6: *Superiority to Rival Hypotheses.* The Hallucination Hypothesis is old hat in German theology, having been expounded notably by Emmanuel Hirsch back in the 1920s; but most critics remain unpersuaded. Berger complains that Lüdemann's book is comprised almost exclusively of warmed-over positions which have dominated the Bultmann school for over 50 years.[66] I think that we can say confidently that the Hallucination Hypothesis has not demonstrated its clear superiority to rival theories, including the Resurrection Hypothesis.

Often the assessment of historical hypotheses is difficult because a hypothesis may be strong relative to certain criteria but weak relative to others. The historian's craft involves assessing the relative weight of these strengths and weaknesses. But the Hallucination Hypothesis does not fare well when assessed by any of our criteria. Its explanatory scope is too narrow, its explanatory power is too weak to account for the phenomena it does seek to explain, it is implausible in certain important respects, it contradicts a number of accepted beliefs, it is *ad hoc*, and it does not outstrip its rivals in meeting the above criteria. The only hope remaining for proponents of the Hallucination Hypothesis is that the Resurrection Hypothesis will fail even more miserably in meeting the same criteria, so that the Hallucination Hypothesis emerges victorious.

The Resurrection Hypothesis

The Resurrection Hypothesis asserts that "God raised Jesus from the dead." While most New Testament scholars agree with the inductive data base sketched above, many, if not most, will have grave reservations about the Resurrection Hypothesis as I have stated it because as historians they believe that they cannot offer supernatural explanations of the facts. This disturbs me not in the least. For in

---

[66] Klaus Berger, "Ostern fällt nicht aus!," p. 21.

the first place, the question of methodological naturalism, in history as in the sciences, is a *philosophical* question, which lies outside the realm of expertise of New Testament scholars. And there are quite a few very fine philosophers who argue that methodological naturalism is unwarranted, especially for one who is a theist.[67] Second, I am quite happy to concede, for the sake of argument if need be, that my hypothesis is not a "strictly historical" conclusion. We may call it a theological hypothesis, if we want. Even if the historian *qua* historian is debarred by some methodological constraint from drawing this conclusion, that does not mean that we (or the historian in his off-hours) cannot, as men and women seeking to discover the truth about life and the world, draw it. I offer the theological hypothesis as the best explanation of the facts and am willing to submit it to the same criteria used to assess any historical hypothesis. And the resurrection Hypothesis does seem to meet McCullagh's criteria successfully:

(a) It has great *explanatory scope*: it explains why the tomb was found empty, why the disciples saw post-mortem appearances of Jesus, and why the Christian faith came into being.

(b) It has great *explanatory power*: it explains why the body of Jesus was gone, why people repeatedly saw Jesus alive despite his earlier public execution, and so forth.

(c) It is *plausible*: given the historical context of Jesus's own unparalleled life and claims, the resurrection serves as divine confirmation of those radical claims.

(d) It is *not excessively* ad hoc or *contrived*: it requires only one additional hypothesis: that God exists. And even that need not be an additional hypothesis if one already believes in God's existence, as Lüdemann and I do.

---

[67] See the very interesting recent discussions about the warrant for methodological naturalism in science, *e.g.*, Paul de Vries, "Naturalism in the Natural Sciences: A Christian Perspective," *Christian Scholar's Review* 15 (1986): 388-396; Alvin Plantinga, Howard J. Van Till, Pattle Pun, and Ernan McMullin, "Symposium: Evolution and the Bible," *Christian Scholar's Review* 21 (1991): 8-109; William Hasker, "Evolution and Alvin Plantinga," *Perspectives on Science and Christian Faith* 44 (1992): 150-162; Alvin Plantinga, "On Rejecting The Theory of Common Ancestry: A Reply to Hasker," *Perspectives on Science and Christian Faith* 44 (1992): 258-263; Alvin Plantinga, "Methodological Naturalism," paper presented at the symposium "Knowing God, Christ, and Nature in the Post-Positivistic Era," University of Notre Dame, April 14-17, 1993; J. P. Moreland, "Theistic Science and Methodological Naturalism," in *The Creation Hypothesis*, ed. J. P. Moreland (Downer's Grove, Ill.: Inter-Varsity Press, 1994), pp. 41-66; J. P. Moreland, Stephen C. Meyer, and Richard H. Bube, "Conceptual Problems and the Scientific Status of Creation Science: a Discussion," *Perspectives on Science and Christian Faith* 46 (1994): 2-25.

(e) It is *in accord with accepted beliefs*. The hypothesis: "God raised Jesus from the dead" does not in any way conflict with the accepted belief that people do not rise *naturally* from the dead. The Christian accepts *that* belief as wholeheartedly as he accepts the hypothesis that God raised Jesus from the dead.

(f) It far outstrips any of its rival theories in meeting conditions (1)-(5). Down through history various alternative explanations of the facts have been offered, for example, the conspiracy theory, the apparent death theory, the hallucination theory, and so forth. Such hypotheses have been almost universally rejected by contemporary scholarship. No naturalistic hypothesis has attracted a great number of scholars.

Thus, the Resurrection Hypothesis fares very well when assessed by the standard criteria used for testing historical descriptions. Its greatest weakness is that it is *ad hoc* in requiring us to assume that God exists. But for those of us who are theists that is not an insuperable problem.

So why, we may ask, does Lüdemann reject the Resurrection Hypothesis? The answer is very simple: the resurrection is a miracle, and Lüdemann denies the admissibility of miracles. He states, "Historical criticism...does not reckon with an intervention of God in history."[68] Thus, the resurrection *cannot* be historical; it goes out the window before we even sit down at the table to look at the evidence.

The problem here can best be understood, I think, as a disagreement over what sort of explanations constitute live options for a best explanation of the facts. According to the pattern of inductive reasoning known as inference to the best explanation, in explaining a body of data, we first assemble a pool of live options and then pick from the pool, on the basis of certain criteria, that explanation which, if true, would best explain the data.[69] The problem at hand is that scientific naturalists will not permit supernatural explanations even to be in the pool of live options. By contrast, I am open to scientific naturalistic explanations in the sense that I include naturalistic explanations in the pool of live options, for I assess such explanations using the standard criteria for being a best explanation rather than dismiss such hypotheses out of hand. But Lüdemann is so sure that supernatural explanations are wrong that he thinks himself justified in no longer being open to them: they cannot even be permitted into the pool of live options.

---

[68] Lüdemann, "Auferstehung Jesu," p. 16.
[69] Peter Lipton, *Inference to the Best Explanation* (London: Routledge, 1991).

But, of course, if only naturalistic explanations are permitted into the pool of live options, then the claim or proof that the Hallucination Hypothesis is the best explanation is hollow. For one could happily admit that of all the naturalistic explanations on tap, the best naturalistic explanation is the Hallucination Hypothesis. But, of course, the question is not whether the Hallucination Hypothesis is the best naturalistic explanation, but whether it is true. After all, we are interested in veracity, not orthodoxy (whether naturalistic or supernaturalistic). So in order to be sure that he is not excluding the true theory from even being considered, Lüdemann had better have pretty good reasons for limiting the pool of live options to naturalistic explanations.

So what justification does Lüdemann give for this crucial presupposition of the inadmissibility of miracles? All he offers is a couple of one-sentence allusions to Hume and Kant.[70] He says, "Hume...demonstrated that a miracle is defined in such a way that 'no testimony is sufficient to establish it'."[71] The miraculous conception of the resurrection, he says, presupposes "a philosophical realism that has been untenable since Kant."[72] Now Lüdemann's procedure here of merely dropping names of famous philosophers is sadly all too typical of theologians. Thomas Morris, a philosopher, comments in his book *Philosophy and the Christian Faith*,

> What is particularly interesting about the references theologians make to Kant or Hume is that most often we find the philosopher merely mentioned..., but we rarely, if ever, see an account of precisely which arguments of his are supposed to have accomplished the alleged demolition.... In fact, I must confess to never having seen in the writings of any contemporary theologian the exposition of a single argument from either Hume or Kant, or any other historical figure for that matter, which comes anywhere near to demolishing...historical Christian doctrine, or...theological realism....[73]

Hume's argument against miracles was already refuted in the eighteenth century by Paley, Less, and Campbell, and most contemporary philosophers also reject it as fallacious, including such prominent philosophers of science as Richard Swin-

---

[70] Notice his failure to interact with Pannenberg's critique of "the all-powerfulness of analogical thinking in historical research and the postulate of the similarity in principle of all events" (Lüdemann, "Zwischen Karfreitag und Ostern," p. 20; cf. Wolfhart Pannenberg, "Die Auferstehung Jesu—Historie und Theologie," *Zeitschrift für Katholische Theologie* 91 [1994]: 318-328).
[71] Lüdemann, *Resurrection of Jesus*, p. 12.
[72] Ibid., p. 249.
[73] Thomas V. Morris, *Philosophy and the Christian Faith*, University of Notre Dame Studies in the Philosophy of Religion 5 (Notre Dame, Ind.: University of Notre Dame Press, 1988), pp. 3-4.

burne and John Earman and analytic philosophers such as George Mavrodes and William Alston.[74] Even the atheist philosopher Antony Flew, himself a Hume scholar, admits that Hume's argument is defective as it stands.[75] As for philosophical realism, this is in fact the *dominant* view among philosophers today, at least in the analytic tradition. So if Lüdemann wants to reject the historicity of miracles on the basis of Hume and Kant, then he has got a lot of explaining to do. Otherwise, his rejection of the resurrection hypothesis is based on a groundless presupposition. Reject that presupposition, and it is difficult to deny that the resurrection of Jesus is the best explanation of the facts.

CONCLUSION

In conclusion, then, we have seen, first, that any adequate historical hypothesis concerning Jesus's fate must explain four established facts: Jesus's honorable burial, the discovery of his empty tomb, his post-mortem appearances, and the origin of the disciples' belief in his resurrection. Second, when assessed by standard criteria used for testing historical descriptions, Lüdemann's Hallucination Hypothesis is seen to have narrow explanatory scope, to have weak explanatory power, to be implausible, to be unacceptably *ad hoc*, to contradict quite a number of accepted beliefs, and not to outstrip its rivals in meeting these tests. By contrast, the Resurrection Hypothesis, when assessed by the same criteria, fares very well. Therefore, we ought to regard the latter as the better explanation of the facts.

---

[74] See George Campbell, *Dissertation on Miracles* (1762; rep. ed.: London: T. Tegg & Son, 1834); Gottfried Less, *Wahrheit der christlichen Religion* (Göttingen: G. L. Förster, 1776); William Paley, *A View of the Evidences of Christianity*, 2 vols., 5th ed. (London: R. Faulder, 1796; reprint ed.: Westmead, England: Gregg, 1970); Richard Swinburne, *The Concept of Miracle* (New York: Macmillan, 1970); John Earman, "Bayes, Hume, and Miracles," *Faith and Philosophy* 10 (1993): 293-310; George Mavrodes, "Miracles and the Laws of Nature," *Faith and Philosophy* 2 (1985): 333-346; William Alston, "God's Action in the World," in *Divine Nature and Human Language* (Ithaca, N. Y.: Cornell University Press, 1989), pp. 197-222.

[75] Antony Flew in *Did Jesus Rise from the Dead*, ed. Terry L. Miethe (San Francisco: Harper & Row, 1987), p. 4.

Appendix D

DALE ALLISON ON JESUS' EMPTY TOMB, HIS POST-MORTEM APPEARANCES, AND THE ORIGIN OF THE DISCIPLES' BELIEF IN HIS RESURRECTION

Dale Allison's essay "Resurrecting Jesus" is one of the most impressive pieces of work I have read in this well-ploughed field. His treatment is commendable for its candor, both about his proclivities toward belief in the physical resurrection and his philosophical misgivings about it, for its rigorous argument, and especially for its dazzling scholarly erudition. One is duly impressed when a fine New Testament scholar evinces a thorough mastery of the literature in his field pertinent to the subject; but it is especially impressive when he begins citing literature in philosophy relevant to problems of personal identity and material constitution and in psychology and parapsychology concerning bereavement visions, collective hallucinations, and the like.

Allison forced me, as no one else has, to re-think the evidence for Jesus' resurrection afresh. Indeed, I've never seen a more persuasive case for scepticism about the historicity of Jesus' resurrection than Allison's presentation of the arguments. He's far more persuasive than Crossan, Lüdemann, Goulder, and the rest who actually deny the historicity of Jesus' resurrection. That Allison should, despite his sceptical arguments, finally affirm the facts of Jesus' burial, empty tomb, post-mortem appearances, and the origin of the disciples' belief in Jesus' resurrection and hold that the resurrection hypothesis is as viable an explanation as any other rival hypothesis, depending upon the worldview one brings to the investigation, is testimony to the strength of the historical case for Jesus' resurrection.

In my response I'm going to limit myself principally to a discussion of Allison's treatment of what I take to be the three central facts undergirding a historical inference to Jesus' resurrection, namely, the discovery of his empty tomb, his post-mortem appearances, and the origin of the disciples' belief that God had raised Jesus from the dead. I shall not be concerned with the question of which hypothesis best explains these three facts but rather with the historicity of the events themselves.

The Empty Tomb

Let's consider first Allison's treatment of the empty tomb. It is noteworthy in this connection that Allison makes a strong case for the historicity of Jesus' entombment by Joseph of Arimathea (Excursus 2, pp. 252-63). One of the ironies of his treatment of the burial and empty tomb narratives--which is apparently unnoticed by Allison--is that virtually the same arguments which lead him to his confident and unqualified verdict of "highly likely" for the burial by Joseph (*e.g.*, multiple attestation, lack of legendary embellishment, embarrassing features of the narrative, use of proper names, public knowledge of the burial and the tomb's location) also support the historicity of the empty tomb, which he deems "with great hesitation" to be "historically likely" (pp. 332, 362)!

There is clearly a double standard operative here, which is born, I think, out of Allison's disdain for material continuity between the mortal body and the resurrection body. He says, "I believe, rightly or wrongly, in a future existence free from the constraints of material corporeality as we have hitherto known them. . . . I do not believe that our life in the world to come in any way depends upon the recovery of our current flesh and bones; and if not for us, why for Jesus?" (pp. 225, 344). Philosophical problems about identity are then exploited in the attempt to justify this proclivity toward platonism. But those problems at the very most show that the resurrection bodies of people whose mortal bodies have been utterly dissolved are duplicates of those bodies rather than the numerically identical bodies. Such problems have no relevance to the case of Jesus of Nazareth. Allison says that then Jesus would be "the exception, an anomaly, an aberration" (p. 225). I think this claim is dubious[1], but

---

[1] In Jewish belief the primary object of the resurrection was the bones of the deceased (hence, the Jewish practice of preserving the bones in ossuaries for the eschatological resurrection), and skeletal remains are amazingly durable, existing even from

never mind: the more important point is that such doctrinal concerns are simply irrelevant to the historian's assessment of the evidence for the historicity of the women's discovery of Jesus' empty tomb. Allison's lack of even-handedness in his treatment of the burial and empty tomb traditions betrays a theological prejudice.

In treating the empty tomb, Allison examines seven arguments for the fact of the empty tomb ranked in order of increasing strength. Before discussing these, we should note a general weakness in Allison's handling of the arguments. He seems to treat each argument as though it had to bear the full weight of the case for the empty tomb, rather than as part of a cumulative case for that fact. If an argument does not make the empty tomb more probable than not, Allison dismisses it. This procedure is all too quick. Even if an argument makes the empty tomb, say, only 10% probable on a particular piece of evidence, that does not imply that the argument is of no value. For probabilities are cumulative. An event can be more probable than not relative to a composite body of evidence even if it is improbable relative to any single component of that body of evidence. In a court of law a case for the prosecution is not infrequently built upon an accumulation of such individually inadequate but cumulatively convincing pieces of evidence. One thinks, for example, of the circumstantial case which led to the conviction of Scott Peterson for the murder of his wife Lacey and their unborn child. In the case of the empty tomb, the fact of the empty tomb could have a probability greater than 0.5 relative to the seven arguments taken together even if no single argument renders it more probable than not.

Let's turn, then, to an examination of the individual arguments Allison scrutinizes.

1. *The earliest Jewish polemic presupposes the empty tomb.* It has been claimed that the Jewish charge that the disciples stole the body presupposes that the body was missing (Matt 28:11-15). Allison disputes this argument because of the uncertainty of the age of the Jewish polemic. He notes that "Some have, to be sure, surmised that the verses bear 'the mark of a fairly protracted controversy,'" but he responds, "why this should

---

prehistoric times. Moreover, the world's population explosion almost guarantees, barring worldwide catastrophe, that there will always be more recently deceased than long deceased. Thus, Jesus' case, involving as it does the raising of the mortal remains, is not atypical. The theological concern here, I suppose, is that Jesus' resurrection must be prototypical for our own. But such theological concerns are just irrelevant to the historian's task.

be so escapes me" (p. 312). In so saying, Allison overlooks, I think, the developing pattern of assertion and counter-assertion in the tradition history that plausibly lay behind Matthew's guard story:

Christian Jew: "The Lord is risen!"

Non-Christian Jew: "No, his disciples stole away his body."

Christian Jew: "The guard at the tomb would have prevented any such theft."

Non-Christian Jew: "No, the guard fell asleep."

Christian Jew: "The chief priests bribed the guard to say this."

In response to the Christian proclamation of Jesus' resurrection, the non-Christian Jewish reaction was simply to assert that the disciples had stolen the body. The idea of a guard could only have been a Christian, not a non-Christian development. At the next stage there is no need for Christians to invent the bribing of the guard; it was sufficient to claim that the tomb was guarded. The bribe arises only in response to the second stage of the polemic, the non-Christian allegation that the guard fell asleep. This part of the story could only have been a non-Christian development, since it serves no purpose in the Christian polemic. At the final stage, the time of Matthew's writing, the Christian answer that the guard were bribed is given. So the story does, I think, show signs of fairly protracted controversy. The story also is peppered with non-Matthean vocabulary, indicative of a prior tradition.[2] I see no reason to think that it does not represent the sort of controversy that went on between Jewish Christians and Jewish non-Christians soon after the message of the resurrection began to be proclaimed in Jerusalem. Given the early date of the pre-Markan Passion story, there is no need to quarrel with Allison's surmise that the controversy arose between Mark and Matthew, so long as by "Mark" we mean Mark's tradition.

2. *There was an absence of veneration of Jesus' tomb*. Given the extraordinary interest shown in the tombs of holy men, this lack of veneration of Jesus' tomb is said to be best explained by the fact that Jesus' bones

---

[2] E.g., several words or expressions which are unique in all the New Testament, such as "on the next day," "the preparation day," "deceiver," "guard (of soldiers)," " to make secure," "to seal." The expression "chief priests and Pharisees" is unusual for Matthew and never appears in Mark or Luke. The expression "on the third day" is also non-Matthean; he always uses "after three days." In general only 35 of Matthew's 136 words in the empty tomb story are found in Mark's 138 words.

no longer lay there. Allison rejects this argument because the location of the tomb was, in fact, preserved in Christian memory; the Church of the Holy Sepulchre has a credible claim to stand on the site (p. 313). But Allison's response seems to miss the point. The point is that there was no place where Jesus' remains were remembered to lie, where they might be preserved and honored. That fact is not in doubt historically. It is best explained by the fact that the tomb no longer contained Jesus' remains. Allison makes sport of the argument by noting that Lüdemann turns it inside out, arguing:

1. If the site of the tomb were known, it would have been venerated.

2. It was not venerated.

3. Therefore, the site of the tomb was unknown.

But, in fact, Lüdemann's logic is impeccable. The problem is that Allison disagrees with Lüdemann that the site of the tomb was unknown. Since the tomb was not venerated, it follows that Lüdemann's first premiss is false: it is not the case that if the site of the tomb were known, it would have been venerated. The correct premiss is

1′. If the site of the tomb were known and Jesus' remains still lay in the tomb, it would have been venerated.

Allison attempts to dispute this premiss by suggesting that the burial place may have been an unwholesome criminals' gravesite and therefore not venerated. But this contradicts his later claim in discussing the burial that people capable of redeeming so shameful an event as the cross could easily have redeemed burial in a trench (p. 354), *e.g.*, the presence of Jesus' bones sanctified the site. (This is just one of the many internal tensions in Allison's treatment of the evidence. He often seems to play the devil's advocate, putting forward arguments which are in tension with his own views elsewhere.) In any case, it seems to me that Allison has esteemed this argument too lightly and that it has an honorable part to play in a cumulative case for the empty tomb.

3. *The formula cited by Paul in I Cor. 15. 3-5 presupposes an empty grave.* Allison thinks that while this consideration shows that Paul may have *believed* in the empty tomb on theological grounds, it does not exclude that he may have done so "without knowing a tradition about its discovery" (p. 316). The weakness of this response is that a comparison

of the four-line formula passed on by Paul with the Gospel narratives on the one hand and the sermons in the Acts of the Apostles on the other reveals that the formula summarizes in its second and third lines the burial and empty tomb stories:

I Cor 15.3-5	Acts 13.28-31	Mk. 15.37-16.7
Christ died ...	Though they could charge him with nothing deserving death, yet they asked Pilate to have him killed.	And Jesus uttered a loud cry and breathed his last.
he was buried ...	they took him down from the tree and laid him in a tomb	And he [Joseph] bought a linen shroud, and taking him down, wrapped him in the linen shroud and laid him in a tomb.
he was raised ...	But God raised him from the dead ...	"He has risen, he is not here; see the place where they laid him."
he appeared ...	... and for many days he appeared to those who came up with him from Galilee to Jerusalem, who are now his witnesses to the people.	"But go, tell his disciples and Peter that he is going before you to Galilee; there you will see him."

This remarkable correspondence of independent traditions is convincing proof that the four-line formula (which, as is evident from the grammatically unnecessary repetition of "and that" (*kai hoti*) at the head of each line, lists sequentially four distinct events) is a summary in outline form of the basic events of Jesus' passion and resurrection, including the discovery of his empty tomb. Curiously, Allison himself recognizes that "1 Cor. 15:3-8 must be a summary of traditional narratives that were told in fuller forms elsewhere" (ibid., p. 235; cf. his footnote 133). This is another example of the many internal tensions in Allison's treatment.

4. *The disciples could not have preached the resurrection in Jerusalem in the face of an occupied tomb.* Here we find Allison's skepticism becoming somewhat desperate. He says that perhaps the disciples were so convinced of Jesus' resurrection that they "never bothered to visit the gravesite" (p. 318). This suggestion is, frankly, fantastic when you think about it (they *never* went back, if not to verify, even to see where the Lord lay?) and contradicts Allison's own point that the site of the tomb was preserved in Christian memory (cf. p. 236, n. 143). Just as fantastic

is Allison's suggestion that the Jerusalem authorities never inspected the tomb because they "just did not care because they did not take the business very seriously or regarded it as nothing more than a minor, transient nuisance" (319) —this despite their engaging Saul of Tarsus to ravage the early Jesus movement!

5. *The empty tomb story lacks theological and legendary embellishment.* Allison agrees; this is also one of the reasons he accepts the historicity of the burial account.

6. *Post-mortem visions alone are insufficient to account for early belief in Jesus' resurrection.* Although Allison makes very heavy weather of visions of recently deceased persons by the bereaved, in the end he admits, "If there was no reason to believe that his solid body had returned to life, no one would have thought him, against expectation, resurrected from the dead. Certainly visions of or perceived encounters with a postmortem Jesus would not by themselves, have supplied such reason" (pp. 324-5). So the tomb was probably found empty.

7. *The tomb was discovered empty by women.* Probably no other factor has proved so persuasive to scholars of the empty tomb's historicity as the role of the female witnesses. Allison is no exception.

Allison concludes that that "a decent case" can be made for the empty tomb (p. 331). We've seen that this is an understatement. The case for the empty tomb is every bit as, if not more powerful than, the case for Jesus' burial.

But Allison thinks that there is also "a respectable case" against the empty tomb (p. 331). I found this assertion surprising. The supposedly respectable case consists of only two arguments: first, "the ability of early Christians to create fictions" and, second, "the existence of numerous legends about missing bodies" (p. 332). But these two considerations show at the very most the possibility that the empty tomb narrative is a legend. That same possibility exists for the crucifixion and burial accounts. This is a possibility we become aware of based on our general background knowledge *prior* to an examination of the specific evidence. These two considerations do nothing to show that, based on an examination of the specific evidence, we ought to judge that the narrative of the empty tomb *is* a fiction or legend. It's shocking to me that Allison could construe such *a priori* possibilities based on general background knowledge as constituting a respectable case against the fact of the empty tomb.

In short, the discovery of Jesus' empty tomb emerges from Allison's scrutiny as very credible historically.

The Post-Mortem Appearances

So now we turn to the post-mortem appearances of Jesus. Allison argues for the historicity of post-mortem appearances of Jesus on the part of Peter, the disciples, Mary Magdalene, and others. I should mainly quibble with him here about details, *e.g.*, his attempt to collapse all the appearances into Galilean appearances, despite multiple, independent attestation of Jerusalem appearances. *Pace* Allison (p. 257), the fact that Mark foreshadows a Galilean appearance (and perhaps narrated only that one, if his ending has been lost) in no wise entails that Jerusalem appearances did not, in fact, occur first. It follows from Mark's foreshadowing that a Galilean appearance alone occurs in Mark's storyworld, just as in Luke's storyworld only Jerusalem appearances take place. The historical question is not thereby settled. Neither Matthew nor Luke thought that Mark's predictions of a Galilean appearance precluded prior appearances in Jerusalem. Why should we? Contrary to Allison (p. 258), the story of the disciples' fishing in John 21 does not represent a return to their old way of life, for neither Thomas nor Nathaniel were fishermen. It does not therefore preclude prior appearances to the disciples, as indicated by the testimony of the Beloved Disciple. As for the Gospel of Peter 12-14, this Gospel, as a compilation based on the four canonical Gospels, provides no independent grounds for thinking that no Jerusalem appearances occurred prior to the disciples' return to Galilee.

But let all this pass. The overriding point is that Allison agrees with the consensus of scholarship concerning the historicity of post-mortem appearances of Jesus to various individuals and groups after his death.

The Origin of the Disciples' Belief in Jesus' Resurrection

Finally, there is the fact of the disciples' coming sincerely and suddenly to believe that God had raised Jesus from the dead. Although Allison doesn't discuss this as a separate point, he recognizes this fact throughout his handling of the evidence. For example, in discussing the third day motif, Allison concludes that we can say with some confidence "that Christians found the three-day language appropriate because they believed that very little time elapsed between Jesus' crucifixion and God's vindication of him. This is some reason to suppose the Gospels correct when they represent Easter faith as emerging very soon, indeed, within a week, after the crucifixion" (p. 232). Again, Allison rejects the suggestion by some that the earliest disciples spoke of Jesus' vindication without using the concept of eschatological resurrection, commenting, "proclamation of his eschatological resurrection must go back to people who knew Jesus himself and were part of the earliest Jerusalem community" (p. 244, n. 180).

So Allison recognizes the three facts which I have elsewhere argued are best explained by the hypothesis that God raised Jesus from the dead.

Explaining the Facts

Allison disagrees, however, with the judgement that "The best historical explanation . . . is that Jesus was indeed bodily raised from the dead" (p. 345). Here Allison's basic complaint is that the evidence for the resurrection cannot challenge the investigator's worldview which he brings to the inquiry. He observes that for the determined naturalist even abduction by space aliens will be thought a better explanation than the resurrection hypothesis. Allison takes this to show that "Probability is in the eye of the beholder. It depends upon one's worldview, into which the resurrection fits, or alternatively, does not fit" (p. 340). Hence, "Arguments about Jesus' literal resurrection cannot establish one's Weltanschauung" (p. 342).

This argument is multiply confused. In the first place, historical apologetics for Jesus' resurrection was traditionally undertaken only *after* some case for theism had been presented. The question then became, given a theistic worldview, what is the best explanation for the evidence? It's not clear what Allison's answer to that question would be. He never interacts directly with the question of how someone who comes to the evidence with a robust natural theology (*e.g.*, R. Swinburne, S. Davis) should assess the competing hypotheses (see p. 341, note 557). I should therefore like to ask him directly, "How would you evaluate the comparative probability of the resurrection hypothesis and the theft *cum* bereavement vision hypothesis given theism and a good understanding of the life, claims, and activities of Jesus of Nazareth leading up to his death?"

Second, Allison confuses the fact that probabilities are *conditional* with their being *subjective*. Probabilities are relative to a body of information, but the fact that probabilities are conditional in no way implies that they "are in the eye of the beholder." The theist will agree with the naturalist that relative to naturalism, the resurrection is hopelessly improbable. The question will then be what justification one has for one's relevant background beliefs. Because Allison thinks that probability is just in the eye of the beholder, his way of determining what belongs in one's background beliefs is to look within and analyze introspectively what one believes. He advises, "we need to scrutinize not just the texts but also ourselves" (p. 343). What he fails to advise is that we scrutinize the evidence and arguments for our background beliefs. Introspection is no substitute for argument.

Third, Allison fails to take into account the differing degrees of conviction or tenacity with which people hold their background beliefs. He tends, again, to consider only the extreme case of people who approach the evidence "with the sure and certain conviction that there is no God" (p. 340). But suppose that the person's atheism is just a cultural veneer, thoughtlessly or lightly held as a result of being raised, for example, in Soviet or Chinese society. Such persons may well be led to abandon their atheism as a result of seeing that the resurrection "does not fit" into such a worldview. If they become convinced that the evidence is better explained by the resurrection hypothesis than by rival hypotheses, then they may well change their worldview in order to accommodate the better explanation.

Or suppose someone is agnostic but open and searching with respect to God's existence. Such a person might also adopt a theistic worldview because he is convinced that the evidence is better explained by the resurrection hypothesis than by rival hypotheses. Not only is this possible, but it in fact happens frequently. Allison has given no good reason for thinking that such a change of worldview must be irrational.

NAME AND SUBJECT INDEX

Aaron, Raymond—vi
Accetta, J. S.—129
Adam, first and second—99-100 pass.
Adler, Allan D.—129
Aland, Kurt—166
Albertz, Martin—5, 137
Allo, Ernst-Bernard—21, 40, 45, 54, 64, 93, 97, 108, 109, 110, 111, 112
Alston, William—380
Alsup, John E.—viii, 41, 52, 153, 161, 162, 187, 189, 191, 194-195, 207, 227-235 pass., 238, 281, 313, 319
Anderson, Hugh—149, 190, 224, 238
angels—45, 54, 94, 196, 231, 232, 233, 234, 236, 237, 242, 250, 251, 265, 292, 302, 316, 318, 322, 337
    angels, angelic visions vs. angelic appearances—292, 317, 374
    angels, at the tomb of Jesus—46, 134, 135, 143, 144, 145, 152, 153, 154, 159, 160, 161-163 pass., 165, 178, 182, 185, 186, 187, 188, 246, 248, 263, 265, 267, 283, 309, 316-317 pass., 336, 338, 356, 357
    angels, bodies of—250-251 pass.
apostles
    appearance to—see resurrection appearances, to all the apostles
    concept of—6-7, 27, 50-51
ascension—51, 59, 145, 183, 184, 187, 197, 198, 213, 221-222 pass., 240, 323

Bailey, Robert E.—112
Bammel, Ernst—3, 5, 8, 40
Barrett, C.K.—15, 54, 64, 75, 108, 109, 111, 135, 139, 149, 150, 175, 206, 207, 212, 214, 217, 220, 247, 248, 264
Barth, Karl—iii, iv, 18-21 pass., 24
Bartsch, Hans-Werner—3, 19, 238, 295
Bauer, J. B.—73
Bauer, K.-A.—86
Baumgart, J. S.—129
Baumgärtel, Friedrich—86, 91, 97
Beasley-Murray, G. R.—197
Behm, Johannes—278
Beloved Disciple—139, 161, 168-178 pass., 184, 185, 203, 204, 206, 207, 210, 215, 217-221 pass., 274, 282, 283, 311, 338, 342
Benoit, Pierre—173, 178, 190, 271
Berger, Klaus—191, 196, 235-236 pass., 263, 299, 317, 359, 360, 376
Bernard, J. H.—150, 210
Bertram, Georg—91
Betz, H.-D.—190, 191
Bickermann, E.—303
Bieder, Werner—97
Black, M.—74
Blackburn, Barry L.—231
Blank, Josef—4, 53, 70, 271
Blinzler, Josef—40, 122, 123, 124, 125, 126, 127, 128, 139, 141, 144, 145, 147, 148, 152, 271
Bode, Edward L.—viii, 35, 53, 71, 73, 74, 75, 76, 81, 82, 85, 121, 122, 148, 149, 150, 163, 164, 166, 170, 174, 188, 255, 256, 264, 268, 271, 356
body, Paul's concept of—85-92 pass., 105, 284-285
bones as the subject of the resurrection—

101-102, 104, 249
Bonsirven, Joseph—67
Borg, Marcus J.—352
Borgen, Peder—59, 249, 312
Bornhäuser, Karl—66-67, 91, 97, 101-102, 112, 243, 324
Bornkamm, Günther—121, 221, 257, 295
Bousset, Wilhelm—7, 72, 73
Bovon, François—29
Bowman, J.—74
Bowman, T.—74
Braaten, Carl—239
Brandenburger, E.—91
Bratcher, R. G.—57
Broer, Ingo—147, 153, 227, 258, 354
Browen, C.—74
Brown, Raymond E.—41, 55, 60, 65, 66, 70, 101, 119, 122, 134, 135, 145, 147, 149, 150, 163, 164, 168, 172, 173, 177, 178, 183, 184, 185, 188, 192, 195, 201, 202, 205, 206, 207, 208, 210, 212, 215, 216, 218, 219, 220, 238, 248, 264, 271, 301, 311, 330, 334, 335, 353
Bruce, A. B.—viii, 291
Bruce, F. F.—329
Bube, Richard H.—377
Bucher, T. G.—21
Bultmann, Rudolph—iii, iv, vi, vii, 18, 19, 21, 63, 86, 87, 88, 89, 90, 91, 92, 100, 102, 108, 110, 121, 127, 145, 146, 162, 164, 169, 170, 174, 191, 193, 195, 202, 206, 208, 210, 212, 218, 228, 238, 239, 245, 246, 257, 289, 295, 297, 331, 376
Burchard, Christoph—29
burden of proof—118-121 pass.
Burhenn, Herbert—304
burial of Jesus—117-141 pass., 256-260 pass.
   in I Cor. 15—25, 26, 36-37, 64-68 pass., 260-262 pass.
   gospel traditions of—117-141 pass., 262-264 pass.
Burkill, T. A.—166
Burkitt, F. C.—74
Byrne, Brenden—176

Cadoux, Cecil—73
Campbell, George—380
Carlson, Jeffrey—340
Carson, D. A.—vi, 45, 218
Cavallin, H. C. C.—297
Cerfaux, L.—8
Charlot, J.—4
Clavier, H.—96, 98, 101

Clemen, Carl—72
Cobb, John B.—249, 274
Conzelmann, Hans—4, 8, 9, 10, 11, 12, 13, 16, 17, 21, 24, 30, 32, 35, 37, 44, 53, 54, 74, 79, 86, 89, 94, 97, 102
Coppens, Joseph—94, 222, 312
Coquerel, Athanase—277
Corinthian opponents of Paul—5-6, 11, 92, 287, 346
Craig, William L.—272, 306, 339, 349, 352, 358
Cranfield, C. E. B.—146, 149, 165, 166
Crossan, John Dominic—327-348 pass., 373
Cullmann, Oscar—5, 8, 41, 85, 95, 101, 102, 109, 111, 113

Dahl, M. E.—103
Davies, W. D.—6, 92, 94, 100, 105, 110, 320
De Kruijf, T. C.—133
De Vries, Paul—377
De Zwaan, J.—28
Deichgräber, R.—8
Deines, Roland—371
Delling, Gerhard—35, 70, 71, 74
Dhanis, Edouard—36, 40, 64, 94, 121, 122, 144, 148, 166, 222, 264, 271, 298, 312, 313, 364
Dibelius, Martin—7, 28, 29, 161, 191, 280
Dickman, Steven—129
dichotomy between history and theology—v-vi, 82, 118-120 pass., 137
Dihle, Albert—91
dissimilarity criterion—120, 304
Docetism—63, 178, 196, 236-245 pass., 287, 309, 317
Dodd, C. H.—5, 15, 17, 21, 28, 29, 41, 58, 74, 192, 225-227 pass., 233, 281, 319
Doeve, J.—74
Donaldson, Terence L.—200
Donfried, Karl P.—41, 172, 192
doubt motif—46, 195-196, 199, 201, 202
dualism, anthropological—87, 91, 111
Dunn, James W. D. G.—46, 53, 54-55, 60, 90-91, 101, 104, 161-162, 184, 187, 197, 237, 243, 247, 271, 302, 312, 313-314, 320, 324
Dupont, Jacques—8, 29, 74

Earman, John—380
Ellis, E. Earle—67, 70, 125, 166, 196, 243, 279-280, 324
Ellis, I. P.—199
empty tomb—143-179 pass., 255-274 pass.,

290, 291, 293, 330-340 pass., 355-361 pass.
  account uncolored theologically—145-146, 262-264 pass.
  alternative explanations of—269-270 pass.
  Gattung for narrative of—235 pass., 263-264, 298
  implicit in resurrection—64-69 pass.
  in kerygma—256
  in pre-Pauline formula—63-84 pass., 256-257 pass.
  inspection by disciples—167-179 pass., 184, 186, 192, 194, 217, 267-268
  Jewish interest in—84, 256, 268-270 pass.
  women's visit to—146-150 pass., 181, 184, 186
Eusebius—49, 50, 78, 124, 217
Evans, C. F.—viii, 5, 29, 59, 66, 74, 112, 161, 164, 187, 197, 225, 249, 297, 312
existentialism—19, 20, 87-88, 90, 103, 119, 239

Farmer, William—121
Fascher, Eric—3
Feine, Paul—278
Field, Frederic—71
Finnegan, Jack—45, 74
Fischer, Karl M.—55, 64, 74, 147, 161, 225, 237, 260, 262, 268, 270, 303
Fitzmeyer, Joseph A.—209, 210
flesh and blood—101-102 pass., 113, 248-251 pass., 342
flesh and bones—101, 237, 247-249
flesh, Paul's concept of—88, 91, 93-94, 96, 104, 319
Flew, Antony—380
flight of disciples to Galilee—137, 168, 176-179 pass., 220, 223, 268, 340, 347, 360
formula(s)
  Christological—4, 9, 15, 23, 36
  pre-Pauline f. in I Cor. 15.3ff—1-37 pass.
    age of—7, 14
    existence of—3-5 pass.
    geographical origin of—7-16 pass.
    length of—5-7 pass.
    purpose of—16-21 pass., 24
    structure of—7-8, 22-38 pass.
    unity and tradition history of—22-38 pass.
Fortna, R. T.—208, 218
Fuller, Daniel P.—iv

Fuller, Reginald H.—5, 14, 20-24 pass., 25, 39, 41, 45, 53, 56, 76, 108, 164, 178, 183, 187, 196, 212, 238, 247, 272, 297, 319
Funk, R. W.—340, 341

Gaechter, Paul—148, 155, 162
Gardner-Smith, Patrick—55, 64, 134, 148, 164, 178, 187, 190, 197, 313
Gasque, W. Ward—28
Gaston, Lloyd—354
Geense, Adriaan—18
Geering, Lloyd—303
Geiselmann, J. R.—8
Gerhardsson, B.—8
Gewiess, J.—8
Gilbert, M.—129
Gilbert, R.—129
Gillman, John—90, 102, 103, 319
Gils, F.—41
Ginzberg, Louis—78
glory of resurrection body—96, 312
Gnilka, Joachim—68, 122, 129, 140, 141, 144
Gnosticism—vi, 240-244 pass., 307-325 pass.
Godet, F.—122, 167
Goguel, Maurice—45, 73, 74, 146
Goppelt, Leonhard—4
Goulder, Michael—265, 266, 367
Grant, Michael—271, 300
Grass, Hans—iii, v, vii, 3, 8, 14, 15, 27, 35, 36, 37, 39, 47, 50, 51, 52, 53, 54, 56, 57, 58, 59, 63, 64, 65, 67, 68, 72, 73, 74, 101, 103, 105, 107, 108, 109, 111, 124, 127, 129, 137, 140, 141, 146, 153, 160, 161, 164, 166, 187, 195, 196, 197, 203, 206, 212, 214, 221, 237, 238, 239, 246, 248, 265, 276, 289, 290, 293, 297, 305, 314, 315, 371
Grässer, Erich—29
Gruenler, Royce G.—278
Grundmann, Walter—122, 124, 147, 148, 149, 152, 153, 154, 164, 165, 168, 188, 191, 195, 197, 198, 210, 237, 249, 271
guard at the tomb—see tomb of Jesus, guard at the
Gundry, Robert H.—viii, 66, 86-90 pass., 91, 97, 100, 102, 105, 114, 149, 152, 154, 198, 209, 271, 319, 321, 329, 336, 337, 339
Guthrie, Donald—277-279 pass.
Güttgemanns, Ehrhardt—10, 11, 12, 35, 89
Gutwenger, E.—iv, 44, 146-147, 164

Haas, N.—259
Haenchen, Ernst—14, 29, 31, 32, 57, 58, 101, 129, 239
Hahn, Ferdinand—vii, 3, 8, 9, 35, 70, 221
hallucinations—52, 272, 275, 284, 286, 289, 290, 291, 293, 300, 301, 302, 341, 349-381 pass.; see also visions
Harrington, Daniel J.—90
Hartmann, Gert—185-186
Hasker, William—377
Hedrick, Charles—58, 59, 313
Heinrici, Georg—48, 54, 68, 93, 94, 97, 108, 110, 250
Heitmüller, Wilhelm—7
Heller, John H.—129
Hengel, Martin—25, 104, 268, 271, 278, 280, 370-371
Héring, Jean—93, 95, 98, 99, 103, 111
Hirsch, Emmanuel—45, 289, 376
Hoffmann, Paul—4, 14, 16, 23, 25, 53, 54, 60, 66, 108, 111, 112, 237, 300, 312
Holl, Karl—3
Holsten, C.—86, 321
Hooke, S. H.—69, 100, 157, 239, 255, 271, 297
Hooker, Morna—120
Hoover, R. W.—340, 341
Hoskyns, E. C.—73, 150
Hughes, P. E.—108, 109, 111
Hume, David—379-380
Hunkin, J. W.—70
Hunter, A. M.—281

Ignatius—243, 244-245
immortality of the soul—85, 89, 92, 95, 104, 114, 244, 246, 286, 342
intermediate state—66, 104, 111-113 pass.
Irenaeus—244

Jacob, Edmond—91
James
  appearance to—see resurrection appearances: to James
  role in primitive church—5-6, 25, 27, 39, 48-50 pass.
Jeremias, Joachim—4, 7, 8, 9, 10, 11, 12, 13, 16, 35, 40, 45, 48, 70, 92, 93, 101, 144, 164, 204, 239, 259, 271, 298, 364
Jerome—48, 215
Jesus's view of resurrection—67
Jewett, Robert—86, 90, 91, 96
Jewish polemic—155, 160-161 pass., 259, 269-270 pass., 273, 334, 358
Johnson, B. A.—150
Johnson, Luke T.—364
Joseph of Arimathea—122-123, 124-127 pass., 130, 141, 258, 259, 266, 269, 273, 332, 333-334, 347, 350-355 pass., 356, 375
Josephus—40, 47, 49, 78, 123, 135, 161, 218, 278, 279, 330, 363, 368
Judaizers—6

Kähler, Martin—28
Käsemann, Ernst—iii, 9, 86
Kant, Immanuel—379
Kattenbusch, Ferdinand—3
Kee, Howard Clark—328
Kessler, Hans—368, 372
kerygma:—4, 5, 8, 9, 10, 13, 14, 19, 22, 24, 25, 26, 28, 29, 30, 31, 32, 33, 34, 40, 65, 68, 71, 118, 145, 146, 157, 162, 163, 192, 196, 240, 260, 262, 264, 346
  competing versions of—23, 29-32 pass.
  empty tomb not mentioned in—65, 68, 146
  naming of witnesses in—5, 6, 16, 17, 18, 19, 20, 21, 22, 24, 25, 26, 28, 34, 39-62 pass., 283, 369
Kilpatrick, G. D.—15
Kingsbury, J. D.—200
Kittel, Gerhard—71, 74
Klappert, Berthold—8, 10, 12, 17, 35, 69, 103, 121, 248, 271, 304
Klein, Günter—5
Kleinknecht, Hermann—97, 99, 100, 319
Koch, Gerhard—69, 107, 137, 148, 154, 161, 166, 238, 245, 272, 295
Kragerud, Alv—169, 173
Kramer, Werner—23, 36
Kratz, R.—153
Kremer, Jacob—4, 8, 64, 66, 70, 74, 107, 137, 145, 149, 150, 162, 163, 164, 167, 170, 173, 177, 183, 189, 191, 197, 198, 214, 215, 233, 237, 264, 265, 271, 272, 273, 359, 369
Kuhn, K. G.—102
Kümmel, Werner G.—6, 8, 21, 45, 51, 54, 71, 86, 97, 109, 278, 302, 321
Künneth, Walther—53, 65, 67, 69, 72, 102, 243-244, 281, 297, 304, 324
Kwiran, Manfred—18

Lagrange, M.-J.—124, 127, 138, 139, 149, 164, 165, 166, 203
Lake, Kirsopp—28, 74, 103, 133, 134, 152, 154, 178, 212, 239, 273, 356

Lampe, G. W. H.—70, 249
Lane, William L.—125, 140, 146, 147, 164, 165, 271
Lang, Friedrich G.—108
Lapide, Pinchas—iv
LeDéaut, R.—79
legends
 inapplicable to I Cor. 15:3-8—42, 44, 264, 275, 340, 368
 insufficient time for—257, 261, 276-280 pass., 282
legitimation—20, 24, 25, 26, 27, 28, 39, 41
Lehmann, Karl—4, 7, 14, 22, 35, 69, 71, 73, 74, 75, 76, 78, 79, 80, 81, 82, 157, 263, 271
Léon-Dufour, Xavier—55, 59, 73, 187, 271, 312-313
Less, Gottfried—380
Lichtenstein, Ernst—3, 8, 35, 69, 70, 82, 271
Lietzmann, Hans—21, 45, 51, 54, 86, 97, 109, 321
Lightfoot, J. B.—217
Lightfoot, R. H.—166
Lilly, J. L.—57
Lindars, Barnabas—73, 74, 157, 169, 203, 208, 210, 311
Lindemann, Andreas—148, 164
Lipton, Peter—378
Lohfink, Gerhard—70, 221
Lohmeyer, Ernst—121, 146, 147, 149, 154, 166, 201, 245, 352
Lohse, Eduard—8, 35, 91, 190
Longenecker, R. N.—278
Longstaff, Thomas R. W.—148
Lord's Supper—31, 59, 64, 190-191, 216-217, 220, 263
Lorenzen, Thorwald—169, 173
Lüdemann, Gerd—349-381 pass.
Lüdemann, Hermann—86, 321
Ludwig, Robert—340

Macalister, R. A. S.—134
Mach, R.—73
MacKinnon, D. M.—70, 249
Mahoney, Robert—123, 128, 150, 162, 167-168 pass., 173, 178, 204, 206, 270
Mandelbaum, Maurice—vi
Mánek, Jindrich—69, 271
Marlé, René—iv
Marshall, I. Howard—viii, 124, 166, 189, 194, 197, 210, 221, 244, 271
Marxsen, Willi—iv, 21, 89, 148, 154, 164, 173, 174, 178, 245-246, 248, 255, 295

Masson, C.—55-56, 70
Matill, A. J.—28
Mavrodes, George—380
McArthur, Harvey K.—263
McCasland, Selby—73
McCullagh, C. B.—365-378 pass.
McGhee, M.—183
McKay, K. L.—46-47
McLeman, James—101, 239, 289
McMullin, Ernan—377
McNeile, A. H.—153, 280
Meier, John P.—359
Menoud, Philippe—204
Messiah
 as a name or title—9, 10, 11, 12
 dying and rising—20, 156, 189, 296, 299, 343, 359, 362, 363, 371
 Jesus as M. for early church—50, 296, 363
Metzger, Bruce M.—73, 74
Meyer, Ben—103, 328
Meyer, H. A. W.—48, 54, 68, 93, 94, 97, 108, 110, 250
Meyer, Rudolf—91
Meyer, Stephen C.—377
Meyers, E. M.—104
Michaelis, Wilhelm—5, 40, 42, 53, 54, 164, 187, 249, 281
Mildenberger, Friedrich—74
Minear, Paul S.—204
miracles—vi, vii, 156, 276, 306, 341-342, 361-362, 378-380
 historiography and—304-306, 354
missionaries
 Jewish—33-34
 preach same gospel—5, 6, 10, 13, 14, 18, 31
Moehring, H. R.—57
Moltman, Jürgen—119
Morgenthaler, Robert—204
Morissette, Rodolphe—92, 99-100, 319-320
Moreland, J. P.—377
Morris, Leon—168, 217, 218, 219
Morris, R. A.—129
Morris, Thomas V.—379-380
Moule, C. F. D.—viii, 35, 64, 67-68, 70, 75, 97, 102, 109, 165, 166, 184, 203, 224-225, 271, 278, 280, 299, 300, 302, 330
Moulton, J. H.—264
Müller, Julius—276, 277, 280
Murphy-O'Connor, Jerome—4, 17
Mussner, Franz—8, 23, 34, 36, 53, 64, 69, 271, 297

Nauck, Wolfgang—69, 145, 271
Naveh, J.—259
Neirynck, Frans—143, 153
Nickelsburg, Jr., G. W. E.—297
Niebuhr, Richard R.—238
Nock, A. D.—73
Norden, Eduard—5
Nötscher, F.—74

Oberlinner, Lorenz—64, 74, 161, 227, 261, 265, 267, 269
O'Collins, Gerald—vii, 32-33, 60, 63, 74, 98, 102, 103, 113, 127, 153-154, 157, 187, 221, 237, 242, 246, 247, 271, 303, 327
Oepke, Albrecht—66
Orr, James—55, 64, 125, 137, 154, 197, 291, 313
Osborne, Grant—vi, 59, 69, 139, 140, 148, 162, 183, 189, 201, 202, 208, 210, 221, 225

Paley, William—380
Pamment, Margaret—97, 103
Pannenberg, Wolfhart—iv, viii, 3, 16, 17, 44, 249, 250, 274, 304, 305, 379
Parousia—6, 17, 32, 89, 101, 102-107 pass., 108, 109, 110, 111, 112, 113, 166, 169, 174, 205, 217, 336, 345, 346, 347
Paul
  apostleship—27-28, 52, 54-55, 59, 61
  contact with early disciples—14-15, 22, 23-24, 27, 42, 43, 48, 49, 53, 61, 83-84 pass., 239, 257, 275, 282, 283
  conversion of—7, 14, 15, 16, 27, 47, 48, 49, 50, 54, 55-61 pass., 83, 236, 312, 366
Pearson, Birger A.—66, 97, 102
Peel, M. L.—324
Pellicori, S. F.—129
Pentecost—45, 47, 50, 51, 53, 55, 62, 224, 362, 368-369, 375
Perkins, Pheme—164, 190, 191, 297
Perrin, Norman—v, 118, 166, 191, 221, 228, 247, 272, 275-276
Perry, Michael—45, 69, 155, 271, 291-293 pass.
Pesch, Rudolph—25, 26, 35, 53-54, 64, 121, 136-137, 138, 140, 143, 144, 164, 165, 208, 239, 258, 261, 263-264, 265, 267, 268, 269, 273, 300-301, 302, 303
Peter
  called Cephas—8, 23, 40, 50, 370
  called Simon—8, 40, 189, 209, 370

P.'s commissioning—172, 193, 214
P.'s denial—41, 137, 172, 177, 193, 267, 340, 341, 371, 375-376
Pfammater, J.—153
Pharisee (Pharisaic)—6, 55, 67, 92, 93, 105, 151, 152, 154, 158, 159, 218, 260, 283, 298, 299, 335, 357, 367, 371
Philo—78, 99, 108, 111, 125
physicalism—52, 62, 196, 222, 236-246 pass. 283-288 pass., 324, 325
Plantinga, Alvin—377
Plein, Ina—11
Plevnik, Joseph—103
Plummer, Alfred—21, 40, 45, 53, 54, 64, 66, 96, 97, 101, 103, 108, 109, 111, 112, 124, 191, 197, 281
pre-Markan passion story—121, 136, 137, 139, 140, 155, 156, 162, 177, 257, 283, 352, 353, 355
  included empty tomb narrative—143-146 pass., 167, 262-264 pass.
  included reference to resurrection appearance—164-166 pass., 187-188
Pun, Pattle—377

Quintillian—119

Ramsey, Michael—40, 75, 98, 157, 165
Reicke, B.—277, 278
Rengstorff, Karl H.—3, 8, 9, 35, 53, 65, 67, 69, 124, 146, 249, 271
resurrection
  appearances—39-62 pass., 275-293 pass.
    at the Sea of Tiberius—182-183, 203-221 pass., 225, 245, 248, 283, 289
    dislocated narratives of—41, 192-194 pass., 207-211 pass.
    distinct from visions—see visions: distinct from resurrection appearances
    Gattung for—191, 225-235 pass.
    Jerusalem vs. Galilee—70, 165-166, 223-225 pass., 283
    of the Son of Man—16, 300-304 pass.
    on the Galilean mountain—43, 45-48 pass., 198-201 pass., 245, 247, 322
    structure of list of—39-40 pass.
    to all the apostles—6, 7, 26, 27, 50-53 pass., 55, 224
    to Emmaus disciples—139, 174, 182, 183, 188-191 pass., 192, 213,

216, 223-224, 225, 226, 227, 230, 231, 233, 247, 248, 250, 301, 317, 343
to 500 brethren—17, 19, 25, 26, 27, 43-48 pass., 50, 52, 53, 55, 60, 61, 201, 224, 275, 283, 293, 361, 368-369 pass., 375
to James—26, 27, 48-50 pass., 53, 224, 283, 302, 368
to Paul—27, 48, 51, 53-61 pass., 62, 68, 114, 241-243 pass., 275, 283, 285, 302, 312, 313
extra-mental aspects—57-61 pass., 62, 242, 284-287 pass., 374
not determinative—55-56 pass., 61, 114, 284-285
to Peter—24, 26, 29, 30, 40-42 pass., 70, 43, 174, 192-193, 195, 282, 302
to the Twelve—24, 25, 26, 30, 41, 42-43 pass., 54, 70, 183, 188, 194-201 pass., 202, 212, 233, 242, 245, 247, 282, 289, 311, 361, 362, 367
to the women—27, 45, 143, 163, 165, 181-188 pass., 189, 201, 237-238, 247, 282, 342, 362, 365, 369
to Thomas—32, 154, 170, 183, 198, 199, 201-203 pass., 206, 224, 226, 242, 244, 245, 247
body—63, 67, 68, 85-114 pass., 154, 175, 236-251 pass., 260, 284, 285, 286, 287, 308, 310, 311, 312, 324, 342, 344
concept of—66, 69-70, 104, 106-107, 246, 260, 290
disciples' belief in—295-297 pass.
Jewish notion of—297-304 pass.
new creation as r.—100, 102, 105, 108-111 pass.
pagan analogies to—72-73 pass.
Pauline analogies to—92-95 pass., 98, 103, 106, 311
predictions of—71, 74, 151, 155-158 pass., 165, 289, 302, 336, 338, 339
Reumann, John—41, 172, 192
Rigaux, Beda—v, 189
Rinaldi, P. A.—129
Robertson, Archibald—21, 40, 45, 53, 54, 64, 66, 96, 97, 101, 103, 281
Robinson, B. P.—190
Robinson, H. Wheeler—67
Robinson, James M.—19-20, 60, 89-90, 94, 99, 101, 113, 118, 119, 120, 237, 241, 242, 243, 248, 307-325 pass.
Robinson, John A. T.—29, 40, 55, 64, 69, 85, 86, 128, 133, 185, 271, 272, 273, 277-280 pass., 289, 291, 313, 354
Rohde, Erwin—91
Roloff, J.—8, 191
Rordorf, Willi—72
Ross, J. M.—266
Ruckstuhl, Eugen—153, 204, 271
Rudolph, W.—74

Sand, Alexander—91, 101, 102
Sanders, J. N.—209
Schelkle, Karl H.—8, 268
Schenke, Ludger—70, 147, 161, 162, 164, 271
Schmauch, Werner—121, 149, 198, 201, 245, 352
Schmithals, Walter—5
Schmidt, C.—322
Schmitt, Joseph—8, 36, 271
Schnackenburg, Rudolf—128, 145, 150, 162, 169, 171, 172, 175, 183, 185, 187, 194, 202, 205, 206, 208, 212, 214, 218, 245, 271, 272, 311
Schneider, Johannes—54
Schottroff, Luise—45-46, 138, 148, 155, 177
Schunack, G.—74
Schwager, Raymund—358
Schwartz, E.—72
Schweizer, Albert—6
Schweizer, Eduard—86, 91, 97, 102, 146, 166, 204, 238, 248
Schwemer, Anna Maria—371
Seeberg, Alfred—3
Seidensticker, Philipp—4, 44, 271
Semitisms
in I Cor. 15—7-13 pass., 22, 79
in Acts sermons—28-31 pass.
sermons in Acts—14, 28-34 pass., 240-241, 262, 344, 351, 352, 357, 359
Sevenster, J. N.—102, 109, 111
Sheol—66, 104, 113
Sherwin-White, A. N.—47, 119, 120, 277, 280
Shroud of Turin—129-133 pass., cf. 122, 123, 128, 135, 140, 143, 173, 175-176 pass., 274, 332, 351
Sider, Ronald J.—93, 98, 102, 103, 105
signs
apostolic—20
Johannine—33

Sjöberg, Eric—97
Smalley, Stephen S.—210
Smith, Joseph L.—93, 105
Smith, Morton—328
Smith, R. H.—134
Solanges, B. de—204
soul—66, 67, 73, 85, 87, 89, 90, 92, 95, 96, 97, 99, 104, 109, 111, 112, 113, 114, 228, 229, 230, 232, 243, 244, 246, 251, 286, 301, 319, 333
Sparks, H. F. D.—28-29
Spirit identified with Risen Christ—99-100, 241-242 pass., 309
spiritual body—86, 90, 95-99 pass., 100, 105, 108-109, 113, 183, 236, 237, 247, 285, 286, 291, 319, 320, 321
Staudinger, Hugo—155
Stauffer, Ethelbert—5, 40, 69
Steck, O. H.—33, 34
Stein, Robert H.—120
Stendahl, Krister—371
Strathmann, Hermann—5
Strauss, David F.—276, 277
Strecker, G.—74
Stuhlmacher, Peter—5, 6, 7, 12, 13, 15, 26, 29, 41, 74, 263-264, 271, 299
Suppe, Frederick—vii
Swete, H.—203
Swinburne, Richard—380

Talbert, Charles H.—239-240
Taylor, Vincent—69, 71, 121, 122, 123, 124, 127, 139, 140, 144, 146, 166, 280, 281
Teeple, Howard M.—218, 289
Tertullian—74
theophanies—54, 231-235 pass., 287
Thiede, Carsten P.—175, 178
third day motif—4, 29, 69-84 pass., 155, 156, 157, 158, 263, 264, 333
Tholuck, F. August—277
Thompson, J. G. S. S.—74
Thrall, M. E.—viii, 273-274, 300
Thüsing, W.—8
Tödt, H. E.—74
tomb of Jesus—133-136 pass., 140, 258, 271
  guard at the t.—127, 150-161 pass., 266, 269, 273, 329, 333, 358
Torrey, C. C.—28
transformation at the resurrection—63, 64, 67, 90, 92, 96, 97, 101, 102-107 pass., 109-111 pass., 112, 113, 238, 260, 286
translation vs. resurrection—54, 221, 230, 234, 235-236, 263, 280, 300, 301-304 pass.
Trilling, Wolfgang—17, 259, 271, 276, 285, 304, 335, 341, 342, 361-362
Trites, Allison A.—32
Tröger, Karl-Wolfgang—91
Twelve, the—6, 14, 24, 25, 26, 30, 32, 39, 41, 42-43 pass., 45, 50-51, 54, 70, 158, 181, 183, 188, 194-201 pass., 202, 212, 218, 220, 233, 242, 243, 245, 247, 282, 289, 311, 322, 323, 361, 362, 367
Tzaferis, V.—259

Van Daalen, D. H.—55, 246, 271, 340
Van der Horst, P. W.—47
Van Till, Howard J.—377
Vermes, G.—79, 272
Vielhauer, Philipp—9
visions
  distinct from resurrection appearances—51-52, 53-54 pass., 57, 60-61, 62, 196, 243, 284-293 pass., 300-304 pass.
  heavenly—52-53, 54, 55, 57, 59, 114, 234, 235, 241-243 pass., 284, 285, 287, 303-304 pass., 370
  objective—iii, 52, 62, 284, 291, 302, 374
  subjective—iii, 52, 272, 284, 289-290 pass., 291, 293, 301-304 pass., 349-380 pass.; see also hallucinations
  veridical—iii, 52, 62, 230, 290-293 pass., 315, 316, 374
Vogel, C.—216
Vögtle, Anton—8, 53-54, 64, 261, 265, 267, 269, 271
Von Campenhausen, Hans F.—3, 8, 26, 35, 40, 69, 153, 166, 271
Von Harnack, Adolf—3, 35, 53, 39, 279, 341
Von Rad, Gerhard—71

Wegenast, Klaus—5
Weiss, Johannes—17, 18, 53, 54, 68, 74, 90, 92, 96, 97, 100, 102, 103, 111, 137, 319
Wendland, H.-D.—74
Wengst, Klaus—4, 12, 13, 24, 51, 76, 79
Wenham, David—viii, 120, 159, 231
Wenham, John—225
Wescott, B. F.—53, 55, 103, 165, 167
White, Morton—vi
Whitely, D. E. H.—97, 103, 110, 112
Whittaker, David—273
Wijngaards, J.—74
Wilckens, Ulrich—3, 14, 15, 22, 23, 24-34

pass., 36, 44, 65, 69, 74, 93, 141, 144, 145, 148, 162, 166, 169-170, 178, 187, 195, 198, 210, 214, 221, 227-228, 244, 246, 248, 263, 265, 271, 272, 273, 297, 299
Wilcox, Max—29
Willems, B. A.—iv
Wilson, Ian—129
Wilson, S. G.—354
Winter, Paul—3, 8, 190
witness motif
   in I Cor. 15:3-8—22, 26
   in John—32-33
   in Luke-Acts—28-33 pass., 239-241 pass.
women
   absence from list in I Cor. 15:3-7—40, 137, 140, 174, 369
   appearance to—see resurrection, appearances, to the women
   at the cross and burial—121, 135, 136-140 pass., 144, 146-148 pass., 235, 240, 258-259, 335, 339, 356, 358
   discoverers of empty tomb—iii, 45, 46, 69, 134-135, 137, 139, 143, 144, 145, 149-150 pass., 154, 156, 161-166 pass., 167, 178, 236, 240, 258-259, 266-267 pass., 272-273, 274, 337, 338, 339, 347, 355, 356, 357, 358, 360, 365, 375
   participants in appearance to disciples—41, 43, 45-46
Wood, J. E.—79
Wright, David F.—159
Wright, N. T.—328, 345, 352, 363

Yamauchi, Makota—166, 198, 199, 304

SCRIPTURE INDEX

Old Testament

Genesis
1:3—61, 312
1:11—93
1:12—93
2:7—97, 99-100, 213, 320
5:24—234, 301
15—81
18—231, 233-234
19:1—196
21:16—9
22—79, 81
22:4—76, 77, 79
25:8—37
34:25—76
35:8—37
40:20—76
42:17—77, 79
42:18—76, 77
50—266

Exodus
3—231
3:8—78
15:21—266
15:22—77
19:11—76
19:16—76, 77

Leviticus
8:18—76
11:1-30—94
21:11—87

Numbers
6:6—87
7:24—76
19:11—128
19:12—76
19:19—76
24:25—167

Deuteronomy
4:49—133
16:3—202
21:22-23—123, 332
21:23—363

Joshua
2:16—77
8:29—123
10:16-27—266
10:26-27—332-333
10:27—123

Judges
3—231
13—231
19:8—76
20:30—76

I Samuel
1:1—124
3—232
3:1-18—235
30:1—76
31:11—67

II Samuel
1:2—76

2:12-14—123
21:10—67

I Kings
4:33—94
12:24—76

II Kings
2:11-18—234, 301
2:16-18—263
2:17—235
6:16-18—250
20:5—74, 76, 77
20:8—76
21—135
23:17—67

II Chronicles
10:12—76
24:16—37

Ezra
8:32—77

Nehemiah
3:3—196
3:16—135
13:16—196

Esther
5:1—76, 77

Job
38:7—251

Scripture Index

Psalms
22—79
16:10—298
37:36—263
38:11-14—266
49:16—298
77:24—99

Isaiah
6:9-10—10
11:16—332
25:8—298
26:19—104, 297
38:12—108
49:16—298
50:6—157
53—8, 9, 31
53:3-10—157
53:4—10
53:5—10, 12
53:12—10, 12

Jeremiah
17:21-22—148
34:5—133

Ezekiel
10—316
26:21—263
37—213, 297
37:1-14—104
37:9—213
47:10—215

Daniel
6:17—266
7—301
7:9—316
8:10—251
10:5-6—316
12:2—104, 251, 297

Hosea
6:1-2—165
6:2—9, 74-82 pass.

Jonah
1:17—74
2:1—77, 79, 82
2:2—77
2:11—77

Zechariah
13:7—165

New Testament

Matthew
1:20—200
2:13—200
3:1—200
3:14—200
3:16—237
3:16-17—200
4:1-2—192
4:8—200
4:17—200
4:18—209
5:1—198
5:22—181
5:23—181
5:24—181
5:44—10
5:47—181
7:3—181
7:4—181
7:5—181
8:1-4—200
8:15—183
8:23-27—200
9:6—200
10:1—32
10:2—32
10:5—32, 43
10:19—32
10:32—305
11:25-30—200
12:40—71, 75, 157
12:46-50—181
12:49-50—45
13—200
13:31-32—93
14:23—198, 200
14:28-33—193
14:31—199
15:22-28—206
15:29—198
15:29-31—200
16:16-19—193
16:17—102
16:17-19—41, 193
16:21—8, 71, 158
17:1—198
17:9-13—200
17:22—158
17:23—71
18—200
18:15—181
18:16—212
18:21—181
18:35—181
20:1-16—200
20:18—71
20:19—158
21:45—152
22—200
22:23-33—298
23:8—45, 181
23:27—67
24-25—107
24:3—198
25:40—181
26:14—43
26:26—190
26:26-29—200
26:28—9, 10
26:32—158
26:47—43
26:58—152
26:61—71, 158
27:40—71, 158
27:52-53—104, 243
27:56—138
27:57—123-124
27:58—127, 352
27:59—128
27:60—124, 134, 135
27:61—136
27:62—152
27:62-66—150
27:63—71, 158
27:64—66, 160, 269, 358
27:65—152
28—45
28:1—71, 149
28:1-7—150
28:2—135
28:2-3—309
28:4—150
28:6—128, 135, 154
28:7—41, 45, 66, 158, 160
28:8—182
28:9—181, 183, 247
28:9-10—181, 182, 225-226, 292, 362
28:10—45, 158, 181
28:11—189
28:11-15—150
28:12—152
28:13—125, 149, 270
28:16—43, 45
28:16-17—362
28:16-20—198, 225-226

Scripture Index

28:17—46, 47, 199
28:18—198
28:18-20—46, 51, 248
28:20—216

Mark
1:14—125
1:15—125
1:16-20—192, 209
1:19—209
1:31—183
3:13-19—200
3:14—43
3:21—49, 368
3:31-35—49, 368
4:10—43
4:35-41—41
5:5—200
5:11—200
6:3—49, 368
6:7—32, 43
6:14—268
6:30—32
6:45-52—41
6:45-8:26—156
6:46—200
6:50—194
8:11—157
8:13—4
8:31—8, 71, 145, 158
8:31-32—165
8:32—156
9:2—200
9:2-8—41, 310
9:4—54
9:9-13—298
9:10—156
9:10-11—156
9:30—158
9:31—4, 71, 145, 158
9:35—43
10:32—43, 136, 137, 145
10:32-33—137
10:32-34—4, 136
10:34—9, 71, 145, 158
10:46—337
10:47—145
11:1—137
11:11—43, 137
11:15—137
11:27—137
12:25—250

12:41—136
13—107, 278
13:2—278
13:3—200
13:26—336
13:31—103
14:2—122
14:3—136, 338
14:3-9—338, 339
14:8—147, 148, 267
14:10—43, 136
14:12—10
14:17—43, 145
14:20—43
14:22—190
14:24—9
14:26-28—200
14:27—164, 165
14:27-31—165
14:28—145, 158, 164-165 pass., 336
14:29—164
14:43—43, 136
14:44—150
14:50—137, 176
14:53—263
14:54—136, 152, 263
14:55—334
14:58—71, 158
14:60—263
14:61—263
14:62—336
14:63—263
14:64—334
14:65—151
14:66-72—340
14:67—145
15:1—136, 145, 334
15:2—133, 136
15:5—136
15:7—136
15:9—133, 136
15:11—136
15:12—133, 136
15:13—133, 145
15:14—145
15:15—136
15:15—136
15:15—145
15:18—133
15:20—145
15:21—136

15:24—145
15:25—145
15:26—133
15:27—126, 145
15:29—71, 158
15:31—133
15:32—126, 133
15:33—145
15:34—145
15:37-16:7—351
15:39—328
15:40—136, 145
15:40-41—43, 136, 339
15:40-16:8—329
15:42—122, 144
15:42-47—144, 335
15:43—124, 127, 144
15:44—121, 144
15:44-45—127, 136, 352
15:45—121, 144
15:46—127, 128, 133, 134, 135, 144, 145, 352
15:47—121, 136, 137, 138-140, 144
16:1—136, 138-140, 144, 145, 337
16:1-8—144-145, 146, 148, 182, 186, 336, 337, 339, 355
16:2—71, 144, 145, 146, 149
16:3—135, 144
16:4—134, 137, 144, 145, 147
16:5—134, 144, 309, 337
16:6—128, 135, 144, 145, 163, 164, 165, 247, 356
16:7—41, 43, 45, 158, 164-166 pass., 177, 187, 318, 336, 362
16:8— vii, 46, 144, 145, 164, 166, 182, 356
16:14-15—226
16:14-18—42
16:21—8

Luke
1:1-4—240
1:4—277
1:11—54

SCRIPTURE INDEX

1:18—176
1:20—176
1:63—175
2:18—175
2:33—175
3:22—237
4:29—200
4:38—209
5—192-193, 208, 209, 210, 211
5:1-11—41
5:4—192
5:4-7—47
5:6—192
5:7—192
5:8—209
6:12-16—200
6:14—209
8:3—138-139
8:32—200
8:49—167
9:22—71, 158
9:28—200
9:32—237
9:37-43—200
9:44—158
11:14—175
11:29-30—157
12:12—99, 320
13:32—71
16:22—36
16:23—167
18:32—9
18:33—71, 158
18:34—157
19:43-44—278
20:3-36—250
21:5-36—107
21:15—99, 320
21:19-20—167
21:20-24—278
21:37—200
22:14—220
22:19—190
22:30—220
22:31—177
22:31-34—165
22:32—193
22:39—200
22:43—54
23:24—149
23:39-43—303
23:43—111
23:49—136, 138, 177

23:50—355
23:50-51—124
23:52-53—127
23:53—122, 128, 134
23:54—124, 146
23:55—136, 147, 240
23:55-56—259
23:56—146
24:1—71, 81, 136, 146, 149
24:2—135
24:3—167
24:4—134, 161, 309
24:5—162
24:6—167
24:6-7—158
24:7—71
24:10—136, 138
24:11—167
24:12—47, 129, 130, 135, 167, 168, 171, 173, 175, 192, 227, 274, 339
24:13—81, 189, 249
24:13-32—190
24:13-35—188-191 pass.
24:14—189
24:15—189
24:16—183, 309
24:18—139
24:19—189
24:21—71, 81
24:22-23—139
24:22-24—189
24:23—237, 240
24:24—47, 167, 168, 171, 192, 339
24:25—189
24:26—71, 222, 248
24:28—189
24:30—190
24:31—183, 189, 309
24:33—42
24:34—8, 10, 40, 41, 176, 192, 195-196, 227, 362, 370
24:36—167
24:36-42—226
24:36-43—42, 240, 362
24:36-49—194
24:37—46, 195, 196
24:38—198, 199
24:39—101, 195, 196, 247
24:39-43—237

24:40—167
24:41—175, 198, 199
24:41-43—190, 216
24:44—197
24:44-49—51, 197, 226
24:44-53—197
24:45—74
24:46—81
24:49—213
24:50-51—51
24:51-52—167
24:52—199

John
1:14—108, 218
1:19—208
1:21—217
1:35-51—218
1:39—218
1:41—11
1:42—205
2:1—9
2:1-11—106
2:11—218
2:13—218
2:16—218
2:17—218
2:19—71
2:19-21—158
2:20—82
2:21-22—218
2:22—75, 170, 205
2:23—218
2:43-51—202
3:1-15—128
3:2—150
3:11—150
3:32—150
3:34—99
4:6—218
4:9—218
4:25—9, 11, 12
4:27—213, 217, 218
4:33—218
4:48—206
4:54—205
5—218
5:10—218
5:27-29—205
5:28—67
5:28-29—104, 243
6:1—205
6:3—200
6:11—216

Scripture Index

6:15—200, 218
6:19—218
6:39—205
6:44—205
6:54—205
6:60-61—218
6:71—220
7—128
7:1-10—49, 368
7:15—217
7:22—218
7:32—152
7:45—152
7:47—218
7:50—128
7:50-52—128
8:1—200
8:25—208
9:31—150
9:38—199
9:47—152
9:57—152
10:3—183
10:4—164
10:27—164
10:38—206
11:2—128
11:13—218
11:16—203, 220
11:24—156, 298
11:44—129
11:47-50—218
11:54—218
12:1—128
12:16—75, 170
12:21—128
12:23—219
12:24—93
12:27-28—219
12:34—296
12:41—213
12:42-43—126
13—169, 174, 217
13:1-20—218
13:2—220
13:26—220
13:30—215
13:36-38—165, 205
14:1-3—107
14:3—205
14:5—150, 203
14:11—206

14:16-17—213
14:18-19—183
14:22—205, 220
14:22-23—213
14:25-26—213
14:27—194
15:26-27—213
15:27—27, 51
16:5-7—213
16:7—218
16:13—213
16:22—183
16:32—172
17:3—152
18:2—218
18:3—151, 152
18:10—218
18:12—151
18:13—218
18:15—172, 177
18:17—172
18:18—148
18:25—172
18:26—218
18:28—154
18:30—151
19—169, 220
19:25—138
19:26-27—170, 172, 174, 178
19:31—122, 141, 335
19:31-37—354
19:34—196
19:35—117, 170, 174, 178, 215, 218
19:38—124, 355
19:40—126
19:41—122, 134, 135
19:42—122
20—169, 171, 211, 212, 342
20-21—203-207 pass.
20:1—71, 134, 135, 136, 149, 168
20:1-2—357
20:1-18—184-187 pass.
20:2—47, 149, 171, 173, 176
20:2-3—171
20:2-10—167, 171, 176, 339, 352
20:3—339

20:4-9—130
20:5—135
20:5-8—135
20:7—129
20:8—171, 175
20:8-9—75, 170
20:8-10—172
20:9—170, 171, 175
20:10—171
20:11—135
20:11-17—362
20:11-18—181, 226
20:12—134
20:14-15—309
20:17—45, 178, 181, 183, 248, 318
20:18—52-53, 189, 201
20:19—71, 175, 198, 201, 309
20:19-20—362
20:19-21—225
20:19-23—42, 194, 226
20:20—46, 196, 202
20:21-23—51, 204
20:22—212-213
20:24—42, 220
20:24-29—201-203 pass.
20:25—53, 196, 218
20:26—175, 309
20:26-29—43
20:26-38—237
20:27—196, 199
20:28—203
20:29—170, 203, 206, 207, 242
20:30—204, 206, 207
20:30-31—203, 206
20:31—204, 205, 206
21—169, 171, 172, 175, 192, 193, 199, 201, 203, 204, 211, 212, 214, 216, 217, 219, 362
21:1—205, 207
21:1-14—43, 207-211 pass.
21:1-23—41
21:2—128, 207, 219, 220
21:3—207, 214, 218
21:4—208, 309
21:5—207, 208, 210
21:6—205, 208

21:7—170, 174, 207, 208, 209, 210, 218, 219
21:8—208
21:9—207, 208
21:9-13—216
21:9-19—174
21:10—205, 207, 208
21:11—208
21:12—208, 213, 216
21:12-13—208
21:13—208, 216
21:14—205, 207, 208, 236
21:15—207
21:15-17—172, 193, 205, 207
21:19—205, 209
21:20—128, 205, 217
21:20-23—174
21:20-24—169
21:22—217
21:22-23—107
21:23—169, 182, 205, 217
21:24—117, 150, 168, 170, 171, 217, 218, 219, 311

Acts
1:1-5:16—28
1:2—51
1:3—20, 43, 197, 199, 249
1:4—240
1:6-7—107
1:6-11—51
1:9—309
1:10—316
1:12—200
1:14—49, 50, 220, 368
1:20—42
1:21—27
1:21-22—51
1:21-23—6
1:22—27
1:25—42
2—368
2:1-13—368
2:3—54, 237
2:4—237
2:7—111
2:23—354
2:24-32—68
2:26-27—243
2:29—36, 359
2:31—243
2:32—20, 296

2:33—237
2:34-36—30
2:36—296, 354
2:38—31
3:12—175
3:15—20
3:19—31
3:20-21—31
4:10—354
4:12—31
4:13—175, 219
5:7—133
5:30-32—20
5:31—31
7:2—54
7:26—54
7:30—54
7:35—54
7:55-56—309, 315, 374
8:14—27
8:17-18—237
8:32-35—31
9—58, 59
9:1-19—55, 309
9:3—56
9:4—56
9:5—310
9:5-6—56
9:7—56, 57, 128
9:10—52, 315
9:12—58
9:13—23
9:17—52
9:17-18—58
9:19-25—56
9:31-11:18—28
10—28, 29, 30
10:1-11:18—53
10:5—209
10:9-17—52
10:18—209
10:28—52
10:32—209
10:40—71
10:41—59, 240
10:42—4, 31
10:43—30, 31
10:44-46—237
11:13—209
11:25-26—15
12:15—233
12:17—27, 49, 368
13—32, 256
13:27-29—335

13:28-31—351
13:29—141, 354
13:29-31—69
13:30—23
13:33—9, 30
13:35-37—243
13:36—359
13:38—32
13:38-39—31
14—30, 31
14:4—51, 59
14:14—51, 59
14:15-17—24
15:13—49
16:6—99, 320
16:7—99, 320
16:9—52, 315
17—30, 31, 32
17:16-34—20
17:22-31—24
17:31—19, 107
17:31-32—344
19:6—237
20:25—279
20:28—31
21—49
21:13—58, 279
21:18—49
22—58
22:3-16—55
22:4-16—309
22:6—56
22:7—56
22:8—56, 310
22:9—56, 57
22:10—56
22:11—56
22:14—52
22:17—52, 315
22:17-21—374
22:20—41
23:6—93
23:8—298
23:9—196
24:14—93
26—58
26:6—93
26:9-18—309
26:9-23—55
26:13—56
26:13-14—57
26:14—56
26:15—310
26:15-18—56

Scripture Index 407

26:19—57
26:21-23—93
27:24—279

Romans
1:1-5—27
1:3—320
1:24—88
2:28—86
3:7—372
3:25—31
4:17—79, 81
4:19—89
4:24-25—23
4:25—10, 30, 35, 79, 81, 296
5:6—9, 10
5:8—10
5:9—31
5:12-14—372
5:12-21—105
6—65
6-8—87
6:1-11—95
6:4—9, 65
6:5—85
6:6—88
6:9—9
6:10—6
6:12—89
6:12-14—88
6:16—88
6:19—88
7:1-3—88
7:4—88
7:5—4
7:7-25—372
7:14—372
7:24—88, 89
7:25—372
8:9-11—99, 320, 344
8:10—9, 88, 89, 95, 105, 110, 216
8:10-11—105, 106
8:11—23, 88, 89, 105, 109, 110, 344
8:12-13—88
8:13—89
8:18—110
8:18-23—102, 103
8:19-24—96
8:22-23—106, 110

8:23—110, 344
8:24-25—110
8:32—79, 81
8:34—221, 320
10:7—111
10:9—23, 66, 296, 305
11:16—85
12:1—88
12:2—88
12:4—88
14:9—9
14:15—9, 10
15:15—27
15:16—27
15:18-19—61
15:19—28
15:25—83
15:28—279
16:7—27

I Corinthians
1:1—27
1:8-10—88
1:11—83
1:12—8, 20
1:17-25—19
1:17-2:13—19
1:31-2:5—20
2:4—20, 61
2:10—60
2:14—96
2:14-15—98
2:14-3:3—91
3:4—20
3:10—27
3:18-21—20
3:22—8
5:3—89, 344
5:3-5—87
6:12-20—88, 106
6:13—106
6:14—106, 109, 110
6:15—106, 372
6:15-18—106
6:16—86
6:17—106
6:19—106
7:4—88
7:31—103
7:34—87
8:11—9

9:1—27, 52, 53, 56, 101, 312
9:1-2—54
9:2—27
9:5—4, 8, 14, 27, 50
9:6—27
9:16—27
9:17—27
9:26—88
9:26-27—86
10:3-4—99
10:29-30—372
11:23—4, 16
11:23-25—263
11:23-26—83, 257
11:24—190
11:25—5
12-13—315
12-14—52
12:1—373
12:13—91
12:28—28
13:1-3—372
13:3—88
14:30—60
15—12, 16, 18, 21, 22, 24, 28, 29, 30, 31, 32, 33, 34, 35, 37, 42, 65, 68, 79, 82, 85, 86, 88, 90, 91, 98, 109, 110, 111, 113, 121, 140, 145, 187, 192, 275, 276, 281, 285, 286, 319, 341, 342, 361, 373
15:1—16, 22
15:1-2—17
15:1-11—19, 341
15:3—4, 9, 10, 11, 12, 13, 14, 23, 25, 74, 330
15:3-5—13, 14, 23, 25, 69, 83, 188, 260, 262, 303, 331, 346, 351
15:3-7—3-37 pass.
15:3-8—20, 23, 24, 313, 373
15:4—4, 10, 25, 54, 72, 74, 78, 157, 165, 192, 256, 257, 264, 333, 359
15:4-8—44
15:5—7, 14, 17, 25, 41, 137, 362, 369, 370

15:5-7—17, 18, 361, 369
15:5-8—4, 21, 236, 342
15:6—5, 6, 7, 16, 17, 19, 25, 35
15:6-7—7, 14, 16
15:7—6, 17, 19, 25, 35, 368
15:8—5, 6, 16, 20, 54, 56, 68, 236, 312, 314, 315, 361, 373
15:8-9—54
15:8-10—28
15:8-11—27
15:9—20, 56
15:11—8, 13, 20, 22, 346
15:12—9, 11, 16, 17, 18, 20, 22, 65-66, 111
15:12-14—4
15:12-23—344
15:13—17
15:14—9, 22, 296
15:15—20, 22, 23
15:16—4
15:17—4, 9, 296
15:20—4, 16, 17, 18, 20, 44, 85, 111, 113, 299
15:20-21—21
15:22—105
15:22-28—21
15:23—107, 320
15:24-28—320
15:29—83
15:29-32—344
15:35—92, 104, 344
15:35-44—87
15:35-57—85-107 pass.
15:36-41—93
15:36-50—92
15:38—93
15:40—100
15:40-41—94, 311
15:41—94
15:42—93
15:42-44—93, 95, 100, 103
15:42-50—95
15:43—94, 309, 312
15:44—100, 105, 241, 260, 310, 320
15:45—99, 100, 310, 319, 320
15:46—100, 320
15:47—94, 95, 100
15:48—95
15:49—100
15:50—98, 101, 102, 103, 237, 342
15:50-55—104
15:51—101, 102
15:51-57—92
15:52—103, 104
15:53—102, 109
15:53-54—95
15:54—109, 110
15:54-57—105
16:3—83
16:22—41

II Corinthians
1:1—27
1:22—110-111
2:17—27
3:7—314
3:12—314
3:17—99, 319, 320
3:17-18—99, 241, 310, 319, 320
3:18—96, 99, 319, 320
4:4—60, 312
4:6—60, 312
4:7—88, 108, 110
4:7-5:10—110
4:10—110
4:10-12—88
4:11—110
4:14—110
4:16—88, 95, 110
4:17—110
5—98, 111, 112
5:1—88, 95, 108, 110
5:1-3—100
5:1-4—96
5:1-5—95
5:1-10—viii, 108-114 pass.
5:2—95, 106, 109, 110
5:3—109
5:4—96, 105, 106, 109, 110
5:5—105, 109, 110
5:6—88, 110, 111
5:6-9—110, 111
5:8—67, 110, 111
5:8-9—88
5:9—112
5:10—110
5:15—10
5:18—27

8-9—83
10-13—19
10:1-2—20
10:10—86, 89
10:12—20
10:18—20
11:1-12:13—28
11:5—4, 54
11:14—316
12—53
12:1—54, 315
12:1-4—111
12:1-5—52, 315
12:1-7—53
12:2-4—61
12:7—86
12:7-10—96
12:11—4, 20, 54
12:12—20, 28, 61
13:4—96

Galatians
1:1—27-28, 54, 66
1:4—4, 10
1:6-9—15
1:11-12—54
1:12—15, 60
1:13—56
1:14—56
1:15—54
1:15-16—54, 56
1:16—56, 60, 102, 312, 342
1:17-21—56
1:18—8
1:18-19—14
1:19—4, 27, 48, 49, 368
1:22-23—23
2:1—27, 52, 83, 315
2:2—31
2:2-10—15
2:9—8, 27, 31, 49
2:11—8, 16, 83
2:12—49
2:13—16
2:14—8, 15
2:15-16—28
2:16—15
2:18-19—372
3:13—9
4:13-14—86, 96
5:1—9
6:17—89

Ephesians
1:7—31
1:13-14—111
1:19—221
2:1—4
3:5—60
3:7-8—28
4:11—28
5:28-29—88
6:12—102, 342

Philippians
1:20—88
1:21—112
1:21-26—111
1:23—67, 95, 112
1:24—88
1:24-25—112
2:6-11—198
2:8—303
3:4-14—372
3:5-6—56
3:6—56, 289-290
3:7—56
3:10-11—96
3:15—60
3:20-21—107, 320
3:21—85, 89, 94, 96, 113, 309, 312
4:5—107

Colossians
1:1—28
1:14—4
1:18—85, 221
1:20—31
1:22—88
1:23-25—28
1:24—96
1:25—56
2:5—89, 344
2:11—88
2:12—23, 65
2:17—86
3:4—107, 320

I Thessalonians
1—29, 31
1:9—22, 24
1:9-10—23
1:10—66
2:4-6—28
2:14-15—32
2:17—89
4—108, 110
4:7—108
4:13—22
4:13-17—22, 67
4:13-18—18
4:14—112
4:15—22, 103
4:16—22, 103, 104
4:16-17—107, 112, 320
4:17—103, 107
5:9-10—10

II Thessalonians
1:7—107
1:7-8—320
1:8—107
1:10—107, 320
2:1—107, 320
2:8—107, 320
3:6—16

I Timothy
3:16—4, 198
6:14—107

II Timothy
2:8—4
4:1—107

Titus
2:13—107
2:14—9
3:18—9

Hebrews
1:3—221
1:5-9—198
1:10-12—103
2:14—102
6—29, 31
7:27—6
8:9—108
9:11—9
9:12—6, 31
10:10—6
10:19—31
10:26—9, 10
10:37—107
11:17-19—79, 81
13:20—221

James
2:21-23—81
3:15—96
5:7—107
5:9—107

I Peter
1:13—107
1:19—31
1:21—23
2:21—9
2:21-25—4
2:24—88
3:18—9, 10
3:18-20—4
4:1—88

II Peter
1:13—108
1:13-14—109
1:16—33
1:16-17—310, 318
3:4—107
3:10—103, 107

I John
1:1—33, 247
1:3—33
2:2—9, 10
2:28—107
3:2—107
3:16—9
4:2-3—244

II John
7—244

Jude
19—96

Revelation
1:5—31
1:10—310
1:10-18—374
1:13-16—60, 241, 309
1:17-18—241
1:20—80, 251
2:7—241, 310
2:8—241
2:11—241, 310
2:17—241, 310

410 SCRIPTURE INDEX

2:29—241, 310
3:6—310
3:13—310
3:22—310
4:4—109, 316
5:9—31
6:1—80
6:11—109
6:14—103
7:9—109
7:13—109
7:14—109
8:2—80
9:13—161
10:1—161, 316
11:3—264
15:1—80
15:7—80
20-21—320
20:11—103
21:1—103
21:14—32

Apocrypha and Pseudepigrapha

Ascension of Isaiah
3:16—153
7:22—109
8:26—109
9—109

I Baruch
5:2—109

II Baruch
21:23—104
30:2-5—104, 112, 298
42:8—104
49:2-3—92
50-51—80, 92, 103
50:1—298
51:1-10—94
51:5—251
51:8-10—251

I Enoch
5:7—297
22:1-14—112, 297
22:13—66
51:1—66, 104, 297
61:5—104, 297
62:15—109
90:33—298
91:1-10—298
91:15-16—80
93—80
100:4-5—298

II Enoch
22:8-10—109

IV Ezra
7:26-44—80, 104, 112, 298

Gospel of Nicodemus
16:6—263

Gospel of Peter
6:23-24—331
8:30—333
8:30-33—331
8:35-42—153
9—161
9:35-10:42—336
14:58-60—212

Gospel of the Hebrews
—48, 301

I Maccabees
7:16-17—74

II Maccabees
3:1-39—56
3:26—161
3:33—161
5:14—80
7:9-42—80, 297
11:18—76, 80
12:43-45—80, 297

IV Maccabees
17:2-6—235

Odes of Solomon
11:11—109
21:3—109
25:8—109

Sirach
7:33—123
14:18—102
17:31—102
38:16—123

Testament of Abraham
—232, 233

Testament of Job
18—235
39-40—263
40—234, 301
40:9—235
40:13-14—235

Testament of the Twelve Patriarchs
Benjamin: 10:6-18—80, 298
Judah: 25:1—80, 298
Judah: 25:4—80, 298
Levi: 16:3—155
Zebulun: 10:2—80, 298

Tobit
1:17-19—123
2:3-7—123
5—232
12—232
12:12-13—123
12:19—196

Wisdom
9:15—108

www.ingramcontent.com/pod-product-compliance
Lightning Source LLC
Chambersburg PA
CBHW071227290426
44108CB00013B/1317